Making Connections

Readings in Relational Communication

Fifth Edition

Kathleen M. Galvin
NORTHWESTERN UNIVERSITY

New York   Oxford
OXFORD UNIVERSITY PRESS
2011

Oxford University Press, Inc., publishes works that further Oxford University's
objective of excellence in research, scholarship, and education.

Oxford   New York
Auckland   Cape Town   Dar es Salaam   Hong Kong   Karachi
Kuala Lumpur   Madrid   Melbourne   Mexico City   Nairobi
New Delhi   Shanghai   Taipei   Toronto

With offices in
Argentina   Austria   Brazil   Chile   Czech Republic   France   Greece
Guatemala   Hungary   Italy   Japan   Poland   Portugal   Singapore
South Korea   Switzerland   Thailand   Turkey   Ukraine   Vietnam

Published by Oxford University Press, Inc.
198 Madison Avenue, New York, New York 10016
http://www.oup.com

Oxford is a registered trademark of Oxford University Press

Library of Congress Cataloging-in-Publication Data
 Making connections: readings in relational communication / Kathleen M. Galvin.—5th ed.
  p. cm.
ISBN 978-0-19-973381-1 (pbk. : acid-free paper)
1. Interpersonal communication. 2. Interpersonal relations. 3. Communication—Psychological
aspects. 4. Sex differences (Psychology)   I. Galvin, Kathleen M.
 BF637.C45M33   2011
 302.2—dc22   2009042478

Printed in the United States of America
on acid-free paper

To Ryan James Wilkinson,
The next generation rises…

CONTENTS

Knapp and Hall describe categories of nonverbal communication and the interrelationships between verbal and nonverbal messages.

communication patterns common to this relational practice.

Welcome to the fifth edition of *Making Connections: Readings in Relational Communication*. This edition continues to rely on the root metaphor of lenses, perspectives through which each of us can view and make sense of our communication interactions and those we observe in the world around us. My core belief is that effective communication depends on knowledge and skills that can be developed; it is not an accident of birth. I also believe human beings are more effective at understanding relationships when they have multiple perspectives through which to view interpersonal interactions. Finally, I believe multiple perspectives lead to alternative ways of creating and sustaining ongoing relationships. Relying on the research and insights of many fine scholars and teachers, I have assembled a timely and challenging set of perspectives on relational communication. This edition continues to offer a mix of theory and practice designed to make clear the connection between communication practices and the development of such significant relationships as friends, romantic partners, family members, and colleagues. This text reflects my belief that gender, culture, and family serve as critical perceptual filters, or lenses, through which human beings view the world; these filters directly affect the ways each of us interprets relational interactions and interacts with others. As you read the chapters, I hope you will examine how your own personal perceptual filters affect the way you interact with others and, in addition, consider how other people rely on their filters for the same purpose.

In *Making Connections* you will encounter concepts and research findings that will provide you with new perspectives on relational communication and, in some cases, give you a new terminology for your intuitive relational knowledge and insights. In addition, you will consider a range of strategies for dealing with communication situations. And, finally, you will explore three primary contexts—family, friends and technology—in which communication knowledge and skills play a significant role. I hope you will consider insights from these readings when making informed personal choices about your own interpersonal interactions in significant relationships while increase your analytical skills as an observer of relational life within the contexts of family, friendship, and digital media use.

NEW TO THE FIFTH EDITION

The fifth edition has been updated and expanded to include ten new articles, four of which are original. Nine articles have been updated, with changes ranging from minor to significant. Based on reviewer feedback certain chapters have been discontinued and others have been added, on topics such as technology as a communication building block, managing difficult conversations and communicating in a connected world, and intimate intercultural conflict. Using the same framework from earlier editions, gender, family, and culture serve as "lenses" through which to view and make sense of relational communication.

The articles in *Making Connections* were selected from the recent work of communication scholars and teachers—with a balance between humanistic and social-science perspectives. The fifth edition continues to:

- offer a well-rounded discussion of the links between communication and relationships, including perception, verbal and nonverbal communication, listening and technological communication.

- feature a developmental approach to relationships addressing initiating, sustaining, and ending relationships.
- reflect direct applications of relational issues within contexts of family, friendships, and technology.
- explore issues relating to technology, specifically, computer-mediated communication.

Each chapter concludes with a set of questions to encourage you to think and talk about your reactions to the chapter content.

STRUCTURE

The text is designed to move you from concepts and theories to applications within specific contexts.

Part I provides an introduction to the communication process as well as to the key concepts of relational culture, dialectical processes, and relational development.

Part II establishes the critical role of perceptual processes in relational communication and presents culture, family, and gender as "lenses" through which we view our relational experiences.

Part III introduces the basic building blocks of communication, which include verbal language, nonverbal messages, listening, and technology skills.

Part IV discusses relational development, emphasizing various models of relational growth, and sustaining relationships, including sharing affection, managing rules and rituals, nagging, and forgiving.

Part V explores the inevitable struggles that surface in significant long-term relationships involving personal differences, lying, and standoffs, and how these can be managed through negotiation, difficult conversations, listening strategies, and constructive conflict practices.

Part VI confronts the reality of relational decline as friends or partners move toward greater individuality, confront their differences and, in some cases, dysfunctional behavior, and construct relational termination narratives.

Part VII demonstrates the effect of context on relational interaction and explores the interpersonal communication issues unique to the contexts of families, friendships, and computer mediated communication or CMC.

An introduction opens each section of the text, previewing some of the concepts that appear in the readings that follow. In addition, an introduction introduces each reading, placing it in a theoretical context and summarizing the chapter highlights. At the end of each reading you will find a set of questions and challenges to help you integrate and apply key points.

I am very excited about the fifth edition and the new and revised chapters included here; some establish major communication concepts, strategies or theories, whereas others represent emerging areas of research and interest to communication professionals. I hope you find the readings thought-provoking and that you will apply the theoretical insights, concepts, and examples to understanding your own personal relationships as well as to understanding others' relational practices.

With each edition I have learned more about relational communication and about myself as a communicator. My hope is that you will be able to say the same after you have reached the last page of this edition!

ACKNOWLEDGMENTS

Revising this book continues to be a relational experience. Many persons contributed to the creation of this edition.

I appreciated the opportunity to examine the responses of persons familiar with the fourth edition, to talk with authors of academic and trade works about their ideas, and to seek out original pieces from both established and emerging scholars.

I am very grateful to the reviewers of this edition for their thoughtful and detailed responses to the fourth edition. These reviewers provided in-depth responses to the last edition, suggesting changes and affirming the value of many pieces. Each person made specific suggestions for changes and additions. And they made many suggestions! These individuals include:

Melissa A. Broeckelman-Post, Ohio University
Bryan K. Crow, Southern Illinois University, Carbondale
Barrie S.T. Mason, North Central College
Kyle Tusing, University of Arizona

I also wish to acknowledge the reviewers and users of all four previous editions who provided extremely helpful formal and informal feedback:

Marcee Andersen, Anoka Ramsey Community College
Theodore Avtgis, West Virginia University
Jennifer Bieselin, Florida Gulf Coast University
Judy Bowker, Oregon State University

Janie Harden Fritz, Dusquesne University
Colleen Garside, Weber State University
James Hasenauer, California State University, Northridge
Stephen Klien, Augustana College
Randall Koper, University of the Pacific
Alan Lerstrom, Luther College
Claire Sullivan, University of Maine

In addition, I relied heavily on the assistance of Northwestern University students for manuscript development. Rebecca Otto provided exceptional ongoing assistance with manuscript preparation, computer expertise, and interpersonal support. Genevieve Szymanski and Lindsay Dhuse made valuable contributions to the fifth edition at varying points in the process.

I am indebted to the professionals at Oxford University Press. Executive Editor Peter Labella served as a strong supporter as well as a valued advisor. Associate Editor Josh Hawkins provided clear direction, immediate responses, and reassurance.

Finally, I need to acknowledge the contributions of Pamela J. Cooper, who co-edited the first three editions with me and helped to set the tone and direction of that first edition that influenced all subsequent editions. I miss our discussions and collaboration.

Kathleen M. Galvin

Ronald B. Adler is a professor in the Department of Communication at Santa Barbara City College.

Janna Anderson is a researcher at the PEW Internet and American Life Project.

Bernard J. Brommel is a professor emeritus in the Department of Communication at Northeastern Illinois University.

Carol J. Bruess is an associate professor in the Department of Theatre Arts and Communication Studies at the University of St. Thomas.

Carma L. Bylund is an Assistant Attending Behavioral Scientist in the Department of Psychiatry and Behavioral Sciences at Memorial Sloan-Kettering Cancer Center.

Daniel J. Canary is a professor in the Hugh Downs School of Human Communication at Arizona State University.

Leeva C. Chung is an associate professor in the Department of Communication Studies and Ethnic Studies at the University of San Diego.

Michael J. Cody is a professor in the Annenberg School for Communication at the University of Southern California.

Pamela J. Cooper is Director of Quality Enhancement Program at the University of South Carolina, Beaufort.

William R. Cupach is a professor in the Department of Communication at Illinois State University.

Anita K. Foeman is a professor in the Department of Communication Studies at West Chester University.

Sheryl Friedley is a professor in the Department of Communication at George Mason University.

Kathleen M. Galvin is a professor in the Department of Communication Studies at Northwestern University.

John Gottman is an emeritus professor of psychology at the University of Washington and founder of the "Love Lab."

Brandon D. Grill is the Assistant Director of Information Technology in the School of Communication at Northwestern University.

Lauren H. Grill is a lecturer in the Department of Communication at the University of Illinois at Urbana-Champaign.

Judith A. Hall is a professor of psychology at Northeastern University.

Dale Hample is a professor in the Department of Communication at the University of Maryland.

Thomas E. Harris is a professor in the Communication Studies Department at the University of Alabama.

Sheila Heen is a partner at Triad Consulting Group and an affiliate of the Harvard Negotiation Project.

Joyce L. Hocker is a clinical psychologist in Missoula, Montana.

David Johnson is a professor in the Department of Educational Psychology at the University of Minnesota and Co-Director of the Cooperative Learning Center.

Jody Koenig Kellas is an associate professor in the Department of Communication Studies at the University of Nebraska, Lincoln.

Douglas L. Kelley is an associate professor of Communication Studies Department at Arizona State University West.

Mark L. Knapp is the Jesse H. Jones Centennial Professor in the College of Communication at the University of Texas, Austin.

Valerie L. Manusov is a professor in the Department of Communication at the University of Washington.

Sandra Metts is a professor in the Department of Communication at Illinois State University.

Courtney Waite Miller is an assistant professor in the Communication Arts & Sciences Department at Elmhurst College.

Elizabeth Munz is a doctoral student in the Department of Communication at Purdue University.

Scott A. Myers is a professor in the Department of Communication Studies at West Virginia University.

Teresa Nance is an associate professor in the Department of Communication at Villanova University.

James Neuliep is a professor in the Department of Communication and Media Studies at St. Norbert's College.

Bruce Patton is a Deputy Director of the Harvard Negotiation Project and a Director of Vantage Partners LLC.

Lee Rainie is the Director at the PEW Internet and American Life Project.

William K. Rawlins is the Stocker Professor in the School of Communication at Ohio University.

Felicia Roberts is an associate professor in the Department of Communication at Purdue University.

George Rodman is a professor in the Department of Television and Radio at Brooklyn College of the City University of New York.

Sai Sato is a doctoral student in the Department of Communication Studies at the University of Nebraska, Lincoln.

John C. Sherblom is a professor of Communication and Journalism at the University of Maine.

Katrina Shonbeck is an Ad Programs Associate at Google in Chicago.

Kari P. Soule is a quantitative research consultant in Charlotte, NC.

Brian H. Spitzberg is a professor in the School of Communication at San Diego State University.

Alan Stewart is a lecturer in the Department of Communication at Rutgers University.

Lea P. Stewart is a professor in the Department of Communication at Rutgers University.

Douglas Stone is a managing partner at Triad Consulting Group and an affiliate of the Harvard Negotiation Project.

Elizabeth Stone is a professor of English Communication and Media Studies at Fordham University.

Stella Ting-Toomey is a professor in the Department of Human Communication Studies at California State University, Fullerton.

Lynn H. Turner is a professor in the Department of Communication Studies at Marquette University.

Anita L. Vangelisti is a Jesse H. Jones Centennial Professor of Communication in the Department of Communication Studies at the University of Texas, Austin.

Kathleen S. Verderber is a professor emeritus in the Department of Communication at Northern Kentucky University.

Rudolph F. Verderber is a professor emeritus in Department of Communication at the University of Cincinnati.

Ethan Watters is a journalist, non-fiction author, and writing teacher.

Richard West is a professor in the Department of Communication Studies at Emerson College.

Charles A. Wilkinson is a retired family therapist and freelance writer.

William W. Wilmot is a professor emeritus in the Department of Communication Studies at the University of Montana.

Steven R. Wilson is a professor in the Department of Communication at Purdue University.

Julia T. Wood is the Lineberger Distinguished Professor of Humanities and a professor in the Department of Communication Studies at the University of North Carolina.

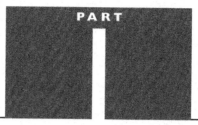

Communication Foundations in Relationships

Introduction

Sustaining relationships is a lifelong concern. Relationships are messy, unpredictable, joyful, frustrating, comforting, painful, and necessary! Each of us treasures our relationships and most of us struggle with our relationships at different points in time. These struggles are captured by the philosopher Arthur Schopenhauer in his famous porcupine dilemma:

> On a wintry day a couple of chilled porcupines huddled together for warmth. They found that they pricked each other with their quills; they moved apart and were again cold. After much experimentation, the porcupines found the distance at which they gave each other some warmth without too much sting. (Quoted in Bellak 1970, 3)

Most human beings find themselves in situations similar to those of the porcupines as they try to manage their relationships with the significant people in their lives. They struggle to find the comfortable distance in each relationship and to adjust to changes in themselves and others over time.

You may be surrounded by people during most of your waking hours but it is the quality of your relationships that significantly influences your state of mind, your personal growth, and even your health. Your relational circles widen as you age, potentially incorporating partners, children, colleagues, classmates, teachers, friends, or neighbors. Some of these individuals represent highly significant relationships, but many of them will engage primarily in functional communication with you. After a certain point many older adults find the circle begins to shrink, making the long-term ties even more critical.

Everyday conversation contains ritualistic, impersonal interactions, such as greetings, small talk, or sharing business information, which may be ritualistic but require very little personal attention. Most of your important relationships involve interpersonal interaction, necessitating attention, emotional involvement, and caring. Sustaining valued relationships involves every-day talk rituals, as well as attempts at openness, assurances, forgiveness, positivity, and presence (Canary, Stafford, & Semic 2002; Foley & Duck, 2006). It may also include disagreeing, showing concern, solving a problem, giving or requesting advice, listening to feelings, or planning for the future. These less ritualized interactions demand effort and attention from all persons involved. Relational life also reveals a dark side, the source of difficult and painful interactions. Occasionally you will find yourself in "turning point" inter-actions, critical conversations that carry great significance for the relationship. Such events may involve revealing something very personal about yourself, asking for help with a serious problem, responding to a friend who is ill or upset, or plan-ning for a major shared life event. They may also involve confronting another with your feelings of anger or hurt that leaves you questioning the rela-tionship's value.

Your psychological well-being depends heavily on managing the relationships in your life in a constructive manner. Yet such effective inter-actions do not "just happen" and effective com-municators are not "born that way." Although there are some people who appear to manage their relationships effortlessly, when you observe them carefully, however, most effective commu-nicators consciously work at their relationships. Interpersonally skilled communicators may come to experience this as natural, but their level of effectiveness was developed with time and effort. Every individual has the opportunity to develop and improve her or his communication effective-ness through a combination of knowledge and strategies that increase competence.

It is important for you to understand the key beliefs about communication that serve as the foundation for this book. They are:

1. There is no "right" way to communi-cate. Communication patterns reflect the unique individuals who bring their cul-tural and personal backgrounds, as well

as relational histories and perceptions of each other, to the interaction. Each signif-icant relationship creates its own identity distinguishing it from similar relation-ships. A relationship that "works" for one set of people may not seem desirable to others.

2. Communication serves to construct as well as reflect relationships. It is through talk that people construct their identities and negotiate their relationships with each other. Their talk serves to reflect the state of their relationship to others.

3. Communication is the process by which individuals work out and share their mean-ings with each other. In close relationships members develop a relational culture—a shared vision of reality, or worldview—that includes deep understandings of the other and unique communication patterns.

4. Interpersonal relationships shift over time as participants respond to changing cir-cumstances. Each relationship develops a life of its own. After the early interac-tions, relationships reinvent themselves over time through the amount and type of participant involvement. Relationships experience various stages of development as they grow and deepen or, in some cases, become less vital or wither away.

5. An individual's communication style is influenced by background factors such as cultural heritage, gender, family interac-tions, and unique life experiences, each of which affects his or her adult interpersonal relationships.

6. Persons in well-functioning interper-sonal relationships nurture their ties. Developing and maintaining strong relationships require putting in effort, or what Duck (1994) calls "relation-shipping." Most relational partners are self-aware; they avoid taking their rela-tionships for granted.

This book opens with an overview of commu-nication concepts and processes, followed by an examination of personal factors that influence communication. You will encounter a range of readings from scholarly books, academic journals, commissioned chapters, trade books, and magazines in order to reflect theory and practice.

Your understanding of communication processes will progress in stages. First, you will encounter an introduction to the knowledge base of relational communication. This involves considering the concepts and research findings as well as providing you with new ways to consider the relational communication process. You will develop new terminology and theories that relate to your intuitive knowledge. Second, the importance of individual perceptions will be addressed. You will appreciate how your background, your culture, gender, family, and individual experiences help you to make sense of communication interactions. You will consider a number of perspectives or "lenses" through which to analyze interpersonal interactions. Finally, you will encounter examples of strategies for managing communicative interactions and read the application pieces that address everyday communication dilemmas and challenges. This information should help you to make informed choices about how to manage a range of interpersonal interactions.

The overall aim of this text is to provide you with a set of *lenses* for analyzing specific communication situations and examples of strategies for action based on your analysis. If you have ever had an eye examination, you will remember the ophthalmologist inserting different lenses into an eyeglass frame while asking you to indicate which lens helped you see most clearly. Each lens provided a slightly different view of the chart; sometimes it took a while to find just the right set of lenses to see most clearly.

Think back to situations when you tried to make sense out of a confusing conversation or problematic interaction. For example, consider that a reasonably friendly co-worker suddenly becomes distant and distracted. If you try on various relational lenses that help you understand an individual's personal experience, you may conclude the silence to be the result of worrying over a child's illness. If you try on lenses illuminating cultural communication styles, you may determine the person's silence reflects an attempt to be polite when dealing with a sensitive topic. In a third alternative you may decide the response reflects a gender pattern; perhaps some of your humor offended her. Each lens illuminates a different perspective. Your view of the situation will affect how you respond. In the second situation you may decide to rephrase a comment in a less assertive manner. Finally, you may become more conscious of gendered humor. In each case you analyze the situation to the best of your ability and then act on the basis of your analysis. And, if that lens and the change in your interaction style does not appear to have the desired effect, you may try another lens. Also, if appropriate, you may address the issue directly with the other person.

This sounds very formal and carefully thought out, yet in many everyday interactions, you instinctively respond in particular circumstances. Your conscious awareness of this process occurs when confronted with a confusing situation or when high stakes are involved in your actions. This occurs because most routine interactions are patterned, requiring little reflection; however, when the patterns shift, attention is refocused on them. In a world of very diverse people, these processes are significant. You cannot assume others view interactions the same way that you do. Or that, when Person X says "I'm frustrated," it means the same thing as when you say "I'm frustrated."

Significant interpersonal relationships must be nurtured. In one case this may mean sharing personal problems and "being there" for each other; in another case it may mean getting together on a regular basis to swap work stories and banter about sports. The goal is to create ways in which both persons feel recognized and connected.

Hopefully you will find the readings in this firth edition of *Making Connections* to be thought provoking and when you put the book down, you will find everyday situations in which to apply the concepts and strategies.

REFERENCES

Bellak, L. (1970). *The porcupine dilemma.* New York, NY: Citadel Press.

Canary, D. J., Stafford, L., & Semic, B. (2002). A panel study of the associations between maintenance strategies and relational characteristics. *Journal of Marriage and the Family, 64,* 395–406.

Duck, S. (1994). Steady as (s)he goes: Relational maintenance as a shared meaning system. In D. J. Canary and L. Stafford (Eds.), *Communication and Relational Maintenance,* (pp. 45–49). San Diego, CA: Academic Press.

Foley, M. K., & Duck, S. (2006). "That dear octopus": A family-based model of intimacy. In R. West & L. H. Turner (Eds.), *The Family Communication Sourcebook* (pp. 183–199). Thousand Oaks, CA: Sage.

The Communication Process: Impersonal and Interpersonal

KATHLEEN M. GALVIN AND CHARLES A. WILKINSON

Communication is a complex, ongoing process that brings us together and maintains the ties with the people in our world. Some people view communication as a straightforward easy and effective exchange of messages between a speaker and a listener—one speaks while the other listens, and vice versa. This is a naïve view. This chapter asserts that communication is a symbolic process of sharing meanings, or a complicated sense-making experience.

To interpret another's communication effectively involves finding the meanings of messages; those meanings are found in people, not in words. Your friend's meaning of "trust" or "happiness" may be quite different than yours. Even a presumably simple, concrete word can create misunderstandings. You may think of "vacation" as personal time spent away from the workplace with no thought of your job. Your boss may think "vacation" implies that employees will be away from the office but continuously available to discuss work-related issues via cell phone, e-mail, or Twitter. The closer both persons' meanings are, the easier it is to communicate effectively.

Communication is a continuous process that begins with a first encounter between people and does not end until the last encounter in their lives, even though years may separate some interactions. These encounters may involve functional messages that serve practical purposes or, in cases of close ties, the encounters may also involve nurturing messages that convey a sense of caring and personal connection. Today, individuals are able to maintain ties with friends and family through digital media, such as Facebook, where messages are directed to a group of "friends," not to an individual, and where updates on another's life are readily visible and may influence future interactions with those who read the public posts. Over time, members of a relationship develop increasingly predictable communication patterns and, if participants become close, create a relational culture or similar worldview.

In the following pages, Kathleen Galvin and Charles Wilkinson address this complex issue, discussing the communication process as an ongoing symbolic interaction of sharing, exchanging, and coordinating meanings. Through various examples, they apply this understanding of the communication process to explain the difference between specific types of communication, such as interpersonal, impersonal, functional, and nurturing *communication. Finally, they explore and discuss the communication dynamics involved in relational culture, a very specific and unique type of interpersonal communication. This chapter lays the initial groundwork for exploring the question "How does communication work?" and establishes a basis of knowledge that prepares you for the chapters to follow. As you read this chapter, begin to formulate your answer to the question: What is communication?*

■

THE COMMUNICATION PROCESS: IMPERSONAL AND INTERPERSONAL

How often have you heard someone say, "We just can't communicate" or "Jack and I are having communication problems" or "Our group struggles with misunderstandings." These expressions occur regularly in everyday conversations as people struggle to solve a problem, start a relationship, manage a conflict, or find new ways to connect in an established relationship. Such struggles occur in all areas of life, in classrooms and offices, at kitchen tables, in board rooms, and on athletic fields. In our society people of different backgrounds come together to create relationships, solve problems or accomplish tasks, and they can find themselves frustrated by "communication breakdowns." Although these dissatisfactions are not new, they are heightened by the fact that we live in an information age in which effective communication is expected and valued in all areas of life.

Over time we have had the opportunity to listen to many different people discuss their interpersonal frustrations in classrooms, community groups, organizational settings, and family therapy sessions. Participants are invested in improving their abilities to manage certain situations, in analyzing their relationships, and developing new relational skills.

As we discuss interpersonal communication with others, we describe the communication process and its elements as well as the specific characteristics of *inter*personal communication that distinguish it from *im*personal communication. We also address the concept of relational culture,

or the development of a highly unique interpersonal relationship characterized by a unique system of meanings created and maintained by the partners or members of a group. Our hope is to encourage participants to develop their knowledge and skills in relationship development and relationship maintenance in various contexts. We will introduce these issues in the following pages.

THE COMMUNICATION PROCESS

Whenever we ask workshop participants how they would define communication we hear responses such as "transmitting ideas," "talking and listening," or "exchanging messages with others." Everyone has some notion of what it means to communicate with another and knows how it feels when communication attempts are successful or unsuccessful, yet many people have not thought deeply about the communication process itself. They assume communication works or it doesn't work, more as a matter of fate than as a process that can be changed or improved.

Because the communication process is so complex, we could list multiple elaborate and highly technical definitions of it. For our purposes, however, a simple phrase is an appropriate starting point. As we view it, communication is *the symbolic process of sharing meanings*. Because this definition is almost deceptively simple, each of these key words needs to be developed.

Symbolic

By saying that communication is symbolic, we mean that symbols are used to transmit messages. Symbols are representations of a person, event, place, or object. Words, or verbal expressions, are the most frequently understood communication symbols, but symbolic actions also include the whole range of nonverbal behaviors: facial expressions, vocal tone, eye contact, gestures, movement, body posture, appearance, context, and spatial distance. In addition, objects, ideas, and visual images serve symbols. For example, friends often exchange gifts, food, or e-mails as symbols of connectedness.

You have learned to use symbols to create and interpret messages. As a speaker (or sender) you create messages by selecting the most appropriate symbols from a range of options in order to reach your intended receivers most effectively. As a listener (or receiver) you attempt to interpret the symbols others convey to you. Although exchanging appropriate symbols appears rather simple and straight forward, we are constantly amazed at the communication breakdowns that occur as symbols (verbal, nonverbal, and visual) are misinterpreted.

Effective communicators select the most appropriate symbols or messages for specific other persons and effectively interpret the intent of symbols exchanged with others. As a child you learned to create, or encode, one message to ask your father for money and another message to request a loan from your best friend. You learned to interpret your brother's gestures in order to determine if he was feeling sad, worried, or exhausted. You have learned who will be enraged if you roll your eyes at them, and who will interpret, or decode, your nonverbal cue as humorous. For effective communication to occur, the speaker and listener, or sender and receiver, must share the same meanings for the messages they exchange.

Process

Relational communication involves a process—dynamic and continuous process.

Each relationship develops its own communication history, an ongoing history that cannot be rewritten. Someone once said, "It's unfortunate you only get one chance to make a first impression." A relationship begins at the first moment of contact, with the first communication exchanged at a party, in a classroom, in a meeting or online. A relationship is initiated in any number of ways: a question, a glance, an introduction, a smile, or a Facebook invitation. Once contact is made, the relationship begins to develop its own unique history which is constructed and reflected in its communication patterns. A relationship's ongoing development may be interrupted by physical or psychological distance; relational partners may move in and out of each others' lives over many months or many years, but, no matter how long the relationship lasts, the history of the relationship builds from that first meeting. Sometimes people say they wish to start over—to wipe out a difficult time period of their relationship or forget a painful argument that occurred. Individuals may choose to emphasize or deemphasize certain communication events throughout their relational history, but they can never go back to "how things used to be," or delete a piece of that history.

Although some models of communication portray it as a circular process, our preferred model for understanding this process comes from the thinking of Frank Dance (1976, Dance and Zak-Dance 1986), who proposed a helical representation. Imagine the form of a helix, in which the continuousness of the process is represented by the infinity sign (Figure 1.1). This model depicts the ever-widening scope of relationships as participants continuously reencounter each other, a process that continues indefinitely.

Whereas a circular model suggests that communication returns to the same place, the helical model implies the ever-changing, progressive, and evolving nature of relational interactions. The helix representation provides support for the concept that "You can't put a relationship into reverse and erase a difficult period of time." We have stopped counting the times we have heard, "If only things

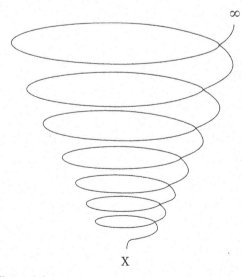

Figure 1-1

could go back to the way they were two years ago." Or "I want to wipe out the last six months of our marriage." In reality each encounter adds experience and meaning to a relationship; this history cannot be denied. People in relationships cannot wipe out a huge hurtful fight, long periods of verbal aggression or silence or, in romantic situations, an affair. Yet most friends, partners, or colleagues can learn to manage their relational history in effective ways, if they are conscious of "working on" or attending to the relationship. Research reveals the importance of relational maintenance efforts such as providing positive messages and assurances, openness, sharing interpersonal networks, sharing tasks, managing conflict, and providing advice and support.

Therefore, a conflictual father and son pair cannot pretend they never hurt one another with words or fists; friends cannot erase sarcastic comments. All they can do is work through the issues that currently keep them from dealing with each other in constructive or caring ways, and attempt to change their present communication patterns as they continue in their relational process. According to the helical model, such constructive interactions should begin to diminish the power of the previous destructive experiences. People can always *choose* to change, to do things differently. Such choices represent one of the most exciting and scary parts of the relational development process.

Sharing

Even though the words "speaker" and "listener" are commonly used to describe communicators, communication is not a process of trading messages. It does not resemble a poor tennis match in which Player A hits the ball and then stands there until Player B hits a return ball, and only then does Player A head toward the spot where the ball might bounce. In a good tennis match both players are always moving, anticipating where the ball might bounce on the return. Symbolic messages do not travel from Person A to Person B and back to Person A again in some turn-taking ritual. Rather, at its most basic level, communication requires mutual and continuous mutual involvement,

sometimes referred to as *the transactional nature of communication*. This mutual influence process is similar to a skilled tennis match in which both players are always in motion based on what they anticipate where the other player's ball will land. Similarly, in communication encounters both parties remain actively involved in the communication process. For example, even though Michael may appear more talkative, Vanessa conveys nonverbally that she is bored or pleased or annoyed, thus influencing Michael's choice of future messages. If Vanessa appears engaged, Michael is likely to continue to talk; if she appears uninterested, he is likely to limit his message. Both are actively and continuously involved in every moment of the interactions thus creating the mutual influence process that characterizes interpersonal interaction. Diagrammed, the transactional nature of communication looks like Figure 1–2.

As relationships develop over time the transactional process becomes more complex. Your perception of another person and that individual's perception of you combine to form a context for your interactions. If you see Person X as warm and supportive, you will relate to him or her in an open manner. Person X is then likely to see you as open and friendly and relate to you with increasing warmth or support. Your perceptions of each other affect each interaction as well as the overall perception of the relationship. The situation can also be reversed, creating a negative context. If you see another person as judgmental or sarcastic, this may lead you to interact in a defensive or combative manner. You both may become caught up in a negative spiral. Every communication exchange occurs within the context of a mutually constructed relationship.

If the definition of a relationship remains relatively unchanged, for example, boss and employee, romantic partners, parent and child, the nature of

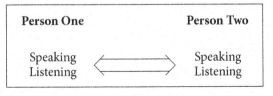

Figure 1-2

the communication process becomes fixed. A boss who constantly relates to staff members as incompetent may stifle their attempts to be innovative. A parent who treats children as responsible fosters their ability to handle new situations. This process is captured in the statement, "Over time we create an image of another person and relate to the image we create." Individuals construct an image of others through their interactions and relate to those realities they constructed. The attempt to understand and adapt to another represents a communication challenge.

Meanings

Although verbal and nonverbal symbols permit us to transmit thoughts and feelings, the symbols must be mutually understood for the meanings to be truly shared. *Common meanings make it possible for us to communicate.* Since there is no absolute standard for all symbols, we are constantly trying to connect with people, even our family members, who do not share exactly the same meanings for the symbols that we use. Therefore it is important to remember the expression "Words don't mean, people do."

Each person's background, including physiological state, individual and family background, and unique experiences, influences how they perceive the world and attach meanings to symbols. The experience of being anxious, nearsighted, athletic, extroverted, dyslexic, artistic, or shy affects how you perceive the world and relate to others. Your family of origin (the family or families in which you were raised) served as your first communication classroom, teaching you how to interpret messages and how to use specific communication strategies to manage key relational issues such as intimacy and conflict. In addition, your gender, cultural background, socioeconomic level, religious, and educational experiences influence your perceptions. Males and females are socialized into various ways to express caring and commitment in relationships. Some cultures value big hugs, multiple-course meals, and shouting voices as symbols of caring; others emphasize restraint and understanding subtle cues. If you grew up in a lower-middle-class neighborhood, you may have different meanings for money than someone who grew up in an affluent community.

Finally, your own unique circumstances influence how you assign meanings. A painful custody battle affects how you consider new romantic relationships. Early school experiences influence how you participate in college classes. Living abroad affects how willing you are to interact with people of different cultures.

Fortunately most people report many similar experiences, but no two people develop the same set of meanings. Each is a unique entity with particular meanings for certain symbols. For you, $100 may represent a *large* purchase for one person, but your partner assumes that only purchases above $500 are *large*. Your nickname for a friend may seem funny to you and insulting to your friend. Avoidance may be viewed as an acceptable or terrible way to resolve conflicts. Breakdowns in communication often occur because of missed meanings. Only with knowledge and empathy can you walk in someone else's shoes, experience the world from a different perspective, and create messages which reflect the other's point of view.

Frequently, communicators focus solely on the words rather than the range of nonverbal messages, which are central to interpreting a speaker's meaning. At any point in time, each communicator contributes to the interaction and experiences the transactional nature of the communication process. Effective communication requires the psychological presence of both parties; their attention and investment in the interaction serves to enhance communication effectiveness.

We find the following simple exercise very useful for demonstrating how individuals may differ in translating the meaning of everyday terms. Imagine yourself saying these phrases to a particular person. Think about exactly what you would hope that other person would respond if you said these words.

I need more *respect* from you.

I feel there is a lack of *trust* in our relationship.

Each of the italicized words receives many different responses. Depending on the speaker, more *respect* may imply: (1) listening to me, (2) asking for my opinion, or (3) following my advice. *Trust* may imply: (1) keeping what I say confidential, (2) telling me your real feelings, or (3) telling me when a painful event happens. These are only examples of the many meanings that people have for the terms "respect" and "trust." Shared meanings are critical because they help to create the context for a relationship in which participants learn to predict how the other will react to particular verbal and nonverbal messages.

INTERPERSONAL COMMUNICATION

Not all communication is truly interpersonal communication. Frequently, you are engaged in impersonal interactions. When you ask for directions, pay for a purchase, or call for a doctor's appointment, you are not automatically involved in interpersonal communication. If you ask a teacher for clarification, discuss a project with a boss, or plan a family reunion with a distant cousin, you may be involved in necessary, functional interactions but you do not share a strong, significant relationship.

Interpersonal communication occurs when two or more people engage in voluntary, ongoing, interdependent interactions that involve meaningful interpretation of verbal and nonverbal messages. This implies that all parties view the relationship as significant, and choose to continue to relate to each other and deepen the relationship over time, making it increasingly unique. Many of these relationships are formed voluntarily, often involving friendships and romantic relationships among peers. In the case of involuntary relationships, such as those with teachers or co-workers, the person with the less power usually adapts to the person in charge, setting up a hierarchical interaction pattern. Yet, even involuntary relationships may develop strong interpersonal ties. You may interact with particular teachers or managers over time, develop a more horizontal interaction pattern, and eventually develop a strong interpersonal relationship.

Relationships move from impersonal to increasingly personal as closeness and trust develops. It is valuable to think about relationships on

Impersonal   **Interpersonal**

Figure 1.3

a continuum from impersonal to interpersonal, understanding that a particular relationship may move forward and backward at different points in time.

Patterns

Communication in ongoing relationships becomes patterned. Some friends can give each other a look, or use a phrase, and their meaning is conveyed. The more intense and personal the relationship, the more unique relational patterns develop. Relational patterns involve verbal and nonverbal communication acts that are recurring and relationship defining. People in highly developed relationships display unique interaction patterns. For example, you may know that you and Tony will joke around when you see each other, whereas you and Alberto will talk about computer games. You may share your romantic problems with Sarah but not with Gail. Observing an ongoing significant relationship, you may see a remarkably complex pattern, similar to a dance, emerge. For example:

X makes a statement, Y answers with a complaint, X makes a joke

A asks for help, B counters with sarcasm, A whines, B assists

C raises a sensitive topic, D looks intently at A, C continues, D listens quietly

In his book *Couplehood* (p. 202), Paul Reiser describes numerous examples of everyday patterns between partners.

Like all businesses, couples engage in endless meetings to discuss areas of management concern and division of labor.

"You know, we really should call the post office and tell them to hold our mail while we're away."

"*We?* You mean *me*, don't you?"

"No, I mean *we*. I didn't say 'you.' I said '*we*.' You *or* me."

"Oh, really? Are *you* going to ever call the post office?"

A moment to think. "No."

"Then you mean 'me,' don't you?"

"Yeah."

Some version of this interaction pattern may occur weekly between these partners as they negotiate tasks.

FUNCTIONAL AND NURTURING COMMUNICATION

Everyday communication tends to be dominated by functional rather than nurturing interactions. *Functional communication* involves managing day to day necessities and exchanging impersonal information such as, getting plans coordinated, meals fixed, schedules arranged—all the details that keep life running smoothly. We estimate that 80 to 90 percent of the communication that goes on between friends or colleagues, parents and children, and even spouses or partners tends to be functional communication. If the necessary and desirable functional interactions are not accompanied by communication that is *more personal*, distance characterizes the impersonal ties.

Nurturing communication occurs when participants exchange messages that are caretaking of the relationship—messages that indicate that the relationship is valued. Such nurturing communication may include intimate relational currencies such as: a hug, a thinking-of-you text message, affectionate teasing, or a label of "best friend." Nurturing communication involves emotional closeness and open conversation. People who nurture each other confirm the other's existence— "You are there; I recognize you."

Everyone needs to experience nurturing messages. Coworkers, friends, and family members can all be involved some level of this supportive communication. Individuals who have been nurtured are likely to be good nurturers; those who have not been nurtured can learn to nurture others, but often this takes conscious effort and hard work. Nurturing communication serves as the life blood of any significant relationship. Without it, the relationship remains static and functional; with it, the relationship renews itself through continual growth.

RELATIONAL CULTURE

Persons in strong, highly developed interpersonal relationships eventually create their own *relational culture*. Julia Wood (2007) captures the essence of a relational culture as "a private world of rules, understandings, meanings, and patterns of acting and interpreting that partners create for their relationship"(p.308). Relational cultures involve a jointly constructed worldview, a personally developed set of understandings that affect the attitudes, actions, and identities of the relational partners. Over time many partners or best friends adapt to each other until they experience an evolving, unique set of meanings that are reflected in their relational culture. These private meanings, conveyed verbally and nonverbally, separate the partnership from other relationships; nicknames, joint storytelling, inside jokes, and code words contribute to the creation of a "world built for two." Relational cultures are constructed, maintained, or changed through communication. A strong relational culture is the hallmark of an intense, intimate interpersonal relationship.

In a world of many stresses and changes, we need our relationships to sustain us and nourish us as human beings. Communication is central to the process of constructing meaningful and fulfilling relational support. The ability to build and nurture such relationships is a critical life skill, one to be learned and valued.

REFERENCES

Dance, F. E. X., & Larson, C. (1976). *The functions of human communication: A theoretical approach.* New York, NY: Holt, Rinehart & Winston.

Dance, F. E. X., & Zak-Dance, C. (1986). *Public speaking.* New York, NY: Harper & Row.

Reiser, P. (1994). *Couplehood.* New York, NY: Bantam Books.

Wood, J. (2007). *Interpersonal communication* (5th ed.). Belmont, CA: Thomson/Wadsworth.

QUESTIONS/THOUGHTS

1. Identify and describe a relationship you have observed that exhibits high levels of nurturing messages. Give examples of three different types and the situations in which these currencies are used.

2. Think about a situation in which two or more differences in the communicator's backgrounds (e.g., gender, culture, age, socioeconomic status, religion) contributed to misunderstandings. Describe one communication breakdown identifying differences that led to misunderstandings or serious problems.

3. How does the helical model of communication relate to your life? Think about communication in a significant relationship in your life that has included difficult or frustrating experiences. Describe how you and the other person have managed to deal with painful or conflictual times in your relational history and continued to move on.

2

Principles of Interpersonal Communication

JULIA T. WOOD

A famous saying asserts, "The last creature to discover water would be a fish." Fish spend their lives
swimming in water, a taken-for-granted environment. Because humans live in a world in which
communication is ubiquitous, or surrounds us,
usually we take it for granted and do not stop to
consider how communication influences our everyday lives and how effectively or ineffectively we
communicate with others in our lives. Yet we also
spend much of our lives watching and listening to
others as we negotiate each day's activities.

Most people seldom stop to consider the complexity of the communication process. If such
moments of reflection do occur, they are likely
brought about by unusual experiences that force
us to stop and reflect on what just happened or
what might happen. Those of you who have grown
up speaking another language than English or who
lived in a non-English speaking country or community for a period of time were forced to think about
communication when you encountered confusion
or difficulty as you interacted with English speakers. You had to reflect on what might account for
the confusion, and what alternative means, such as
nonverbal signals or a local interpreter, you could

use to accomplish your goals. You had to attend to
the communication process.

In addition to issues of language use, there are
moments of wonder or frustration created through
communication interactions that also catch our
attention. This may include a first social encounter
with a friend of a friend that lasted for hours because
you identified so many similarities in backgrounds,
interests, or beliefs that your conversation flowed
easily and with excitement. The reverse may occur
also. You could find yourself discussing a serious
issue, such as immigration or religion, with a good
friend when sharp differences emerge and you find
your friend's position totally unpredictable and
unacceptable. You may be left wondering how this
friendship could have developed without recognizing
such areas of difference. In either case, the communication process emerges as an area of reflection.

Many individuals believe communication just
happens naturally; there is no need to study it or think
about it. Yet, in our current world we are surrounded
by communication breakdowns among individuals,
groups, and nations that necessitate extensive informal or formal interactions aimed at reducing the tensions that endanger relationships and, in some cases,

lives. Communication breakdowns between professionals and clients result in patients who receive poor levels of medical care or students who misunderstand teachers' expectations. Friends and family members encounter countless confusions due to unclear or unexpressed expectations or demands.

Today, increasing numbers of students are enrolling in graduate and undergraduate communication classes because they recognize the needs for such a background due to experiences in their workplace or in their personal lives. They are not looking for simple answers or simple tricks; rather they are searching for ways to think about human interaction, for theories and concepts to help them analyze communicative situations, and for a set of communication competencies that will serve them well in the future. These students hope to be better pediatricians, science teachers, office managers, and travel agents. They need to work well in professional groups as they design bridges, create computer applications and tend to patients. Some hope to improve communication with their parents or their children, partners, or close friends.

Some of these students become fascinated with the concept of metacommunication, or communication about communication, because they never really thought about the skill of "going to the meta level," talking with a boss or child about the way communication in their relationship is working. Others learn to appreciate the complexity of meaning and learn to pay close attention to the context or learn to ask for feedback on their communication attempts. Many students had not considered the issues of interpersonal ethics and the impact that their messages might have on another person. Essentially these students become much more reflective about their communication as well as more skilled in interaction. Finally, some students come to believe that they can learn to change the ways they interact with others, instead of just reacting to situations without considering the impact of their messages.

In the following chapter the author, Julia Wood, describes eight principles of communication, some of which may surprise you or challenge your beliefs about the communication process. She begins by reminding you that communication is ubiquitous, a constant in life, and ends with the hopeful assertion that interpersonal communication effectiveness can be learned. In between, you will understand the critical importance of metacommunication and the ongoing importance of interpersonal across your lifespan, among other ideas. These principles will serve you well as you move through the later chapters in the text.

Our first look at interpersonal communication suggests eight basic principles for effectiveness.

PRINCIPLE 1: WE CANNOT NOT COMMUNICATE

Whenever people are together, they communicate. We cannot avoid communicating when we are with others, because they interpret what we do and say as well as what we do and don't say. Even if we choose to be silent, we're communicating. What we mean by silence and how others interpret it depend on cultural backgrounds.

Because Westerners typically are more verbal than many cultural groups, they are likely to regard silence as a signal of lack of knowledge, anger, or disinterest. Some Native Americans and members of many Eastern cultures might interpret some silence as thoughtfulness or respect. Either way, silence communicates.

Even when we don't intend to communicate, we do so. We may be unaware of a grimace that gives away our disapproval or an eye roll that shows we dislike someone, but we are communicating nonetheless. Unconscious communication often occurs on the relationship level of meaning as we express feelings about others through the subtle, often nonverbal communication. Regardless of whether we aim to communicXate and whether others understand our intentions, we continuously, unavoidably communicate.

PRINCIPLE 2: INTERPERSONAL COMMUNICATION IS IRREVERSIBLE

Perhaps you have been in heated arguments in which you lost your temper and said something you later regretted. It could be that you hurt someone or revealed something about yourself that you meant to keep private. Later, you might have tried to repair the damage by apologizing, explaining what you said, or denying what you revealed. But you couldn't erase your communication; you couldn't unsay what you said. You may have had similar experiences when communicating by email. Perhaps you read a message that made you mad, and you dashed off a pointed reply, sent it, and then wished you could unsend it. The fact that communication is irreversible reminds is that what we say and do matters. It has impact. Once we say something to another person, our words become part of the relationship. Remembering this principle keeps us aware of the importance of choosing when to speak and what to say—or not to say!

PRINCIPLE 3: INTERPERSONAL COMMUNICATION INVOLVES ETHICAL CHOICES

Ethics is the branch of philosophy that focuses on moral principles and codes of conduct. Ethical issues concern right and wrong. Because interpersonal communication is irreversible and affects others, it always has ethical implications. What we say and do affects others: how they feel, how they perceive themselves, how they think about themselves, and how they think about others. Thus, responsible people think carefully about ethical guidelines for communication. For instance, should you not tell someone something that might make him less willing to do what you want? If you read a message in a chat room that makes you angry, do you fire off a nasty reply, assuming that you will never meet the person and so won't face any consequences? Do you judge another person's communication from your own individual perspective and experience? Or do you try to understand her communication on her terms and from her perspective? In work settings, should you avoid giving negative feedback because it cold hurt others' feelings? In these and many other instances, we face ethical choices.

Richard Johannesen (1996) has devoted most of his career to studying the ethical aspects of human communication. He says that ethical communication occurs when people create relationships of equality, when they attend mindfully to each other, and when their communication demonstrates that they are authentic, empathic, supportive, and confirming of each other. Because interpersonal communication affects us and others, ethical considerations are always part of our interactions. Throughout this book, we note ethical issues that arise when we interact with others. As you read, consider what kinds of choices you make and what moral principles guide your choices.

PRINCIPLE 4: PEOPLE CONSTRUCT MEANINGS IN INTERPERSONAL COMMUNICATION

Human beings construct the meanings of their communication. The significance of communication doesn't lie in words and nonverbal behaviors. Instead, meaning arises out of how we interpret communication. This calls our attention to the fact that humans use symbols, which sets us apart from other creatures.

Symbols, such as words, have no inherently true meanings. Instead, we must interpret them. What does it mean if someone says, "You're sick"? To interpret the comment, you must consider the context (a counseling session, a professional meeting, after a daredevil stunt), who said it (a psychiatrist, a supervisor, a subordinate, a friend, an enemy), and the words themselves, which may mean various things (a medical diagnosis, a challenge to your professional competence, a compliment on your zaniness, disapproval).

In interpersonal communication, people continuously interpret each other. Although typically we're not aware that we assign meanings, inevitably we do so. Someone you have been dating suggests some time away from each other, a friend turns down invitations to get together, or your supervisor at work seems less open to conversations with you than in the past. The meanings of such communications are neither self-evident nor inherent in the words. Instead, we construct their significance. In close relationships, partners gradually coordinate meanings so that they share understandings of issues and feelings important to their connection. When a relationship begins, one person may regard confrontation as healthy, and the other may avoid arguments. Over time, partners come to share meanings for conflict—what it is, how to handle it, and whether it threatens the relationship or is a path to growth.

The meanings we attribute to conflict and other aspects of communication are shaped by cultural backgrounds. Because standing up for your own ideas is emphasized in the United States, many people who were born and raised in this country value confrontation more than do many Asians who were raised in traditional Asian families. Conflict means different things to each group.

> BYRON: Sometimes my buddies and I will call each other the "boy" or even "black boy," and we know we're just kidding around. But if a white calls me "boy," I get real mad. It doesn't mean the same thing when they call is "boy" that it does when we call ourselves "boy."

Even one person's meanings vary over time and in response to experiences and moods. If you're in a good mood, a playful gibe might strike you as funny or as an invitation to banter. The same remark might hurt or anger you if you're feeling down. The meaning of the gibe, like all communication, is not preset or absolute. Meanings are created by people as they communicate in specific contexts.

PRINCIPLE 5: METACOMMUNICATION AFFECTS MEANINGS

The word *metacommunication* comes from the prefix *meta*, meaning "about," and the root word *communication*. Thus, *metacommunciation* is communication about communication. For example, during a conversation with your friend Pat, you notice that Pat's body seems tense and her voice is sharp. You might say, "You seem really stressed." Your statement metacommunicates about Pat's nonverbal communication.

Metacommunication may be verbal or nonverbal. We can use words to talk about other words or nonverbal behaviors. If an argument between Joe and Marc gets out of hand, and Joe makes a nasty personal attack, Joe might say, "I didn't really mean what I just said. I was so angry it came out." This metacommunication may soften the hurt caused by the attack. If Joe and Marc then have a productive conversation about their differences, Marc might conclude by saying, "This has really been a good talk. I think we understand each other a lot better now." This comment verbally metacommunicates about the conversation that preceded it.

We also metacommunicate nonverbally. Nonverbal metacommunication often reinforces verbal communication. For example, you might nod your head while saying, "I really don't know what you mean." Or you might move away from a person after you say, "I don't want to see you anymore." Yet, not all nonverbal metacommunication reinforces verbal messages. Sometimes, our nonverbal expressions contradict our verbal messages. When teasing a friend, you might wink to signal you don't mean the teasing to be taken seriously. Or you might smile when you say to a friend who drops by, "Oh rats—you again!" The smile tells the friend you welcome the visit despite your comment to the contrary.

Metacommunication can increase understanding. For instance, teachers sometimes say, "The next point is really important." This comment signals students to pay special attention to what follows. A parent might tell a child, "What I said may sound harsh, but I'm only telling you because I care about you." The comment tells the child how to interpret a critical message. A manager tells a subordinate to take a comment seriously by saying, "I really mean what I said. I'm not kidding." On the other hand, if we're not really sure what we think about an issue, and we want to try out a stance, we might say, "I'm thinking this through as I go, and I'm not really wedded to this position, but what I tend to believe right now is…." This preface to your statement tells listeners not to assume that what you say is set in stone.

We can also metacommunicate to check on understanding: "Was I clear?" "Do you see why I feel like I do?" "Can you see why I'm confused about the problem?" Questions such as these allow you to find out whether another person understands what you intend to communicate. You may also metacommunicate to find out whether you understand what another person expresses to you. "What I think you meant is that you are worried. Is that right?" "If I follow what you said, you feel trapped between what you want to do and what your parents want you to do. Is that what you were telling me?" You may even say, "I don't understand what you just told me. Can you say it another way?" This question metacommunicates by letting the other person know you did not grasp her message and that you want to understand.

Effective metacommunication also helps friends and romantic partners express how they feel about their interactions. Linda Acitelli (1988, 1993) has studied what happens when partners in a relationship talk to each other about how they perceive and feel about their interaction. She reports that women and men alike find metacommunication helpful if there is a conflict or problem that must be addressed. Both sexes seem to appreciate knowing how the other feels about their differences; they are also eager to learn how to communicate to resolve those differences. During a conflict, one person might say, "I feel like we're both being really stubborn. Do you think we could each back off a little from our positions?" This expresses discontent with how communication is proceeding and offers an alternative. After conflict, one partner might say, "This really cleared the air between us. I feel a lot better now."

> TARA: I never feel like an argument is really over and settled until Andy and I have said that we feel better for having thrashed out whatever was the problem. It's like I want closure, and the fight isn't really behind us until we both say, "I'm glad we talked," or something to say what we went through led us to a better place.

Acitelli also found that women are more likely than men to appreciate metacommunication when there is no conflict or immediate problem to be resolved. While curled up on a sofa and watching TV, a woman might say to her male partner, "I really feel comfortable snuggling with you." This comments on the relationship and on the nonverbal communication between the couple. According to research by Acitelli and others (Wood, 1997, 1998), men generally find talk about relationships unnecessary unless there is an immediate problem to be addressed. Understanding this gender difference in preferences for metacommunication may help you interpret members of the other sex more accurately.

PRINCIPLE 6: INTERPERSONAL COMMUNICATION DEVELOPS AND SUSTAINS RELATIONSHIPS

Interpersonal communication is the primary way we build, refine, and transform relationships. Partners talk to work out expectations and understandings of their interaction, appropriate and inappropriate topics and styles of communicating, and the nature of the relationship itself. Is it a friendship or a romantic relationship? How much and in what ways can we count on each other? How do we handle disagreements—by confronting them, ignoring them, or using indirect strategies to restore harmony? What are the bottom lines, the "shalt not" rules for what counts as unforgivable betrayal? What counts as caring—words, deeds, both? Because communication has no intrinsic meanings, we must generate our own in the course of interaction.

Communication also allows us to construct or reconstruct individual and joint histories. For instance, when people fall in love, they often redefine former loves as "mere infatuations" or "puppy love" but definitely not the real thing. When something goes wrong in a relationship, partners may work together to define what happened in a way that allows them to continue. Marriage counselors report that couples routinely work out face-saving explanations for affairs so that they can stay together in the aftermath of infidelity (Scarf, 1987). Partners often talk about past events and experiences that challenged the, and ones that were joyous. The process of reliving the past reminds partners how long they have been together and how much they have shared.

As partners communicate thoughts and feelings, they generate shared meanings for themselves, their interaction, and their relationship.

Communication is also the primary means by which intimates construct a future for themselves, and a vision of shared future is one of the most powerful ties that link people (Dixson & Duck, 1993; Wood, 2006). Romantic couples often dream together by talking about the family they plan and how they'll be in 20 years. Likewise, friends discuss plans for the future and promise reunions if they must move apart. Communication allows us to express and share dreams, imaginings, and memories and to weave all of these into the joint world of relational patterns.

> KAREN: I love talking about the future with my fiancé. Sometimes, we talk for hours about the kind of house we'll have and what our children will be like and how we'll juggle two careers and a family. I know everything won't work out exactly like we think now, but talking about it makes me feel so close to Dave and like our future is real.

PRINCIPLE 7: INTERPERSONAL COMMUNICATION IS NOT A PANACEA

As we have seen, we communicate to satisfy many of our needs and to create relationships with others. Yet it would be a mistake to think communication is a cure-all. Many problems can't be solved by talk alone. Communication by itself won't end hunger, abuses of human rights around the globe, racism, intimate partner violence, or physical diseases. Nor can words alone bridge irreconcilable differences between people or erase the hurt of betrayal. Although good communication may increase understanding and help us solve problems, it will not fix everything. We should also realize that the idea of talking things through is distinctly Western. Not all societies think it's wise or useful to communicate about relationships or to talk extensively about feelings. Just as interpersonal communication has many strengths and values, it also has limits, and its effectiveness is shaped by cultural contexts.

PRINCIPLE 8: INTERPERSONAL EFFECTIVENESS CAN BE LEARNED

It is a mistake to think that effective communicators are born, that some people have a natural talent and others don't. Although some people have extraordinary talent in athletics and writing, all of us can become competent athletes and writers. Likewise, some people have an aptitude for communicating, but all of us can become competent communicators. This book and the course you are taking should sharpen your understandings of how interpersonal communication works and should help you learn skills that will enhance your effectiveness in relating to others.

QUESTIONS/THOUGHTS

1. Describe three situations in which you heard a communicator use metacommunication. Briefly explain the circumstances, describe what the individual said that called for metacommunication, and the impact of metacommunication on the effectiveness of the ongoing interactions.

2. Under what conditions have you observed others attempting to make ethical choices about what they are saying? Describe one situation and explain what you believe was the effect of such an attempt. Under what circumstances do you find yourself having to consider the ethical impact of your messages?

3. What is your position on the following claim: "Great communicators are born, not made." Give reasons for your position.

REFERENCES

Acitelli, L. (1993). You, me, and us: Perspectives on relationship awareness. In S. W. Duck (Ed.), *Understanding relationship processes: Vol. 1. Individuals in relationships* (pp. 144–174). Newbury Park, CA: Sage.

Acitelli, L. (1998). When spouses talk to each other about their relationship. *Journal of Social and Personal Relationships, 5,* 185–199.

Dixson, M., & Duck, S. W. (1993). Understanding relationship processes: Uncovering the human search for meaning. In S. W. Duck (Ed.), *Understanding relationship processes: Vol. 1. Individuals in relationships* (pp. 175–206). Newbury Park, CA: Sage.

Johannesen, R. (1996). *Ethics in human communication* (4th ed.). Prospect Heights, IL: Waveland.

Scarf, M. (1987). *Intimate partners*. New York, NY: Random House.

Wood, J. T. (1997). Clarifying the issues. *Personal Relationships, 4*, 221–228.

Wood, J. T. (1998). *But I thought you meant…: Misunderstandings in human communication*. Mountain View, CA: Mayfield.

The Relational Perspective

WILLIAM W. WILMOT

Metaphors provide a lens for viewing relationships. In his writings, communication scholar William (Bill) Wilmot frequently uses a dance metaphor to capture the dynamics of relational communication. Edna Rogers (2008), who also uses a dance metaphor for understanding relationships, asserts that "individual message behaviors are an essential "part" in the creation of an interpersonal dance..." (p. 336). In the following piece, William Wilmot suggests that "a relationship exists when the participants construct a mental view of it." Without the relational conceptions of both people, there is no way to know what type of relationship exists or even if one exists at all. These perceptions contribute to the creation of a relational world.

One of the ways to understand relationships is to think about the language people use to describe and discuss them. Wilmot writes about relational minicultures in ways that will remind you of the concept of relational culture. He stresses the importance of metaphors, narratives, and idioms as tools for understanding relationships.

Metaphors provide a way of talking about very complex and abstract ideas. A relationship depicted as a "rock" conveys a very different message from

one described as a "house of cards." Relationship narratives or stories help both participants and outsiders to make sense of their world. In addition, "People build and communicate their relationships, cultures, and identities, in part, through the stories they tell" (Koenig Kellas, 2008, p. 241). Stories reflect where the relationship has been; they also have an impact on the future of the relationship. The use of idioms reinforces the special nature of the relationship and conveys this to the outside world. Finally, participants in a relationship can understand that relationship better by examining the symbols of relational identity, for example, activities, places, or artifacts.

In this chapter William Wilmot discusses what relationships are, how one can learn to define them, and ways in which to conceptually think of them. He describes relationships as "private minicultures," which, through metaphors, narratives, idioms, and symbols of identity, take shape and provide meaning for the individuals involved. Combining theory with examples, the author illustrates the complex role that the relationship plays in relational communication. As you read this chapter consider the following question: What is a metaphor or mental image that you would use to describe each of three relationships in your life?

REFERENCES

Koenig Kellas, J. (2008). Narrative theories. In L. A. Baxter & D. O. Braithwaite (Eds.), *Engaging theories in interpersonal communication* (pp. 241–254). Thousand Oaks, CA: Sage.

Rogers, L. E. (2008). Relational communication theory. In L. A. Baxter & D. O. Braithwaite (Eds.), *Engaging theories in interpersonal communication* (pp. 335–347). Thousand Oaks, CA: Sage.

Relationships are like a dance. The two partners dance close some times, far apart at others. When they are doing the same dance (like cowboy swing) it works fine. And, similarly to a dance, each relationship has its own form, flow, challenges, disruptions, and recoveries. With relationship partners in synchrony, the flow and synergistic energy elevate both. The dance becomes a thing of beauty to watch, and it looks easy. Often, however, one partner wants to do cowboy swing while the other insists on the foxtrot. And if both insist on doing their own dance, they will struggle, flounder, and fall.

For most of us, our personal relationships with family, friends, work colleagues, and romantic partners sometimes flow and sometimes trip us up—they are among the most fulfilling and frustrating events of our lives. This is reflected by college students, for example, in that the most frequent topic of conversation is romantic relationships (Haas & Sherman, 1982). Our personal relationships ebb and flow throughout our entire life span, yet our knowledge about them is often not equal to the challenges they bring us....

WHAT *IS* A RELATIONSHIP?

In the 1800s, not much time was spent by people discussing the "state of our relationship," whereas these days relationships are discussed over coffee and lunch, in college courses, and in the mass media. Just scan the magazines in the grocery store and you'll see articles on "how to make love last," "moving from lovers to friends," and "getting your

family to talk to you." Whether people openly discuss relationships or not, participants are in a relationship when they have a "sense of being in a relationship" (Duck, 1988, p. 2). The crucial difference isn't whether some outside social scientist thinks you are in a relationship by some academic criteria (Hinde, 1979), but *a relationship exists when the participants construct a mental view of it.* Those mental images of the relationship occur on many levels.

At the most basic level, Level I, a relationship occurs when there is a mutual recognition of being perceived. Whether it is someone across the aisle in a theatre, or having coffee with a best friend, we become aware of being in a relationship when communication processing is reciprocal. At this first level, a "relationship" is formed when:

1. You and another are behaving;
2. You are aware of his/her behavior, and at the same time
3. The other is aware of your behavior;
4. As a result,
   a. you are aware that the other is aware of you
   b. the other is aware that you are aware of him/her.

People are in a relationship when each *has the perception of being perceived*—when both persons can say "I see you seeing me."

At the more complex level, Level II, relationship awareness occurs over and above the specific cues being sent and received—you treat the relationship as having a *past, present, and future.* As Leatham and Duck (1990) say, "You have a relationship when the partners believe in the *future* of it." A relationship emerges from its history and continually reemerges and transforms over time—continually changing. Thus, you may not be sending messages to your parents, nor they to you, but you would say that you are "in a relationship" with them. You name the relationship by things such as "I am her son" or some other relationship marker to signify its existence. Level II awareness arises from cumulative interactions with a particular person so that you "name" the relationship—it becomes a reality that transcends the particular communication messages being sent. At Level II, people speak of relationships "declining," "improving," and "being flat"—clearly relationships are conceptual realities.

Understanding a relationship is much like reading a short story or novel. As we move through time, new information is integrated into our interpretation of the events of the past and makes a difference in the present and our projections about the future. Relationship processing, however, is much more complex, because our interpretations of ongoing events affect how we respond and how others respond to us. As Fletcher and Fincham (1991a) say, "Thus, participants' interpretations of events are part of the changing flux of events as individuals mutually influence each other" (p. 79).

When we enter into a relational world, it is no longer exclusively our own—the other person is considered in the acts we do; there is no such thing as individual behavior not influenced by the relational context from which it springs. Each person's perceptions influence the relationship, because each participant affects and is affected by the other. At Level II, we integrate previous communication exchanges by constructing a view of them and projecting into the future. Thus, while relationships are derived from previous communicative exchanges, it is our mental images of them that create their reality for us. One young man who lives alone has a girlfriend in a small town out of state. She is an incredibly good shopper who can find bargains. When he goes to the local discount store to buy food, as he cruises the aisles looking for bargains and comes upon an item, he can imagine her saying, "Now, *that* is a good value." He brings his past experiences of shopping with her and pushes them forward in time to the current shopping trip. An example of this sort of "carrying the relationship with you" occurs when you imagine the reaction of parents or friends to something you have done. Whenever you think about someone's reaction, you are drawing upon past experience and pulling it forward in time.

RELATIONSHIPS AS MINICULTURES
Relationships are "private minicultures" where participant perceptions of the relationship are

its reality (Fitzpatrick & Indvik, 1982). The perceived reality of relationships builds over time for the participants. And, further, as we move to new relationships, different aspects of ourselves are activated. In a true sense, each relationship is unique, calling forth diverse elements from each participant.

Relationship participants need to "make sense" of their relationships, because relationships are more than the sum of the individual parts. When two people have a relationship, there is a "third party"—the relationship itself—which has a life of its own. This synergistic creation is built by the participants yet goes beyond them. As Humphreys says, "There is no such thing as two, for no two things can be conceived without their relationship, and this makes three" (Humphreys, 1951).

Each relationship is a "miniculture," with its own norms and rules (Morton & Douglas, 1981). In all pairings, such as teacher-student, mother-son, friend-friend, or doctor-patient, the participants have their own conception of the relationship, their own "relational miniculture" that encompasses what they do and who they are to one another. These created "relational minicultures" are particular to the relationship and are more rich and complex than the general labels we all learn (such as "friend," "romantic partner," "family member"). The relationship partners develop a label, or metaphor, for their relationship, replete with its own system of obligations and rights (Hinde, 1979). There are times, of course, when one partner sees the relationship one way and the other another way—and these contrasting or *asymmetric* definitions also comprise the miniculture (Neimeyer & Neimeyer, 1985). Sometimes, a continual disagreement about the nature of a relationship (I want to be friends/I want to be lovers) may be a central feature of the relationship.

Metaphors for Relationships
People's metaphors about relationships supply meaning for those relationships. We use metaphors when we compare one thing to something else. For example, if you are in a "stormy" romantic relationship, you are comparing the relationship to the weather, emphasizing the bad weather at

times. Describing a work relationship or marriage as a "battleground" conveys a different image than the metaphor "game" or "partnership."

When an ongoing relationship does *not* have an agreed-upon definition, it brings conflict and discord. Jackson says that "in a pathologic relationship we see…a constant sabotaging or refusing of the other's attempts to define the relationship" (Jackson, 1959). And Weick notes the same effects in organizations: "One of the major causes of failure in organizations is a shortage of images concerning what they are up to, a shortage of time devoted to producing these images, and a shortage of diverse actions to deal with changed circumstance" (Weick, 1979). Some overlap in the definitions is necessary so the participants can have coordinated action, a sense of common purpose, and agreement about "who they are."

The choice of metaphor or image for a relationship evokes a feel for the dynamics of a relationship. If a man describes his marriage as an "endangered species," it conveys a fragile, close-to-extinction nature of the relationship. Themes that emerge in ongoing relationships have been explored by Owen. He notes that thematic interpretation becomes a way to understand "relational life." For instance, "A male and female meet as 'friends,' become 'daters,' then 'lovers,' perhaps finally becoming a 'married couple' making transitions to the different relationship states or definitions primarily through communication." In his study composed of married couples, romantic dating partners, sets of relatives, sets of live-in friends, and groups of friends not living together, Owen identified some central determinants that participants use to make interpretative sense of relationships (Owen, 1984a). The participants saw their relationships illustrating the following:

1. *Commitment*—dedication to this particular relationship in spite of difficult times.
2. *Involvement*—some relationships, such as marriage and family relationships, demand more involvement than others.
3. *Work*—relationships require more "work" to keep them functioning in a healthy manner.

4. *Unique-Special*—this bolsters the belief that the participants have "beat the odds" and survived a "breakup."
5. *Fragile*—for dating couples, the fragile nature of the relationship is paramount, whereas for married couples it helps them feel they have "held it together."
6. *Consideration-Respect*—married couples primarily saw respect as an important gauge of the relationship, whereas others did not.
7. *Manipulation*—women who were dating especially noted that the person might be "playing games" or "using others" in dates (Owen, 1984a).

Owen notes that relationships vary according to these themes—they are the dimensions the participants use to make "sense" out of the relational experience. And it has been suggested by Wilmot and Hocker (1993) that actively working to alter couples' metaphors can help bring change into a married relationship.

One other piece of work on metaphors for relationships has been offered by Baxter (1992b). She classified people's descriptions of heterosexual couples into four root metaphors. People saw their relationships as (1) work-exchange, (2) journey-organism, (3) force-danger, and (4) game. If you characterize your cross-sex romance as work-exchange, it connotes a process of effort and coordination, whereas seeing it as journey-organism suggests an ever-changing process of growth. Characterizing a relationship in terms of force-danger implies that it is a risky undertaking where you can be hurt and have limited control, whereas seeing it as a game suggests that romance is a set of scripts where you can win or lose (Baxter, 1992).

The parties to a relationship also reflect their "miniculture" by manifesting (1) narratives, (2) relationship idioms, and (3) symbols of relationship identity.

Relationship Narratives

People share narratives or stories about their relationships. Whether a fellow is complaining about his boss, celebrating his newfound love, or wanting to be closer to his brother, he talks about relationships in many ways. When you say, "Gee, she sure isn't the friend I thought she was. When she left me downtown, I had to walk home," you are providing a story or a narrative about a relationship.

What is a narrative? It is a story, telling about a unique event or series of events (Van Kijk, 1985). Narratives organize and synthesize a jumbled set of events into an understandable sequence and come in many forms. Narrative texts are such things as short stories, diaries, and even novels or biographies. For our purposes here, however, we will focus on oral narrative—when you talk about a relationship to someone else. The relationship narratives we share with others usually are conversational stories about important events (Polanyi, 1985)—the struggle with your sister, the special time with your parents, the exhilaration of a new love relation, the fun times you had with your friends over spring break, or the breakup of a love affair. I would guess (since there is scant research on it right now) that most narratives are about turmoil and trouble—how to deal with the difficult boss, how to get freedom from your parents (or children), what to do when you fall out of love, or how to cope when someone you love suddenly stops seeing you without any explanation....

Narratives not only reflect your reaction to a relationship, they also impact the future course of it. When you say, "It was a fine vacation—we love going to the North Fork," it tends to reinforce the positive features of the relationship. Similarly, if one spends a great deal of time criticizing a love relationship partner, that tends to further solidify your negative view of it. In the most dramatic cases, when an ex-spouse says, "My ex-husband and I are enemies since the divorce," it not only reflects the current reality but reinforces this view each time she complains about him.

Not only do our experiences of the relationship change, our accounts and representations of it also change. Relationships tend to flow like the wind—ever changing. To bring some order to the ever-fluctuating reality, people activate "memory structures" about their relationships. They can generate and write down typical communication events and order their relationships across time

(Honeycutt, Cantril, & Greene, 1989). Further, the narratives about the relationship change across time. The person who has fallen wildly in love gives you a far different picture of the relationship today than he or she [will] a year following the breakup. We reformulate our memories about our relationships quite dramatically (Duck, 1988). In the Duck and Miell (1986) studies comparing contemporary accounts of first meetings with subsequent retrospective accounts, they found people giving different accounts of where they first met. And as Duck (1988, p. 112) says, "Surra reports that about 30 percent of one of her samples of married couples were in disagreement with their own partner by more than one year about when they first had sexual intercourse together!" And, of course, when a breakup occurs people tend to alter their representation of the entire history of the relationship....

Narratives, being so commonplace, obviously serve important functions for the participants. First, they serve functions *for the storyteller*. By "telling our story" we come to understand our own confusing experiences (Surra, 1987; Veroff, 1993). In fact, some people state, "I don't know what I feel until I talk about it!" In a sense, *all* stories can be seen as "narratives of the self." Telling a story (1) reinforces your view of yourself, (2) contrasts you to others ("he is such a scumbag; I can't believe he stole money from his mother"), and (3) allows you to transform yourself by talk. It is well known that people in crisis "need to talk"— they have to tell their story, to "let it out" and start the process of adjustment to the changes....

Second, in addition to "saving face" for the storyteller, narratives create "*acceptable public and private accounts*" of the events. In the case of romantic breakups, Duck (1982) argues that verbal accounts serve as "grave dressing." When the relationship is over, one of the last stages you go through is "telling a story," a narrative, about the relationship. You do that to both save face and bring further changes for yourself, *and* to create public versions of the relationship for the consumption of others.

Farrell (1984) suggests that the narratives are designed to "delight, instruct, or move the listener" (p. 174). Grandparents who tell stories to their grandchildren can be seen as passing on family values and history. The tried-and-maybe-true story of the parents or grandparents walking through the blizzard to make it to the schoolhouse is a way to tell the progeny about the importance of getting an education—even in a blizzard. My father used to tell me about "going to town" when he was a child twice a year from the homestead in Wyoming and having five cents to spend on candy. Clearly, relationship narratives (or "accounts," as the social science researchers prefer to call them), are "presentational"—they serve as a way to present an event (Duck & Pond, 1991).

As a listener to a narrative, you too have a communication role to perform. You need to (1) agree to hear the story, (2) refrain from taking a turn except to make remarks about the relationship under discussion, and (3) at the end of the storytelling, demonstrate your understanding of it (Polanyi, 1985). In a sense, the active listener ("Yeah, I see; then what did he say to you?") participates as a "co-author," urging the other on (Mandelbaum, 1989).

What about the accuracy of narratives? Rather than ask about accuracy, it is more informative to focus on the degree of overlap in the two people's narratives. If Russell and Susan tell similar stories about their romantic relationship, that is evidence that they have some agreement about important relationship marker events. If both, for example, tell about the time they went winter camping and didn't take enough food and both laugh about it, then it indicates how they are "together" in this view. If the story is a "collaborative effort" (Veroff et al., 1993), it indicates the cooperation between the two. On the other hand, if they have relational difficulties or break up, you can rest assured that Russell will tell one story and Susan another. The "narrative overlap" is an indicator of the "we-ness" of the relationship; conjoint stories indicate more closeness and agreement, while divergent stories indicate people who are defining themselves as more separate and independent. One of the differences between men and women is that, in recalling past events in relationships, women tend to have more vivid memories, which, of course, makes it difficult to have conjoin[t] stories that are

perfectly in tune (Ross & Holmberg, 1993). In sum, narratives can be seen as varying between these two poles: (1) individual, divergent accounts; and (2) conjointly agreed-upon accounts....

Listening closely to others' narratives will give you a window into [their] desire to save face and be seen as acceptable, and will also give you information about how they got [to] the state of their relationship. The narrative serves as both a reflection of the relationship and a force for the future of the relationship. And, finally, listen to your own narratives—and see where you are in your own relationships. Are you stuck and frustrated? Do you tell the same story over and over, unable to change over time? Does the narrative correspond with what the other would say? These and related questions about how you talk about your own relationships can give you insight into your reactions to the current situation.

Idioms in Relationship

Part of the narrative of a relationship involves personal idioms. They tend to develop in concert with the intimacy of a relationship (Bell, Buerkel-Rothfuss, & Gore, 1987) and are part of the "personalized" language used in close relationships. For example, saying "my honey" or "sweetykins" for your romantic partner cues both you and outsiders to the idea that the relationship is something special. Idioms are used both in private and in public, and come into being only after there is a certain degree of intimacy in the couple pairing (Hopper, Knapp, & Scott, 1981). Once used, they tend to both (1) reflect the degree of intimacy and (2) facilitate continued escalation of intimacies (Bell, Buerkel-Rothfuss, & Gore, 1987). Idioms are used in many types of close relationships, for example, among friends and family members, and between romantic partners.

Couples' idioms can be discussed as falling into the following categories (the categories and examples come from Hopper, Knapp, & Scott, 1981, and Bell, Buerkel-Rothfuss, & Gore, 1987):

Partner Nicknames: Where the partners refer to one another by special names only fully understood by the couple....

Expressions of Affection: These idioms express love, reassurance or praise to one's partner....

Labels for Others Outside the Relationship: These are nicknames for specific people who are not in the relationship.... The labels allow the couple to discuss others in public, usually in pejorative ways.

Confrontations: These idioms show criticism of the partner or displeasure about him or her....

Requests and Routines: These are ways to signal the partner. One common situation is when you let the other know you want to leave a party....

Sexual References and Euphemisms: Idioms that make a reference to sexual techniques, birth control, intercourse, breasts, or genitals....

Sexual Invitations: These idioms become code words for proposing sexual intercourse.

Teasing Insults: These idioms are used to derogate our partner, but in a spirit of play....

In the Hopper et al. (1981) study and the Bell et al. (1987) studies, respectively, 57 percent and 43 percent of the idioms were used exclusively in private. About half the idioms used by couples, therefore, are not used or understood by outsiders. Friends, however, more often use idioms in public, and in the research by Bell and Healey (1992), friends' idioms were used 65 percent of the time by their other friends. So friends' idioms are less private and more public than those of couples.

Research has not yet uncovered the specific use of idioms in other close relationships, but we know they exist. One daughter, for example, used to send electronic mail (e-mail) to her father and address it to "Poppy." He picked up on this and started addressing her e-mail to "poppyseed," and they now refer to one another with these interlocked idioms. If this father-daughter relationship parallels those used by friends, other family members may soon learn of the new form of address.

Symbols of Relational Identity

Baxter (1987b) probed how participants construct relationship meanings. She found that relationship symbols are "concrete metacommunicative 'statements' about the abstract qualities of intimacy, caring, solidarity, etc. which the parties equate with their relationships. The symbols give the parties a sense of 'history' about the relationship; they serve to link the past to the 'forces of novelty and change'" (Baxter, 1987b). In addition, the symbols allow them to test their common conception of their experience and see if the two of them have agreement on the relationship. Baxter found five types of relational symbols, listed in the order of frequency, for same-sex friendships and opposite sex romantic relationships.

1. *Behavioral actions* are actions the participants do. They have three subtypes:
   a. Jointly enacted activities—such as hiding Valentine's Day stuffed hearts from one another, playing sports, or other things jointly created.
   b. Interaction routines unique to the pair, such as jokes and teasing.
   c. Others such as nicknames, affection terms, or code words to refer to sexual matters.
2. *Events or times that held special meaning* were very diverse but all "held special meaning as distinguishing the relationship as unique." Many of them represented "firsts"—first meeting, first time they "really go to know one another," and so on.
3. *Physical objects* include an even more diverse set of examples. Everything from "strawberries, to a stuffed buffalo, to a broken string from a violin, to assorted pieces of jewelry" (Baxter, 1987, p. 269).
4. *Symbolic places* were of two types. Some were symbolic because they were visual metaphors of the partner or something in the history of the relationship, such as a restaurant or coffee shop. Others were symbolic because they served as a meeting place for the partners, such as Kalispell, Montana.

5. *Symbolic cultural artifacts* were things such as songs, music, books, and films that are part of the surrounding culture that have symbolic meaning for the two people.

Baxter then assessed the symbolic functions of the relationship symbols. She asked the participants what meaning these symbols had that made them feel the relationship was unique and special. The following nine functions [e]merged in order of frequency:

1. *Recollection Prompt*—to remind them about past events or thinking about the other in her/his absence.
2. *Intimacy Indicators*—signs of closeness, trust, or affection.
3. *Communication Mechanism*—promoting togetherness or sharing between the two.
4. *Stimulation/Fun*—offsetting boredom or excessive seriousness.
5. *Seclusion Mechanism*—to physically separate themselves from others.
6. *Exclusivity Indicator*—providing psychological seclusion for the relationship.
7. *Management of Difference/Conflict*—using locations that were conducive to discussion or joking or teasing as a way to deal with difficult issues.
8. *Public Tie-Sign*—giving others a signal that the parties were in a relationship.
9. *Endurance Index*—testifying to the relationship's endurance or strength in withstanding adversity.

This research establishes what we already know intuitively—that relationships contain symbolic elements. The meanings of events in a relationship, while showing some general patterns, are seen as unique and special by the two people involved. Once a symbolic marker begins being used in the relationship, people can make shorthand references to it. A romantic couple, for example, only need say, "Ah, Kalispell," to serve as a symbolic remembrance of events important to them.

One final finding is worthy of note. Baxter found that, even though males and females did not differ in the type or quantity of relationship symbols, "females regarded their relationship symbols more positively than was the case for males. Further, there was a trend towards females finding their relationship symbols more important than was the case for relationship symbols reported by men" (Baxter, 1987b, p. 279). This is consistent with the often-noted finding that females value their close relationships more than do men....

REFERENCES

Baxter, L. A. (1987). Symbols of relationship identity in relationship cultures. *Journal of Social and Personal Relationships, 4*, 261–280.

Baxter, L. A. (1992a). Forms and functions of intimate play in personal relationships. *Human Communication Research, 18*, 336–363.

Baxter, L. A. (1992b). Root metaphors in accounts of developing romantic relationships. *Journal of Social and Personal Relationships, 9*, 253–275.

Bell, R. A., Buerkel-Rothfuss, N. L., & Gore, K. E. (1987). Did you bring the yarmulke for the Cabbage Patch Kid? The idiomatic communication of young lovers. *Human Communication Research, 14*(1), 47–67.

Bell, R. A., & Healy, J. G. (1992). Idiomatic communication and interpersonal solidarity in friends' relational cultures. *Human Communication Research, 18*, 307–335.

Duck, S. W. (1982) A topology of relationship disagreement and dissolution. In S. W. Duck (Ed.), *Personal relationships: Vol. IV. Dissolving personal relationships* (pp. 1–30). New York, NY: Academic Press.

Duck, S. W. (1988). *Relating to others.* Chicago, IL: The Dorsey Press.

Duck, S. W., & Miell, D. E. (1986). Charting the development of personal relationships. In R. Gilmour & S. W. Duck (Eds.), *Emerging field of personal relationships* (pp. 133–144). Hillsdale, NJ: LEA.

Duck, S. & Pond, K. (1991, May). *On public display of private intimacy: An analysis of Valentine's Day messages.* Paper presented to third conference of the International Network on Personal Relationships, Normal/Bloomington, IL.

Farrell, T. B. (1984). Narrative in natural discourse: On communication and rhetoric. *Journal of Communication, 34*, 109–127.

Fisher, W. R. (1987). *Human communication as narration: Toward a philosophy of reason, value, and action.* Columbia: University of South Carolina Press.

Fitzpatrick, M. A., & Indvik, J. (1982). Implicit theories in enduring relationships: Psychological gender differences in perceptions of one's mate. *Western Journal of Speech Communication, 46*, 311–325.

Fletcher, G. J. O., & Fincham, F. D. (Eds.). (1991a). *Cognition in close relationships,* (pp. 7–35). Hillsdale, NJ: Lawrence Erlbaum.

Haas, A., & Sherman, M. A. (1982). Reported topics of conversation among same-sex adults. *Communication Quarterly, 30*, 332–342.

Hinde, R. A. (1979). *Towards understanding relationships.* London, England: Academic Press.

Hollihan, T. A., & Riley, P. (1987). The rhetorical power of a compelling story: A critique of a "toughlove" parental support group. *Communication Quarterly, 35*, 12–35.

Honeycutt, J. M., Cantrill, J. G., & Greene, R. W. (1989). Memory structures for relational escalation: A cognitive test of the sequencing of relational actions and stages. *Human Communication Research, 16*, 62–90.

Hopper, R., Knapp, M. L., & Scott, L. (1981). Couples' personal idioms: Exploring intimate talk. *Journal of Communication, 31*, 23–33.

Humphreys, C. (1951). *Buddhism.* Harmondsworth, England: Penguin Books.

Jackson, D. D. (1959). Family interaction, family homeostasis and some implications for conjoint family psychotherapy. In J. H. Masserman (Ed.), *Individual and familial dynamics.* New York, NY: Grune and Stratton.

Leatham, G., & Duck, S. (1990). Conversations with friends and the dynamics of social support. In S. Duck (Ed.), *Personal relationships and social support* (pp. 1–29). London, England: Sage.

Mandelbaum, J. (1989). Interpersonal activities in conversational storytelling. *Western Journal of Speech Communication, 53*, 114–126.

Morton, T. L., & Douglas, M. A. (1981). Growth of relationship. In S. Duck & R. Gilmour (Eds.), *Personal relationships* 9 (pp. 563–584).

Neimeyer, G. J., & Neimeyer, R. A. (1985). Relational trajectories: A personal construct contribution. *Journal of Social and Personal Relationships, 2*, 325–349.

Owen, W. F. (1984a). Interpretive themes in relational communication. *Quarterly Journal of Speech, 70*, 274–287.

Polanyi, L. (1985). Conversational storytelling. In T. A. van Kijk (Ed.), *Handbook of discourse analysis: Vol. 3* (pp. 183–201). New York, NY: Academic Press.

Ross, M., & Holmberg, D. (1993). Are wives' memories for events in relationships more vivid than their husbands' memories? *Journal of Social and Personal Relationships, 9*, 585–604.

Surra, C. A. (1987). Reasons for changes in commitment: Variations by courtship type. *Journal of Social and Personal Relationships, 4*, 17–33.

Van Kijk, T. A. (Ed.). (1985). *Handbook of discourse analysis.* New York, NY: Academic Press.

Veroff, J., Sutherland, L., Chadiha, L., & Ortega, R. M. (1993). Newlyweds tell their stories: A narrative method for assessing marital experiences. *Journal of Social and Personal Relationships, 10*, 437–457.

Weick, K. E. (1979). *The social psychology of organizing* (2nd ed.). Reading, MA: Addison-Wesley.

Wilmot, W. W., & Hocker, J. L. (1993). Couples and change: Intervention through discourse and images. In N. Coupland & J. F. Nussbaum, *Discourse and lifespan development* (pp. 262–283). Hillsdale, NJ: Lawrence Erlbaum.

QUESTIONS/THOUGHTS

1. Choose two important relationships in your life. How would you describe the miniculture of each relationship? What are the two major differences between them?

2. Choose one of the relationships in Question 1. Keep a journal about this relationship for one week. Based on your journal entries, would you still use the same mental image and metaphor to

describe it? What new insights did you gain about the miniculture of this relationship?

3. Observe a real or media romantic relationship that you believe is very strong and caring. Look for the patterns of interaction that might resemble ongoing dance movements. Describe some of the ways that the partners' verbal interactions seem to weave in and out as they hold conversations.

Reprinted from William W. Wilmot, "The Relational Perspective." In *Relational Communication Reader*, 4th ed., pp. 1–12. Published by McGraw-Hill. Copyright © 1995 by William W. Wilmot. Reprinted with permission of the author.

Theories of Relational Communication

LYNN H. TURNER AND RICHARD WEST

Relational theories grow out of the questions we ask ourselves about the interactions of others, the issues we confront in our own interactions with another, or from the observations of others on interaction patterns. If you have ever been puzzled about someone's behavior and asked yourself, "Why did he say or do that?" and then tried to figure out the answer to the question, you have engaged in theory building.

Theories serve several functions. They organize and explain our experiences. Because we cannot focus on every detail of every event, a theory suggests which details are the most important. Toulmin (1961) calls theories "intellectual spectacles" (p. 104). Like a pair of tinted sunglasses, the theory we use to explain a communication event colors that event. Depending on which theory is used, the explanation of events may differ.

In addition to organizing our experience, theories extend our knowledge. They enable us to go beyond what we observe and expand our knowledge to consider events we have not yet encountered. If we observe a friend in one situation when arguing with another person, we can make predictions about how our friend will react in similar situations.

Finally, theories stimulate and guide future research. This function is called the heuristic function of theory. As we test our theories, we modify them in order to better explain the events we observe.

A good theory meets certain criteria. First, it is logically consistent; it cannot contain contradictory propositions. For example, social exchange theory suggests that we desire relationships that benefit our self-interest, or relationships in which our rewards are greater than our costs. To be logically consistent, the theory cannot suggest that we desire relationships in which the costs outweigh the rewards.

Second, the theory needs to be consistent with accepted facts. If we observe that people generally do not stay in costly relationships, then social exchange theory makes sense. If, on the other hand, we observe that individuals generally do maintain costly relationships, the theory is not consistent with fact.

Third, as is often said, nothing is as practical as a good theory. In other words, theories need to be useful—relevant to your life. You need to be able to use the theory to explain and, if necessary, change *your own behavior. The theory's advice should be helpful to your own life.*

In their text, Engaging Theories in Interpersonal Communication, *Leslie Baxter and Dawn Braithwaite (2008), separate theories into individual-centered theories, discourse/interaction-centered theories, and relationship-centered theories. The following chapter focuses heavily on the relationship-centered theories. In later chapters you will see reference to theories such as narrative theory, face theory, and uncertainty management theory.*

This is the linchpin chapter of this book because its content directly affects how you will respond to many of the later chapters. The authors, Lynn Turner and Richard West, introduce several interpersonal theories alluded to throughout this reader. You will encounter a description and application of the following theories: symbolic interaction, uncertainty reduction, social penetration, social exchange, and relational dialectics. As you consider these theories, apply the criteria of a good theory to each. In addition, try to imagine the application of these theories to your everyday life by answering the question: What is one example of how each theory plays out in a familiar relationship?

REFERENCES

Baxter, L. A., & Braithwaite, D.O. (2008). *Engaging theories in interpersonal communication.* Thousand Oaks, CA: Sage.

Toulmin, S. (1961). *Foresight and understanding: An inquiry into the aims of science.* New York, NY: Harper Torchbooks.

Communicating with relational partners can be exciting, complex, and confusing. Even though we spend so much time talking and listening to others, we are often perplexed by what they say, how they react to what we say, or what happens as a result of our conversations. Researchers believe that theories offer help in clarifying these complexities. In 1986, Jonathan H. Turner defined theory as "a process of developing ideas that can allow us to explain how and why events occur" (p. 5). Theoretical thinking can be applied to

any question: how the world began, how people develop their personalities, what causes cancer, or why we communicate the way we do, to list a few. The theories discussed in this chapter help us make sense of questions about our own communication behavior and the behavior of our relational partners.

We are discussing theory as professional researchers use it in their work, yet all of us in daily life think like researchers, using implicit theories to help us understand confusing questions concerning communication. Fritz Heider (1958) used the term "naive psychologists" to describe people puzzling over theoretical issues in their everyday life. Whenever we think about our relational communication and question its direction and meaning, we are engaging in theoretical thinking; that is, we are applying theoretical concepts to make sense of relational communication.

Researchers struggle to develop and agree on explanations for communication behavior. But this process is complicated and people make so many different assumptions about others, that there is no one definitive theory that all researchers use. In fact, there is not even a short list of interpersonal communication theories. The possibilities for theorizing about the communication process remain extensive. Furthermore, most researchers don't t try to come up with a theory that addresses all interpersonal communication. Many theories only attempt to explain a small segment of the process, such as attraction, listening, conflict, or relational development.

In this chapter, the following theories are presented: symbolic interaction, uncertainty reduction, social penetration, social exchange, and relational dialectics. You will see the variety in what they attempt to explain, their format, and their assumptions about human behavior. As you read the other chapters in the book, you should see where each of the theories might be applied to explain a part of relational communication. You should remember, however, that these theories are only a few among many that we could use in explaining communication practices. Nonetheless, the five theories reviewed here offer a useful introduction to how theory can help us unravel communication questions. We begin with Symbolic Interaction Theory, which tries to explain the general question of how people make meaning.

SYMBOLIC INTERACTION THEORY (SI)

Overview

Symbolic Interaction Theory (SI) originated in the works of the sociologist George Herbert Mead, although he did not publish much about his ideas himself. After he died, his students put together a book, *Mind, Self, and Society* (1934), based on his lectures detailing SI's theoretical framework. As its name suggests, Symbolic Interaction Theory centers on symbols and interactions. Ralph LaRossa and Donald C. Reitzes (1993) state that Symbolic Interactionism is "essentially…a frame of reference for understanding how humans, in concert with one another, create symbolic worlds and how these worlds, in turn, shape human behavior" (p. 136). This statement echoes Mead's belief in individuals as active, reflective beings.

Assumptions

LaRossa and Reitzes (1993) examined SI as it relates to families. They note that seven central assumptions ground the theory. These assumptions include the following:

1. Humans act toward others on the basis of the meanings those others have for them.
2. Meaning is created in interaction between people.
3. Meanings are modified through an interpretive process.
4. Individuals develop self-concepts through interaction with others.
5. Self-concepts provide an important motive for behavior.
6. People and groups are influenced by cultural and social processes.
7. Social structure is worked out through social interaction.

The first assumption focuses on people as choice makers, rejecting the notion that human behavior is predestined. The second assumption stresses Mead's belief that meaning only exists when people share common interpretations of the symbols they exchange in interaction. According to SI, meanings are seen as "social products" or "creations that are formed in and through the defining activities of people as they interact" (Blumer 1969, 5). Therefore, two people from different cultures, or even different regions, have difficulty creating shared meaning.

The third assumption, that meanings are modified through an interpretive process, has two parts. First, people notice the things that have meaning. This involves people in conversation with themselves. When you mull over the possible meanings your friend might have had for canceling a dinner with you, you are engaging in this part of the process. The second step consists of selecting, checking, and transforming the meanings in a particular context. The contextual cues such as your culture, your idiosyncratic knowledge of your friend, and so forth will aid you as you decide why you think your friend canceled. The same behavior practiced by two different friends may have different meanings for you.

The fourth assumption states that it is only through contact with others that we develop a sense of self. We are not born with self-concepts, we learn them through interactions and in relationship with others. The fifth assumption focuses on the importance of the self-concept as a motive for behavior. This assumption relates to the process of self-fulfilling prophecy, or the expectations of self that cause a person to behave in such a way that the expectations are realized. Your prediction that you will have fun at a party, for example, often results in behaviors on your part that ensure you do have a good time.

The sixth assumption recognizes that social norms constrain individual behavior. For instance, when you meet your significant other's parents for the first time, you probably choose clothing that is appropriate for the occasion, not necessarily what you would most prefer wearing. The context and your desire to make a good impression influence your choices. Additionally, culture influences our choices. Thus, what would be appropriate clothing to wear for meeting your future in-laws in India differs from what it would be in the United States. Yet, people are able to adopt a multicultural perspective and learn to value traits not endorsed by their own culture of origin. When people attend college in a new country they might begin to value attitudes and behaviors of their host country, for instance.

The last assumption of SI acknowledges that although our choices are influenced by social structure, as the previous assumption states, the opposite is true as well. Individuals can modify social situations through interactions. For example, even though you might want to make a good first impression, you might justify wearing jeans to meet the parents by noting that is just how you are and people need to accept your individuality. You could tell your significant other to explain that to the parents.

Key Concepts

Mead's book title, *Mind, Self, and Society*, reflects the three key concepts of SI. Mead defined mind as the ability to use symbols that have common meanings.

According to Mead, one of the most critical activities that people accomplish with their minds is role-taking, or the ability to symbolically place oneself in someone else's situation. Whenever we try to imagine how another person might view something or when we try to behave as we think another would, we are role-taking. Mead suggested that role-taking helps us develop our self-concept and allows us to develop empathy with others.

Mead defined self as the ability to reflect on ourselves as others would. For Mead, the self developed from a particular kind of role-taking, that is, imagining how we look to others. This is described as the looking-glass self, or our ability to see ourselves in the reflection of another (Cooley 1972).

Further, Mead argued that people have the ability to be both subject and object to themselves. As subject we act and as object we observe ourselves acting. Mead called the subject or acting self "I," and the object or observing self "ME." The "I" is spontaneous, impulsive, and creative

while the "ME" is more reflective and socially aware. The "I" might want to scream and yell during an argument with a roommate, while the "ME" realizes that this would be counterproductive and offers some reasoned arguments instead. Mead saw the self as a process that integrated the "I" and the "ME."

Mead defined society as the network of social relationships humans establish. People engage in society through behaviors that they choose actively and voluntarily. Society and the individual exist in a reciprocal relationship. First, society exists prior to the individual and so exerts influence on individuals. But society is also shaped and influenced by the individual acting in concert with others. Mead thought that two specific parts of society affect the mind and the self: Particular Others, or the individuals in society who are significant to us, and the Generalized Other, which refers to social standards as a whole. We look to Particular Others to get a sense of social acceptability and a sense of self. The Generalized Other provides information about roles, rules, and attitudes shared by the community; this information is influential in developing a social conscience.

Application

Because Symbolic Interaction Theory is such a broad explanation, providing an understanding of how people develop a sense of self, many studies have used its tenets. Recently, Margie Edwards (2004) examined how women work to create a sense of family identity using principles of SI. Edwards interviewed working class women from two rural trailer park communities and she also observed their family routines and interactions.

She concluded that, as SI predicts, women's work consists, in large part, of managing and developing family identity. Further, women in these rural trailer parks believed that an important part of their work was connecting their family's identity with the community. In this way they were able to link the family to the larger community and secure help for the family when it was needed. Edwards stated that SI helped understand the meanings that women assign to their labor within the family as well as how women's work supports the family.

SI provides a starting point for understanding relational communication. It explains how people see themselves and others and how they make meaning of their observations. It is a general, broad theory that explores the intersection of the self and its relationship to others. We now turn to a much more specific theory, which focuses the uncertainty that occurs in the beginning of relational development.

UNCERTAINTY REDUCTION THEORY (URT)

Overview

Uncertainty Reduction Theory (URT) was conceptualized by Charles Berger and Richard Calabrese in 1975. Their goal was to explain how communication reduces uncertainties between strangers engaging in initial interactions. URT is a theory geared toward understanding the very beginning stages of a relationship. Berger and Calabrese thought that people want to predict and explain what goes on in their initial interactions with strangers. Prediction is the ability to define in advance what we or a relational partner will do or say. Explanation refers to our interpretation of these behaviors. These two concepts—prediction and explanation—comprise the major subprocesses of uncertainty reduction.

After Berger and Calabrese (1975) originated their theory, it was later elaborated (Berger 1979; Berger and Bradac 1982). The final version added the idea that there are two types of uncertainty in initial encounters: cognitive and behavioral. Cognitive uncertainty refers to the degree of uncertainty associated with one's own beliefs and attitudes. (Do I like her?) Behavioral uncertainty, on the other hand, pertains to the extent of certainty associated with behavioral practices: what people do and say. (Why did she interrupt me?) Because we have cultural rituals for small talk, strangers have some certainty about how to behave when they first meet. If these rituals are violated by engaging in inappropriate self-disclosure (revealing intimate information about one's

self to another), for example, then behavioral uncertainty increases.

URT has been described as an example of original theorizing in the field of communication (Miller 1981) because it centers on concepts like information seeking and nonverbal behaviors that are specifically relevant to studying communication.

Assumptions

1. People experience uncertainty in interpersonal settings.
2. Uncertainty is an aversive state, generating cognitive stress.
3. When strangers meet, their primary concern is to reduce their uncertainty or to increase predictability.
4. Interpersonal communication is a developmental process that occurs through stages.
5. Interpersonal communication is the primary means of uncertainty reduction.
6. The quantity and nature of information that people share change through time.

Axioms and Theorems

URT is an axiomatic theory, which means that it begins with a series of truisms drawn from past research and common sense. These axioms require no further proof as they are accepted as truth. Each axiom presents a relationship between uncertainty (the central theoretical concept) and one other concept. URT rests on seven axioms.

Axiom 1: As the amount of verbal communication between strangers increases, the level of uncertainty for each person in the relationship will decrease. As uncertainty is further reduced, the amount of verbal communication will increase. (The more two strangers talk, the more certainty they will feel.)

Axiom 2: As nonverbal expressiveness increases, uncertainty levels will decrease and vice versa. (The more you and your partner do things like smile, the more certainty you will both feel.)

Axiom 3: High levels of uncertainty cause increases in information-seeking behavior. As uncertainty levels decline, information-seeking behavior decreases. (The more two strangers feel uncertain, the more questioning they will do.)

Axiom 4: High levels of uncertainty in a relationship cause decreases in the intimacy level of communication content. Low levels of uncertainty produce high levels of intimacy. (The more two strangers feel uncertain, the less intimate their conversation will be.)

Axiom 5: High levels of uncertainty produce high rates of reciprocity. Low levels of uncertainty produce low levels of reciprocity. (High uncertainty brings with it a concern to reciprocate what the other does, such as exchange like information: "What's your major?" "Biology. What's yours?" "English.")

Axiom 6: Similarities between persons reduce uncertainty, while dissimilarities produce increases in uncertainty. (The more similar two strangers appear to each other, the less uncertainty they will feel.)

Axiom 7: Increases in uncertainty level produce decreases in liking; decreases in uncertainty produce increases in liking. (The more uncertainty you feel around a stranger, the less you like him or her.)

Axiomatic theories proceed by pairing two axioms together to produce a theorem. While the axioms are assumed to be true, the resulting theorems are theoretical and have to be tested. The process follows deductive logic: If A = B, and B = C, then A = C. Berger and Calabrese combined all seven axioms in every possible pairwise combination to derive 21 theorems. For instance, because verbal communication is negatively related to uncertainty (Axiom 1) and intimacy is also negatively related to uncertainty (Axiom 4), verbal communication and intimacy levels are positively related (resulting thereom). You can generate the other 20 theorems by combining the axioms using the deductive formula above.

You need to use the rule of multiplication for multiplying positives and negatives: If two variables have a positive relationship with a third, they have a positive relationship with each other. If one variable has a positive relationship with a third while the other has a negative relationship with the third, they should have a negative relationship with each other. Finally, if two variables have a negative relationship with a third they should have a positive relationship with each other.

Application

Although many studies investigate how uncertainty operates in initial interactions, as Berger and Calabrese intended the theory to be applied, newer research attempts to expand URT. For instance, a recent study (Powell & Afifi, 2005) tested how well URT could explain the process of uncertainty management that adoptees engage in about their birth parents. First, the researchers note that adoptees may experience different levels of uncertainty about their birth parents, although 70% of their respondents expressed moderate to high levels of uncertainty.

In 21 face-to-face interviews and 32 telephone interviews, the researchers generated data about how adoptees managed uncertainty in this situation which they termed the ambiguous loss of their birth parents. This was the case, because for most of the respondents, the birth parents were presumed to be still living. Although they were not currently in the adoptees' lives, it was theoretically possible to locate them and engage in contact. Thus, their loss was termed ambiguous.

The study concludes that URT may treat uncertainty too simplistically, not acknowledging that in some cases, people would rather remain uncertain. The researchers note that ignorance of potentially unpleasant information may be bliss for some people and reducing uncertainty is only one strategy that people employ.

URT takes a narrow, but common, experience in relational life—uncertainty—and attempts to clearly and completely explain how communication is used to manage it. We will now discuss a theory that examines a much larger aspect of relational communication, the process of relationship development.

SOCIAL PENETRATION THEORY (SPT)

Overview

Social Penetration Theory (SPT), articulated by Irwin Altman and Dalmas Taylor (1973), moves beyond the initial encounters that URT tries to explain, and attempts to understand overall relational development. The term social penetration refers to the movement from superficial communication to more intimate communication during the process of relationship development. In their discussion of SPT, Altman and Taylor utilize an onion metaphor. They believe that the layers of an onion represent various aspects of a person's personality. On the outer layer is an individual's public image. As more and more layers are revealed through interaction, the private self is revealed.

Altman and Taylor (1973) acknowledge that relationships vary. From married couples to supervisor-employee to business partners to friends, relationships "involve different levels of intimacy of exchange or degree of social penetration" (p. 3). Regardless of variation, however, Altman and Taylor believed that all relationships follow some predictable trajectory, or pathway.

Assumptions

1. Relationships progress from nonintimate to intimate.
2. Relational development is generally systematic and predictable.
3. Relational development includes depenetration and dissolution.
4. Self-disclosure is at the core of relationship development.

The first assumption presumes that relational communication begins at a nonintimate level and then moves along a continuum to a more intimate level. Initial conversations may at first appear trivial, yet such conversations allow individuals to size each other up and give them a chance to think about prospects for a future. Not all relationships are simply nonintimate or intimate. In fact, most of our relationships fall somewhere in the middle. Many times, we want only a moderately close relationship. The theory does not argue that all relationships have to move to an intimate stage.

The second assumption of SPT pertains to predictability. Specifically, social penetration theorists argue that relationships progress fairly systematically and predictably. Some people may have difficulty with this assertion because they know that relationships are dynamic and ever-changing. Yet, according to SPT, even dynamic relationships follow some standard pattern of development. Social penetration processes are rather organized and predictable. Of course, a number of other events and variables (time, personality, and so forth) affect the way relationships progress so relationships are never completely predictable.

The third assumption of SPT is that relational development includes depenetration and dissolution. Altman and Taylor liken the process to a film shown in reverse. Just as communication allows a relationship to move forward toward intimacy, communication can also move a relationship back toward nonintimacy. Some researchers refer to this depenetration process as the return of the stranger. Social penetration theorists think that depenetration—like the penetration process—is systematic. If a relationship depenetrates, it does not mean that it will inevitably dissolve. Niall Bolger and Shannon Kelleher (1993), for example, note that stress may cause depenetration, but most couples manage the stress before the relationship dissolves.

The final assumption contends that self-disclosure is at the core of relationship development. According to Altman and Taylor (1973), the way that nonintimate relationships progress toward intimacy is through self-disclosures. Self-disclosure allows people get to know each other. Self-disclosure helps shape a relationship, and, as Altman and Taylor observe, "making self accessible to another person is intrinsically gratifying" (p. 50).

The Social Penetration Process

The social penetration has two dimensions: breadth and depth. Breadth refers to the number of topics discussed in the relationship and depth refers to the degree of intimacy guiding topic discussions. In the initial stages, most relationships have narrow breadth and shallow depth. As relationships move toward intimacy, a wider range of topics is discussed (more breadth), with several of those topics marked by depth.

Breadth and depth issues affect relationship development. For instance, shifts or changes in central layers (of the onion) have more of an impact on relationships than shifts in outer or peripheral layers. For example, if you change your hair color, your relationship with a significant other would be less affected than if you changed your opinion about a core value, such as the importance you place on money.

SPT asserts that the process of relationship development follows a stage model consisting of four stages: orientation, exploratory affective exchange, affective exchange, and stable exchange. The earliest stage of interaction, orientation, occurs at the public level. During this stage, comments usually reflect superficial aspects of individuals. People act in socially desirable ways, smile pleasantly, and react politely. Taylor and Altman (1987) note that people tend not to evaluate or criticize during the orientation stage.

The second stage, the exploratory affective exchange stage, represents an expansion in which people progress beyond public level information. Taylor and Altman describe relationships with casual acquaintances and friendly neighbors as being in this stage. In this stage, people use phrases that are idiosyncratic to the relationship, there is more spontaneity in communication, more touch behavior, and more nonverbal expression of emotions. The researchers note that many relationships stay at this stage.

The affective exchange stage includes those interactions that are more "freewheeling and casual" (Taylor and Altman 1987, 259), meaning that communication is spontaneous and individuals say what they think without fearing that it will end the relationship. The affective exchange stage represents further commitment to the other individual; both interactants are comfortable with one another. The stage includes those aspects of a relationship that make it unique, for example

the use of personal idioms (Hopper, Knapp, and Scott 1981), which are private ways of expressing a relationship's intimacy—through words, phrases, and/or behaviors. Idiomatic expressions—such as "rabbit running" or "honey bubbles"—carry unique meaning for two people in a relationship.

The final stage, stable exchange, is reached in few relationships. It involves open expression of thoughts, feelings, and behaviors, which result in much spontaneity and relational uniqueness. Social penetration theorists believe that there are relatively few misinterpretations in communication meaning at this stage because both partners have had numerous opportunities to clarify any previous ambiguities and have established their own personal system of communication. As a result, communication—according to Altman and Taylor—is efficient.

Application

Social Penetration Theory has been used to frame many studies. For instance, Zhong, Myers, and Buerkel (2004) examined the central variable in Social Penetration Theory: self-disclosure. They surveyed 123 sons and 118 of their fathers investigating relational intimacy between the pairs. They presented participants a number of surveys that examined perceptions of self-disclosure and trust. Among their conclusions were two relevant to SPT: First, there were no significant differences in perceptions of relationship intimacy between fathers and sons. Second, with respect to self-disclosure, fathers were found to self-disclose more intentionally than their sons.

Zhong and associates suggest that the differences in self-disclosure may be the result of fathers wanting to maintain positive relationships with their sons. Second, the researchers contend that children are usually not accustomed nor willing to self-disclose, particularly to their fathers. Therefore, a willingness to self-disclose on the part of fathers seems to be an effort to establish closeness with sons. The study concludes with a call for research on the implications of self-disclosure (among other communication traits) in mother-child relationships to assess whether similar findings exist.

SPT approaches relationships as a series of exchanges. It borrows that notion from another theoretical framework called social exchange, which we will now discuss.

SOCIAL EXCHANGE THEORY (SET)

Overview

Social Exchange Theory (SET) is based on the notion that people think about their relationships in economic terms, adding up the costs involved and comparing those costs to the available rewards. Costs are those aspects of relational life that provide negative value to a person, like having to listen to your best friend talk at length when you need to do other things. Rewards are those things providing positive value to a person, like having your best friend listen to your problems when you need to talk them through. Social exchange theorists argue that people assess their relationships in terms of costs and rewards. The social exchange perspective argues that people calculate the overall worth of a relationship by subtracting its costs from the rewards it provides.

Positive relationships are those in which the rewards exceed the costs. Relationships where the worth is a negative amount (i.e., with greater costs than rewards) tend to be negative ones. Social exchange theory predicts that the worth of a relationship influences whether people will continue the relationship or terminate it. Positive relationships are expected to endure while negative relationships probably will not. The situation is a bit more complex than this simple explanation implies, but it does reveal essentially what exchange theorists argue. As Ronald Sabatelli and Constance Shehan (1993) note, the social exchange approach views relationships through the metaphor of the marketplace, where each person acts out of a self-oriented goal of profit-taking.

So far, we have been talking in general about exchange theories or the overall framework of social exchange, but there are several distinct theories of social exchange. Michael Roloff (1981) discusses five different theories in his book, *Interpersonal Communication: The Social Exchange Approach*. Roloff observes that while these theories differ in several significant respects, they are connected by the central argument that relational partners act on the basis of their self-interest. Additionally, he notes that these theories do not assume that self-interest is a negative thing but, rather, that it may actually enhance a relationship. It is beyond our purposes here to distinguish among all social exchange theories. We will concentrate on explicating what may be the most popular version of social exchange, the theory of interdependence created by John Thibaut and Harold Kelley in 1959.

Assumptions

All social exchange theories are built upon common assumptions about human beings and about the nature of relationships. Some of these assumptions are probably quite clear to you after the introduction to this theory. Many of these assumptions flow from the notion that people view life as a marketplace. More specifically, Thibaut and Kelley focused on human nature and the social exchange (or relationship) between two people. Thus, the assumptions they make also fall into these two categories.

The assumptions that social exchange theory makes about human nature include the following:

1. Humans seek rewards and avoid punishments.
2. Humans are rational beings.
3. The standards that humans use to evaluate costs and rewards vary over time and from person to person.

The assumptions that social exchange theory makes about the nature of relationships include these:

1. Relationships are interdependent.
2. Relational life is a process.

Evaluating Relationships

As we mentioned earlier, SET is more complex than the simple equation stating that worth = rewards minus costs. When people calculate the worth of their relationships and make decisions about staying in them, they are concerned with a few other issues as well. One of the most interesting parts of Thibaut and Kelley's theory is their explanation of how people evaluate whether or not to leave a relationship. Thibaut and Kelley stated that this evaluation rests on two types of comparisons, which they call comparison level and comparison level for alternatives. The comparison level (CL) is a standard representing what rewards people feel they should receive and what costs they expect to pay in a specific relationship. Your CL is shaped by all past relationships, by family members' advice, and by popular culture such as TV and film representations of relationships.

Comparison levels vary among individuals because they are subjective assessments. Yet, because we often interact with people who are subjected to similar messages about relationships from the popular culture, we have many relational expectations in common (Rawlins 1992). Thus, people in the same culture overlap somewhat in their general expectations for relationships, and their CLs may not be totally different from each other's.

Thibaut and Kelley's theory asserts that our satisfaction with a relationship derives from comparing its rewards and costs to our CL. If the relationship meets or exceeds our CL, the prediction is that we will be satisfied with it. Yet people sometimes leave relationships that meet their CL and stay in ones that do not seem to meet it. Thibaut and Kelley explain this type of situation with their second standard of comparison, the comparison level for alternatives (CLalt). This standard refers to how people evaluate a relationship compared to the realistic alternatives to that relationship. CLalt provides a measure of stability rather than of satisfaction. Thus, if you felt you had few chances to make new friends, you might evaluate your current friends more positively than you would if you thought it would be relatively easy to make new friends. If people see no alternatives to an existing relationship, and fear being alone more than being in the relationship, SET predicts they will stay. Some who have written about women in abusive relationships have used this theoretical reasoning to explain why women stay with violent

men (Walker 1984). Thibaut and Kelley were also interested in how people adjust their behaviors when interacting with their relational partners. Thibaut and Kelley suggested that people are goal directed in their interaction behaviors. This fits with their assumption that human beings are rational. According to Thibaut and Kelley, people engage in what they termed behavioral sequences, or a series of actions designed to achieve a goal. These sequences are at the core of what Thibaut and Kelley consider social exchange. Behavioral sequences depend on issues of interdependence and power.

All interpersonal relationships are interdependent and their interdependence results in two types of power: fate control and behavior control. Fate control is the ability to affect another person's outcomes. For example, if your friend normally helps you study and then decides that she no longer has time to do so, she controls, to an extent, how well you may do on your next exam. Behavior control is the power to change a partner's behavior by changing one's own behavior. If you are talking to a friend who suddenly stops talking, you will probably change your behavior in response. You may stop talking too or you might question your friend to find out if something is wrong.

To cope with power differentials and to deal with the costs associated with exercising power, Thibaut and Kelley state that people develop patterns of exchange. These patterns, made up of behavioral rules or norms, indicate how people attempt to maximize rewards and minimize costs. Thibaut and Kelley describe three different matrices that exist in social exchange: the given matrix, the effective matrix, and the dispositional matrix. The given matrix represents the behavioral choices and outcomes that are determined by a combination of factors external to the relationship (like the environment) with factors that are internal (like the specific skills the relational partners possess). When two people engage in an exchange, the environment may make some options more difficult than others. Romeo and Juliet's love was doomed by their families' feud, for instance. Further, the given matrix depends on the skills people bring to the social exchange. If people lack skills for downhill skiing, for example, that makes it unlikely that they will spend time skiing together.

To some extent people are restricted by the given matrix, but they are not completely trapped by it. By changing their behaviors, acquiring new skills, and creatively managing their environment, they can transform the given matrix into the effective matrix, which expands possible behaviors and/or outcomes. If two people did not know how to ski, for example, they could take lessons and learn how, transforming their given matrix into the effective matrix. If a couple found that their families were restricting their relationship too much, they could engage in conflict with them until they changed their families' minds. Or they could stop talking about each other at home and keep their affair secret so that they could avoid their families' negative sanctions.

The final matrix, the dispositional matrix, represents how people believe rewards ought to be exchanged. If one member of a couple thought that it was critical for family to approve of their romance, that would affect their dispositional matrix. Some people view exchanges as competition, and this belief would be reflected in their dispositional matrix.

Thibaut and Kelley's Social Exchange Theory states that knowing the kinds of dispositions a person has (the dispositional matrix) and the nature of the situation (the given matrix) in which they are relating will allow us to predict the transformations they will make (the effective matrix) to affect the social exchange. The dispositional matrix guides the transformations people make to their given matrix, which leads to the effective matrix, which determines the social exchange.

In their theory, Thibaut and Kelley do not explicitly deal with communication behaviors, yet some of their discussion about the three matrices implies that self-disclosure plays an important role in social exchange. Michael Roloff (1981) observes:

> Self-disclosure would seem to imply the communication of two things: (1) the dispositions one has, and (2) the transformations (strategy) one is

going to employ in this exchange. Since dispositions affect a person's strategy, we might assume that knowledge of dispositions might well allow us to predict the transformations. (p. 77)

If people know how their partner transforms the given matrix, that could give them an edge in social exchanges. An understanding of how the matrices affect communication behavior is an important reason why communication researchers are interested in SET.

Application

Social exchange principles frame many studies. For instance, Kramer (2005) explored two volunteer groups involved in community theatre musicals. The researcher was interested in knowing what benefits and costs (two Social Exchange concepts) people obtain by participating in the groups. Over 50 participants completed a questionnaire asking about their summer productions. Several categories of benefits emerged from the analysis, including Social Interaction, Peer Support, Playfulness, and Performing for an Audience (Response). Among the costs cited were Complaints about a Lack of Organization, Personality Conflicts, and Challenging Roles (or Parts). The experiences articulated by theatre group members were discussed employing the "sometimes overlooked" (p. 177) aspects of Social Exchange Theory, namely cost benefit ratios. Kramer concludes that social exchange theorists have often looked at tangible exchanges of costs and rewards. This study provides less-tangible evidence such as "the exchange of affect and status" and its relationship to commitment and satisfaction.

SET supposes a rational, even calculating, side to interpersonal relationships. The final theory we will discuss, Relational Dialectics, takes a much different perspective on the life of a relationship.

RELATIONAL DIALECTICS THEORY (RDT)

Overview

This theory maintains that what characterizes relational life is ongoing tensions between contradictory desires. While that sounds messy, researchers who use Relational Dialectics Theory (RDT) believe it accurately depicts people's experience. RDT claims that although we are not always able to resolve contradictions, we can be comfortable believing inconsistent things about relationships. For example, the old folk adage that "opposites attract" seems to coexist easily with its opposite, "birds of a feather flock together."

Leslie Baxter and Barbara Montgomery (1996) formulated a complete statement of the theory in their book, *Relating: Dialogues and Dialectics*. Baxter and Montgomery's work was influenced by Mikhail Bakhtin, a Russian philosopher. Social life for Bakhtin was a dialogue among many voices espousing different perspectives and viewpoints. According to Bakhtin, the self was only possible in context with another. Bakhtin's ideas relate to Symbolic Interaction Theory because they both focus on the importance of interaction for meaning making.

Dialectic thinkers maintain that in all contradictions multiple points of view interact. Although we think of a contradiction as involving polar opposites, dialectics states that the resulting situation expands beyond these two poles. As Baxter and Montgomery (1996) observe, "dialectical thinking is not directed toward a search for the 'happy mediums' of compromise and balance, but instead focuses on the messier, less logical, and more inconsistent unfolding practices of the moment" (p. 46).

Assumptions

RDT is grounded in four main assumptions about relational life:

1. Relationships are not linear.
2. Relational life is characterized by change.
3. Contradiction is the fundamental fact of relational life.
4. Communication is central to organizing and negotiating relational contradictions.

The most significant assumption that grounds this theory is the first one. Rather than being linear (as Social Penetration Theory implies with its stages), dialectical researchers think that relationships consist of oscillations between contradictory desires. Baxter and Montgomery (1996) suggest rethinking the phrase "relational development" because it connotes linear movement or forward progress. Progress implies "either/or" thinking. Relationships that progress are pictured as having more of certain elements such as intimacy, self-disclosure, certainty, and so forth than relationships that do not progress. Either/or thinking frames a relationship as either intimate, open, certain or not. In the dialectic perspective, the concept of "both/and" replaces either/or.

The second assumption of RDT focuses on the notion of process or change while not necessarily framing change as linear progress. Thus, you and your friend are different today than you were when you first met. But that difference is not a linear move toward intimacy as much as it is simply changes in the way you express togetherness and independence.

The third assumption states that these tensions between opposing desires never go away. People manage to live with tensions and oppositions, and they are constants in relational life. This approach differs from other types of relational theories in that it considers stability to be unnatural—change and transformation are characteristic of relational life in the dialectic perspective (Montgomery 1992).

The final assumption of RDT gives a central position to communication. The communicative practices enacted in relational life organize the three central dialectics that are discussed in the following section: autonomy and connection; openness and protection; and novelty and predictability (Baxter 1990).

Central Dialectical Tensions

The dialectic between autonomy and connection refers to our simultaneous desires to be independent and to be bonded with significant others. Relational life is filled with conflicting desires to be both close to and separate from relational partners. Baxter and Montgomery (1996) discuss how couples' private communication codes illustrate the presence of both connection and autonomy in relationships. For instance, nicknames celebrate something inherently individual and also indicate a relational closeness in that casual friends do not call each other by affectionate "pet" names.

A second important tension pervading relational life has to do with openness and protection. The openness and protection dialectic focuses on our conflicting desires to be open and vulnerable to our relational partners while at the same time to be strategic and self-protective in our communication. Katherine Dindia (1994) argues for what she calls an "intrapersonal dialectic" of disclosure. This involves a gradual and incremental process of disclosure, ranging from concealment to full revelation. We do not have much research focusing on the actual communication practices that allow relational partners to simultaneously disclose personal information and to protect themselves from hurt that might arise from their partners' knowledge of their vulnerabilities.

The dialectic between novelty and predictability refers to our desire for both the comfort of stability and the excitement of change. Uncertainty Reduction Theory assumes that people move toward certainty and away from uncertainty as their relationship develops. The dialectic position sees the interplay of certainty and uncertainty in relationships. A couple's planning behavior illustrates this interplay. When they make a plan together, they are accomplishing at least two things with reference to predictability. First, their plan self-defines them as in a relationship, because planning is a relational activity. It also establishes a routine so they know what they will be doing in the short-term future. Yet if they leave the plan a bit open-ended, they can also allow for creativity and novelty. As with the openness/protection dialectic, not much research has uncovered the specific communication behaviors used to manage novelty and predictability.

Coping With Dialectical Tensions

While dialectical tensions are always present in relationships, people do find ways to manage them. Baxter (1988) identified four main management strategies: (1) cyclic alternation, (2) segmentation, (3) selection, and (4) integration. In cyclic alternation people alternate between two opposites at different times in their relationship. For instance,

when brothers are very young they may be inseparable, highlighting their closeness. As adolescents they may favor autonomy in their relationship, seeking separate identities. Later, when they are adults, perhaps living near each other and confronting caretaking responsibilities for their aging parents, they may again favor closeness.

Segmentation means identifying separate arenas for emphasizing each of the opposites. For example, a married couple who work together might stress predictability in the working relationship, but novelty while at home. The third strategy, selection, refers to making a choice between the opposites. Friends who choose to be close at all times, ignoring their needs for autonomy, use selection.

Finally, integration involves a synthesis. Integration takes three forms: neutralizing, disqualifying, or reframing the polarities. Neutralizing means compromising between the polarities. People who choose this strategy find "a happy medium" between opposites. Disqualifying neutralizes the dialectics by exempting certain issues from the general pattern. If you are very open with your best friend on all topics but one, that exemplifies disqualifying.

Reframing refers to transforming the dialectic so that it no longer seems to contain an opposition. Julia Wood and her colleagues (1994) discuss how couples in their study reframed. These couples defined connection as including differences, stating that they felt closer to their partner when they could share their different perspectives on life. Thus, they reframed what it meant to be close so they could incorporate distance in the definition.

Application

In an interpretive study, Leslie Baxter, Dawn Braithwaite, and Leah Bryant (2004), examined children's perceptions' of the contradictions that framed their interactions with stepparents who lived with them in their primary household. Baxter, Braithwaite, and Bryant were interested in seeing how Relational Dialectics Theory helped to understand the relationship between stepchildren and their stepparents. They begin by noting that step relationships are well suited to an analysis guided by RDT because they are relationships freighted with tensions.

In fact, after conducting in depth interviews with stepchildren resulting in 802 pages of double-spaced interview transcripts, the authors found that three dialectics characterized the relationship. These dialectics are similar to the central dialectics we discussed previously, but they are tailored a bit more specifically to the stepchild-stepparent relationship. The researchers found that stepchildren spoke about tensions of integration, status, and expression. Integration referred to their simultaneous desires for closeness and distance while status concerned the tension between labeling the stepparent as a legitimate or an illegitimate authority for them. Finally expression focused on stepchildren's desires for candor and concurrent concerns for discretion in what they told their stepparent.

CONCLUSION

We live in relationship with others and interact with them in myriad ways. These interactions create many questions about why things occur the way they do. The five theories discussed in this chapter help us see patterns in relational communication and provide a starting place for answering our questions and posing new questions. Two critical aspects in using theory should be clear from the chapter. First, some theories are more suited to our personal outlooks than others. This is the case because of the underlying assumptions of the theories. Thus, some researchers may not be comfortable using Social Exchange Theory because they do not agree with the calculating picture of humans that it posits. Second, fitting the right theory to a communication question is also a matter of understanding the boundaries and limits of each theory. A theory like Uncertainty Reduction Theory may be better suited for questions about initial encounters between strangers than to marital interaction, although some researchers have tried to extend the theory's axioms to developed relationships (Planalp and Honeycutt 1985; Turner, 1989). Third, we cannot (and should not) ignore the fact that now people may establish relationships online,

sustain their intimacy via electronic means, and often have acquired an understanding of another's beliefs and values prior to a face-to-face meeting. When we think about these changes in relational life, we have to question how they affect the utility of theories created before technology's impacts.

We might conclude that these five theories are still useful because many of the same issues and concerns in face-to-face relationships operate in relationships initiated and maintained by technology (Pauley & Emmers-Sommer, 2007). Fostering identity and sustaining intimacy, for example, are key parts of (face-to-face) relationship building and both are also critical in electronic relationships. But, alternatively we may believe that new theory is needed because of some critical differences between online and face-to-face relational communication. Online relationships, for instance, are less random (Shin, 2003) and more "hyperpersonal" (High & Caplan, 2008; Walther, 1996; 2009), meaning that technology allows people to exploit it and manipulate their identity and manage others' impressions to attain desired goals.

As we gain experience with theoretical thinking, we can use it to help us answer many perplexing questions about communication in relational life.

REFERENCES

Altman, I., & Taylor, D. A. (1973). *Social penetration: The development of interpersonal relationships.* New York, NY: Holt, Rinehart and Winston.

Baxter, L. A. (1988). A dialectical perspective on communication strategies in relationship development. In S. Duck (Ed.), *Handbook of personal relationships* (pp. 257–273). New York, NY: Wiley.

Baxter, L. A. (1990). Dialectical contradictions in relationship development. *Journal of Social and Personal Relationships, 7,* 69–88.

Baxter, L. A., Braithwaite, D. O., & Bryant, L. (2004). Stepchildren's perceptions of the contradictions in communication with stepparents. *Journal of Social and Personal Relationships, 21,* 447–467.

Baxter, L. A., & Montgomery, B. M. (1996). *Relating: Dialogues and dialectics.* New York, NY: Guilford Press.

Berger, C. R. (1979). Beyond initial interaction: Uncertainty, understanding, and the development of interpersonal relationships. In H. Giles & R. St. Clair (Eds.), *Language and social psychology* (pp. 122–144). Oxford, England: Blackwell.

Berger, C. R., & Bradac, J. J. (1982) *Language and social knowledge: Uncertainty in interpersonal relations.* London, England: E. E. Arnold.

Berger, C. R., & Calabrese, R. J. (1975). Some explorations in initial interaction and beyond: Toward a developmental theory of interpersonal communication. *Human Communication Research, 1*, 99–112.

Blumer, H. (1969). *Symbolic interactionism: Perspective and method.* Englewood Cliffs, NJ: Prentice Hall.

Bolger, N., & Kelleher, S. (1993). Daily life in relationships. In S. Duck (Ed.), *Social context and relationships* (pp. 100–108). Newbury Park, CA: Sage.

Cooley, C. H. (1972). *Human nature and social order.* Glencoe, IL: Free Press.

Dindia, K. (1994). The intrapersonal-interpersonal dialectical process of self-disclosure. In S. Duck (Ed.), *Dynamics of relationships* (pp. 27–56). Thousand Oaks, CA: Sage.

Edwards, M. L. K. (2004). We're decent people: Constructing and managing family identity in rural working class communities. *Journal of Marriage and Family, 66*, 515–529.

Heider, F. (1958). *The psychology of interpersonal relations.* New York, NY: Wiley.

High, A., & Caplan, S.E. (2008). *Social anxiety and computer-mediated communication during initial interactions: Implications for the hyperpersonal perspective.* Paper presented at the annual meeting of the International Communication Association, Montreal, Canada.

Hopper, R., Knapp, M. L., & Scott, L. (1981). Couples' personal idioms: Exploring intimate talk. *Journal of Communication, 31*, 23–33.

Kramer, M. W. (2005). Communication and social exchange processes in community theatre groups. *Journal of Applied Communication Research, 33*, 159–182.

LaRossa, R., & Reitzes, D. C. (1993). Symbolic interactionism and family studies. In P. G. Boss, W. J. Doherty, R. LaRossa, W. R. Schumm, & S. K. Steinmetz (Eds.), *Sourcebook of family theories and methods: A contextual approach* (pp. 135–163). New York, NY: Plenum.

Mead, G. H. (1934). *Mind, self and society: From the standpoint of a social behaviorist.* (Charles W. Morris, ed.). Chicago, IL: The University of Chicago Press.

Miller, G. R. (1981). 'Tis the season to be jolly: A yuletide 1980 assessment of communication research. *Human Communication Research, 7*, 371–377.

Montgomery, B. M. (1992). Communication as the interface between couples and culture. *Communication Yearbook, 15*, 475–507.

Pauley, P. M., & Emmers-Sommer, T.M. (2007). The impact of technologies on primary and secondary romantic relationships development. *Communication Studies, 58*, 411–427.

Planalp, S., & Honeycutt, J. M. (1985). Events that increase uncertainty in personal relationships. *Human Communication Research, 11*, 593–605.

Powell, K. A., & Afifi, T. D. (2005). Uncertainty management and adoptee's ambiguous loss of their birth parents. *Journal of Social and Personal Relationships, 22*, 129–151.

Rawlins, W. K. (1992). *Friendship matters: Communication, dialectics, and the life course.* New York, NY: Aldine De Gruyter.

Roloff, M. E. (1981). *Interpersonal communication: The social exchange approach.* Beverly Hills, CA: Sage.

Sabatelli, R. M., & Shehan, C. L. (1993). Exchange and resource theories. In P. G. Boss, W. J. Doherty, R. LaRossa, W. R. Schumm, & S. K. Steinmetz (Eds.), *Sourcebook of family theories and methods: A contextual approach* (pp. 385–411). New York, NY: Plenum.

Shin, L. (2003, May 9). Ah, sweet mystery of email. *New York Times*, D2.

Taylor, D. A., & Altman, I. (1987). Communication in interpersonal relationships: Social penetration processes. In M. E. Roloff & G. R. Miller (Eds.), *Interpersonal processes: New directions in communication research* (pp. 257–277). Newbury Park, CA: Sage.

Thibaut, J., & Kelley, H. (1959). *The social psychology of groups.* New York, NY: Wiley.

Turner, J. H. (1986). *The structure of sociological theory* (4th ed.). Chicago, IL: Dorsey.

Turner, L. H. (1989). *The relationship between communication and marital uncertainty* (Unpublished doctoral dissertation). Northwestern University, Evanston, IL.

Walker, L. (1984). *The battered woman syndrome*. New York, NY: Springer.

Walther, J. B. (1996). Computer-mediated communication: Impersonal, interpersonal and hyperpersonal interaction. *Communication Research, 23,* 3–43.

Walther, J. B. (2009). Theories, boundaries, and all of the above. *Journal of Computer Mediated Communication, 14,* 748–752.

Wood, J. T., Dendy, L. L., Dordek, E., Germany, M., & Varallo, S. M. (1994). Dialectic of difference: A thematic analysis of intimates' meanings for differences. In K. Carter & M. Prisnell (Eds.), *Interpretive approaches to interpersonal communication* (pp. 115–136). New York, NY: SUNY Press.

Zhong, M., Myers, S. A., & Buerkel, R. (2004). Communication and intergenerational differences between Chinese fathers and sons. *Journal of Intercultural Communication Research, 33,* 15–27.

QUESTIONS/THOUGHTS

1. Your answers to the following questions will serve as a basis for your worldview about human nature and will help to explain when you are attracted to certain theories more than others.

   To what extent do you believe human nature is based on nature or nurture?

   How strongly do you believe human behavior is guided by self-interest?

   How predictable do you find human behavior to be?

   After reading this chapter, pick on of the theories and explain how your worldview influences how you evaluate that theory.

2. Identify and explain two questions or two of your personal theories about relationships that were not addressed in the five theories covered by this chapter.

3. Discuss social exchange theory with three friends. Ask them if they analyze their relationships using an economic model. If they keep a list of rewards and costs in their heads, how does this affect their relationships? If not, what other way do they determine if the relationship is effective? Discuss your findings in class.

4. Consider how social penetration theory might have been altered in recent years as new technologies provided opportunities for many initial encounters to take place without a face-to-face meeting? Write a page describing the extent to which you develop many new relationships with or without extensive face-to-face contact.

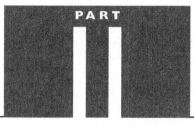

Building Blocks

Introduction

The ability to speak and hear does not ensure communicative success. Effective communication depends on the knowledge, skill, and sensitivity of the speakers and listeners. People who communicate effectively are referred to as *competent communicators*; they appear to know what to say or do in almost every situation. Competent communicators do not possess a secret formula or magical power; they follow a set of steps that allows them to increase their effectiveness with each encounter of an ongoing relationship. The goals of the Building Blocks section are to help you understand what it means to be a competent communicator and to encourage you to make efforts to increase your communication competence.

The term *communication competence* refers to a person's knowledge of how to use verbal and nonverbal language appropriately in a range of communication situations. When people work to develop communication competence, they are concerned with "putting language to work" in the following ways (Wood 1977; Galvin and Terrell 2001).

1. Enlarging a personal repertoire of communication strategies.
2. Establishing criteria and choosing one of more communication strategies from the repertoire. Analyzing options and determining the best one for this situation.
3. Implementing the communication strategies chosen. Acting on the chosen option.
4. Evaluating the effectiveness of the strategies. Reviewing results of the encounter.

STAGES OF COMPETENCE DEVELOPMENT

Enlarging the Repertoire of Communication Strategies

The term "communication strategies" refers to the specific verbal and nonverbal messages created to reach a certain goal when interacting with one or more specific other persons. To be effective, communicators must be able to imagine and perform a range of communication strategies appropriate to: the conversation, the other person(s), the setting, and the communicative goal. The more you observe interpersonal interactions carefully, the more ways you can envision for responding to communication difficulties or unpredictable interactions. For example, as a student you may have four strategies for requesting an extension on an assignment, although a few years ago you only had one or two strategies. You enlarge your communicative repertoire by observing others; you see multiple strategies for handling certain communication situations, you learn to implement new strategies and you reflect on ways you might have handled difficult situations more effectively. A competent communicator always considers a number of possible ways he or she might deal with a situation; alternatives are crucial to this process.

Selecting a Strategy

Communication effectiveness is based on the appropriateness of the alternative chosen from the communicative repertoire. The competent communicator carefully weighs the factors of the situation, including:

1. WHO—What do you know about the people involved in the interaction? What tends to make this person defensive or what makes him laugh? Think about your past relationship and the possible future relationship with the individual.
2. WHERE—How does the setting or context—the time, privacy, and place, or presence of specific other people—affect your interaction?
3. WHAT—How important is the subject matter or situation to the other person or yourself? Who is most highly knowledgeable about the topic? How important is it for the other person to save face?
4. TASK—What is the purpose or goal of the interaction? To solve a problem, reduce

interpersonal tensions, or just have a good time?

Competent communicators select from their extensive repertoires of communication strategies—those that they perceive to be the most appropriate, given the situational factors. The goal of the selection step is to provide an opportunity to identify and sharpen the criteria used in choosing communication strategies. It helps you develop an immediate communication plan. For example, "I'm going to joke around to break the tension" or "I'm going to say it was my fault so she saves face."

Acting on the Choice

How often have you known what you should say or do in a particular situation, but you didn't act on this knowledge? Once people have made communication choices for a particular situation, they must possess skills and the willingness to enact their communication plan. Selecting a strategy creates no benefit unless you act on it. It is one thing to plan to tell a friend that she hurt your feelings and another thing to actually talk to the person about it. Just as skilled athletes spend time visualizing their every move on the field, skilled communicators visualize difficult situations in their minds and mentally rehearse how to handle them. Often, they may try out strategies with a "safe" person before confronting the "difficult" person. These planning procedures help build confidence to act on, or implement, the selected strategy.

Evaluating the Relational Effects

The final step involves making a judgment about the effectiveness of the strategy you implemented. You need to evaluate your communication in terms of its relational outcome. As people develop communicative competence, they make more informed judgments about their message effectiveness. These judgments are based on feedback from others, as well as from your personal assessment.

By evaluating each encounter in terms of appropriateness and satisfaction, communicators gain valuable information and develop new criteria for future interactions. Your goal is to sharpen critical awareness of self and others ("Did my plan work?" "What is the effect of my chosen strategy?" "How did the other person appear to feel?" "What would I do in a future similar situation?"). When you communicate in important situations, you need to examine the interaction's effect in order to decide whether you would repeat the strategy in a similar situation or try something different.

Communication competence contributes to successful and satisfying personal relationships. Competent communicators are more likely to reach their goals (Canary, Cody, and Manusov, 2008). As later readings in this text suggest, there is little question that communication competence is an important ingredient in the development of friendship, family, and workplace relationships.

This section will address the building blocks, the foundation of the communication process—verbal communication, nonverbal communication, listening. As you read each of the articles, consider how an understanding of each can help you become a more competent communicator.

REFERENCES

Canary, D. J., Cody, M. J., & Manusov, V. L. (2008). *Interpersonal communication: A goals-based approach* (4th ed). Boston, MA: Bedford/St. Martin's.

Galvin, K. M., & Terrell, J. (2001). *Communication works!* Columbus, OH: Glencoe Press.

Wood, B. (Ed.). (1977). *Development of functional communication skills: Grades 7–12.* Urbana, IL: ERIC and Speech Association.

Elements of Language

RUDOLPH F. VERDERBER AND KATHLEEN S. VERDERBER

A word is a symbol but, as these authors indicate, it is not a thing. Stop reading for a moment and write down your description for the word "frog." What did you write? A tailless amphibian? A small holder placed in a vase to hold flower stems in position? A hoarseness in your throat? A mass of elastic substance found in the middle of a horse's foot? An ornament for fastening the front of a coat? All these are correct definitions of "frog." It's all in the meaning you had in mind.

Words, in addition to being symbolic, are also arbitrary. They derive their meaning from the people who use them. Linguists Ogden and Richards created the "semantic triangle," or "triangle of meaning," to graphically illustrate this symbolic, arbitrary nature of words:

The symbol (lower left-hand corner) is a word. The apex of the triangle is the thought—the concept you have of an object, idea, or event. The referent (lower right-hand corner) is the actual object or thing being perceived. For example, you see a chair and say "chair." The word you speak is the symbol, the thought is your image of the chair, and the referent is the actual chair. Notice that the line connecting the symbol and the referent is broken.

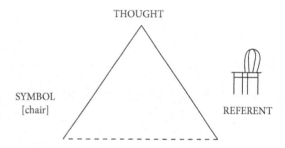

Figure 5-1

This indicates that the symbol and the referent have no connection except that which you make in your mind—in your thoughts.

As language changes rapidly in a technological world, words have migrated into the world of the Internet where they acquire completely new meanings. Consider simple words such as mouse, cookie, or nickname. The Internet has spawned a whole new vocabulary that only certain users understand quite well. Terms related to social media, such as Web 2.0, blog, wiki, tweet, and viral messaging were unknown a few years ago, and remain unknown to certain individuals, especially those with limited access to, or interest in, the Internet. Our language and behavior is caught up in a groundswell, or "A social trend in which people use technologies to get the things they need from each other, rather than from traditional institutions like corporations" (Li & Bernoff, 2008). And this groundswell includes a whole new vocabulary.

In this chapter on language, the authors describe the importance of meaning and how meanings change across time and subgroups. In addition, they suggest ways to speak more clearly and to be sensitive to cultural and gender differences. Excellent guidelines for language use are included. Research on verbal aggression between spouses (Stamp and Sabourin 1995) reveals that men who abuse their wives experience their spouses' verbal aggression as having physical force, such as "It was a real blow." In some cases they responded to this attack with physical force. Other research reveals the negative effects of hostile parent messages on children (Vissing and Baily 1996). Such aggression, often called verbal abuse, includes disparaging terms, insults, belittling, ridiculing, sarcasm, and threats.

On a lighter note, think about the words that are used in everyday language but which derive from the game of poker. For example, you talk about being "passing the buck" and "standing pat" without thinking about the gaming origin of the words. Consider how you use words strategically to affect relationships and how others do the same to you.

Through careful definitions and examination of how words shape meaning depending on culture and context, this chapter looks at communication from a technical standpoint: highlighting uses of grammar, syntax, connotation, and denotation in everyday speech. First illustrating the universal purposes of language, authors Verderber and Verderber describe how someone's use of language can sometimes change or confuse meanings, and they offer strategies for speaking more clearly, precisely, and accurately. As you read this chapter consider the question: How conscious are you of changing your language as you move from one circumstance to another, such as from a classroom to an athletic field or from an office to a family dinner?

REFERENCES

Li, C., & Bernoff, J. (2008). *Groundswell*. Boston, MA: Harvard Business Press.

Ogden, C. K., & Richards, I. A. (1923). *The meaning of meaning*. New York, NY: Harcourt Brace.

Stamp, G., & Sabourin, T. (1995). Accounting for violence: An analysis of male spousal abuse narratives. *Journal of Applied Communication Research*, 23, 284–307.

Vissing, Y., & Baily, W. (1996). Parent-to-child verbal aggression. In D. Cahn & S. Lloyd (Eds.), *Family violence from a communication perspective.* (85–107). Thousand Oaks, CA: Sage.

THE NATURE OF LANGUAGE

Language is the body of words and the systems for their use that are common to the people of the same language community.

Uses of Language

Although language communities vary in the words that they use and in their grammar and syntax systems, all languages serve the same purposes.

1. *We use language to designate, label, define, and limit.* Thus, when we identify a house as a "Tudor," we are differentiating it from another that may be identified as an "A-frame."

2. *We use language to evaluate.* Through language we give positive or negative slants. For instance, if you see Hal taking more time than others to make a decision, you could describe Hal positively as "thoughtful" or negatively as "dawdling."

3. *We use language to discuss things outside our immediate experience.* Language enables us to speak hypothetically, to talk about past and future events, and to communicate about people and things that are not present. Thus, we can use language to discuss where we hope to be in five years, to analyze a conversation two acquaintances had last week, or to learn about the history that shapes the world we live in.

4. *We can use language to talk about language.* We can use language to discuss how someone phrased a statement and whether better phrasing would have resulted in

a clearer meaning or a more positive response. For instance, if your friend said she would see you "this afternoon," but she didn't arrive until 5 o'clock, when you ask her where she's been, the two of you are likely to discuss the meaning of "this afternoon."

Language and Meaning

On the surface, the relationship between language and meaning seems perfectly clear: We select the correct word, and people will interpret our meaning correctly. In fact, the relationship between language and meaning is not nearly so simple for two reasons: Language must be learned, and the use of language is a creative act.

First, we are not born knowing a language. Rather, each generation within a language community learns the language anew. We learn much of our language early in life from our families; much more we learn in school. But we do not all learn to use the same words in the same way.

A second reason the relationship between language and meaning is complicated is that even though languages have systems of syntax and grammar each utterance is a creative act. When we speak, we use language to create new sentences that represent our meaning. Although on occasion we repeat other people's sentence constructions to represent what we are thinking or feeling, some of our talk is unique.

A third reason language and meaning is so complicated is that people interpret the meaning of words differently. Words have two kinds of meaning: denotative and connotative. Thus, when Melissa tells Trish that her dog died, what Trish understands Melissa to mean depends on both word denotation and connotation.

Denotation. The direct, explicit meaning a language community formally gives a word is its *denotation*. Word denotation is the meaning found in a dictionary. So, denotatively, when Melissa said her dog died, she meant that her domesticated canine no longer demonstrates physical life. In some situations the denotative meaning of a word may not be clear. Why? First, dictionary definitions reflect current and past practice in the language community; and second, the dictionary

uses words to define words. The end result is that words are defined differently in various dictionaries and often include multiple meanings that change over time.

Moreover, meaning may vary depending on the context in which the word is used. For example, the dictionary definition of *gay* includes both having or showing a merry, lively mood and homosexual. Thus, *context*, the position of a word in a sentence and the other words around it, has an important effect on correctly interpreting which denotation of a word is meant. Not only will the other words and the syntax and grammar of a verbal message help us to understand the denotative meaning of certain words, but so will the situation in which they are spoken. Whether the comment "He's really gay" is understood to be a comment on someone's sexual orientation or on his merry mood may depend on the circumstances in which it is said.

Connotation. The feelings or evaluations we associate with a word represent the *connotation* and may be even more important to our understanding of meaning.

C. K. Ogden and I. A. Richards (1923) were among the first scholars to consider the misunderstandings resulting from the failure of communicators to realize that their subjective reactions to words are based on their life experiences. For instance, when Melissa tells Trisha that her dog died, Trisha's understanding of the message depends on the extent to which her feelings about pets and death—her connotations of the words—correspond to the feelings that Melissa has about pets and death. Melissa, who sees dogs as truly indispensable friends, may be trying to communicate a true sense of grief, but Trish, who has never had a pet and doesn't particularly care for dogs, may miss the sense of Melissa's statement.

Word denotation and connotation are important because the only message that counts is the message that is understood, regardless of whether it is the message you intended.

Meaning Varies Across Subgroups in the Language Community

As we mentioned earlier, within a larger language community, subgroups with unique cultures are sometimes formed. These subgroups develop variations on the core language that enable them to share meanings unique to their subcultural experience. People from different subcultures approach the world from different perspectives, so they are likely to experience some difficulty sharing meaning when they talk with each other....

In addition to subgroups based on race, religion, and national origin, there are also subgroup cultures associated with generation, social class, and political interests. The need for awareness and sensitivity in applying our communication skills does not depend on someone's being an immigrant or from a different ethnic background. Rather, the need for being aware of potential language differences is important in every type of communication. Developing our language skills so that the messages we send are clear and sensitive will increase our communication effectiveness in every situation.

SPEAKING MORE CLEARLY

Regardless of whether we are conversing, communicating in groups, or giving speeches, we can speak more clearly by reducing the ambiguity and confusion. Compare these two descriptions of a close call in an automobile: "Some nut almost got me with his car a while ago" versus "An older man in a banged-up Honda Civic crashed the light at Calhoun and Clifton and came within inches of hitting me last week while I was waiting to turn left at the cross street." The differences are in clarity. In the second example, the message used language that was specific, concrete, and precise as well as statements that are dated and indexed.

Specificity, Concreteness, and Precision in Language Use

Specific words clarify meaning by narrowing what is understood from a general category to a particular item or group within that category. Thus saying "It's a Honda Civic" is more specific than saying "It's a car." *Concrete words* are sense-related. In effect we can see, hear, smell, taste, or touch concrete words. Thus we can picture that "banged up" Civic. Abstract ideas, such as justice, equality, or

fairness, can be made concrete through examples or metaphors. *Precise words* are those that most accurately express meaning—they capture shades of difference. It is more precise to note that the Civic came "within inches of hitting me" than it is to say "some nut almost got me."

Often, as we try to express our thoughts, the first words that come to mind are general, abstract, and imprecise. The ambiguity of these words makes the listener choose from many possible images rather than picturing the single focused image we have in mind. The more listeners are called on to provide their own images, the more likely they are to see meanings different from what we intend....

As we move from general to specific, we also move from abstract to concrete. Consider the word *speak*. This is a general, abstract term. To make it more concrete, we can use words such as *mumble, whisper, bluster, drone, jeer,* or *rant*. Say these words aloud. Notice the different sound of your voice when you say *whisper* as opposed to *bluster, jeer,* or *rant*.

Finally, we seek words that are precise—those that most accurately or correctly capture the sense of what we are saying. In seeking the most precise word to describe Phillip's speech, at first we might say, "Phillip blustered. Well, to be more precise, he ranted." Notice that we are not moving from general to specific; both words are on roughly the same level of abstraction. Nor are we talking about abstract versus concrete; both words are concrete. Rather, we are now concerned with precision in meaning. *Blustering* means talking in a way that is loudly boastful; *ranting* means talking in a way that is noisy or bombastic. So, what we are considering here is shades of meaning: Depending on how the person was talking, *blustering* or *ranting* would be the more precise word....

Although specific, concrete, and precise words enable us to reduce ambiguity and sharpen meaning through individual words, sometimes clarity is best achieved by adding a detail or an example. For instance, Linda might add, "He never criticizes a friend behind her back." By following up her use of the abstract concept of loyalty with a concrete example, Linda makes it easier for her listeners to "ground" their idea of this personal quality in a concrete or "real" experience....

Developing the Ability to Speak More Clearly

Being able to speak more clearly requires us to build our working vocabulary and to brainstorm to generate word choices from our active vocabulary.

Vocabulary building. As a speaker, the larger your vocabulary, the more choices you have from which to select the word you want. As a listener, the larger your vocabulary, the more likely you are to understand the words used by others.

One way to increase your vocabulary is to study one of the many vocabulary building books on the shelves of most any bookstore, such as *Merriam Webster's Vocabulary Builder* (Cornog, 1998). You might also study magazine features such as "Word Power" in the *Reader's Digest*. By completing this monthly quiz and learning the words with which you are not familiar, you could increase your vocabulary by as many as twenty words per month.

A second way to increase your vocabulary is to make note of words that you read or that people use in their conversations with you and look them up. For instance, suppose you read or hear, "I was inundated with phone calls today!" If you wrote inundated down and looked it up in a dictionary later, you would find that "inundated" means *overwhelmed* or *flooded*. If you then say to yourself, "She was inundated—overwhelmed or flooded—with phone calls today," you are likely to remember that meaning and apply it the next time you hear the word. If you follow this practice, you will soon notice the increase in your vocabulary.

Mental brainstorming. Having a larger vocabulary won't help your speaking if you do not have a procedure for using it. One way to practice accessing choices from your memory is to brainstorm during practice sessions and later in conversation. *Brainstorming* is an uncritical, nonevaluative process of generating alternatives. Suppose someone asked you about how well preregistration was working. You might initially say, "Preregistration is awful." If you don't think that *awful* is the right word, you might be able to quickly brainstorm the words *frustrating, demeaning, cumbersome*, and *annoying*. Then you could say, "What I really meant to say is that preregistration is overly cumbersome."...

Dating Information

Because nearly everything changes with time, it is important that we *date* the information we communicate by telling when it was true. Not dating leads to inaccuracies that can be dangerous. For instance, Parker says, "I'm going to be transferred to Henderson City." Laura replies, "Good luck—they've had some real trouble with their schools." On the basis of Laura's statement, Parker may worry about the effect his move will have on his children. What he doesn't know is that Laura's information about this problem in Henderson City is five years old! Henderson City still may have problems, but then, it may not. Had Laura replied, "Five years ago, I know they had some real trouble with their schools. I'm not sure what the situation is now, but you may want to check," Parker would look at the information differently.

Let's consider two additional examples:

Undated: Professor Powell brings great enthusiasm to her teaching.

Dated: Professor Powell brings great enthusiasm to her teaching—at least she did *last quarter* in communication theory.

Undated: You think Mary's depressed? I'm surprised. She seemed her regular high-spirited self when I talked with her.

Dated: You think Mary's depressed? I'm surprised. She seemed her regular high-spirited self when I talked with her *the day before yesterday*.

To date information, (1) consider or find out when the information was true and (2) verbally acknowledge it. We have no power to prevent change. Yet we can increase the effectiveness of our messages through verbally acknowledging the reality of change if we date the statements we make.

Indexing Generalizations

Generalizing—drawing a conclusion from particulars—enables people to use what they have learned from one experience and apply it to another. For instance, when Glenda learns that tomatoes and squash grow better if the ground is fertilized, she generalizes that fertilizing will help all of her vegetables grow better. Glenda has used what she learned from one experience and applied it to another.

Indexing generalizations is the mental and verbal practice of acknowledging that individual cases can differ from the general trend while still allowing us to draw on generalization. For instance, we may have a generalized concept of "men." But we must recognize that although Fred, Darnell, and William are all men, they are likely to have individual differences. So, how do we index in ordinary speaking? Let's consider two examples:

Generalization: Because men are stronger than women, Max is stronger than Barbara.

Indexed Statement: In general men are stronger than women, so _Max is probably stronger_ than Barbara.

Generalization: Your Chevrolet should go 50,000 miles before you need a brake job; Jerry's did.

Indexed Statement: Your Chevrolet may well go 50,000 miles before you need a brake job; Jerry's did, _but of course, all Chevrolets aren't the same._

To index, (1) consider whether what you want to say is about a specific object, person, or place, or whether it is a generalization about a class to which the object, person, or place belongs. (2) If what you want to say is a generalization about the class, qualify it appropriately so that your assertion does not go beyond the evidence that supports it. All people generalize at one time or another, but by indexing statements we can avoid the problems that hasty generalization sometimes creates.

Cultural Differences in Verbal Communication

Cultures vary in how much meaning is embedded in the language itself and how much meaning is interpreted from the context in which the communication occurs.

In _low-context cultures_, such as in Northern Europe or the United States, meaning (1) is embedded mainly in the messages transmitted and (2) is presented directly. In low-context cultures, people say what they mean and get right to the point (Gudykunst & Matsumoto, 1996, pp. 29–30). So, in a low-context culture, "Yes" means "Affirmative, I agree with what you have said." In _high-context cultures_, such as Asian or Middle Eastern countries, meaning is interpreted based on the physical, social, and relational context. High-context culture people expect others to use context cues to interpret meaning. As a result, they present meanings indirectly. In a high-context culture, "Yes" may mean "Affirmative, I agree with what you have said," or it may mean "In this setting it would embarrass you if I said 'No,' so I will say 'Yes,' to be polite, but I really don't agree and you should know this, so in the future don't expect me to act as if I have just agreed with what you said." People from high-context cultures expect others to understand unarticulated feelings and subtle nonverbal gestures that people from low-context cultures don't even process. As a result, misunderstandings often occur.

The United States has a low-context national culture, as described previously. But the United States is a country of immigrants, and we know that individual Americans differ in whether they are high or low context in their approach to language. So, although knowing the characteristics of a national culture or culture of origin may be useful, we still need to be aware that people may or may not behave in line with their ethnic cultures (Adamopoulos, 1999, p. 75). Then why mention these differences at all? Because they give us a clue to how and why people and cultures may differ. An essential aspect of communication is being sensitive to needs and differences among us, so we must be aware of what the nature of those differences might be.

Gender Differences in Verbal Communication

Over the last two decades, stirred by such book titles as _Men Are from Mars, Women Are from Venus_, people have come to believe gender differences in verbal messages are genetic. Yet research strongly states that differences in gender behaviors are learned rather than biological and that the differences are not nearly as large as portrayed (Wood & Dindia, 1998, pp. 34–36).

There is no evidence to suggest that the differences that have been identified between women's message construction patterns and those of men cause "problems" for either group (Canary & Hause, 1993, p. 141). Nevertheless, a number of specific differences between women's and men's speech patterns have been found, and understanding what has led to them has intrigued scholars. Mulac (1998) notes two differences in language usage between men and women that seem to have the greatest support (pp. 133–134):

1. *Women tend to use both more intensifiers and more hedges than men.* Intensifiers are words that modify other words and serve to strengthen the idea represented by the original word. So, according to studies of the actual speech practices of men and women, women are more likely to use words such as *awfully, quite,* and *so* (as in "It was quite lovely" or "This is so important"). Hedges are modifying words that soften or weaken the meaning of the idea represented by the original word. According to the research, women are likely to make greater use of such words as *somewhat, perhaps,* or *maybe* (as in "It was somewhat interesting that…" or "It may be significant that…").

2. *Women ask questions more frequently than men.* Women are much more likely to include questions like "Do you think so?" and "Are you sure?" In general, women tend to use questions to gain more information, get elaboration, and determine how others feel about the information.

But are these differences really important? Mulac goes on the report that "our research has shown that language used by U.S. women and men is remarkably similar. In fact, it is so indistinguishable that native speakers of American English cannot correctly identify which language

examples were produced by women and which were produced by men" (p. 130). If this is so, then why even mention differences? Even though the differences are relatively small, they have judgmental consequences: "Observers perceive the female and male speakers differently based on their language use" (p. 147). Female speakers are rated higher on *socio-intellectual status* and *aesthetic quality.* Thus people perceive women as having high social status, being literate, and being pleasant as a result of perceived language differences. Men rated higher on *dynamism.* That is, people perceive men to be stronger and more aggressive as a result of their language differences. These judgments tend to be the same whether observers are male or female, middle-aged or young (p. 148).

Julia Wood (1997) explains these differences in language usage as resulting from differences in the basic psychological orientation each sex acquires in growing up. Women establish gender identity by seeing themselves as "like" or connected to mother. They learn to use communication as a primary way of establishing and maintaining relationships with others (p. 167). Men establish their gender identity by understanding how they are different or "separate" from mother. Thus they use talk as a way to "exert control, preserve independence, and enhance status" (p. 173).

SPEAKING APPROPRIATELY

During the last few years, we have had frequent discussions and disagreements in the United States about "political correctness." Colleges and universities have been on the forefront of this debate. Although several issues germane to the debate on political correctness go beyond the scope of this chapter, at the heart of this controversy is the question of what language behaviors are appropriate—and what language behaviors are inappropriate.

Speaking appropriately means choosing language and symbols that are adapted to the needs, interests, knowledge, and attitudes of listeners in order to avoid language that alienates them. Through appropriate language, we communicate our respect and acceptance of those who are different from us. In this section, we discuss specific strategies that will help you craft appropriate verbal messages.

Formality of Language

Language should be appropriately formal for the situation. Thus, in interpersonal settings, we are likely to use more informal language when we are talking with our best friend and more formal language when we are talking with our parents. In a group setting, we are likely to use more informal language when we are talking with a group of our peers and more formal language when we are talking with a group of managers. In a public-speaking setting, we are likely to use more formal language than in either interpersonal or group settings....

Jargon and Slang

Appropriate language should be chosen so that _jargon_ (technical terminology) and _slang_ (informal, nonstandard vocabulary) do not interfere with understanding. We form language communities as a result of the work we do, our hobbies, and the subcultures with which we identify. But we can forget that people who are not in our same line of work or who do not have the same hobbies or are not from our group may not understand language that seems to be such a part of our daily communication. For instance, when Jenny, who is sophisticated in the use of cyberlanguage, starts talking with her computer-illiterate friend Sarah about "Social MUDs based on fictional universes," Sarah is likely to be totally lost. If, however, Jenny recognizes Sarah's lack of sophistication in cyberlanguage, she can work to make her language appropriate by discussing the concepts in words that her friend understands. In short, when talking with people outside your language community, you need to carefully explain, if not abandon, the technical jargon or slang.

PROFANITY AND VULGAR EXPRESSIONS

Appropriate language does not include profanity or vulgar expression. There was a time when uttering "hell" or "damn" would have resulted in severe punishment for children and social isolation for adults. Today we tend to tolerate commonplace profanities and vulgarities, and there are many subcultures where the use of profanity and vulgarity are commonplace. Under the influence of film and television writers who aim to scintillate and entertain, we have become inoculated to these expressions. In fact, it is common to hear elementary schoolchildren utter strings of "four letter" words in school hallways, lunchrooms, and on playgrounds....

Sensitivity

Language is appropriate when it is sensitive to usages that others perceive as offensive. Some of the mistakes in language that we make result from using expressions that are perceived to be sexist, racist, or otherwise biased—that is, any language that is perceived as belittling any person or group of people by virtue of their sex, race, age, handicap, or other identifying characteristics. Two of the most prevalent linguistic uses that communicate insensitivity are generic language and nonparallel language.

Generic language. Generic language uses words that may apply only to one sex, race, or gender as though they represent both sexes, races, or genders. Such use is a problem because it linguistically excludes part of the group of people it ostensibly includes. Let's consider some examples.

Traditionally, English grammar called for the use of the masculine pronoun _he_ to stand for the entire class of humans regardless of sex. So, in the past, standard English called for such usage as, "When a person shops, _he_ should have a clear idea of what _he_ wants to buy." Even though these statements are gramatically correct, they are now considered sexist because they inherently exclude females. Despite traditional usage, it would be hard to maintain that we picture people of both sexes when we hear the masculine word _he_.

One way to avoid this problem is to recast the sentence using plurals. Instead of "Because a doctor has high status, his views may be believed regardless of topic," you could say "Because doctors have high status, their views may be believed regardless of topic." Alternatively, you can use both male and female pronouns: "Because a doctor has high status, his or her views may be believed regardless of topic." These changes may seem small, but they may mean the difference between alienating and not alienating the people with whom you are speaking. Stewart, Cooper, Stewart, and Friedly (1998) cite research to show that using "he and she," and to a lesser extent "they," gives rise to listeners' including women in their mental images, thus increasing gender balance in their perceptions (p. 63).

A second problem results from the traditional reliance on the use of the generic *man*. Many words have become a common part of our language that are inherently sexist because they seem to apply to only one gender. Consider the term *manmade*. What this really means is that a product was produced by human beings, but its underlying connotation is that a male human being made the item. Some people try to argue that just because a word has "man" within it does not really affect people's understanding of meaning. But research has demonstrated that people usually visualize men (not women) when they read or hear these words. Moreover, when job titles end in "man," their occupants are assumed to have stereotypically masculine personality traits (Gmelch, 1998, p. 51)....

Nonparallel language. Nonparallel language occurs when terms are changed because of the sex, race, or other characteristic of the individual. Because it treats groups of people differently, nonparallel language is also belittling. Two common forms of nonparallelism are marking and unnecessary association.

Marking means adding sex, race, age, or other designations unnecessarily to a general word. For instance, saying "female" doctor or "black" lawyer would be marking. Marking is offensive to some people because the speaker appears to be trivializing the person's role by emphasizing an irrelevant characteristic. For instance, this usage seems to imply that Jones is a good doctor for a woman or Smith is a good lawyer for a black person. Because you would be very unlikely to ever say "Jones is a good male doctor" and "Smith is a good white lawyer," leave sex, race, age, and other markers out of your labeling.

Another form of nonparallelism is to emphasize one person's association with another when you are not talking about the other person. Very often you will hear a speaker say something like this: "Gladys Thompson, whose husband is CEO of Acme Inc., is the chairperson for this year's United Way campaign." In response to this sentence, you might say that the association of Gladys Thompson with her husband gives further credentials to Gladys Thompson. But using the association may be seen to imply that Gladys Thompson is important not because of her own accomplishment but because of her husband's. If a person has done or said something noteworthy, you should recognize it without making unnecessary associations.

Very few people can escape all unfair language. By monitoring your usage, however, you can guard against frustrating your attempts to communicate by assuming that others will react to your language the same way you do, and you can guard against saying or doing things that offend others and perpetuate outdated sex roles, racial stereotypes, and other biased language.

How can you speak more appropriately? (1) Assess whether the word or phrase used is less appropriate than it should be; (2) pause to mentally brainstorm alternatives; and (3) select a more appropriate word....

SUMMARY

Language is a system of symbols used for communicating. Through language, we designate, label, and define; evaluate; talk about things outside our immediate experience; and talk about language itself.

You will be a more effective communicator if you recognize that language symbols are arbitrary, that language is learned and is creative, and that language and perception are interrelated....

REFERENCES

Adamopoulos, J. (1999). The emergence of cultural patterns of interpersonal behavior. In

J. Adamopoulos & Y. Kashima (Eds.), *Social psychology and cultural context* (pp. 63–76). Thousand Oaks, CA: Sage.

Canary, D. J., & Hause, K. (1993). Is there any reason to research sex differences in communication? *Communication Quarterly, 41,* 129–144.

Cornog, M. W. (1998). *Merriam Webster's vocabulary builder.* Springfield, MA: Merriam Webster.

Gmelch, S. B. (1998). *Gender on campus: Issues for college women.* New Brunswick, NJ: Rutgers University Press.

Gudykunst, W. B., & Matsumoto, Y. (1996). Cross-cultural variability of communication in personal relationships. In W. B. Gudykunst, S. Ting-Toomey, & T. Nishida (Eds.), *Communication in personal relationships across cultures* (pp. 19–56). Thousand Oaks, CA: Sage.

Mulac, A. (1998). The gender-linked language effect: Do language differences really make a difference? In D. J. Canary & K. Dindia (Eds.), *Sex differences and similarities in communication: Critical essays and empirical investigations of sex and gender in interaction* (pp. 127–154). Mahwah, NJ: Erlbaum.

Ogden, C. K., & Richards, I. A. (1923). *The meaning of meaning.* London, England: Kegan, Paul, Trench, Trubner.

Stewart, L. P., Cooper, P. J., Stewart, A. D., & Friedley, S. A. (1998). *Communication and gender* (3rd ed.). Boston, MA: Allyn & Bacon.

Wood, J. T. (1997). *Gendered lives: Communication, gender, and culture* (2nd ed.). Belmont, CA: Wadsworth.

Wood, J. T., & Dindia, K. (1998). What's the difference? A dialogue about differences and similarities between women and men. In D. J. Canary & K. Dindia (Eds.), *Sex differences and similarities in communication: Critical essays and empirical investigations of sex and gender in interaction* (pp. 19–40). Mahwah, NJ: Erlbaum.

QUESTIONS/THOUGHTS

1. List as many meanings of the words *fork, contact, burn, cool,* as you can. Compare your list with some of your classmates'. How are the definitions similar? Different? How would those similarities and differences affect communication?

2. What have you learned about adjusting your language across subgroups of peers? Give two examples of adjustments you regularly make.

3. Write a paragraph describing the language choices and use by someone you consider highly skilled in a specialized area. Include two or three examples of that person's effectiveness when talking with other experts and when talking with people unfamiliar with the area.

4. How is the language associated with new media (IM, tweets, etc.) moving into everyday spoken and written language. Give examples.

Listening and Feedback:
The Other Half of Communication

THOMAS E. HARRIS AND JOHN C. SHERBLOM

Author and diarist James Boswell once said that talking isn't everything. It's only half of a communication skill—the other half is listening. In reality, research indicates that listening is actually more than half. Yet for all its importance, you spend little time learning to listen. No parent waits eagerly for a child to learn to listen. Rather, the emphasis is on learning to talk. In their study of how engineers describe the importance of oral communication, Ann Darling and Deanna Dannels (2003) found that 50 percent of the respondents indicated that public speaking was the most important oral communication genre. When asked about the importance of specific oral communication skills, 37 percent listed message construction, 27 percent noted interpersonal interaction, and 27 reported public speaking/delivery skills. Clearly these engineers valued communication skills. Yet, only 7 percent of these engineers prioritized listening! This is consistent with the belief that listening just happens naturally. In reality, listening is the least taught but the most used skill. The engineers reported on the importance of learning how to talk to people but never reflected on how much time they spent listening to their colleagues.

Listening is like physical exercise. Everyone knows it is important, but many find it difficult to do on a regular basis. Listening is hard work. Listening is a complex activity involving four elements:

- Hearing—the physiological process of receiving aural stimuli.
- Interpretation of sound waves—leading to understanding or misunderstanding.
- Evaluation—deciding how to use the information.
- Response—reacting to information.

If any of these steps is missing, listening has not occurred. There are no shortcuts to effective listening. It is an active, difficult, time-consuming process.

One of the reasons listening is difficult is physiological in origin. Although we are capable of understanding speech rates up to 500 or 600 words per minute, the average speaker speaks between 100 and 140 words per minute. Thus, we have a lot of "spare time" to spend thinking while the other person is talking. Too often, rather than spending this time focusing on the other person, we allow ourselves to be distracted. These distractions may be physical (a hot room, uncomfortable clothing, *loud or annoying noises), mental (focusing on ourselves—what we'll say next, our own needs—or allowing our preconceived attitudes to prematurely determine the value of what the other person is saying), semantic (reacting emotionally to the words), and factual (listening for facts rather than the main ideas and feelings of the message).*

Listening is part of the transactional process of communication. The receiver's responses have a direct impact on the direction of the conversation. The key is to become active listeners rather than passive ones. Active listening involves providing feedback that clarifies and extends a speaker's message. Active listening attempts to reflect rather than direct another's message. As an active listener you seek to draw out the speaker's feelings and thoughts rather than focusing on adding your own ideas.

A variety of studies suggest that active listening is essential for parents, couples, teachers, managers, and supervisors (Wolvin and Coakley 1991). Renowned marital researcher, John Gottman (1999) emphasizes the importance of listening in stress-reducing conversations and provides a seven step process for couples to follow. In short, active listening enhances both personal and professional relationships. It is an approach to listening that involves suspending judgment, withholding evaluation, and striving to hear both the surface message and underlying meanings.

In this chapter Thomas Harris and John Sherblom discuss the importance of listening in communication. After laying out the four components of listening: sensing (hearing the message), interpretation, evaluation and response, they explain strategies for becoming a more active listener, and subsequently, a better communicator. Finally, they discuss styles of feedback and response, including both how to provide feedback constructively, and receive feedback from others. As you read this chapter consider the following question: To what extent is listening an innate talent or a skill that can be improved?

REFERENCES

Darling, A. A. L., & Dannels, D. P. (2003). Practicing engineers talk about the importance of talk: A report on the role of oral communication in the workplace. *Communication Education, 52,* 1–16.

Gottman, J. M. (1999). *The seven principles for making marriage work.* New York, NY: Three Rivers Press.

Wolvin, A., & Coakley, C. G. (1991). A survey of the status of listening training in some Fortune 500 corporations. *Communication Education, 40,* 152–164.

In any human communication process, effective listening is equally as important as clear, articulate speaking. Sensitive, articulate expression of ideas is one half of communication; careful, effective listening is the other. Receiving the message being sent by the other person and accurately assigning meanings to that message are required for understanding and for any real communication to take place. Abbott and Costello's "Who's on First?" misunderstanding can bring a smile to your face, but small group misunderstandings are not usually as funny....

Research indicates ... that while about half of our communication time is spent listening (Johnson, 1996), most of us are not very good listeners (Alessandra & Hunsaker, 1993). Many physicians, for example, do not listen carefully enough to their patients' stories to make accurate diagnoses (Nyquist, 1996). It has been argued that the average college student listens effectively to only about 50 percent of what is said and remembers only 25 percent of that content after two days (Wolvin & Coakley, 1985). Indeed, most individuals listen at about 25 percent effectiveness level. In addition, the 50 percent I hear may not be the 50 percent you thought was the most important, and the 25 percent I remember is unlikely to be the 25 percent you intended as your main message.

Why are we such poor listeners? Some scholars have suggested that, while we have all been encouraged to talk, few of us have been taught how to listen. As Johnson (1996, p. 91) puts it, "No parent waits eagerly for a child to learn to listen. Rather, the emphasis is on learning to talk." We tend to believe that talking is the same thing as communicating. Yet, as the expression goes, "God gave you two ears and one mouth."

We incorrectly identify talking with leading and following with listening. Often, listening is the more important skill (Ray, 1999). A transcript from an actual radio conversation of a U.S. Navy ship with Canadian authorities off the coast of Newfoundland in October 1995—released by the Chief of Naval Operations on October 10, 1995—makes the point.

> CANADIANS: Please divert your course 15 degrees to the South to avoid a collision.
>
> AMERICANS: Recommend you divert your course 15 degrees to the North to avoid a collision.
>
> CANADIANS: Negative. You will have to divert your course 15 degrees to the South to avoid a collision.
>
> AMERICANS: This is the Captain of a U.S. Navy ship. I say again, divert YOUR course.
>
> CANADIANS: No, I say again, divert YOUR course.
>
> AMERICANS: This is the aircraft carrier USS *Lincoln*. The second largest ship in the United States 92 Fleet. We are accompanied by three destroyers, three cruisers, and numerous support vessels. I demand that you change YOUR course 15 degrees north. I say again, that is one five degrees north, or countermeasures will be taken to ensure the safety of this ship.
>
> CANADIANS: This is a lighthouse. Your call.

Listening can be a critical leadership skill.

Mediators, negotiators, and other individuals who are trained to work through problems must first learn to listen effectively. In negotiator training seminars, for example, the negotiator trainees are reminded that they never learned anything while they were talking and that they cannot succeed in a negotiating session until they fully understand the other side (Asherman & Asherman, 1990). When they are talking, they are sending messages but are not developing much insight into how other people think or feel.

In *The Seven Habits of Highly Effective People*, Covey (1989) identifies one of the seven habits as: "Seek first to understand, and only then to be understood." Ineffective people, he explains, are eager to be heard but often do not take the time to understand the other person's perspective before speaking. Highly effective people place understanding the other person first, and that understanding comes only through listening.

Motivation

No one becomes a better listener without the motivation to do so. Essentially, we all ask, "What's in it for me?" . . . .

Listening has been shown to be a vital skill for successful managers, supervisors, and professional employees, taking over 60 percent of their average day on the job (Peters, 1987; Wolvin & Coakley, 1985). In addition, the rewards of good listening include many life-enhancing experiences, such as learning, building relationships, being entertained, making intelligent decisions, saving time, enjoying conversations, settling disagreements, getting the best value, preventing accidents and mistakes, asking intelligent questions, and making accurate evaluations (Bone, 1988). Finally, good listeners get a great deal more out of small group membership and are more appreciated by their fellow members . . . .

FOUR COMPONENTS OF LISTENING

Listening involves four sequential components experienced in rapid succession. We must sense or hear the message, interpret or provide meaning to the message, evaluate the content of the message, and retain and respond to the message in the context of an ongoing communication event. Each of these components is in itself a complex process. For this reason, a more detailed examination of each follows.

Sensing (Hearing the Message)

Hearing the sounds, and even being able to repeat the words, is not the same thing as sensing, or hearing, the message. Hearing is the involuntary "physiological process of receiving aural stimuli" (Johnson, 1996, p. 91). Thus, the act of hearing the sounds is nonselective. Sensing or hearing the message, on the other hand, is a voluntary act whereby we choose certain sounds and noises to pay attention to, while avoiding others. This is an important part of listening and happens as a result of our decision to attune to certain messages. Hearing and listening to the message are influenced by selective attention and the amounts of external and internal noise.

Selective attention. Choosing one message over another is called *selective attention.* The messages we attune to are the ones that have some "pre-programmed" importance for us. If I am an avid football fan, for example, I will be drawn toward football-related messages. If I am a quilter, I will selectively attend to messages related to quilting. If I am committed to social justice, I am more likely to pay attention when civil rights issues are discussed. On the other hand, if I don't follow the soap operas on TV, I am not likely to pay attention to someone discussing the latest gossip about one of the stars.

There are several reasons we engage in this practice of selective attention. To start, some things are simply more important to us. For example, when someone calls our name, we are more likely to respond. With the barrage of stimulation that assaults us from all directions in our daily lives, we must learn to discriminate those stimuli that are necessary either to our survival or to our well-being from those that make little difference to us in our ongoing lives. Because we cannot possibly process all the stimulation that surrounds us, we have learned to pay attention to those stimuli that are familiar to us and that have particular significance for us. These can range from issues of crucial importance to those that appear trivial. They can include basic survival, our jobs, our relationships, popular cultural icons, or any number of other stimuli in our environments....

When messages contradict or challenge our way of thinking, we may tend to reject them. Prejudices, stereotypes, and preconceived ideas can prevent us from fully hearing issues and alternative viewpoints on topics. If, for example, we hold preconceived ideas about the place of women in our society, assume that older people have little to contribute to the economic base of our society, make assumptions about the general characteristics of people based on their racial or ethnic backgrounds, hold stereotypes about gay people,

or believe adamantly in one side of an issue, such as the right to die or the right to choice, then it becomes difficult for us to hear other people's views on these topics when they oppose or even question our own.

In addition, we make conscious decisions to pay attention to some messages and ignore others. As we become more expert in a particular subject we may tend to dismiss what we consider unsophisticated viewpoints....

Finally, difficult material may discourage us from listening carefully. If we feel we don't understand the issue in question, we may simply drop out of the discussion, assuming we have nothing to offer to it anyway....

Noise. Noise is a useful term for the interference that occurs between the spoken message and hearing. There are two types of noise: external and internal. External noise includes distractions that make it difficult to hear the other person.

...[T]hese can include extraneous sounds, a telephone ringing, bad acoustics, poor visibility between the speaker and the listener, an uncomfortable physical environment, other people talking, coughing, or moving around, or any number of other physical distractions....

Internal noise includes a preoccupation with personal issues, charged-up emotional states, stereotyping, and prejudice toward the sender or toward his or her message, or distractions from other aspects of our lives. All of these interfere with our hearing. We are not blank slates that unconditionally accept all incoming verbal and nonverbal message. If we do not make a conscious effort or are not trained in active listening, we frequently allow noise to interfere with our hearing.

Interpreting the Message

Assigning meaning to someone's message is a complex task. In hearing the message and choosing to pay attention, we accept the message into our memory system. Interpreting the message is the next step. Our goal in this should be to understand the other person's meaning. We are all limited in our perspective and understanding, however, by our perceptions of others' verbal and nonverbal communication. As I listen to someone else, I filter my interpretation of their message through my own attitudes, assumptions, needs, values, past and present experiences, knowledge, expectations, fears, goals, educational background, and emotional involvement. Thus, we each bring our own particular limitations to hearing and accurately interpreting someone else's message.

A much cited story provides an example of the preconceptions we frequently bring to our interpretations. A little boy is involved in a serious automobile accident in which his father, who was driving the car, is killed instantly. The boy is rushed to the hospital in critical condition. The emergency room doctor takes one look at the boy and shouts: "Oh my God, it's my son!" How is this possible? For some of us, the answer is not immediately apparent. Our implicit assumption that doctors are ordinarily men can make the interpretation process difficult. In this case, the doctor is the boy's mother. Recognizing our assumptions are interpretations can be tricky business....

Evaluating the Message Content

This stage involves forming an opinion or making a judgment regarding the messages. We are asking ourselves if the "facts" support the points being made or justify the positions being taken. It is a quality-control step, which poor listeners frequently overlook in their rush to judgment. Too often we don't stop to make certain that all the information is carefully gathered and weighed.

When we are asked to serve on a jury, we are admonished by the judge to refrain from making any final decision until all the evidence has been heard. This is a reminder of the importance of the evaluation stage of listening. Evaluation is the process of taking in various inputs, filtering out those that we consider unimportant, interpreting those that are important in our schema, and then making decisions about how to deal with them. In the decision-making process, it is important not to evaluate before collecting enough information....

ACTIVE LISTENING

Active, effective listening is hard work. When we engage in active listening, we respond verbally and nonverbally to the other group members, letting them know we are paying attention. We become part of the transaction and take responsibility for understanding their meanings. These active listening behaviors and skills are not intuitive and do have barriers to their effective achievement. We present eight of those barriers (Golen, 1990).

Barriers to Active Listening

Lack of interest. The first barrier has to do with lack of interest in the subject matter, either because we find it inherently uninteresting or because we have determined it is too difficult for us to understand.... This can lead to boredom, impatience with the speaker, daydreaming, or becoming preoccupied with something else instead of listening.

Distracting delivery. A second barrier to good listening is our tendency to judge the speaker's personal characteristics. If someone fidgets, refuses to be efficient in his or her comments, seems disorganized, speaks in an accent or cadence different from our own, dresses in an unusual way, or behaves in any number of other ways distracting to us, we may become impatient and inattentive, or begin concentrating on the speaker's mannerisms or delivery, rather than on the message (Pearson & Davilla, 1993)....

Eternal and internal noise. In line with distracting delivery is the third barrier—external and internal noise. As we discussed earlier under "Noise," this can prevent us from hearing the messages conveyed during a small group session. During any conversation, a phone ringing, a lawn mower running, or someone hammering nearby is a distraction. Whether the noise is external or internal, it is up to each of us to make an effort to hear past it—to concentrate on the message....

Arrogance and disrespect. The fourth barrier relates to our emotional responses to behaviors that show arrogance or disrespect. People with know-it-all attitudes or who use generalizations such as "you always," or "you never" may create hostility in us. If we are attacked personally or treated with disrespect, we are less likely to listen carefully to what is being said....

Pre-programmed emotional responses. A fifth barrier to effective listening comes when a group member touches on an issue to which we have a strong emotional reaction. Frequently, the more important the topic, the more likely group members are to respond from a pre-programmed point of view than from a rational response to the issue at hand....

Listening for facts. A sixth barrier to effective listening is getting past our training in school, which was to listen only for the facts in order to recall them for a test.... Deliberative listening, or listening only for facts, can actually blind us to the overall point being made by the sender. Understanding comes from sensing the other person's point, not just from developing a catalog of the facts presented....

Faking attention. The seventh barrier to effective listening—faking attention—may also have its genesis in our school training. Usually some time around second or third grade, we are singled out by a teacher who admonishes us to "Pay attention!" After that, we become quite adept at faking attention, and before long we fake more than we listen....

Thought speed. Thought speed is the eighth barrier to careful listening. Because we can think three to four times faster than anyone can talk, our temptation is to make use of the "free" time by allowing ourselves to wander around mentally. We may formulate our responses to what we think is being said; we may be triggered into thoughts on totally unrelated subjects; or we may simply feel bored and stop listening altogether....

Other barriers. Other barriers to active listening are: laziness or tiredness (avoiding a subject because it is complex or difficult or because it takes too much time); and insincerity (avoiding eye contact while listening and paying attention only to the speaker's words, rather than to the speaker's meaning).

Active Listening Response Methods

Active listeners take advantage of the opportunity to listen carefully and understand each person...Four response methods that active listeners use are paraphrasing, expressing understanding, asking questions, and using nonverbal communication.

Paraphrasing. Considered one of the secrets of effective listeners, paraphrasing is stating in our own words what we think the speaker intended to say. The description should be objective. Essentially, we are responding to the verbal and nonverbal signals given by the speaker.

Among other things, paraphrasing is an excellent way to fight daydreaming. If we are concentrating on developing an internal summary of another individual's thoughts and ideas, we do not have time to daydream (Wolvin & Coakley, 1985). We can paraphrase verbally to the speaker or simply paraphrase internally by mentally summarizing the other person's points....

Expressing understanding. At times, it may seem more appropriate to focus on the feelings of the speaker, rather than to restate the content of the message. This type of statement of understanding allows the group to assess more accurately how well the speaker's feelings have been perceived and understood, and this may permit the speaker to view her or his own feelings more accurately, as well....

Asking questions. Part of paraphrasing and expressing understanding is the effective use of questions. This is a skill rarely taught and frequently used in ways that discourage, rather than enhance, discussion. Questions can be seen as challenges to our honesty or position on an issue, or they can be seen as manipulative. A question such as: "You don't really believe those people, do you?" does not invite an open discussion of the respondent's point of view.... [T]he goal of questioning should be to clarify the other person's perspective, open up the discussion, or follow up on a previous idea....

Using nonverbal communication. Since more than 50 percent of all meaning is communicated nonverbally, effective listeners make use of nonverbal gestures. Making eye contact, nodding our heads, and sitting in an attentive manner all indicate that we are interested and listening, and they encourage the speaker to continue talking. Fidgeting, frowning, looking at our watches, reading our own notes, or behaving in other distracting ways gives the opposite message.

FEEDBACK: RESPONDING TO THE MESSAGE

Listening is an active process. Feedback is built on and requires this active process of listening to be effective. Since we cannot not communicate, no response is nonetheless a response. After carefully listening to the message as openly and completely as we can, we are in a position to respond to what was communicated. Feedback plays an important role in the effective listening process, but it is intricately tied to the first three components: hearing the message, interpreting it, and evaluating its content. The most effective feedback should indicate to the sender that we are listening to the content of the message, interpreting it accurately, and understand it....

Providing Constructive Feedback

When offering feedback, use descriptive statements without judgment, exaggeration, labeling, or attribution of motives. State the facts as specifically as possible. Tell how the behavior affects you. Say why you are affected that way and describe the connection between the facts you observed and your feelings. Let the other person respond. Describe the change you want the other person to consider. Describe why you think the change will alleviate the problem. Listen to the other person's response. Be prepared to discuss options and to compromise to arrive at a solution, rather than argue specific points. For example: "When you are late for meetings, I get angry because I am a busy person and dislike wasting time sitting and waiting for you to arrive. Is there another time that we could schedule our meetings so that you could get here on time?" will probably be more effective than: "You are always late for meetings. I'm tired of you being so irresponsible and wasting my time like that. When will you ever grow up, learn to take your commitments seriously, and take some responsibility for being places on time?"

Talk first about yourself, not the other person. Use "I" not "you" as the subject of your feedback statement....

Phrase the issue as a statement, not a question. Questions appear controlling and manipulative and can cause people to become defensive and angry. Consider the difference between: "Can you stop that so we can get down to business?" and "I would like to get on with our meeting and business."

Restrict your feedback to things you know for certain. Don't present opinions as facts. Speak only of what you saw and heard and what you feel and want.

Provide positive feedback as well as negative. Many people take good work for granted and give feedback only when there are problems. People are more likely to pay attention to your complaints if they have also received your compliments. It is important to remember to tell people when they have done something well....

Understand the context. An important characteristic of feedback is that it is always in a context. You never simply walk up to a person, deliver a feedback statement, and then leave. Before you give feedback, review the actions and decisions that led to that moment. Determine if the moment is right. You must consider more than your own need to give feedback. Constructive feedback can happen only within a context of listening to and caring about the person. Do not give feedback when you don't know much about the circumstances of the behavior or will not be around long enough to follow up on your feedback. "Hit and run" feedback is not fair.

Don't use labels. Describe the behavior. Be clear, specific and unambiguous. Calling someone a "Fascist"; a "Male Chauvinist Pig!"; or an "Unthinking Politically Correct Clone" are labels that are likely to be taken as insults rather than as legitimate feedback.

Be careful not to exaggerate. Be exact. An exaggeration will invite an argument from the feedback receiver rather than dealing with the real issue. Saying "You're always late for meetings" invites a defensive response of "Well, not always," or "I'm not usually very late," rather than a thoughtful one.

Don't be judgmental. Evaluative words like "good," "bad," and "should" make implicit judgments that make the content of the feedback difficult to hear.

Receiving Feedback

When you are receiving feedback, the first thing to do is to breathe. Receiving feedback is stressful, and our bodies react by getting tense. Taking slow, full, deep breaths helps our body relax and allows our brain to maintain greater alertness. Listen carefully. Don't interrupt. Don't discourage the feedback-giver. Ask questions for clarity or for specific examples. Acknowledge the feedback. Paraphrase the message in your own words to let the person know you heard and understood what was said. Acknowledge the valid points and agree with what is true. Acknowledge the other person's point of view and try to understand his or her reaction. Then take time to sort out what you have heard....

REFERENCES

Alessandra, T., & Hunsaker, P. (1993). *Communicating at work*. New York, NY: Simon & Schuster.

Asherman, I., & Asherman, S. (1990). *The negotiation sourcebook*. Amherst, MA: Human Resource Development Press.

Bone, D. (1988). *The business of listening*. Los Altos, CA: Crisp.

Covey, S. R. (1989). *The seven habits of highly effective people*. New York, NY: Simon & Schuster.

Furmanek, B., & Palumbo, R. (1991). *Abbott and Costello in Hollywood*. New York, NY: Putnam.

Golen, S. (1990). A factor analysis of barriers to effective listening. *Journal of Business Communication, 27*, 25–36.

Johnson, D. (1996). Helpful listening and responding. In K. M. Galvin & P. J. Cooper (Eds.), *Making connections: Readings in relational communication* (pp. 94–100). Los Angeles, CA: Roxbury.

McIntyre, R. M., & Salas, E. (1995). Measuring and managing for team performance: Emerging principles from complex environments. In R. A. Gauzzo, E. Salas, & Associates (Eds.), *Team effectiveness and decision making in organizations*. San Francisco, CA: Jossey-Bass.

Nyquist, M. (1996). Learning to listen. In K. M. Galvin & P. J. Cooper (Eds.), *Making connections: Readings in relational communication*. Los Angeles, CA: Roxbury.

Pearson, J. C., & Davilla, R. A. (1993). The gender construct. In L. P. Arliss & D. J. Borisoff (Eds.), 1–4 *Women & men communicating: Challenges and changes*. Orlando, FL: Harcourt Brace Jovanovich.

Peters, T. (1987). *Thriving on chaos*. New York, NY: Knopf.

Ray, R. G. (1999). *The facilitative leader*. Upper Saddle River, NJ: Prentice-Hall.

Sashkin, M., & Kiser, K. J. (1993). *Putting total quality management to work*. San Francisco, CA: Berrett-Koehler.

Scholtes, P. R. (1988). *The team handbook*. Madison, WI: Joiner Associates.

Stewart, J., & Thomas, M. (1990). Dialogic listening: Sculpting mutual meanings. In J. Stewart (Ed.), *Bridges not walls* (5th ed., pp. 192–210). New York, NY: McGraw-Hill.

Wheelan, S. A. (1999). *Creating effective teams*. Thousand Oaks, CA: Sage.

Wolvin, A. D., & Coakley, C. G. (1985). *Listening* (2nd ed.). Dubuque, IA: Brown.

Zemke, R., & Schaaf, D. (1989). *The service edge*. New York, NY: New American Library.

QUESTIONS/THOUGHTS

1. Write a description of an interpersonal experience in which a breakdown in listening played an important part. Then write an analysis of how the problem could have been avoided through effective listening.

2. Keep a one-day journal of your listening behavior. How would you describe the times you spend listening in various contexts?

3. How can you tell when someone is listening to you? Recount a conversation you've had with someone when you *knew* you were being heard. What did that person do to let you know he or she was listening?

4. Try a reflective listening approach when you find yourself in an uncomfortable or difficult conversation. Clarify what the other person has said, before you respond. For example, "If I heard you correctly, you believe that ..." or "You're saying, we should never..." Let the person either confirm or correct the message before you state your belief or position.

Describe this encounter in a couple of paragraphs indicating how you felt in the situation and the impact of your attempt to be reflective.

Reprinted from Thomas E. Harris and John C. Sherblom, "Listening and Feedback: The Other Half of Communication."

In *Small Groups and Team Communication*, 2nd ed., pp. 124–143. Published by Allyn and Bacon, Boston, MA. Copyright © 2002 by Pearson Education. Reprinted with permission.

Helpful Listening and Responding

DAVID JOHNSON

Effective listening is a critical life skill, impacting your personal and work life on a daily basis. Improving your listening skills is hard work. Numerous environmental barriers serve to make effective listening difficult. These include: physical distractions, such as noise or heat; problems in the communication channel, such as lack of face-to-face interactions; message overload, multiple messages competing for attention (Adler & Elmhorst, 2008). Cooper and Simonds (2003) suggest several ways to improve listening:

1. ***Remove, if possible, the physical barriers to listening****. You might simply move to another room or move the furniture in the room, turn the thermostat up or down, or close the door to your classroom. Manipulate your environment to fit your needs.*
2. ***Focus on the speaker's main idea****. You can always request specific facts and figures later. Your initial purpose as a listener should be to answer the question, What is this person's main idea?*
3. ***Listen for the intent, as well as the content, of the messages****. Ask yourself, Why is this person saying this?*

4. ***Give the other person full hearing****. Do not begin your evaluation until you have listened to the entire message. When a student tells you that his homework is not finished, allow the student to complete his explanation before you respond. Too often, as listeners we spend our listening time creating our messages rather than concentrating on the content and intent of the other's message.*
5. ***Remember the saying that meanings are in people, not in words****. Try to overcome your emotional reactions to words. Focus on what you can agree with in the message and use this as common ground as you move into more controversial issues.*
6. ***Concentrate on the other person as a communicator and as a human being****. All of us have ideas, and we have feelings about those ideas. Listen with all your senses, not just with your ears. The well-known admonition to "stop, look, and listen" is an excellent one to follow when listening. Focus on questions such as these: What does she mean verbally? Nonverbally? What's the feeling behind the message? Is this message consistent with*

those she has expressed in previous conversations?

Listening to another person discuss his or her problems is something that almost everyone does in their relationships, but, according to author David Johnson, not everyone does it in a way that facilitates growth and open communication in the relationship. In this chapter, types of listening and responding styles are discussed in great detail, illustrating the ways in which each can be potentially misinterpreted, or ineffectively delivered. Through multiple examples, Johnson then indicates the ways in which to use conversational skills like probing responses, supportive responses, and interpretive responses, to help another sort out their difficulties in a way that is most beneficial to the development of the relationship. Finally, a detailed discussion of how to phrase such responses wraps up the section. As you read this chapter think about the following question: Think about the last time a friend came to you with a serious problem with which you tried to help. Which types of Johnson's response styles did you tend to rely on? Which type might have been more helpful?

REFERENCES

Adler, R. B., & Elmhorst, J. M. (2008). *Communicating at work.* Boston, MA: McGraw-Hill.

Cooper, P. J., & Simonds, C. (2003). *Communication for the classroom teacher* (7th ed.). Boston, MA: Allyn & Bacon.

RESPONDING TO ANOTHER PERSON'S PROBLEMS

When someone is talking to you about something deeply distressing or of a real concern to her, how should you listen and respond in order to be helpful? How do you answer in ways that will both help the person solve her problem or clarify her feelings and at the same time help build a closer relationship between that person and yourself?

Perhaps the most important thing to remember is that you cannot solve other people's problems for them. No matter how sure you are of what the right thing to do is or how much insight you think you have into their problems, the other people must come to their own decisions about what they should do and achieve their own insights into the situation and themselves. So how do you listen and respond to ensure that other people will make their own decisions and gain their own insights?

In listening and responding to other people's messages, there are two basic things that help determine the effectiveness of your help:

1. Your intentions and attitudes as you listen and give your response.
2. The actual phrasing of your response.

Your intentions are the most important single factor in helping other people to solve their problems. The appropriate phrasing of your response involves considerable skill, but skill alone is not enough. It is only when the skills in phrasing responses reflect your underlying attitudes of acceptance, respect, interest, liking, and desire to help that your response will be truly helpful. Your response is helpful when it helps the other person explore a problem, clarify feelings, gain insight into a distressing situation, or make a difficult decision....

Intentions Underlying the Responses

When other people want to discuss a problem or concern of theirs with you, there are at least five ways in which you can listen and respond:

1. Advising and evaluating
2. Analyzing and interpreting
3. Reassuring and supporting
4. Questioning and probing
5. Paraphrasing and understanding

Each of these alternative ways of responding communicates certain intentions. All of them, at one time or another, will be helpful. None of the responses can be labeled as good or bad, effective or ineffective. All have their place in helping other people solve their problems and gain insight into their difficulties. But some of the above responses are more helpful than others in building friendships and helping people explore further their feelings and thoughts. In exploring the intentions underlying the responses...the person with the problem will be called the sender and the person giving the response will be the receiver.

Advising and Evaluating (E)

Giving advice and making a judgment as to the relative goodness, appropriateness, effectiveness, and rightness of what the sender is thinking and doing are among the most common responses we make when trying to help others. These responses communicate an evaluative, corrective, suggestive, or moralizing attitude or intent. The receiver implies what the sender *ought* or *might* do to solve the problem. When advice is timely and relevant, it can be helpful to another person. Most often, however, when you give advice and evaluation you build barriers that keep you from being helpful and developing a deeper friendship.

For one thing, being evaluative and giving advice can be threatening to other people and make them defensive. When people become defensive they may closed-mindedly reject your advice, resist your influence, stop exploring the problem, and be indecisive. Why? Because giving advice and passing judgment often communicate that the receiver is assuming that her judgment is superior to that of the sender's. When a person has a problem, she does not want to be made to feel inferior. For another thing, being evaluative often seems to be a way of avoiding involvement with another person's concerns and conflicts. While it is quick, fast, and easy, it also allows the receiver to generalize about the sender's problems, and this communicates that the receiver does not care to take the time to understand the sender's problems fully. In addition, advice can encourage people not to take responsibility for their own problems. Even when praise is used to influence others, it can communicate that the sender must meet certain expectations before she is of value. Finally, advice and evaluation often tell more about the giver's values, needs and perspectives than about the receiver's problems. Thus, if you wish to be helpful and further a relationship, you should usually avoid such phrases as "If I were you…" "One good way is…" "Why don't you…" "You should…" "You ought to…" "The thing to do is…" and "Don't you think…"

It is important to avoid giving advice and evaluation in the early stages of helping other people understand and solve their problems and difficulties. There is a place for advising and evaluating, but there are other responses that are usually more helpful.

Analyzing and Interpreting (I)

When analyzing or interpreting the sender's problems and difficulties, the receiver's intentions are to teach, to tell the sender what his or her problem means, to inform the sender how the sender really feels about the situation, or to impart some psychological knowledge to the sender. In interpreting the sender's problems, the receiver implies what the sender might or ought to think. Analyzing or interpreting attempts to point out some deeper hidden reasons that makes the sender do the things he or she does. It attempts to give the person some additional insight through an explanation. Through such statements as, "Ah, Ha! Now I know what your problem is," or, "The reason you are upset is…" the receiver tries to teach the sender the meaning of the sender's behavior and feelings.

This suggestion will often make the sender defensive and will discourage her from revealing more thoughts and feelings for fear that these will be also interpreted or analyzed. Most of us react negatively when someone else implies that he knows more about us than we do.

When the receiver tries to analyze or interpret the sender's behavior, thought, and feelings, the receiver may communicate "I know more about you than you know yourself." People will usually respond better when you help them think about themselves and their feelings than if you try to figure out what causes them to do the things they do. It also frees you from being an "expert" on human behavior.

Reassuring and Supporting (S)

Supportive and reassuring responses indicate that the receiver wants to reassure, be sympathetic, or reduce the intensity of the sender's feelings. When the receiver rushes in with support and reassurance, this often denies the sender's feelings.

Statements such as, "It's always darkest just before the dawn," and "things will be better tomorrow," frequently end up communicating a lack of interest or understanding. Supportive statements are, however, frequently used by people trying to help a friend, student, or child. It's distressing to see a friend depressed, so all too often a person will communicate, "Don't be depressed," rather than listening carefully and helping clarify the causes and potential solution for the depression. While there are times when other people need to be reassured as to their value and worth or supported in their reactions and feelings, reassurance and support are often ways of saying, "You should not feel as you do."

Questioning and Probing (P)

Probing by asking questions indicates that the receiver wants to get further information, guide the discussion along certain lines, or bring the sender to a certain realization or conclusion the receiver has in mind. In asking a question, the receiver implies that the sender ought or might profitably develop or discuss a point further. Questioning is, however, an important skill in being helpful to people who wish to discuss their problems and concerns with you. In using questions skillfully, it is necessary to understand the difference between an open and closed question and the pitfalls of the "why" question. An *open question* encourages other people to answer at greater length and in more detail. The *closed question* usually asks for only a simple yes or no answer. An example of an open question is, "How do you feel about your job?" while an example of a closed question is, "Do you like your job?" Because open questions encourage other people to share more personal feelings and thoughts, they are usually more helpful.

When you intend to deepen a relationship or help other people understand and solve their problems, it is usually recommended that you avoid why questions. To encourage people to give a rational explanation for their behavior may not be productive because most people do not fully know the reasons they do the things they do. Being asked why can make people defensive and encourages them to justify rather than explore their actions. Why questions are also often used to indicate disapproval or to give advice. For example, the question, "Why did you yell at the teacher?" may imply the statement, "I don't think you should have yelled at the teacher." Because criticism and advice tend to be threatening, people may feel less free to examine the reasons that led them to a particular action or decision. Instead of asking people to explain or justify their actions through answering why, it may be more helpful to ask what, where, when, how, and who questions. These questions help other people to be more specific, precise, and revealing.... Asking questions skillfully is an essential part of giving help to other people who are discussing their problems and concerns with you. But questions, while they communicate that you are interested in helping, do not necessarily communicate that you understand. It may sometimes be more effective to change questions into reflective statements that encourage the person to keep talking. An example is changing the questions, "Do you like swimming?" to a reflective statement, "You really like swimming." Reflective statements, which are discussed in the next section, focus on clarifying and summarizing without interrupting the flow of communication because they don't call for an answer.

Paraphrasing and Understanding (U)

An understanding and reflecting response indicates that your intent is to understand the sender's thoughts and feelings. In effect, this response asks the sender whether you, the receiver, have understood what the sender is saying and how she is feeling.... There are three situations in which you will want to use the understanding response. The first is when you are not sure you have understood the sender's thoughts and feelings. Paraphrasing can begin a clarifying and summarizing process that increases the accuracy of understanding. The second is when you wish to ensure that the sender hears what he has just said. This reflection of thoughts and feelings often gives the sender a clearer understanding of himself and of the implications of his present feelings and thinking. Finally, paraphrasing reassures the sender that you are trying to understand his thought and feelings.

In order to be truly understanding, you may have to go beyond the words of the sender to the feelings and underlying meanings that accompany the words. It is the true meaning of the statement and the sender's feelings that you paraphrase....

HELPING PEOPLE SOLVE THEIR PROBLEMS

There are many times when a friend or acquaintance will wish to discuss a problem or concern with you. People do not often get very far in understanding their experiences and deciding how to solve their problems unless they talk things over with someone else. There is nothing more helpful than discussing a problem with a friend who is an effective listener. The first rule in helping other people solve their problems and understand distressing situations is to remember that all insights, understandings, decisions, and solutions occur within the other people, not within you. No matter how convinced you are that you know what the other people should do, your goal in helping must be to assist them in reaching their own decisions and forming their own insights.

The second rule in helping others solve their problems is to differentiate between an internal frame of reference (how the other person sees and feels about the situation) and an external frame of reference (how you see and feel about the other person's situation). You are able to give help to the extent that you understand and respond to the sender's frame of reference rather than imposing your frame of reference on the problem situation. It is not what makes you angry that is important, it is what makes the other person angry. It is not how you see things that matters, it is how the other person sees things. Your ability to be helpful to another person is related directly to your ability to view the situation from the other person's perspective.

Listening and responding in ways that help you understand the other person's perspective or frame of reference is always a tentative process. Many times the other person will not fully understand or be able to communicate effectively her perspective. While you are clarifying your own understanding of the other person's perspective, you will also be helping the other person understand herself better.

LISTENING AND RESPONDING ALTERNATIVES

The exercise on listening and responding alternatives is based on the work of Carl Rogers, a noted psychologist. Several years ago he conducted a series of studies on how individuals communicate with each other in face-to-face situations. He found that the categories of evaluative, interpretative, supportive, probing, and understanding statements encompass 80 percent of all the messages sent between individuals. The other 20 percent of the statements are incidental and of no real importance. From his observations of individuals in all sorts of different settings—businessmen, housewives, people at parties and conventions, and so on—he found that the responses were used by individuals in the following frequency: (1) evaluative was most used, (2) interpretative was next, (3) supportive was the third most common response, (4) probing the fourth, and (5) understanding the least. Finally, he found that if a person uses one category of response as much as 40 percent of the time, then other people see him as *always* responding that way. This is a process of oversimplification similar to stereotyping.

The categories of response are in themselves neither good nor bad. It is the overuse or underuse of any of the categories that may not be functional or the failure to recognize when each type of response is appropriate that interferes with helping the sender and building a better friendship. If, in analyzing your own listening behavior, you use only one of two of the responses, it may be that you overuse some types of responses while you underuse others. You can easily remedy that by becoming more aware of your responses and working to become proficient in using all five types of responses when they seem appropriate.

When is each response appropriate? From your own experience and from listening to the discussion of your group, you may have some good ideas. In terms of what is appropriate in the early stage of forming a friendship, two of the possible responses to be most sensitive to are the understanding and the evaluative responses. Basically, the understanding response revolves around the notion that when an individual expresses a message and that message is paraphrased in fresh words with no change of its essential meaning, the sender will expand upon or further explore the ideas, feelings, and attitudes contained in the message and achieve a recognition of previously denied meanings or feelings or movie on to express a new message that is more meaningful to him. Even when the receiver has misunderstood and communicated a faulty understanding of the sender's ideas and feelings, the sender will respond in ways that will clarify the receiver's incorrect response, thus increasing the accuracy and clarity of communication between the two individuals.

It is the understanding response that is most likely to communicate to the sender that the listener is interested in the sender as a person and has an accurate understanding of the sender and of what he is saying, and it is this same response that most encourages the sender to go on and elaborate and further explore his problem. The understanding response may also be the most helpful for enabling the receiver to see the sender's problem from the sender's point of view. Many relationships or conversations are best begun by using the understanding response are rather simple…and anyone who takes the time and effort can become quite skillful in their use.

…[T]he major barrier to mutual understanding is the very natural tendency to judge, evaluate, approve, or disapprove or the messages of the sender. For this reason you should usually avoid giving evaluative responses in the early stages of a relationship or of a conversation about the sender's problems. The primary reaction to a value judgment is another value judgment (for example, "You say I'm wrong, but I think I'm right and you're wrong"), with each person looking at the issue only from his own point of view. This tendency to make evaluations is very much heightened in situations in which feelings and emotions are deeply involved, as when you are discussing a personal problem. Defensiveness and feelings of being threatened are avoided when the listener responds with understanding rather than with evaluative responses. Evaluative responses, however, may be helpful when you are specifically asked to make a value judgment or when you wish to disclose your own values and attitudes.

There will be times when another person tries to discuss an issue with you that you do not understand. *Probing responses* will help you get a clear definition of the problem before you respond. They may also be helpful if you do not think the sender is seeing the full implications of some of her statements. *Supportive responses* are useful when the person needs to feel accepted or when she needs enough support to try to engage in behavior aimed at solving her problem. Finally, *interpretive responses* are sometimes useful in confronting another person with the effect of her behavior on you…. Interpretation, if carried out with skill, integrity, and empathy, can be a powerful stimulus to growth. Interpretation leads to insight, and insight is a key to better psychological living. Interpretation is one form of confrontation….

PHRASING AN ACCURATE UNDERSTANDING RESPONSE

The second important aspect of listening with understanding is the phrasing you use to paraphrase the message of the sender. The phrasing of the response may vary in the following ways:

1. *Content*. Content refers to the actual words used. Interestingly enough, responses that are essentially repetitions of the sender's statements do not communicate the receiver's understanding to the sender. It seems that repeating a person's words actually gets in the way of communicating an understanding of the essential meaning of the statement. It is more effective if the receiver paraphrases the sender's message in the receiver's own words and expressions.

2. *Depth*. Depth refers to the degree to which the receiver matches the depth of

the sender's message in his response. You should not respond lightly to a serious statement, and correspondingly, you should not respond seriously to a shallow statement. In general, responses that match the sender's depth of feeling or that lead the sender on to a slightly greater depth of feeling are most effective.

3. *Meaning.* In the receiver's efforts to paraphrase the sender's statements, he may find himself either adding meaning or omitting meaning. Some of the obvious ways in which meaning can be added are (1) completing a sentence or thought for the sender, (2) responding to ideas the sender has used for illustrative purposes only, and (3) interpreting the significance of the message. Perhaps the most obvious way meaning can be omitted is by responding only to the last thing the sender said.

4. *Language.* The receiver should keep the language he uses in his response simple in order to ensure accurate communication.

QUESTIONS/THOUGHTS

1. Think about the last time you had a problem that you tried to discuss with someone to gain some help, but they simply were no help whatsoever. What made their efforts to help ineffective? What could they have changed in their style that would have been more helpful for you?

2. Select the response style that you find most difficult to implement and indicate why you believe this is the case? What keeps you from being effective at that style?

3. Interview someone whose career involves high level listening skills? Ask that person to describe their listening style, the conscious choices they make while listening at work, and how they have improved their listening skills over time.

Reprinted from David Johnson, "Helpful Listening and Responding." In *Reaching Out*, 4th ed., 181–201. Published by Allyn & Bacon, Boston, MA. Copyright © 1990 by Allyn & Bacon. Reprinted with permission.

Elements of Nonverbal Communication

MARK L. KNAPP AND JUDITH A. HALL

Nonverbal communication may be defined as "those behaviors and characteristics that convey meaning without the use of words" (Floyd, 2009, p. 209). The nonverbal portion of any message is extremely important but often overlooked. Although scholars have disputed the exact percentages, there is overall agreement that nonverbal messages are critical to conveying meaning accurately.

The nonverbal part of a message contains a high percentage of the relational portion of a message. For example, a woman tells her husband, "We need to talk," and the husband says, "Okay," but continues to talk on e-mail to a friend. In other words, the nonverbal message contradicts the verbal message and carries the moment. It is important to note that in general, when the nonverbal message contradicts the verbal, people tend to put great emphasis on what is done rather than what is said. Nonverbal communication has multiple functions. It can repeat the verbal message (a wave while saying "goodbye"), substitute for the verbal (a silent wave goodbye), regulate the verbal (a vocal intonation), or complement and accent the nonverbal (a finger circling the ear to signal that "he's crazy").

What are the differences between verbal and nonverbal messages? Verbal messages use a single channel—you cannot say two words simultaneously. Nonverbal messages do not arrive in a sequential manner. Rather, they bombard you simultaneously through a variety of channels. You observe people's facial expressions, how they are dressed, and their gestures as you hear their vocal intonation and quality. Verbal messages are discrete—they have clear beginnings and endings. Unlike the spoken word, nonverbal messages are continuous. While you usually think about what you are going to say, most nonverbal messages are not deliberate. They are often unconscious. For example, although you might smile because you want to appear happy, your slumped shoulders might "give it away." There are just too many nonverbal channels to be able to think about and control all of them. Finally, verbal and nonverbal messages differ in their degree of ambiguity. In general, nonverbal messages are more ambiguous. What does it mean when the teacher smiles at your answer in class? Is the smile a signal of approval or is your answer wrong but amusing? The best way to find out is to ask for verbal clarification.

Skilled communicators can use nonverbal messages to deceive others. Not surprisingly, expressive communicators are more successful at deception than more unexpressive people because they control their communication behaviors more effectively (Floyd, 2009). Nonverbal communication may be designed to create discomfort or fear in the intended recipient of the message. For example, "Personal space intrusions are violations of "private" bodily proximity boundaries" (Cupach & Spitzberg, 2004, p. 82) that may occur in cases of stalking. Nonverbal intimidation often involves objects that convey a sense of threat or may include staring at a victim with malevolent facial expressions. (Cupach & Spitzberg, 2004). For example, in a laboratory study of handholding when faced with a possible threat of electric shock, women were asked to hold the hand of a stranger, their husband, or no one. The researchers found that both stranger hand-holding and spousal hand-holding reduced subjective unpleasantness and arousal: spousal hand-holding was particularly powerful (Coan, Schaefer, & Davidson (2006).

In the article that follows, Knapp and Hall describe the three primary types of nonverbal communication that provide a continuous flow of messages. They stress the importance of physical context as well as the physical characteristics of communicators and their behaviors. Finally, they elaborate on how each of these types of nonverbal communication can contradict, repeat, substitute for, regulate, and complement the verbal messages. In addition, remember that nonverbal messages across cultures so crossed fingers in one culture may have a very different meaning in another one. As you read this chapter ask yourself the following question: Am I satisfied with my skills at interpreting others' nonverbal messages and, if not, how can I begin to improve my competence?

REFERENCES

Coan, J. A., Schaefer, H. S., & Davidson, R. J. (2006). Lending a hand: Social regulation of the neural response to threat. *Pathological Science, 17*, 1032–1038.

Cupach, W. R., & Spitzberg, B. H. (2004). *The dark side of relationship pursuit.* Mahwah, NJ: Lawrence Erlbaum.

Floyd, K. (2009). *Interpersonal communication: The whole story.* Boston, MA: McGraw-Hill.

CLASSIFYING NONVERBAL BEHAVIOR

The theory and research associated with nonverbal communication focus on three primary units: the environmental structures and conditions within which communication takes place, the physical characteristics of the communicators themselves, and the various behaviors manifested by the communicators. A detailed breakdown of these three features follows.

THE COMMUNICATION ENVIRONMENT

Physical Environment

Although most of the emphasis in nonverbal research is on the appearance and behavior of the persons communicating, increasing attention is being given to the influence of nonhuman factors on human transactions. People change environments to help them accomplish their communicative goals; conversely, environments can affect our moods, choices of words, and actions. Thus this category concerns those elements that impinge on the human relationship but are not directly a part of it. Environmental factors include the furniture, architectural style, interior decorating, lighting conditions, colors, temperature, additional noises or music, and the like, amid which the interaction occurs. Variations in arrangements, materials, shapes, or surfaces of objects in the interacting environment can be extremely influential on the outcome of an interpersonal relationship. This category also includes what might be called *traces* of *action*. For instance, as you observe cigarette butts, orange peels, and wastepaper left by the person you will soon interact with, you form an impression that will eventually influence your meeting. Perceptions of time and timing comprise another important part of the communicative environment. When something occurs, how frequently it occurs, and the tempo or rhythm of actions are clearly a part of the communicative world even though they are not a part of the physical environment per se.

Spatial Environment

Proxemics is the study of the use and perception of social and personal space. Under this heading is a body of work called *small group ecology*, which concerns itself with how people use and respond to spatial relationships in formal and informal group settings. Such studies deal with seating and spatial arrangements as related to leadership, communication flow, and the task at hand. On an even broader level, some attention has been given to spatial relationships in crowds and densely populated situations. Personal space orientation is sometimes studied in the context of conversation distance and how it varies according to sex, status, roles, cultural orientation, and so forth. The term *territoriality* is also used frequently in the study of proxemics to denote the human tendency to stake out personal territory (or untouchable space) much as wild animals and birds do.

THE COMMUNICATORS' PHYSICAL CHARACTERISTICS

This category covers things that remain relatively unchanged during the period of interaction. They are influential nonverbal cues that are not visibly movement bound. Included are physique or body shape, general attractiveness, height, weight, hair, skin color or tone, and so forth. Odors (body or breath) associated with the person are normally considered part of a person's physical appearance. Further, objects associated with the interactants also may affect their physical appearance. These are called *artifacts* and include things such as clothes, lipstick, eyeglasses, wigs and other hairpieces, false eyelashes, jewelry, and accessories such as attaché cases.

BODY MOVEMENT AND POSITION

Body movement and position typically includes gestures, movements of the body (limbs, hands, head, feet, and legs), facial expressions (smiles), eye behavior (blinking, direction and length of gaze, and pupil dilation), and posture. The furrow of the brow, the slump of a shoulder, and the tilt of a head are all considered body movements and positions. Specifically, the major areas are gestures, posture, touching behavior, facial expressions, and eye behavior.

Gesture

There are many different types of gestures (and variations of these types), but the most frequently studied are the following:

Speech independent. These gestures are not tied to speech, but they have a direct verbal translation or dictionary definition, usually consisting of a word or two or a phrase. There is high agreement among members of a culture or subculture on the verbal "translation" of these signals. The gesture used to represent "A-OK" or "Peace" (also known as the "V-for-Victory" sign) are examples of speech-independent gestures for large segments of the U.S. culture.

Speech related. These gestures are directly tied to, or accompany, speech—often serving to illustrate what is being said verbally. These movements may accent or emphasize a word or phrase, sketch a path of thought, point to present objects, depict a spatial relationship, depict the rhythm or pacing of an event, draw a picture of a referent, depict a bodily action, or serve as commentary on the regulation and organization of the interactive process.

Posture

Posture is normally studied in conjunction with other nonverbal signals to determine the degree of attention or involvement, the degree of status relative to the other interactive partner, or the degree of liking for the other interactant. A forward-leaning posture, for example, has been associated with higher involvement, more liking, and lower status in studies where the interactants did not know each other very well. Posture is also a key indicator of the intensity of some emotional states, for example, the drooping posture associated with sadness or the rigid, tense posture associated with anger. The extent to which the communicators mirror each other's posture may also reflect rapport or an attempt to build rapport.

Touching Behavior

Touching may be self-focused or other focused. Self-focused manipulations, not usually made for purposes of communicating, may reflect a person's particular state or a habit. Many are commonly called *nervous mannerisms.* Some of these actions are relics from an earlier time in life—times when we were first learning how to manage our emotions, develop social contacts, or perform some instructional task. Sometimes we perform these manipulations as we adapt to such learning experiences, and they stay with us when we face similar situations later in life, often as only part of the original movement. Some refer to these types of self-focused manipulation as *adaptors.* These adaptors may involve various manipulations of one's own body such as licking, picking, holding, pinching, and scratching. Object adaptors are manipulations practiced in conjunction with an object, as when a reformed male cigarette smoker reaches toward his breast pocket for the nonexistent package of cigarettes. Of course, not all behaviors that reflect habitual actions or an anxious disposition can be traced to earlier adaptations, but they do represent a part of the overall pattern of bodily action.

One of the most potent forms of nonverbal communication occurs when two people touch. Touch can be virtually electric, but it also can irritate, condescend, or comfort. Touch is a highly ambiguous form of behavior whose meaning often takes more from the context, the nature of the relationship, and the manner of execution than from the configuration of the touch per se. Some researchers are concerned with touching behavior as an important factor in the child's early development; some are concerned with adult touching behavior. Subcategories include stroking, hitting, greetings and farewells, holding, and guiding another's movements.

Facial Expressions

Most studies of the face are concerned with the configurations that display various emotional states. The six primary affects receiving the most study are anger, sadness, surprise, happiness, fear, and disgust. Facial expressions also can function as regulatory gestures, providing feedback and managing the flow of interaction. In fact, some researchers believe the primary function of the face is to communicate, not to express emotions.

Eye Behavior

Where we look, when we look, and how long we look during interaction are the primary foci for studies of gazing. *Gaze* refers to the eye movement we make in the general direction of another's face. *Mutual gaze* occurs when interactants look into each other's eyes. The dilation and constriction of our pupils also has interest to those who study nonverbal communication because it is sometimes an indicator of interest, attention, or involvement.

Vocal Behavior

Vocal behavior deals with *how* something is said, not what is said. It deals with the range of nonverbal vocal cues surrounding common speech behavior. Generally, a distinction is made between two types of sounds:

1. The sound variations made with the vocal cords during talk that are a function of changes in pitch, duration, loudness, and silence.
2. Sounds that result from physiological mechanisms other than the vocal cords, for example, the pharyngeal, oral, or nasal cavities.

Most of the research on vocal behavior and its effects on human interaction has focused on the pitch level and variability; the duration of sounds (clipped or drawn out); pauses within the speech stream and the latency of response during turn exchanges; loudness level and variability; resonance; precise or slurred articulation; rate; rhythm; and intruding sound during speech such as "uh" or "um." The study of vocal signals encompasses a broad range of interests, from questions focusing on stereotypes associated with certain voices to questions about the effects of vocal behavior on comprehension and persuasion. Thus even specialized sounds such as laughing, belching, yawning, swallowing, moaning, and the like, may be of interest to the extent that they may affect the outcome of interaction.

NONVERBAL COMMUNICATION IN THE TOTAL COMMUNICATION PROCESS

Even though this [chapter] emphasizes nonverbal communication, don't forget the inseparable nature of verbal and nonverbal signals. Ray Birdwhistell, a pioneer in nonverbal research, reportedly said that studying only *nonverbal* communication is like studying *noncardiac* physiology. His point is well taken. It is not easy to dissect human interaction and make one diagnosis that concerns only verbal behavior and another that concerns only nonverbal behavior. The verbal dimension is so intimately woven and subtly represented in so much of what has been previously labeled *non*verbal that the term does not always adequately describe the behavior under study. Some of the most noteworthy scholars associated with nonverbal study refuse to segregate words from gestures and hence work under the broader terms of *communication* or *face-to-face interaction* (McNeill, 2000). Kendon (1983, pp. 17, 20) puts it this way:

> It is a common observation that, when a person speaks, muscular systems besides those of the lips, tongue, and jaws often become active.... Gesticulation is organized as part of the same overall unit of action by which speech is also organized....Gesture and speech are available as two separate modes of representation and are coordinated because both are being guided by the same overall aim. That aim is to produce a pattern of action that will accomplish the representation of a meaning.

Because verbal and nonverbal systems operate together as part of the larger communication process, efforts to distinguish clearly between the two have not been very successful. One common misconception, for example, assumes nonverbal behavior is used solely to communicate emotional messages, whereas verbal behavior is for conveying ideas. Words can carry much emotion—we can talk explicitly about emotions, and we also communicate emotion between the lines in verbal nuances. Conversely, nonverbal cues are often used for purposes other than showing emotion; as examples, people in conversation use eye movements to help tell each other when it is time to switch speaking turns, and people commonly use hand gestures while talking to help convey their ideas (McNeill, 2000).

Argyle (1988) has identified the following primary functions of nonverbal behavior in human communication as follows:

1. Expressing emotion.
2. Conveying interpersonal attitudes (like/dislike, dominance/submission, etc.).
3. Presenting one's personality to others.
4. Accompanying speech for the purposes of managing turn taking, feedback, attention, and so on.

Argyle also notes that nonverbal behaviors are important in many rituals, such as greeting. Notice that none of these functions of nonverbal behavior is limited to nonverbal behavior alone; that is, we can express emotions and attitudes, present ourselves in a particular light, and manage the interaction using verbal cues, too. This does not suggest, however, that in any given situation we might not rely more heavily on verbal behavior for some purposes and on nonverbal for others.

We also need to recognize that the ways we attribute meanings to verbal and nonverbal behavior are not all that different either. Nonverbal actions, like verbal ones, may communicate more than one message at a time—for example, the way you nonverbally make it clear to another person that you want to keep talking may simultaneously express your need for dominance over that person and, perhaps, your emotional state. When you grip a child's shoulder during a reprimand, you may increase comprehension and recall, but you may also elicit such a negative reaction that the child fails to obey. A smile can be a part of an emotional expression, an attitudinal message, part of a self-presentation, or a listener response to manage the interaction. And, like verbal behavior, the meanings attributed to nonverbal behavior may be stereotyped, idiomatic, or ambiguous. Furthermore, the same nonverbal behavior performed in different contexts may, like words, receive different attributions of meaning. For example, looking down at the floor may reflect sadness in one situation and submissiveness or lack of involvement in another. Finally, in an effort to identify the fundamental categories of meaning associated with nonverbal behavior, Mehrabian (1970, 1981) identified a threefold perspective resulting from his extensive testing:

1. *Immediacy.* Sometimes we react to things by evaluating them—positive or negative, good or bad, like or dislike.
2. *Status.* Sometimes we enact or perceive behaviors that indicate various aspects of status to us—strong or weak, superior or subordinate.
3. *Responsiveness.* This third category refers to our perceptions of activity—slow or fast, active or passive.

In various verbal and nonverbal studies over the past three decades, dimensions similar to Mehrabian's have been reported consistently by investigators from diverse fields studying diverse phenomena. It is reasonable to conclude, therefore, that these three dimensions are basic responses to our environment and are reflected in the way we assign meaning to both verbal and nonverbal behavior. Most of this work, however, depends on subjects translating their reactions to a nonverbal act into one identified by verbal descriptors. This issue has already been addressed in our discussion of the way the brain processes different pieces of information. In general, then, nonverbal signals, like words, can and do have multiple uses and meanings; like words, nonverbal signals have denotative and connotative meanings; and like words, nonverbal signals play an active role in communicating liking, power, and responsiveness. With these in mind, we can now examine some of the important ways verbal and nonverbal behavior interrelate during human interaction. Ekman (1965) identified the following: repeating, contradicting, complementing, substituting, accenting/moderating, and regulating.

Repeating

Nonverbal communication can simply repeat what was said verbally. For instance, if you told a person he or she had to go north to find a newspaper stand and then pointed in the proper direction, this would be considered repetition.

Conflicting

Verbal and nonverbal signals can be at variance with one another in a variety of ways. They may communicate two contradictory messages or two messages that seem incongruous or in conflict with one another. In both instances two messages that do not appear to be consistent with one another are perceived. It is quite common (and probably functional) to have mixed feelings about some things. As a result, incongruous verbal and nonverbal messages may be more common than we realize. But it is the more dramatic contradictions we are more likely to notice. Perhaps it is the parent who yells to his or her child in an angry voice, "Of course I love you!" Or the public speaker, who, with trembling hands and knees and beads of perspiration on the brow, claims, "I'm not nervous."

Why do these conflicting messages occur? In some cases it is a natural response to a situation in which communicators perceive themselves in a bind. They do not want to tell the truth, and they do not want to lie. As a result, their ambivalence and frustration produce a discrepant message (Bavelas et al., 1990). Suppose you have just given a terrible presentation, and you ask me how you did. I may say you did fine, but my voice, face, and body may not support my words. In other situations, conflicting messages occur because people do an imperfect job of lying. On still other occasions, conflicting messages may be the result of an attempt to communicate sarcasm or irony, saying one thing with words and the opposite with vocal tone and/or facial expression. The term *coy* is used to describe the display of coexisting signals that invite friendly contact with those that signal rejection and withdrawal. We live in a complex world that makes feelings of ambivalence or mixed emotions a much more common experience in everyday life than we sometimes acknowledge (Weigert, 1991).

These displays of incongruous or conflicting signals may occur in a variety of ways. Sometimes two nonverbal signals may manifest the discord (e.g., vocal with visual), but verbal and nonverbal signals can combine in several ways: positive voice/negative words, negative voice/positive words, positive face/negative words, negative face/positive words.

When confronted with conflicting verbal and nonverbal messages that matter to us, how do we react? Leathers (1979) has identified a common three-step process:

1. The first reaction is confusion and uncertainty.
2. Next, we search for additional information that will clarify the situation.
3. If clarification is not forthcoming, we will probably react with displeasure, hostility, or even withdrawal.

Responses to conflicting messages are often ambiguous themselves. Some believe a constant barrage of inconsistent messages can contribute to a psychopathology for the receiver. This may be particularly true when people have a close relationship and the receiver has no other people he or she can turn to for discussion and possible clarification of the confusion. Some research finds that parents of disturbed children produce more messages with conflicting cues (Bugental, Love, Kaswan, & April, 1971). Other work suggests that the differences are not in conflicting cues but in negative messages; that is, parents with disturbed children send more negative messages (Beakel & Mehrabian, 1969). The combination of negativity, confusion, and punishment can be very harmful if it is a common style of communication directed toward children. Date rape is another situation in which testimony often centers around the extent to which the signals of rejection were unequivocal.

We do not wish to give the impression that all forms of discrepancy are harmful. Our daily conversations are probably peppered with instances where gestures and speech do not exactly match one another—for example, a speaker telling a story about someone climbing up a pipe while simultaneously gesturing like he or she was climbing a ladder (McNeill, Cassell, & McCullough, 1994). Sometimes these discrepancies go unnoticed, and many are cognitively "resolved" without overtly discussing the mismatch. Even contradictions with more important implications for the conversants may not, in some situations, be considered very harmful. Moreover, as stated earlier, discrepancy is *required* for achieving certain effects: Sarcasm occurs when the words are pleasant and the voice quality is unpleasant; when the words are unpleasant but the tone of voice is pleasant, we are likely to communicate the message "just joking."

Finally, some discrepancies may be helpful in certain situations. In an experiment, teachers used mixed messages while teaching a lesson to sixth-grade pupils. When the teachers combined positive words with a negative nonverbal demeanor, pupils learned more than with any other combination (Woolfolk, 1978). Similarly, a study of doctors talking with patients found that the combination of positive words said in a negative voice tone was associated with the highest levels of patient satisfaction with the visit (Hall, Roter, & Rand, 1981). Possibly the positive verbal/negative nonverbal combination is perceived in classrooms and doctors' offices as serious and concerned and, therefore, makes a better impression.

Some research has questioned whether we trust and believe nonverbal signals more than verbal when we are confronted with conflicting messages (Bugental, 1974; Mehrabian, 1972; Stiff, Hale, Garlick, & Rogan, 1990). Burgoon (1980, p. 184), after surveying numerous studies in this area, concluded, "the nonverbal channels carry more information and are believed more than the verbal band, and...visual cues generally carry more weight than vocal ones."

Burgoon goes on to discuss some important reservations about this general conclusion. It is often assumed that nonverbal signals are more spontaneous, harder to fake, and less likely to be manipulated—hence, more believable. It is probably more accurate to say, however, that some nonverbal behaviors are more spontaneous and harder to fake than others and that some people are more proficient than others at nonverbal deception. With two conflicting cues (both of which are nonverbal) we predictably place our reliance on the cues we consider harder to fake. One research team found that people tended to rely primarily on visual cues in visual/auditory discrepancies, but when the discrepancy was great, people tended to rely on the audio signals (DePaulo, Rosenthal, Eisenstat, Rogers, & Finkelstein, 1978).

Credibility of the information presented is also an important factor in determining which cues to believe most in inconsistent messages. If the information being communicated in one channel lacks credibility, we are likely to discount it and look to other channels for the "real" message (Bugental, 1974). Sometimes we are faced with the difficult dilemma of perceiving the meaning communicated by hard-to-fake cues that do not seem credible. If a person says, "This is really great" with a sad tone of voice upon receiving a gift you know was long desired, you are likely to search for other explanations—for example, something else may be bothering the person.

Interestingly, young children seem to give less credence to certain nonverbal cues than adults do when confronted with conflicting verbal and nonverbal messages (Bugental, Kaswan, Love, & Fox, 1970; Bugental, Love, & Gianetto, 1971; Volkmar & Siegel, 1982). Conflicting messages in which the speaker smiled while making a critical statement were interpreted more negatively by children than adults, particularly when the speaker was a woman.

Other work casts a further shadow on the "reliance on nonverbal cues in conflicting message situations" theory. Shapiro (1968) found that student judges differed as to whether they relied on linguistic or facial cues when asked to select the affect being communicated by incongruent sketched faces and written messages and to be consistent in their choices. Vande Creek and Watkins (1972) extended Shapiro's work by using real voices and moving pictures. The stimulus persons were portraying inconsistencies in the degree of stress in verbal and nonverbal channels. Again, they found some respondents tended to rely primarily on verbal cues, some tended to rely on nonverbal cues, and some responded to the degree of stress in general regardless of the channels manifesting

it. The cross-cultural research of Solomon and Ali (1975) suggests that familiarity with the verbal language may affect our reliance on verbal or nonverbal cues. They found, for instance, that persons who were not as familiar with the language used to construct the contradictory message relied on the content for judgments of affective meaning. Those who knew the language well were more apt to rely on the vocal intonation for the affective meaning. So it appears some people rely more heavily on the verbal message, whereas others rely on the nonverbal.

We do not know all the conditions that affect which signals people look to for valid information. As a general rule, people tend to rely on those signals they perceive harder to fake, but this will most likely vary with the situation; so the ultimate impact of verbal, visual, and vocal signals is best determined by a close examination of the people involved and the communication context.

Complementing

Nonverbal behavior can modify, or elaborate on, verbal messages. When the verbal and nonverbal channels are complementary, rather than conflicting, our messages are usually decoded more accurately. Some evidence suggests that complementary nonverbal signals also may be helpful in remembering the verbal message. A student who reflects an attitude of embarrassment when talking to a professor about a poor performance in class assignments is exhibiting nonverbal behavior that complements the verbal. When clarity is of utmost importance (as in a job interview or when making up with a loved one after a fight), we should be especially concerned with making the meanings of verbal and nonverbal behavior complement one another.

Substituting

Nonverbal behavior can substitute for verbal messages. It may indicate more permanent characteristics (sex, age), moderately long-lasting features (personality, attitudes, social group), and relatively short-term states. In the latter case, we may find a dejected and downtrodden executive (or janitor) walk into his or her house after work with a facial expression that substitutes for the statement, "I've had a rotten day." With a little practice, people soon learn to identify a wide range of these substitute nonverbal displays—all the way from "It's been a fantastic, great day!" to "Oh, God, am I miserable!" We do not need to ask for verbal confirmation of our perception.

Sometimes, when substitute nonverbal behavior fails, the communicator resorts to the verbal level. Consider the woman who wants her date to stop trying to become physically intimate with her. She may stiffen, stare straight ahead, act unresponsive and cool. If the suitor still does not stop, she might say something like, "Look, Larry, please don't ruin a nice friendship."

Accenting/Moderating

Nonverbal behavior may accent (amplify) or moderate (tone down) parts of the verbal message. Accenting is much like underlining or *italicizing* written words to emphasize them. Movements of the head and hands are frequently used to accent the verbal message. When a father scolds his son about staying out too late, he may accent a particular phrase with a firm grip on the son's shoulder and an accompanying frown. In some instances, one set of nonverbal cues can accent or moderate other nonverbal cues. The intensity of a facial expression of emotion, for example, may be revealed by observing other parts of the body.

Regulating

Nonverbal behavior is also used to regulate the verbal behavior. We do this in two ways:

1. Coordinating our own verbal and nonverbal behavior in the production of our messages.
2. Coordinating our verbal and nonverbal messages behavior with those of our interaction partner(s).

We regulate the production of our own messages in a variety of ways. Sometimes we use nonverbal signs to segment units of interaction. Posture changes may demarcate a topic change; a gesture may forecast the verbalization of a particular idea; pauses may help in organizing spoken information into units. When we speak of a series of things, we may communicate discreteness by linear, staccato movements of the arm and hand; for example, "We must consider A, B, and C." When we insert one of these chopping gestures after each letter, it may suggest a separate consideration of each letter; a single chop after C might indicate either a consideration of all three (as a group) or just C in particular.

We also regulate the flow of verbal and nonverbal behavior between ourself and an interactant. This may manifest itself in the type of behavior two interactants elicit from one another (e.g., every time one person gets mad and yells, the other behaves in a solicitous manner) or in less obvious ways (e.g., the signals of initiation, continuation, and termination of interaction). The way one person stops talking and another starts in a smooth, synchronized manner may be as important to a satisfactory interaction as the content. After all, we do make judgments about people based on their regulatory skills (for example, "Talking to him is like talking to a wall" or "You can't get a word in edgewise with her"). When another person frequently interrupts or is inattentive, we may feel this person is making a statement about the relationship, perhaps one of disrespect. There are rules for regulating conversations, but they are generally implicit. It is not written down, but we seem to know that two people should not talk at the same time, that each person should get an equal number of turns at talking if he or she desires, that a question should be answered, and so forth. Wiemann's (1977) research found that relatively minute changes in these regulatory behaviors (interruptions, pauses longer than 3 seconds, unilateral topic changes, etc.) resulted in sizeable variations in how competent a communicator was perceived to be. As listeners, we are apparently attending to and evaluating a host of fleeting, subtle, and habitual features of another's conversational behavior. There are probably differences in the actual behaviors used to manage conversational flow across cultures. As children are first learning these rules, they use less subtle cues, for example, tugging on clothing, raising a hand, and the like. Children are also less skilled in accomplishing smooth turn taking, as you will have noticed if you have conversed with a young child on the telephone.

Conversational regulators involve several kinds of nonverbal cues. When we want to indicate we are finished speaking and the other person can start, we may increase our eye contact with the other person. This is often accompanied by the vocal cues associated with ending declarative or interrogative statements. If the other person still does not figuratively pick up the conversational ball, we might extend silence or interject a "trailer," for example, "you know…" or "so, ah…" Keeping another from speaking in a conversation means we have to keep long pauses from occurring, decrease eye contact, and perhaps raise the volume if the other tries to speak. When we do not want to take a speaking turn, we might give the other some reinforcing head nods, maintain attentive eye contact, and, of course, refrain from speaking when the other begins to yield. When we do want the floor, we might raise our index finger or enact an audible inspiration of breath with a straightening of the posture as if ready to take over. Rapid nodding may signal the other to hurry up and finish, but, if we have trouble getting in, we may have to talk simultaneously for a few words or engage in stutter starts that, we hope, will be more easily observed cues to signal our desire.

Conversational beginnings and endings also act as regulatory points. When we are greeting others, eye contact indicates that the channels are open. A slight head movement and an *eyebrow flash* of recognition (a barely detectable but distinct up-and-down movement of the eyebrows) may be present. The hands are also used in greetings for salutes, waves, handshakes, handslaps, emblematic signals such as the peace or victory sign, a raised fist, or thumbs-up. Hands may also perform grooming activities (running fingers through one's hair) or be involved in various touching activities such as kissing, embracing, or hitting another on the arm. The mouth may form a smile or an oval shape, as if one were ready to start talking (Krivonos & Knapp, 1975).

Saying good-bye in semiformal interviews was shown, in one study, to elicit many nonverbal behaviors. The most common included the breaking of eye contact more often and for longer periods of time, positioning one's body toward an exit, leaning forward and nodding. Less frequent, but very noticeable, were accenting behaviors that signaled, "This is the termination of our conversation, and I don't want you to miss it!" These accentors included explosive hand and foot movements such as raising the hands and/or feet and bringing them down with enough force to make an audible slap while simultaneously using the hands and feet as leverage to catapult the interactant out of his or her seat. A less direct manifestation was placing hands on thighs or knees in a leveraging position (as if one was preparing to catapult), hoping that the other person picked up the good-bye cue (Knapp, Hart, Friedrich, & Shulman, 1975).

REFERENCES

Argyle, M. (1988). *Bodily communication* (2nd ed.). London, England: Methuen.

Bavelas, J. B., Black, A., Chovil, N., & Mullett. J. (1990). *Equivocal communication*. Newbury Park, CA: Sage.

Beakel, N. G., & Mehrabian, A. (1969). Inconsistent communications and psychopathology. *Journal of Abnormal Psychology, 74*, 126–130.

Bugental, D. E. (1974). Interpretations of naturally occurring discrepancies between words and intonation: Modes of inconsistency resolution. *Journal of Personality and Social Psychology, 30*, 125–133.

Bugental, D. E., Kaswan, J. W., Love, L. R., & Fox, M. N. (1970). Child versus adult perception of evaluative messages in verbal, vocal, and visual channels. *Developmental Psychology, 2*, 367–375.

Bugental, D. E., Love, L. R., & Gianetto, R. M. (1971). Perfidious feminine faces. *Journal of Personality and Social Psychology, 17*, 314–318.

Bugental, D. E., Love, L. R., Kaswan, J. W., & April, C. (1971). Verbal-nonverbal conflict in parental messages to normal and disturbed children. *Journal of Abnormal Psychology, 77*, 6–10.

Burgoon, J. K. (1980). Nonverbal communication research in the 1970s: An overview. In D. Nimmo (Ed.), *Communication yearbook !79–197* New Brunswick, NJ: Transaction.

DePaulo, B. M., Rosenthal, R., Eisenstat, R., Rogers, P. L., & Finkelstein, S. (1978). Decoding discrepant nonverbal cues. *Journal of Personality and Social Psychology, 36*, 313–323.

Ekman, P. (1965). Communication through nonverbal behavior: A source of information about an interpersonal relationship. (390–442) In S. S. Tomkins & C. E. Izard (Eds.), *Affect, cognition, and personality.* New York, NY: Springer.

Hall, J. A., Roter, D. L., & Rand, C. S. (1981). Communication of affect between patient and physician. *Journal of Health and Social Behavior, 22*, 18–30.

Kendon, A. (1983). Gesture and speech: How they interact. In J. M. Wiemann & R. P. Harrison (Eds.), *Nonverbal interaction.* (pp. 13–46_ Beverly Hills, CA: Sage.

Knapp, M. L., Hart, R. P., Friedrich, G. W., & Shulman, G. M. (1975). The rhetoric of goodbye: Verbal and nonverbal correlates of human leave-taking. *Speech Monographs, 40*, 182–198.

Krivonos, P. D., & Knapp, M. L. (1975). Initiating communication: What do you say when you say hello? *Central States Speech Journal, 26*, 115–125.

Leathers, D. G. (1979). The impact of multichannel message inconsistency on verbal and nonverbal decoding behaviors. *Communication Monographs, 46*, 88–100.

McNeill, D. (Ed.). (2000). *Language and gesture.* New York, NY: Cambridge University Press.

McNeill, D., Cassell, J., & McCullough, K. E. (1994). Communicative effects of speech-mismatched gestures. *Research on Language and Social Interaction, 27*, 223–237.

Mehrabian, A. (1970). A semantic space for nonverbal behavior. *Journal of Consulting and Clinical Psychology, 35*, 248–257.

Mehrabian, A. (1972). Inconsistent messages and sarcasm. In A. Mehrabian (Ed.), *Nonverbal communication.*(pp.104–132) Chicago, IL: Aldine-Atherton.

Mehrabian, A. (1981). *Silent messages* (2nd ed.). Belmont, CA: Wadsworth.

Shapiro, J. G. (1968). Responsivity to facial and linguistic cues. *Journal of Communication, 18*, 11–17.

Solomon, D., & Ali, F. A. (1975). Influence of verbal content and intonation on meaning attributions of first-and-second language speakers. *Journal of Social Psychology, 95*, 3–8.

Stiff, J. B., Hale, J. L., Garlick, R., & Rogan, R. G. (1990). Effect of cue incongruence and social normative influences on individual judgments of honesty and deceit. *Southern Communication Journal, 55*, 206–229.

Vande Creek, L., & Watkins, J. T. (1972). Responses to incongruent verbal and nonverbal emotional cues. *Journal of Communication, 22*, 311–316.

Volkmar, F. R., & Siegel, A. E. (1982). Responses to consistent and discrepant social communications. In R. S. Feldman (Ed.), *Development of nonverbal behavior in children. (pp. 231–255).* New York, NY: Springer-Verlag.

Weigert, A. (1991). Ambivalence as a social reality. In A. J. Weigert (Ed.), *Mixed emotions: Certain steps toward understanding ambivalence* (pp. 33–58). Albany, NY: SUNY Press.

Wiemann, J. M. (1977). Explication and test of a model of communicative competence. *Human Communication Research, 3*, 195–213.

Woolfolk, A. (1978). Student earning and performance under varying conditions of teacher verbal and nonverbal evaluative communication. *Journal of Educational Psychology, 70*, 87–94.

QUESTIONS/THOUGHTS

1. Interview someone from different culture to learn how nonverbal codes differ between the two cultures. Ask that person what confuses him or her about nonverbal messages in your culture. Together, develop a list of ways you could violate unstated but important rules about nonverbal communication in each of the following categories: gestures, eye contact, touch, and personal space.

2. Interview a close friend to find out what nonverbal cues he/she uses to interpret your feelings when you talk. How can that person tell when you are frustrated, sad or angry? If any

of the descriptions surprised you, explain your reaction.

3. Think about a close relationship you share with a friend or sibling. How are you able to communicate your private thoughts, wishes or feelings nonverbally when you are in a group of other people? Are these nonverbal message deliberately developed or have they emerged over time.

4. What nonverbal cues do you rely on to decide if someone is lying to you? Give an example of how you detected a lie from nonverbal cues? If you confronted the other person, how did they respond?

Adapted from Mark L. Knapp and Judith A. Hall, "Elements of Nonverbal Communication." In NONVERBAL COMMUNICATION IN HUMAN INTERACTION, 5th ed., pp. 7–18. Copyright © 2002 Wadsworth, a part of Cengage Learning, Inc. Reproduced by permission. www.cengage.com/permissions

From Telex to Twitter: Relational Communication Skills for a Wireless World

BRANDON D. GRILL

The world of communication technology continues to explode. In 2001 Marc Prensky published an essay entitled "Digital Natives, Digital Immigrants" in which he argued that current students, or Digital Natives, think and process information fundamentally differently from previous generations of students because they are "native speakers" of the language of digital technologies. They tend to live much of their lives online, without making a distinction between the offline and online worlds (Palfrey & Gasser, 2008). He refers to those not born in this digital era as Digital Immigrants, who rely heavily on analog forms of communication. At a later date the concept of Digital Settlers was introduced (Palfrey & Gasser, 2008). Settlers are persons who, although not natives to the digital environment, have contributed to its development. These persons, born before 1980, have a foot in both worlds.

On the other hand, some technology experts argue that not all young people born after 1980 are Digital Natives. They assert that Digital Natives share a common global culture that is defined by how they interact with information technologies, information itself, one another, and other people

(Palfrey, & Gasser, 2008). Therefore Digital Natives are more likely to appear in countries with high levels of broadband access, high rates of literacy and educational systems that value critical thinking.

Although verbal communication skills, nonverbal communication skills and listening skills remain critical to the development of communication competence, the explosion in digital technology requires that basic communication skills be expanded to include digital technology communication skills. Experts argue that Digital Natives are developing thinking patterns and processing information differently than those in previous generations (Palfrey & Gasser, 2008). Persons living and working in this digital age need to be conscious of the different interaction patterns and skills needed to interact using various technologies. They need to develop their repertoire of digital communication skills needed to interact effectively when connecting through digital technology.

Although many of you are highly proficient communicating in a digital world, some of you find yourselves to be Immigrants or Settlers in need of some explicit guidance in CMC (computer-mediated communication). Even some Digital Natives tend to ignore certain online conventions for interaction or forget to adapt to various audiences who may not be as proficient or knowledgeable about technology. Internet lingo may work well for some people, but not for others. Digital Immigrants may not be able to translate certain emoticons, or may find a smiling face in a memo to be inappropriate. They may need to learn to check Facebook regularly if the charity they volunteer at sends out announcements in this manner. On the other hand, Digital Natives may need to monitor their use of certain media, such as Facebook, because Digital Settlers may check their job applicants' Facebook pages to gain more personal information.

The following chapter represents a significant new addition to the Building Blocks section of this book. It reviews a number of commonly used CMC technologies and addresses some adaptations to verbal and listening skills required in order to communicate effectively using new technologies. Finally it elaborates on the many changes in nonverbal communication.

REFERENCES

Palfrey, J., & Gasser, U. (2008). *Born digital.* New York, NY: Basic Books.

Prensky, M. (2001). Digital natives, digital immigrants. *On the Horizon, 9*(5), p.1.

INTRODUCTION

Technology changes interpersonal communication. Whether the modifications are as simple as moving to an electronic medium or as complex as a completely new set of syntax and grammar rules, the widespread public adoption of new technology changes the way people communicate with each other. This technology-based communication revolution started as early as 1837, with the invention of the electrical telegraph and the corresponding required language of Morse code. While modern telegraphy no longer requires electrical pulses to be sent over wires, the principle remains the same: Twitter, Facebook, and instant and text messaging,

are all forms of computer-mediated communication (CMC) that use drastically different language rules and syntax from more conventional means of interpersonal communication. Whereas old-fashioned telegraphs and Morse code generally required people trained in their operation, current CMC technologies are available to everyone. This ubiquitous integration of CMC into daily life is not fully addressed in current interpersonal communication theory, which is designed around building relational communication skills face-to-face.

This chapter will examine current selected CMC technologies that impact relational communication, analyze traditional relational communication skills and how they must be adjusted for CMC, and synthesize new nonverbal skills for communication that incorporate the requirements of modern technology.

CURRENT CMC TECHNOLOGIES

There are many different technologies that are all designed to facilitate interpersonal communication as well as build and maintain relationships. Some forms of CMC that you may think are quite common are not mentioned. Due to the rapid growth of technology-based communication, your common form of CMC might not have been adopted at the time this chapter was written. The skills discussed in this chapter, though, are not specific to any one type of technology; they can be applied in many different situations with many different types of CMC.

Twitter: Started in 2006, Twitter is a real-time short messaging service that works over multiple networks and devices. What differentiates Twitter from other messaging technologies is the character limit and the ease of access. Twitter postings, or "tweets" are limited to 140 characters in length (including spaces) and can be updated from any cell phone or Internet-enabled computer. While the character limit may appear to be a significant restraint, the purpose of Twitter is for people to make several postings a day, each a one-sentence update on the day. The ability to tweet from virtually any device makes this technology one of the easiest to use. Most recently, corporations have started using Twitter to push out updates to their followers on product release dates, new software and many other headlines.

Facebook: Originally a private, collegiate-based social networking company founded in 2004, Facebook has since grown to over 250 million users worldwide (Facebook.com, 2009). While Facebook remains primarily a medium for social networking (meeting new people, reconnecting with old friends, etc.), it has added modules that provide functionality very similar to Twitter (see above), blogs (see below), and IM (see below), in an effort to stay competitive with a rapidly expanding social technology market. While at the onset, Facebook users were comprised primarily of 18–24-year old students, currently the fastest-growing demographic is those over the age of 35, with over 67% of Facebook users outside of college (Facebook.com, 2009).

Blogs: A contraction of the term "weblog," blogs are websites that are typically maintained by an individual on a regular basis. The content of these sites are generally text-based, though it is not uncommon for them to include video and pictures. The subject matter addressed by blogs ranges from professional discussions to personal diaries, typically listed in reverse chronological order. According to the 2008 "State of the Blogosphere" report by Technorati Media, blogs had 77.7 million unique visitors in the U.S. alone, of a total internet audience of 188.9 million. A March 2008 Universal McCann study also found that there are over 184 million distinct blogs worldwide (26.4 million based in the United States) (Technorati Media, 2009). Typically, blogs are multiple paragraphs in length, making the preferred medium for updating them a laptop or desktop computer. Due to this technological tethering, blogs are not typically updated as often as Twitter or Facebook, but are usually much more detailed than postings to either of those services.

Instant Messenger (IM): One of the original forms of CMC, this service allows people from around the world to communicate with each other in a real-time, text-based environment. Pioneered by the Internet Relay Chat (IRC) protocol in 1988 (De Hoyos, 2009), IM is now available from most major software companies, including Yahoo!, Microsoft, Google, and AOL. The most recent advancements in instant messenger technology come from the merger between text and both voice and video protocols. It is now common for IM to be combined with the ability to voice chat or have a point-to-point videoconference with another person; features not available through Twitter, Facebook, or blogs. While both voice and video services are usually constrained to a traditional computing environment, text-based IM is commonplace on cell phones and other mobile devices. Although IM is one of the oldest forms of CMC, it remains one of the most popular because it is one of the few synchronous forms of CMC.

Text Messaging: Formally known as short messaging service (SMS), text messages are essentially mobile email that is limited to 160 characters. Unlike instant messaging, Facebook, or Twitter, which rely on proprietary protocols, SMS was adopted in 1986 as the standard messaging protocol by the Global System for Mobile Communications (GSM) (Milian, 2009). While traditionally text-only, the more recent multimedia messaging service (MMS) allow pictures, video, and audio to be embedded within the messages.

CONNECTIONS TO LANGUAGE AND LISTENING SKILLS

When looking at language and listening skills in relational communication, there are four fundamental elements: the elements and nature of the language itself, listening, responding, and feedback. Each of these pieces, however, is grounded with the assumptions that interpersonal communication is both synchronous (responses received in real-time) and occurs with two people in relative physical proximity. While not all CMC is contrary to these assumptions, it does create an addendum of rules that require different skills to become proficient.

Before addressing the differences between CMC-based languages and traditional verbal language, it's important to recognize that the purpose and uses of language remain the same. CMC-based languages are still used to label and define, as well as to evaluate and discuss things outside our immediate experience. Where technology-based languages begin to differ, however, are in the notions of denotation and specificity.

The denotation of a word is simply the formal meaning of a word; it is a word's definition in the dictionary. While many of the words found in CMC are the same as those used in spoken and written communication, the explosive growth of CMC has led to a much broader word base; many that cannot be found in a dictionary at the moment. These words are more than just traditional slang, but rather nouns, verbs, and adjectives that are representative of the adoption of new technology. It took eight years for "Google" to have an official denotation (Associated Press, 2006) and there are hundreds of other terms that are found in common parlance but have no denotation. CMC also creates different denotations from commonplace words. It is only since 1998 that "text" has been defined as a verb, to "send text messages from one cell phone to another," even though the denotation of the noun has existed since the 14th century (Text, 2009). In order to be successful with CMC, you must keep an open mind to terminology that isn't yet well defined.

The second element of language that is changed by CMC is the notion of specificity. Whether it's spoken or written, precise words are those that most accurately express meaning. Using specific and precise verbal language is incredibly helpful, as it allows you to construct for the listener the exact same senses and emotions that you felt and experienced yourself. Nevertheless, in many forms of CMC, specificity must be sacrificed for brevity. For example, imagine that you would like to describe the perfect steak that you had for dinner

at a restaurant. If you were talking to a friend the next day, you might extol the deliciousness of the dish for several minutes, using words such as "tender," "juicy," or "mouth-watering" to aid your friend in conjuring up sensations that closely mimicked your own the night before. If describing this steak to a friend over Twitter, which has a character limit of 140, you might be constrained to simply say "I went to an amazing restaurant with Joe last night and had a really incredible steak." Without room for specific descriptors, you instead rely on superlatives and other measures of degree to express your satisfaction with your meal. Thus, it becomes a great skill to have the ability to accurately and precisely describe your experience under the strict character limits that many forms of CMC dictate. With such restrictions on the number of adjectives you can use to describe your experiences, you must rely on metaphors and common experiences that draw intense memories from your electronic audience. Although that tweet (Twitter posting) would not use more precise language, it would evoke a much more powerful reaction from your friends reading it.

Another important communication skill involves appropriate listening. Although there are several critical components of listening, there are three specific aspects that change when using CMC: hearing, feedback, and retention of the message. In addition to these three components, the process of active listening is also different through electronic media. While well-honed listening skills are essential for the maintenance of relationships— whether romantic, personal or professional, each of the three components of listening are based on face-to-face interaction. As such, each component needs to be modified slightly to incorporate the skills necessary to become a competent *electronic* listener (or receiver).

"Hearing" messages is a much different process with CMC than it is in traditional verbal communication. Most importantly, most forms of CMC are text-based, and are consequently low-context, where information is presented directly; body language and other traditional nonverbal cues with which to establish context are not available. You can re-read a friends' email or blog posting as many times as necessary, and you can read it as slowly or quickly as you'd like. The permanence of text-based communication gives you additional time for the next two stages in listening: interpreting and evaluating the communication. While when talking to someone in-person, you might have only a few seconds to interpret the message and evaluate the context, asynchronous electronic communication ensures that you have significantly more time to compare the statements to your previous experience and decide how you would like to respond.

Although an instantaneous response is not required in most forms of CMC, there are social norms as to the timeliness of the feedback. Just like sitting by the phone waiting for someone to call you back, you can sit by your computer hitting "refresh," waiting and hoping for the reply to show up in your inbox. The maximum length of time that is generally socially acceptable for responding to a message is directly correlated to the accessibility of the technology. Responses to text messages, the most ubiquitous form of CMC usually need to be sent within a few hours, whereas email responses or comments on blog postings, which generally require access to a computer, should be sent a maximum of one or two days after initial receipt of the message. Unlike traditional interpersonal communication, the amount of time elapsed between receipt of a message and your response can be interpreted as your interest in the other person. For example, when using online dating tools, where email is your primary (and sometimes only) method of getting to know someone, taking several days to respond to a message can be interpreted as a lack of interest in getting to know the other person better. While expected response times do vary with the form of CMC used, late responses results in negative feelings (such as sad, angry or rejected) across all CMC media (Tu, 2002).

Although remembering the sender's message is critical during face-to-face interaction, the act is mitigated by the built-in archiving of CMC media. As the available amount of storage on email accounts continues to expand, there is no need to delete messages or conversations. Text messages can be saved on phones and even transferred from one cell phone to another. Blog entries, Twitter postings, instant messenger logs—all of these forms of CMC can be archived almost indefinitely, which allows you to precisely reference any electronic communication. An argument provides an example of how CMC archiving is different from remembering a face-to-face interaction. In a face-to-face disagreement, the listener can rarely repeat sections of the conversation verbatim; memory of the verbal interaction is heavily influenced by the listener's emotional state. Therefore, your comment of "Sometimes you have mannerisms very similar to your mother" becomes "You're just like your mother!" With an electronic archive, however, a quick look at the log is all that is necessary to concretely demonstrate exactly what was said and the context of the conversation.

Active listening is a critical element in building relationships and is one of the few tenets of listening that does not change substantially in CMC. Paraphrasing, clarifying, expressing understanding and asking questions are all actions that can be directly translated to IM, text messages, email, Facebook, and Twitter. Furthermore, each of these active listening skills serve the same purpose and have the same value in CMC as they do in traditional interpersonal interaction: they let the other person know you're paying attention and allow you to take responsibility for understanding the meaning of the conversation.

NONVERBAL CMC SKILLS

While many aspects of relational communication simply need to be modified slightly to include the skills necessary for electronic communication, there are other nonverbal skills that are unique to CMC. Acronyms, emotional expression (including gender differences), body language, and privacy are examples of nonverbal communication that have a different set of rules and symbols than their traditional relational communication counterparts.

The first nonverbal skill for CMC is learning the language set common for that media. While it's not uncommon for email and blogs to contain full sentences, punctuation, and proper grammar, media that require brevity, such as IM, SMS, Facebook, or Twitter use many different acronyms and shorthand phrases to express more complicated thoughts. A quick look through your cell phone, IM log, or Twitter.com reveals several common acronyms: LOL (laughing out loud), BRB (be right back), and BTW (by the way). Although many acronyms are more common than others, new acronyms appear and are adopted consistently. In 2009, the user-contributed online dictionary NetLingo recorded over 1,700 distinct acronyms and text message shorthand, including more obscure phrases such as @TEOTD (At the End of the Day) and ISH (Insert Sarcasm Here) (NetLingo, 2009).

With so many different combinations of acronyms and phrases, it's extremely difficult to keep track of their definitions. Despite NetLingo's relatively expansive list, it does not necessarily include the shorthand you'll experience in your daily electronic communication with others. While a simple Internet search may indeed reveal the definition of an acronym that you don't know, the most common method of learning the rules behind using shorthand language is from friends (Hoffman & Vance, 2005). In a culture where language is not standardized, but rather created by an enormous Internet-enabled community, the best place to learn is from your peers, friends, and colleagues.

Another fundamental aspect of CMC is the expression of emotion. Text, by its nature, is a cold and unemotional medium. Authors often add warmth and emotion to their stories by adding third-person adverbs and adjectives; protagonists respond "warmly" to a question, or a character might answer "quietly, looking dejected." While this descriptive language is quite helpful in allowing readers to become emotionally attached to a character and more involved in a novel, it is not the way we express emotion in the first person. You're not simply telling a story to another person electronically, you're trying to make your electronic conversations as emotionally involved as face-to-face communication. Instead of traditional adjectives and adverbs, CMC users insert emotional icons (emoticons), or other typographical symbols to express emotion. Despite the pervasive use of emoticons in modern CMC, emotional typography is not a new concept. It was found that as early as 1982, "computer conferees also find ways to overcome the lack of personal contact [in text]. [Users] have even devised ways of sending computerized screams, hugs, and kisses" (Walther & D'Addario, 2001). Thus, emoticons exist to overcome the impersonal nature of text-based communication. Similar to CMC shorthand, there is no set dictionary of emoticons or how to express emotions via text. Even a symbol as simple as a smiling face has many variations; common forms are :-), :) and :o). In fact, these symbols have become so ubiquitous in common parlance than modern instant message and word processing applications automatically convert the sideways gesture into a graphic image: ☺. Thus, it is up to you to decide the emoticon syntax with which you're most comfortable; each CMC user picks a style that suits his or her personality and face-to-face interactive style.

Although emotional and nonverbal expression in text-based media is commonplace with both men and women, there are gender differences. Similar to studies on in-person emotional expressiveness, women are found to use more emoticons and other forms of text-based emotion than men (Wolf, 2000). However, a study on Internet newsgroups found that men adopt the female standard of expressing more emotion with communicating with females, and women express less emotion with electronically communicating with men (Wolf, 2000). Thus, the degree of emotion expressed within CMC media depends not only on your gender, but also on the gender of the person (or people) with whom you're communicating.

In addition to expressing emotion, it is necessary to translate body language, such as facial expressions, posture and touching, and other nonverbal communication to CMC. In IM, SMS, Twitter, and Facebook, putting a word or phrase in asterisks (*) or triple colons (:::) generally denotes the in-person equivalent action. For example, you might send your friend the following text message on his/her first day at a new job: "Thinking of you on your first day! I know you'll be great! *hug*" In this example, asterisks are used to differentiate the word "hug" from the rest of the message and expresses more precisely the equivalent conversation that would have occurred in-person. Another example would during an IM conversation. If you were IMing a friend who asked if you had completed your section of the group's homework assignment, you might respond, "No... :::looks guilty::: I've been really busy and haven't gotten to it yet." Although not analogous to an in-person action, the triple colons allow you to demonstrate the remorse you feel for not completing your part of the homework. Without adding :::looks guilty:::, the sentence might read as if you simply don't care about the assignment or friend.

One of the most important challenges regarding CMC is negotiating how to effectively protect yourself and your private conversations. In traditional face-to-face communication, your conversations are relatively secure. More importantly, it is up to you to decide with whom to disclose your private information. This level of privacy is simply not as readily available in an Internet-connected world. Many people post personal information about themselves, their coworkers, friends, and family to their blogs, describing events and conversations in such detail that it is the equivalent to posting pages from a private diary to the public Internet (Nardi, Schiano, & Gunbrecht, 2004). The information you post in text, pictures, and video is not simply your private information; you're sharing personal data about your friends, family, and coworkers as well—often without their permission. The misappropriation of data on Facebook, Twitter, and blogs can have disastrous effects in the business world as well. It is commonplace to look up someone's blog or their Facebook profile during the interview process to find out more information about the applicant; corporations search through Twitter and blogs to find any detail about a competitor's product from one

of their employees. Many people forget that the information, pictures, and videos that they post to the web are public information (regardless of their attempts to make it private). Thus, you must carefully consider the implications of everything you say in an email, over IM, or post to Twitter, Facebook, or your blog.

CONCLUSIONS

For the 150 years, relational communication has been continually shaped by the advancement of technology. The progression of computer-mediated communication has allowed people to communicate faster and more efficiently than ever before. As a result, many additions to traditional relational communication skills need to be made in the areas of elemental language, listening, and feedback to incorporate CMC technology. Furthermore, there are additional skills necessary to become an effective electronic communicator, ranging from emotional expression to privacy management. These skills will become increasingly important as communication technology converges in the next 5 to 10 years. The widespread adoption of Wi-Max will blanket cities in high-speed broadband Internet service, increasing the multimedia capabilities of mobile CMC. Additionally, the technology gap between "smart" phones (such as Blackberries, iPhones, etc.) and laptops will continue to close. Notebook computers will continue to decrease in size and phones will have greater capability for both personal and professional applications. More forms of communication will begin to converge—home phones will be connected to cell phones and office phone, which in turn will be connected to email, text messages, or Twitter-like services. The growth and convergence of technology will allow people greater access to more forms of communication—from anywhere—than ever before. Furthermore, the millions of blog authors, Facebook members, and Twitter subscribers will continue to grow, as more children are raised with CMC technology in their daily life. Physical separation will also be mitigated by an increase in videoconference technology availability. In short, the revolution witnessed in the last decade in communication technology show no indications of slowing, and as the technology continues to progress, the skills necessary to communicate effectively in an online world will evolve in turn.

REFERENCES

Associated Press. (2006, July 6). "Google," "unibrow" added to dictionary. *USA Today*. Retrieved from http://www.usatoday.com

De Hoyos, B. (2009). IM: A brief history. *About.com*. Retrieved August 21, 2009, from http://im.about.com/od/imbasics/a/imhistory.htm

Facebook.com. (2009). Facebook statistics. Retrieved August 22, 2009, from http://www.facebook.com/press/info.php?statistics

Hoffman, M. E., & Vance, D. R. (2005). Computer literacy: What students know and from whom they learned it. In *Proceedings of the 36th SIGCSE Technical Symposium on Computer Science Education* (pp. 356–360). New York, NY ACM.

Milian, M. (2009, May 3). Why text messages are limited to 160 characters. [Web log message]. Retrieved from http://latimesblogs.latimes.com/technology/2009/05/invented-text-messaging.html

Nardi, B. A., Schiano, D. J., & Gunbrecht, M. (2004). Blogging as social activity, or, would you let 900 million people read your diary? In *Proceedings of the 2004 ACM Conference on Computer Supported Cooperative Work* (pp. 222–231). New York, NY ACM.

NetLingo. (2009). The largest list of text message shorthand found on the Web. *NetLingo*. Retrieved August 27, 2009, from http://www.netlingo.com/acronyms.php

Technorati Media. (2009). State of the blogosphere 2008. *Techorati*. Retrieved August 24, 2009, from http://technorati.com/blogging/state-of-the-blogosphere

Text. (2009). In *Merriam-Webster's Online Dictionary*. Retrieved August 28, 2009, from http://www.merriam-webster.com/dictionary/text DOES This do it?

Tu, C.-H. (2002). The impacts of text-based CMC on online social presence. *Journal of Interactive Online Learning, 1*(2), 1–24.

Walther, J. B., & D'Addario, K. P. (2001). The impacts of emoticons on message interpretation in computer-mediated communication. *Social Science Computer Review*, 19 324–347.

Wolf, A. (2000). Emotional expression online: Gender differences in emoticon use. *CyberPsychology and Behavior, 3*(5), 823–834.

QUESTIONS/THOUGHTS

1. Identify three people in your life who are quite different demographically (age, gender, socioeconomic status, educational level, etc.). Categorize each as a Digital Native, Digital Settler, or Digital Immigrant. Describe each person's use of social media in terms of the technology used, the amount of time spent using digital technology and levels of proficiency. Explain how each person's relational life is different because of his or level of involvement with social media.

2. Imagine you had to instruct someone unfamiliar with the technology in the use of one of the CMC Technologies described in this chapter. Write out the directions and then try to teach that person to use the technology. Describe how well your student did at learning the basic skills and any points at which there was confusion or frustration with the process.

3. Imagine you are writing the next edition of this chapter. Identify one technology that has developed since the chapter was written and write a one paragraph description of the technology and two paragraphs on how to use this new technology. Assume your reader is not highly skilled in social media.

4. Interview an individual over the age of 50. Ask that person to tell you how he or she learned to use on of the following: text messaging, Instant Messenger, blogging, or Twitter. Try to identify points of confusion or frustration that your interviewee experienced.

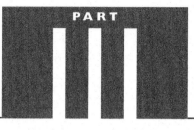

Perceptual Processes and Communication

A. Perception and Self-Concept

INTRODUCTION

How many confusing conversations have you experienced in the past week? Why did these communication breakdowns occur? As discussed in Chapter 1, communication involves the negotiation of shared meanings; if meanings are not held in common, confusion and misunderstanding occur.

But how do you gain meaning? Your set of meanings develops through your perceptual processes. According to Julia Wood (2007), "Perception is the active process of creating meaning by selecting, organizing, and interpreting people, objects, events, situations, and other phenomena" (p. 73). Perception is the means by which you create a meaningful picture of the world; it is a sense-making process. Remember the lenses metaphor discussed in the opening of the book. Each person develops a set of lenses or filters through

which he or she views the world. No two people see the world exactly the same, nor do people see absolutely everything differently (see Figure 1).

The degree of shared or common meanings affects how accurately we can communicate with another person. Meanings continually emerge as information passes through your physical and social filter systems. Your physical state and sensory processes, such as sight, hearing, touch, smell, and taste, constitute the first set of filters. Perceptions are also filtered through your social system, including the way you use language and the socially constructed conventions of your society, such as gender, culture, and family experiences. When you develop perceptions of people, you are engaging in interpersonal perception processes (see Figure 3).

Your language limits and shapes the ways in which you construct messages and the meanings

How People See the World

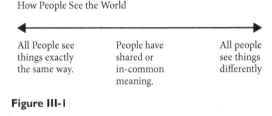

| All People see things exactly the same way. | People have shared or in-common meaning. | All people see things differently |

Figure III-1

Kinch's Model of the Relationship Between Self-Concept and Communication

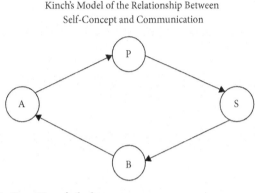

P = Perception of other's responses

S = Self-concept

B = Behavior

A = Actual responses of others

Figure III-2

you are able to interpret. The current pressure to use inclusive language reflects a belief that those persons excluded by some language forms, such as women or minorities, develop less powerful images of themselves arising from their experiences with non-inclusive linguistic cues. For example, proponents of nonsexist language believe that the self-perceptions of women are altered positively by the use of inclusive language.

Your sense of yourself affects your perceptions and, therefore, your communication effectiveness. How you communicate depends to a great extent upon how you define yourself (self-concept) and how you evaluate yourself (self-esteem). Your definitions and evaluation emerge from your communication with others.

Think back to the transactional process of communication that was discussed in Chapter 1. Over time, feedback from others influences your self concept, which may affect your self esteem. For example, if another's feedback is consistently positive, your self esteem may increase and you will engage more actively and comfortably in those interactions; if the feedback is negative, your self esteem may decline and you will become defensive or you may attempt to withdraw from the interactions. Such messages must occur over time from multiple sources for a significant change in self concept or self esteem to occur. But, even some negative feedback can influence your participation in a particular interaction. The reverse is also true. You have the power to influence another's self concept and self esteem if you consistently interact with them in a particular way. But, because communication is a transactional process, your perceptions of others with whom you are interacting are influenced by the way you are interacting with them and vice versa.

As a student, you can impact the self-concepts of teachers and classmates by the nature of the communication you direct toward them. As a parent or child you influence the self-concepts of other family members, just as they influence yours. In general, the way you perceive the communication you receive from others influences your self-concept and your subsequent communication (Cooper and Simonds, 2007).

One of the major ways self-concept affects communication is through self-fulfilling prophecies. Self-fulfilling prophecies are predictions that come true because, consciously or not, an individual believes in the prediction and acts on that belief over a period of time. For example, if Martin perceives himself as having difficulty getting to know others, he sees himself as more introverted than extroverted. Before attending a party, he says to himself, "I'm going to have a lousy time tonight." Because he fears meeting new people, he is reluctant to introduce himself to others. As a result he spends most of his time standing by himself observing others having fun. He does indeed have a miserable time. He tends to fulfill his own prophecy in this situation and many other ones.

Perception is a powerful factor in our communication effectiveness. It undergirds your sense of yourself and affects your relational development and ability to construct and interpret messages effectively. In this section you will read about perception processes and self-concept. In the second section of Part II you will encounter the role of culture, gender, and family experiences in shaping our worldviews and our communication patterns.

REFERENCES

Cooper, P., & Simonds, C. (2007). *Communication for the classroom teacher* (8th ed.). Boston, MA: Allyn & Bacon.

Cooper, P., Stewart, L., & Gudykunst, W. (1982). Relationship with instructor and other variables influencing evaluation of instruction. *Communication Quarterly, 30,* 308–315.

Kinch, J. (1963). A formalized theory in self-concept. *American Journal of Sociology, 68,* 481–486.

Wood, J. T. (2007). *Interpersonal communication* (5th ed.). Belmont, CA: Thomson/Wadsworth.

Perceiving the Self

RONALD B. ADLER AND GEORGE RODMAN

I am me.
In all the world, there is not one exactly like me.
There are people who have some parts like me but no one
adds up exactly like me. Therefore, everything that
comes out of me is authentically mine because I alone
choose it.

—*Virginia Satir*

How people communicate depends to a great extent on how they define themselves (self-concept) and how they evaluate themselves (self-esteem). In this piece on self-perception and communication, communication scholars Ronald Adler and George Rodman explore how people perceive themselves and how those perceptions affect their communication with others.

As adults, this connection may be difficult to recognize, since fully formed self-concepts don't always appear to be terribly vulnerable to communication from others. If someone insults your intelligence, for instance, and you've always thought of yourself as smart, you are not likely to question this concept of yourself. Yet as the authors illustrate, children are not born with a self-concept, and therefore, must use the influence and feedback from others to conceive an understanding of themselves. In this way, people learn to depend upon others to reinforce a certain self-image.

The authors develop an argument for understanding how the communication of others influences how you see yourself. The concept of reflected appraisal describes how you develop an image of yourself from the way you think others view you; in

other words, you construct your sense of self through your relationships with other people. Therefore, self-concept comprises the physical and social perceptions that individuals have of themselves that they have gained through their interactions with others. A self-concept tends to be stable but not necessary permanent (West & Turner, 2009). Yet the key point involves the interactive nature of building a self-concept. An individual selectively incorporates the feedback of others; the messages that really count come from significant others, those whose opinions are valued. Sadly enough, you may value the opinions of some people who may not think highly of you; in such cases, you encounter a struggle between accepting yourself or trying to change yourself in order to please another who does not have your best interests at heart.

By first defining the complex nature of the self-concept, Adler and Rodman explain why and how we form the image of ourselves, concluding with the role of personality in shaping both the self-concept and the degree of influence that communication plays in its development and maintenance. As you read this article consider the question: What person or persons have significantly impacted my image of myself and what messages did I receive that I incorporated into my view of myself?

REFERENCES

Satir, V. (1993). My declaration of self-esteem. In J. Canfield & M. V. Hansen (Eds.), *Chicken soup for the soul*. Pp. 74–75 Deerfield Beach, FL: Health Communications.

West, R., & Turner, L. H. (2009). *Understanding interpersonal communication* (2nd ed.). Boston, MA: Wadsworth/Cenage Learning.

SELF-CONCEPT DEFINED

The *self-concept* is a set of relatively stable perceptions each of us holds about ourselves. The self-concept includes our conception about what is unique about us and what makes us both similar to, and different from, others. To put it differently, the self-concept is rather like a mental mirror that reflects how we view ourselves: not only physical features, but also emotional states, talents, likes and dislikes, values, and roles.

We will have more to say about the nature of the self-concept shortly, but first you will find it valuable to gain a personal understanding of how this theoretical construct applies to you. You can do so by answering a simple question: "Who are you?"

How do you define yourself? As a student? A man or woman? By your age? Your religion? Occupation?

There are many ways of identifying yourself. Take a few more minutes and list as many ways as you can to identify who you are. You'll need this list later in this [chapter], so be sure to complete it now. Try to include all the characteristics that describe you:

- your moods or feelings
- your appearance and physical condition
- your social traits
- talents you possess or lack
- your intellectual capacity
- your strong beliefs
- your social roles

Even a list of twenty or thirty terms would be only a partial description. To make this written self-portrait complete, your list would have to be hundreds—or even thousands—of words long.

Of course, not every item on such a list would be equally important. For example, the most significant part of one person's self-concept might consist of social roles, whereas for another it could consist of physical appearance, health, friendships, accomplishments, or skills.

You can begin to see how important these elements are by continuing this personal experiment. Pick the ten items from your list that describe the most fundamental aspects of who you are. Rank these ten items so that the most fundamental one is in first place, with the others following in order of declining importance. Now, beginning with the tenth item, imagine what would happen if each characteristic in turn disappeared from your makeup. How would you be different? How would you feel?

For most people, this exercise dramatically illustrates just how fundamental the self-concept is. Even when the item being abandoned is an unpleasant one, it's often hard to give it up. And when they are asked to let go of their most central feelings or thoughts, most people balk. "I wouldn't be *me* without that," they insist. Of course, this proves our point: The self-concept is perhaps our most fundamental possession. Knowing who we are is essential, for without a self-concept it would be impossible to relate to the world.

COMMUNICATION AND DEVELOPMENT OF THE SELF

So far we've talked about what the self-concept is; but at this point you may be asking what it has to do with the study of human communication. We can begin to answer this question by looking at how you came to possess your own self-concept.

Newborn babies come into the world with very little sense of self. In the first months of life infants have no awareness of their bodies as being separate from the rest of the environment. At eight months of age, for example, a child will be surprised when a toy grabbed from the grip of another child "resists." Not until somewhere between their first and second birthday are most children able to recognize their own reflections in a mirror. The lack of self-concept in very young children helps explain why toddlers are so difficult to control. Since they lack any sense of individuality, they don't recognize themselves as the target of disapproval by their caretakers. Neither do they experience emotions such as remorse, guilt, or shame that come from being criticized. We can amuse very young children through play; frighten them by speaking loudly and harshly; and comfort them with hugs, songs and soft speech; but we can't influence self-esteem until children have a sense of self.

How do we develop the kind of rich, multidimensional self-concept described in the preceding section? Our identity comes almost exclusively from communication with others. As psychologists Arthur Combs and Donald Snygg put it:

> The self is essentially a social product arising out of experience with people.... We learn the most significant and fundamental facts about ourselves from..."reflected appraisals," inferences about ourselves made as a consequence of the ways we perceive others behaving toward us.

The term *reflected appraisal*, coined by Harry Stack Sullivan, is a good one, for it metaphorically describes the fact that we develop an image of ourselves from the way we think others view us. This notion of the "looking-glass self" was first introduced in 1902 by Charles H. Cooley, who suggested that we put ourselves in the position of other people and then, in our mind's eye, view ourselves as we imagine they see us.

As we learn to speak and understand language, verbal messages—both positive and negative—also contribute to the developing self-concept. These messages continue later in life, especially when they come from what social scientists term *significant others*—people whose opinions we especially value. A teacher from long ago, a special friend or relative, or perhaps a barely known acquaintance who you respect can all leave an imprint on how you view yourself. To see the importance of significant others, ask yourself how you arrived at your opinion of you as a student...as a person attractive to the opposite sex...as a competent worker...and you will see

that these self-evaluations were probably influenced by the way others regarded you.

Research supports the importance of reflected appraisals. One study identified the relationship between adult attitudes toward children and the children's self-concepts. The researcher first established that parents and teachers expect children from higher socioeconomic backgrounds to do better academically than socioeconomically disadvantaged youngsters. In other words, parents and teachers have higher expectations for socioeconomically advantaged students. Interestingly, when children from a higher socioeconomic class performed poorly in school their self-esteem dropped; but children from less advantaged backgrounds did not lose self-esteem. Why was there this difference? Because the parents and teachers sent messages about their disappointment to the higher status children, whereas no such messages went to their less-advantaged counterparts.

Later in life the influence of significant others is less powerful. The evaluations of others still influence beliefs about the self in some areas, such as physical attractiveness and popularity. In other areas, however, the looking glass of the self-concept has become distorted, so that it shapes the input of others to make it conform with our existing beliefs. For example, if your self-concept includes the element "poor student," you might respond to a high grade by thinking "I was just lucky" or "The professor must be an easy grader."

You might argue that not every part of one's self-concept is shaped by others, insisting there are certain objective facts that are recognizable by self-observation. After all, nobody needs to tell you that you are taller than others, speak with an accent, can run quickly, and so on. These facts are obvious.

Though it's true that some features of the self are immediately apparent, the *significance* we attach to them—the rank we assign them in the hierarchy of our list and the interpretation we give them—depends greatly on the opinions of others. After all, there are many of your features that are readily observable, yet you don't find them important at all because nobody has regarded them as significant.

Recently we heard a woman in her eighties describing her youth. "When I was a girl," she declared, "we didn't worry about weight. Some people were skinny and others were plump, and we pretty much accepted the bodies God gave us." Compare this attitude with what you find today: It's seldom that you pick up a popular magazine or visit a bookstore without reading about the latest diet fads, and television ads are filled with scenes of slender, happy people. As a result, you'll find many people who complain about their need to "lose a few pounds." The reason for such concern has more to do with the attention paid to slimness these days than with any increase in the number of people in the population who are overweight. Furthermore, the interpretation of characteristics such as weight depends on the way people important to us regard them. We generally see fat as undesirable because others tell us it is. In a society where obesity is the ideal (and there are such societies), a heavy person would feel beautiful. In the same way, the fact that one is single or married, solitary or sociable, aggressive or passive, takes on meaning depending on the interpretation society attaches to those traits. Thus, the importance of a given characteristic in your self-concept has as much to do with the significance you and others attach to it as with the existence of the characteristic....

THE SELF-CONCEPT, PERSONALITY, AND COMMUNICATION

While the self-concept is an internal image we hold of ourselves, the personality is the view others hold of us. We use the notion of *personality* to describe a relatively consistent set of traits people exhibit across a variety of situations. We use the notion of personality to characterize others as friendly or aloof, energetic or lazy, smart or stupid, and in literally thousands of other ways. In fact, one survey revealed almost 18,000 trait words in the English language that can be used to describe a personality. People do seem to possess some innate personality traits. Psychologist Jerome Kagan reports that ten percent of all children appear to be born with a biological disposition toward shyness. Babies who stop playing when a stranger enters the room, for example, are more likely than others to be reticent and introverted as adolescents. Likewise, Kagan found that another ten percent of infants seem to be born with especially sociable dispositions. Research with twins also suggests that personality may be at least partially a matter of physical destiny. Biologically identical twins are much more similar in sociability than are fraternal twins. These similarities are apparent not only in infancy but also when the twins have grown to adulthood, and are noticeable even when the siblings have had different experiences.

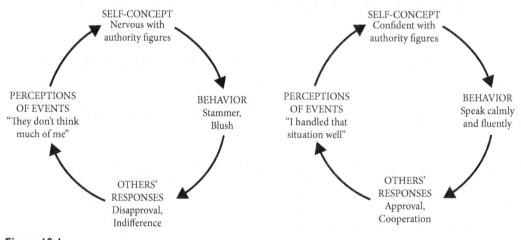

Figure 10-1

The Self-Concept Communications: A Cyclic Process

Despite its common use, "personality" is often an oversimplification. Much of our behavior isn't consistent. Rather, it varies from one situation to another. You may be quiet around strangers and gregarious with friends and family. You might be optimistic about your schoolwork or career and pessimistic about your romantic prospects. The term "easygoing" might describe your behavior at home, while you might be a fanatic at work. This kind of diversity isn't only common; it's often desirable. The argumentative style you use with friends wouldn't be well received by the judge in traffic court when you appeal a citation. Likewise, the affectionate behavior you enjoy with a romantic partner at home probably wouldn't be appropriate in public.... [A] wide range of behaviors is an important ingredient of communication competence. In this sense, a consistent personality can be more of a drawback than an asset—unless that personality is "flexible."

Figure 10-1 pictures the relationships between the self-concept and behavior. It illustrates how the self-concept both shapes much of our communication behavior and is affected by it. We can begin to examine the process by considering the self-concept you bring to an event. Suppose, for example, that one element of your self-concept is "nervous with authority figures." That image probably comes from the evaluations of significant others in the past—perhaps teachers or former employers. If you view yourself as nervous with authority figures like these, you will probably behave in nervous ways when you encounter them in the future—in a teacher-student conference or a job interview. That nervous behavior is likely to influence how others view your personality, which in turn will shape how they respond to you—probably in ways that reinforce the self-concept you brought to the event. Finally, the responses of others will affect the way you interpret future events: other job interviews, meeting with professors, and so on. This cycle illustrates the chicken-and-egg nature of the self-concept, which is shaped by significant others in the past, helps to govern your present behavior, and influences the way others view you.

REFERENCES

Allport, G. W., & Odbert, H. W. (1936). Trait names, a psychological study. *Psychological Monographs*, *47*. (1, Whole No. 211).

Combs, A. W., & Snygg, D. (1959). *Individual behavior* (Rev. ed.). New York, NY: Harper & Row.

Cooley, C. H. (1902). *Human nature and the social order*. New York, NY: Scribner's.

Kagan, J. (1989). *Unstable ideas: Temperament, cognition, and self*. Cambridge, MA: Harvard University Press.

Keltikangas, J. (1990). The stability of self-concept during adolescence and early adulthood: A six-year follow-up study. *Journal of General Psychology*, *117*, 361–369.

Lewis, M., & Brooks, J. (1978). Self-knowledge and emotional development. In M. Lewis & L. A. Rosenblum (Eds.), *The development of affect*. New York, NY: Plenum.

McCroskey, J. C., & Richmond, V. (1980). *The quiet ones: Communication apprehension and shyness*. Dubuque, IA: Gorsuch Scarisbrick.

Ryce-Menuhin, J. (1988). *The self in early childhood*. London, England: Free Association Books.

Smith, M. D., Zingale, A., & Coleman, J. M. (1978). The influence of adult expectations/child performance discrepencies upon children's self-concepts. *American Educational Research Journal*, *15*, 259–266.

Steinfatt, T. M. (1987). Personality and communication: Classical approaches. In J. C. McCroskey & J. A. Daly (Eds.), *Personality and interpersonal communication*. Newbury Park, CA: Sage.

Stipek, D. J., Gralinski, J., & Kopp, C. B. (1990). Self-concept development in the toddler years. *Developmental Psychology*, *26*, 972–977.

Sullivan, H. S. (1953). *The interpersonal theory of psychiatry*. New York, NY: Norton.

QUESTIONS/THOUGHTS

1. Number a piece of paper from 1 to 10. Then answer this question: Who am I? List the characteristics that you think define you. Then, take a moment to rank the top three that you think are most important or crucial to your self concept. Why are these most important to you? What feedback have you received from others on these characteristics?

2. Identify three people who have contributed to the development of your self-concept, positively or negatively, through the process of reflected appraisal. Why are these persons important to you? What have they helped you to understand about yourself? How did their communication affect your self-concept?

3. Relying on the authors' suggestions, develop a list of the many ways you identify yourself. Star the ones that are most important to you. Identify three characteristics you would like to add to this list in the next few years and note one way to work on each of those characteristics.

4. How have you contributed to the self-concept of another person? What messages have you conveyed that influenced how that person developed a self-concept?

Four Important Cognitive Processes

DANIEL J. CANARY, MICHAEL J. CODY, AND VALERIE L. MANUSOV

Social cognition is the study of mental processes and structures used to make sense of, remember, and think about people and interactions. Cognitive structures are processes that influence our perceptions of people and events. These perceptions in turn affect our communication. Social cognition enables you to categorize individuals and make sense of social interactions. Trenholm and Jensen (2008) indicate that there are four key social cognition questions for any given communication:

1. *How does each participant view the situation? What type of event or activity does each think he or she is participating in?*
2. *What impressions do the participants have of each other?*
3. *What kind of relationship have the participants enacted? Do they both view the relationship as having the same status (for example, friends or casual acquaintances)?*
4. *What explanations do the participants provide to account for their own and each other's behavior? (p. 158).*

Every person sees the world differently, and therefore, has a slightly different process of perception, remembering and thinking about others' interactions. In this chapter, authors Canary, Cody and Manusov explain social cognition, starting with a discussion of different knowledge structures, or schemata, and elaborate upon the four specific cognitive processes that determine how you react and respond to different situations. Citing relevant research and examples, they depict each of the four processes—interpersonal expectancies, attributions, person perception, and stereotypes—revealing their impact on communication. As you read this chapter explore the question: How do my social cognition processes appear to be similar to, and /or different from, those of a close friend?

REFERENCE

Trenholm, S., & Jensen, A. (2008). *Interpersonal communication* (6th ed.). New York, NY: Oxford University Press.

In the film *He Said/She Said*, two directors portray the relationship of Lorie Bryor and Dan Hanson, one from the perspective of Lorie and the other from the perspective of Dan. The portrayal follows the opening scene in which Lorie throws a coffee mug at Dan on their TV show, "He Said/She Said." Dan, who believes that the mug-throwing incident is "just the way we are," presents a very positive "almost perfect" view of their relationship. Lorie, who feels their relationship is over, gives a less glowing view; she talks about Dan as an unreliable womanizer and herself as an insecure individual who thinks marriage will help quiet her fears. At the end of the film, the audience is left guessing whose version of events is more accurate.

...Most researchers believe that people are relatively strategic in their communication with others. To better understand the dynamics of interpersonal communication, it is helpful to know more about how the mind works when people interact with others and when they think about their own behavior. To do this, we focus...on several processes that are part of **social cognition** (the mental processes and structures used to make sense of, remember, and think about people and interactions)....

In the [above] example, the two characters were looking back on their relationship in very different ways. Dan, who did not want the relationship to end, remembered events in one way. Lorie, who was very unhappy at the time, remembered the same events quite differently. Their memories, "one of the cognitive processes important to interpersonal communication," were affected by their feelings, backgrounds, personalities, and fears. Each had memories of a very different reality.

What "really" happened was probably not exactly what either of the characters recalls—because we tend to remember very selectively. Indeed, we remember only certain parts of events or only some events and not others. In addition, what we do remember tends to be in a different form than what may have happened originally. We may do this because we are not able to notice everything, so we (usually unconsciously) make choices about what, and where, we will focus attention. This is known as *selective attention*.

The operation of **selectivity** in perception is important, because it shows that we each interact with others and with the world in a way that is different from others. This is natural yet inherently

problematic: Because no two people will ever perceive events or situations in exactly the same way, the discrepancy has the potential to increase communication errors. Our goal in this chapter is to explain some of the perception processes that we all use in our interpersonal interactions as we attempt to achieve our communication goals. We hope that a better understanding will make the influences of those processes more apparent.

KNOWLEDGE STRUCTURES AND COMMUNICATION

When people communicate with others or try to make sense of their own behavior, they do so within the constraints of a certain way of viewing the world. Over their lifetimes, people develop knowledge structures, or **schemata**, that they carry with them, and these structures help them interpret, remember, and organize new information. Schemata are influenced by the culture in which people live...and the personal experiences people have. So, when you see someone act in a certain way, you process the observations through existing schemata. You are likely to take something that was potentially ambiguous (i.e., the observed behavior) and make sense of it with an already established way of viewing the world.

One the first day of class, for example, you probably entered your classroom, sat down in a seat, and waited for the instructor. You may have talked to others in the class whom you knew already or asked other students you did not know brief questions about the class. It is likely that your instructor distributed a syllabus and talked about what the class would involve. Without knowledge structures, you would not have known how to act, and little of what your instructor did would have made any sense. Instead, however, you relied on established schemata to help you process the situation and communicate with others.

Different types of schemata exist. Fiske and Taylor (1984) discuss four:

1. *Self-schemata* reflect peoples' views of themselves and guide how they process information about themselves. These are discussed later in this chapter.

2. *Event schemata*, also called scripts, help people recognize the typical ways in which a sequence of actions tends to unfold (e.g., the particular events that are likely to occur on the first day of a class and the order in which they occur).

3. *Role schemata* provide information about appropriate behavior based on social categories (e.g., age, race, sex, and occupation) (Fiske & Taylor, 1984). Scholars often refer to these as stereotypes.

4. *Person schemata* reflect peoples' understanding of individuals they know (e.g., "my husband Chuck") and/or particular "types" of people (e.g., happy people). This knowledge guides interactions with others.

Planalp (1985) argues that people also have a fifth schemata, a *relational schemata* to make sense of their love, friendship, family, and work bonds. Relational schemata help predict, interpret, expect, and remember things for these different types of relationships. Fitzpatrick and Ritchie (1994) describe some of the relational schemata that are particular to families and their communication patterns. According to Fitzpatrick and Ritchie, people form one of the following schemata about what families are or should be like: *pluralistic* families, in which communication is open and discussion is encouraged; *consensual* families, in which there is strong pressure toward agreement and children are supposed to be involved in the family without disturbing the family's power structure; *laissez-faire* families, in which little direction comes from parents to children and children are influenced more by people outside the family; and *protective families*, in which obedience is highly valued and the family is focused internally. Like other types of knowledge structures, these family schemata are thought to affect the ways in which people think and communicate.

FOUR IMPORTANT COGNITIVE PROCESSES

Researchers have identified some important processes involved when people communicate that are all connected to knowledge structures. Four particularly important processes for understanding how people communicate and ultimately achieve their interpersonal goals are (1) interpersonal expectancies, (2) attributions, (3) person perception, and (4) stereotyping.

Interpersonal Expectancies

When people communicate with others, they usually bring along a set of *interpersonal expectancies* for how they think the interaction (or the relationship they have or hope to have with another) will proceed. Like relational schemata, expectancies guide our communication with others; but expectancies focus particularly on how we think people will or ought to communicate with us. They may also be reflected in our behavior as we act in ways that adapt to the expectations we have for others. In turn, our behaviors may affect others' communication.

One of the best-known interpersonal expectancies is the *self-fulfilling prophecy*, discussed originally by Merton in 1948. "[A] self-fulfilling prophecy is, in the beginning, a *false* definition of the situation evoking a new behavior which makes the originally false conception come *true*" (Merton, 1948, p. 195). Thus, if you believed, incorrectly, that another student was not likely to be friendly, you may have acted toward him or her *as if* he or she were unfriendly. A self-fulfilling prophecy would have occurred if that student reacted in an unfriendly way *rather than* how he or she might have otherwise. Because of your actions, you brought about what you had expected would occur. Merton also discussed the *self-disconfirming prophecy*. This happens when the beliefs that we have about others make them act in ways that would counter the expectancy (e.g., they would act particularly friendly). If another responds to our friendliness with friendliness—and this is not how he or she would have behaved had we not acted as we did—a self-disconfirming prophecy would have occurred. Our "opposite" behaviors helped bring about behaviors that went against how we expected the other to act.

Another type of prophecy effect is the *Pygmalion effect*. According to this prophecy, if people believe something will take place, they behave in ways that ensure that it will occur. Rosenthal and Rubin (1978) first used the term to define the potential influence of teachers' expectancies on students' performance. According to Miller and Turnbull (1986), in Rosenthal and Rubin's initial study,

> Teachers in an elementary school were told that a new IQ test administered to their students indicated that certain students, "bloomers," should show a marked increase in intellectual competence over the course of the school year. In actuality, the label "bloomer" was assigned randomly by the researchers. All students were given an IQ test at both the beginning and the end of the school year. The results indicated that students labeled "bloomers" showed a significantly greater gain in IQ than other pupils. (p. 235)

Rosenthal and Rubin concluded that the expectancies the teachers had for the students affected how the teachers treated the students. This treatment in turn had significant outcomes: higher IQ. Although subsequent studies have found mixed support for the Pygmalion effect (and for the other types of prophecies), there has been enough research to document and sometimes expectancies have an effect on another's behavior.

Expectancies can take different specific forms. One such type of expectancy entails how a romance develops. Honeycutt and his colleagues concluded that people have a knowledge structure that reflects their expectations for how they think a relationship is likely to grow....

Honeycutt (1995) found that people's awareness of how they think relationships ought to progress affects the ways in which they practice or "imagine" future interactions with their partner. A recent study shows that people also use their expectancies of a romance to determine what compliance-gaining strategies they might use to convince their partner to move forward to another stage (Honeycutt, Cantrill, Kelly, & Lambkin, 1998).

People in relationships also develop expectancies for the actual and desired behaviors they think or want their romantic partners to use

with them. Kelley and Burgoon (1991) proposed that people enter relationships with *relational expectancies*, beliefs about what behaviors their partners will and should use.... [P]eople's communication reflects the kind of relationship that they have with one another. For example, if a relationship is defined to be unequal (i.e., one person has more power), this inequality may be shown through the behaviors used (e.g., one person may speak more and control the conversation in other ways). Relational expectancies are those knowledge structures that mirror the beliefs we have for how our interaction partner will (or should) act.

Like the imagined interactions discussed earlier, relational expectancies become particularly important for communication, because they may influence how we act with others. A recent study by Manusov, Trees, Liotta, Koenig, and Cochran (1999) showed, for example, that relational expectancies affected whether married couples reciprocated or compensated their partners' behaviors.... Specifically, when one couple member expected the other to act dominantly, he or she was more likely to compensate (act different from) the partner. When high levels of intimacy were expected, some reciprocity of intimacy cues was most likely. This is a clear case of how expectancies can affect communication behavior.

The preceding studies demonstrate that we have expectancies and that we act in ways that are influenced by our expectancies for others. Of course, those others do not always act as we expect them to. When people notice that someone has violated their beliefs about how they thought the other would act (e.g., acted more or less involved in the conversation than they would expect normally), they try to make sense of the violation (Burgoon & Hale, 1988). One way that people do this is to consider the person who committed the violation. If they judge that person to be "high reward" (e.g., they think well of that person or that person is attractive or has power), people assume that he or she violated their beliefs for a good reason. This judgment actually makes others evaluate the "violator" better than if he or she had acted "normally." Those who are judged to be "low reward," however, are thought to have less positive reasons for violating beliefs. In that case, the violation of expectations results in a lower evaluation than would have occurred if she or he had not committed the violation....

Attributions

When we perceive others and make judgments about them or about ourselves, we are making *attributions* about their behavior. The term *attribution* refers to assessments of the *cause* of an action or behavior (i.e., our thoughts about why someone acted as he or she did or what caused us to act in a certain way).

Fritz Heider (1958) was one of the first researchers to study attributions in any depth. He asserted that people act as "naïve scientists" (i.e., untrained but active psychologists) who study others' (and their own) actions in order to determine why people behave in certain ways. Finding a cause (even an incorrect one) helps put unexpected behavior in order and make sense of the world.

Causes can be either *internal* to a person (e.g., a person's disposition, mood, or other character trait), *external* to him or her (e.g., environmental or situational factors), or both. Heider called these dimensions of attributions *causal loci* or the *sources* of observed behavior. For example, if you see someone who is walking across campus suddenly trip, you may attribute the cause to the person ("She fell because she's clumsy"), to something outside of the person ("A crack in the pavement must have caused her to fall"), or to a combination ("There must be a crack, but only clumsy people would trip on cracks"). Other dimensions besides causal locus differentiate attributions (e.g., responsibility for the stability of the cause), and these factors help reflect the great variety of causes that can be found for any communication behavior.

In an extension of Heider's work, Jones and Davis (1965) argued that human behavior has the potential to be more or less meaningful depending on the *level of intention* inferred for a behavior. Accordingly, one of the most important considerations for making an attribution is deciding whether or not another person acted with intent. Those behaviors judged to be intended are thought to say more about the person (i.e., to be

more meaningful) than those thought to have occurred without intent (i.e., on a whim or under conditions that could not have been controlled). Importantly, Jones and Davis argued that people will judge a behavior to be intended under specific conditions: (1) the other had *knowledge* about the potential effects of his or her action, and (2) he or she had the *ability to enact the actions*.

What else beyond level of intention determines our attributions of actions to internal or external causes? Three features of observing others may influence such judgments: distinctiveness, consistency, and consensus (Kelley, 1973). *Distinctiveness* is whether or not a person's behavior is clearly different in one situation than in other situations. For example, if a friend of yours got good grades in all of her classes but one, you are likely to make an external attribution: the one class is too difficult or is taught poorly. However, if your friend received poor grades in all her classes, you would be more likely to make an internal attribution: she is not very smart and/or she is not very motivated.

Consistency is the extent to which a person's behavior is the same over time. Highly consistent behavior means, using the preceding example, that your friend has always received high grades or has always received low grades. If your friend has in the past demonstrated the ability and motivation to get good grades, you would probably look for external causes for a recent bout of bad grades. Perhaps this semester she had tough professors, or other things going on in her life are distracting her from her coursework.

Consensus is the perception of similar others in similar situations (e.g., how well your friend is doing in one class relative to other similar students in the same class). High consensus means that all students in particular classes receive poor grades. When all students get poor grades, you would probably attribute your friend's poor grades to an external cause, such as the professor's grading or the difficulty of the material. Consensus is low, however, when other students are receiving high marks, but your friend is one of the few who are not. Overall, according to Kelley, people are likely to believe that a person's behavior is caused by external factors when distinctiveness, consistency, and consensus are high....

The *fundamental attribution error*, for instance, suggests that people are more likely to assume that another's actions were caused by something internal rather than external (Ross, 1977). Rather than going through the steps of one of the attribution models listed earlier, a person may just believe that some personality trait or intention was the cause of the action. This may occur because it is earlier to find an internal cause—there are fewer of them and the observer is already focused on the person. The *ultimate attribution error* asserts that peoples' tendency to assume another's actions were caused by something internal is particularly likely when another's behavior is negative. Conversely, people are less likely to assume an internal explanation with positive behaviors. So, if a stranger acted nice to you, you might assume that he was just following social rules (i.e., an external explanation). If he acted rudely, you would be more likely to think that his actions were due to something about him (e.g., "he's a snob").

Other errors or biases depend on our "place" in an interaction. The *actor-observer bias* refers to people's tendency to see their own behaviors as less negative overall than others' actions (Jones & Nisbett, 1972). For example, if you decided to turn down a job, you could easily say that the cause of your behavior was your belief that taking the job would hurt your school performance. If someone else had done the same thing, however, you might attribute his or her actions to laziness ("He or she didn't want to have to work hard").

The *negativity and positivity biases* (Kellermann, 1984) are also due to one's perspective in an interaction. If people are watching someone from afar, they tend to make relatively negative judgments of the other's actions (the negativity bias) at least when compared to what they do when they try to make sense of the same behavior while interacting with that person. It appears that having a chance to actually talk with another person helps us focus on more positive attributes (positivity bias). Some researchers say that we do this because *we* can now be seen as the cause of

the other's actions ("She acted that way because she likes me"). We may label other people and/or their behavior positively (rather than negatively as we do with strangers) because we want to think that we would cause others to take only positive actions.

Attributions may also be biased by people's feelings for each other. In one study, Manusov (1990) had couples play the game "Trivial Pursuit." One of the couple members had been asked to become a part of the study, and his or her cards were marked. About a third of the way into the game, he or she received a marked card that told him or her to start acting unusually positive or negative. Watching the videotape of the interactions after they were complete, the "naïve" partner was asked to explain any unusual behaviors. Manusov found that, for most couples, negative behaviors were more likely to prompt attribution-making than were positive behaviors (not all behaviors make us think about their causes). For positive behaviors, however, the nature of the attributions differed based on couples' satisfaction level. Couples who were happy with one another attributed positive behaviors to something internal to their partner, whereas unhappy couples made more external attributions.

Manusov's study was only one of many that have looked for biases in the attributions made by couples. Indeed, it is so common for unhappy couples to assume that their partners are responsible for negative actions and for happy couples to attribute internal causes for positive behaviors that these tendencies have names. The tendency for unhappy couples to "see the worst" is known as the *distress-maintaining bias*; whereas the inclination for happy couples to "see the best" is called the *relationship-enhancing bias* (Holtzworth-Munroe & Jacobson, 1985)....

Attributions are important for understanding interpersonal communication in that the causes we give for behaviors are part of the *meaning* we derive from them. This meaning is a fundamental part of what is communicated in an interpersonal interaction. As well, the attribution we decide on for another's behavior helps influence how we communicate with him or her.

Person Perception

The positivity and negativity biases just discussed reflect a larger social cognition process: *person perception*. Every day as we communicate with others, we attempt to determine what those others are like and whether we like them. Person perception is therefore a communicative goal in itself and/or it is used as we attempt to pursue other goals (e.g., we try to figure out what someone is like in order to know best how to ask them to comply with a request).

As noted earlier, people create person schemata that guide their actions and thoughts regarding (1) people they know, and (2) certain "types" of people (i.e., people who are in particular groups with characteristics people think they can identify). Thus schemata for *specific* friends, family, and co-workers (e.g., the authors have schemata for one another) and for "types" of people such as friends, family, and co-workers (e.g., the authors have schemata for what "co-authors" are like) are part of person perception. People also have general person schemata that are based in personality traits such as shyness, humorousness, and kindness. These are called *prototypes.*

Sometimes general perception categories are very broad and influenced by factors out of our awareness. Monahan (1998) argues that people make quick and often automatic judgments of whether another person is good or bad. Interestingly, these views of others can be instigated in a number of ways. Monahan had her participants watch some slides prior to viewing a videotape of a young man whom they were going to judge. Some of the participants saw presentations that included subliminal (quickly shown, out of awareness) slides of the young man smiling. Those participants who had been "primed" to see the young man positively evaluated him as more attractive and more likeable than did those who did not receive the subliminal slides. Further, those who saw the slides evaluated *others* more positively as well. This suggests that person perception processes may be affected by factors unknown to the perceiver (e.g., mood, temperature, and even time of year)....

In addition to the perceptions we form of others, we also have *self-perceptions* and generally work equally hard to maintain them. Swann (1987) explains that, as part of their primary task of making sense of the world, children watch their own behavior and how others react to them and form a view of self. As their self-views become clearer, children try to find ways to maintain them, even if the self-perceptions are negative. According to Swann (1990), "people want to confirm their self-views *not* as an end in itself, but as a means of bolstering their perception that the world is predictable and controllable" (p. 414). We tend to seek out, notice, and remember those things that are consistent with our self-views. These "stabilizing processes" cause us often to have what Swann calls a "chronic view of self," one that is particularly unlikely to change.

How we view ourselves is important for several reasons. First, who we see ourselves to be and how we evaluate ourselves (i.e., self-esteem) likely influence what goals we set and whether or not we pursue them. Second, self-views affect the choices of others with whom we wish to interact or form relationships. Third, the way we see ourselves is also likely to influence how we interpret others' behaviors in regard to us and our relationship with them. So, in *He Said/She Said*, the example at the beginning of this chapter, Lorie's view of her relationship with Dan was made more negative by her own belief that she was largely unlovable. As was seen, however, Dan's view reflected a very different reality (i.e., that Lorie was interesting and dynamic and a person whom he could love).

The processes of person perception are key to our communication. Our perceptions of others affect how we will communicate with them—or even if we will communicate with them at all. Our perceptions of self also influence how we will communicate and in what contexts as well as the types of relationships we develop.

Stereotypes

In addition to creating a view of ourselves (and of those around us), we also tend to use categories for others. Lakoff (1987) states that,

> [T]here is nothing more basic than categorization to our thought, perception, action, and speech.

Every time we see something as a *kind* of thing, for example, a tree, we are categorizing. Whenever we reason about *kinds* of things—chairs, nations, illnesses, emotions, any kind of things at all—we are employing categories. (pp. 5–6)

When categories are about people and are based on their group membership, they are called **stereotypes.** "People categories" may include ethnic or cultural groups, gender groups, and social groups, and stereotypes include beliefs about the characteristics common to all members of that group (e.g., "All basketball players are tall"). As Lakoff suggests, stereotypes, as a type of categorization, are a common way to make sense of people and objects and in this regard are thought of as important to communication. Stereotypes are also, however, sometimes incorrect and always only partially reflect the complexities of the group; thus they may hurt our ability to communicate with others.

As a type of category or knowledge structure, stereotypes help people process information. When one person sees another person act in a particular way, the observer may do so in light of a stereotype of the other person's group. But using a stereotype, like any other form of perception, means that people see things *in a certain way*, and that way is usually consistent with the stereotype they hold. For example, if you notice someone from another group (e.g., you are a college student, and you are watching someone who is not a student), and that person is doing something that does not fit your stereotype (e.g., reading a textbook), you probably will not even notice the behavior because it doesn't fit with your image of things. If you do pay attention to it (and sometimes this is actually *more* likely because the behavior may seem so extraordinary), you probably will try to make it fit with your existing stereotype. Thus you may say that the person you observed was an "exception" or that he or she was enacting the behavior for a reason that allows it to fit with your view (e.g., you may offer an external attribution that means something else besides the person was responsible for the behavior). In other words, you will usually try to make what you observe fit with your pre-existing views if possible.

We do, of course, change our stereotypes or even let go of them completely in favor of other categorizations. As noted earlier, a person's behaviors (i.e., "individuating information") can often become more important than expectancies in judging that person. If enough people from a group act inconsistently with our preconceptions, we may change our stereotypes for the group. Having the opportunity to interact with people from an "out-group" (i.e., a group that is not our own) may allow us to see more similarities than differences with their group and thus no longer categorize them.

More commonly, however, an individual's behaviors do not affect views of a group as a whole, but they do influence how he or she is judged and how we communicate with him or her (Jussim, 1990). Manusov, Winchatz, and Manning (1997), for instance, paired up students from the United States with students from other countries. Before interacting, the authors asked the participants to evaluate how positively or negatively they viewed people from the other group. After talking for ten minutes, some "residual," or leftover, effects of the initial stereotype remained (e.g., if participants expected a positive interaction, they judged their partner more positively no matter how the partner behaved). Still, it was clear that in the majority of the evaluations people made, how their partner *actually acted* more strongly influenced participants' assessments. So, even if the initial stereotype led them to think they would *not* enjoy the conversation, if they thought their partner acted positively, the study participants were likely to evaluate their partners well (or if they had high expectations that were not met, they judged their partners more negatively than their initial stereotype would have led them to do). . . .

SUGGESTED READING

Schemata and Expectancies

Fitzpatrick, M. A., & Ritchie, L. D. (1994). Communication schemata within the family: Multiple perspectives on family interaction. *Human Communication Research, 20,* 275–301.

Kelley, D. L., & Burgoon, J. K. (1991). Understanding marital satisfaction and couple type as functions of relational expectations. *Human Communication Research, 18,* 40–69.

Planalp, S. (1985). Relational schemata: A test of alternative forms of relational knowledge as guides to communication. *Human Communication Research, 12,* 3–29.

Rosenthal, R., & Rubin, D. B. (1978). Interpersonal expectancy effects: The first 345 studies. *Behavioral and Brain Sciences, 3,* 377–415.

Attributions

Heider, F. (1958). *The psychology of interpersonal relations.* New York, NY: Wiley.

Kelley, H. H. (1973). The processes of causal attribution. *American Psychologist, 28,* 107–128.

Manusov, V. (1990). An application of attribution principles to nonverbal behavior in romantic dyads. *Communication Monographs, 57,* 104–118.

Stereotypes and Person Perception

Jussim, L. (1990). Social reality and social problems: The role of expectancies. *Journal of Social Issues, 46,* 9–34.

Manusov, V., Winchatz, M. R., & Manning, L. M. (1997). Acting out our minds: Incorporating behavior into models of stereotype-based expectancies for cross-cultural interactions. *Communication Monographs, 64,* 119–139.

Swann, W. B. (1987). Identity negotiation: Where two roads meet. *Journal of Personality and Social Psychology, 53,* 1038–1051.

REFERENCES

Burgoon, J. K., & Hale, J. L. (1988). Nonverbal expectancy violations: Model elaboration and application to immediacy behaviors. *Communication Monographs, 55,* 58–79.

Cooper, P. (1995). *Communication for the classroom teacher* (5th ed.). Scottsdale, AZ: Gorsuch Scarisbrick.

Dansereau, F., & Markham, S. E. (1987). Superior-subordinate communication: Multiple levels of analysis. In F. M. Jablin, L. L. Putnam, K. H. Roberts, & L. W. Porter (Eds.), *Handbook of organizational communication: An interdisciplinary perspective* (pp. 343–388). Newbury Park, CA: Sage.

Fiske, S. T., & Neuberg, S. L. (1990). A continuum of impression formation, from category-based to individuating processes: Influences of information and motivation on attention and interpretation. In M. P. Zanna (Ed.), *Advances in experimental psychology: Vol. 23* (pp. 1–74). San Diego, CA: Academic Press.

Fiske, S. T., & Taylor, S. E. (1984). *Social cognition.* New York, NY: Random House.

Fitzpatrick, M. A., & Ritchie, L. D. (1994). Communication schemata within the family: Multiple perspectives on family interaction. *Human Communication Research, 20,* 275–301.

Gross, B., & O'Hair, H. D. (1988). *Communicating in interpersonal relationships.* New York, NY: Macmillan.

Heider, F. (1958). *The psychology of interpersonal relations.* New York, NY: Wiley.

Holtzworth-Munroe, A., & Jacobson, N. S. (1985). Causal attributions of married couples: When do they search for causes? What do they conclude when they do? *Journal of Personality and Social Psychology, 48,* 1398–1412.

Honeycutt, J. M. (1995). Predicting relational trajectory beliefs as a consequence of typicality and necessity rating of relationship behaviors. *Communication Reports, 12,* 3–14.

Honeycutt, J. M., Cantrill, J. G., & Greene, R. W. (1989). Memory structures for relational escalation: A cognitive test of the sequencing of relational actions and stages. *Human Communication Research, 16,* 62–90.

Honeycutt, J. M., Cantrill, J. G., Kelly, P., & Lambkin, D. (1998). How do I love thee? Let me consider my options: Cognition, verbal strategies, and the escalation of intimacy. *Human Communication Research, 25,* 39–63.

Johnson, D. (1996). Helpful listening and responding. In K. M. Galvin & P. Cooper (Eds.), *Making connections: Readings in relational communication* (pp. 91–97). Los Angeles, CA: Roxbury.

Jones, E. E., & Davis, K. (1965). From acts to dispositions: The attribution process in person perception. In L. Berkowitz (Ed.), *Advances in experimental social psychology: Vol. 2* (pp. 219–267). New York, NY: Academic Press.

Jones, E. E., & Nisbett, R. E. (1972). The actor and the observer: Divergent perceptions of the causes of behavior. In E. E. Jones, D. E. Kanouse, H. H. Kelley, R. E. Nisbett, S. Valins, & B. Weiner (Eds.), *Attributions: Perceiving the causes of behavior* (pp. 79–94). Morristown, NJ: General Learning Press.

Jussim, L. (1990). Social reality and social problems: The role of expectancies. *Journal of Social Issues, 46,* 9–34.

Kellermann, K. (1984). The negativity effect and its implications for initial interaction. *Communication Monographs, 51,* 37–55.

Kelley, D. L., & Burgoon, J. K. (1991). Understanding marital satisfaction and couple type as functions of relational expectations. *Human Communication Research, 18,* 40–69.

Kelley, H. H. (1973). The processes of causal attribution. *American Psychologist, 28,* 107–128.

Kelly, L. (1972). Empathic listening. In J. Stewart (Ed.), *Bridges not walls: A book of interpersonal communication* (pp. 222–227). Reading, MA: Addison-Wesley.

Kirtley, M. D., & Honeycutt, J. M. (1996). Listening styles and their correspondence with second guessing. *Communication Research Reports, 13,* 174–182.

Lakoff, G. (1987). *Women, fire, and dangerous things: What categories reveal about the mind.* Chicago, IL: University of Chicago Press.

Manusov, V. (1990). An application of attribution principles to nonverbal behavior in romantic dyads. *Communication Monographs, 57,* 104–118.

Manusov, V., Trees, A. R., Liotta, A., Koenig, J., & Cochran, A. T. (1999, May). *I think therefore I act: Interaction expectations and nonverbal adaptation in couples' conversations.* Paper presented to the Interpersonal Division of the International Communication Association, San Francisco, CA.

Manusov, V., Winchatz, M. R., & Manning, L. M. (1997). Acting out our minds: Incorporating behavior into models of stereotype-based expectancies for cross-cultural interactions. *Communication Monographs, 64,* 119–139.

McComb, K. B., & Jablin, F. M. (1984). Verbal correlates of interviewer empathic listening and employment outcomes. *Communication Monographs, 51,* 353–371.

Merton, R. K. (1948). The self-fulfilling prophecy. *Antioch Review, 8,* 193–210.

Miller, D. T., & Turnbull, W. (1986). Expectancies and interpersonal processes. *Annual Review of Psychology, 37,* 233–356.

Monahan, J. L. (1998). I don't know it but I like you: The influence of nonconscious affect on person perception. *Human Communication Research, 24,* 480–500.

Nyquist, M. (1996). Learning to listen. In K. M. Galvin & P. Cooper (Eds.), *Making connections: Readings in relational communication* (pp. 98–100). Los Angeles, CA: Roxbury.

Planalp, S. (1985). Relational schemata: A test of alternative forms of relational knowledge as guides to communication. *Human Communication Research, 12,* 3–29.

Rosenthal, R., & Rubin, D. B. (1978). Interpersonal expectancy effects: The first 345 studies. *Behavioral and Brain Sciences, 3,* 377–415.

Ross, L. (1977). The intuitive psychologist and his shortcomings: Distortions in the attribution process. In L. Berkowitz (Ed.), *Advances in experimental social psychology: Vol. 10* (pp. 173–220). New York, NY: Academic Press.

Stiff, J. B., Dillard, J. P., Somera, L., Kim, H., & Sleight, C. (1988). Empathy, communication, and prosocial behavior. *Communication Monographs, 55,* 198–213.

Swann, W. B. (1987). Identity negotiation: Where two roads meet. *Journal of Personality and Social Psychology, 53,* 1038–1051.

Swann, W. B. (1990). To be adored or to be known: The interplay of self-enhancement and self-verification. In E. T. Higgins & R. M. Sorrentino (Eds.), *Handbook of motivation and cognition: Vol. 2, Foundations of social behavior* (pp. 408–448). New York, NY: Guilford Press.

Thompson, T. (1994). Interpersonal communication and health care. In M. L. Knapp & G. R. Miller (Eds.), *Handbook of interpersonal communication* (pp. 696–725). Beverly Hills, CA: Sage.

QUESTIONS/THOUGHTS

1. Think of a situation in which you and a friend have viewed the exact same event or situation in two very different ways. Why did this happen? List 3 reasons why you think your perceptions and opinions differed.

2. How do stereotypes help people process information? How do they hinder information processing? Give an example.

3. What role do interpersonal expectancies have in the perception process?

4. Identify a self-fulfilling prophecy that you have experienced or witnessed. Explain how the expectations created by others influenced the perceptions that were developed.

B. Perceptual Filters

INTRODUCTION

Social experience frames your world. Your group identifications and your significant experiences serve to construct perceptual filters used to view the world. An older married Hispanic mother of six perceives certain issues and experiences differently than a male Caucasian teenager with a single father and a twin brother. Life experiences significantly influence how one views the world. Although there are many factors, such as religion, money, or health, that contribute to a world view, this section focuses on three powerful social perceptual influences—culture, your gender, and your family. Each will be addressed in this section. Hopefully you will think about your personal worldview as you read about the experiences of others.

Culture is "that set of values and beliefs, norms and customs, rules and codes, that socially define groups of people, binding them to one another and giving them a sense of commonality" (Trenholm and Jensen 2008, p. 373). Culture represents a collective answer to such fundamental questions as: "Who am I?" "Where do I fit in this world?" "How should I live my life?", and "How do I make sense out of the behaviors of others?" Although each person ultimately answers these questions individually, your culture affects your personal viewpoints.

Whereas culture used to be viewed as uniquely related to ethnicity, geographic locations and languages, today there are multiple understandings of culture. Terms such as disability culture, technology culture, or youth culture are commonly discussed.

How does culture affect communication? First, culture affects perceptions; it influences what you experience and how you interpret it. It affects whether you view the world as individual or as part of a collective society. For example, the typical Western perspective presumes people are unique individuals who control their own destinies. Children may be viewed as having equal rights to express opinions to adults. This is unlike the typical Eastern worldview that is more communal, including extended family members and organizational colleagues. In the latter case, the behavior of specific members reflects directly on the entire family or an organization, a reality that influences many decisions. What one says or does reflects directly on many other people because one is part of a collective society.

Second, culture affects verbal and nonverbal language codes. Language is the primary tool a culture uses to transmit its values and beliefs. The Sapir-Whorf hypothesis suggests that your language determines how you view the world. If this is true, then people who speak different languages will experience the world differently. For example, in English speakers use "you" regardless of the status or age of the person addressed. In German, however, there are two words: "du" for informal use and "Sie" for formal use—for strangers, those of high status, and older persons. Some ethnic cultures have no words for illnesses recognized in other cultures; what are symptoms in one culture may have different meanings in another one (Fadiman, 1997). Members of the technology culture tend to be younger and more technologically skilled; they communicate in a language that is unintelligible to those less technologically savvy.

Third, culture affects role identity. The value placed on birth order, gender, or family position affects communication. In addition, the roles of children or elders vary across cultures. In some cultures children are expected to remain unobtrusive when adults are talking; in other cultures children are the center of attention for the adults and are welcomed into conversation. The United States is experiencing a generational role reversal as young people become the "experts" on buying and using new technologies. Young members of immigrant families may serve as language brokers for elder family members who depend on them for translation help in areas related to medicine,

social services or education (Galvin, Bylund & Brommel, 2008).

Culture and communication are interdependent. In order to communicate effectively, it is necessary to be sensitive to cultural differences. Cultural norms establish acceptable communication practices and culture is transmitted and maintained through communication. Persons raised in multiple cultures are able to see the world through multiple cultural lenses and adapt to the communication styles of others and engage in meaningful interactions cross-cultural interactions.

A second major perceptual filter is gender. Males and females tend to be socialized differently, although the differences tend to be less distinct than in previous generations. For example, in our society males are more likely socialized to be successful, aggressive, sexual, and self-reliant, whereas females are socialized to be nurturing, sensitive, interdependent, and concerned with appearance (Stewart et al. 2003; Wood, 2007). Because of these socialization experiences, males and females tend to view the world somewhat differently; such differences are reflected in their communication styles. Until recently, men were discouraged from expressing feelings directly, whereas women were permitted to express theirs. Wood and Inman (1993) developed masculine models of closeness, which emphasize sharing joint activities or doing things for others, approaches that differ from the more feminine pattern of self-disclosure.

In addition to culture and gender, families provide members with perceptual filters. All families have rules, themes, roles, and boundaries that influence members' communication. The family, or families, that you grew up in, sometimes referred to as your "family of origin," taught you a great deal about communication practices such as, sharing affection, expressing anger, making decisions, and trusting others. These beliefs, in turn, affect your perceptions and communication. For example, if you grew up in a family with prescribed and rigid gender roles, your perception of what constitutes appropriate mother-child interaction will differ from someone raised in a family with flexible gender roles. You may be amazed at the way a friend argues with his mother, or confides in her, because that may not be comfortable for you. In addition, the family lessons about expressing emotions carry into all parts of your life. If your family taught you to express anger directly, you may have difficulty with a roommate who learned to keep anger inside or express it indirectly. If your new romantic partner grew up in a family that expressed affection openly, you may feel uncomfortable if your family was reserved about expressing feelings.

These three powerful forces—culture, gender, and family—are among those that shape your worldview and, hence, your communication patterns. The more fully you understand your own cultural, gendered and family background, the more effectively you will be able to make sense or your current communication experiences.

REFERENCES

Stewart, L., Cooper, P., Stewart, A., & Friedley, S. (2003). *Communication between the sexes* (4th ed.). Boston, MA: Allyn & Bacon.

Fadiman, A. (1997). *The spirit catches you and you fall down*. New York, NY: Farrar, Straus & Giroux.

Galvin, K. M., Bylund, C.L. & Brommel, B. J. (2008). *Family communication: Cohesion and change*. Boston, MA: Allyn & Bacon.

Trenholm, S., & Jensen, A. (2008). *Interpersonal communication* (6th ed.). New York, NY: Oxford University Press.

Wood, J. (2007). *Gendered lives* (7th ed.). Belmont, CA: Wadsworth.

Wood, J., & Inman, C. (1993). In a different mode: Masculine styles of communicating closeness. *Journal of Applied Communication*, 21(3), 279–295.

The Necessity of Intercultural Communication

JAMES NEULIEP

If you have lived or traveled in different parts of the world, you know the joys and frustrations of intercultural communication. In a diverse society, such as the United States, you regularly encounter individuals and groups with strong cultural traditions different from your own. Because most people view the world through the labels, categories, and concepts that are products of their culture, it can be difficult to communicate effectively outside that culture.

Several dimensions have been used to discuss cultural characteristics that might affect intercultural communication (Samovar & Porter, 2001). The first dimension concerns ways in which members of a particular culture deliver messages. A low-context culture, such as that found in the United States, relies heavily on language to express thoughts, feelings, and ideas as clearly and logically as possible. Verbal fluency is admired, and a direct statement of opinions and desires is valued. In high-context cultures, such as that found in China or Japan, important information is carried in contextual and nonverbal cues (such as time, place, relationship between speakers, and situation). Relational harmony is valued, so communicators rely on a less direct verbal style. They rely heavily on contextual, nonverbal cues to convey important messages.

A second dimension involves the difference between individualistic and collectivistic cultures. A culture that values the individual believes that each person is a separate, unique individual who should be independent and self-sufficient. Such is the case in the United States, where value is placed on autonomy, youth, individual security, equality, and personal achievement. Many cultures in Latin America and Asia are collective. These cultures have a "we" rather than an "I" orientation. A high value is placed on order, duty, traditions, age, group security, and hierarchy. People are identified by their membership in extended families, and sometimes in their workplaces, and are expected to reflect a "we" orientation. High value is placed on acting as a group member rather than as an individual.

The third dimension, power distance, refers to the degree to which members of a society accept an unequal distribution of power. Cultures with low power distance believe in minimizing the differences between social classes. The culture of the United States is generally considered a low power distance *culture. Low power distance cultures believe that challenging authority is acceptable, even desirable. High power distance cultures honor a strong hierarchy and the role of authority.*

Classes in intercultural communication used to focus extensively on international cultural diversity. Today, the focus is much broader because, "As we enter the twenty-first century, direct contact with culturally different people in our neighborhoods, community, schools, and workplaces is an inescapable part of life" (Ting-Toomey & Chung, 2005). Most people in the United States find themselves in some type of intercultural communication on a daily basis.

The word "culture" is a highly complex term, which, like "communication" is easily recognized for what it is, but not as easily defined. Because culture plays a large role in shaping communicative practices, author James Neuliep defines intercultural communication and describes four components of a definition of culture. Next, he introduces a model for understanding the contexts in which intercultural communication take place, including cultural, microcultural, environmental, perceptual, and sociorelational contexts. Overall, this chapter provides further explanation for the occurrence of varying, and sometimes conflicting perceptions on the part of different people, especially in situations involving intercultural participants with different backgrounds, values, beliefs, rules, and practices.

As you read this article, consider your own intercultural communication experiences and address the question: How do my cultural experiences affect my interactions with people from backgrounds different than my own?

REFERENCES

Samovar, L., & Porter, R. (2001). *Communication between cultures.* Belmont, CA: Wadsworth.

Ting-Toomey, S. & Chung, L. C. (2005). *Understanding intercultural communication.* New York, NY: Oxford University Press.

THE BENEFITS OF INTERCULTURAL COMMUNICATION

Although the challenges of an increasingly diverse world are great, the benefits are even greater.

Communicating and establishing relationships with people from different cultures can lead to a host of benefits, including healthier communities; increased international, national, and local commerce; reduced conflict; and personal growth through increased tolerance. Joan England (1992) argues that genuine community is a condition of togetherness in which people have lowered their defenses and have learned to accept and celebrate their differences. England contends that we can no longer define equality as "sameness" but instead must value our differences with others, whether they be differences of race, gender, ethnicity, lifestyle, occupation, or professional discipline. Healthy communities are made up of individuals working collectively for the benefit of everyone, not just their own group. Through open and honest intercultural communication people can work together to achieve goals that benefit everyone, regardless of group or cultural orientation. According to M. Scott Peck (1987), the overall mission of human communication is (or should be) reconciliation. He argues that effective communication can ultimately lower or remove the walls and barriers of misunderstanding that separate human beings from one another. Peck states that the rules for community building are the same as the rules for effective communication.

Communication is the foundation of all human relationships. Moreover, argues Peck, the principles of community are applicable to any situation in which two people are gathered together, including the global community, the home, business, or neighborhood. Healthy communities support all community members and strive to understand, appreciate, and acknowledge each member....

As you communicate with people from different cultures, you learn more about them and their way of life, including their values, history, habits, and the substance of their personality. As your relationships with people from other cultures develop, you start to understand them better, perhaps even empathizing with them. One of the things you will learn eventually is that although your cultures are different, you have much in common. As humans we all have the same basic needs and desires—we just have different ways of achieving them. As we learn that our way is not the only way, we develop a tolerance for difference....

THE NATURE OF CULTURE

Like communication, culture is ubiquitous and has a profound effect on humans. Culture is simultaneously invisible and pervasive. As we go about our daily lives, we are not overly conscious of our culture's influence on us. How often have you sat in your dorm room or classroom and consciously thought about what it means to be an American? As you stand in the lunch line, do you say to yourself, "I am acting like an American?" As you sit in your classroom do you say to yourself, "The professor is really acting like an American?" Yet most of your thoughts, emotions, and behaviors are culturally driven. One need only step into a culture different from one's own to feel the immense impact of culture.

Culture has a direct influence on the physical, relational, and perceptual environment. The next time you enter your communication classroom, consider how the room is arranged physically, including where you sit and where the professor teaches, the location of the chalkboard, windows, and so forth. Does the professor lecture from behind a podium? Do the students sit facing the professor? Is the chalkboard used? Next, think about your *relationship* with the professor and the other students in your class. Is the relationship formal or informal? Do you interact with the professor and students about topics other than class material? Would you consider the relationship personal or impersonal? Finally, think about your *perceptual disposition*—that is, your attitudes, motivations, and emotions about the class. Are you happy to be in the class? Do you enjoy attending? Are you nervous when the instructor asks you a question? To a great extent, the answers to these questions are contingent on your culture. The physical arrangement of classrooms, the social relationship between students and teachers, and the perceptual profiles of the students and teachers vary significantly from culture to culture.

Like communication, culture is difficult to define. Australian anthropologist Roger Keesing (1974, p. 73) argues that:

> Culture does not have some true and sacred and eternal meaning we are trying to discover, but that like other symbols, it means whatever we use it to mean; and that as with other analytical concepts, human users must carve out—and try to partly agree on—a class of natural phenomena it can most strategically label.

Just about everyone has a definition of culture. To be sure, over forty years ago two well-known anthropologists, Alfred Kroeber and Clyde Kluckhohn (1993), found and examined three hundred definitions of culture, none of which were the same....

Although there may not be a universally accepted definition of culture, there are a number of properties of culture upon which most people agree describe its essence. In this textbook, culture is defined as *an accumulated pattern of values, beliefs, and behaviors, shared by an identifiable group of people with a common history and a verbal and nonverbal symbol system.*

Culture as an Accumulated Pattern of Values, Beliefs, and Behaviors

Cultures can be defined by their value and belief systems and by the actions of their members. People who exist in the same culture generally share similar values and beliefs.... In the United States, individuality is highly valued. An individual's self-interest takes precedence over group interests. Americans believe that people are unique. Moreover, Americans value personal independence. Conversely, in Japan, a collectivistic and homogeneous culture, a sense of groupness and group harmony is valued. Most Japanese see themselves as members of a group first, as individuals second. Where Americans value independence, Japanese value interdependence. Norwegians value conformity. Norwegian children are taught to put the needs of society above their own. Cultural aspects of conformity are embodied in what Norwegians call *Janteloven*, which denotes the fear of individuality, of standing out in a crowd. Although the Norwegian literacy rate is among the highest in the world, Norwegian schools do not have accelerated programs for gifted and talented students. Norwegians believe that to divide students on the basis of intellectual ability would disrupt the social cohesion (Yurkovich and Halverson, 1993).

The values of a particular culture lead to a set of expectations and rules prescribing how people should behave in that culture. Although many Americans prefer to think of themselves as unique individuals, most Americans behave in similar ways. Most work forty hours a week, receive some form of payment for their work, and pay some of their earnings in taxes. Most spend their money on homes and cars. Almost every home in the United States has a television. Observe the students around you in your classes. Although you may think that you are very different from your peers, you are really quiet similar to them. Most of them follow a daily behavioral pattern very similar to your own, attending classes, taking examinations, going to lunch, studying, partying, writing papers, and so forth.

Culture as an Identifiable Group of People With a Common History

Because the members of a particular culture share similar values, beliefs and behaviors, they are identifiable as a distinct group. In addition to their shared values, beliefs, and behaviors, the members of a particular culture share a common history. Any culture's past inextricably binds it to the present and guides its future. At the core of any culture are traditions that are passed on to future generations. In many cultures, history is a major component of the formal and informal education systems. To learn a culture's history is to learn that culture's values. One way children in the United States develop their sense of independence is by learning about the Declaration of Independence, one of this country's most sacred documents. Elementary school children in Iran learn of the historical significance of the political and religious revolution that took place in their culture in the 1970s and 1980s. Russian children are taught about the arts in Russian history, including

famous Russian composers such as Tchaikovsky, Rachmaninoff, and Stravinsky. The arts of the past help Russians remember their culture as they face the disrupting social and political crises of the present. Such historical lessons are the glue that binds people to one another (Westfahl, Koltz, and Manders, 1993).

Culture as a Verbal and Nonverbal Symbol System

One of the most important elements of any culture is its communication system. The verbal and nonverbal symbols with which the members of a culture communicate are culture bound. To see the difference between the verbal codes of any two cultures is easy. The dominant verbal code in the United States is English whereas the dominant verbal code in Mexico is Spanish. Two cultures that share the same verbal code may have dramatically different verbal styles, however. Most white Americans use a very direct, instrumental, personal style in speaking English. Many Native Americans use an indirect, impersonal style in speaking English and may prefer the use of silence instead of words (Basso, 1990).

Nonverbal code systems vary significantly across cultures also. Nonverbal communication includes the use of body language, gestures, facial expressions, the voice, smell, personal and geographical space, time, and artifacts. Body language can communicate a great deal about one's culture. When adults interact with young children in the United States, it is not uncommon for the adult to pat the head of the child. This nonverbal gesture is often seen as a form of endearment and is culturally acceptable. In Thailand, however, where the head is considered the seat of the soul, such a gesture is unacceptable. Belching during or after a meal is viewed by most Americans as rude and impolite, perhaps even disgusting. But in parts of Korea and the Middle East, belching after a meal might be interpreted as a compliment to the cook (Axtell, 1991)....

Microcultural Groups

Within most cultures there are groups of people, or *microcultures*, that coexist within the mainstream society. Microcultures exist within the broader rules and guidelines of the dominant cultural milieu but are distinct in some way, perhaps racially, linguistically, or through their sexual orientation, age, or even occupation. In some ways, everyone is a member of some microcultural group. Often microcultures may have histories that differ from the dominant cultural group. In many cases, microcultural groups are subordinate in some way, perhaps politically or economically....

A CONTEXTUAL MODEL OF INTERCULTURAL COMMUNICATION

Intercultural communication occurs whenever a minimum of two persons from different cultures or microcultures come together and exchange verbal and nonverbal symbols. A central theme throughout this book is that intercultural communication is contextual. A contextual model of intercultural communication is shown in Figure 12-1.

According to the model, intercultural communication occurs within a variety of contexts, including (1) cultural, (2) microcultural, (3) environmental, (4) perceptual, and (5) sociorelational contexts. A context is a complex combination of a variety of factors, including the setting, situation, circumstances, background, and overall

framework within which communication occurs. The largest, outer circle of the model in Figure 6–1 represents the *cultural context*. This is the largest circle because the dominant culture permeates every aspect of the communicative exchange, even the physical geography. All communicative exchanges between persons occur within some culture....

The next-largest circle in the model is the *microcultural context*. As mentioned earlier, within most cultures, separate groups of people coexist. These groups, called microcultures, are in some way different from the larger cultural milieu. Sometimes the difference is ethnicity, race, or language. Often microcultures are treated differently by the members of the larger culture....

The next-largest circle in the model is the *environmental context*. This circle represents the physical, geographical location of the interaction. While culture prescribes the overall rules for communication, the physical location indicates when and where the specific rules apply. For example, in the United States there are rules about yelling. Depending on the physical location, yelling can be prohibited or encouraged. In church, yelling is generally prohibited, whereas at a football game, yelling is the preferred method of communicating. The physical environment includes the physical

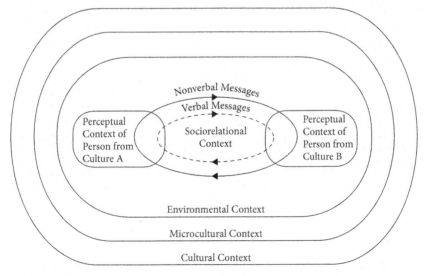

Figure 12-1

geography, architecture, landscape design, and even the climate of a particular culture. All of these environmental factors play a key role in how people communicate....

The two circles in the model on either side of the sociorelational context represent the *perceptual* contexts of the individuals interacting. The perceptual context refers to the individual characteristics of the interactants, including their cognitions, attitudes, dispositions, and motivations. How an individual perceives the environment and gathers, stores, and retrieves information is uniquely human but also culturally influenced. How an individual develops attitudes about others, including stereotypes, varies from culture to culture....

The circle intersecting the perceptual contexts in the model is the *sociorelational context*—that is, the relationship between the interactants. Whenever two people come together and interact, they establish a relationship. Within this relationship each person assumes a role. Right now, you are assuming the role of student. The person teaching your communication class is assuming the role of teacher. Roles prescribe how people should behave. Most of the people with whom you interact are related to you through your role as student. The reason you interact with so many professors is because you are a student. What you interact about—that is, the topic of your interaction—is also defined by your role as student. You and your professors interact about courses. How you interact with your professor—that is, the style of talk (for example, polite language)—is also prescribed by your role as student. The language and style of your talk with your professor is probably very different from the language and style of talk you use when you go back to your dorm room and interact with your friends. Probably the last ten people with whom you interacted were directly related to you through your role as student. When you go back to your hometown during semester break and step into the role of son or daughter, or brother or sister, you are assuming a different role, and your interaction changes accordingly. Your interaction varies as a function of the role you assume.

Roles vary from culture to culture. Although in just about every culture there are student/teacher role relationships, how those roles are defined varies significantly. What it means to be a student in the United States is very different from what it means to be a student in Japan. In Japan, students go to school six days a week. Japanese teachers are highly respected and play a very influential role in the Japanese student's life. What it means to be a mother or father also varies considerably from one culture to another. In the Masai culture of Kenya, a woman is defined by her fertility. To be defined as a mother in Masai culture, a woman must endure circumcision (clitoridectomy), an arranged marriage, and wife beating (Angeloni, 1995). One's roles prescribe the types of verbal and nonverbal symbols that are exchanged.

In the model in Figure 12–1, the sociorelational context is graphically represented by two circles labeled "nonverbal messages" and "verbal messages." The nonverbal circle is larger of the two and is represented by a continuous line. The verbal circle is smaller and is represented as a series of dashes. The nonverbal-message circle is larger than the verbal-message circle because the majority of our communicative behavior is nonverbal. Whether we are using words or not, we are communicating nonverbally though eye contact, bodily stance, and space. In addition, our nonverbal behavior is ongoing—we cannot not behave. The verbal message circle is portrayed as a series of dashes to represent the *digital* quality of verbal communication. By digital, we mean that, unlike our nonverbal communication, our verbal communication is made up of words that have recognizable and discrete beginning and ending points. A word is like a digit. We can start and stop talking with words. Our nonverbal behavior goes on continuously, however....

REFERENCES

Angeloni, E. (Ed.). (1995). *Mystique of the Masai.* Guilford, CT: Dushkin.

Axtell, R. (1991). *Gestures: Do's and taboos of body language around the world.* New York, NY: Wiley.

Basso, K. (1990). To give up on words: Silence in western apache culture. In D. Carbaugh (Ed.), *Cultural communication and intercultural contact* (pp. 303–320). Hillsdale, NJ: Erlbaum.

England, J. T. (1992). Building community for the 21st century. *ERIC Digest.* Retrieved from http://www.eric.ed.gov/ERICDocs/data/ericdocs2sql/content_storage_01/0000019b/80/28/ee/3f.pdf

Gayle, A. R., & Knutson, K. P. (1993). Understanding cultural differences: Jenteloven and social conformity in Norway. *Et cetera, 50,* 449.

Keesing, R. (1974). Theories of culture. In B. J. Siegel (Ed.), *Annual review of anthropology.* (pp. 73–87)/ Palo Alto, CA: Annual Reviews.

Kroeber, A. I., & Kluckhohn, C. (Eds.). (1954). *Culture: A critical review of concepts and definitions.* New York, NY: Random House.

Peck, M. S. (1987). *The different drum: Community making and peace.* New York, NY: Touchstone.

Resnick, A. (1993). *The commonwealth of independent states.* Danbury, CT: Children's Press.

Seelye, H. N. (1993). *Teaching culture: Strategies for intercultural communication* Lincolnwood, IL: National Textbook Company.

Westfahl, G., Koltz, R., & Manders, A. (1996). *Ethnic Russian culture and society.* Unpublished student manuscript, St. Norbert College, De Pere, WI.

Yurkovich, D., Pliscott, K., & Halverson, R. (1996). *The Norwegian culture.* Unpublished student manuscript, St. Norbert College, De Pere, WI.

QUESTIONS/THOUGHTS

1. Define the word "culture" for yourself. Ask 10 other people to define "culture." What are the similarities and differences in the definitions? What does this suggest about intercultural communication?

2. Think about an intercultural interaction you had that was difficult. After reading this chapter, what things might you do differently if you found yourself in a similar situation?

3. An old adage suggests, "When in Rome, do as the Romans do." Based on this article, is that sound advice? Why or why not? What might be a difficulty in following this adage?

4. What have you learn about yourself on the basis of intercultural interactions? Give two specific examples.

Reprinted from James Neuliep, "The Necessity of Intercultural Communication." In *Intercultural Communication: A Contextual Approach,* 4/e, pp. 2–28. Copyright © 2009. Reprinted by permission of Sage Publications.

Family-of-Origin Influences

KATHLEEN M. GALVIN, CARMA L. BYLUND, AND
BERNARD J. BROMMEL

Your experiences in your family-of-origin serve as a perceptual filter as you enter into new relationships, close friendships, and romantic partnerships. Family-of-origin refers to the family or families in which a person is raised and is generally thought to be the earliest and most powerful influence in one's personality. Families-of-origin provide blueprints for the communication of future generations. Initially, a child learns to communicate within the home, and, throughout life, the family setting provides a major testing ground for new communication skills or strategies. Young people leaving families-of-origin to form new families take with them a set of conscious and unconscious ways of relating to people.

Family relationship models act as a guide for children's behavior and become central to their interpretation of others' behavior. For instance, if you have lived in a stepfamily, you may have witnessed the stress involved in integrating your stepparent's family of origin influences into a system with communication patterns that already reflected two other families of origin.

Although family of origin issues focus on parent-to-child transmissions, recently, greater

emphasis has been placed on influences across generations. In recent years family scholars and researchers have focused more directly on the effect of multigenerational systems. Some of the issues that may be used to examine multigenerational matters include how gender roles are played out; how families deal with losses; how ethnic patterns affect interactions; how affection is shared; how family boundaries are managed; and how members deal with conflict. These issues are viewed across three or four generations to see how patterns are passed down, consciously or unconsciously.

Although the United States is viewed as a melting pot, "Cultural meanings may persist many generations after migration and after people have ceased to be aware of their heritage." (McGoldrick, Giordano & Garcia-Preto, 2005, p. 11). Values, beliefs, and behaviors often traverse generations without being recognized as having their origins in ethnic patterns.

Yet, although patterns do move across generations, changes also occur. Mormon and Floyd (2002) suggest that "At the beginning of the 21ˢᵗ Century, evidence is mounting that a 'changing culture of fatherhood' is well underway, as men attempt to gain a more positive perspective on their role as fathers." (p. 395) Although this statement reflects changes in overall life patterns for many men, due to societal shifts, individuals in earlier generations may have chosen not to follow in their fathers' footsteps because they rejected specific behaviors, such as treating female children as unimportant. Floyd and Morman (2006) found that some sons modeled their fathers whereas others behaved in opposite ways with their children, thus compensating for their upbringing.

Many of you may desire a family life different from the one in which you grew up, yet you find yourself re-creating similar patterns in a new relationship. Because parental socialization serves as a major factor in determining children's family-formation behavior, children often establish marriages similar to their parents', not because of heredity, but because they are following family patterns.

This chapter discusses the ways in which families shape your self-understanding, values, attitudes, roles and habits. Through a careful discussion of family influence and impact, the author also emphasizes the need to take personal responsibility for one's own actions and choices. Family background, therefore, can be seen and used as a learning tool, and an important resource; not as an excuse for undesirable behaviors or lifestyle choices. As you read this chapter, ask yourself the following: What is one communication related pattern from your family of origin that you anticipate maintaining in your life?

REFERENCES

Floyd, K., & Morman, M. T. (2006). The good son: Men's perceptions of the characteristics of sonhood. In K. Floyd & M. T. Morman (Eds), *Widening the family circle: New research in family communication (37–55).* Thousand Oaks, CA: Sage.

McGoldrick, M., Giordano, J., & Garcia-Preto, N. (2005). Overview: Ethnicity and family therapy. In M. McGoldrick, J. Giordano, N. Garcia-Preto (Eds.), *Ethnicity and family therapy* (pp. 1–40). New York, NY: Guilford Press.

Mormon, M. T., & Floyd, K. (2002). A "changing culture of fatherhood": Effects on affectionate communication, closeness, and satisfaction in men's relationships with their fathers and their sons. *Western Journal of Communication, 66,* 395–411.

FAMILY-OF-ORIGIN INFLUENCES ON THE NEXT GENERATION

"My son's a Kaplan, all right. He'll walk up and talk to anyone without a trace of shyness." "My grandparents and parents always fought by yelling at each other and then forgetting about it. My wife doesn't understand this." These statements indicate family-of-origin influences on communication patterns in new family systems. *Family-of-origin* refers to the family or families in which a person is raised and is generally thought to be the earliest and most powerful source of influence on one's personality (Bochner & Eisenberg, 1987).

The term *family-of-origin influences* refers to how current relational experiences reflect a unique combination of (1) unique multigenerational transmissions and (2) the ethnic heritages represented within the family-of origin. The multigenerational and ethnic background that each person brings to a relationship creates a significant social influence on their partnership and their children. You may desire a family life different from the one you experienced, yet you find yourself re-creating similar patterns in a new relationship. Paternal socialization serves as a major factor in determining children's family-formation behavior (Dixson, 1995). People often create marriages similar to that of their parents, because they are following a family pattern.

Multigenerational Transmissions

Families-of-origin may provide blueprints for the communication of future generations. Initially, communication is learned in the home, and, throughout life, the family setting provides a major testing ground for new communication skills or strategies. Each young person who leaves the family-of-origin to form a new system takes with him or her a set of conscious and unconscious ways of relating to others. For example, the idiosyncrasies and culturally based communication patterns of the current Watson family may be passed on to generations of children.

My husband gets crazy with all the odd-words my family uses, especially around children. I came from a family of 12 kids and there were always words someone couldn't say or codes for things. So I talk to our kids about "I-box" (ice-cream), doing a "zip-perino" (getting dressed), or "the throne" (toilet).

Just as simple language terms travel across the generations, more significant attitudes and rule-bound behaviors move from a family-of-origin to a newly emerging family system. The family-of-origin serves as the first communication classroom.

Differences in family-of-origin experiences can lead to a communication breakdown in a couple's system. In the following example, a wife describes the differences in nonverbal communication in her family-of-origin from that of her husband.

It was not until I became closely involved with a second family that I became conscious of the fact that the amount and type of contact can differ greatly. Rarely, in Rob's home, will another person reach for someone else's hand, walk arm in arm, or kiss for no special reason. Hugs are reserved for comfort. When people filter into the den to watch television, one person will sit on the couch, the next on the floor, a third on a chair, and finally the last person is forced to sit on the couch. And always at the opposite end! Touching, in my home, was a natural, everyday occurrence. Usually, the family breakfast began with "good morning" hugs and kisses. Even as adults, no one ever hesitated to cuddle up next to someone else, run their hands through another person's hair, or start tickling whoever happens to be in reaching distance.

When you consider your parent's relationship, you can find instances of this situation in which the rules or networks affect how and what communication occurs. Models of relationships can act as a guide for children's behavior and become central to their interpretation of others' behavior (Dixson, 1995). For instance, if you have lived in a stepfamily, you may have witnessed the stress involved by integrating your stepparent's family-of-origin influences into a system with

communication patterns that already reflected two families-of-origin.

Frequently, family-of-origin patterns have been used to study abusive or harsh parenting. Chen and Kaplan (2001) examined the continuity of supportive parenting across generations and found positive patterns. The results of their longitudinal study report modest intergenerational continuity tied to factors such as interpersonal relations, social participation, and role modeling. This is consistent with Simons, Beaman, Conger, and Chao's (1993) findings on the connection between early experiences of supportive parenting to later adoption of similar parenting.

Although family-of-origin issues may be discussed as parent-to-child transmissions, greater emphasis has been placed on transmission across multiple generations. In recent years family researchers have focused more directly on the effect of multigenerational systems, suggesting, "Evidence indicates a link between the parenting children receive and their subsequent behaviors" (Buerkel-Rothfuss, Fink, & Buerkel, 1995, p. 63). Following are the basic assumptions inherent in such an approach.

Multigenerational systems:

- Influence, and are influenced by, individuals who are born into them
- Are similar to, but more complex than, any multiperson ecosystem are developmental in nature
- Contain patterns that are shared, transformed, and manifested through intergenerational transmission
- Contain issues that may appear only in certain contexts and may be at unconscious levels
- Have boundaries that are hierarchical in nature
- Develop functional and dysfunctional patterns based on the legacy of previous generations and here-and-now happenings. (Hoopes, 1987, pp. 198–204)

One way to envision intergenerational transmissions is through genograms (McGoldrick, Gerson,

& Schellenberger, 1999). A genogram is a multi-generational family tree that plots familial relationships and visually records information about social relationships and biological and physiological issues in the family across three or more generations (*www.genograms.org*)....

I have come to learn that my problem of behavior was a reaction to my mother's alcoholism, and to her emotional distance during my infancy and childhood. Likewise, my mother's behaviors had a similar origin. Handicapped by her own mother's chronic depression, my mother never received the affirmation she needed and desired. Yet, having been reared by an alcoholic mother, my grandmother was in no better position to be an effective mother or role model for intimacy. With such unavailable models, the women in my family were perpetually unable to develop this essential capacity. Consequently, my own mother built our relationship from a faulty blueprint.

Such patterns are not usually so dramatic. According to Duck (1986), relationships that have major effects on people are of this perpetual but dormant kind: "They are part of the unchallenged and comfortable predictability of lives made up of routine, regular conversation, and assumptions that most of tomorrow will be based on the foundation of today (p. 91). Yet, although patterns do move across generations, changes also occur. In their study of grandfather-father-son relational closeness patterns, Buerkel-Rothfuss, Fink, and Buerkel (1995) conclude, "Males use communication behaviors similar to those of their fathers and in many cases, their grandfathers, but father-son relationships may be evolving into a more positive form" (p. 80).

Some of the factors that may be used to examine multigenerational issues include the following: how gender roles are played out; how families deal with losses; how ethnic patterns affect interactions; how certain people are linked, such as through names or physical similarities; how themes are played out; how rigid or open the boundaries are; and how members deal with conflict. These and other related issues are viewed across three or four generations to see how patterns are passed down, consciously or unconsciously. Yet, further research is needed on numerous issues, such as why some children in problematic families continue the tradition, while others create well-functioning adult familial relationships. In his analysis of family psychosocial risk factors, Rutter (2002) states, "Some children seem to escape most serious ill effects (although that does not mean that they have been totally unaffected or unscarred) whereas others succumb to lasting psychopathology" (p. 335). In addition, mutual influence must be better understood because parents and children interact and mutually influence each other; this occurs in a bidirectional manner as opposed to a unidirectional manner (Saphir & Chaffee, 2002).

The effects of significant traumas may be transmitted to future generations. Studies of children of Holocaust survivors identified issues faced by some of them; these included impaired self-esteem and identity problems; catastrophic expectations and preoccupation with death; anxiety, feelings of loss and increased vulnerability; exaggerated attachments or exaggerated independence; and difficulty with intimate relationships (Kellerman, 2001).

Biological/Genetic Factors Current genetic studies will influence thinking in this area over the next few decades. Many of the family problems have recognized intergenerational components (Daly et al., 1999). Some of these issues are genetically linked. Booth, Carver, and Granger (2000) propose the importance of the following biological topics with direct links to family interaction: (1) behavioral endocrinology, (2) behavioral genetics, (3) evolutionary psychology, and (4) behavioral psychopharmacology. The impact on physiology, genetics, and evolution on interaction patters gained attention in the past decade with renewed attention to biological contributions to individual communication practices and discussion of a communibiological paradigm (Beatty, McCroskey, & Valencic, 2001; Floyd & Haynes, 2006).

Although knowledge of the effects of complex sets of genes on behavior is limited, established lines of research are exploring passive, reactive, and active influences related to behaviors of parents and children. For example, a way in which genes influence environmental risk exposure is though their effects on children's behavior. Thus, adoptee studies have shown that the adoptive parents of children born to, but not reared by antisocial parents, are more likely to exhibit negative forms of control than are parents of children who lack that biological risk (Rutter, 2002). The mediation in this case comes about through the genetic effects on the children's disruptive behavior, which in turn influences their interactions with their adoptive parents who are rearing them. Animal studies suggest the quality of mothering appears to be maintained across generations not only through genetics, but also through "early experiences of maternal sensory, perceptual and recognition mechanisms that affect later responsiveness to offspring" (Fleming et al., 2002).

The importance of a family-of-origin is summarized well by Kramer (1985) in her depiction of its influence in a child's view of the world:

(The child) observes the environment he inhabits, partakes of its ambiance. He forms values and beliefs, develops assumptions about how marriages and families are and should be, ad learns about life cycles, including how to handle the changes of maturation and of aging and death. He learns about power and control and about the consequences of emotions, both his own and others. He is schooled in patterns of communication: what role to take in triangles; how to handle secrets; how to respond to pressure. (p. 9).

Such a description captures the power of a child's family experiences to influence his or her entire life.

ETHNICITY

The role of ethnicity in multigenerational patterns often is overlooked, yet its influence can be powerful, since ethnic values and identification are retained for many generations after immigration (McGoldrick, 1994). Ethnicity describes people by their supposed common ancestry, language, and cultural ancestry. Coontz (1999) argues that ethnicity is a product bit just of the traditions brought by immigrants but if the particular immigrant group's class origins and occupational skills interacting with the historically or regionally specific

jobs, housing stock, and political conditions they meet (p. xvi).

Ethnic family issues may be reflected in issues such as age, gender, roles, expressiveness, birth order, separation, or individuation. In their examination of Italian families, Giordano and McGoldrick (1996) highlight the families' cultural enjoyment of celebrating, loving, and fighting and their orientation toward social skills, including cleverness, charm, and graciousness. They place heavy emphasis on how actions affect the family honor. In addition, Italian families function within a network of other relatives, *gumbares* (old friends), and godparents from whom mutual support is expected. This orientation stresses parental role distinction, with the father as the undisputed head of the family and mother as the heart.

This generalization about the Italian heritage comes into sharp contrast with descriptions of Scandinavian family patterns, which generally stress the importance of emotional control and the avoidance of open confrontation (Erickson & Simon, 1996). Within the Norwegian family, words are likely to be used sparingly; inner weaknesses are kept secret; aggression is channeled into teasing, ignoring, or silence. A marriage of persons reflecting these two ethnic backgrounds has the potential for misunderstanding unless differences are addressed. Such differences may never be resolved because of the strength of the family pattern, or compromises may be necessary as the whole family is influenced by social forces.

African American families emphasize extended kinship bonds, African roots, strong three-generation systems, religion, and spirituality (Hines & Boyd-Franklin, 1996). African American parent-child interaction patterns involve parents as cultural advisors, coaches, and participants, given unique needs of racial socialization (Socha, Bromley, & Kelly, 1995). Specifically, African American patterns exhibit the "imperative mode" or directive communication as a protective authority (Daniel & Daniel, 1999).

A family's ethnic heritage may dictate norms for communication, which are maintained for generations. For example, an emphasis on keeping things "in the family," or the way in which such subjects re discussed may pass from generation to generation, reflecting individual and cultural influences. An examination of communication patterns through three generations of an extended Irish American family revealed great similarities across generations in terms of culturally predictable communication patterns (Galvin, in press). Whereas the Irish family sets strong boundaries, the following description of Arabic family life portrays a different picture.

Growing up in an Arab household, our immediate family and our extended family reflected the strong patriarchal influence and a theme of "family is family," which implied active support of many relatives. We lived by the Arabic proverb "A small house has enough room for one hundred people who love each other" and we shared joys, sorrows, money, and things among and across generations.

Although a growing number of studies address different ethnic patterns, few studies address ethnic patterns that occur as the result of remarriages and stepfamilies, or most transnational adoptions (particularly of older children), or transracial domestic adoption or foster care.

To date, much of this related research presumes family communication issues are similar across ethnic groups; unique issues have been overlooked or underrepresented. The attention placed on the "traditional" family has led some authors to proclaim, "The psychology of marriage as it exists is really a psychology is European American middle class marriage" (Flanagan et al., 2002, p. 109). Few would disagree that the unique family patterns and the ethnic heritage combine to create a powerful lineage that influences generations.

The family-of-origin plays a significant role in creating and developing its members' communication patterns, tied to the primary functions of cohesion, adaptability, and the secondary function of images, themes, boundaries, and biosocial issues. Taken together, all these factors combine to create a framework for examining family communication.

REFERENCES

Beatty, M. J., McCroskey, J. C., & Valencic, K. M. (2001). *The biology of communication: A communibiological perspective.* Cresskill, NJ: Hampton Press.

Bochner, A. P., & Eisenberg, E. (1987). Family process: System perspectives. In C. Berger & S. Chaffee (Eds.), *Handbook of communication science* (pp. 540–563). Beverly Hills, CA: Sage.

Booth, A., Carver, K., & Granger, D. (2000). Biosocial perspectives on the family. *Journal of Marriage and the Family, 62,* 1018–1034.

Buerkel-Rothfuss, N., Fink, D. S., & Buerkel, R. A. (1995). Communication in the father-child dyad: The intergenerational transmission process. In T. J. Socha & G. H. Stamp (Eds.), *Parents, children and communication* (pp. 63–85). Mahwah, NJ: Lawrence Erlbaum.

Chen, Z., & Kaplan, H. B. (2001). Intergenerational transmission of constructive parenting. *Journal of Marriage and the Family, 63,* 17–31.

Coontz, S. (1999). Introduction. In S. Coontz, M. Parson, & G. Raley (Eds.), *American families: A multicultural reader* (pp. ix–xxxiii). New York, NY: Routledge.

Daly, M., Farmer, J., Harrop-Stein, C., Montgomery, S., Itzen, M., Costalas, J. W., Rogatko, S. M., Balshem, A., & Gillespie, D. (1999). Exploring family relationships in cancer risk counseling using the genogram. *Cancer, Epidemiology, Biomarkers & Prevention, 8,* 393–398.

Daniel, J., & Daniel, J. (1999). African-American child rearing: The context of the hot stove. In T. J. Socha & R. C. Diggs (Eds.), *Communication, race and family: Exploring communication in black, white, and biracial families* (pp. 25–43). Mahwah, NJ: Lawrence Erlbaum.

Dixson, M.D. 1995. Models and perspectives of parent-child communication. In T. J. Socha & G. H. Stamp (Eds.), *Parents, children and communication* (pp. 433–462). Mahwah, NJ: Lawrence Erlbaum.

Duck, S. (1986). *Human relationships: An introduction to social psychology.* London, England: Sage.

Erickson, B. M., & Simon, J. S. (1996). Scandinavian families: Plain and simple. In M. McGoldrick, J. Giordano, & T. K. Pearce (Eds.), *Ethnicity and* family therapy (2nd ed., pp. 595–608). New York, NY: Guilford Press.

Flanagan, K. M., Clements, M. L., Whitton, S. W., Portney, M. J., Randall, D.W., & Markman, H. J. (2002). Retrospect and prospect in the psychological study of marital and couple relationships. In J. P. McHale & W. S. Grolnick (Eds.), *Retrospect and prospect in the psychological study of families* (pp. 99–128). Mahwah, NJ: Lawrence Erlbaum.

Fleming, A. S., Kraemer, G. W., Gonzalez, A., Loric, V., Rees, S., & Melo, A. (2002). Mothering begets mothering: The transmission of behavior and its neurobiology across generations. *Pharmacology, Biochemistry and Behavior, 73*, 61–75.

Floyd, K., & Haynes, M. T. (2006). The theory of natural selection: An evolutionary approach to family communication. In D. O. Braithwaite & L. A. Baxter (Eds.), *Engaging theories in family communication* (pp. 325–340). Thousand Oaks, CA: Sage.

Giordano, J., & McGoldrick, M. (1996). Italian families. In M. McGoldrick, J. Giordano, & T. K. Pearce (Eds.), *Ethnicity and family therapy* (2nd ed., pp. 567–582). New York, NY: Guilford Press.

Hines, P. M., & Boyd-Frankin, N. (1996). African-American families. In M. McGoldrick, J. Giordano, & T. K. Pearce (Eds.), *Ethnicity and family therapy* (pp. 66–84). New York, NY: Guilford Press.

Hoopes, M. (1987). Multigenerational systems: Basic assumptions. *American Journal of Family Therapy, 15*, 195–205.

Kellerman, N. P. (2001). Transmission of Holocaust trauma–An integrative view. *Psychiatry, 64*, 256–267.

Kramer, J. (1985). *Family interfaces: Transgenerational patterns.* New York, NY: Brunner-Mazel.

McGoldrick, M., Gerson, R., & Shellenberger, S. (1999). *Genograms: Assessment and intervention.* New York, NY: Norton.

Rutter, M. (2002). Family influences on behavior and development: Challenges for the future. In J. P. McHale & W. S. Grolnick (Eds.), *Retrospect*

and prospect in the psychological study of families (pp. 321–351). Mahwah, NJ: Lawrence Erlbaum.

Saphir, M. N., & Chaffee, S. H. (2002). Adolescents' contributions to family communication patterns. *Human Communication Research, 28*(1), 86–108.

Simons, R. L., Beaman, J., Conger, R. D., & Chao, W. (1993). Stress, support, and antisocial behavior trait as determinants of emotional well-being and parenting practices among single mothers. *Journal of Marriage and the Family, 55*, 385–398.

Socha, T. J., Bromley, J., & Kelly, B. (1995). Invisible parents and children: Exploring African-American parent-child communication. In T. J. Socha & G. H. Stamp (Eds.), *Parents, children and communication* (pp. 127–145). Mahwah, NJ: Lawrence Erlbaum.

QUESTIONS/THOUGHTS

1. To what extent do you believe individuals develop communication patterns similar to those used by members of their families-of-origin? Give two examples of specific individuals to support your position.

2. In what ways do you believe you, or your siblings, influenced your parents' communication practices through reciprocal parent-child interaction?

3. What is one communication pattern from your family-of-origin that you would hope to carry into your parenting practices? What pattern would you choose not to replicate?

4. To what extent to you believe cultural communication patterns are carried through three to four generations? Support your position with examples.

Growing Up Masculine, Growing Up Feminine

JULIA T. WOOD

What does it mean to be masculine or feminine in our society? The family introduces the child to the definitions, meanings, and values of gender in the child's culture. The majority of males and females embody these definitions, meanings, and values in their own communication, thus perpetuating existing social and cultural views of gender.

Gender identity is believed to begin at an early age. The year between a child's second and third birthdays is the time during which gendered perceptions of toys, clothing, household objects, games, and work are acquired (Fagot, Leinbach, and O'Boyle, 1992). During this time period, children learn to identify others as boys and girls and to become aware that they themselves belong in one category or the other.

Today, two approaches dominate understanding of gendered family communication. Historically, scholars conceptualized gender as role bound, with women and men playing distinct parts in response to socialization and particular settings or circumstances in which their roles were embedded. From this role perspective, men and women "are seen as enacting roles that are separable, often complementary, and necessary elements to the integrity of

the social settings or structures in which the roles are embedded" (Fox & Murry, 2000, 1163). This approach reifies difference between the sexes and suggests that gender-specific socialization of boys and girls both takes place in and reproduces different masculine and feminine speech communities. Such communities are purported to represent different cultures—"people who have different ways of speaking, acting, and interpreting, as well as different values, priorities, and agendas" (MacGeorge et al., 2004, 144). For example, Martin, Wood, and Little (1990) argue that gender ideologies develop through a series of stages:

> *Children in the first stage learn what kinds of things are directly associated with each sex, such as "boys play with cars, and girls play with dolls." Around the ages of 4–6, children seem to move to the second stage, where they begin to develop the more indirect and complex associations for information relevant to their own sex but have yet to learn these associations for information relevant to the opposite sex. By the time they are 8, children move to the third stage, where they have also learned the associations relevant to the opposite*

sex. These children have mastered the gender concepts of masculinity and femininity that link information within and between the various content domains. (1893)

The alternative approach views gender as a social construct that embodies cultural meanings of masculinity and femininity; essentially, gender is conceived as "a constituent element of social structures, intricately interwoven with other elements of social structures such as class and race, and tied to the social distribution of societal resources" (Fox & Murry 2000, 1164). This approach assumes that "gender is disengaged from norms based on heterosexuality and power differences between men and women, and relationships are thought of in terms of equality rather than gender differences" (Knudson-Martin & Laughlin 2005, 110). No matter how you choose to view gender, the rapidly changing world in which you live will present you with increasingly ambiguous data.

Given the increasing diversity of family life, the social construction lens may be an increasingly valuable way to view gender in families. In other words, many children no longer experience a dress rehearsal that prepares them for future family or relational life. Rather, more adults will have to "make it up as they go along" because, as the possibilities expand, so does the nature of gendered family experiences (Galvin, 2006). Recent research suggests that mothers and daughters develop unique communication patterns and turning points in their ongoing relationships(Fisher & Miller-Day, 2006).

In the following article, Wood presents themes of growing up for both males and females. She provides the different socially understood expectations for most males and females in this society, and raises the issue of what happens when people do not adapt to these gendered themes. Finally, the question of growing up outside these conventional roles is addressed. Consider your own growing up as you read these themes, and consider this question: To what extent are these gendered themes consistent with your youthful experience?

REFERENCES

Fagot, B., Leinbach, M., & O'Boyle, C. (1992). Gender labeling, gender stereotyping, and parenting behaviors. *Developmental Psychology, 28,* 225–230.

Fisher, C., & Miller-Day, M. (2006). Communication over the life span: The mother-adult daughter relationship. In K. Floyd & M. T. Morman (Eds.), *Widening the family circle: New research on family communication* (pp. 3–19). Thousand Oaks, CA: Sage.

Fox, G. L., & Murry, V. M. (2000). Gender and families: Feminist perspectives and family research. *Journal of Marriage and the Family, 62,* 160–172.

Galvin, K. M. (2006). Gender and family interaction: Dress rehearsal for an improvisation? In B. Dow & J. T. Wood (Eds.), *The SAGE handbook of gender and communication* (pp. 41–55). Thousand Oaks, CA: Sage.

Knudson-Martin, C., & Laughlin, M. J. (2005). Gender and sexual orientation in family therapy: Toward a postgender approach. *Family Relations, 54,* 101–115.

MacGeorge, E. L., Graves, A. R., Feng, B., Gillihan, S. J., & Burleson, B. R. (2004). The myth of gender cultures: Similarities outweigh differences in men's and women's provision of and responses to supportive communication. *Sex Roles, 50,* 143–175.

Martin, C. L., Wood, C. H., & Little, J. K. (1990). The development of gender stereotype components. *Child Development, 61,* 1891–1904.

THE PERSONAL SIDE OF THE GENDER DRAMA

What does it mean to us as individuals to grow up masculine or feminine in present-day America? To answer this question, we'll translate the research we've considered into personal portraits of becoming gendered in our society.

GROWING UP MASCULINE

What does it mean to be masculine in the United States in the 21st century? To understand the advantages, challenges, and issues of masculinity, let's consider what five college men say. In their commentaries, Pete, Charles, Aaron, Derek, and Steve focus as much on the pressures, expectations, and constraints of manhood as its prerogatives and privileges. In his book *The Male Experience*, James A. Doyle (1997) identifies five themes of masculinity, which are woven throughout the commentaries of these six men. We will consider each of these elements of the male role, as well as a sixth that seems to have emerged since Doyle made his analysis.

Don't be female seems to be the most fundamental requirement for manhood. Early in life most boys learn they must not think, act, or feel like girls and women. Any male who shows sensitivity or vulnerability is likely to be called a sissy, a crybaby, a mama's boy, or a wimp (Kantrowitz & Kall, 1998; Pollack, 2000). The antifemale directive is at least as strong for African American men as for European American men.

When a young boy wants to hurt another boy, he is likely to call him by a name associated with femininity directly (*girly*) or indirectly (*sissy*). Even as adults, a favorite means of scorning or putting down men is to suggest that they are feminine, or like women. During the 2004 elections, Republicans labeled Democratic vice presidential candidate John Edwards "the Breck girl" while linking incumbents George W. Bush and Dick Cheney with real men who "fight for America."

The second element of the male role is to *be successful*. Men are expected to achieve status in their professions, to "make it." Warren Farrell (1991) writes that men are regarded as "success objects," and their worth as marriage partners, friends, and men is judged by how successful they are at what they do. Training begins early with sports, where winning is stressed (Messner, 2000). Peer groups pressure males to be tough, aggressive, and not feminine (Lobel & Bar, 1997; Ponton, 1997).

…[T]he theme of success translates not just into being good at what you do but into being better than others, more powerful than peers, pulling in a bigger salary than your neighbors, and having a more expensive home, car, and so on than your friends. Most men today…think that being a good provider the primary requirement for manhood—an internalized requirement that appears to cut across lines of race and economic class (Eagly, 1996; Ranson, 2001).

A third injunction for masculinity is to *be aggressive*. Even in childhood, boys are often rewarded for being daredevils and roughnecks (Cohen, 1997). They are expected to take stands and not run from confrontations (Newburger, 1999; Pollack, 2000). Later, sports reinforce early training by emphasizing aggression, violence, and toughness (Messner, 2000). Coaches psych teams up with demands that they "make the other team hurt, hurt, hurt" or "make them bleed." The masculine code tells men to fight, inflict pain on others, endure pain stoically themselves, and win, win, win. Dr. Michael Miller (2003) says that many men don't seek help when they are depressed because their gender identity is "tied up with strength, independence, efficiency, and self-control" (p. 71).

Men's training in aggression may be linked to violence (Gordon, 1988; Kivel, 1999; Messner, 1997a, 1997b), especially violence against women. Because masculine socialization encourages aggression and dominance, some men think they are entitled to dominate women. This belief surfaces in studies of men who rape women (Costin & Schwartz, 1987; Scott & Tetreault, 1987) and men who abuse girlfriends and wives (Gelles & Straus, 1988, Wood, 2001b, 2004). One study (Thompson, 1991) reports that both college women and men who are violent toward their dates have masculine gender orientations, reminding us again that *gender* and *sex* are not equivalent terms.

A fourth element of the male role is captured in the injunction to *be sexual*. Men should be interested in sex—all the time, anytime. They are expected to have a number of sexual partners; the more partners a man has, the more of a stud he is (Jhally & Katz, 2001). During rush, a fraternity recently sent out invitations with the notation "B.Y.O.A.", which one of my students translated for me: Bring your own ass. Defining sexual conquest as a cornerstone of masculinity encourages men to view and treat women as sex objects rather than as multidimensional human beings (Brownmiller, 1993; French, 1992).

Finally, Doyle says the male sex role demands that men *be self-reliant*. A "real man" doesn't need others, particularly women. He depends on himself, takes care of himself, and relies on nobody. Autonomy is central to social views of manliness. As we noted earlier, male self-development typically begins with differentiation from others, and from infancy most boys are taught to be self-reliant and self-contained (Newberger, 1999; Thompson & Pleck, 1987). Men are expected to be emotionally controlled, not to let feelings control them, and not to need others.

In addition to the five themes of masculinity identified by Doyle, a sixth seems to have emerged. This theme highlights the mixed messages about being men that confront many boys and men today: *Embody and transcend traditional views of masculinity*....

For many men today, the primary source of pressure to be conventionally masculine is other men who enforce what psychologist William Pollack (2000) calls the "boy code." Boys and, later, men encourage each other to be silent, tough, and independent and to take risks. Boys and men who don't measure up often face peer shaming ("You're a wuss," "Do you do everything she tells you to do?"). At the same time, many men feel other pressures—often from romantic partners, female friends, and mothers—to be more sensitive and emotionally open and to be a full partner in running a home and raising children. It's hard to be both traditionally male and not traditionally male. Just as women in the 1960s and 1970s were confronted with mixed messages about being traditionally female and not, men today are negotiating new terrain and new ways of defining themselves.

What happens when men don't measure up to the social expectations of manhood? Some counselors believe men's striving to live up to social ideals of masculinity has produced an epidemic of hidden male depression (Kahn, 1997). Terrence Real is a psychotherapist who specializes in treating depressed men. According to Real (1997), male depression is widespread, and so is society's unwillingness to acknowledge it, because it is inconsistent with social views of masculinity. Whereas depressed women suffer the social stigma of having emotional problems, Real says men who admit they are depressed suffer the double stigma of having emotional problems and being unmanly by society's standards.

These first five themes of masculinity clearly reflect gender socialization in early life and lay out a blueprint for what being a man means. Yet, we also see a sixth theme that points out and challenges the contradictions in traditional and emerging views of masculinity. Individual men have options for defining and embodying masculinity, and many men are crafting non-traditional identities for themselves....

GROWING UP FEMININE

What does it mean to be feminine in the United States in the 21st century? Casual talk and media offer us two quite different versions of the modern women. One suggests that women now have it all. They can get jobs that were formerly closed to them and rise to the top levels of their professions; they can have egalitarian marriages with liberated men and raise nonsexist children. At the same time, our culture sends us the quite different message that women may be able to get jobs, but fewer than 20% will actually be given opportunities to advance to the highest levels of professional life. Crime statistics warn us that the incidence of rape is rising, as is battering of women. We discover that married women may have careers, but more than 80% of them still do most of the housework and child care. And media relentlessly carry the message that youth and beauty are women's tickets to success. Prevailing images of women are conflicting and confusing.... We can identify five themes in current views of femininity and womanhood.

The first theme is that *appearance* still *counts*....women are still judged by their looks (Greenfield, 2002; Haag, 2000). To be desirable, they are urged to be pretty, slim, and well dressed. The focus on appearance begins in the early years of life, when girls are given dolls and clothes, both of which invite them to attend to appearance. Gift catalogues for children regularly feature makeup kits, adornments for hair, and even wigs so that girls learn early to spend time and effort on looking good. Dolls, like the ever-popular Barbie, come with accessories such as extensive wardrobes, so girls learn that clothes and jewelry are important.

Teen magazines for girls are saturated with ads for makeup, diet aids, and hair products. Central to current cultural expectations for women is thinness, which can lead to harmful and sometimes fatal eating disorders (Davies-Popelka, 2000; Pike & Striegal-Moore, 1997)....

The ideals of feminine appearance are communicated to women when they enter retail stores. Most mannequins in stores are size 0, 2, or 4, which does not reflect the average size of real-life women. Social prescriptions for feminine beauty are also made clear by the saleswomen, who are often hired because of their looks, not their experience or skills. Stores that market to young women like to hire people who are young, sexy, and good looking. According to Antonio Serrano, a former assistant store manager for Abercrombie and Fitch, he and other employees were told by upper management "to approach someone in the mall who we think will look attractive in our store. But if someone came in who had lots of retail experience and not a pretty face, we were told not to hire them at all" (Greenhouse, 2003, p. 10 YT). Elysa Yanowitz, who was a regional sales manager for L'Oreal stores, says she was pressured to hire physically attractive saleswomen and once told to fire a top-performing employee who was "not hot enough" (Greenhouse, 2003, p. 10 YT). The Equal Employment Opportunity Commission has brought suit against a number of companies for discriminating against people who do not meet the current ideals for attractiveness.

At Abercrombie and Fitch, The Gap, and throughout society in general, cultural ideals of feminine beauty continue to reflect primarily White standards (Lont, 2001). Women of color may be unable to meet White standards of beauty on the one hand and, on the other, to reject the standards that the culture prescribes (Garrod, Ward, Robinson, & Kilkenny, 1999; Haag, 2000). In a critique of Blacks' acceptance of White standards of beauty, bell hooks (1995) describes the color caste system among Blacks whereby lighter skin is considered more desirable. She also points out that some Black children learn early to devalue dark skin, and many Black men regard biracial women as the ideal. In a society as ethnically diverse as

ours, we need to question and challenge standards that reflect and respect only the identities of some groups.

Women athletes sometimes feel special pressure to look feminine. Female Olympic competitors, despite being competitive and strong, are described by commentators in terms of feminine ideals (Clasen, 2001). Jenny Thompson posed nude in *Sports Illustrated*, a resoundingly clear declaration of her femininity (Reilly, 2000). She was followed by other female athletes as Katarina Witt and Brandi Chastain, who posed nude or nearly nude (Reilly, 2000). Florence "FloJo" Griffith-Joyner was highly muscular and also wore dazzling iridescent fingernail polish.

A second cultural expectation of women is to *be sensitive and caring*. Women feel pressure to be nice, deferential, and helpful in general, whereas men are not held to the same requirements (Simmons, 2002; Tavris & Baumgartner, 1983). In addition, girls and women are supposed to care about and for others. From assuming primary responsibility for young children to taking care of elderly, sick, and disabled relatives, women do the preponderance of hands-on caring (Cancian & Oliker, 2000; Ferguson, 2000).

By the time girls enter puberty, society, peers, and sometimes family encourage them to focus on pleasing others (Lally, 1996). Girls are encouraged to lose weight, to dress well, and to use makeup so that others will find them attractive. They're taught to soften their opinions and to accommodate others, particularly males.... For many girls, adolescence means shifting attention from developing and asserting identity to pleasing others.

At the opening of this chapter, I asked you what an ideal day would be like for you 10 years in the future. When psychologist Barbara Kerr (1997, 1999) asks this question of undergraduates in her classes, she reports a striking sex difference in responses. College men tend to describe their perfect day like this:

"I wake up and get into my car—a really nice, rebuilt '67 Mustang—and then I go to work—I think I'm some kind of manager of a computer firm—then I go home, and when I get there, my

wife is there at the door (she has a really nice figure), she has a drink for me, and she's made a great meal. We watch TV or maybe play with the kids." (p. B7)

Contrast the men's perfect day with this typical description for college women:

"I wake up, and my husband and I get in our twin Jettas, and I go to the law firm where I work. Then after work, I go home, and he's pulling up in the driveway at the same time. We go in and have a glass of nice wine, and we make an omelet together and eat by candlelight. Then the nanny brings the children in and we play with them until bedtime." (p. B7)

Note that the typical male scenario features wives who work but who also have drinks and a meal ready for husbands. Fewer and fewer college women see this as an ideal day—or life. Yet, women's fantasy of shared responsibilities for home and family are not likely to be met unless there are major changes in current patterns. A majority of both women and men share the breadwinner role relatively equally, but few have managed to share the homemaker and parenting role equally (Coontz, 2005; Tyre & McGinn, 2003).

A third persistent theme of femininity for women in Western cultures is *negative treatment by others*. Men students in my class sometimes challenge this as a theme of femininity. They say women are treated *better* than men. They point out that women—but not men—get free drinks at "Ladies' Night," they get their meals paid by dates, and they can cry their way out of speeding tickets. However, these rather small advantages of being female don't compensate for more significant disadvantages such as being more subject to sexual assault, more likely to live in poverty, and more likely to face job and salary discrimination.

Early in life, many children learn how society values each sex. In the United States, sons are preferred, although the preference is less strong than in former eras (Starling-Lyons, 2003). In some cultures the preference for males is so strong that female fetuses are often aborted, and female infants are sometimes killed after birth (French,

1992; Hegde, 1999a, 1999b; Pollitt, 2000). In other cultures, female and male children are equally valued; in still others, females are more valued (Cronk, 1993; Lepowsky, 1998).

Devaluation of femininity is not only built into cultural views but typically is internalized by individuals, including women. Negative treatment of females begins early and can be especially intense in girl's peer groups (Chesler, 2001; Lamb, 2002; Simmons, 2002; Tavris, 2002). Girls can be highly critical of other girls who are not pretty, thin, and otherwise feminine.

Research (Simmons, 2002, 2004; Underwood, 2003) shows that many young girls engage in social aggression toward other girls. As the term implies, social aggression involves attacking others using social, rather than physical, strategies. Unlike physical aggression, social aggression is usually indirect, even covert. It takes forms of spreading hurtful rumors, excluding a girl from groups, and encouraging others to turn against a particular girl. Social aggression among girls reflects their internalization of negative social views of females. For instance, one of the most damaging forms of aggression is spreading the rumor that one of the girls is a slut. All these tactics rupture the relational network of the girls who are the targets of social aggression. Social aggression peaks in girls between the age of 10 and 14 (Simmons, 2002).

Why do young girls rely on indirect strategies of aggression? One reason appears to be that, even at young ages, girls understand that they are supposed to be nice and everyone, so they fear that being overtly mean to others would lead to disapproval or punishment (Simmons, 2002). Instead of learning how to work through feelings of anger, dislike, and so forth, young girls learn to hide those feelings and express them only indirectly.

To be superwoman is a fourth theme emerging in cultural expectations of women. Jana's sense of exhilaration at "being able to have it all" is tempered by the realization that the idea that women *can* have it all appears to be transformed into the command that they must have it all. It's not enough to be just a homemaker and mother or to just have a career—young women seem to feel they are expected to do it all.

Women students talk with me frequently about the tension they feel trying to figure out how to have a full family life and a successful career. They tell me that they want both careers and families and don't see how they can make it all work. The physical and psychological toll on women who try to do it all is well documented (Coltrane & Adams, 2001; Galvin, 2006; Greenberg, 2001; Orenstein, 2000), and it is growing steadily as women find that changes in the workplace are not paralleled by changes in home life. Perhaps it would be wise to remember that Wonder Woman, like Superman, is a comic-book character, not a viable model for real life. Instead of trying to have it all, simultaneously, maybe it's better to aim to have some of it all—some career, some family—or all of some—full-time family focus or full-time career focus.

A final theme of femininity in the 1990s is one that reflects all of the others and the contradictions inherent in them: *There is no single meaning of feminine anymore.* A woman who is assertive and ambitious in a career is likely to meet with approval, disapproval, and curiosity from some people and to be applauded by others. At the same time, a woman who chooses to stay home while her children are young will be criticized by some women and men, envied by others, and respected by still others...there are many ways to be feminine, and we can respect all of them.

Prevailing themes of femininity in North America reveal both constancy and change. Traditional expectations of attractiveness and caring for others persist, as does the greater likelihood of negative treatment by others. Yet, today there are multiple ways to define femininity and womanhood, which may allow women with different talents, interests, and gender orientations to define themselves in diverse ways and to chart life courses that suit them as individuals.

GROWING UP OUTSIDE CONVENTIONAL GENDER ROLES

Not every male and female grows up identifying with the gender society prescribes for him or her. For people who do not identify with and embody the prescribed gender role, growing up is particularly difficult. Gay men are often socially ostracized because they are perceived as feminine, while lesbians are scorned for being masculine.

Social isolation also greets many people who are (or are thought to be) transgendered...[Some material dropped]. They find themselves trapped in a society that rigidly pairs males with masculinity and females with femininity. There are no in-between spaces; there is no room for blurring those rigid lines; there are no binary choices of male/female and masculine/feminine. For people who do not fit the conventional sex and gender roles, it is hard to find role models and equally difficult to find acceptance from family, peers, and society (Berlant & Warner, 1998; Fausto-Sterling, 2000; Feinberg, 1996; Glenn, 2002)....

REFERENCES

Berlant, L., & Warner, M. (1998). Sex in public. *Critical Inquiry, 24*, 547–566.

Brownmiller, S. (1993, January 4). Making female bodies the battlefield. *Newsweek*, 37.

Cancian, F., & Oliker, S. (2000). *Caring and gender.* Thousand Oaks, CA: Sage.

Chesler, P. (2001). *Woman's inhumanity to woman.* New York, NY: Thunder's Mouth Press/Nation Books.

Clasen, P. R. W. (2001). The female athlete: Dualisms and paradox in practice. *Women and Language, 24*, 36–41.

Cohen, L. (1997). Hunters and gatherers in the classroom. *Independent School*, 28–36.

Coltrane, S., & Adams, M. (2001). Men, women and housework. In D. Vannoy (Ed.), *Gender mosaics* (pp. 145–154). Los Angeles, CA: Roxbury.

Coontz, S. (2005). *Marriage: A history.* New York, NY: Viking Adult.

Costin, F., & Schwartz, N. (1987). Beliefs about rape and women's social roles: A four-nation study. *Journal of Interpersonal Violence, 2*, 46–56.

Cronk, L. (1993). *What our mothers didn't tell us: Why happiness eludes the modern woman.* New York, NY: Simon & Schuster.

Davies-Popelka, W. (2000). Mirror, mirror on the wall: Weight, identity and self-talk in women. In D. O. Braithwaite & J. T. Wood (Eds.), *Case* studies in interpersonal communication (pp. 52–60). Belmont, CA: Wadsworth.

Doyle, J. (1997). The male experience (3rd ed.). Dubuque, IA: William C. Brown.

Eagly, A. H. (1996). Differences between women and men. American Psychologist, 51, 158–159.

Farrell, W. (1991, May/June). Men as success objects. Utne Reader, 810–884.

Fausto-Sterling, A. (2000). Sexing the body: Gender politics and the construction of sexuality. New York, NY: Basic Books.

Feinberg, L. (1996). Transgender warriors: Making history from Joan of Arc to RuPaul. Boston, MA: Beacon.

Ferguson, S. (2000). Challenging traditional marriage: New married Chinese-American and Japanese-American women. Gender and Society, 14, 136–159.

French, M. (1992). The war against women. New York, NY: Summit.

Galvin K. M. (2006). Gendered communication in families. In B. Dow & J. T. Wood (Eds.), Sage handbook of gender and communication (4155–). Thousand Oaks, CA: Sage.

Garrod, A., Ward, J., Robinson, T., & Kilkenny, R. (Eds.). (1999). Souls looking back: Life stories of growing up Black. New York, NY: Routledge.

Gelles, R., & Straus, M. (1988). Intimate violence. New York, NY: Simon & Schuster.

Glenn, D. (2002, November 22). Practices, identities, and desires. Chronicles of Higher Education, pp. A20–A21.

Greenberg, S. (2001, January 8). Time to plan your life. Newsweek, 54–55.

Greenfield, L. (2002). Girl culture. San Francisco, CA: Chronicle Books.

Greenhouse, S. (2003, July 13). Going for the look, but risking discrimination. The New York Times International, p. 10YT.

Haag, P. (2000). Voices of a generation: Teenage girls report about their lives today. New York, NY: Marlowe.

Hegde, R. (1999a). Sons and m(others): Framing the fraternal body and the politics of reproduction in a South Indian context. Women's Studies in Communication, 22, 1–20.

Hegde, R. (1999b). Marking bodies, reproducing violence: A feminist reading of female infanticide in south India. Violence against Women, 5, 507–524.

hooks, b. (1995, August). Appearance obsession: Is the price too high? Essence, 26, 69–71.

Jhally, S., & Katz, J. (2001). Big trouble, little pond: Reflections on the meaning of the campus pond rapes. UMass, 26–31.

Kahn, J. (1997, April 11). Therapist says male depression widespread and widely denied. Raleigh News and Observer, p. 5D.

Kantrowitz, B., & Kall, C. (1998, May 11). How to build a better boy. Newsweek, 55–60.

Kerr, B. (1997). Smart girls: A new psychology of girls, women, and giftedness. Scottsdale, AZ: Gifted Psychology Press.

Kerr, B. (1999, March 5). When dreams differ: Male-female relations on campuses. Chronicle of Higher Education, pp. B7–B8.

Kindlon, D., & Thompson, M. (1999). Raising Cain: Protecting the emotional life of boys. New York, NY: Ballantine.

Kivel, P. (1999). Boys will be men: Raising our sons for courage, caring and community. Gabriola Island, Canada: New Society Press.

Lally, K. (1996, January 7). For girls now, adolescence a perilous rite. Richmond Times Dispatch, pp. G1, G2.

Lamb, S. (2002). The secret life of girls: Sex, play, aggression, and their guilt. New York, NY: Free Press.

Lepowsky, M. (1998). The influence of culture on behavior and the case of aggression: Women, men, and aggression in an egalitarian society. In D. Anselmi & A. Law (Eds.), Questions of gender: Perspectives and paradoxes, pp. 159–172. New York, NY: McGraw-Hill.

Lobel, T., & Bar, E. (1997). Perceptions of masculinity and femininity of kibbutz and urban adolescents. Sex Roles, 37, 283–289.

Lont, C. (2001). The influence of media on gender images. In D. Vannoy (Ed.), Gender mosaics (pp. 114–122). Los Angeles, CA: Roxbury.

Messner, M. (1997a). Boyhood, organized sports, and the construction of masculinities. In E. Disch

(Ed.), *Reconstructing gender* (pp. 57–73). Mountain View, CA: Mayfield.

Messner, M. (1997b). *Politics of masculinities: Men in movements.* Thousand Oaks, CA: Sage.

Messner, M. (2000). Barbie girls versus sea monsters: Children constructing gender. *Gender and Society, 7,* 121–137.

Miller, M. (2003, June 16). Stop pretending nothing's wrong. *Newsweek,* 71–72.

Newberger, E. (1999). *The men they will become: The nature and nurture of male character.* Cambridge, MA: Perseus Books.

Orenstein, P. (2000). *Flux: Women on sex, work, love, kids and life in a half-changed world.* New York, NY: Doubleday.

Pike, K., & Striegel-Moore, R. (1997). Disordered eating and eating disorders. In S. Gallant, G. Keita, & R. Royak-Schaler (Eds.), *Healthcare for women.* (pp. 97–114). Washington, DC: American Psychological Association.

Pollack, W. (2000). *Real boys: Rescuing ourselves from the myths of boyhood.* New York, NY: Owl Books.

Pollitt, K. (2000, May 1). Abortion history 101. *The Nation,* 8.

Ponton, L. (1997). *The romance of risk: Why teenagers do the things they do.* New York, NY: Basic Books.

Ranson, G. (2001). Men at work: Change or no change in the era of the "new father"? *Men and Masculinities, 4,* 3–26.

Real, T. (1997). *I don't want to talk about it: Overcoming the secret legacy of male depression.* New York, NY: Scribner's.

Reilly, R. (2000, September 4). Bare in mind. *Sports Illustrated,* 112–113.

Scott, R., & Tetreault, L. (1987). Attitudes of rapists and other violent offenders toward women. *Journal of Social Psychology, 127,* 375–380.

Simmons, R. (2002). *Odd girl out: The hidden culture of aggression in girls.* New York, NY: Harcourt.

Starling-Lyons, K. (2003, October 21). The gender game. *Raleigh News & Observer,* pp. 1E, 3E.

Tavris, C. (2002, July 5). Are girls really as mean as books say they are? *Chronicle of Higher Education,* pp. B7–B9.

Tavris, C., & Baumgartner, A. (1983, February). How would your life be different? *Redbook,* 92–95.

Thompson, E. H., Jr. (1991). The maleness of violence in dating relationships: An appraisal of stereotypes. *Sex Roles, 24,* 261–278.

Thompson, E. H., Jr., & Pleck, J. H. (1987). The structure of male role norms. In M. S. Kimmel (Ed.), *Changing men: New directions in research of men and masculinity* (pp. 25–36). Newbury Park, CA: Sage.

Tyre, P., & McGinn, D. (2003, May 12). She works, he doesn't. *Newsweek,* 44–54.

Underwood, M. (2003). *Social aggression among girls.* New York, NY: Guilford Press.

QUESTIONS/THOUGHTS

1. How might you wish to socialize a child born today into what it means to be a male or female in this society? How might this socialization differ from your childhood messages regarding gender? How are male and female socialized into media use in families?

2. To what extent do you think the themes presented by Wood remain relevant in the social contexts in which you find yourself? Are they more visible in one context than in another?

3. Interview a person from a culture other than your own about her or his culture's views of masculinity and femininity. How are these views similar to those of your culture? How are they different?

4. Think of a family you know. How does family storytelling reflect gender beliefs in that family? Do adult males and females tell different types of stories? Do male or female children hear different stories? What does an important family story say about members' gender beliefs?

Developing and Sustaining Relationships

Introduction

Every new face holds the potential for a future interpersonal connection, yet only a small percentage of those you meet will become significant persons in your life. Friends, romantic pairs, and some colleagues collaboratively create unique relational cultures that represent their understandings of each other and the world. Relational culture is fundamentally a product of communication—it arises out of communication, is maintained and altered through communication, and is dissolved through communication. Within these relational cultures, intimacy and closeness develop at levels consistent with the individuals' previous relational, cultural, and family-of-origin experiences.

All developing relationships reflect history-building processes. There are multiple perspectives on the relationship-building process, the most common of which involves stage theories.

These theories are developed on the assumption that all relationships exhibit points of initiation, maintenance, and possible dissolution. However, issues raised by the dialectical perspective have called into question some of the assumptions of stage models. (Chapter 4, "Theories of Relational Communication," introduced these theories but they will be explained again briefly).

DEVELOPING RELATIONSHIPS

Numerous scholars have proposed models of relationship development based on stages through which the partners move as they draw closer (Knapp and Vangelisti, 2005; Altman and Taylor, 1973). These are called linear models. Psychologists Irwin Altman and Dalmas Taylor created a linear model, *social penetration*, which depicts the stages of relational development. They hypothesize that interpersonal exchange gradually progresses from superficial, non-intimate topics to more intimate, deeper layers of the self; people assess the interpersonal costs and rewards gained from their interactions as they move through the stages. Altman and Taylor propose a four-stage model of relational movement, relying on eight characteristics of a developed relationship; each dimension becomes more apparent as the relationship moves through stages toward the highest point. Movement through these stages also depends on the perceived costs or rewards of interactions as estimated by each person in the relationship.

The model is best understood by picturing a continuum (Figure 1) with guidelines for movement through these stages. The levels represent where the relationship is at a given time, even if one or the other person involved wishes it were different.

The *orientation stage* represents the first meeting, when strangers tend to follow traditional social rules, try to make a good first impression, and attempt to avoid conflict. They try to reduce uncertainty about the other person and increase their ability to imagine future reactions. Adult family relationships, such as partners or in-laws, start at this point, although some previous information may be known about the "other." Such meetings may involve face-to-face, and/or online interactions.

The second stage, *exploratory affective exchange*, refers to the relationship between casual acquaintances or friendly neighbors. By this point, the relationship contains some honest sharing of opinions or feelings that are not too personal, but no real sense of commitment exists.

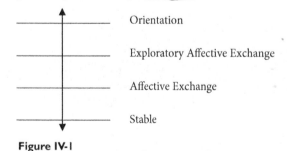

Figure IV-1

Orientation

Exploratory Affective Exchange

Affective Exchange

Stable

Most relationships do not go beyond this casual exploratory stage.

The third stage, *affective exchange*, encompasses the experiences of close friendships or dating relationships, in which people know each other well and have a fairly extensive history of association based on reciprocity. Their connections may be built over a long time or through numerous intense and important shorter interactions. Communication practices include sharing positive and negative personal messages, including interpersonal evaluations as well as high levels of self-disclosure. Many marriages or long term committed relationships continue indefinitely at the affective exchange level, and partners remain either satisfied or disappointed. Numerous people find this level of intimacy to be quite sufficient.

Finally, some relationships enter the fourth, or *stable*, stage which involves committed, intimate friendships or very strong familial relationships. This stage is characterized by high interdependence, open sharing and a strong, shared relational worldview. Yet, even these relationships require extensive effort to maintain their closeness. Individuals who share a stable relationship are aware of each other's needs and changes; they are willing to work consistently to maintain their relationship.

Relationships do not follow the four stages easily and simply. Some relationships may speed through certain stages; others may remain at one stage for years. Certain relationships move up and down the levels as the partners' lives change. The theorists suggest that the stages are experienced in reverse as a relationship declines, unless one person discontinues any contact.

Other stage models provide variations on the theme. For example, in a following article, Knapp and Vangelisti (2005) propose a model of interaction stages in relationships that details five coming-together and coming-apart stages. This model has a unique "bonding" stage, which occurs when the partners undergo a public ritual announcing to the world a relational contract or commitment.

THE DIALECTICAL PERSPECTIVE

Some theorists question the value of stage models, believing that they appear too linear and static; that is, they depict a linear, predictable upward and downward movement while implying that relationships may remain static, or in the same place, for a long time. A dialectical approach recognizes that relationships begin, develop, and deteriorate, but it stresses the ongoing "background noise" or the struggles that characterize the overall life of a relationship rather than a linear, stage approach (Baxter & Braithwaite, 2008). This perspective highlights the continual tensions that relationships must manage, or the non-linear nature of relational life. This approach does not mean that a relationship experiences constant struggle or tension but suggests that relationships are constantly at some level of flux, although the movement may be very slight. At critical times when relational struggles move to the forefront of a relationship's life, there are more times when the dialectical tension serves as the background of an ongoing relationship. In other words:

> Dialectics may work backstage in a relationship beyond partners' mindful awareness or ability to identify and describe them, but still contribute a sense of unsettledness or instability in the relationship. (Montgomery 1993, 206)

Yet the initiation and maintenance of relationships rests entirely in the premise that people acknowledge each other as human beings.

SUSTAINING RELATIONSHIPS

Sustaining relationships is not easy, because *sustaining* relationships implies proactive efforts to invest emotionally in the relational ties and struggle through major changes and crises. Commitment is critical to sustaining ongoing relationships. The stronger the commitment level, and the fewer good alternatives that exist, the more likely a relationship will continue (Rusbult, Drigotas, and Verette 1994). People remain in relationships for various reasons. Frequently people remain in relationships due to strong emotional

attachments. However, some relationships continue because one person desires to control the other or feels responsible for the other.

Some relational ties are maintained through inertia; change seems like too much effort so partners maintain lifeless relationships. Certain relationships are continued out of convenience; finding a new roommate or tennis partner may involve too much effort. Frequently marital relationships are maintained "for the sake of the children." Divorces and separations are financially and emotionally costly; therefore couples stay together to avoid other problems. Fear motivates some people to stay together—fear of being lonely, of social criticism ("What would people say?"), or of violating a religious, cultural, or parental norm.

How do individuals keep relationships vital over the years? Several researchers have focused on the strategies people use to sustain various relationships. For example, Dindia and Baxter (1987) suggest four general types of strategies:

1. Prosocial behaviors: being friendly and polite, avoiding criticism, and compromising.
2. Ceremonial behaviors: celebrating birthdays and anniversaries, eating at a favorite restaurant, and discussing past pleasurable times.
3. Communication behaviors: sharing feelings, talking honestly and openly, and calling just to say, "Hi, how are you?"
4. Togetherness behaviors: including spending time together, visiting friends, and doing specific things as a couple.

In a study of marital life, Canary, Stafford, and Semic (2002) describe marital resilience as a process in which people purposefully engage in *maintenance strategies* to repair and protect their connections. They discuss the following five relational maintenance strategies: positivity, openness, assurances, managing social networks, and sharing tasks.

As you read the following articles, notice that many of the articles use the term "maintaining" relationships, a common expression, although "sustaining" is a preferable term. Montgomery

(1993) points that "sustaining relationships" is a more desirable term because "maintaining" sounds like an attempt to create a steady state rather than to acknowledge the ongoing inevitable tensions.

As you read these chapters, remember that each new relationship represents a potential adventure, a chance to discover new parts of yourself and to connect with a significant other person. This chapter focuses on everyday relational life, the issues you confront and the communication strategies you use to sustain a relationship once you have moved through the early stages of development. These articles should make you consider how much thought and effort you devote to nurturing the relationships in your life.

REFERENCES

Altman, I., & Taylor, D. (1973). *Social Penetration*. New York, NY: Holt, Rinehart and Winston.

Baxter, L. A., & Braithwaite, D. O. (2008). Relational dialectics theory. In L. A Baxter & D. O. Braithwaite (Eds.), *Engaging theories in interpersonal communication* (pp. 349–361). Los Angeles, CA: Sage.

Canary, D., Stafford, L., Hause, K., & Wallace, L. (1993). An inductive analysis of relational maintenance strategies: Comparisons among lovers, relatives, friends and others. *Communication Research Reports, 10,* 5–14.

Canary, D. J., Stafford, L., & Semic, B. A. (2002). A panel study of the association between maintenance characteristics and relational characteristics. *Journal of Marriage and Family, 64,* 395–406.

Dindia, K., & Baxter, L. (1987). Strategies for maintaining and repairing marital relationships. *Journal of Social and Personal Relationships, 4,* 143–158.

Knapp, M., & Vangelisti, A. (2005). *Interpersonal communication and human relationships* (5th ed.). Boston, MA: Allyn & Bacon.

Montgomery, B. (1993). Relationship maintenance versus relationship change: A dialectical perspective. *Journal of Social and Personal Relationships, 10,* 205–223.

Rusbult, C. E., Drigotas, S. M., & Verette, J. (1994). The investment model: An interdependence analysis of commitment processes and relationship maintenance phenomena. In D. J. Canary & L. Stafford (Eds.), *Communication and relational maintenance* (pp. 115–140). San Diego, CA: Academic Press.

Relationship Stages:
A Communication Perspective

MARK L. KNAPP AND ANITA L. VANGELISTI

Relationships are not static; they change and shift slightly or greatly over the years. An intense relationship may become more distant; a superficial relationship may deepen. In this chapter, Knapp and Vangelisti create a stage model for developing, maintaining, and terminating relationships. Although some of the stage characteristics could apply to three persons (a triad) simultaneously developing a relationship, this model focuses primarily on a two person (dyadic) relationship.

This model assumes that the relationship is built extensively through face-to-face interactions. A recent study of Facebook use on campus (Haspels, 2008) reveals that Facebook helps to build and promote face-to face relationships. According to one student, Facebook can serve as a first meeting because, "You can get over initial insecurity. You can get the meeting-someone stage out of the way all on the tidbits of information" (p. 48). Some of you may have met your freshman roommate on Facebook before school opened, or you may have stumbled upon your lab partner's profile and learned about their "interests" before you ever even met face-to-face. Consider the role of online interactions as you read the about the stage model.

Remember that movement through these stages is somewhat predictable and that it occurs over time. The following generalizations will help you see the underlying assumptions of such a stage model.

1. *Movement through stages is generally systematic and sequential.* This is true, according to Knapp and Vangelisti, because each stage contains groundwork for the following stage. Progressing in sequence makes predicting behavior in the next stage easier, and skipping steps is an uncertain gamble caused by a lack of information that would have been learned in the skipped step. Sometimes it is easier to think about the stages as points on a continuum so you can imagine the early intensifying point and the late intensifying point,

2. *Movement may be forward.* As people "come together," they evaluate the rewards and costs in moving the relationship forward. Any movement toward greater intimacy is a move forward within the coming together stages.

3. *Movement may be backward.* A movement toward less intimacy is a movement backward. Two people might decide to "step back" from

intensifying to experimenting, such as when one person gets involved with an all-consuming interest that the other does not share.

4. **Movement is always to a new place**. Once something has been talked through, the relationship is different. The continuous nature of communication implies that friends or partners cannot go back to the way they were. This is because communication is a process—irreversible and unrepeatable. This concept is best represented by the helical model of communication that you found in the Part 1 introduction.

5. **Movement may be rapid or slow**. If there is daily positive interaction with a new person the relationship's movement will be more rapid than if there is weekly or monthly contact. In addition, movement is usually faster during the early stages or when time is short (for example, summer romances or week-long retreats). Movement will be slower when only one person desires to move forward.

6. **Dialectical tensions serve as background to each stage**. At all times ongoing tensions or struggles between goals, such as autonomy-connection or openness-closedness, will be present in each stage.

The ideas presented in this chapter are based upon the notion that there are separate stages in the development and decline of relationships. Authors Knapp and Vangelisti elaborate upon 5 stages of relationship growth: initiating, experimenting, intensifying, integrating and bonding; and within each description, they site examples for the types of communication behavior expected. (In Chapter 29 you will encounter their stages of decline). As you read this chapter consider the question: At what stage would you locate a highly significant relationship in your life and how does your relationship display characteristics of that stage?

REFERENCES

Haspels, M. (2008, May 1). Will you be my Facebook friend? In *Proceedings of the 4th Annual GRASP Symposium*. Elliott School of Communication, Witchita State University, Wichata KS.

A MODEL OF INTERACTION STAGES IN RELATIONSHIPS

Scientists are forever seeking to bring order to a seemingly chaotic world of overlapping, interdependent, dynamic, and intricate processes. Frequently, the process of systematizing our life and environment is discussed in terms of stages of growth, stages of deterioration, and the forces that shape and act on this movement through stages. For instance, developmental psychologists recount regularized patterns of behavior accompanying stages of infancy, childhood, adolescence, maturity, and old age. Anthropologists and geologists plot the evolutionary stages of human beings and human environments. Biologists note similarities in the life processes of such seemingly diverse organisms as trees and fish. Physical and social scientists talk about affinity and attraction, weak and strong interactions, friction, repulsion, and splitting-up as basic forces acting on matter and people. Rhetorical critics often dissect spoken messages by noting patterns regularly occurring during the introduction, development toward the main points, transitions, and conclusion.

The idea that there are stages in the development of relationships that are characterized by certain patterns of communication is not new.[1] We tried to synthesize as well as expand on this previous work in the development of the model presented in Table 15-1.

Before each stage is described in greater detail, several preliminary remarks about the model are in order. First, we should resist the normal temptation to perceive the stages of coming together as "good" and those of coming apart as "bad." It is not "bad" to terminate relationships nor is it necessarily "good" to become more intimate with someone. The model is descriptive of what seems to happen—not what should happen.

We should also remember that in the interest of clarity the model simplifies a complex process. For instance, the model shows each stage adjacent to the next—as if it was clear when a communicating couple left one stage and entered another. To the contrary. Each stage contains some behavior from other stages. So stage identification becomes a matter of emphasis. Stages are identified by the

Table 15-1

A Model of Interactive Stages

Process	Stage	Representative Dialogue
	Initiating	"Hi, how ya doin" "Fine. You?"
	Experimenting	"Oh, so you like to ski . . . So do I." "You do? Great, where do you go?"
Coming Together	Intensifying	"I . . . I think I love you." "I love you too."
	Integrating	"I feel so much a part of you." "Yeah, we are like one person. What happens to you happens to me."
	Bonding	"I want to be with you always." "Let's get married."
	Differentiating	"I just don't like big social gatherings." "Sometimes I just don't understand you. This is one area where I'm certainly not like you at all."
	Circumscribing	"Did you have a good time on your trip?" "What time will dinner be ready?"
Coming Apart	Stagnating	"What's there to talk about?" "Right, I know what you're going to say and you know what I'm going to say."
	Avoiding	"I'm so busy, I just don't know when I'll be able to see you." "If I'm not around when you try, you'll understand."
	Terminating	"I'm leaving you . . . and don't bother trying to contact me" "Don't worry."

proportion of one type of communication behavior to another. This proportion may be the frequency with which certain communication acts occur, or proportion may be determined by the relative weight given to certain acts by the participants. For example, a couple at the Intensifying Stage may exhibit behaviors that occur at any of the other stages, but their arrival at the Intensifying Stage is because: (1) the most frequent communication exchanges are typical of the Intensifying Stage and/or (2) the exchanges that are crucial in defining the couple's relationship are statements of an intensifying nature. The act of sexual intercourse is commonly associated with male-female romantic couples at the Intensifying or Integrating Stages, but it may occur as an isolated act for couples at the Experimenting Stage. Or it may occur regularly for a couple at the Experimenting Stage, but remain relatively unimportant for the couple in defining the closeness of their relationship. Thus, interaction stages involve both overt behavior and the perceptions of behavior in the minds of the parties involved. During the formation of a romantic relationship, the couple's overt behavior (to each other and in front of others) may be a good marker of their developmental stage. During periods of attempted rejuvenation of a relationship, we may find that the overt behavior is an effective marker of the stage *desired*. However, in stable or long-established relationships, overt behavior may not be a very accurate indicator of closeness. Instead it is the occasional behavior or memories of past behaviors that are perceived by the couple as crucial in defining their relationship. For example, the married couple of fifteen years may spend much of their interaction time engaging in small talk—behavior typical of an early developmental stage. And even though the small talk does play an important role in maintaining the relationship, it is the less frequent but more heavily weighted behavior that the couple uses to define their relationship, as at the Integrating Stage. Similarly, close friends may not engage in a lot of talk that outside observers would associate with closeness. In some cases, friends are separated for long periods of time and make very little contact with one another. But through specific occasional acts and the memory of past acts, the intimacy of the friendship is maintained.

The dialogue in the model is heavily oriented toward mixed-gender pairs. This does not mean the model is irrelevant for same-gender pairs. Even at the highest level of commitment, the model may apply to same-gender pairs. The bonding ceremony, for instance, need not be marriage. It could be an act of becoming "blood brothers" by placing open wounds on each other to achieve oneness. Granted, American cultural sanctions against the direct expression of high-level intimacy between same-sexed pairs often serve to inhibit, slow down, or stop the growth of relationships between same-sexed pairs. But when such relationships do develop, similar patterns are reported.[2]

The model…also focuses primarily on relationships where people voluntarily seek contact with, or disengagement from, one another. But the model is not limited to such relationships. All people drawn into, or pulled out of, relationships by forces seemingly outside their control will like or not like such an event and communicate accordingly. For instance, a child's relationship with his or her parent (involuntary) may, at some point, be very close and loving, at another time be cold and distant, and at another time be similar to relationships with other friends.

Our model of relationship development is primarily focused on the interaction patterns of the relationship partners. Nevertheless, we should not forget that these relationships are nested within a network of other social relationships which affect communication patterns manifested by the partners.[3] Friends, co-workers, and/or kin make up the larger social system which influences and is influenced by any single relationship. Sometimes these networks are small, sometimes large; sometimes they are influential on one issue or at one point in time and not so on other issues or at another point in time; sometimes these other relationships tend to serve one relationship partner, and at other times they serve both. What role do social networks play as we develop and maintain a relationship? The people who comprise these networks give us feedback, advice, and support; they act as a sounding board; they help mediate problems; they offer consultation and

engage in persuasion. They may, of course, fail to provide these things when they are expected. In short, social networks are comprised of coaches who can dramatically affect our communicative performance as relationship partner. In addition, they are sources of a social identity which extends beyond the pair bond.

Finally…we would expect the Initiating and Terminating Stages to be characterized by communication that is more narrow, stylized, difficult, rigid, awkward, public, hesitant, and with overt judgments suspended; the stages of Integrating, Bonding, and Differentiating should show more breadth, uniqueness, efficiency, flexibility, smoothness, personalness, spontaneity, and overt judgments given. In short, it is proposed that we communicate within a prescribed range of content, style, and language at different levels of intimacy.…

INTERACTION STAGES

Initiating

This stage incorporates all those processes enacted when we first come together with other people. It may be at a cocktail party or at the beach; it may be with a stranger or with a friend. As we scan the other person we consider our own stereotypes, any prior knowledge of the other's reputation, previous interactions with this person, expectations for this situation, and so on. We are asking ourselves whether this person is "attractive" or "unattractive" and whether we should initiate communication. Next, we try to determine whether the other person is cleared for an encounter—is he or she busy, in a hurry, surrounded by others. Finally, we search for an appropriate opening line to engage the other's attention.

Typically, communicators at this stage are simply trying to display themselves as a person who is pleasant, likable, understanding and socially adept. In essence, we are saying: "I see you. I am friendly, and I want to open channels for communication to take place." In addition, we are carefully observing the other to reduce any uncertainty we might have—hoping to gain clarification of mood, interest, orientation toward us, and aspects of the other's public personality. Our conscious awareness of these processes is sometimes very low. "Morning, Bob. How ya doin'?" "Morning, Clayton. Go to hell." "Fine, thanks." ....

Experimenting

Once communication has been initiated, we begin the process of experimenting—trying to discover the unknown. Strangers trying to become acquaintances will be primarily interested in name, rank, and serial number—something akin to the sniffing ritual of animals. The exchange of demographic information is frequent and often seems controlled by a norm that says: "If you tell me your hometown, I'll tell you mine." Strangers at this stage are diligently searching for an integrating topic, an area of common interest or experience. Sometimes the strain of this search approaches the absurd: "Oh, you're from Oklahoma. Do you know...?" Obviously, the degree to which a person assists another in finding this integrating topic shows the degree of interest in continuing the interaction and the willingness to pursue a relationship ....

Small talk is the *sine qua non* of experimenting. It is like exercising; we may hate it, but we may also engage in large quantities of it every day. If we hate it, why do we do it? Probably because we are vaguely aware of several important functions served by small talk:

1. It is a useful process for uncovering integrating topics and openings for more penetrating conversation.
2. It can be an audition for a future friendship or a way of increasing the scope of a current relationship.
3. It provides a safe procedure for indicating who we are and how another can come to know us better (reduction of uncertainty).
4. It allows us to maintain a sense of community with our fellow human beings.

Relationships at this stage are generally pleasant, relaxed, overtly uncritical, and casual. Commitments are limited. And, like it or not, *most of our relationships probably don't progress very far beyond this stage.*

Intensifying

When people achieve a relationship known as "close friends," indicators of the relationships are intensified. Active participation and greater awareness of the process typify this stage when it begins. Initial probes toward intensification of intimacy are often exercised with caution, awaiting confirmation before proceeding. Sitting close, for instance, may precede hugging; holding hands will generally precede holding genitals. Requests for physical or psychological favors are sometimes used to validate the existence of intensity in a relationship ....

The amount of personal disclosure increases at this stage, and we begin to get a glimpse of some previously withheld secrets—that my father was an alcoholic, that I masturbate, that I pretend I'm a rhino when I'm drunk, and other fears, frustrations, failures, imperfections, and prejudices. Disclosures may be related to any topic area, but those dealing most directly with the development of the relationship are crucial. These disclosures make the speaker vulnerable—almost like an animal baring its neck to an attacker.

Verbally, a lot of things may be happening in the intensifying stage:

1. Forms of address become more informal—first name, nickname, or some term of endearment.
2. Use of the first person plural becomes more common—"*We* should do this" or "*Let's* do this." One study of married couples found that the use of "we" was more likely to be associated with a relationship orientation, while the use of "I" was more likely to be associated with a task orientation or the functional requirements and accomplishments of marriage.[4]
3. Private symbols begin to develop, sometimes in the form of a special slang or jargon, sometimes using conventional language forms that have understood, private meanings.

Places they've been together, events and times they've shared; and physical objects they've purchased or exchanged; all become important symbols in defining the nature of developing closeness.[5] Such items or memories may be especially devastating and repulsive reminders if the relationship begins to come apart unless the symbols are reinterpreted ("I like this diamond ring because it is beautiful, not because he gave it to me.") or put in a different perspective ("It really was fun when we did _____, but in so many other ways he was a jerk.").

4. Verbal shortcuts built on a backlog of accumulated and shared assumptions, expectations, interests, knowledge, interactions, and experiences appear more often; one may request a newspaper be passed by simply saying, "paper."

5. More direct expressions of commitment may appear—"We really have a good thing going" or "I don't know who I'd talk to if you weren't around." Sometimes such expressions receive an echo—"I really like you a lot." "I really like you, too, Elmer."

6. Increasingly, one's partner will act as a helper in the daily process of understanding what you're all about—"In other words, you mean you're…" or "But yesterday, you said you were…"

Sophistication in nonverbal message transmission also increases. A long verbalization may be replaced by a single touch; postural congruence may be seen; clothing styles may become more coordinated; possessions and personal space may be more permeable.

As the relationship intensifies, each person is unfolding his or her uniqueness while simultaneously blending his or her personality with the other's.

Integrating

The relationship has now reached a point where the two individual personalities almost seem to fuse or coalesce, certainly more than at any previous

stage. Davis discusses this concept, which he calls *coupling*

> The extent to which each intimate tries to give the other his own self-symbols or to correct the other's self-symbols measures the degree to which he wants to increase their communion.[6]

…Verbal and nonverbal manifestations of integrating may take many forms:

1. Attitudes, opinions, interests, and tastes that clearly distinguish the pair from others are vigorously cultivated—"We have something special; we are unique."

2. Social circles merge and others begin to treat the two individuals as a common package—one present, one letter, one invitation.

3. Intimacy "trophies" are exchanged so each can "wear" the other's identity—pictures, pins, rings.

4. Similarities in manner, dress, and verbal behavior may also accentuate the oneness.

5. Actual physical penetration of various body parts contributes to the perceived unification.

6. Sometimes common property is designated—"our song," a joint bank account, or a co-authored book.

7. Empathic processes seem to peak so that explanation and prediction of behavior are much easier.[7]

8. Body rhythms and routines achieve heightened synchrony.[8]

9. Sometimes the love of a third person or object will serve as glue for the relationship—"Love me, love my rhinos."

Obviously, integration does not mean complete togetherness or complete loss of individuality. Maintenance of some separate and distinct selves is critical, and possible, due to the strength of the binding elements. One married woman of ten years told us: "I still hold some of myself back from John because it's the only part of me I don't share, and it's important to have something that is uniquely mine."

Thus, we can see that as we participate in the integration process we are intensifying and minimizing various aspects of our total person. Consequently, when we commit ourselves to integrating with another, we also agree to become another individual.

Bonding

Bonding is a public ritual that announces to the world that commitments have been formally contracted. It is the institutionalization of the relationship. There are many kinds of bonding rituals and they characterize several stages of the mixed-sex relationship—going steady, engagement, and ultimately marriage. American society has not sanctioned similar rituals for same-sexed romantic pairs, although some exist.

Since bonding is simply the contract for the union of the pair at any given stage of the relationship, one might question why it has been designated as a separate stage. It is because the act of bonding itself may be a powerful force in changing the nature of the relationship "for better or for worse." The institutionalization of the relationship hardens it, makes it more difficult to break out of, and probably changes the rhetoric that takes place without a contract. The contract becomes, either explicitly or implicitly, a frequent topic of conversation. Communication strategies can now be based on interpretation and execution of the commitments contained in the contract. In short, the normal ebb and flow of the informal relationship can be, and often is, viewed differently....

NOTES

1. Representative works include: F. Lacoursiere, *The Life Cycle of Groups* (New York: Human Sciences Press, 1980); R. Thornton and P. M. Nardi, "The Dynamics of Role Acquisition," *American Journal of Sociology* 80 (1975): 870–885; I. Altman and D. A. Taylor, *Social Penetration: The Development of Interpersonal Relationships* (New York: Holt, Rinehart, & Winston, 1973); B W. Tuckman, "Developmental Sequence in Small Groups," *Psychological Bulletin* 63 (1965): 384–399;

S. W. Duck, *Personal Relationships and Personal Constructs: A Study of Friendship Formation* (New York: John Wiley & Sons, 1973); M. S. Davis, *Intimate Relations* (New York: Free Press, 1973); T. M. Newcomb, *The Acquaintance Process* (New York: Holt, Rinehart, & Winston, 1961); C. B. Broderick, "Predicting Friendship Behavior: A Study of the Determinants of Friendship Selection and Maintenance in a College Population" (Doctoral diss. Cornell University, 1956); G. M. Phillips and N. J. Metzger, *Intimate Communication* (Boston: Allyn & Bacon, 1976), pp. 401–403; C. R. Berger and R. J. Calabrese, "Some Explorations in Initial Interaction and Beyond: Toward a Developmental Theory of Interpersonal Communication," *Human Communication Research* 1 (1975): 99–112; C. R. Rogers, "A Process Conception of Psychotherapy," *American Psychologist* 13 (1958): 142–149; G. Simmel, *The Sociology of George Simmel*, trans. K. Wolff (New York: Free Press, 1950); K. Lewin, "Some Social Psychological Differences Between the United States and Germany," *Character and Personality* 4 (1936): 265–293; J. T. Wood, "Communication and Relational Culture: Bases for the Study of Human Relationships," *Communication Quarterly* 30 (1982): 75–83; D. P. McWhirter and A. M. Mattison, *The Male Couple* (Englewood Cliffs, NJ: Prentice-Hall, 1984); W. J. Dickens and D. Perlman, "Friendship over the Life Cycle." In S. Duck and R. Gilmour, eds., *Personal Relationships: 2. Developing Personal Relationships* (New York: Academic Press, 1981); C. A. VanLear, Jr., and N. Trujillo, "On Becoming Acquainted: A Longitudinal Study of Social Judgment Processes," *Journal of Social and Personal Relationships* 3 (1986): 375–392; J. M. Honeycutt, J. G. Cantrill, and R. W. Greene, "Memory Structures for Relational Escalation: A Cognitive Test of the Sequencing of Relational Actions and Stages," *Human Communication Research* 16 (1989): 62–90; J. M. Honeycutt, J. G. Cantrill, and T. Allen, "Memory Structures for Relational Decay: A Cognitive Test of Sequencing of Deescalating Actions and Stages," *Human Communication Research* 18 (1992): 528–562; and J. M. Honeycutt, "Memory Structures of the Rise and Fall of Personal Relationships." In

S. Duck, ed., *Individuals in Relationships* (Newbury Park, CA: Sage, 1993).

2. McWhirter and Mattison, *The Male Couple*. S. M. Haas and L. Stafford, "An Initial Examination of Maintenance Behaviors in Gay and Lesbian Relationships," *Journal of Social and Personal Relationships* 15 (1998): 846–855.

3. T. L. Albrecht, M. B. Adelman, and Associates, *Communicating Social Support* (Newbury Park, CA: Sage, 1987). M. R. Parks and M. B. Adelman, "Communication Networks and the Development of Romantic Relationships: An Expansion of Uncertainty Reduction Theory," *Human Communication Research* 10 (1983): 55–79. R Klein and R. M. Milardo, "Third-Party Influence on the Management of Personal Relationships." In S. Duck, ed., *Social Context and Relationships* (Newbury Park, CA: Sage, 1993), pp. 55–77. G. Allan, *Friendship: Developing a Sociological Perspective* (Boulder, CO: Westview, 1989). M. R. Parks, "Communication Networks and Relationship Life Cycles." In S. Duck, ed., *Handbook of Personal Relationships*. 2nd ed. (New York: John Wiley & Sons, 1997).

4. H. L. Rausch, K. A. Marshall, and J. M. Featherman, "Relations at Three Early Stages of Marriage as Reflected by the Use of Personal Pronouns," *Family Process* 9 (1970): 69–82.

5. L. A. Baxter, "Symbols of Relationship Identity in Relationship Cultures," *Journal of Social and Personal Relationships* 4 (1987): 261–280.

6. M. S. Davis, *Intimate Relations* (New York: The Free Press, 1973), p. 188.

7. W. Ickes, ed., *Empathic Accuracy* (New York: Guildford, 1997).

8. H. C. Davis, D. J. Haymaker, D. A. Hermecz, and D. G. Gilbert, "Marital Interaction: Affective Synchrony of Self-Reported Emotional Components," *Journal of Personality Assessment* 52 (1988): 48–57; and K. Grammar, K. B. Kruck, and M. S. Magnusson, "The Courtship Dance: Patterns of Nonverbal Synchronization in Opposite-Sex Encounters," *Journal of Nonverbal Behavior* 22 (1998): 3–29.

QUESTIONS/THOUGHTS

1. Choose a friendship relationship in which you find yourself currently. According to Knapp and Vangelisti's model, what stage is it in? What predictions would you make concerning movement to the next stage? Why?

2. Watch a movie such as *(500) Days of Summer*, or *The Sisterhood of the Traveling Pants* in which two characters develop a strong relationship. Discuss the relationship development terms of Knapp and Vangelisti's stages.

3. Think about which stage into which most of your important friendship relationships fall. Are they closer to the beginning stages? Closer to the more intimate stages? How satisfied are you with the level?

4. Analyze a relationship that has relied heavily on new technologies for developing the ties between the friends or romantic pair. How closely did they mirror the model described above? How did technology aid or hinder the relational development?

Adapted from Mark L. Knapp and Anita L. Vangelisti, "Stages of Relationships." In *Interpersonal Communication and Human Relationships*, 5th ed., pp. 36–49. Published by Allyn & Bacon, Boston, MA. Copyright © 2005 by Pearson Education. Reprinted with permission.

From Miscegenation to Multiculturism: Perceptions and Stages of Interracial Relationship Development

ANITA K. FOEMAN AND TERESA NANCE

In the not too distant past, interracial marriages were prohibited in the United States. In fact, it was only in 1967 that the Loving vs. Virginia Supreme Court decision abolished all statutes prohibiting interracial marriage. As a result, much of the original research on interracial marital relationships was developed in the 1960s and 1970s. Researchers did not examine interracial marriage again in any depth until the 1990s.

In a discussion of interracial dialogue, Houston and Wood (1999) identify reasons why marital relationships between Whites and African Americans face challenges that are not experienced in marital relationships of same-race couples; these are presented as generalizations because each marriage is different and some couples may not encounter these issues. One issue involves differing values. For example, Whites may emphasize individualism—an emphasis on "I" rather than "we." African Americans are less individualistic, placing greater emphasis on family and community. Such differences in orientation can lead to misunderstanding in the marriage relationship. How much time should be spent with family, how

much monetary support should be given to family members, and "who comes first" are all issues to be negotiated. Orbe and Harris (2001) suggest that interracial marriage "may become an option when people have more in common with those from a different racial/ethnic group than their own" (p. 178).

Second, differing communication styles can lead to misunderstandings. For example, African Americans tend to be more confrontational and forceful in conversations among themselves than most Whites. Thus, the authors suggest, Whites sometimes perceive African Americans as rude and African Americans sometimes perceive Whites as unfeeling. Certainly, all married couples confront issues of differing values and communication styles. However, according to many researchers, these issues are greater in interracial marriages.

In a recent study of marital dissolution Zhang and Van Hook (2009) examined instability of interracial marriage among Whites, Blacks, Hispanics and Asians. They report that, "Overall, although marital dissolution was found to be strongly associated with race or ethnicity, the results failed to *provide evidence that interracial marriage per se is associated with an elevated risk of marital dissolution" (p. 104). The researchers did find that "Mixed marriages involving Blacks were the least stable...." (p. 104).*

Although there are universal challenges that all relationships encounter, interracial couples have a series of extra obstacles to overcome in order to maintain a successful relationship. Assuming these differences, Foeman and Nance present a relationship development model of African American/ White couples. The authors suggest that because of the unique issues interracial couples face, the way the relationship develops may differ from the way the relationships of same-race couples develop.

Based on couples' experiences, the authors developed a "new model" for examining these relationships. Their model identifies four stages of development: racial awareness, coping, identity awareness and maintenance, which lead to the establishment of long-term commitment. Throughout this chapter, each stage is carefully identified and described, laying out the framework for a new way to understand and view interracial relationships. As you read this chapter reflect on the question: What communication skills are critical for persons entering an interracial romantic partnership?

REFERENCES

Houston, M., & Wood, J.T. (1999). Difficult dialogues, expanded horizons: Communicating across race and class. In J.T. Wood (Ed.), *Gendered relationships* (pp. 39–56). Mountain View, CA: Mayfield.

Orbe, M. P., & Harris, T. M. (2001). *Interracial communication: Theory into practice.* Belmont, CA: Wadsworth/Thomson Learning.

Zhang, Y., & Van Hook, J. (2009). Marital dissolution among interracial couples. *Journal of Marriage and the Family, 71*, 95–107.

A NEW MODEL OF INTERRACIAL RELATIONSHIP DEVELOPMENT

Researchers have begun to look at the success strategies of interracial couples, the ways in which their relationships are functional and the reasons for their steady increase (Hall 1980; Jeter 1982;

Poston 1990; Poussaint 1984). These researchers' developing work begins to suggest specific stages of relationship evolution. It is important to know that interracial couples are working through these stages, in addition to all those any other couple must negotiate, as they move toward establishing a long-term commitment to each other. The following framework stems from past work, but evolves theoretically toward a new view of interracial families. Briefly, the stages include (a) racial awareness, (b) coping, (c) identity emergence, and (d) maintenance.

Stage 1: Racial Awareness

Awareness for an interracial couple is an interpersonal and cultural experience. As any two individuals become acquainted, they must become familiar with the similarities and differences between them and develop a shared belief that a relationship is possible. For same-group couples, growing awareness may require a subtle process of learning individual patterns and idiosyncrasies and making intentions known. To the extent that a couple does not share similar group membership (i.e., religious, socioeconomic, political), the process may be more tentative, even grinding. When the couple is of different races, differences are immediately obvious.

Interracial couples that survive likely learn in this early stage to develop an awareness of at least four concurrently operating sets of perspectives: (a) their own, (b) their partner's, (c) their collective racial group's, and (d) their partner's racial group's. Even if the couple decides not to discuss or even acknowledge one or more of these perspectives, they may influence early decisions that the couple makes (like where or whether to dine out, or which friends to socialize with). Motoyoshi (1990) describes the source of the interracial couple's challenge, stating that "In the United States, the racial stratification system is caste; that is, a person is either white or non-white" (pp. 85–86). This being the case, individuals of two different races will likely experience and respond to the world and each other in different ways (e.g., the majority partner may develop a more trusting nature than the minority one). Furthermore, outsiders will likely view the partners in different ways. The couple may also feel pressure to frame their relationship in terms of traditional social roles and attitudes. At this phase of the relationship, communication functions to bring about and articulate a common perspective on the role of race in their initial interpersonal attraction (e.g., "I liked a man who happened to be Black" versus "I am often attracted to Black men") and to highlight or downplay race as an influencing factor (e.g., "Let's just eat in tonight" versus "I didn't like the way they treated us at the restaurant last night"). Interracial couples work their way through the awareness stage by engaging in communication behaviors related to their mutual attraction and sensitivity.

Attraction. Interpersonal attraction for partners of different races may not be unlike attraction for single race couples. Interracial couples, however, have the added dimension of acknowledging the volatility of their interracial attraction in the social context. If, for example, a Black male partner admires his White lover's blond hair, the cultural implications take on an added dimension. If a White man admires aloud a Black woman's full lips, the society may view the statement as offensive. And, of course, in this context the individuals themselves may question their own attraction to one another (e.g., "Is there something wrong with me for being attracted to this person?").

Sensitivity. The awareness of this stage is also produced by emerging sensitivity to the racial place of the other. Racial place is the way that members of a racial group are treated in society, what is seen as their natural role and profile. The discovery of the other's racial place may occur in a number of different ways. It may be revealed in discussion as the couple talks directly about race, or revealed indirectly as a couple addresses daily life. For example, the White partner could talk about experiences revealing cultural privilege (the assumption of neutral or positive regard in public places). The minority person may respond in a defensive or suspicious manner to poor treatment in a new situation. Suddenly, each member may find that he or she has to make explicit life-long assumptions (regarding how one deals with new

situations, what it means to be a man or woman, how to interact with strangers, how to expect to be treated, etc.). Both partners must explain their thinking and perspective to a sometimes unfamiliar but intimate other. Both must develop sensitivity to a sometimes uncomfortable alternate perspective. In-group patterns, ranging from music and eating habits to ways of talking about the other, come under new scrutiny in this context. Both must learn new sets of public responses they are likely to receive when they are out together.

Emerging racial sensitivity is an important subphase, because it fosters the development of racial consciousness that previously would have been unattainable to either partner in a single race relationship. Such insight will probably change each partner's view of the world, regardless of the future course of the relationship.

Each interracial couple must resolve issues of racial awareness in their own time and manner. And, of course, individual partners' past experience in interracial relationships and mixed race situations will shape the manner in which this phase unfolds. In any case, the couple's communication at this early stage reflects their ability to adequately address awareness that forms the foundation for later stages. Success at this initial stage begins to build a base of trust and dialogue for the interracial couple.

Stage 2: Coping With Social Definitions of Race

Most people would agree that a couple from different races has additional ongoing challenges, as well as unique benefits to their relationship, both from without and from within. Should the couple find satisfaction in their initial interactions and choose to move forward, the next task is to manage these challenges. At the end of the awareness stage, interracial couples recognize their attraction for each other and their increased sensitivity to the function of race in their lives. They must now decide how to integrate this new information into their long-term relationship.

It is interesting to note that many couples are actually forced into the coping phase by an unaccepting society. Ironically, whereas a couple from different cultures may need more time to work through their complex attraction, they may be pushed into deeper commitment than they had intended. Those around them may predict negative outcomes or challenge the couple's choices and, in response, the couple may draw together to learn to respond to these assaults.

During the coping stage, the couple develops proactive and reactive strategies. The couple learns to insulate itself when possible from people and situations that are potentially harmful. For example, the couple may choose not to attend a family reunion. They will also learn to negotiate potentially threatening situations when necessary. To appease a parent, one partner might agree to attend a family reunion without the other-race companion.

As the couple begins to become proficient in the process of insulation and negotiation, they begin to work together to establish sets of characteristic responses to a variety of situations. They may select public places that are more diverse and welcoming, or learn to respond to questions about their group loyalty in a deescalating or curtailing manner. For example, in response to a comment like, "You must think you are Black/White," the recipient might say in jest, "Look at me, how could I not know I'm Black/White?" or "If I leave my Black/White spouse, will you marry me?" Or more provocatively, when questioned about the choice to date a White woman, a Black partner might ask, "Do you want to go back to the days when Black men were lynched for dating White women?"

The couple may learn to avoid racially hot issues or language in public settings. They may learn to read the code in phrases like "What about the children?" as a thin mask for a deeper felt discomfort. They may learn to ignore people who insist that their every problem is because of race. They may learn where to turn for support and common perspective or to develop new networks. They will probably learn that "Not everyone has to like me—and if they dislike me for racist reasons, that is their problem." They may join a support group.

Communication will function at this stage to relay strategies and enact them as necessary. As couples work their way through these issues, they draw closer together. If the couple cannot or will not face these challenges together and to their own satisfaction, they will likely feel pressure to split. It is reasonable to speculate that success in the coping process will build on success in the attraction phase and increase the likelihood for success of the relationship, helping the couple grow stronger. The couple begins to establish a culture common to them.

The coping stage can be summarized as a time for generating sets of reactive strategies to ensure the survival of the relationship. This is essentially a defensive posture. The couple stands ready to protect itself. But whereas safety is important, healthy family life demands more than simple defense from a racially biased culture. Healthy family life requires that restrictive and inaccurate descriptions of interracial couples and individuals be reframed and/or redefined.

Although most of the literature helps us to understand the awareness and coping phases of relationship development, the most positive and transforming ones have yet to be fully explored. We suggest that these are identity emergence and relationship maintenance, and begin to outline them here.

Stage 3: Identity Emergence
Redefinition occurs as the interracial couple and individual take control over images of themselves. For example, children may learn to answer questions like "Are you Black or White?" with "I am 100% both" or "I am biracial." In the emergence stage, couples begin to develop behaviors that are self-sustaining. Instead of looking at their differences as obstacles to be overcome, interracial couples view the unique racial configuration of their families as a positive source of strength (e.g., "Being biracial is a gift").

Interracial couples are also in a position to reframe their experience for the culture at large. They may learn to deconstruct statements like "I would never date a person outside my race and I think anyone who would is sick" by questioning its foundation: "If you say you would never date a person outside your race, how could you possibly understand the motivations of someone who would?"

Interracial couples or individuals may choose to see themselves as exceptional or different but, ultimately, as existing in their own right and on their own terms rather than as an inadequate subset of what is deemed desirable by others. Communication functions to provide the voice and words to recast their world: We are the inevitable family of a truly multicultural society. Successful interracial couples develop skills to resolve problems that threaten the very foundation of our society. They have perspective that escapes others and the wherewithal to define themselves where no set guidelines exist. These are skills that will be needed in the multicultural society of the future. Interracial families can see themselves as at the head of a trend.

Stage 4: Maintenance

As couples emerge with effective strategies and perspectives, they may feel energized to share their views. Over a lifetime together, an interracial couple will have more or less need at any given time to focus on race or to evolve as an interracial couple. Literature and experience tell us that the stages suggested here are not lock step. Individuals and couples may revisit steps at different points in their lives.

Although each couple will probably begin with their own awareness, individuals within couples may be at different beginning points. One partner may have addressed issues in earlier interracial relationships and have to revisit them with a new partner. Another couple may enter a relationship with the posture that race is not an issue and only much later be forced to overtly address racial awareness. If and when couples begin to rear interracial children, they may need to recycle through stages in light of their children's experiences as well as their own. Essentially, each phase of a couple's life together brings new opportunities for racial awareness, development of new coping strategies, emergence as a reconstructed unit, and ongoing relationship maintenance....

REFERENCES

Hall, C. C. I. (1980). *The ethnic identity of racially mixed people: A study of Black-Japanese* (Unpublished doctoral dissertation). University of California, Los Angeles.

Jeter, K. (1982). Analytic essay: Intercultural and interracial marriage. *Marriage and Family Review, 5*, 105–111.

Motoyoshi, M. M. (1990). The experience of mixed-race people: Some thoughts and theories. *Journal of Ethnic Studies, 18*, 77–94.

Poston, W. S. C. (1990). The biracial identity development model: A needed addition. *Journal of Counseling and Development, 69*, 152–155.

Poussaint, A. (1984). Study of interracial children presents positive picture. *Interracial Books for Children Bulletin, 15*, 9–10.

QUESTIONS/THOUGHTS

1. Compare the states of relationship presented by Foeman and Nance to those of Knapp and Vangelisti in the previous chapter. How are they similar? How are they different? What reasons can you posit for the similarities and differences?

2. What media images exist of interracial relationships? Are these images generally positive or negative? Select one film or television show and indicate what these images indicate about society's view of interracial relationships?

3. What type of communication situations might members of an interracial couple encounter that same-race partners never face? What communication skills would help them to deal with the situation(s)?

4. Why might the research by Zhang and Van Hook, noted in the introduction, have found that, "Mixed marriages involving Blacks were the least stable..." (p. 104)? How might couple or family communication play a role in these findings?

Expressing Affection:
A Vocabulary of Loving Messages

CHARLES A. WILKINSON AND LAUREN H. GRILL

Although sharing affection is central to relational maintenance, many well-intended attempts at displaying affection miss their mark. The intended recipient of the caring message misinterprets the messages, wishes for a different sign of affection or does not respond in the desired way. In his book, Gifts from the Heart, *Randy Fujishin examines the many ways to share affection. He asserts that body language provides the most powerful form of communicating caring, and says "whether it's the reassuring pat on the back from a friend, the gentle kiss of a mother, or the familiar touch or a lover, body language conveys an important message—the gift of showing you care" (1998, p. 102). In* Hold Me Tight, *a book intended to help couples build stronger emotional ties, therapist Sue Johnson (2008) argues that the way to enhance a relationship is to reestablish the emotional connection through openness and to be responsive and attuned to the other person. This good advice succeeds only if both partners can work together to make this emotional connection.*

In the following article, Charles Wilkinson and Lauren Grill discuss the various ways people express affection to others and the difficulty that can arise when you can't construct loving messages

in the way your partners or friends need to hear them. These authors describe the many good, well-meaning individuals who experience relationship problems because they "don't speak the same language" as their friend or romantic partner. In other words, they do not share the same meanings for what counts as affection.

If you think of your family-of-origin as your first communication classroom, as described in Chapter 13 you will realize how much you learned about how to share or withhold affection. This background, coupled with your cultural heritage, your gender socialization and individual experiences, provided a solid base from which to construct your "affection vocabulary" or the ways in which you would expect to express and receive affection.

But your goals are not always reached. For example, painful relational breakdowns occur when Partner A tries so hard to indicate caring by giving gifts or making special meals while Partner B waits for a hug. The situation becomes even more complex when Partner B reaches out through touch and caring words and Partner A doesn't reciprocate.

In the following piece, the authors develop a set of various communication strategies that can indicate caring; they range from direct verbal statements to doing favors. They assert that the key to success depends on the similarity of the relational participants' values; any loving behavior is valid, if both parties interpret and value it in similar ways. After briefly describing the many ways in which people share affection, Wilkinson and Grill develop three specific relational currencies—direct relational statements, self-disclosure, and gifts. Each of these is commonly used to send "I care" messages, with very different effects.

As you read this piece, consider how participants in a particular relationship try to reach out to each other and evaluate their effectiveness. As you read this chapter consider the question: How satisfied am I with the ways I share affection in friendship and family relationships and what changes might I wish to make in how I use relational currencies?

REFERENCES

Fujishin, R. (1998). *Gifts from the heart.* San Francisco, CA: Acada Books.

Johnson, S. (2008). *Hold me tight.* New York, NY: Little, Brown and Company.

INTRODUCTION

How did you know you were loved as a child? Did someone tease you, give you a backrub, surprise you with a present, fix your meals, listen to your troubles, hug you goodnight? Every family implicitly and explicitly teaches its members specific ways to show caring for others and to accept caring from others. Growing up, we all learn specific nurturing behaviors. You learned to use and expect certain behaviors and not to use or to expect others. You were taught the rules for how affection should or should not be shared, and how intensely it should be expressed. In addition you learned appropriate nurturing messages for males and females, older and younger persons, immediate family and friends. Some of these lessons reflected your family's cultural background. In short, part of growing up consisted of a series of family lessons on communicating affection. Thus everyone, knowingly and unknowingly, develops a specific set of acceptable ways of sharing affection

within his or her family-of-origin, the first words of a vocabulary of caring. It is important to note that, although many people follow their family-of-origin patterns, others deliberately choose to alter them. For example, in their study of father-son affection Floyd and Morman (2000) found that men who were most affectionate with their sons had fathers who were either highly affectionate or highly unaffectionate. In such cases sons either followed their fathers' modeling or compensated for the lack of affection by demonstrating strong affection when they became fathers.

Verbal and nonverbal messages which carry meaning about the caring dimension of human relationships may be called "relational currencies." Although the concept of "currency" reflects an economic model of investing or trading, within a communication framework, relational currencies can be considered part of a symbolic exchange process. As partners share relational currencies, they form understandings about "what counts for what"; this either strengthen or limit their relationship worldview. When the same currencies are equally valued, this agreement enhances attempt to communicate affection.

The ways you learned to show affection to friends and relatives are not necessarily similar to what other people learn. Growing up, you gradually became aware that others expressed caring differently, and you also learned to appreciate and use some of the nurturing messages taught to you by others. Occasionally you also have been surprised or angered by the insensitive ways others expressed caring, resisting their intensity or their actions.

Friends from different cultures can value different ways of sharing affection. One may be very expressive, physically hugging and touching; another may be very reserved but brings you wonderful gifts of food. Cross-gender relationships are sources of confusion regarding the most comfortable ways to show affection (Wood & Inman 1993). These differences may have broadened your ways of thinking about affection.

One of the most frustrating relational experiences occurs when someone you care about does not respond with the intensity you expect or becomes silent or distant. It hurts when another does not understand your attempts to show affection and when you feel unloved by the responses from someone you care about.

The most painful experiences in some partnerships occur when members value different ways of sharing affection. Many husbands and wives feel unloved because their spouses never seem to do the "right thing"—to send the expected or desired caring message. According to Dr. Gary Chapman, author of *The Five Love Languages*, when couples are in the dating phase of their relationship, they often shower each other with a variety of loving messages and gestures to accommodate the needs of their partner to feel special and loved. Over time, however, partners reduce the frequency and variety of these messages, usually favoring the messages that mean the most to themselves, and not necessarily their partners or spouses. As each person grew up learning a different set of loving behaviors from their families, their "I care" messages may look and feel very different from each other. Naturally, when members move away from their families they carry their relational currency patterns with them. When these patterns are not shared over time between romantic partners, their loving vocabularies bypass each other.

In their early work on relational communication, Villard and Whipple (1976) discuss intimate and economic relational currencies, or communication behaviors that convey affection. Proponents of transactional analysis also discuss currencies for expressing affection (Berne 1964). In his discussion of communication skills in loving relationships, Fujishin (1998) refers to them as ways of showing caring. Just as children learn verbal language and expand their vocabularies as they encounter new objects, people, and ideas, so too, they learn a vocabulary of loving behaviors which should expand as they mature and encounter new people and ideas. The vocabulary learned initially in the family-of-origin influences greatly any development of a lifetime loving vocabulary.

Being conscious of such a vocabulary helps individuals identify their particular patterns of expressing affection, and examine how those patterns fit or miss the needs of their significant others—partners, parents, children, extended

Direct relational statement	Gifts
Positive verbal statements	Money
Self-disclosure	Food
Listening	Favors
Staying in touch	Service
Nonverbal expressiveness	Time together
Touch	Access rights
Sexuality	
Aggression	

(Adapted from Villard & Whipple, 1976.)

Figure 17-1

families, and friends. In more emotionally distanced families each member has a small number of loving behaviors which coordinate with the specific relational currencies used or valued by the others. There are many possible patterned messages for conveying affection.

Each of the following (Figure 17-1) represents one way of sharing affection. The use of each must be considered within the contexts of gender, culture, and developmental stage (McGoldrick, Giordano, & Garcia-Preto, 2005; Wood, 2007).

OVERVIEW OF CURRENCIES
Direct Relational Statements
Such statements include oral and written messages that directly indicate love or caring. In some relationships, people express affection easily, saying "I love you" directly and frequently. Others may view such directness as unacceptable, preferring to save such words for special occasions (weddings, homecomings) or crisis situations. A study of statements of love within birthday cards reveals that the recipients of such affectionate messages are most often female relatives (Mooney & Brabant 1988).

Positive Verbal Statements
Such statements include oral and written messages that directly or indirectly indicate support, praise, or liking. Compliments, encouragement, indications, pleasure, involvement ("I'm really glad

you decided to come, I missed you") may convey liking or affection. A "Thinking of you" card or a phone call or e-mail to "touch base" also conveys involvement and caring.

Self-Disclosure

Voluntarily telling someone personal information about yourself that the other is unlikely to discover from other sources serves as a means of deepening understanding and trust between people. To be considered a relational currency, self-disclosure must be intentionally meant to demonstrate caring and investment in a relationship.

Listening

A frequently underappreciated communication behavior, listening carries a message of involvement with, and attention to, another person. More than any other currency, it communicates *presence*. True empathetic listening requires focused energy and practice. "It's a mental habit at which one has to work" (Ryan & Ryan, 1982, p. 44). Listening may be taken for granted unless the speaker is sensitive to the listener's careful attention.

Staying in Touch

Staying in touch implies efforts to maintain important relational ties, often across significant distances. Traditionally, this process involved sending cards and gifts or long-distance phone calls. Today, however, many friends and family members remain in close connection through the use of cell phones, e-mail, and the Internet. Dating partners may IM or text message each other 4 or 5 times a day; parents and college students may check in regularly over e-mail. Many grandparents are getting online to participate in the family's round-robin e-mails or check updates on the family website. Facebook has also changed the ways friends and family members may stay in touch online, reading each other's status updates and posting on each other's walls. The ease of everyday interaction has helped to maintain many friendships or extended family ties that might have frayed in the past. Even if the words are not affectionate, the effort to stay in touch is symbolic of caring.

Nonverbal Expressiveness

Spontaneous displays of affection, best characterized as love "in that 'eyes lighting up' sense" (Malone & Malone, 1987, p. 14) are referred to as nonverbal expressiveness. Nonverbal symbols such as facial expressions, outstretched arms, or general exuberance convey delight at the other's presence.

Touch

Touch is the language of physical intimacy. Positive physical contact carries a range of messages about friendship, concern, love, or sexual interest. Touch may serve as a significant indicator or "tie sign" (Goffman, 1959) of interpersonal connection to outsiders. Because touching behaviors vary greatly across genders and cultures they may be easily misinterpreted.

Sexuality

For adult partners, sexuality provides a unique opportunity for intimacy. The discourse surrounding intercourse and the act itself combine to create a powerful message of affection as long as both partners interpret the meaning of their sexual exchange in the same way.

Aggression

Aggression connotes actions usually thought to be incompatible with affection. Yet aggressive actions may serve as the primary emotional connection between members of certain families, especially within sibling relationships. Some people find it difficult to express intimacy directly; in these cases, verbal or physical aggression can serve as a means to feel connected and thus can be a sign of caring. For example, some friends and relatives may use sarcasm, teasing, tickling, or put downs as attempts at staying connected with others. Some conflictual couples may maintain their contact through bickering and disagreements. An individual who typically avoids conflict may indicate caring by engaging in an argument with a loved one as a way to stay connected.

Gifts

Gifts are symbols of affection that may be complicated by issues of cost, appropriateness, and reciprocity. Gifts may signal of a person's intentions about future investment in a relationship (Camerer 1988). The thought and consideration involved in the process of identifying, selecting, and presenting the gift communicates the degree of caring and love symbolized in the gift (Chapman, 2004).

Money
Dollars and cents symbolize the economic nature of an exchange of currencies. Money must be given or loaned as a sign of affection and not an obligation if the act is to convey caring.

Food
A symbol of nurturing in many cultures, food preparation has emerged as a sign of caring in romantic and immediate family relationships, in addition to its historical place in inter-generational methods of affection.

Favors
Performing helpful acts for others may be complicated by norms of reciprocity and equality. Favors, to be considered signs of affection, must be performed willingly rather than in response to a friend, partner or relative's order. The underlying message of an action may be missed if the effort behind the favor is not appreciated.

Service
Service implies that a favor has evolved into a habitual behavior. Driving the carpool, making the coffee in the morning, or maintaining the checkbook may have begun as favors and moved into routines. People often continue such habits out of caring and consideration of others' needs, yet such services frequently go unnoticed or are taken for granted, thus negating the underlying message of affection.

Time Together
Being together, whether it's just "hanging out" or voluntarily accompanying someone on a trip or errand carries the message "I want to be with you." This is a subtle message with potential for being overlooked, although it is particularly important for maintaining many close relationships. "Staying in touch" is a variation on this relational currency.

Access Rights
Allowing another person to use or borrow things you value conveys affection when the permission is intended as a sign of caring. The key to this relational message is the exclusive nature of granting permission, the underlying assumption being that not "just anyone" can have access to your belongings, only people you care about.

Clearly some of these categories overlap, and they also may vary based upon cultural heritage, personal experiences and observations. You may think of caring behaviors that do not seem to fit with these categories. Yet, for most people, these specific behaviors represent major ways of showing affection or of receiving affection. Some of these behaviors will send a more direct message than others—but all can be powerful indicators of caring and affection if intended and interpreted properly.

Any or all of these behaviors can be used to manipulate another or to gain power in a relationship. They serve as nurturing messages only when they communicate a genuine attitude that says "I honestly care" and carry the intention of maintaining or deepening the relationship. A closer look at three key aspects of this vocabulary demonstrates the subtleties and complexities of any currency.

DIRECT RELATIONAL STATEMENTS
Verbal statements of affection are not always easy to express. In *Fiddler on the Roof*, Teyve asks his wife Golda, "Do you love me?" Her reply takes the form of a list of all the things she'd done for him over the years. She says: "For twenty-five years I've washed your clothes, cooked your meals, cleaned your house, given you children, milked the cow. After twenty-five years why talk about love right now?" Clearly for Golda feelings of love are not talked about directly. Yet Teyve really wants a direct statement of caring, and reluctantly Golda finally admits, "I suppose I do." Teyve, to be safe, replies, "And I suppose I love you too."

Each of us can recall wondering about another's affection for us and thinking "Does he really love me?" or "How much does she really care about me?" Many adults wonder how much their parents loved them because they never heard words such as "I love you" or "You're very special to me" while they were growing up. In some households direct statements of affection and caring occur with great frequency, and may even lose some potency through such regularity, whereas in other homes direct verbal affection does not occur or it occurs sparingly during special family occasions. In these families one seldom hears "I'm glad you are my daughter" or "I missed you" even though in many relationships such statements serve to clarify and strengthen the bond between individuals.

If you grew up in a family that was highly verbal about its affection, it may be hard to appreciate just how difficult it is for others to put affection into words. Some people think that it isn't necessary to talk about how you feel. Others will be able to tell by your actions. Many men have learned it is "masculine" to withhold feelings. In today's society, greeting card companies have made fortunes by writing the caring messages so all the customer has to do is select the right card. This process serves as a buffer for verbalizing deep feelings. Humorous cards often allow people to avoid sharing their feelings directly because the joke serves as a functional remembrance of the occasion. Sometimes, expressing verbal affection can best be done in writing. One man left love notes on his wife's mirror, even after nineteen years of marriage. A student bemoaned the fact that her parents lived near her college and so she never got letters; the only way her father expressed his feelings was by writing and he wrote such wonderful letters about how much he missed her when she was away at camp.

One wife said in the presence of her husband, "We've been married eleven years and in all that time, never once, not ONCE has he ever said to me, 'I love you!'" Asked if that was so, he replied, "Well, I take care of her, she's very special." When asked, "But have you ever said the words 'I love you' to her?" he said, "Not really, I guess." And even then he couldn't add, "but I do love you, Hon."

Most people have a deep need to talk about caring. Witness the letters to advice columnists grieving the death of a family member with "If only I had told him how much I loved him before he died."

Alternatively, some people can nurture others through direct, caring statements but cannot accept such statements comfortably. In a society that teaches many people to put themselves down, direct statements of caring can be unsettling and may be met with averted eyes, a flip remark or a disclaimer such as "Oh, you tell everyone that."

Direct statements of affection, spoken and written, are essential to all healthy relationships, especially within families whose primary function is to nurture.

SELF-DISCLOSURE

Carl Sandburg once wrote: "Life is like an onion: You uncover it a layer at a time and sometimes you weep." Relationships are also like onions. The surface, onion-skin stuff is there for all to see. But as layer after layer is peeled away, the deeper truths of any relationship can cause its members to laugh, cry, appreciate, discover, despair, grow and expand, or cling to the safe and known. People, like onions, grow from the inside out; that growing edge is at the core of one's being. And sharing the growing edge with another, inviting another "in," is a powerful way of saying "I care about you."

Closely related to direct verbal statements of caring, self-disclosure implies voluntarily telling others private/personal information that they are not likely to discover from another source. This personal/private information may involve your feelings for the other person or it may involve information about yourself. Either way the message is: "I trust you and am willing to share this information with you as a symbol of my caring for you and for our relationship."

True self-disclosure involves some degree of risk because the other person learns information which, if misused, could be hurtful to you. For example, the person could throw the information back at you in anger or reveal to others what you have shared. Still, despite the risks, many individuals self-disclose to establish bonds between themselves and to deepen their relationships.

For this reason, although a verbal statement of caring for another is one type of self-disclosure, statements about yourself constitute the primary type of self-disclosure. How often have you heard, "I'm only telling this to you," or "Only a very few people know this about me." Such statements designate the listener as "special" and "trusted" and make the information privileged.

The decision to self-disclose is tied to personal history with another. For example, you may find yourself thinking, "I've reached a point in my relationship with Sarah where I can talk about my mother's illness or my fears of losing my job." Or you may think "John is a close enough friend to know about the breakup of my first marriage." What this really says is that the relationship is secure enough and mature enough to handle such information appropriately. Sarah or John, although they may be surprised or upset by the information, will not withdraw from the relationship based on the disclosure because the growth of the relationship allows such risks to be taken.

One of the most intriguing aspects of self-disclosure is how differently it is interpreted by various individuals. One person may consider a conversation to contain deep self-disclosure, yet the other may not. Allen may sit and talk for hours about his sexual exploits and think nothing of it while Rick would never be comfortable discussing his sexual life, except in a very special relationship. Jamie may share her poetry easily but struggles when it comes to talking about her inner feelings. Julie may be just the opposite. Self-disclosure is valued in certain cultures and not in others; women are socialized to value this vocabulary more than men in our society (Wood, 2005; Wood and Inman 1993).

Occasionally self-disclosure conjures up an image of telling another person all the bad stuff—the pain, the negative scary feelings, the dark side of self. This is partially true since that's where the risk may be perceived as the greatest. In most long-term relationships there are times when one or both members are too vulnerable to take such

risks. Experiences such as illness, job loss, or death of a loved one may render one partner unable to accept difficult self-disclosure from the other.

Self-disclosure is not only about planned revelation. It's also about responding to the moment. If you suddenly hear a piece of music that has emotional meaning for you—share that meaning. If you encounter a stranger who reminds you fondly of your former roommate—tell your college friend you miss her. Seize the moment to tear down walls rather than building them up through silence or distance. Healthy self-disclosure involves being alive to the current state of a relationship and being willing to take risks to foster future growth. All relationships have the potential for deepening, no matter how old, static, locked-in they are. Oftentimes all it takes is for one or the other to take the risk of saying "I need to talk" or "I need you to know something."

Finally, self-disclosure is not intended to be unidirectional. It doesn't work for one person in a relationship to take all the risks of sharing while the other listens. Self-disclosure develops through reciprocity. Over time both parties must share with each other or relational growth stagnates. The deepening of intimacy must be incremental and shared.

GIFTS

In some relationships how much you are loved reflects directly on the gifts you receive. A gift is "a visual symbol of love...something you can hold in your hand and say 'Look, he was thinking of me,' or 'Look, she remembered me'" (Chapman, 2004, p. 82–83). At this symbolic level, "Gifts become containers for the being of the donor" (Csikszentmihalyi and Rochberg-Halton 1981, 37). In some relationships gifts are the most commonly used vocabulary for conveying affection; in others, gifts play a minor role. Love letters, cards, or a kiss may substitute adequately for presents; what counts is the caring thought underlying the presentation of the gift.

The importance of shared or "recognized as different" attitudes toward gift giving cannot be overestimated. More holidays have been ruined, often annually, because one person or another felt ignored or discounted by the lack of gifts or the type of gift received from a loved one.

Often gift-giving raises the issue of reciprocity. The tit-for-tat social rule is so strong the gift giving process becomes filled with scorekeeping. Reciprocity becomes extremely complicated, however, because the value of a gift may be judged at several different levels. Some people may judge a gift's significance based upon how much it costs; others care more about how personal the gift is, or how perfectly it suits them, because only someone who truly knew them and loved them could pick out such a perfectly tailored gift. On the other hand, the phrase "it's the thought that counts" became popular because some people measure the quality of a gift based upon the time and thought put into it. So, when you want to show someone how much you care with a gift, how do you select the right item? By price? Sentimentality? Time and effort?

Not an easy thing, this ritual of gifting another! Because it may appear "silly" or "unimportant" many people never express their real wishes around the subject of presents when, if the wishes were known, others would cheerfully change their behavior. Many individuals expect others to mind read-believing that "If you really loved me you would know I want." This creates a frustrating and futile trap for both parties, one easily resolved by openness and honesty about one's expectations and desires.

MEANINGS AND CURRENCIES

The meanings attached to a specific vocabulary of relational caring have direct impact on relationship development. Interaction may be viewed as an exchange process in which actors are invested in trading meanings. When meanings are shared, rewards are experienced; when meanings are missed, costs are experienced (Stephen 1984). Therefore, over a period of time, intimate partners will create common assumptions about the importance of parts of a relational vocabulary and develop high levels of symbolic interdependence.

Although messages of affection may be exchanged with the best intentions, accurate interpretation occurs only when both parties agree upon the meaning of the act. Usually, the meanings you apply to another's messages are those you would use in a familiar situation. For example:

> Each of us tends to identify as loving those expressions of love that are similar to our own. I may express my love…by touching you, being wonderfully careless with you, or simply contentedly sitting near you without speaking. You may express an equally deep love feeling by buying me a gift, cooking the veal, working longer hours to bring us more monetary freedom, or simply fixing the broken faucet. These are obviously different ways of loving. (Malone and Malone 1987, 74)

In the previous example, the question remains: Does the contented silent partner know that a veal dinner or a fixed faucet is a way of showing love? When you think about your relationships, you may find that you are apt to see others as more loving if they express their affection the same way you do. Such a similarity adds to a growing sense of symbolic interdependence.

What happens if family members want to share affection but seem unable to exchange the currencies desired by others? After interviewing married couples, Villard and Whipple concluded that spouses with similar affection exchange behaviors were more likely to report (a) high levels of perceived equity and (b) high levels of relationship satisfaction. Thus, they experienced greater relationship rewards. Nonetheless, accuracy in predicting (i.e. understanding) each other's choice of vocabulary did not raise relational satisfaction level. If spouses were accurate at predicting how their partners would respond to certain loving behaviors, they still reported low marital satisfaction if they were dissimilar in their own preferred affection behaviors. Unfortunately, as this study also found that wives were more likely to use more intimate communication than husbands, it suggests that many marriages may face "unhappiness, unfulfillment, conflict and/or divorce because of socialized differences between men and women in how they share 'who they are' and how they manifest 'affection'" (Millar, Rogers-Millar, & Villard, 1978, p. 15). Being able to share affections provides definite advantages. Floyd (2002) found that high-affection communicators receive advantages in psychological, emotional, mental, social and relational characteristics compared to low-affection communicators. He reports, "They were more likely to have a secure attachment style and less likely to have a fearful/avoidant style. They received more affection from others." (p. 147). Additionally, high-affection communicators tended to have higher self-esteem than low affection communicators, which rendered them more likely to achieve greater levels of social and economic success.

Personal meaning placed on relational currencies changes over time. As relationships mature, members may change how they share affection because of new experiences, pressures, or expectations. For example, in a study of fathers and their adult sons, Floyd, Sargent and Di Corcia (2004) found that fathers change their loving behaviors with their sons as their sons mature; specifically, as their sons reach adulthood, fathers shift their communication of affection away from direct verbal statements or nonverbal gestures, preferring instead to engage in more supportive activities.

Economic conditions also affect the exchange of certain currencies. Financial stressors may result in fewer gifts exchanged among family members, but may also lead to greater sharing and favors. When a family member or friend loses a job, he may increase self-disclosure—sharing feelings and frustrations—which could deepen the intimacy of his significant relationships. Once re-employed, however, he may not have the time or inclination to continue this level of self-disclosure, and his relationships may revert to former patterns.

The process of exchanging affectionate messages significantly affects relational levels of intimacy. The greater similarity in individuals' exchange processes, the higher the levels of symbolic interdependence and satisfaction in the relationship. Thus, persons with an expanded vocabulary of loving messages have a greater chance of connecting with others in satisfying ways.

REFERENCES

Berne, E. (1964). *Games people play.* New York, NY: Grove.

Camerer, C. (1988). Gifts as economic signals and social symbols. *American Journal of Sociology, 94,* S180–S214.

Chapman, G. (1995). *The five love languages: How to express heartfelt commitment to your mate.* Chicago, IL: Northfield Publishing.

Csikszentmihalyi, M., & Rochberg-Halton, E. (1981). *The meaning of things: Domestic symbols and the self.* Cambridge, England: Cambridge University Press.

Floyd, K. (2002). Human affection exchange: V. Attributes of the highly affectionate. *Communication Quarterly, 50,* 135–152.

Floyd, K., & Morman, M. T. (2000). Affection received from fathers as a predictor of men's affection with their own sons: Tests of the modeling and compensation hypotheses. *Communication Monographs, 67,* 347–361.

Floyd, K., Sargent, J., & Di Corcia, M. (2004). Human affection exchange: vi. Further tests of reproductive probability as a predictor of men's affection with their adult sons. *Journal of Social Psychology, 144*(2), 191–206.

Fujishin, R. (1998). *Gifts from the heart.* San Francisco, CA: Acada Books.

Goffman, E. (1959). *The presentation of self in everyday life.* New York, NY: Doubleday.

Malone, T., & Malone, P. (1987). *The art of intimacy.* New York, NY: Prentice-Hall.

McGoldrick, M., Anderson, C., & Walsh, F. (Eds.). (1989). *Women in families: A framework for family therapy.* New York, NY: Norton.

McGoldrick, M., Giordano, J., & Garcia-Preto, N. (Eds.). (2005). *Ethnicity and family therapy* (3rd ed.). New York, NY: Guilford Press.

Millar, F., Rogers-Millar, L. E., & Villard, K. (1978, April). *A proposed model of relational communication and family functioning.* Paper presented at the Central States Speech Association Convention, Chicago, IL.

Mooney, L., & Brabant, S. (1988). Birthday cards, love, and communication. *Social Science Research, 72,* 106–109.

Ryan, K., & Ryan, M. (1982). *Making a marriage*. New York, NY: St. Martin's Press.

Villard, K., & Whipple, L. (1976). *Beginnings in relational communication*. New York, NY: Wiley.

Wood, J. T. (2007). *Gendered lives: Communication, culture and gender* (7th ed.). Belmont, CA: Thomson/Wadsworth.

Wood, J. T., & Inman, C. (1993). In a difficult mode: Masculine styles of communicating closeness. *Journal of Applied Communication*, 21(30), 279–294.

QUESTIONS/THOUGHTS

1. Think about the ways you express affection. Which of the relational currencies discussed in the chapter are you comfortable using? Which currencies are difficult for you to accept form others? Give an example of how your repertoire of relational currencies has changed in the last few years.

2. Describe a person who tries to reach out to others to be a friend, but who seems to have difficulty "speaking the same language" as those others. Indicate what you might suggest to that person in order to be more effective.

3. What relational currencies did you think about that the reading does not include? Describe two of them and indicate examples of how and by whom they are likely to be exchanged.

4. Describe the ways in which people use two of the following for exchanging caring messages—IM, Twitter, cell phones, texting. Give examples.

Face Management in Interpersonal Communication

WILLIAM R. CUPACH AND SANDRA METTS

Sociologist Erving Goffman (1967) described face as the favorable social impression that a person wants others to have of him or her. In other words, face represents the concept of self that each person displays in interactions with others. Face is not how people think of themselves, but what they want others to think of them. When someone makes an effort to protect his or her face, this is called "facework," which occurs only in a relational context. Facework is "about the verbal and nonverbal strategies that we use to maintain, defend, or upgrade our own social self image and attack or defend (or "save") the social images of others (Ting-Toomey & Chung, 2005, p. 268). One can only gain or lose face through actions that are known and interpreted by others. The concept of face is meaningful only when considered in relation to others in the social context.

Facework represents an ongoing process, often unconscious, that .permeates interpersonal interactions. What is critical is that the process of face management seems to be as enduring as human social existence. In the very act of communicating individuals are continuously adapting to others and attempting to influence their impressions.

This impression may not be shared by everyone and may differ from a person's own self-image. To maintain face, you engage in facework in order to convince others to act toward you with respect, regardless of their "real" impression of you. Facework is the communication designed to counteract face threats to self or others. In their study of workplace communication, Carson and Cupach (2000) found that a perceived face threat was negatively correlated with perceptions of the other's interactional fairness and communicative competence. Finally, face relates to the positive social attributes that people want others to acknowledge. Negative attributes are concealed and protected from judgment. For example, communicators may use euphemisms to avoid negative judgments of others (McGlone & Batchelor, 2003).

Apologies represent common areas of facework. In her analysis of the apologies of leaders, Kellerman (2006) claims that they are very strategic choices: "Leaders will publicly apologize if and when they calculate the costs of doing so to be lower than the costs of not doing so" (p. 75). She concludes that "Most apologies are motivated by self interest"(p. 81). Essentially, leaders choose to save face in certain situations by behaving in a way that threatens their face.

In their examination of everyday facework among friends, Agne and White (2004) found that people who were seeking support, and thus engaging in facework, were more satisfied when the persons providing the support minimized the imposition of giving advice and showed an appreciation for the other's problem. They also felt more satisfied when the person in need of support asked directly for help—not always easy if the person is trying to save face.

In most relationships, there are moments in which you completely embarrass yourself, and others in which you make yourself proud. These moments of pride or embarrassment are examined in this chapter, in the context of face management, in which embarrassment means "losing" face, and pride means "sustaining" face. In the following article Cupach and Metts integrate Goffman's facework theories into their discussion of the ways in which people use communication to manage face. Throughout the chapter, they discuss face needs, threats, facework, and finally, the reasons why managing face is important for the development and maintenance of interpersonal relationships. As you read this article, consider how this concept of face relates to your own interpersonal communication. Ask yourself, "How do I tend to manage my face in new situations and how do I adapt to face threats in these circumstances?"

REFERENCES

Agne, R. R., & White, C. H. (2004). The nature of facework in discussion of everyday problems between friends. *Southern Communication Journal, 70*(1), 1–14.

Carson, C. L., & Cupach, W. R. (2003). Facing corrections in the workplace: The influence of perceived face threat on the consequences of managerial reproaches. *Journal of Applied Communication Research, 28*, 215–234.

Goffman, E. (1967). *Interaction ritual: Essays on face-to-face behavior.* Garden City, NY: Anchor Books.

Kellerman, B. (2006, April). When should a leader apologize and when not? *Harvard Business Review*, 73–81.

McGlone, M., & Batchelor, J. A. (2003). Looking out for number one: Euphemism and face. *Journal of Communication, 53*, 251–264.

Ting-Toomey, S. & Chung, L.C. (2005). *Understanding intercultural communication.* Los Angeles, CA: Roxbury.

FACE MANAGEMENT IN INTERPERSONAL RELATIONSHIPS

"I was so embarrassed!" Have you ever found yourself recounting a story of how you stumbled and fell while trying to impress a new date with your dancing talents? Have you ever expressed in much more somber tones a time when you felt great shame because you violated a trust that you and your partner shared about sexual exclusivity? If you have felt embarrassment, or shame, then you have experienced the effects of losing face. If, on the other hand, you have felt pride, or validation, or respect, then you have experienced the effects of sustaining face, even, perhaps, during awkward situations. This [article] is about gaining and losing face in close relationships. The notion of face, and related concepts, is used to explain the role of communication in managing the course of interpersonal relationships.

COMMUNICATION AND THE MANAGEMENT OF FACE

Face and Face Needs

The conception of self that each person displays in particular interactions with others is called face. When a person interacts with another, he or she tacitly presents a conception of who he or she is in that encounter, and seeks confirmation for that conception. In other words, the individual offers an identity that he or she wants to assume and wants others to accept. In social scientific terms, face refers to "socially situated identities people claim or attribute to others" (Tracy, 1990, p. 210).

According to Goffman (1967), whatever the context in which communication occurs, and whatever the relationship shared by interactants, it is assumed that each person's face is supported and maintained during interaction. Out of self-respect, communicators are emotionally invested in the presentation and preservation of their own face; out of considerateness, communicators exert effort to save the feelings and maintain the face of other people. Goffman characterizes an individual who can experience his or her own face loss without distress as "shameless" and an individual who can unfeelingly observe others lose face as "heartless."

Under normal circumstances, then, individuals reciprocate face support and cooperate to ensure that each other's face is protected. Indeed, when any person's face is threatened during an interaction, all participants are motivated to restore it because not doing so leaves them open to the discomfort and embarrassment that arises from a disrupted interaction.

This mutual cooperation in the maintenance of face is so ordinary and pervasive that it is considered a taken-for-granted principle of interaction. People do it automatically—unless the intent is to embarrass someone playfully or to discredit someone contemptuously. Generally, face is not a conscious concern of communicators. The everyday goals of expressing one's beliefs, ingratiating others, seeking advice, eliciting information, and so on "are typically pursued in such a way as to be consistent with the maintenance of face" (Goffman, 1967, p. 12).

Thus maintaining face is an underlying motive in all social encounters, but it is not usually a strategic objective. It is only when some event, action, or comment discredits face or threatens to discredit face that strategies to minimize the occurrence and consequences of face threat come into consciousness. The next subsection deals with face threats and ways of coping with them.

Threats to Face

Face threats occur when a person's desired identity in a particular interaction is challenged. Given that it is virtually impossible to avoid all face threats at all times, any interaction is potentially face-threatening (Tracy, 1990). Even the most skillful and well-intended communicator sometimes finds him- or herself in the position of having spoken an inappropriate comment or having felt diminished by receiving a complaint or criticism from someone else. And as we will

see later, some types of interaction episodes, such as terminating a relationship, are by their very nature face-involving situations.

A particularly interesting explication of how face is threatened is offered by Penelope Brown and Stephen Levinson (1987). Drawing from their analysis of 13 societies in various areas of the world, they present a theory based on two types of universal face needs: positive face needs and negative face needs. Positive face refers to the desire to be liked and respected by the significant people in our lives. Positive face is supported when messages communicate value for the things we value, appreciation for us as competent individuals, and solidarity with us (Lim & Bowers, 1991). Positive face is threatened when one's fellowship is devalued or one's abilities are questioned. Negative face pertains to the desire to be free from constraint and imposition. Messages respecting one's autonomy are supportive of negative face, whereas messages interfering with one's desired actions are threatening to negative face.

Brown and Levinson's description of positive and negative face is interesting because of the dilemma it exposes for people trying to meet both types of face needs for themselves and other people. Essentially, the dilemma is that satisfying one type of face need often threatens the other. Consider this just within an individual. Karen Tracy (1990) gives an example of a college professor who values teaching very highly and wants to cultivate his students' potential. However, the cost of this desire is that students make daily demands on his time and drain his energy. His positive face needs are satisfied at the cost of his negative face needs.

To understand this dilemma at the relationship level, think for a moment about what you do when you like someone: You spend time with the person, teasing and complimenting, self-disclosing, borrowing money or clothes; you drop by the person's home unexpectedly, and so forth. You do what comes naturally when you care about and value someone. You are, in these behaviors, showing regard for the individual's positive face. However, consider how these actions might threaten negative face. This other person may feel it an imposition to have to stop his or her activity to visit with you, or may not be comfortable with your self-disclosures, or may find it tiring to entertain you when he or she would prefer to do something else. These responses are natural because your friend's negative face is being constrained at the very same time his or her positive face is being validated. In fact, sometimes your own negative face may feel threatened because you simply don't want to be pleasant, or funny, or supportive toward your friend; you may even want to be free of the sense of obligation that the friendship implies. Leslie Baxter (1988) eloquently captures the dialectical nature of these competing forces:

> No relationship can exist by definition unless the parties sacrifice some individual autonomy. However, too much connection paradoxically destroys the relationship because the individual identities become lost (Askham, 1976). Simultaneously, an individual's autonomy can be conceptualized only in terms of separation from others. But too much autonomy paradoxically destroys the individual's identity, because connections with others are the "stuff" of which identity is made (Lock, 1986). (p. 259)

The dilemma of satisfying positive and negative face at the same time may seem like a no-win situation, but it is not. It is a matter of balancing the natural tension between being connected to someone and being independent. As we will discuss below, facework and politeness are communication mechanisms that allow us to manage this dilemma.

Facework

Facework is communication designed to counteract face threats to self and others (Goffman, 1967). On many occasions, face-threatening acts can be avoided or minimized before they occur through the use of preventive facework. On other occasions, face threats are not anticipated and the loss of face must be remediated through corrective facework. We will spend the next few pages discussing each of these types of facework. We then close this chapter with discussion of a third type

of facework unique to close relationships that is contained in a couple's personal idioms.

Preventive Facework. Avoiding face threat is often accomplished by such tactics as avoiding face-threatening topics, changing the subject of conversation when it appears to be moving in a face-threatening direction, and pretending not to notice when something face-threatening has been said or done. In addition, individuals employ linguistic devices such as "disclaimers" (Hewitt & Stokes, 1975) and "politeness" (Brown & Levinson, 1987) to minimize the negative implications that might be made about them when they know they are about to threaten someone's face.

Disclaimers are statements people use to minimize the negative attributions that might be ascribed to their motives or character because they are about to violate expectations for appropriate behavior. Hewitt and Stokes (1975) identify five types of disclaimers:

1. *hedging*: indicates uncertainty and receptivity to suggestions ("I may be wrong, but...")
2. *credentialing*: indicates that there are good reasons and appropriate qualifications for engaging in a sanctionable action ("I'm your husband; I have every right to read your mail.")
3. *sin license*: indicates that this is an acceptable occasion for rule violation and should not be taken as a character defect ("What the hell, this is a special occasion.")
4. *cognitive disclaimer*: indicates that the impending behavior is reasonable and under cognitive control, in spite of appearances ("I know this sounds crazy, but...")
5. *appeal for suspended judgment*: request to withhold judgment for a possibly offensive act until it has been fully explained ("Hear me out before you get upset.")

In essence, disclaimers are used by speakers to save their own face; they signal a message something like, "Please recognize that I am aware of social appropriateness and I ask your indulgence while I act inappropriately; I am not merely rude or stupid." Politeness strategies, on the other hand, are more directly focused on the face of the recipient of the threat. They signal a message something like, "Please recognize that I regard your face needs very highly and would not threaten them if it were not necessary to do so; I am not merely selfish and insensitive to your needs."

Politeness strategies allow people to walk a fine line between being totally indirect and possibly never getting their point across (e.g., "Gee, there's a great movie playing downtown tonight…hmm, well, hope you enjoy it."), and being unexpectedly blunt and direct (e.g., "Take me to the movie tonight because I want to see it"). Very intimate partners can be a bit more indirect than social acquaintances because they are attuned to each other's hints. And intimate partners can be a bit more direct than social acquaintances because they know that the relationship is based on mutual positive regard even when it is not demonstrated in one or two particular interactions. However, frequent and repeated disregard for each other's face may eventually lead a couple to feel the foundation of mutual regard in their relationship may be weakening.

Thus it is no accident that people have developed an elaborate system of politeness strategies to use when they want to reach a goal efficiently but do not want to appear insensitive to the face concerns of the other person. Brown and Levinson (1987) describe the general strategies of positive and negative politeness that are respectively directed toward the positive and negative face needs of the partner. Positive politeness expresses appreciation for the value of another person and expresses affiliation with that person. Positive politeness includes messages showing that the partner's desires are known and considered to be important, that he or she is viewed as a member of an in-group, a friend, or a valued other. For instance: "Hey buddy! You're really doin' great in calculus class. How 'bout sharing some of your talent with me?" Negative politeness offers assurances that the partner's freedom will not be unnecessarily curtailed and that he or she has options. These messages are characterized by self-effacement and formality, permitting the partner to feel that his or her response was not obligatory or coerced. For example: "John, I hate to bother you, but if you are not too busy, would it be possible to get a lift to campus?"

Corrective Facework. In an effort to repair face damage that has occurred because of a transgression, corrective facework is employed. Corrective behaviors may be defensively offered by the actor responsible for creating face threat, may be protectively offered by other people who witness the loss of face, or may be offered by the person who has lost face as he or she attempts to regain lost social identity.

The facts that facework can be performed by observers and participants, that it can be accepted or rejected, and that its effectiveness depends on the features of a particular situation underscore how challenging problematic events can be. The restoration of lost face and the smooth realignment of a disrupted episode are truly cooperative accomplishments. We describe below several types of strategies used during the remediation process.

Although we present them separately, it is important to remember that people often use several of them in various orderings as the process of restoring face unfolds (Cupach & Metts, 1990).

A large class of behaviors intended to contain or control the extent of damage to face is called avoidance. The principle underlying avoidance is that in some face-threatening situations, drawing explicit attention to the face threat may be counterproductive. If only one's own face has been modestly threatened but the face of others remains largely intact, then the benefit of saving one's own face might be at the expense of threatening the face of others (Cupach & Metts, 1990). Belaboring a minor infraction can create inconvenience for others and possibly induce them to feel embarrassment. Similarly, if an observer notes that one has committed an error, he or she may overlook it. People routinely gloss over their own and each other's mistakes when they are relatively minor. This is accomplished by acting as if face has not been threatened. Gracefully continuing with social interaction following a minor predicament demonstrates one's poise and minimizes the extent to which other people become embarrassed or annoyed. Of course, when abashment is intense, one may exhibit an extreme form of avoidance by physically fleeing the embarrassing or shameful encounter (Cupach, Metts, & Hazleton, 1986).

Humor is frequently a response to predicaments, partly because some predicaments are intended to be comical (such as teasing; Argyle, Furnham, & Graham, 1981; Knapp, Stafford, & Daly, 1986; Sharkey, 1991) and some are inherently funny in their consequences. Argyle et al. (1981) found, for example, that rule-breaking episodes are characterized by a fundamental underlying dimension ranging from humorous to irritating. Similarly, affective reactions to rule-breaking episodes are characterized by the dimension of laughter versus anger. If the face-threatening event involves a harmless accident or flub, then laughter allows the release of nervous tension and signals that the problematic circumstances need not be taken too seriously. Making a joke can show that the offending person acknowledges blameworthiness (as with a simple excuse or apology) and can also allow the person to demonstrate poise and social competence (Edelmann, 1985; Fink & Walker, 1977).

Apologies admit blame and seek atonement for untoward behavior (Goffman, 1967; Schlenker, 1980; Tedeschi & Riess, 1981). The form of an apology can range from a simple statement, such as "I'm sorry," to more elaborate forms including one or more of the following elements: (a) expression of regret or remorse, (b) requests for forgiveness, (c) self-castigation, (d) promises not to repeat the transgression in the future, and (e) offers of restitution (Goffman, 1971; Schlenker & Darby, 1981).

The nonverbal display of anxiety or discomfort can function much like an apology insofar as it demonstrates to others that the offending person acknowledges the impropriety of his or her own behavior. Merely appearing to be chagrined (by blushing or grimacing) can show one's self-effacement and thereby mitigate negative attributions that might be ascribed by observers (Castelfranchi & Poggi, 1990; Edelmann, 1982; Semin & Manstead, 1982).

Accounts are verbal explanations given to explain inappropriate or awkward behavior (Buttny, 1985, 1987; Scott & Lyman, 1968). Two general classes of accounts are excuses and justifications. Excuses attempt to minimize the actor's responsibility for an event ("I didn't mean it"; "I couldn't help it"; "It's not my fault"); justifications reframe an event by downplaying its negative implications ("It's not so bad"; "It's for your own good"). There are numerous varieties of excuses and justifications. Several authors have described a wide range of types of excuses and justifications (Schlenker, 1980; Schonbach, 1980, 1990; Scott & Lyman, 1968; Snyder, Higgins, & Stuckey, 1983; Tedeschi & Riess, 1981)....

Physical remediation involves behavioral (nonverbal) correction or repair of physical damage (if any has occurred) associated with a loss of face. This includes such acts as adjusting clothing (zipping up one's pants), cleaning up a spill, and fixing a broken toy (Metts & Cupach, 1989; Semin & Manstead, 1982; Sharkey & Stafford, 1990).

Most of the remedial facework strategies employed by a person creating face loss can also be utilized by observers on the person's behalf. Observers can offer physical assistance following a pratfall, and can make various types of positive comments to assist a face-threatened individual, including attribution of guilt or responsibility for the occurrence of the event to persons other than the embarrassed person, positive comments on the embarrassed person's conduct during the failure event (e.g., expressing understanding, appeasement, friendly advice), and positive comments on the embarrassed person's liability for the consequences of the failure event (exoneration, waiving of claims, pardon, compassion, offers of help) (Schonbach, 1990). Humor is also a common strategy, although it entails some risk, as the inferred line between laughing "with" the person and laughing "at" him or her can be blurry (Cupach & Metts, 1990). Similarly, attempts to avoid calling attention to an untoward act are expected, particularly for minor infractions. However, such inattention can exacerbate discomfort on some occasions. By not overtly attempting to repair the awkward encounter, individuals remain somewhat uncertain about whether or not they have demonstrated efforts commensurate with expectations to repair face.

Observers also have unique remedial responses at their disposal that can be particularly effective in diminishing the discomfort felt by the person who has lost face. In fact, one study found that observers were much more effective than transgressors in ameliorating the transgressor's embarrassment following a face-threatening predicament (see Cupach & Metts, 1990). In particular, observers can offer help by expressing empathy, communicating to the distressed person that his or her predicament is not unique or uncommon. They can also offer support through indications of positive regard in spite of the predicament. We found in one study that approximately half of all remedial responses offered by observers were such displays of empathy and support (Metts & Cupach, 1989b).

THE IMPORTANCE OF FACEWORK IN INTERPERSONAL RELATIONSHIPS

For several reasons, the management of face is particularly relevant to the formation and erosion of interpersonal relationships. First, the ability to manage one's own and others' face is fundamental to interpersonal competence (Cupach & Imahori, 1993a; Weinstein, 1969; Wiemann, 1977). In order for people to achieve their own goals, they must be able to establish and maintain desired identities for each other when they interact. Succinctly stated, getting ahead ordinarily entails getting along, which in turn necessitates sensitivity to the face needs of others. As Goffman (1967) suggests, in our society, the ability to engage in appropriate facework is tantamount to "tact, *savoir-faire*, diplomacy, or social skill" (p. 13).

Second, face support is identity confirming. Situational identities constitute important sources of rewards and costs for social actors (Weinstein, 1969). The importance of confirmation is magnified as the intimacy of the relationship between partners escalates. Indeed, Weinstein (1969) contends that "it is only in the most impersonal encounters that the situational identities of the parties are not a principal nexus of rewards and

costs. Often, they are precisely and completely that" (p. 757).

Third, effective facework fosters mutual respect and buttresses against contempt (see Penman, 1990). This supports the ritual order of social interactions, allowing encounters between people to be relatively smooth and enjoyable, rather than disruptive and distressing. Moreover, facework is integral to managing the challenges and dilemmas of relationships. At its best, effective face support permits us to achieve (however fleeting) relationship nirvana. At its worst, persistent face loss can create bitter enmity and personal agony.

REFERENCES

Argyle, M., Furnham, A., & Graham, J. A. (1981). *Social situations*. Cambridge, England: Cambridge University Press.

Baxter, L. A. (1988). A dialectical perspective on communication strategies in relationship development. In S. Duck (Ed.), *Handbook of personal relationships: Theory, research, interventions* (pp. 257–273). London, England: Wiley.

Brown, P., & Levinson, S. (1987). *Politeness: Some universals in language usage.* Cambridge, England: Cambridge University Press.

Buttny, R. (1985). Accounts as a reconstruction of an event's context. *Communication Monographs, 52,* 57–77.

Buttny, R. (1987). Sequence and practical reasoning in accounts episodes. *Communication Quarterly, 35,* 67–83.

Castelfranchi, C., & Poggi, I. (1990). Blushing as discourse: Was Darwin wrong? In W. W. Crozier (Ed.), *Shyness and embarrassment: Perspectives from social psychology* (pp. 230–251). Cambridge, England: Cambridge University Press.

Cupach, W. R., & Imahori, T. T. (1993). Identity management theory: Communication competence in intercultural episodes and relationships. In R. L. Wiseman & J. Koester (Eds.), *Intercultural communication competence* (pp. 112–131). Newbury Park, CA: Sage.

Cupach, W. R., & Metts, S. (1990). Remedial processes in embarrassing predicaments. In J. A. Anderson

(Ed.), *Communication Yearbook* 13 (pp. 323–352). Newbury Park, CA: Sage.

Cupach, W. R., Metts, S., & Hazleton, V. (1986). Coping with embarrassing predicaments: Remedial strategies and their perceived utility. *Journal of Language and Social Psychology, 5,* 181–200.

Edelmann, R. J. (1985). Social embarrassment: An analysis of the process. *Journal of Social and Personal Relationships, 2,* 195–213.

Edelmann, R. J. (1987). *The psychology of embarrassment.* Chichester, England: Wiley.

Fink, E. L., & Walker, B. A. (1977). Humorous responses to embarrassment. *Psychological Reports, 40,* 475–485.

Goffman, E. (1967). *Interaction ritual: Essays on face-to-face behavior.* New York, NY: Pantheon.

Goffman, E. (1971). *Relations in public.* New York, NY: Basic Books.

Hewitt, J., & Stokes, R. (1975). Disclaimers. *American Sociological Review, 40,* 1–11.

Knapp, M. L., Stafford, L., & Daly, J. (1986). Regrettable messages: Things people wish they hadn't said. *Journal of Communication, 36,* 40–58.

Lim, T. S., & Bowers, J. W. (1991). Facework: Solidarity, approbation, and tact. *Human Communication Research, 17,* 415–450.

Lock, A. J. (1986). The role of relationships in development: An introduction to a series of occasional articles. *Journal of Social and Personal Relationships, 3,* 89–100.

Metts, S., & Cupach, W. R. (1989. Situational influence on the use of remedial strategies in embarrassing predicament. *Communication Monographs, 56,* 151–162.

Penman, R. (1990). Facework and politeness: Multiple goals in courtroom discourse. *Journal of Language and Social Psychology, 9,* 15–38.

Schlenker, B. R. (1980). *Impression management: The self-concept, social identity, and interpersonal relations.* Monterey, CA: Brooks/Cole.

Schlenker, B. R., & Darby, B. W. (1981). The use of apologies in social predicaments. *Social Psychology Quarterly, 44,* 271–278.

Schonbach, P. (1980). A category system for accounts please. *European Journal of Social Psychology, 10,* 195–200.

Schonbach, P. (1990). *Account episodes: The management or escalation of conflict.* Cambridge, England: Cambridge University Press.

Scott, M. B., & Lyman, S. M. (1968). Accounts. *American Sociological Review, 33,* 46–62.

Semin, G. R., & Manstead, A. S. R. (1982). The social implications of embarrassment displays and restitution behavior. *European Journal of Social Psychology, 12,* 367–377.

Semin, G. R., & Manstead, A. S. R. (1983). *The accountability of conduct: A social psychological analysis.* London, England: Academic Press.

Sharkey, W. F. (1991). Intentional embarrassment: Goals, tactics, and consequences. In W. R. Cupach & S. Metts (Eds.), *Advances in interpersonal communication research* (Proceedings of the Western Speech Communication Association Interpersonal Communication Interest Group) (pp. 105–128). Normal: Illinois State University, Personal Relationships Research Group.

Sharkey, W. F., & Stafford, L. (1988, November). *I've never been so embarrassed: Degree of embarrassment and its effect upon communicative responses.* Paper presented at the annual meeting of the Speech Communication Association, New Orleans, LA.

Synder, C. R., Higgins, R. L., & Stuckey, R. J. (1983). *Excuses: Masquerades in search of grace.* New York, NY: Wiley.

Tedeschi, J., & Riess, M. (1981). Verbal strategies in impression management. In C. Antaki (Ed.), *The psychology of ordinary explanations of social behavior* (pp. 271–309). New York, NY: Academic Press.

Tracy, K. (1990). The many faces of facework. In H. Giles & W. P. Robinson (Eds.), *Handbook of language and social psychology* (pp. 209–226). New York, NY: Wiley.

Weinstein, E. A. (1969). The development of interpersonal competence. In D. A. Goslin (Ed.), *Handbook of socialization theory and research* (pp. 753–775). Chicago, IL: Rand McNally.

Wiemann, J. M. (1977). Explication and test of a model of communicative competence. *Human Communication Research, 3,* 195–213.

QUESTIONS/THOUGHTS

1. Consider a relationship in which you are very conscious of personally engaging in facework. How would you characterizes this relationship? What are examples of the effects of you facework efforts?

2. Describe a relationship in which you do not experience a strong need to manage your face. Do you believe the other person engages in facework with you? How would you characterize the communication that takes place in this relationship?

3. Describe an example of corrective facework that you found memorable. How did the person who stood to lose face try to manage the situation and maintain his or her face?

4. How is facework managed online in Facebook or on MySpace? Describe three strategies you have observed or used.

Adapted from William R. Cupach and Sandra Metts, "Face Management in Interpersonal Communication." In *Facework*, pp. 1–16. Copyright © 1994 by Sage Publications.

Belly Button Fuzz and a Wicky-Wacky Cake: Rituals in Our Personal Relationships

CAROL J. BRUESS

Rituals serve as a powerful way to bond individuals in developing or establishing relationships. Although generations of scholars in varied fields have studied rituals, only recently have communication scholars turned their attention to the role of rituals in sustaining and deepening interpersonal relationships. Most people think of rituals as major ceremonial acts or events such as weddings, birthdays, or holiday celebrations. Such a view is correct but narrow. Another way to conceptualize rituals is to see them as customary, repeated acts that are commonplace. Therefore, patterned greetings or partings, ways of expressing affection, and unique conversational expressions may be considered rituals. Such acts serve as the focus for communication scholars. This approach is in keeping with Duck's (1994) call for a focus on everyday or mundane interactions, Baxter's (1987) suggestion that communication rituals are linked to the development of relational cultures and Gottman's (1999) assertion that rituals are one of the primary ways couples develop shared meanings.

The nature of rituals varies across contexts—family, friendship—and in terms of intensity of meaning. For example, in their extensive exploration of family rituals, Leslie Baxter and Dawn Braithwaite (2006) define a family ritual as a voluntary, recurring, patterned communication event whose jointly enacted performance by family members pays homage to what they regard as sacred, thereby producing and reproducing a family's identity and its web of social relations. Some family rituals may appear less than "sacred" in their nature but, if tampered with or changed, may result in great discontent among family members. Likewise, some friendship rituals may feel sacred because they reaffirm very powerful ties over and over again.

In the following piece, Carol Bruess presents her perspective on the role of rituals within interpersonal relationships, including friendships and romantic pairs. Beginning with a description of a ritual from her childhood, the author depicts the importance of rituals in relationships. She defines relational rituals, discusses ritual types and addresses the roles rituals play in our lives. She stresses the commonplace and everyday aspect of rituals which may be taken for granted but which serve an important function in sustaining interpersonal relationships. As you read this chapter *consider the question: How would you explain the link between relational rituals and relational currencies?*

REFERENCES

Baxter, L. (1987). Symbols of relationship identity in relationship cultures. *Journal of Social and Personal Relationships, 4,* 261–280.

Baxter, L. A., & Braithwaite, D. O. (2006). Family rituals. In L. H. Turner & R. West (Eds.), *The family communication sourcebook* (pp. 259–280). Thousand Oaks, CA: Sage.

Duck, S. (1994). Steady as (s)he goes: Relational maintenance as a shared meaning system. In D. Canary & L. Stafford (Eds.), *Communication and relational maintenance.* New York, NY: Academic Press.

Gottman, J. M., & Silver, N. (1999). *The seven principles for making marriage work.* New York, NY: Three Rivers Press.

INTRODUCTION: ME AND RITUAL

My name is Carol Bruess (last name rhymes with "peace"). I teach communication studies and direct a family studies program at a small Catholic University in St. Paul, MN just 172 steps from the home I share with my partner/husband Brian, our two kids, and our ferocious (not really) five-pound dog Fred. About 14 years ago I earned my Ph.D. in Interpersonal Communication and have enjoyed every single second since then teaching undergraduates, like you, about relationships and the communication that makes them good, bad, beautiful, ugly, and everything in between.

All of this personal disclosure might seem an unusual way to begin a book chapter. Yet, I think it's important to remind you that research, like that which you have been reading about in this book, is conducted by average and curious people, not too different from yourself. My research, for instance, is about something I have experienced in my own marriage of seventeen years and in my family of origin. As one of my colleagues often says, research is "me search;" we often study what we experience or want to know more about personally. I'll admit I do. I study the kinds of interactions that I've

enjoyed for decades with my life-long friend Sarah and my BFF Molly. And those I cherish in my marriage. And those I share with my kids.

The studies I'm about to summarize also reflect something I simply find fascinating: how communication in our marriages, families, and friendships helps us create a "relationship culture" in which we develop our own language, symbols, jokes, patterns of talking, and ways of behaving and thinking. In essence, our relational cultures are reflected in our daily routines and rituals. So in the next few pages, let's explore, specifically, the way both celebratory and mundane rituals shape our interpersonal relationships.

When I was growing up, my entire family (mom, dad, sister Lynn and brother Greg, both older than me) would hop in the family station wagon shortly after church on Sunday and make the few-mile journey out to my grandparents' farm. Without fail the day was delightfully predictable; the memories, etched vividly in my mind, are so clear I can almost see them in my brain—like watching a familiar movie over and over again—nearly four decades later. Here's how a typical Sunday unfolded in our simple lives:

> *Our slightly rusted brown Chevy station wagon would wind its way, my dad behind the wheel, through the quiet rural roads of Southern Wisconsin. The trip, although brief now when I make the trek today in our more modern family wagon, seemed painfully long as I bounced along in the backseat next to my brother and sister. We each would fidget with anticipation. As we scaled the last big hill, we took a collective deep breath, hoping to be the first to spot the shiny top of the silo sitting adjacent to Grandpa's bright red barn.*
>
> *The farm was a place of great adventure for kids. My three cousins lived on the adjoining farm, less than a mile down the road. They inevitably and annoyingly would arrive first, greeting us in the yard or on Grandma's sofa. Without missing a second we joined together in a large group for an afternoon of exploring the woods, climbing the hay loft, or skipping rocks across the pond; of following the muddy cow trails or digging in Grandma's attic, sewing bench and closets for unknown treasures*

like dolls and hats and buttons and beads. In warm weather we'd play "PIG" and "HORSE" on the hand-painted court, basketball hoop attached to the side of the big red barn. Our uncle Bill would teach us how to properly feed calves, wash cars and tractors, water tomato plants, and clear cross-country ski trails for the fast-approaching winter. When winter did arrive, the back of our wagon was packed with ice skates, wool mittens, and metal saucer sleds. For much of those snowy afternoons we would slide down the massive hill (which now seems unusually small when I stand atop it telling stories of my childhood to my own somewhat unimpressed children), ski through the pine trees (trading boots and skis each time around so the next kid could give it a try) and ice skate on the pond if the weather that year had gifted us a smooth and glassy finish. When our feet were frozen and our noses red and runny, we would each—usually in pairs—trek back up to Grandma's kitchen table where a steaming mug of hot cocoa awaited us. Each cup was, of course, overflowing with mini-marshmallows; Grandma never limited our intake of those fluffy bits of goodness.

Then, winter or summer—it didn't matter the season—we would all convene (3 cousins, 3 uncles/aunts, grandma, grandpa, and our family of 5) in grandma's kitchen for a familiar feast: barbeque—known in many regions as "sloppy joes"—on white burger buns next to Pringles chips and a few peanut butter sandwiches (made for for my youngest cousin Jeff who did not care for the offered meal) and lemonade. For dessert we devoured ice cream with a dash of chocolate syrup and splash of milk, and Grandma's homemade chocolate chip cookies. No one makes cookies quite like Grandma's. Maybe it was her signature mini-chocolate chips?

By about 6 p.m., as 60 Minutes appeared on television and while my mother and aunts helped Grandma wash the dishes, my grandparents were happily ready for all of us to go home. And we did. Every Sunday. Without question. That was our ritual.

YOU AND RITUAL

I'll bet everyone reading this chapter could tell a similar story about a ritual in your family. Maybe it wasn't a weekly ritual. Maybe it was a dinnertime ritual, one that your family shared at the holidays, or at a certain time of year (Summer camping? Fall pumpkin gathering? First snow fall?). Maybe it was a bedtime ritual or Saturday morning breakfast ritual. Whatever its shape, form, or frequency, your rituals played and continue to play very important roles in your relationships. You likely know—intuitively or instinctually—that rituals are important. Or maybe someone in your family has stated explicitly the importance of sustaining a cherished family gathering. But the purpose of this chapter is to explain exactly how important rituals are, what they look like in our relationships, and the many roles rituals play in our lives and relationships.

The goal is to raise your awareness about this very important aspect of interpersonal communication, a kind of daily interaction we often take for granted. To do so, I'd like to share the results of my own research on rituals, conducted by interviewing and surveying married couples about the rituals in their relationships, and about the rituals they shared with their friends. I think you'll find the stories of these people funny and interesting. I anticipate you'll also find a slightly new understanding of the term "ritual" as well as how they function in your relationships. As author Robert Fulghum (1995, p. 113) smartly states:

> *Nobody lives without rituals. Rituals do not live without somebody.*

Rituals, indeed, are valuable dynamics in relationships. We all have them. And we need them. Without them, we would be alone, or at least lonely. With and through them, we develop and maintain relationships, including our families, partnerships, and friendships. Rituals serve so many positive functions you'll find an entire section below outlining their many roles in our relationships. It might seem that their utility is quite obvious, or just common sense. But in fact researchers haven't been studying rituals in relationships for all that long and are just starting to understand the intricate, delicate, and powerful ways rituals play central roles in our relationships. Originally the topic of rituals was that of anthropologists, particularly those interested in religious rituals (Durkheim, 1965). The study of ritual often focused on—and thus the term often connoted—magic, myth, taboo, or other mystical practices (Bossard & Boll, 1950). However, research by family and relationship scholars have helped reveal the common and essential place of rituals in our personal relationships, especially family and friendships (Bossard & Boll, 1950; Fiese, 2006; Wolin & Bennett, 1984). But what exactly is a ritual?

WHAT ARE RITUALS? DEFINING THE CONCEPT

On the surface, ritual seems like an easily understood concept. As two prominent ritual researchers note: "Ritual itself is an elusive concept, on the one hand transparent and conspicuous in its enactment, on the other, subtle and mysterious in its boundaries and effects on participants" (Wolin & Bennett, 1984, p. 401). Some scholars define rituals as repetitive, symbolic behaviors or practices shared by members of a relationship (Allen, 1993; Wolin & Bennett, 1984). Others distinguish between rituals and more mundane repetitious patterns of interaction. For instance, Wise (1986) believes *routines* are activities or behaviors predictably enacted by family members; *rituals* are routines that have symbolic meaning. For example, routines in this instance would be characterized by their functional aspect, such as eating breakfast, washing the dishes every evening, or taking weekly trips to the grocery store. Rituals would have significance beyond the activity itself, such as dining out on Friday evenings without the children, baking someone's favorite cake every year for her birthday, meeting friends for coffee on Saturday mornings at a local restaurant, or taking summer family vacations. However, Wise (1986) notes that any routine behavioral pattern, (i.e., eating) can become a ritual when the routine is viewed by the participants as somehow relationally or symbolically significant (i.e., when dinner time is not simply for feeding, but is cherished as a time to talk with children and to share the day's events). According to Goffman (1967), rituals are

communicative enactments that pay homage to a person or object which is sacred.

Goffman's (1967) definition is the one I use in my own study of rituals. I find it useful because it acknowledges that rituals are "symbolically" significant; no ritual is special until it is ascribed meaning or value—even implicitly—by the relationship members. For instance, is taking your friend out to lunch for her birthday a ritual? It depends. Does the lunch have value for you and your friend? Does it symbolize something about your relationship? Because the lunch has been taking place for 15 years and you have accorded it meaning in its long history, the lunch ritual probably pays homage to—symbolically reinforces the importance of—something unique to the character of your friendship. To another set of friends, a birthday lunch might be a one-time event that while indeed important, is probably not yet "ritual." As you can start to see, the question of what counts as ritual is not entirely a clear one. But the nature of symbolic significance and repetition are key concepts to keep in mind when defining ritual.

WILL I KNOW ONE IF I SEE ONE? TYPES OF RITUALS

At this point in the chapter I hope you are already beginning to think of the rituals in your own relationships. When I first started my own research on ritual I had a hunch that people in relationships—particularly marriages and friendships, because these relationships are often our most intimate—had a variety of rituals. I guessed they ranged in form and type from the daily to the annual to the periodic. What I didn't realize, however, is just how many or how diverse (and how amusing) they would be. I could not have predicted that people would tell me about their belly button fuzz, their butt-cheek kisses, or their exchanges of flamingo lawn art with neighbors. It seems there were rituals for every occasion, big and small.

Early research on ritual revealed some ritual types. Wolin and Bennett (1984), for instance, suggested that family rituals come in three varieties: celebrations, traditions, and patterned family interactions. Family celebrations are family rituals created and enacted in conjunction with more standardized culture celebration such as holidays or rites of passage. Included would be Thanksgiving, New Year's Eve, weddings, funerals, and bar mitzvahs. Family traditions are more idiosyncratic to each family and less culturally influenced. Annual family vacations, family reunions, customary birthday celebrations, family meetings, and visits to extended family members are a few common examples of family traditions. Often, family traditions are created to serve a special family need or solve problems (i.e., family meetings) (Wolin & Bennett). Of the three types of family rituals, patterned family interactions are "the least deliberate and the most covert" (Wolin & Bennett, p. 406). Such are the rituals that organize daily life; often they are mundane daily routines that involve little conscious planning. Dinnertime, bedtimes, general evening or morning routines, and other patterned family rules for interaction (i.e., seats at the table) are examples. Wolin and Bennett note that patterned interactions are often not recognized as ritualistic because of their mundane and routine nature.

In my own research (see Bruess & Pearson, 1997, 2002) of married couples and of friendship rituals, individuals and couples reported ritualizing many aspects of their daily married lives, everything from sharing romance to sharing household tasks to sharing annual outings and get togethers. I was primarily interested in two questions: What kinds of rituals did married couples have? And what purpose did they serve? I'll answer the first of these questions here. The second question is answered in a later section of this chapter (What Good Are They?).

To find answers I set out to interview and/or survey 99 married couples (25 were interviewed, the rest were sent open-ended surveys), asking them to tell me about rituals in their marriages. I also asked each spouse to tell me about the rituals in their separate (and/or joint) friendships. The couples I studied were mostly from the Midwest and were married an average of 19 years, anywhere from married just one month to married over 53 years. The average age of participants was 49. The 25 interviews I conducted lasted between 20

minutes to 4 ½ hours. The biggest news was that the 198 individuals in the study reported over 1000 different types of rituals in their marriages and friendships!

To help make sense of all the ritual examples, I grouped similar rituals into categories. For married couples, rituals ended up grouping into seven distinct types or categories: 1) Enjoyable Activities, Togetherness Rituals, and Escape Episodes, 2) Favorites, Private Codes, and Play Rituals, and Celebration Rituals, 3) Daily Routines and Tasks, 4) Intimacy Expressions, 5) Communication Rituals, 6) Patterns/Habits/Mannerisms, and 7) Spiritual Rituals.

One woman, for example, explained a ritual in the category "Favorites." She described the long-standing ritual in her marriage which clearly pays homage to her husband via one of his favorite treats:

> His favorite cake is wicky-wacky chocolate. It's a chocolate-out-of-scratch cake, an old family recipe.... So when I really, really, really, really, like him, and he's really, really, really, really, made me happy, I bake him a wicky-wacky cake. He knows I'm really happy with him when he gets a wicky-wacky cake.

Another couple shared details of their Play rituals called "A Game of Elephants" which includes two players: "Marco" (husband) and "Simba" (wife), and involves "quick trunk movements made with the arms accompanied by appropriate elephant noises." They reveal: "[it] is used to indicate private playfulness."

Samples of other couple rituals include the married couples who developed "Private Code Rituals." One couple reported ritualistically saying to each other "Honey, you make me hotter than Georgia asphalt," a line from a movie they saw together. Another couple explained their idiomatic ritual for indicating how they are feeling about one another on any given day:

> ...Whoever goes in and brushes their teeth first always puts toothpaste on the other's toothbrush.... If we're upset with one another we might set the tube next to the brush, not put paste on it. This is sort of a sign of "how ya feeling today about one another?"

Couples reported many creative, playful rituals. An example is this couple's ritual:

> I would check my husband's belly button for fuzz on a daily basis at bedtime. It originated when I noticed some blanket fuzz in his belly button one day and though it was funny....We both found it funny and teased often about the fuzz. If there wasn't any fuzz for a few days my husband would put some in his belly button for me to find. It's been happening for about 10 years now.

Idiomatic games and contests were also ritualized by couples, exemplified by the couple that created a game called the "Happy Anniversary Contest":

> We were married on the 26th day of May. We have a monthly contest to see who says "Happy Anniversary" first on the 26th day of every month. Rules are: no waking spouse, said anytime after midnight, and must be person to person (in other words no written messages or answering machine messages). This originated the first month after we were married. It is on going since 1968 (305 months), we never missed a month, and we don't keep score.

Not all rituals were necessarily as playful or fun, yet were equally important. For instance, many couples reported celebration rituals for holidays, birthdays, or anniversaries. Often the rituals were simple yet important in their symbolic value, paying homage to the relationship's history or to relational members. For instance, one couple reported a ritual for celebrating their relationship by returning to the same restaurant where they shared their first date. Other rituals included those of daily tasks and routines, revealed by the couple who explained: "usually one washes and one dries the dishes." These are just a few of the hundreds of examples married couples reported when asked to share their rituals.

What I also discovered by talking to couples is that rituals play a central role in their friendships, too. People reported sharing rituals with most of their friends and around a number of activities, everything from annual celebrations to daily phone calls. Similar to the marriage categories, six types of friendship rituals emerged

in our study, including: 1) Enjoyable Activities, Getting Together Rituals, Established Events, Escape Episodes, 2) Celebration Rituals, Play Rituals, Favorites, 3) Communication Rituals, 4) Share/Support/Vent Rituals, 5) Tasks/Favors, and 6) Patterns/Habits/Mannerisms.

Regular phone calls were common among friends, representing what were categorized as Communication Rituals. A good example is the monthly calling ritual one woman reported she and her friend have maintained "for 21 years and over five continents." They call one another every month, and have done this for over two decades and as they have each moved around the world. Many college aged friends report texting rituals including private phrases or characters that have meaning just between the friends (a cute boy walks by and you send your friend a text that simply states "cb.")

Rituals among friends in my studies were often mundane and even spontaneous, as in the Getting-Together ritual explained by one male. He simply shares a ritual of regularly "having a beer with my neighbor." Others represented rituals of shared activities, such as the female who reported her ritual of meeting with friends once a month for a "Stitch and Bitch Club" where "we learn crafts, work on some holiday gifts, visit, and have dessert." Many friends, especially those who work and have children, develop annual rituals that pay homage to their shared interests. One man explained a ritual developed among some of his buddies. They call the event "Tough-Guys' Night Out." Once a year during the Golden Gloves Boxing Match the men in this group enjoy a steak dinner, cigars, and watch the boxing match together.

Similar to the marriage rituals, some friendship rituals were playful, silly, and/or represented "inside jokes" or private codes. Illustrative is the ritual shared among the couple-friends in one neighborhood: "We have a collection of flamingo lawn art that we put in the neighbors' yard when they least expect it. Then eventually the items return!" They talked about this on-going game as a ritual lasting many years and providing a playfulness promoting the group's closeness as friends.

The examples and stories of rituals reported by people in these studies are endless. The point in sharing them is that rituals take a variety of forms. Our studies (Bruess & Pearson, 1997, 2002) attempted to further sort out some of the questions about ritual forms and functions. Recall, the two questions that guided our research were 1) What kinds of rituals did they (friends and couples) have? And 2) what purpose or function do they serve? We'll explore the second question next.

WHAT GOOD ARE THEY? THE ROLE OF RITUALS

Based on just the few examples above, it's not hard to imagine why rituals are important in relationships. It's probably obvious that rituals provide chances to connect or be together, foster a sense of "we-ness," or a private culture between relationship members, and often provide opportunities for fun and play. All true. But that's not all. Based on years of research, we know rituals serve a whole host of functions in our relationships, some which might surprise you.

For instance, rituals play an essential role in the positive development of individuals and families (Baxter & Braithwaite, 2006; Fiese, Tomcho, Douglas, Josephs, Poltrock, & Baker, 2002). Especially in the early years of marriage, repetitive symbolic actions affirm and establish commitment among partners (Weigel, 2003) and help maintain most types of relationships over time (Bruess & Pearson, 1997, 2002; Fiese, et al., 2002; Homer, Freeman, Zabriskie, & Eggett, 2007). In fact, a lack of patterned interactions might actually signal relational dissatisfaction (Aylor & Dainton, 2004).

In families, rituals help create intergenerational bonds and preserve a sense of meaningfulness (Schvaneveldt & Lee, 1983). They transmit family values, attitudes and beliefs (Bossard & Boll, 1950), are related to family strength (Meredith et al., 1989), provide members with a sense of belonging (Wolin, Bennett, Noonan, & Teitelbaum, 1980), serve to bond and promote closeness (Meredith, 1985), help families maintain and perpetuate a paradigm or shared belief systems (Reiss, 1982), create and maintain family cohesion (Wolin & Bennett,

1984), and provide means for maintaining family contact (Meredith, 1985). They even protect alcoholic families from the generational recurrence of alcoholism (Wolin et al., 1980) and facilitate the general health and well-being of members (Compan, Moreno, Ruiz, & Pascual, 2002).

Bossard and Boll (1950) best capture the importance of family rituals:

Just as those religions with the most elaborate and pervasive rituals best retain the allegiance of their members, so families that do things together prove to be the most stable ones. (foreword)

We also know that the importance of ritual extends beyond the family. Rituals are important in all kinds of our interpersonal relationships. In friendship, for instance, rituals help develop a shared understanding of what is important in the friendship and provide a shared history (Oring, 1984). Baxter (1987) found that rituals among friends provide fun and stimulation, opportunities for sharing, and express closeness or intimacy.

In all relationships, rituals play a role in sustaining and maintaining them. In the 1950s, classic ritual researchers Bossard and Boll made the poignant suggestion that ritual is "the core of family culture." Most research since that time has verified that rituals, indeed, are central to relational cultures in all types of relationships, functioning to transmits relational goals, attitudes, and values.

In my own research on marriage and friendship rituals, the multivocal and multilayered meanings of rituals were evident. Interviews revealed rich insights into the many ways rituals contribute to both personal and relational well-being. In the words of one couple: "A relationship needs rituals and routines to function properly. In this day and age with our fast-moving society, rituals are the one constant." In marriages, rituals appear to function as masons, building and cementing the marriage, in the management of everyday life, and in providing enjoyment and fun, togetherness, and communication among partners. Rituals among adult friends function in the maintenance and affirmation of the friendship, and as important events of personal support and self-affirmation, as well as means of personal-improvement and escape.

Specifically, I discovered that rituals in marriage function as *Relational Masonry*, or in the building and cementing of a bond, commitment, and a sense of security in marriage. Couples reported how rituals "reinforce our love and commitment," "help us build a solid relationship," and "bond a couple together." Rituals also function in *Relational Maintenance*, contributing to marital satisfaction and representing the core of the relationship culture. As one couple said: "Sometimes I think they (rituals) are what makes our marriage work and what makes us special." Another individual succinctly observed: "Rituals are the foundation of a marriage."

The third ritual function discovered by talking with the married couples was *Life Management*; rituals make married life easier, provide organization, and define roles in marriage. Couples noted how rituals: "...provide a sense of control over the random happenings of the week," and "...simply make life easier." One couple noted: "Rituals serve as a clock for our inner lives; they give us a rhythm." Rituals also function as *Fun/Enjoyment*, providing stress-relief, enjoyment, and recreation. As one couple said: "It's communication that builds a relationship, but the rituals which add the spice." Rituals also provide *Togetherness*, bringing couples closer together and providing shared time together. In the words of one couple: "They provide us with structured time together." Couples reported that rituals also function simply as providing time to communicate, or as *Talk-Time*.

A very small number of couples reported the potentially negative aspect of rituals, such as "making our lives too boring" or "allowing us to be lazy about our relationship." The few negative indications of rituals might be a factor of the positive connotations of the term ritual as it is used in most research and practice. As one couple in our study observed: "I think the rituals in my life are positive. If they weren't, I'd probably call them bad habits." Negative associations with ritual might also indicate the changing needs or desires of individual relational members (Kudak, Pearson, & Bruess, 2009) which could be remedied by adapting the ritual to meet new life stages.

Similar to marriage, friendship rituals also serve multiple functions, both personal and relational. We uncovered seven different functions from the hundreds of ritual functions reported by participants about their friendships. First, friendship rituals play a role in *Personal & Relational Stimulation*. For instance, rituals stimulate and maintain friendships by fostering loyalty and keeping friends in touch, and provide stimulation for relational members in the form of fun, humor, and "something to look forward to." Friends observed: "without the ritual there is a sense of loss," "without them we wouldn't be as good of friends," "rituals establish a reliable-ness in your friends and a certain amount of trust," and "they (rituals) provide a sense of security, something to count on and look forward to." According to one woman, and not unlike the comments of many others, sharing rituals "...has simply made the friendship stronger."

According to the participants in our study, rituals among friends also provide opportunities for *Personal-Improvement*, or as arenas of personal enhancement in such forms as time management, spiritual and skill development, and networking. For instance, individuals reported that rituals shared between friends helped them "grow as a person," and "learn new skills," and that rituals provided needed "relaxation, both mentally and emotionally." One man observed how certain of his friendship rituals "build me spiritually." Others found that rituals function in networking; "our rituals provide times for meeting new people, and just networking in the community."

Relational Affirmation was another reported function of friendship rituals; rituals reinforce and/or reaffirm the exigencies of friendship such as trust, common interests, and shared experiences. Friends reported how "rituals seem to start friendships and kept them going," "with rituals, you know who your real friends are," "rituals give you something common forever," and "rituals seem to serve as anchors during the ups and downs of friendship." Rituals also "create a history" in many friendships. For one woman, "rituals are reminders of where you began, or what you've shared." According to another, "rituals kept our friendship alive."

Support was yet another function of friendship rituals; rituals appear to offer opportunities for receiving and giving support and advice from friends. Friends observed that their rituals "help us realize we're not alone," "provide emotional support," and "provide physical, financial and spiritual support." As one woman reported, "rituals give me the opportunity to sort out my thoughts." In the words of another, "I need them just to get through my weeks."

Another function of friendship rituals was *Self-Affirmation*; friendship rituals are opportunities for individuals, and their ideas, to be supported. Rituals are often therapeutic, allowing friends to share ideas and compare thoughts. One man reported how certain rituals serve as "a kind of therapy session." Another reported that rituals in friendship serve as "a means of finding people with the same ideas and attitudes." One woman observed: "I like my rituals of talk with other women; it makes me realize I'm not the only one who has problems."

Friendship rituals also appear to function as *Escape*, providing freedom and privacy from spouses, family, work and/or the pressures of life. One woman reports of her friendship rituals: "they provide my own sort of independence." Others reported how their rituals "give us a break from the kids," "give you an outlet from the family," and are simply "an escape…a time for not dealing with family anything during those moments."

Friendship rituals, like family and couple rituals, are diverse in form and function. They are centralizing forces and serve individuals and their friendships in many important ways. According to Duck (1992), a relationship researcher, "taken-for-granted routines build in ways that we do not always realize until they are removed. Their loss takes away unspoken and unrealized parts of ourselves," (p. 86), and probably our relationships too. The contribution of rituals to our personal lives, as well as our relationships, is significant.

CONCLUSION
Hopefully, while reading, you have begun reflecting on some of the rituals in your own relationships and have started a new appreciation for the value they have both for you personally, and for the health and well-being of your relationships. As researchers, we have only just started to fully understand the dynamics and nature of rituals in our personal relationships. The inherent paradoxes of ritual—as both predictable yet dynamic, individual yet coordinated, as both new yet familiar, as both created from, and expressive of, communication in relationships—make them inherently interesting questions about interpersonal interactions and relationships. I hope that you will begin to ask questions—of yourself and/or of your class members—about rituals and relationships. You might start by wondering about their power as a central force in many of our relationships. One of the interesting things about ritual and its study is that rituals are both incredibly visible, yet almost invisible, relational dynamics; members often take them for granted to the point of not recognizing them. They are so tightly woven into the tapestry of everyday living and relational management they are what we might call subtly pervasive. Whatever they are, you have them. Hopefully, this chapter has helped you further understand them.

*For more extensive reports on this research, see Bruess and Pearson (1997; 2002).

REFERENCES
Allen, J. (1993, February). The incredible healing power of family rituals. *McCalls, 120*, 68.

Aylor, B., & Dainton, M. (2004). Biological sex and psychological gender as predictors of routine and strategic relational maintenance. *Sex Roles, 50,* 689–697.

Baxter, L. A. (1987). Symbols of relationship identity in relationship cultures. *Journal of Social and Personal Relationships, 4,* 261–280.

Baxter, L. A., & Braithwaite, D. O. (2006). Family rituals. In L. Turner & R. West (Eds.), *The family communication sourcebook* (pp. 259–280). Thousand Oaks, CA: Sage.

Bossard, J. H. S., & Boll, E. S. (1950). Ritual in family living. *American Sociological Review, 14,* 463–469.

Bruess, C. J., & Pearson J. C. (1997). Interpersonal rituals in marriage and adult friendship. *Communication Monographs, 64*, 25–46.

Bruess, C. J., & Pearson, J. C. (2002). The function of mundane ritualizing in adult friendship and marriage. *Communication Research Reports, 19*, 314–326.

Compan, E., Moreno, J., Ruiz, M. T., & Pascual, E. (2002). Doing things together: Adolescent health and family rituals. *Journal of Epidemiology & Community Health, 56*, 89–94.

Duck, S. (1992). *Human relationships* (2nd ed.). London, England: Sage.

Durkheim, E. (1965). *The elementary forms of religious life*. New York, NY: Free Press.

Fiese, B. H. (2006). *Family routines and rituals*. New Haven, CT: Yale University Press.

Fiese, B. H., Tomcho, T., Douglas, M., Josephs, K., Poltrock, S., & Baker, T. (2002). A review of 50 years of research on naturally occurring routines and rituals: Cause for celebration? *Journal of Family Psychology, 16*, 381–390.

Fulghum, R. (1995). *The rituals of our lives: From Beginning to End*. New York, NY: Villard.

Goffman, E. (1967). *Interaction ritual: Essays on face-to-face behavior*. Garden City, NY: Anchor.

Homer, M. M., Freeman, P. A., Zabriskie, R. B., & Eggett, D. L. (2007). Rituals and relationships: Examining the relationship between family of origin rituals and young adult attachment. *Marriage and Family Review, 42*, 5–28.

Kudak, A. D. H., Pearson, J. C., & Bruess, C. J. (2009). Belly Button Fuzz and a Wicky-Wacky Cake: Rituals in Our Personal Relationships.Submitted for publication.

Meredith, W. H. (1985). The importance of family traditions. *Wellness Perspectives, 2*, 17–19.

Meredith, W.H., Abbott, D., Lamanna, M., & Sanders, G. (1989). Rituals and family strengths. *Family Perspectives, 23*, 75–83.

Oring, E. (1984). Dyadic traditions. *Journal of Folklore Research, 21*, 19–28.

Reiss, D. (1982). The working family. A researcher's view of health in the household. *American Journal of Psychiatry, 139*, 1412–1428.

Schvaneveldt, J. D., & Lee, T. R. (1983). The emergence and practice of ritual in the American family. *Family Perspective, 17*, 137–143.

Weigel, D. J. (2003). A communication approach to the construction of commitment in the early years of marriage: A qualitative study. *Journal of Family Communication, 3*, 1–19.

Wise, G. (1986). Family routines, rituals, and traditions: Grist for the family mill and buffers against stress. In S. Van Zandt (Ed.), *Family strengths: Vol. 7. Vital connections* (pp. 32–41). Lincoln, NE: Center for Family Strengths.

Wolin, S. J., & Bennett, L. A. (1984). Family rituals. *Family Process, 23*, 401–420.

Wolin S,J,, Bennett, L.A., Noonan, D.L., & Teitelbaum, M.A. (1980). Disrupted family rituals: A factor in the intergenerational transmission of alcoholism. *Journal of Studies in Alcohol, 41*, 99–214.

QUESTIONS/THOUGHTS

1. Describe two communication rituals you have developed in a friendship or romantic relationship that are unique to that relationship and have helped to deepen the relational culture you share. Note the type and function of each ritual in your answer.

2. Over time certain rituals change or disappear because they no longer seem to meet the needs of the relationship. Under what circumstances have your friendship rituals changed over the past five years and what has been the effect of the change? Give specific examples.

3. Although Bruess' research primarily uncovered rituals which could be considered positive or neutral, what negative rituals have you seen in a relationship with which you are familiar? (These might include unpleasant teasing, name-calling, or negative physical contact.)

4. To what extent do you believe persons in close relationships should consciously attempt to create rituals? What might be the pros and cons of such a practice?

The What, When, Who, and Why of Nagging in Interpersonal Relationships

KARI P. SOULE

A particular communication ritual occurs in many relationships, creating responses ranging from humor to exasperation to anger. That interpersonal ritual is nagging. Yet, the term nagging seldom appears in interpersonal communication or conflict textbooks. It appears that "nagging" is commonly used in everyday conversation but it rarely makes it into academic print. A traditional understanding of the word suggests, "to annoy by constant scolding, complaining or urging." An online contest for the best description of nagging revealed this winner— "Whenever you open your mouth, you are either criticizing or complaining about me or something to do with me." (Yahoo! Answers, 2009)

If you read newspaper cartoons or watch sitcoms regularly, you are very familiar with examples of nagging. You may also experience it in your friendships or family relationships, situations in which you may be the nagger or the naggee. Everyone has stereotypical information on who nags or is nagged, how nagging is interpreted, and the function it plays in a relationship; these generalizations are reinforced by popular culture. But few research studies have addressed nagging behaviors.

Currently a large body of communication research, including work on self-presentation theory, perceptual contrast theory, and indebtedness theory, attempts to explain why people comply when others make requests of them. Self-presentation theory suggests that, when asked to do something for others, people monitor the image that others will have of them. They may feel bad about not complying. If so, they are motivated to comply in order to avoid being judged negatively.

Perceptual contrast theory is based on two principles—anchoring and contrast (Cialdini, 1993). When people experience a certain amount of something (e.g. money or happiness) and then expect that amount as typical or normative, they have "adapted" to that level. Essentially we anchor our expectations to our experiences. After such an anchor is established, a contrast effect occurs when one judges others against his or her standard for characteristics such as wealth, intelligence, politeness, and is disappointed. Essentially the other is displaced away from the anchor. Language creates expectations for how people anchor experience to expectations. Contrast *effects are common in relationships. Consider the following example:*

> A: *"Honey, could you do me a really big favor?"*
> B: *"What?" (Expecting a really major request to be stated.)*
> A: *"Could you bring in the mail when you come back from the store?"*

No doubt B will comply with this request. After all, in contrast to what B was expecting to be asked, bringing in the mail is a small favor.

Indebtedness theory utilizes the idea of reciprocity (Bell, Cholerton, Davison, Frazcek & Lauter (1996). This theory is based on the idea that we come to feel indebted (a felt obligation to repay another) when that person has done something for us. If B brings in the mail, perhaps A will feel indebted and comply with B's next request. Obviously, there is a level of equality here. A might feel obligated to get B a soda from the refrigerator but not to buy B a new car.

What if the person does not comply with such a request? What are the options then? Research by Kari Soule suggests that one of the options is to nag the other person. She suggests that nagging is a fairly common phenomenon in attempting to gain compliance. In one of the first attempts to examine the pattern of nagging in close relationships, Soule categorizes nagging as "persistent persuasion" and tries to discover how it is similar to or different from other types of ongoing persuasion. She studied nagging experiences of friends and marital partners; her findings are contained in the following piece.

As you read this, you will see that some respondents believe nagging indicates caring while others view it as a way to get partner compliance. We have included nagging in this section of the book because it is frequently viewed as a type of caretaking communication. Although nagging might be considered a negative and controlling interpersonal behavior, Soule presents nagging as a method of persuasion, with sequential, logical steps involved. From this perspective, she discusses the circumstances under which nagging occurs and explains that it is a product of the actions of both parties (the nagger and the naggee). The chapter concludes with an emphasis on the function of

nagging in relationships, why it occurs, and both its positive and negative impacts.

As you read this chapter think about how you interpret or enact nagging. Consider your general reaction to being nagged. Under what conditions are you more or less likely to comply with a first request? If you wish to avoid complying, you may wish to consider the importance of nondefensive responses to nagging, such as taking responsibility, avoiding the "summarizing-self syndrome," or reframing the message (Gottman, 1994). Ask yourself the question: To what extent should I reconsider the messages contained within nagging behavior in my family or friendship relationships?

REFERENCES

Bell, R. A., Cholerton, M., Davison, V., Fraczek, K. E., & Lauter, H. (1996). Making health education self-funding: Effectiveness of pregiving in an AIDS fundraising/education campaign. *Communication Quarterly, 8,* 331–352.

Cialdini, R. B. (1993). *Influence, science, and practice* (3rd ed.). New York, NY: HarperCollins.

Gottman, J. (1994). *Why marriages succeed or fail.* New York, NY: Simon and Schuster.

"Take out the trash."
"I asked you to take out the trash."
"When are you going to take out the trash?"
"I need you to take out the trash now."

Does this sound familiar? Though your experience with this type of communication may not be in the context of taking out the trash, I am sure that you are familiar with its pattern. In fact, it is probable that someone with whom you share an interpersonal relationship has nagged you just as I have described, or that you may have been the one doing the nagging. While you may be quite familiar with nagging, have you ever really thought much about it, besides perhaps to make jokes or laugh about it? (Just think how many cartoons and comics you have probably been exposed to depicting an aggressive wife nagging a browbeaten husband.) My goal in this essay is to make you more aware of this everyday behavior and the purpose it may serve in your interpersonal relationships. To this end, I am going to answer four basic questions about nagging, particularly the what, when, who, and why of nagging. I turn to "What is nagging?" first.

WHAT IS NAGGING?

As you can tell from the above description of someone nagging another person to take out the trash, the goal of nagging is to persuade someone to perform or, depending on the situation, stop performing some behavior. So an easy way to think of nagging is as a form of persuasion. We can further categorize nagging as an example of persistent persuasion. Persistent persuasion implies that a persuader tries several times to get another to comply. In effect, the person receiving these persuasive attempts is not doing what the persuader wants, so the persuader keeps trying to gain his or her compliance. This may be your experience when you try to persuade someone to do something; people rarely do what we want the first time we try to influence them. Indeed, in this chapter's opening description of a nagging interaction, the persuader made not just one request to get the trash taken out but four.

So what exact form of persistent persuasion does nagging take? Kozloff (1988), a researcher, helps to answer this question by identifying the sequential steps that occur in a nagging interaction. These steps are as follows:

1. A nagger gives a naggee a signal to perform (or stop performing) a specific behavior (such as asking him or her to take out the trash).
2. The naggee does not cooperate or comply with the nagger.
3. In response, the nagger repeats his or her initial signal in a further effort to gain the naggee's compliance.
4. The naggee again responds by being noncompliant.

Kozloff argues that this exchange of the nagger's signal to comply and the naggee's noncompliance continues until either the nagger gives up and stops trying to persuade the naggee or the naggee eventually gives in and does what the persuader wants.

There are several important processes that Kozloff identifies in his description of a nagging interaction. The first is that a naggee does not immediately comply with a nagger. Noncompliance is necessary for a persuader to be persistent, since once a naggee complies there is no need for a persuader to continue trying to influence him or her. The second, as was previously discussed, is that a persuader reacts to this noncompliance by being persistent or continuing to try to influence a naggee; he or she does not at first give up. However it is *how* the persuader is persistent in a nagging interaction that is interesting. Specifically, the nagger repeats the initial message. Now this is not to say that a nagger repeats the previous message word for word. It is likely, as shown in the example of someone nagging another to take out the trash, that subsequent attempts will be worded differently but will still communicate the same essential message. Moreover, a nagger may also change paralinguistic cues, such as beginning to whine or to speak in a pleading tone.

A persuader choosing to be persistent by repeating himself or herself is at odds with research indicating that individuals often become more aggressive when trying to influence someone who will not comply (deTurck 1985, 1987). Particularly, persuaders usually start trying to influence someone using polite strategies, such as asking them to do something. However, when polite strategies are not successful, persuaders may become more aggressive by making threats, harassing the other, or, in rare cases, turning to violence (Pruitt, Parker, and Mikolic 1997). Throughout your life, you have probably seen examples of a persuader "escalating" to more aggressive strategies. Just think of a parent trying to persuade a child to pick up toys. The parent probably starts out by using requests or by asking the child several times to pick up the toys. When this strategy does not work, the parent may threaten the child with a time out or spanking if the child does not cooperate. If the child still does not comply, the parent may then follow through on his or her threat.

Through my research I sought to determine whether nagging could be differentiated from other instances of persuader persistence by a nagger repeating himself or herself rather than escalating to more aggressive strategies. I asked two different groups of people to complete a questionnaire about nagging. The first group was composed of 103 students at a Midwestern university (63 females and 40 males, ranging in age from 19 to 49). The second group included 101 married couples (202 individuals whose ages ranged from 25 to 84 years; the number of years the couples had been married ranged from 1 to 59 years). Consistent with what was expected, both groups described nagging as more repetitious than aggressive (Soule 2001).

Let us turn back to the original question of "What is nagging?" The answer is that nagging is a form of persistent persuasion that involves a persuader repeating himself or herself rather than escalating to a more aggressive persuasive strategy. You may now be asking yourself, why would a persuader choose to be repetitive rather than become more aggressive? It probably seems an annoying and less successful way to try to persuade someone. The answer to why a nagger relies on repetition may lie in the actions of the person being persuaded; when this individual behaves in a specific manner, a persuader replies by nagging. Thus, we next turn to the question "When does nagging occur?"

WHEN DOES NAGGING OCCUR?

You are aware that people's communicative behaviors do not occur in a vacuum; rather, they are affected by and in turn affect the communicative behaviors of others; thus, a persuader may nag in response to the actions of a naggee. Indeed, we already know that a naggee must be noncompliant in order for a persuader to continue nagging. However, just as it is *how* a persuader is persistent that differentiates nagging from other types of persuader persistence, *how* a naggee reacts to a persuader's initial and subsequent influence messages can bring about and continue nagging behavior.

An individual who is not complying with a persuader can enact this noncompliance in one of two ways. The first is that he or she can be verbally noncompliant. Verbal noncompliance involves a persuasive target telling a persuader through words

that he or she will not comply. For example, when asked to take out the trash, a verbally noncompliant person could simply say "No," or "It is not my job to take out the trash." On the other hand, this individual could be behaviorally noncompliant. When being behaviorally noncompliant, an individual does not necessarily verbalize an intent not to comply; he or she simply does not do what the persuader wants. For example, when asked to take out the trash, a behaviorally noncompliant person may just calmly say nothing and continue the activity in which he or she was engaged, such as watching TV or reading. Moreover, being behaviorally noncompliant could also be accompanied by a verbal agreement to comply without actually doing so. For example, when asked to take out the trash, a behaviorally noncompliant person might simply say "Okay" or "All right" without doing what the persuader wants. This individual could also communicate a plan to take out the trash in the future (perhaps without intending to do so) by saying "I'll do it in a minute," or "I'll take it out at the next commercial break" when watching TV.

When thinking back to your own experiences with nagging, you can probably guess which type of noncompliance, behavioral versus verbal, most often occurs in nagging interactions. If you said behavioral, your response would be consistent with the results of my research. When I asked the sample of married couples to think about a nagging interaction they have had with their spouse, most of them indicated that the naggee's most common response was behavioral noncompliance (Soule 2001).

Why do nagging interactions more often entail behavioral rather than verbal noncompliance? The answer to this question may have to do with the repetitive nature of nagging. By not making a verbal refusal to a persuader, a behaviorally noncompliant person makes it difficult for a persuader to use a more aggressive or less polite method of persuasion. Indeed, if a behaviorally noncompliant individual has apparently agreed to do what the persuader wants (e.g., says "I'll do it in a minute"), a persuader may feel that it is inappropriate to use a more aggressive strategy (such as threats or harassment). In effect, the persuader may believe that this person has seemingly done nothing to deserve such a response. Even if a person simply says nothing when being behaviorally noncompliant, a persuader may feel (either consciously or unconsciously) that it is not appropriate to use a more aggressive strategy in response. As a result, since escalating to a more aggressive influence method seems inappropriate, a persuader is left with no choice but to repeat the original message and therefore nag.

Thus, nagging occurs as a product of the actions of both the nagger and naggee. When a naggee responds to a persuader's initial influence attempts with behavioral noncompliance, a persuader is ostensibly left with no other option than to nag. This reasoning suggests that nagging may not always occur because someone is simply a nag or nags because it is his or her personality to do so, but rather as a result of the situation. You may have made this assumption (i.e., that nagging is a personality trait) about some of the people in your life, for example stating that "My husband/wife is such a nag," or "All my mother/father knows how to do is nag." If nagging is in part a result of the actions of a naggee, this would suggest that a variety of people might nag. To further investigate this idea, the next question is "Who nags?"

WHO NAGS?

Think for a moment about the numerous interpersonal relationships you share with the variety of people in your life. In which ones do you and/or the other person in the relationship nag? Many of you may think that this behavior only occurs in intimate relationships, such as with a spouse, boyfriend/girlfriend, or your parents. Though this may be the case for some, the results of my research indicate that a large variety of people nag one another.

I asked the sample of students to list the people who nag them and the people they nag, indicating the relationship they share with each. For example, participants could list their father, roommate, friend, and so forth. Surprisingly, the persons in this study listed a large assortment of people. Among those whom they nag, participants included not only the people we would expect, such

as significant others (i.e., boyfriends, girlfriends, spouses, ex-boyfriends and girlfriends) but also persons in less obvious relationships. For example, several participants indicated that they nagged superiors (e.g., professors, teachers, bosses at work, and coaches), roommates, friends, best friends, coworkers, siblings, neighbors, and subordinates (e.g., the children they babysit). When participants indicated who nags them, many of the same people were listed, such as roommates, friends, superiors, and significant others. In addition, participants indicated that their parents, grandparents, aunts, and uncles were likely to nag them.

Thus, it appears that nagging occurs in a wide variety of interpersonal relationships. But when you think of nagging, with whom do you most often associate this behavior, men or women? Turning back to the opening of this chapter, which depicts someone nagging another to take out the trash, did you picture a man or woman saying these words? If you pictured a woman as the nagger, your perception may be consistent with that of many people in Western culture. We often stereotype nagging as a feminine behavior and believe that women are more likely to nag than men. To gain a greater understanding of sex differences in nagging, I first examined whether most people really do view nagging as a feminine behavior. The point was not to look at which sex actually nags most but whether society views nagging in general as more feminine or masculine. Thus, I asked individuals in both of the samples (the married couples and students) whether they perceive or think of nagging as a more feminine or more masculine behavior. Not too surprisingly, both samples viewed nagging as more feminine than masculine (Soule 2001).

Though many people may view nagging as more feminine, I was curious as to whether one sex is more likely than the other to nag. In effect, I wanted to see whether the perception of nagging as a more feminine behavior is accurate; specifically, do women really nag others more than men? An examination of the lists generated by the sample of students concerning whom they nag and who nags them indicated that nagging not only depends on the sex of the nagger but on that of the naggee as well. Specifically, women were found to nag similar numbers of men and women, whereas men were more likely to nag other men than women (Soule 2001). Therefore, it appears that both sexes engage in nagging behavior, but men tend to be more selective than women in that they are more likely to nag other men.

It appears, then, that a variety of people in a variety of interpersonal relationships nag. Moreover, though we may think of nagging as a more feminine than masculine behavior, men do nag, although they are more likely to nag other men than women. Perhaps this is why nagging is perceived to be feminine. Since women nag a greater variety of people, we may tend to stereotypically associate this behavior with them. We now have an idea of who nags; however, we still do not know exactly why nagging occurs in such a diverse group of relationships or why men tend to nag other men rather than women. Thus the last question is, "Why nag?"

WHY NAG?

Think back to the opening of this chapter; why do you think the persuader is nagging another to take out the trash? The persuader's motive may seem obvious—he or she simply wants the trash taken out. Thus, the most apparent answer to the question "Why nag?" is to influence another. Indeed, when asked why they nag their spouse, the majority of subjects in the sample of married couples reported that it was to gain the naggee's (their spouse's) compliance (Soule 2001). However, nagging may serve several other important functions in our interpersonal relationships. Think back to instances where you have nagged someone you care about. Though your primary goal may have been to gain compliance, did you also nag this person out of feelings of concern or love? Perhaps you even used nagging as a means of showing your affection. For example, nagging your significant other about calling you when he or she stays out late may be a way for you to express how you worry about this person's safety and well-being. In the context of parent/child relationships, Youniss and Smollar (1985) found that many children and adolescents view

their parents' nagging as annoying and intrusive. Surprisingly, they also view it as a sign of caring, concern, and love. Rosenfeld (1985) interviewed a 17-year-old boy who complained about his mother's nagging but then added that it showed her concern for him, since, "You only nag someone you care about." In my own research, when I asked married participants to describe something about which they nag their spouse, their responses appeared to be motivated by love and a concern for their spouse's well-being (Soule 2001). For example, several of these individuals reported that they nagged their spouse about taking his or her medicine, going to the doctor, stopping smoking, or starting to exercise for health reasons.

In addition to showing affection, another function of nagging may be to avoid becoming aggressive toward a relational partner. As noted earlier, nagging is different from other instances of persuader persistence in that a persuader repeats himself or herself rather than escalating to a more aggressive influence strategy (such as angry and abusive statements, threats, or even physical violence). Though a persuader may not consciously choose to nag in order to avoid hurting a naggee, it might be a way to be a persistent persuader while avoiding conflict, destructive statements, or even violence. This reasoning may explain why men tend to nag other men rather than women. Indeed, men may choose to nag other men as a way to avoid conflict. Since men are thought to be more aggressive than women (e.g., Clarke-Stewart, Friedman, and Koch 1985; Maccoby and Jacklin 1980), a persistent male persuader who escalates to a more aggressive strategy to try to influence another male could cause a verbal conflict or even a physical fight. Moreover, since women have traditionally held less power than men in society, they may be likely to comply immediately with a male persuader. As a result, men may rarely have to resort to nagging with a female naggee.

Thus, nagging may serve a variety of functions in our interpersonal relationships. It may allow us not only to influence someone but also to show caring and to avoid acting aggressively. These functions indicate that nagging may play an important role in helping to maintain harmony in a variety of relationships. However, it should be noted that interactions involving nagging are not always positive. Repeatedly nagging another person could cause him or her to feel irritation or annoyance. In extreme cases, a naggee could become irritated enough to respond to a nagger with violence (Gelles 1972). Though nagging may be an important part of most healthy relationships, in some cases it can cause problems.

CONCLUSION

I trust that this chapter has given you a greater understanding of nagging in your own interpersonal relationships. Though you might not have given much thought to nagging (besides to wish that a nagger would go away or that a naggee would just comply), you may now recognize what constitutes this behavior and how the actions of both the nagger and naggee can cause and continue a nagging interaction. Moreover, not only may nagging occur in a variety of our relationships, but it might also serve several important functions, such as showing affection and helping us to avoid acting aggressively. Therefore, as strange as this idea may have seemed to you at first, everything we do in our interpersonal relationships has meaning and serves a purpose, even nagging.

REFERENCES

Clarke-Stewart, A., Friedman, S., & Koch, J. (1985). *Child development: A topical approach.* New York, NY: Wiley.

deTurck, M. A. (1985). A transactional analysis of compliance-gaining behavior: Effects of non-compliance, relational contexts, and actors' gender. *Human Communication Research, 1,* 54–78.

deTurck, M. A. (1987). When communication fails: Physical aggression as a compliance-gaining strategy. *Communication Monographs, 54,* 106–112.

Gelles, R. J. (1972). *The violent home: A study of physical aggression between husbands and wives.* Thousand Oaks, CA: Sage.

Kozloff, M. A. (1988). *Productive interaction with students, children, and clients.* Springfield, IL: Charles C. Thomas.

Maccoby, E. E., & Jacklin, C. N. (1980). Sex differences in aggression: A rejoinder and reprise. *Child Development, 51,* 964–980.

Pruitt, D. G., Parker, J. C., & Mikolic, J. M. (1997). Escalation as a reaction to persistent annoyance. *International Journal of Conflict Management, 8,* 252–270.

Rosenfeld, A. A. (1985). Parents who nag. *Human Sexuality, 19,* 133–142.

Soule, K. P. (2001). Persistence in compliance-gaining interactions: The role of nagging behavior (Unpublished doctoral dissertation). Northwestern University, Evanston, IL.

Youniss, J., & Smollar, J. (1985). *Adolescent relations with mothers, fathers, and friends.* Chicago, IL: The University of Chicago Press.

QUESTIONS/THOUGHTS

1. Define "nagging." in your own words and give a clear example. Ask five other people to define it as well, including an example. What are the similarities in the definitions? The differences?

2. Describe two different patterns of nagging you have witnessed in close friendships or romantic relationships. How do the targets of the nagging differ? (For example, a child, partner, employee). How do you interpret the goals of the naggers? What is the effect on their relationships with the naggees?

3. Are there some "nagging lessons" or conclusions you can draw from considering who nags you and who you nag? Design your own list of five recommendations to break a nagging pattern.

4. How might nagging appear in relationships in the digital age? Give examples of how nagging may occur online or through other communication media. How might it change the perception of nagging?

Communicating Forgiveness

DOUGLAS L. KELLEY

People do and say hurtful things to each other, particularly in the context of close relationships (Kowalski, Walker, Wilkinson, Queen & Sharpe, 2003). Yet, frequently the words "I am sorry" are difficult to speak to another and difficult to accept from another. Forgiveness is not, as Douglas Kelley suggests in this article, an easy thing—whether you are the person who needs to offer forgiveness or the person who needs to be forgiven.

What is forgiveness? Vince Waldron and Douglas Kelley (2008) consider it to be a relational process in which a wrong is identified and the partners renegotiate the relationship. The process involves the possibility of reconciliation. These authors suggest that forgiveness has the potential to: repair broken relationships, restore individual well being, serve as an expression of continued love and commitment, recognize conciliatory behavior, and restore relational justice.

One step toward forgiveness is an apology. Apologies can help repair relationships. Cody and McLaughlin (1990) review a number of studies that suggest apologies help reduce both the punishments the perpetrator receives and the anger the victim experiences. In their study of forgiveness

McCullough, Worthington and Rachal (1997) stress the importance of empathy because empathizing with a significant other raised the probability of maintaining closeness and lowered the possibility of avoidance and revenge.

Even after the words are spoken and accepted, and time has passed, true forgiveness is difficult. As Smedes (1984) suggests:

> There are some hurts that we can leave behind which float away like debris on rushing water. But, there are others which rivet themselves into our memory. Deep hurts we never deserved flow from a dead past into our living present. A friend betrays us; a parent abuses us; a spouse leaves us in the cold—these hurts do not heal with the coming of the sun. (p. 11)

In the following article, Douglas Kelley addresses a significant concept that has received little attention in the communication literature. He suggests that forgiveness is a concept that most everyone has attempted, but few have actually accomplished. Part of this problem, according to Kelley, is the fact that very few people have a real definition of what forgiveness is. To this end, the first section of this chapter provides a detailed look at different ideas or "types" of forgiveness, subsequently specifying a comprehensive definition. The next section discusses the interpersonal aspects of forgiveness, using several examples to illustrate the complex dynamics involved in the process. The final section reviews the role of communication in forgiveness, assessing both the motivation for forgiveness, and strategies for expressing such feelings appropriately. Overall, Kelley places emphasis on the complex and transactional nature of forgiveness, specifically, asserting that forgiving is based not only upon the feelings and actions of the forgiver, but also on the responses of the offender. Further, he notes that the consequences (both positive and negative) of the decision to forgive (or not to forgive) impact both parties as well. As you read this chapter think about your experience with forgiveness and ask yourself the question:"What criteria do I tend to use when deciding if I need to ask for forgiveness or to expect forgiveness from another person?"

REFERENCES

Cody, M. J., & McLaughlin, M. L. (1990). Interpersonal accounting. In H. Giles & P. Robinson (Eds.), *Handbook of language and social psychology* (pp. 227–255). London, England: Wiley.

Kowalski, R. M., Walker, S., Wilkinson, R. Queen, A., & Sharpe, B. (2003). Lying, cheating, complaining, and other aversive interpersonal behaviors: A narrative examination of the darker side of relationships. *Journal of Social and Personal Relationships, 20*, 471–490.

McCullough, M. E., Worthington, E. L., & Rachal, K. C. (1997). Interpersonal forgiving in close relationships. *Journal of Personality and Social Psychology, 73*, 321–336.

Smedes, L. (1984). *Forgive and forget: Healing the hurts we don't deserve.* New York, NY: Pocket Books.

Waldron, V. R., & Kelley, D. L. (2008). *Communicating forgiveness.* Thousand Oaks, CA: Sage.

"I cried some, too, then, holding him in my arms, kissing his hair.... All the same I knew I was forgiving him. I had that miraculous clarity for an instant and so I understood that the forgiveness itself was strong, durable, like strands of a web, weaving around us, holding us."

Alice—*A Map of the World,* (p. 390)

Just last week, as I was preparing to write this chapter, someone in our office said to me, "Forgiveness is tough. If anyone thinks it's easy, then they haven't really tried it." She went on to say, "I realized that at first I didn't really want things to get better. I wanted to hurt the other person like they had hurt me." Her comments made me think about the first marriage workshop I conducted in which I included information about forgiveness. I had completed about ninety minutes worth of material on working through conflict in marriage and was finishing with ten minutes on forgiveness. I actually thought that talking about forgiveness would be a "nice" way to end the session—you know, after we had been talking about the heavy stuff, now each partner could forgive the other and go back to marital bliss. I was very surprised when most of the questions during the question-and-answer period were about forgiveness. "Should you forgive if you think they may do it again?" "Should you forgive if they have apologized?" "How do you forgive someone? I'm trying, but it doesn't seem to be working."

In order to answer these questions, we need to understand something about the nature of forgiveness. Contemporary definitions of forgiveness vary in terms of their complexity and their etiology. For example, Hargrave (1994a), a marriage and family therapist, offers the following general definition of forgiveness: "Generally, the word *forgive* means to cease to feel resentment against an offender" (p. 339). Hargrave's definition is parsimonious and succinct and easy to grasp by couples and family members. On the other side of the coin, Enright et al. (1992) reviewed ancient writings and modern philosophies, in order to provide a more comprehensive understanding of what forgiveness includes. They concluded that the idea of forgiveness generally includes "the casting off of deserved punishments, the abandonment of negative reactions, the imparting of love toward the other person, self-sacrificial nature, the potential restoration of the relationship, and positive benefits for the forgiver" (p. 88).

Some of you may be thinking, "Whoa, hold the boat! It's one thing to cease having negative feelings toward offenders. It's a whole other thing to feel positively toward them"—and you would be right. Enright et al. provide a very ambitious definition of forgiveness. However, if you think their definition is unrealistic, I invite you to consider the following story about Marietta Jaeger (Jaeger 1998). Marietta and her family (her husband, five children, and her parents) were camping for a full month in Montana. One night, as she tucked the children into bed, she could barely reach Susie, her 7-year-old. Marietta stretched over all of the kids to reach Susie, but could barely reach her cheek to kiss her goodnight. Marietta recalls Susie exclaiming, "'Oh no, Mama,!' and she crawled out of her sleeping bag and over her sister to kneel right in front of me.' She hugged me hugely and kissed me smack on the lips. 'There, Mama, that's the way it should be!'" This was the last time Marietta was ever to see her little girl. During the night Susie was discovered missing—a hole had been slashed in the tent next to where she had lain.

I can hardly do justice in this short amount of space to Marietta's emotional journey, but let me summarize her process to forgiveness as well as I can. Shortly after the event she felt that, "Even if the kidnapper were to bring Susie back, alive and well, this very moment, I could still kill him for what he has done to my family. I believed I could have done so with my bare hands and a big smile on my face, if only I knew who he was." I think most of us would agree that Marietta had every right to feel that way. However, she soon realized that this mindset violated her own value system, and that nurturing her hatred was not psychologically healthy. Eventually she made a decision to forgive the kidnapper, whoever he was, and she finally slept soundly for the first time since Susie's abduction.

A year after Susie's kidnapping, after a newspaper article was written in which Marietta expressed her concern for Susie's abductor, the kidnapper called to taunt her. Marietta, ever since her intellectual decision to forgive this man, had

been working at her forgiveness. She had repeated, again and again, "that, however I felt about the kidnapper, in God's eyes he was just as precious as my little girl...that, even if he wasn't behaving like one, this man was a son of God...that, as a Christian, I am called to pray for my enemies." However, now, one year to the day after Susie's disappearance, her forgiveness was put to the test by a phone call. Her response? Marietta looked past his smug taunting and asked him how she could help him. His response? He broke down and wept, "I wish this burden could be lifted from me." During the course of their conversation this broken man revealed enough information to allow the FBI to locate him. After his conviction for kidnapping and murder, Marietta could have asked for the death penalty, yet she believed that she better honored Susie, "not by becoming that which I deplored, but by saying that all life is sacred and worthy of preservation."

Marietta Jaeger's courageous story demonstrates in dramatic fashion that turning negative feelings to positive ones is possible. Yet her story also helps us understand what forgiveness is not. In understanding the forgiveness process, it is crucial to realize that forgiveness is distinct from the concepts of forgetting, condoning, excusing, and denying. Each of these concepts fails to recognize a person's responsibility for a relational transgression and therefore eliminates the need for forgiveness. Forgetting implies that memories of the offense are gone. Yet, as Desmond Tutu (1998) states, "Forgiveness does not mean amnesia" (p. xiv). If we no longer remember the transgression, then there is no longer forgiveness. Similarly, condoning justifies an infraction by denying that any wrong took place. Excusing implies that the wrongdoer had a good reason for the offense and thereby removes responsibility from wrongdoers for their actions. Likewise, denying is a refusal to recognize a transgression.

What seems clear, from analyzing what forgiveness is not, is that for something to count as forgiveness, a wrong must be recognized. In Marietta Jaeger's case, the wrongdoing was not excused, condoned, denied, or forgotten. Rather, the wrong was experienced and acknowledged and was, of course, remembered. But in light of this, Marietta made a decision to move beyond her hatred.

North's (1987) work emphasizes this need to move beyond negative feelings by making a willful decision to forgive. She states, "Forgiveness is a matter of a willed change of heart, the successful result of an active endeavor to replace bad thoughts with good, bitterness and anger with compassion and affection" (p. 506). I like the way that Enright, Freedman, and Rique (1998) put it when they define forgiveness as "a willingness to abandon one's right to resentment, negative judgment, and indifferent behavior toward one who unjustly hurt us, while fostering the undeserved qualities of compassion, generosity, and even love toward him or her" (pp. 46–47). Forgiveness, at its best, is "abandoning" the negative, and "fostering" the positive.

INTERPERSONAL ASPECTS OF FORGIVENESS

Stories like Marietta Jaeger's help us realize the powerful reality of forgiveness (many other forgiveness stories can be found by studying conflictual settings around the world, such as the Truth and Reconciliation process in South Africa or the conflict in Northern Ireland). However, as poignant as these stories are, what most of us need is to understand how forgiveness is managed in our day-to-day lives. Studying the communication of forgiveness in daily interactions requires us to focus on the transactional nature of forgiveness interactions, that is, the mutual influence that forgiver and offender exert on one another, and to emphasize the potential of forgiveness to restore hurting relationships.

North (1987) moves forgiveness from a purely intrapersonal experience to an interpersonal experience by placing forgiveness in the role of restoring damaged relationships. She recognizes the importance of internal change but also argues that internal change may lead to outward expression:

> Typically an act of wrongdoing brings about a distancing of the wrongdoer from the one he has harmed....Forgiveness is a way of healing the damage done to one's relations with the wrongdoer, or at least a first step towards a full reconciliation. (North 1984, 502–503)

Although little social scientific research has been done to study directly the interpersonal dynamics of the forgiveness process, certain researchers have developed theoretical models that address issues of importance in understanding the interpersonal nature of forgiveness. Enright and the Human Development Study Group (1991) offer a model of forgiveness that includes the need for the forgiver to respond behaviorally to the offender. This model focuses on the forgiver and begins with the initial injury. At this point the injured party experiences negative psychological consequences, such as emotional pain. This leads to the need to resolve the conflict in some way, namely, to choose between two basic strategies: justice and mercy. Justice takes the form of legal action, seeking personal fairness, or revenge. Mercy involves the options we discussed previously, such as condonation, excuse, and denial, or it takes on a more active response, such as forgiveness. Various motives lead the offended party to make the cognitive decision to forgive the injurer, which leads to eventually changing the way the injury or injurer is viewed. Finally, the injured individual recognizes the need for some type of behavioral response that will bring about either reconciliation or release. Both of these options result in less negative, and more positive, affect experienced toward the offender. Release occurs if reconciliation is deemed impossible or unwise.

Similar to Enright et al.'s description of the various ways that mercy can be given is Hargrave's distinction between exonerating and forgiving. Exonerating involves gaining *insight* and *understanding* into the offending person's situation. This perspective change results in the offended party no longer holding the offender accountable for his or her actions. In contrast, forgiveness provides the offender *opportunity to provide compensation*. This means that the offending party is held accountable for his or her wrongdoing. In contrast to Enright et al.'s distinction between justice and mercy, forgiveness is conceptualized as providing the wrongdoer with an opportunity to engage in restorative justice. Hargrave also includes in his discussion an *overt act of forgiving*. This overt act involves renegotiating the relationship to restore a sense of fairness or balance.

One aspect of Hargrave's (1994a, 1994b) perspective that I find particularly interesting is his belief that there are three prerequisites before the two parties renegotiate the relationship covenant. First, both parties must agree about what constituted the infraction. This may seem like an obvious step, but often individuals in conflict do not agree on what the conflict is really about. Second, there has to be a mutual recognition of the damage that the wrongdoing caused. Finally, there must be some type of apology from the offender for the damage caused.

Interestingly, these three prerequisites parallel the phases that individuals go through when giving an account of a wrong action (Cody and McLaughlin 1988; Schonbach and Kleibaumhuter 1990). For example, the account process begins by one party experiencing what is termed *a failure event*. Failure events can involve an action that is viewed as an offense or an omission of a behavior that was expected or required. Once the offended party experiences the offense, they reproach the perceived offender by behaving in some way that indicates that they feel wronged. Some time after experiencing the reproach, the offender responds either by giving a mitigating response, such as conceding or confessing guilt, or by giving an aggravating response, such as denying responsibility for the wrong done. Finally, the offended person assesses the veracity of the account, the offense in light of the account, and the characteristics of the perceived offender.

Hargrave's (1994a, 1994b) suggestion that an apology is needed before the relationship is renegotiated is also consistent with the accounts research indicating that more mitigating strategies, such as concession (of which apology is one type), are more likely to bring mitigating responses (Cody and McLaughlin 1988), such as forgiveness of the offense. Several other studies have also found a close relationship between apology and forgiveness. For example, McCullough, Worthington,

and Rachal (1997) tested the relationship between apology, empathy, and forgiveness, and found strong evidence for the relationship between apology and forgiveness. Likewise, Emmers and Canary (1996) conceptualized forgiveness and apology as related constructs. In a study examining the effect of young couples' communication strategies on relational repair, they found that individuals listed forgiveness when asked to describe what was done to repair the relationship after a negative event. Forgive was defined as "forgave" or "accepted apology" (Emmers and Canary 1996, 174). Forgiveness was one of many interactive strategies reported by respondents. Interactive strategies are those that involve directly interacting with the other person (Baxter and Wilmot 1984). Walters (1984) offers an interesting perspective on actually interacting with the one who has hurt us. For Walters, forgiveness often involves "follow-through"; that is, at times you simply need to talk to the person being forgiven.

COMMUNICATING FORGIVENESS

In order to better understand how forgiveness is communicated day to day, I conducted a study wherein participants were asked to write about three forgiveness stories: a time they were forgiven, a time they forgave, and a time they asked for forgiveness. After collecting 304 stories, my staff and I analyzed them for themes related to forgiveness motivations, forgiveness strategies, and relational consequences. The stories the participants shared were mostly about family relationships, dating relationships, and friendships.

Forgiver Motivation

Participants' forgiveness stories primarily described five different reasons for forgiving someone: love, well-being, restoring the relationship, strategy of the other, and reframing. The first dimension, *love*, was often mentioned as follows: "I forgave him, primarily because I love him...." Likewise, one of our participants who was on the receiving end of forgiveness stated, "I guess the reason I was forgiven was because he loves me."

The second dimension, *well-being*, included forgiving in order to restore well-being to oneself or to the offender. One individual realized that her negative emotions were damaging to her own self: "I began to realize that this anger was not only torturing him, but myself as well. It was eating me up inside and making me more of an angry person. Why should I suffer for what he has done? So I wrote him...." The following statement demonstrates how motivations were often multifaceted, arising from both the motivations of love and well-being of the other: "I forgave him because I love him and he needed my forgiveness to make himself feel better."

The third dimension focused on *restoring the relationship*. Responses in this dimension were grouped three ways. Sometimes individuals simply mentioned that they desired to forgive the other so that the relationship would continue. Other times, individuals mentioned that the nature of the relationship prompted the giving of forgiveness. Participants who reported this aspect of forgiveness motivation indicated, at times, that there were implicit or explicit obligations because of the relationship type, for example, "I forgave her because she is my friend of 12 years...." The third grouping represented statements that compared the severity of the infraction to the worth of the relationship. For example, "I forgave the person because it was not a major problem that a tape was destroyed. It was not worth risking a friendship over."

The fourth motivation dimension was *strategy of the other*. Here forgivers' motivations were seen to be influenced by how the offender responded to his or her own infraction. Of course, this was no surprise to us given the previous research that demonstrated the close relationship between apology and forgiveness. It was common for individuals to mention the importance of hearing an apology. Additional strategies mentioned were a show of responsibility and a demonstration of remorse. The following example demonstrates both apology and responsibility: "He said he forgave me but only because I apologized and admitted I was wrong."

The final dimension of forgiver motivation was entitled *reframing*. This concept is consistent with several of the more psychologically based models of forgiveness (Cunningham 1985; Enright et al. 1991). Reframing often took the shape of claiming to understand why the other person engaged in the offending behavior; viewing the offender as not responsible for his or her actions; viewing the offender's act as unintentional; or diminishing the perceived significance of the offending behavior. One female participant describes her motivation as based on reframing her boyfriend's character: "I forgave him, primarily because I love him and I know that what occurred was not part of his normal character. He comes from a great family, he's a Christian, and I knew he wasn't the cheating kind." Another respondent was forgiven because his friend reframed the significance of the infraction: "He forgave me because it was a small issue to him."

Offender (Forgiveness-Seeking) Motivation

While less varied than forgiver motivations, it is clear that not all forgiveness seeking comes from the same motives. The two primary motives for individuals seeking forgiveness were *well-being* and *restoring the relationship*. One respondent described his response to his mother, which was designed to restore *well-being* when things had become too uncomfortable: "When I could not stand this behavior any more, or needed her forgiveness, I started visiting her more frequently...."

Offenders who desired forgiveness in order to *restore the relationship* handled things differently than did their forgiving counterparts. As with forgivers, this dimension represented a sense of obligation to obtain forgiveness in certain relationships. For offenders, however, restoring the relationship was also associated with restoring trust and with a simple desire to maintain the relationship, for example: "I feel that we lost that friendship.... After I talked to him, I explained to him that I hoped he could forgive me and we could remain friends."

FORGIVENESS-GRANTING STRATEGIES

Forgiveness was granted using any of three main strategies: direct, indirect, and conditional. Many of our respondents reported giving forgiveness by *directly* addressing the transgression with the offender. Direct strategies included such things as discussing the issue; the forgiver telling the offender that he or she understands; directly telling the other, "I forgive you"; and using a third party to mediate the issue. For example, one respondent reported, "I told him I understood, but would hope he would be more up front with problems. I told him of course I forgave him."

Indirect strategies included a wide variety of tactics. For example, some individuals used humor or tried to diminish the perceived effect of the infraction by saying something like, "It was no big deal." Many people used nonverbal behavior such as hugging, touching, eye contact, changes in vocal patterns, and shows of emotion. Sometimes the nonverbal behaviors accompanied a more direct strategy, while at other times the nonverbal elements were meant to carry the whole meaning. A number of narratives reported "returning to normal" as a way of showing the offender they had been forgiven. In these cases nothing was really said, but the return to normal behavior signaled that all had been forgiven. Similarly, some described how the forgiveness was "just understood." For example, one respondent describes forgiving his father: "The forgiveness was spontaneous but not vocalized, it was understood."

A third way in which individuals granted forgiveness was *with conditions*. This could best be described as "forgiveness if...," that is, I will forgive you if you adhere to certain stipulations. One typical narrative describes a child-father discussion, wherein the father asks forgiveness as part of his alcohol recovery; forgiveness is given in the following way: "I told him I would accept his apology; however, we both knew that there was the stipulation that he stay off of the booze."

Offender (Forgiveness-Seeking) Strategies

Forgiveness-seeking strategies are used by offenders in order to gain forgiveness from the person they injured. The dimensions identified here were the same as for the forgiver; however, specific tactics within each dimension differed when it was forgiveness-seeking rather than

forgiveness-granting. For example, *conditions* that were placed on the forgiveness as they related to the offenders' strategies were not set by the forgiver but offered instead by the offender.

Direct strategies used by the offender involved discussion, as they did for the forgiver, but the focus was not on the forgiver understanding but rather on the offender explaining. Also, direct requests for forgiveness were reported (e.g., "Will you forgive me?"), as was the use of third parties to help solve the problem. Paralleling the forgiver motivation category, individuals also reported such elements as apologizing, taking responsibility for their actions, and showing remorse. These types of behavior were deemed direct because they focused specifically on dealing with the infraction; for example, "I apologized to him over and over. I told him I didn't deserve him and that I took him for granted." Taking responsibility and apologizing were an effective combination in the following description: "At this time he apologized and explained that he felt responsible for my leaving.... At the time I forgave him...."

Indirect forgiveness-seeking strategies included such elements as humor, nonverbal displays of acceptance or emotion, using one's social network to communicate remorse or apology (e.g., having a friend tell the injured person that you are sorry), ingratiation, or returning to normalcy. One common example of nonverbal display of emotion was summed up like this: "I was crying because I was truly sorry for my action." In the following quote, the offender sought forgiveness by using a combination of strategies: "After not talking for two days I came home from work one day with a funny belated birthday card for her and a gift certificate to her favorite restaurant.... We went to dinner and in a joking manner, I expressed to her how sorry I was...."

Relational consequences took place in two basic ways: relational change and return to normalcy. The most common form of relational consequence was to experience some type of change in the relationship. In fact, 72 percent of the narratives reporting relational consequences described some type of change, while 28 percent reported a return to normalcy. Relational change consisted of a variety of responses. Some relationships changed in type, such as from dating partners to "just friends." The following quote from a father-son scenario describes a rather interesting change in type: "The typical father/son relationship we had prior to the separation is gone and has been replaced by one where we exist more as friends rather than father/son."

Some relationships did not change in type but rather strengthened, as is illustrated in this work scenario: "My forgiveness was appreciated. The relationship seemed to improve slightly, as evidenced by more casual talk and sharing of what's going on in our lives." However, other relationships were not so lucky: "I apologized and asked him to forgive me and he did. After a while he did, and we were still friends, but not as good of friends." A final type of relationship change involved behavior or rules. One participant's story demonstrates this well: "No name-calling's become a rule in our relationship and we stand by it. It's helped us fight fairly."

Those individuals who did not report relational change often noted that the relationship required a *return to normalcy*. One of our participants succinctly sums this up: "After I forgave her things returned to normal." Returning to normal included the way the individuals communicated, interacted, or the kinds of tasks they could do (e.g., after a fender bender, Dad still trusts you to take his truck to the store).

Time

Often the participants described the forgiveness process as taking time. This could be described as taking time to be ready to forgive (motivation), taking time to actually work through the forgiveness (strategy), or taking time for the full effect of the forgiveness to become evident (relational consequences). It was not uncommon for time to play a role in more than one of these aspects of the forgiveness process: "It took probably ten months for her to get over my disappointing her (my mom). She finally forgave me when she found out that I was pregnant with my first child." While it is evident that time is a factor, it is not clear as to whether time is primarily influencing motivation, strategy,

relational consequence, or some combination of the three. What is obvious, however, is that time is often an important component of the forgiveness process.

I was also interested in how the forgiveness process might vary depending on the type of relationship. To explore this question I used chi-square analysis which compared my actual data with what I would have expected for each relationship type, if all the relationship types were equal. What I found was that, compared with the expectation that all relationship types are the same, family members were less likely to be motivated by love or to restore the relationship, and were less likely to experience deterioration of the relationship; dating individuals were more influenced by love and friends had a greater tendency to experience a deterioration of the relationship. Other results compared with this expectation showed there was a tendency for family members to be less motivated to forgive because of the strategy of the offender; dating couples were more likely to be motivated by a desire to restore the relationship or by the strategy of the offender when deciding to forgive someone, and as the offender they were more likely to seek forgiveness to restore well-being. Dating couples were the only relationship to experience change in relationship type more than expected; friends were less motivated to forgive by love, but were more motivated than expected by a desire to restore the relationship; in addition, friends were less motivated to seek forgiveness in order to restore well-being.

SOME FINAL THOUGHTS ON THE FORGIVENESS PROCESS

It is evident that forgiveness, while certainly a psychological process, often has interpersonal dimensions and that these dimensions are important to the overall forgiveness process. For example, the strategy the offenders in the study chose affected the decision to forgive, as individuals noted that they forgave because the other apologized, took responsibility for his or her actions, or showed remorse. Thus, this influence of the offenders' strategies on the decision to forgive demonstrates the need to conceptualize forgiveness as a dynamic interpersonal process.

The dimensions generated as possible motivations in this study both consolidate and build upon previous research. Of particular interest is the concept of reframing. Reframing, in the current investigation, includes such elements as understanding, recognizing that the other person did not mean to hurt you, or realizing that the offender cannot be held responsible for his or her actions. This perspective also represents what Hargrave (1994b) refers to as exoneration. That is, once one reframes the infraction, the incident is no longer viewed as a violation; the offender is no longer held accountable; and subsequently he or she is no longer in need of forgiveness. It is important to realize that while the distinction between exoneration and forgiveness is an important one, the individuals who participated in this study believe that all of the events they reported involved forgiveness. However, understanding the difference between exoneration and forgiveness may account for differences in individuals' forgiveness experiences and relational outcomes.

The important emphasis placed on reframing raises interesting questions regarding attribution and account processes. It can be argued from an attribution theory perspective that the most effective strategies with which to secure forgiveness would involve making external attributions for the cause of a relational transgression ("I was late because of an accident on the freeway"), since individuals are only accountable for an infraction if it can be attributed to internal causes ("You were late because you are insensitive") (Jellison 1990; Sillars 1982). This argument is consistent with current findings indicating that individuals were often motivated to forgive because they reframed the infraction and concluded that the perceived offender was not responsible for his or her actions or did not intend to inflict harm—in other words, the cause of the infraction was located outside of the offending party. This reframing of the infraction from internal to external causes could be the result of the offender offering excuses. As was found by McLaughlin, O'Hair, and Cody (1983), "Excuse was by far the most popular mode of failure

management and may simply reflect the fact that most people in judging their own behavior attribute failure to the circumstances of the situation rather than to their own bad intentions" (p. 222). However, although excuses may be quite effective in certain circumstances, concession, including apology, has been conceptualized as a more mitigating strategy than excuse (McLaughlin, O'Hair, and Cody 1983) and therefore could be more effective in achieving forgiveness. Concession can be understood as applying internal causal attributions to the offender's actions. Clearly in the present investigation, apologizing, taking responsibility for one's actions, and expressing remorse were related to the offended party's motivation to forgive. As such, it appears that both internal and external attributions can be effective when seeking to achieve forgiveness or manage a relational failure. This conclusion is consistent with research suggesting that apologies, excuses, or an "excuse-apology" hybrid are most effective when deflecting blame in interpersonal settings (Cody and McLaughlin 1990). In spite of these findings, however, it remains to be seen under what conditions internal and external attributions of behavior may be most effective in securing forgiveness.

Forgiveness strategies, in the present study, were either direct, engaging the other specifically about the issue, or indirect, wherein the issue is never explicitly dealt with. Direct strategies for offenders were characterized by discussion and often by further explanation of the infraction, direct requests for forgiveness, using a third party to intervene, apologies, taking responsibility for one's actions, and showing remorse. Indirect strategies involved humor, nonverbal behaviors and displays of emotion, using the social network to communicate the offender's feelings to the forgiver, and treating the injured party as he or she would normally be treated.

Interestingly, forgiver direct and indirect strategies largely paralleled offender strategies. Offender direct strategies included discussion, which often led to the forgiver understanding the offender's position, statements of forgiveness ("I forgive you"), and use of third-party mediators. Indirect strategies involved the use of humor, diminishing the perceived effect of the infraction ("It was no big deal"), nonverbal behaviors and emotional displays, a return to normalcy, and a sense that the other was forgiven and it was just "understood." These findings are interesting in light of the fact that Hargrave (1994b) believes that forgiveness requires an overt expression. Only a little over one-half of the scenarios in this study that identified a forgiver strategy mentioned the forgiver using direct strategies. If Hargrave is correct, this would mean that "true forgiveness" was not experienced in almost half of the participants' stories. To address this issue, it will eventually be necessary for forgiveness researchers to study dyads where partners' perceptions of forgiveness can be compared and contrasted; however, it is important to note here that our participants considered these stories to be stories of forgiveness.

Two additional strategy issues involve forgiving conditionally and time. Both forgivers and offenders were described as using conditional forgiveness at times. For instance, the forgiver might forgive the other as long as he or she promised that the transgression was never to happen again. Sometimes the offender initiated this condition when they were asking for forgiveness by promising never again to commit such a wrong. Also, both forgiver and offender mentioned that forgiveness took time. That is, while forgiveness can be a one-time act, it often involves a process of discussion and repeated requests for forgiveness. As we saw in Marietta Jaeger's story, it can take time to decide to forgive, and then often, once the decision is made, it takes time and effort to practice acting in a forgiving manner.

This study has also identified a variety of relational consequences that are associated with interpersonal forgiveness. The central dimensions are change and return to normalcy. Participants' narratives revealed that relationships can change in type, strengthen, deteriorate, or develop new behavior or rules in response to forgiveness. A common response that served as both a relational consequence and a type of forgiver indirect strategy was returning the relationship to normal. Many participants indicated that treating each other "normally" was the way that they knew they

had been forgiven. Also, respondents noted that time played a role in the relational effects. Time, as it is understood as part of relational consequences, typically referred to the process of relationship healing. Individuals indicated that even after forgiveness was imparted to the other person, it could still take time to restore the relationship.

It was also interesting to find that forgiveness motivations, strategies, and relational consequences vary by relationship type. Possibly because family relationships are not voluntary relationships, family members reported being less motivated to give forgiveness because of love, to restore the relationship, or because of what the other person might do to seek forgiveness. This obligatory quality of family relationships may also account for the fact that family members reported their relationships being weakened fewer times than was expected. This may be because the involuntary nature of these relationships creates a sense of stability and resiliency in the relationship.

In the voluntary relationships, both dating and friendship, there was more of a tendency for individuals to be motivated to forgive in order to restore the relationship. In both of these relationship types there are fewer social constraints to hold individuals in a relationship. However, dating relationships and friendships differed in that dating individuals were motivated to forgive by love, well-being, and the forgiveness-seeking strategy of their partner. Friends, however were less inclined to be motivated by love or well-being, but were more likely to report a deterioration of the relationship. It was interesting that dating individuals were the only ones to show a higher likelihood than expected of changing relationship type as a consequence of the infraction and forgiveness process. Here we are aware of the proverbial "let's just be friends" in response to some violation in the relationship. That is, I may forgive you, but I've also learned through the process that I no longer want to seriously date you. Friendships evidently can also be weakened but do not as often change relationship type.

The information presented here emphasizes the transactional nature of the forgiveness process as it demonstrates that the decision to forgive may be based on how the offender reacts after he or she realizes that the other person has been injured. It is important to consider the role of both the offender and the forgiver. This discussion also highlights the complex nature of the offender/offended relationship and the interrelationships between relationship type, motivation, strategy, and relational consequences. Perhaps most important, it is evident that forgiveness plays an important role in relational repair and personal well-being. As Walters (1984) puts it, "When we have been hurt we have two alternatives: be destroyed by resentment, or forgive. Resentment is death; forgiving leads to healing and life" (p. 366).

REFERENCES

Baxter, L. (1991). Content analysis. In B. M. Montgomery & S. Duck (Eds.), *Studying interpersonal interaction* (pp. 239–254). New York, NY: Guilford Press.

Baxter, L. A., & Wilmot, W. W. (1984). "Secret test": Social strategies for acquiring information about the state of the relationship. *Human Communication Research, 11,* 171–201.

Cody, M. J., & McLaughlin, M. L. (1988). Accounts on trial: Oral arguments in traffic court. In C. Antaki (Ed.), *Analysing everyday explanation: A casebook of methods* (pp. 113–126). London, England: Sage.

Cody, M. J., & McLaughlin, M. L. (1990). Interpersonal accounting. In H. Giles & W. P. Robinson (Eds.), *Handbook of language and social psychology* (pp. 227–255). Chichester, England: Wiley.

Cunningham, B. R. (1985). The will to forgive: A pastoral theological view of forgiving. *Journal of Pastoral Care, 39,* 141–149.

Emmers, T. M., & Canary, D. J. (1996). The effect of uncertainty reducing strategies on young couples' relational repair and intimacy. *Communication Quarterly, 44,* 166–182.

Enright, R. D., Eastin, D. L., Golden, S., Sarinopoulos, I., & Freedman, S. (1992). Interpersonal forgiveness within the helping professions: An attempt to resolve differences of opinion. *Counseling and Values, 36,* 84–103.

Enright, R. D., Freedman, S., & Rique, J. (1998). The psychology of interpersonal forgiveness. In R. D. Enright & J. North (Eds.), *Exploring forgiveness* (pp. 46–62). Madison: University of Wisconsin Press.

Enright, R. D., & the Human Development Study Group. (1991). The moral development of forgiveness. In W. Kurtines & J. Gewirtz (Eds.), *Handbook of moral behavior and development* (pp. 123–152). Hillsdale, NJ: Erlbaum.

Freedman, S. R., & Enright, R. D. (1996). Forgiveness as an intervention goal with incest survivors. *Journal of Consulting and Clinical Psychology, 64,* 983–992.

Hamilton, J. (1994). *A map of the world.* New York, NY: Anchor Books/Doubleday.

Hargrave, T. D. (1994a). *Families and forgiveness.* New York, NY: Brunner/Mazel.

Hargrave, T. D. (1994b). Families and forgiveness: A theoretical and therapeutic framework. *Family Journal: Counseling and Therapy for Couples and Families, 2,* 339–348.

Jaeger, M. (1998). The power and reality of forgiveness: Forgiving the murderer of one's child. In R. D. Enright & J. North (Eds.), *Exploring forgiveness* (pp. 9–14). Madison: University of Wisconsin Press.

Jellison, J. M. (1990). Accounting: Societal implications. In M. J. Cody & M. L. McLaughlin (Eds.), *The psychology of tactical communication* (pp. 283–298). Philadelphia, PA: Multilingual Matters.

McCullough, M. F., & Worthington, E. L., Jr. (1994). Encouraging clients to forgive people who have hurt them: Review, critique, and research prospectus. *Journal of Psychology and Theology, 22,* 3–20.

McCullough, M. F., Worthington, E. L., & Rachal, K. C. (1997). Interpersonal forgiving in close relationships. *Journal of Personality and Social Psychology, 73,* 321–336.

McLaughlin, M. L., O'Hair, H. D., & Cody, M. J. (1983). The management of failure events: Some contextual determinants of accounting behavior. *Human Communication Research, 9,* 208–224.

North, J. (1987). Wrongdoing and forgiveness. *Philosophy, 62,* 499–508.

Schonbach, P., & Kleibaumhuter, P. (1990). Severity of reproach and defensiveness of accounts. In

M. J. Cody & M. L. McLaughlin (Eds.), *The psychology of tactical communication* (pp. 229–243). Philadelphia, PA: Multilingual Matters.

Sillars, A. L. (1982). Attribution and communication: Are people "naïve scientists" or just naïve? In M. E. Roloff & C. R. Berge (Eds.), *Social cognition and communication* (pp. 73–106). Beverly Hills, CA: Sage.

Tutu, D. (1998). Foreword: Without forgiveness there is no future. In R. D. Enright & J. North, eds., *Exploring forgiveness* (pp. xiii–xiv). Madison: University of Wisconsin Press.

Walters, R. P. (1984). Forgiving: An essential element in effective living. *Studies in Formative Spirituality*, 5, 365–374.

QUESTIONS/THOUGHTS

1. What is your reaction to the five reasons to forgive mentioned in the introduction to the chapter? Do you believe all of them are equally significant? What do you see as the most important reason to forgive another person?

2. Describe an episode of forgiveness in your own life. Which of the forgiveness-granting or forgiveness-seeking strategies described in this article did you use or witness? What was their effect on the relationship?

3. Brainstorm several occasions upon which you have decided to forgive someone, either a member of your family, a friend, and/or a dating partner. What enabled you to forgive them? To what extent are your strategies or reasons for forgiveness different depending upon the relationship?

4. Do you believe it is really forgiveness if the individual doing the forgiving is doing it for his or her own sake? They may say, "I have to let go of this anxiety." or "I will feel better if I forgive him."

Struggling in Relationships

Introduction

"If you have to work at a relationship, there is something wrong with it." Many people have expressed this "throwaway" response, reflective of a fast-paced environment—"if it doesn't work, toss it." Fortunately, maturity and a history of relational losses have convinced most people that a relationship is not an old gym shoe; relationships have to be nurtured and renegotiated over time for them to continue to grow. When discussing relationships, many writers use a gardening metaphor that evokes images of caretaking—seeding, watering, and weeding.

The writings in this section are supported by the concepts of dialectical tensions and dialectical management. The ideas tie back to Bellak's porcupine dilemma: "How can we live together without hurting each other too much?" This question is reflective of the tensions that all significant relationships must manage. The term *dialectic* implies opposition, change, and interconnection. As people develop relationships, they encounter

struggles that are normal and predictable but that may feel frustrating or frightening. Managing these struggles usually takes attention and effort. Some tensions emerge from the natural differences among persons; others develop as a result of individual developmental changes or a crisis, such as illness, which affects the relationship. No matter what the source, tensions must be faced and managed. Many people cannot accept that conflict is inevitable but because no two people see the world in exactly the same way, our needs and goals vary. Even people you love may frustrate you, just as you frustrate them sometimes. Those who are aware of such predictable struggles often attempt to nurture their relationships to reduce or limit the tensions.

Many factors compete for attention in your life. Meeting your responsibilities at home, work, and school while maintaining multiple relationships, takes tremendous time and effort. The nurturing of friendships, work ties, or family relationships often receives the time and energy that is "left over," a minimal amount at best. Yet, unless relational ties receive high priority, relationships will "go on automatic pilot" and eventually stagnate or deteriorate (Galvin Bylund & Brommel, 2008).

The most difficult part of managing a relationship is addressing relational differences. It is easier to avoid a conflict, and remain frustrated or unhappy, than to address the issue directly. Such avoidance places relationships into a pattern of stagnation—creating off-limits topics and predictable silences—that eventually results in relationship dissolution. In her research on hurtful messages Vangelisti (1994) describes their negative effect on relationships, concluding, "If hurtful messages are sometimes associated with positive relational outcomes, partners must have (or develop) ways to minimize their feelings of hurt" (p. 53). Therefore, learning to manage conflict directly and constructively is part of relational struggle for many individuals.

In our diverse society, differences abound. Ethnicity, social status, religion, as well as gender, culture, and family-of-origin patterns create a multicolored quilt for each of us. We are wrapped in our backgrounds and we must try to explain ourselves to others with whom we interact. Conversely, we must try to understand the quilts that envelope others and encourage them to explain themselves so that we know them better. This is not an easy process but, over time, it can lead to significant rewards. These are the struggles of humanity.

Differences or conflicts may not be resolved, even in long term strong relationships. Noted marital researcher, John Gottman (1999), asserts that some problems are solvable and others create gridlock. Some issues are irresolvable because of beliefs or values that cannot be reconciled; all individuals can do is continue an open dialogue, listening to each others dreams and needs and trying to find areas of flexibility.

As you read the following selections consider your willingness to engage in conflict, rather than avoid it, to take responsibility for your part of a problem and to put forth explicit effort to repair relational difficulties.

REFERENCES

Galvin, K. M., Bylund, C. L., & Brommel, B. J. (2008). *Family communication: Cohesion and change* (7th ed.). Boston, MA: Allyn & Bacon.

Gottman, J. (1999). *The seven principles for making marriage work.* New York, NY: Three Rivers Press.

Vangelisti, A. L. (1994). Messages that hurt. In W. R. Cupach & B. H. Spitzberg (Eds.), *The dark side of interpersonal communication* (pp. 53–82). Hillsdale, NJ: Lawrence Erlbaum.

Collaborative Negotiation

JOYCE L. HOCKER AND WILLIAM W. WILMOT

Relational conflict is inevitable. No two people perceive the world in exactly the same way; differences characterize relational life. Hocker and Wilmot define conflict as "an expressed struggle between at least two interdependent parties who perceive incompatible goals, scarce rewards, and interference from the other party in achieving their goals," thus highlighting the interconnection of the communicators. By this definition, one quietly seething individual and a partner who is unaware of the anger, are not considered to experience interpersonal conflict. Although conflict cannot be eliminated, it can be managed effectively. Hocker and Wilmot suggest that the way to manage conflict effectively is through collaborative negotiation. As you read this article, keep in mind that two important communication behaviors are inherent in the collaborative negotiation process—argumentativeness and confirmation.

Agumentativeness is important in conflict situations. This may seem strange, as often being argumentative is associated with verbal aggression. However, argumentativeness implies your willingness to argue for a point of view, to speak your mind. Infante (1988) suggests several ideas

for preventing argumentativeness from turning to aggressiveness:

- *Treat disagreements as objectively as possible; avoid assuming that, because someone takes issue with your position or interpretation, they are attacking you as a person.*
- *Avoid attacking the other person (rather than the person's arguments), even if the attack would give you a tactical advantage; center your arguments on issues rather than personalities.*
- *Reaffirm the other person's sense of competence; compliment the other person as appropriate.*
- *Avoid interrupting; allow the other person to state her or his position fully before you respond.*
- *Stress equality and stress the similarities you have with the other person; emphasize areas of agreement before attacking the disagreements.*
- *Express interest in the other person's position, attitude, and point of view.*
- *Avoid presenting your arguments too emotionally; using an overly loud voice or*

interjecting vulgar expressions will prove offensive and eventually ineffective.

⊙ Allow the other person to save face; never humiliate the other person.

Confirmation is critical to collaborative negotiation. A confirming message communicates "you exist," or "you matter." Disconfirming messages communicate the opposite—"you don't exist," or "you don't matter." Confirming messages aid conflict management because they convey interpersonal respect even though there is disagreement.

Confirming messages occur on three levels (Cissna and Sieberg 2006):

1. Recognition—the most fundamental confirming message is to recognize the other person. Often we don't do this. When we fail to return a phone message, visit a friend, make eye contact, or approach someone we know, we fail to recognize them.

2. Acknowledgment—when we acknowledge the feelings or ideas of others, we send a stronger confirming message than when we simply recognize them. Listening to another or asking them questions are two ways to acknowledge them. So is paraphrasing—feedback that restates, in your own words, the message you thought the speaker sent.

3. Endorsement—this is an agreement message and is the strongest type of confirming message. Often we don't agree with everything the person said, but we can usually find something in the message that we can endorse.

In addition, collaborators have dual concerns for themselves and for others, sometimes called an integrative approach. Essentially, persons using this style are "assertive and try to find new and creative solutions to problems by focusing both on their own needs and the needs of their partners" (Guerrero, Andersen, and Afifi, 2001, 378).

In the following article Joyce Hocker and William Wilmot address the critical topic of collaborative negotiation, a highly valuable approach to problem solving. The authors lay out the assumptions underlying this approach, describe the

communication patterns and principles associated with this approach and then note the difficulty of using it. As you read this chapter think about your usual pattern for addressing conflicts and ask the question: What approaches are contained in this article that I can use to expand my repertoire of conflict management skills?

REFERENCES

Cissna, K. N. L., & Sieberg, E. (2006). Patterns of interactional confirmation and disconfirmation. In J. Stewart (Ed.), *Bridges not walls* (9th ed.). (pp.429–439) New York: McGraw-Hill.

Guerrero, L. K., Andersen, P. A., & Afifi, W. A. (2001). *Close encounters.* Mountain View, CA: Mayfield.

Infante, D. A. (1988). *Arguing constructively.* Prospect Heights, IL: Waveland Press.

Miller, S., Nunnally, W., & Wackman, D. (1975). *Alive and aware: How to improve your relationships through better communication.* Minneapolis, MN: Interpersonal Communication Programs.

Negotiation requires ongoing back-and-forth use of reflective listening and assertion skills by one or both parties. Management of conflict through effective negotiation requires listening to the other party; indicating that you understand his or her concerns; expressing your feelings; stating your points in a firm but friendly manner; linking your points to points expressed by the other party; and working toward a joint resolution that builds on the ideas of both parties and addresses all concerns.

—Umbreit, Meditating Interpersonal Conflict

Competitive, or distributive, negotiations assume that what one person wins the other loses. Integrative, or collaborative, bargaining, on the other hand, assumes that the parties have both (1) diverse interests and (2) common interests and that the negotiation process can result in both parties' gaining something. There are mixed motives—separate needs and interdependent needs. Whereas the competitive model assumes that someone loses and someone wins, **collaborative negotiation** assumes that creativity can transcend the win/lose aspect of competitive negotiations.

One classic example, often repeated in a variety of forms, comes from Mary Parker Follett (1940), who coined the term *integrative*. She illustrates an integrative solution to a conflict that at first appears to be competitive.

> In the Harvard Library one day, in one of the smaller rooms, someone wanted the window open, I wanted it shut. We opened the window in the next room, where no one was sitting. This was not a compromise because there was no curtailing of desire; we both got what we really wanted. For I did not want a closed room, I simply did not want the north wind to blow directly on me; likewise the other occupant did not want the particular window open, he merely wanted more air in the room. (32)

Although she doesn't detail her bargaining process, the result was clearly integrative—it integrated the needs of both parties. Integrative, or collaborative, negotiations emphasize maximizing joint benefits for both parties, often in creative ways (Bazerman, Magliozzi, and Neale 1985). Such bargaining places value on the relationship between the conflict parties, requires trust, and relies on full disclosure of relevant information (Walker 1988).

One of the assumptions of collaborative, or integrative, negotiation is that polar opposites are not necessarily in conflict. For example, if two people are negotiating, sometimes they can reach a satisfactory solution precisely because they want different things. Fisher, Ury, and Patton (1991, 74)

list some of the polar opposites that can be reconciled in integrative negotiation:

> …We suggested that conflict parties often specialize in certain goals. If you are most concerned about "getting things done" (results) and your work associate is more concerned about "looking good" (prestige, reputation), your needs are not necessarily incompatible. For instance, you may want to make sure the work is done for your campus committee and the other may want to make sure there is newspaper coverage of the event you are sponsoring. He can help you get the job done, and you can put him in touch with a reporter you know. Collaborative approaches treat assumed opposites as connected and not incompatible.

Follett (1940) relates yet another story that provides insight into collaborative, or integrative, negotiations. Two sisters were fighting over an orange and, after much acrimony, agreed to split the orange in half—a compromise. One sister used her half of the orange for juice and the other sister used the peel of her half of the orange for a cake. They overlooked the integrative, or collaborative, elements of negotiations. They each could have had a full orange since they wanted different parts! Unlike the sisters, collaborative negotiators engage in joint problem solving, jointly devising solutions that maximize benefits for both parties.

ASSUMPTIONS

Just as the competitive model of negotiations has basic assumptions, so does the integrative, or

Table 22-1

One party cares more about	Other party cares more about
form, appearance	substance
economic considerations	political considerations
internal considerations	external considerations
symbolic considerations	practical considerations
immediate future	more distant future
ad hoc results	the relationship
progress	respect for tradition
precedent	this case
prestige, reputation	results
political points	group welfare

collaborative, model of negotiation. The process presumes the following:

- The negotiating world is controlled by enlightened self-interest.
- Common interests are valued and sought.
- Interdependence is recognized and enhanced.
- Limited resources do exist, but they can usually be expanded through cooperation.
- The resource distribution system is integrative (joint) in nature.
- The goal is a mutually agreeable solution that is fair to all parties and efficient for the community. (Murray 1986)

As you can see, the collaborative approach has very different assumptions about the world than does the competitive approach. Rather than taking a dog-eat-dog view, it presumes that we can, even in the midst of conflict, work from "enlightened self-interest." We then get what we need from others but do it in such a way that also helps them achieve some of their goals. The collaborative bargainer is interested in preserving the relationship with the other. Therefore, driving a hard bargain at the expense of the other is not seen as a victory. Collaborative bargainers must maintain some interest in the other while holding out for their own goals. Unlike a win/lose situation, a collaborative agreement allows both of you to come away from the negotiation with an intact relationship, willing to trust and work with each other in the next bargaining situation.

COMMUNICATION PATTERNS

The obvious next question is, "How does one *do* collaborative negotiations?" Unless we can specify communication behaviors that can activate a collaborative negotiation set, the basic principles won't take us very far.... Also worthy of note are some specific techniques that lead to collaborative outcomes. If you want more lengthy treatment of these techniques, consult Rubin, Pruitt, and Kim (1994) and Lewicki and Litterer (1985).

Expanding the pie encourages collaborative outcomes because most conflicts are based on the perception of scarce resources; expanding the resources alters the structure of the conflict. For example, if Jane wants to go to the mountains and Sandy wants to go to the seashore, they might collaborate to find a mountainous seashore. Although it won't be the perfect mountain and the shore may have some limitations, they will get to spend their vacation together—they have expanded the pie. Often, children squabble with one another because of the perception that there is not enough parental care and consideration to go around. They fight, say mean things to one another, and struggle over the available love. As the parent, if you refuse to "parcel out" the love and attention, giving each child attention and focus without leaving out the other, you have expanded the pie. Whether the "pie" is actual or metaphoric, its expansion alters the conflict.

Nonspecific compensation, a process in which one of the parties is "paid off" with some other form of compensation, could also help break a competitive spiral and begin a collaborative set. For instance, the boss could have offered extra time off after the project was finished or offered to move up Caitlin's evaluation, which would result in the possibility of an early promotion. If two roommates are bargaining over use of the car, one may say, "OK, you can have my car, but I get to have the apartment for an all-night party after graduation."

Another example is looking to purchase a house and discovering that the owner is more interested in moving rapidly than in getting the stated purchase price. Your cousin owns a moving company, so you arrange to have the house owner moved at no cost. Your cousin charges you less than the going rate, and you get the house for less money than was originally asked. If the deal is sealed, you have created a form of nonspecific compensation. You have found some dimension that is valued by the other and have made an offer to offset your gains in the negotiation.

Logrolling is similar to creating nonspecific compensation, only one offers to "trade off" issues that are the top priority for the other. The parties have to find multiple issues in the conflict (for example, time is of the essence to you, money to him). Then, you arrange agreements so that each of you gets that top priority item while giving on the lower priority item. You "roll the logs" and shuffle issues until the top priority issues come to the top of the pile. In one organization the supervisor wanted more work from a particular employee. The employee wanted a fairer evaluation at the end of the year. With the help of an outsider, they negotiated so that (1) the evaluation process would involve discussion before memos were sent and (2) the employee would take on some extra work. Each received acknowledgement of his main concern and gave on the item that was vitally important to the other.

Cost cutting minimizes the other's costs for going along with you. For example, you want to go skiing with your friend. She is overloaded with work, so you offer to ski only half a day and not let her incur the "cost" of missing all her work time. Alternatively, you are negotiating with your romantic partner about going on vacation. He is tied up and feels he can't take off so many days, yet you both want to vacation together. So, you offer to drive your car to the resort you wish to visit, giving you the "decompression time" that you value, and suggest he fly to join you two days later. You shorten his total vacation time yet make it possible for the two of you to vacation together at the resort you want to visit.

Bridging invents new options to meet the other side's needs. You want to rent an apartment, but it is too expensive. You discover that your landlord is concerned about the appearance of the property. So you offer her a rent somewhat below what she wants but agree to do 15 hours of "fix-it-work" each month. She receives property improvements, and you receive reduced rent. Everyone gains!

In collaborative negotiations, parties brainstorm to invent new and creative options to meet everyone's needs. For example, Sally is negotiating with her work partner. She is frustrated about the job not being done, and Chuck is feeling that the work intrudes too much on his personal time. So, she offers to do more of the work on the spreadsheet if he will bring her coffee and sandwiches. Chuck gains more free time, Sally sees the project moving ahead, and both of them contribute to the task while maintaining their working relationship.

Bargainers who employ collaborative approaches view negotiation as being complex; thus, they find creative ways to "package" agreements and invent new options (Raiffa 1982). The collaborator moves from "fighting" to "conferring" (Follett 1940), assuming that working with the other will bring joint benefit. Information serves as fact-finding material for the bargainers rather than as a wedge that drives between the two parties. With information, one problem solves, explores causes, and generates alternative solutions (Lewicki and Litterer 1985).

Disadvantages

As with competitive tactics, collaborative approaches have some disadvantages. Probably the biggest overall difficulty is that they require "a high order of intelligence, keen perception and discrimination, and, more than all, a brilliant inventiveness" (Follett 1940, 45). If it hasn't been modeled in the home or on the job, collaboration may require specific training. Unless the beginning bargainer (whether an attorney, spouse, friend, or co-worker) has some level of training, the usual approach is to equate "good" bargaining with competitive tactics.

Murray (1986) has provided a comprehensive list of the disadvantages of collaborative, problem-solving, integrative bargaining approaches. According to Murray, collaborative negotiation

- Is strongly biased toward cooperation, creating internal pressures to compromise and accommodate that may not be in one's best interests.
- Avoids strategies that are confrontational because they carry the risk of impasse, which is viewed as failure.
- Focuses on being sensitive to others' perceived interests; increases vulnerability to deception and manipulation by a competitive opponent; and increases the possibility that the settlement may be more favorable to other side than fairness would warrant.
- Increases the difficulty of establishing definite aspiration levels and bottom lines because of the reliance on qualitative (value-laden) goals.

- Requires substantial skill and knowledge of the process to do well.
- Requires strong confidence in one's own assessment powers (perception) regarding the interests and needs of other side and other's payoff schedule. (184)

Collaborative negotiations, then, are not a panacea to be used in every conflict. They require considerable skill on the part of the negotiator, who strives to keep the negotiations from disintegrating into a win/lose approach....

THE LANGUAGE OF COLLABORATION

...No specific set of techniques will assure collaboration. Collaboration is both a mind-set and a set of techniques. If one does not believe that energetic cooperation will provide better solutions that competitive techniques, all the language of collaboration that could be memorized will not ultimately produce collaboration. Sometimes, however, you may get stuck looking for the right phrase to help a negotiation move toward collaboration. If so, consider some of the following phrases.

- I know this is difficult, but we can work it out.
- I can understand why you want to "split the difference," but let's try for some creative alternatives.
- I certainly appreciate your stance. Let's also talk about what I need to be satisfied.
- Your threat tells me how important this issue is to you, but it will work better with me not to threaten. Can we back this up and come at it another way?
- I don't see any conflict between us both getting more of what we want, but we have been acting as if what we each get the other is loses.
- I really do want a fair and durable settlement for both of us. That requires, of course, more direct information about what we each want. Let's explore that awhile."
- I will discuss with you as long as it takes to reach a settlement that will work for both of us.

- Yes, I see that you think that is the best solution. Remember, however, that there are two of us here. Let's see if both of us can be satisfied with the outcome.

Most people approach negotiating from a competitive frame of mind—assuming both sides have to lose part of the pie. The competitive or collaborative approaches are more a function of the bargainers than of any other factors. In fact, you can be in a negotiation where one person takes a cooperative and the other a competitive stance—a cooperative negotiation (Walker 1988). If you take a competitive approach, whether you are negotiating about how to spend the evening with a friend or buying a house, the negotiation process will probably be a competitive, win/lose experience. On the other hand, if you stick firmly to a collaborative approach, you will find creative options that someone with a competitive approach simply would not find. Creative options are often available (Fogg 1985), but unless the negotiators believe them possible and work to jointly produce those options, the negotiations will begin and end on a win/lose footing. Having had experience negotiating and serving as third party interveners, we are always gratified by how many creative, jointly satisfying options are available and constantly are reminded of how difficult they are for the parties to initially see.

Work by Kolb and Putnam (1997) and Putnam (1996) suggest that collaborative "moves" are not analyzed as genuinely collaborative if the intent is still, as in a competitive system, to promote self-interest at the expense of the other. Kolb and Putnam rightly point out the difference between a relational approach used for personal gain, which is manipulative, and true collaboration. As long as predetermined goals benefiting the self are pursued, the underlying assumptions of both competitive and collaborative modes are

- Self-interest
- Competitiveness
- Rationality
- An individualistic focus
- The exchange model

These underlying assumptions limit the transformative potential of negotiation. Transformation creates something new from what existed before. New ways to cooperate emerge, new feelings arise, and new solutions become possible. The transformative approach to negotiation rests on

- Community concerns
- Cooperativeness
- Subjectivity
- Intuition
- Emotion (Putnam 1996)

A negotiator following such a set of assumptions would focus on relationships, using connectedness, transformation, dialogue, and storytelling (Kolb and Putnam 1997). Such approaches reflect a relational unit of analysis (Wilmot 1995), which transcends the individualistic "I have to have mine," or seeing the self as separate from the other. The unit of analysis would not be the individual but rather the ongoing exchange produced from the joint actions of the participants. The Kolb and Putnam approach highlights many aspects of negotiation taken for granted even in collaborative approaches and is worthy of consideration, argumentation, and examination....

You may be thinking, "Why negotiate from a shared perspective?' When relationships are ongoing and the current dispute is just one of a series to be solved over time, no one gains from a narrowly focused, self-interested perspective. A common phrase from the ecology movement is "we are all downstream from each other," referring to the fact that there is no safe place for toxic wastes or pollutants to be dumped—someone will be adversely affected. Many conflicts are like this: downstream of the current conflict, another will surface, and if the relationship becomes polluted, the entire future will be poisoned.

REFERENCES

Bazerman, M. H., Magliozzi, T., & Neale, M. A. (1985). Integrative bargaining in a competitive market. *Organizational Behavior and Human Decision Processes, 35,* 294–313.

Fisher, R., Ury, W., & Patton, B. (1991). *Getting to yes* (2nd ed.). New York, NY: Penguin Books.

Fogg, R. W. (1985). Dealing with conflict: A repertoire of creative, peaceful approaches. *Journal of Conflict Resolution, 29,* 330–358.

Follett, M. P. (1940). *Dynamic administration: The collected papers of M. P. Follett* (H. C. Metcalf & L. Urwick, Eds.). New York, NY: Harper and Brothers.

Kolb, D., & Putnam, L. (1997). Through the looking glass: Negotiation theory refracted through the lens of gender. In S. Gleason (Ed.), *Frontiers in dispute resolution in industrial relations and human resources* (pp. 231–257). East Lansing: Michigan State University Press.

Lewicki, R. J., & Litterer, J. A. (1985). *Negotiation.* Homewood, IL: Irwin.

Murray, J. A. (1986). Understanding competing theories of negotiation. *Negotiation Journal, 2,* 179–186.

Putnam, L. L. (1996, September 26). A gendered view of negotiation. Address to Communication Studies Department, University of Montana, Missoula.

Raiffa, H. (1982). *The art and science of negotiation.* Cambridge, MA: Harvard University Press, Belknap Press.

Rubin, J. Z., Pruitt, D. G., & Kim, S. H. (1994). *Social conflict: Escalation, stalemate and settlement* (2nd ed.). New York, NY: McGraw-Hill.

Umbreit, M. S. (1995). *Mediating interpersonal conflicts.* West Concord, MN: CPI.

Walker, G. B. (1988). Bacharach and Lawler's theory of argument in bargaining: A critique. *Journal of the American Forensic Association, 24,* 218–232.

Wilmot, W. W. (1995). *Relational communication.* New York, NY: McGraw-Hill.

QUESTIONS/THOUGHTS

1. Reconstruct a recent disagreement you had with a close friend. Write down as completely as possible who said what in what sequence. Analyze the conflict using Hocker and Wilmot's ideas. To what extent did you use collaborative negotiation? Which of these strategies did you use, or might you have used?

2. Transcribe an argument from a movie with which you are familiar. Analyze the strategies used by the participants. Prepare a list of suggestions you would make to them in order to develop a more collaborative style.

3. Identify someone you believe demonstrates good communication skills. Carefully listen to that person engage in a problem solving discussion. What communication principles or skills did he or she employ to help solve the problem?

Difficult Conversations:
How to Discuss What Matters Most

DOUGLAS STONE, BRUCE PATTON, AND SHEILA HEEN

Conversations can be very difficult, especially when you are emotionally invested in an issue, you are interacting with a person with whom you have "a history," or you have a "hidden agenda." In each of these cases, the "you" gets in the way of the "we" creating major roadblocks on the road to reflective and open exchanges between individuals.

Most people have "hot button" topics or issues that are emotionally charged and which trigger very strong reactions when beliefs or commitments are challenged. If you are highly committed to environmental causes, it may be incredibly frustrating to discuss global warming with individuals who believe the issue is exaggerated by politicians and scientists and who see meeting the needs of the current population as more critical than looking toward the future. If you and your brother have a history is colored by his belief that you were always the "favorite" child and that you deliberately tried to outshine him in every situation, it will be very difficult to hold conversations in which you feel comfortable taking a strong stand because that will trigger a set of remarks about the old patterns. Finally, if you have a hidden agenda, such as showing up a colleague or gaining acceptance into a

certain group, your interactions with another individual will be colored by the "alternative audience" you are really addressing. This may lead you to try to win or upstage the other. Such situations may arise among colleagues, friends and family members. In these circumstances, each individual sees the other is "the problem" to be fixed or conquered.

Many of these difficult interactions become patterned over time; whenever a certain topic arises or one person makes a certain comment or exhibits a particular nonverbal action, such as a smirk or eye roll, the pattern kicks in and each party falls into the old pattern. And these are tough patterns to change! Yet, some conflict experts believe there are many ways to change such patterns but such changes take commitment and work. For example, Randy Fujishin (1998), a family therapist, suggests that a commitment to communicating for connection, accepting others and listening for understanding, will change the dynamics of a problematic relationship. Marital therapist John Gottman and Nan Silver (1999) talk about "overcoming gridlock" by moving to dialogue. In the following selection Douglas Stone, Bruce Patton, and Sheila Heen, experts in negotiation and conflict resolution, address similar issues but for much wider audiences. They work with governments, businesses, universities, and other organizations to help members solve problems, manage conflicts, and negotiate issues and move proactively through complex situations. In their book, Difficult Conversations, *the authors address three key "conversations" that characterize complex problem solving. These are: the "what happened?" conversation, the feelings conversation, and the identity conversation. The goal is to turn difficult conversations into learning conversations and in the process, to hold learning conversations as individuals learn from each other as they work through difficult issues. The following segment focuses on how to explore each other's stories instead of arguing about who is right.*

REFERENCES

Fujishin, R. (1998). *Gifts from the heart.* San Francisco: Acada Books.

Gottman, J. M. & Silver, N. (1999). *The seven principles for making marriage work.* Three Rivers Press, NY:NY.

Michael's version of the story is different from Jack's:

> In the past couple of years I've really gone out of my way to try to help Jack out, and it seems that one thing or another has always gone wrong. And instead of assuming that the client is always right, he argues with me! I just don't know how I can keep using him.
>
> But what really made me angry was the way Jack was making excuses about the chart instead of just fixing it. He knew it wasn't up to professional standards. And the revenue graphs were the critical part of the financial presentation.

One of the hallmarks of the "What Happened?" Conversation is that people disagree. What's the best way to save for retirement? How much money should we put into advertising? Should the neighborhood boys let your daughter play stick ball? Is the brochure up to professional standards?

Disagreement is not a bad thing, nor does it necessarily lead to a difficult conversation. We disagree with people all the time, and often no one cares very much. But other times, we care a lot. They won't agree with what we want them to agree with and they won't do what we need them to do. Whether or not we end up getting our way, we are left feeling frustrated, hurt, or misunderstood. And often the disagreement continues into the future, wreaking havoc whenever it raises its head.

When disagreement occurs, arguing may seem natural, even reasonable. But it's not helpful.

WHY WE ARGUE, AND WHY IT DOESN'T HELP

Think about your own difficult conversations in which there are important disagreements over what is really going on or what should be done. What's your explanation for what's causing the problem?

We Think *They* Are the Problem

In a charitable mood, you may think, "Well, everyone has their opinion," or, "There are two sides to every story." But most of us don't really buy that. Deep down, we believe that the problem, put simply, is *them.*

- **They're selfish.** "My girlfriend won't go to a couple's counselor with me. She says it's a waste of money. I say it's important to me, but she doesn't care."
- **They're naïve.** "My daughter's got these big ideas about going to New York and 'making it' in the theatre. She just doesn't understand what she's up against."
- **They're controlling.** "We always do everything my boss's way. It drives me crazy, because he acts like his ideas are better than everyone else's, even when he doesn't know what he's talking about."
- **They're irrational.** "My Great Aunt Bertha sleeps on this sagging old mattress. She's got terrible back problems, but no matter what I say, she refuses to let me buy her a new mattress. Everyone in the family tells me, 'Rory, Aunt Bertha is just crazy. You can't reason with her.' I guess it's true."

If this is what we're thinking, then it's not surprising that end up arguing. Rory, for example, cares about her Aunt Bertha. She wants to help, and she has the capacity to help. So Rory does what we all do: If the other person is stubborn, we assert harder in an attempt to break through whatever is keeping them from seeing what is sensible. ("If you would just try a new mattress, you'd see how much more comfortable it is!")

If the other person is naïve, we try to educate them about how life really is, and if they are being selfish or manipulative, we may try to be forthright and call them on it. We persist in the hope that what we say will eventually make a difference.

But instead, our persistence leads to arguments. And these arguments lead nowhere. Nothing gets settled. We each feel unheard or poorly treated. We're frustrated not only because the other person is being so unreasonable, but also because we feel powerless to do anything about it. And the constant arguing isn't doing the relationship any good.

Yet we're not sure what to do instead. We can't just pretend there is no disagreement, that it doesn't matter, or that it's all the same to us. It *does* matter, it's *not* all the same to us. That's why we feel so strongly about it in the first place. But if arguing leads us nowhere, what else can we do?

The first thing we should do is hear from Aunt Bertha.

They Think *We* Are the Problem

Aunt Bertha would be the first to agree that her mattress is indeed old and battered. "It's the one I shared with my husband for forty years, and it makes me feel safe," she says. "There are so many other changes in my life, it's nice to have a little haven that stays the same." Keeping it also provides Bertha with a sense of control over her life. When she complains, it's not because she wants answers, it's because she likes the connection she feels when she keeps people current on her daily comings and goings.

About Rory, Aunt Bertha has this to say: "I love her, but Rory can be a difficult person. She doesn't listen or care much about what other people think, and when I tell her that, she gets very

angry and unpleasant." Rory thinks the problem is Aunt Bertha. Aunt Bertha, it seems, thinks the problem is Rory.

This raises an interesting question: Why is it always the *other* person who is naïve or selfish or irrational or controlling? Why is it that we never think we are the problems? If you are having a difficult conversation, and someone asks you why you disagree, how come you never say, "Because what I'm saying makes absolutely no sense"?

We Each Make Sense in Our Story of What Happened

We don't see ourselves as the problem because, in fact, we aren't. What we are saying *does* make sense. What's often hard to see is that what the other person is saying *also* makes sense. Like Rory and Aunt Bertha, we each have different stories about what is going on in the world. In Rory's story, Rory's thoughts and actions are perfectly sensible. In Aunt Bertha's story, Aunt Bertha's thoughts and actions are equally sensible. But Rory is not just a character in her own story, she is also a visiting character in Aunt Bertha's story. And in Aunt Bertha's story, what Rory says seems pushy and insensitive. In Rory's story, what Aunt Bertha says sounds irrational.

In the normal course of things, we don't notice the ways in which our story of the world is different from other people's. But difficult conversations arise at precisely those points where important parts of our story collide with another person's story. We assume the collision is because of how the other person is; they assume it's because of how we are. But really the collision is a result of our stories simply being different, with neither of us realizing it. It's as if Princess Leia were trying to talk to Huck Finn. No wonder we end up arguing.

Arguing Blocks Us from Exploring Each Other's Stories

But arguing is not only a *result* of our failure to see that we and the other person are in different stories—it is also a part of the *cause*. Arguing inhibits our ability to learn how the other person sees the world. When we argue, we tend to trade conclusions—the "bottom line" of what we think: "Get a new mattress" versus "Stop trying to control me." "I'm going to New York to make it big" versus "You're naïve." "Couples counseling is helpful" versus "Couples counseling is a waste of time."

But neither conclusion makes sense in the other person's story. So we each dismiss the other's argument. Rather than helping us understand our different views, arguing results in a battle of messages. Rather than drawing us together, arguing pulls us apart.

Arguing Without Understanding Is Unpersuasive

Arguing creates another problem in difficult conversations: it inhibits change. *Telling* someone to change makes it less rather than more likely that they will. This is because people almost never change without first feeling understood.

Consider Trevor's conversation with Karen. Trevor is the financial administrator for the state Department of Social Services. Karen is a social worker with the department. "I cannot get Karen to turn in her paperwork on time," explains Trevor. "I've told her over and over that she's missing the deadlines, but it doesn't help. And when I bring it up, she gets annoyed."

Of course we know there's another side to this story. Unfortunately, Trevor doesn't want to know what it is. Trevor is telling Karen what she is supposed to do, but has not yet engaged her in a two-way conversation about the issue. When Trevor shifts his purposes from trying to change Karen's behavior—arguing why being late is wrong—to trying first to *understand* Karen, and then to be understood by her, the situation improves dramatically.

Karen described how overwhelmed and overworked she is. She puts all of her energy into her clients, who are very needy. She was feeling like I didn't appreciate that, which actually, I really didn't. On my end, I explained to her how I have to go through all kinds of extra work when she submits her paperwork late, and I explained the extra work in detail to her. She felt badly about

that, and it was clear that she just hadn't thought about it from my perspective. She promised to put a higher priority on getting her work in on time, and so far she has.

Finally, each has learned something, and the stage for meaningful change is set.

To get anywhere in a disagreement, we need to understand the other person's story well enough to see how their conclusions make sense within it. And we need to help them understand the story in which our conclusions make sense. Understanding each other's stories from the inside won't necessarily "solve" the problem, but as with Karen and Trevor, it's an essential first step.

DIFFERENT STORIES: WHY WE EACH SEE THE WORLD DIFFERENTLY

As we move away from arguing and toward trying to understand the other person's story, it helps to know why people have different stories in the first place. Our stories don't come out of nowhere. They aren't random. Our stories are built in often unconscious but systematic ways. First, we take in information. We experience the world—sights, sounds, and feelings. Second, we interpret what we see, hear, and feel; we give it all meaning. Then we draw conclusions about what's happening. And at each step, there is an opportunity for different people's stories to diverge.

Put simply, we all have different stories about the world because we each take in different information and then interpret this information in our own unique ways.

In difficult conversations, too often we trade only conclusions back and forth, without stepping down to where most of the real action is: the information and interpretations that lead each of us to see the world as we do.

1. We Have Different Information

There are two reasons we all have different information about the world. First, as each of us proceeds through life—and through any difficult situation—the information available to us is overwhelming. We simply can't take in all of the sights, sounds, facts, and feelings involved in even a single encounter. Inevitably, we end up noticing some things and ignoring others. And what we each choose to notice and ignore will be different. (Second,) we each have access to different information.

We Notice Different Things

Doug took his four-year-old nephew, Andrew, to watch a homecoming parade. Sitting on his uncle's shoulders, Andrew shouted with delight as football players, cheerleaders, and the school band rolled by on lavish floats. Afterward, Andrew exclaimed, "That was the best truck parade I've ever seen!"

Each float, it seems, was pulled by a truck. Andrew, truck obsessed as he was, saw nothing else. His Uncle Doug, truck indifferent, hadn't noticed a single truck. In a sense, Andrew and his uncle watched completely different parades.

Like Doug and Andrew, what we notice has to do with who we are and what we care about. Some of us pay more attention to feelings and relationships. Others to status and power, or to facts and logic. Some of us are artists, others are scientists, others pragmatists. Some of us want to prove we're right; others want to avoid conflict or smooth it over. Some of us tend to see ourselves as victims, others as heroes, observers, or survivors. The information we attend to varies accordingly.

Of course, neither Doug nor Andrew walked away from the parade thinking, "I enjoyed my particular perspective on the parade based on the information I paid attention to." Each walked away thinking, "I enjoyed *the* parade." Each assumes that what he paid attention to was what was significant about the experience. Each assumes he has "the facts."

In a more serious setting, Randy and Daniel, coworkers on an assembly line, experience the same dynamic. They've had a number of tense conversations about racial issues. Randy, who is white, believes that the company they work for has a generally good record on minority recruitment and promotion. He notices that of the seven people on his assembly team, two are African Americans and one is Latino, and that the head of the union is Latino. He has also learned that his supervisor is originally from the Philippines. Randy believes in the merits of a diverse workplace and has noticed approvingly that several people of color have recently been promoted.

Daniel, who is Korean American, has a different view. He has been on the receiving end of unusual questions about his qualifications. He has experienced several racial slurs from coworkers and one from a foreman. These experiences are prominent in his mind. He also knows of several minority coworkers who were overlooked for promotion, and notices that a disproportionate number of the top executives at the company are white. And Daniel has listened repeatedly to executives who talk as if the only two racial categories that mattered were white and African Americans.

While Randy and Daniel have some information that is shared, they have quite a bit of information that's not. Yet each assumes that the facts are plain, and his view is reality. In an important sense, it's as if Randy and Daniel work at different companies.

Often we go through an entire conversation—or indeed an entire relationship—without ever realizing that each of us is paying attention to different things, that our views are based on different information.

We Each Know Ourselves Better
Than Anyone Else Can

In addition to *choosing* different information, we each have *access* to different information. For example, others have access to information about themselves that we don't. They know the constraints they are under; we don't. They know their hopes, dreams, and fears; we don't. We act as if we've got access to all the important information there is to know about them, but we don't. Their internal experience is far more complex than we imagine.

Let's return to the example of Jack and Michael. When Michael describes what happened, he doesn't mention anything about Jack's staying up all night. He might not know that Jack stayed up all night, and even if he does, his "knowledge" would be quite limited compared to what Jack knows about it. Jack was there. Jack knows what it felt like as he struggled to stay awake. He knows how uncomfortable it was when the heat was turned off at midnight. He knows how angry his wife was that he had to cancel their dinner together. He knows about the anxiety he felt putting aside other important work to do Michael's project. Jack also knows how happy he felt to be doing a favor for a friend.

And there is plenty that Jack is not aware of. Jack doesn't know that Michael's client blew up just that morning over the choice of photograph in another brochure Michael had prepared. Jack doesn't know that the revenue figures are a particularly hot topic because of questions about some of the client's recent business decisions. Jack doesn't know that Michael's graphic designer has taken an unscheduled personal leave in the midst of their busiest season, affecting not just this project but others as well. Jack doesn't know that Michael has been dissatisfied with some of Jack's work in the past. And Jack doesn't know how happy Michael felt to be doing a favor for a friend.

Of course, in advance, we don't know what we don't know. But rather than assuming we already know everything we need to, we should assume that there is important information we don't have access to. It's a good bet to be true.

2. We Have Different Interpretations

"We never have sex," Alvy Singer complains in the movie *Annie Hall*. "We're constantly having sex," says his girlfriend. "How often *do* you have sex?" asks their therapist. "Three times a week!" they reply in unison.

A second reason we tell different stories about the world is that, even when we have the same information, we interpret it differently—we give it different meaning. I see the cup as half empty; you see it as a metaphor for the fragility of humankind. I'm thirsty; you're a poet. Two especially important factors in how we interpret what we see are (1) our past experience and (2) the implicit rules we've learned about how things should and should not be done.

We Are Influenced by Past Experiences

The past gives meaning to the present. Often, it is only in the context of someone's past experience

that we can understand why what they are saying or doing makes any kind of sense.

To celebrate the end of a long project, Bonnie and her co-workers scraped together the money to treat their supervisor, Caroline, to dinner at a nice restaurant. Throughout the meal, Caroline did little but complain: "Everything is overpriced," "How can they get away with this?" and "You've got to be kidding. Five dollars for dessert!" Bonnie went home embarrassed and frustrated, thinking, "We knew she was cheap, but this is ridiculous. We paid so she wouldn't have to worry about the money, and still she complained about the cost. She ruined the evening."

Though the story in Bonnie's head was that Caroline was simply a cheapskate or wet blanket, Bonnie eventually decided to ask Caroline why she had such a strong reaction to the expense of eating out. Upon reflection, Caroline explained:

> I suppose it has to do with growing up during the Depression. I can still hear my mother's voice from when I was little, getting ready to go off to school in the morning. "Carrie, there's a nickel on the counter for your lunch!" she'd call. She was so proud to be able to buy my lunch every day. Once I got to be eight or nine, a nickel wasn't enough to buy lunch anymore. But I never had the heart to tell her.

Years later, even a moderately priced meal can feel like an extravagance to Caroline when filtered through the images and feelings of this experience.

Every strong view you have is profoundly influenced by your past experiences. Where to vacation, whether to spank your kids, how much to budget for advertising—all are influenced by what you've observed in your own family and learned throughout your life. Often we aren't aware of how these experiences affect our interpretation of the world. We simply believe that this is the way things are.

We Apply Different Implicit Rules

Our past experiences often develop into "rules" by which we live our lives. Whether we are aware of them or not, we all follow such rules. They tell us how the world works, how people should act, or how things are supposed to be. And they have a significant influence on the story we tell about what is happening between us in a difficult conversation.

We get into trouble when our rules collide. Ollie and Thelma, for example, are stuck in a tangle of conflicting rules. As sales representatives, they spend a lot of time together on the road. One evening, they agreed to meet at 7:00 the next morning in the hotel lobby to finish preparing a presentation. Thelma, as usual, arrived at 7:00 sharp. Ollie showed up at 7:10. This was not the first time Ollie had arrived late, and Thelma was so frustrated that she had trouble focusing for the first twenty minutes of their meeting. Ollie was frustrated that Thelma was frustrated.

It helps to clarify the implicit rules that each is unconsciously applying. Thelma's rule is "It's unprofessional and inconsiderate to be late." Ollie's rule is "It is unprofessional to obsess about small things so much that you can't focus on what's important." Because Thelma and Ollie both interpret the situation through the lens of their own implicit rule, they each see the other person as acting inappropriately.

Our implicit rules often take the form of things people "should" or "shouldn't" do: "You should spend money on education, but not on clothes." "You should never criticize a colleague in front of others." "You should never leave the toilet seat up, squeeze the toothpaste in the middle, or let the kids watch more than two hours of TV." The list is endless.

There's nothing wrong with having these rules. In fact, we need them to order our lives. But when you find yourself in conflict, it helps to make your rules explicit and to encourage the other person to do the same. This greatly reduces the chance that you will be caught in an accidental duel of conflicting rules.

3. Our Conclusions Reflect Self-Interest

Finally, when we think about why we each tell our own stories about the world, there is no getting around the fact that our conclusions are partisan, that they often reflect our self-interest. We look for

information to support our view and give that information the most favorable interpretation. Then we feel even more certain that our view is right.

Professor Howard Raiffa of the Harvard Business School demonstrated this phenomenon when he gave teams of people a set of facts about a company. He told some of the teams they would be negotiating to buy the company, and others that they would be selling the company. He then asked each team to value the company as objectively as possible (not the price at which they would offer to buy or sell, but what they believed it was actually worth). Raiffa found that sellers, in their heart of hearts, believed the company to be worth on average 30 percent more than the independently assessed fair market values. Buyers, in turn, valued it at 30 percent less.

Each team developed a self-serving perception without realizing they were doing so. They focused more on things that were consistent with what they wanted to believe and tended to ignore, explain away, and soon forget those that weren't. Our colleague Roger Fisher captured this phenomenon in a wry reflection on his days as a litigator: "I sometimes failed to persuade the court that I was right, but I never failed to persuade myself!"

This tendency to develop unconsciously biased perceptions is very human, and can be dangerous. It calls for a dose of humility about the "rightness" of our story, especially when we have something important at stake.

MOVE FROM CERTAINTY TO CURIOSITY

There's only one way to come to understand the other person's story, and that's by being curious. Instead of asking yourself, "How can they think that?!" ask yourself, "I wonder what information they have that I don't?" Instead of asking, "How can they be so irrational?" ask, "How might they see the world such that their view makes sense?" Certainty locks us out of their story; curiosity lets us in.

Curiosity: The Way into Their Story

Consider the disagreement between Tony and his wife, Keiko. Tony's sister has just given birth to her first child. The next day Keiko is getting ready to visit the hospital. To her shock, Tony says he's not going with her to visit her sister, but instead is going to watch the football game on TV. When Keiko asks why, Tony mumbles something about this being a "big game," and adds, "I'll stop by the hospital tomorrow."

Keiko is deeply troubled by this. She thinks to herself, "What kind of person thinks football is more important than family? That's the most selfish, shallow, ridiculous thing I've ever heard!" But she catches herself in her own certainty, and instead of saying, "How could you do such a thing?" she negotiates herself to a place of curiosity. She wonders what Tony knows that she doesn't, how he's seeing the world such that his decision seems to make sense.

The story Tony tells is different from what Keiko had imagined. From the outside, Tony is watching a game on TV. But to Tony it's a matter of his mental health. Throughout the week, he works ten hours a day under extremely stressful conditions, then comes home and plays with his two boys, doing whatever they want. After the struggle of getting them to bed, he spends time with Keiko, talking mostly about her day. Finally, he collapses into bed. For Tony, watching the game is the one time during the week when he can truly relax. His stress level goes down, almost as if he's meditating, and this three hours to himself has a significant impact on his ability to take on the week ahead. Since Tony believes that his sister won't care whether he comes today or tomorrow, he chooses in favor of his mental health.

Of course, that's not the end of the issue. Keiko needs to share her story with Tony, and then, once everything is on the table, together they can figure out what to do. But that will never happen if Keiko simply assumes she knows Tony's story, no matter how certain she is at the outset that she does.

What's *Your* Story?

One way to shift your stance from the easy certainty of feeling that you've thought about this from every possible angle is to get curious about what you don't know about *yourself*. This may sound like an odd thing to worry about. After all,

you're with yourself all the time; wouldn't you be pretty familiar with your own perspective?

In a word, no. The process by which we construct our stories about the world often happens so fast, and so automatically, that we are not even aware of all that influences our view. For example, when we saw that Jack was really thinking and feeling during his conversation with Michael, there was nothing about the heat being turned off, or about his wife's anger at canceling their dinner plans. Even Jack wasn't fully aware of all the information behind his reactions.

And what implicit rules are important to him? Jack thinks to himself, "I can't believe the way Michael treated me," but he is unaware that this is based on an implicit rule of how people "should" treat each other. Jack's rule is something like "You should always show appreciation to others no matter what." Many of us agree with this rule, but it is not a truth, just a rule. Michael's rule might be "Good friends can get angry with each other and not take it personally." The point isn't whose rule is better; the point is that they are different. But Jack won't know they're different unless he first considers what rules underlie his own story about what happened.

Recall the story of Andrew and his Uncle Doug at the parade. We referred to Andrew as "truck obsessed." This description is from his uncle's point of view. Uncle Doug is aware of "how Andrew is," but he is less aware of how he himself "is." Andrew is truck obsessed if we use the baseline his Uncle Doug's level of interest in trucks, which is zero. But from Andrew's point of view, Uncle Doug might be considered "cheerleader obsessed." Among the four-year-old crowd, Andrew's view is more likely the norm.

Embrace Both Stories: Adopt the "And Stance"

It can be awfully hard to stay curious about another person's story when you have your own story to tell, especially if you're thinking that only one story can really be right. After all, your story is so different from theirs, and makes so much sense to you. Part of the stress of staying curious can be relieved by adopting what we call the "And Stance."

We usually assume that we must either accept or reject the other person's story, and that if we accept theirs, we must abandon our own. But who's right between Michael and Jack, Ollie and Thelma, or Bonnie and her boss, Caroline? Who's right between a person who likes to sleep with the windows open and another who prefers the window closed?

The answer is that the question makes no sense. Don't choose between the stories; embrace both. That's the And Stance.

The suggestion to embrace both stories can sound like double-talk. It can be heard as "Pretend both of your stories are right." But in fact, it suggests something quite different. Don't pretend anything. Don't worry about accepting or rejecting the other person's story. First work to understand it. The mere act of understanding someone else's story doesn't require you to give up your own. The And Stance allows you to recognize that how you *each* see things matters, that how you each feel matters. Regardless of what you end up doing, regardless of whether your story influences theirs or theirs yours, both stories matter.

The And Stance is based on the assumption that the world is complex, that you can feel hurt, angry, and wronged, *and* they can feel just as hurt, angry, and wronged. They can be doing their best, *and* you can think that it's not good enough. You may have done something stupid, *and* they will have contributed in important ways to the problem as well. You can feel furious with them, *and* you can also feel love and appreciation for them.

The And Stance gives you a place from which to assert the full strength of your views and feelings without having to diminish the views and feelings of someone else. Likewise, you don't need to give up anything to hear how someone else feels or sees things differently. Because you may have different information or different interpretations, both stories can make sense at the same time.

It may be that as you share them, your stories change in response to new information or different perspectives. But they still may not end up the same, and that's all right. Sometimes people have honest disagreements, but even so, the most useful question is not "Who's right?" but "Now that we really understand each other, what's a good way to manage this problem?"

QUESTIONS/THOUGHTS

1. Select a relationship in which you might be thought of as "the problem." Describe the other person and give an example of how he or she makes you feel like the problem. What might be that person's explanation for continuing to hold that belief?

2. Identify a person who regularly frustrates you creating a situation in which you perceive him or her as "the problem"? What reason might that person give to others about the way you are perceived? What would it take for you to change that perception?

3. Think about an older person you know well. What appear to be that person's "implicit rules"? For example, "A gift must be acknowledged with a formal "thank you-note or phone call" or "families must be together for all holidays." How do that person's rules influence some of the disagreements or difficulties her or she has with others?

4. Select a person with whom you disagree frequently. During your next interaction try to enact the "And Stance". Work to understand that person's story in order to help you recognize how you each see things matters and how you each feel matters. Describe the interaction and what, if anything, you learned from the experience.

I Can't Talk About It Now

JULIA T. WOOD

When friends, colleagues or partners reflect different styles of relational conflict, tension rises the minute a tough subject must be discussed or one party acts a certain way. Many people are raised to believe that conflict should be avoided, however researchers suggest that conflict in relationships is not only unavoidable, but they are a necessary part of highly effective relationships. For example, Knapp and Vangelisti (2005) suggest that conflict can produce a greater understanding of the two parties and their relationship, clarify the similarities and differences between them, help the two learn better methods for handling future conflict, and reveal areas in which communication can be strengthened. In his classic book, Getting Together: Building Relationships As We Negotiate, Fisher (1988) suggests that it is how people negotiate conflict that determines whether the conflict will be beneficial or destructive to the relationship.

Frequently males and females are socialized differently toward conflict. Boys may be encouraged to be expressive, aggressive and active in their responses, girls may learn to be gentle, indirect, and adaptive. When ending family conflicts, mothers are more likely to work toward compromise;

daughters tend to work toward compromise more actively than fathers or sons (Stewart, Cooper, Stewart, & Friedley, 2003). Research with adult males and females reveals physiological differences in response to conflict. Women are likely to experience more negative physiological changes as a result of negative conflict interactions than men (Jones, Beach, & Jackson, 2004). Marital disagreements are associated with women's higher blood pressure and heart rates (Kiecolt-Glaser & Newton, 2001) due to the effects of conflict.

In the following article, Julia Wood presents a model of conflict response and relates this model to gender differences in conflict response. She presents an example of a difficult discussion in which romantic partners use very different conflict management styles. This is followed by an overview of varied responses to conflict, a consideration of the influence of gender and suggestions for improving communication.

As you read this article, think about the differences discussed between how men and women handle conflict. Consider the question: To what extent does my experience confirm or deny the significant of gender in the development of conflict styles?

REFERENCES

Fisher, R. (1988). *Getting together: Building relationships as we negotiate.* New York, NY: Penguin.

Jones, D. J., Beach, S. R. H., & Jackson, H. (2004). Family influences on health: A framework to organize research and guide intervention. In A. Vangelisti (Ed.), *Handbook of family communication* (pp. 647–672). Mahwah, NJ: Lawrence Erlbaum.

Kiecolt-Glaser, J. K., & Newton, T. L. (2001). Marriage and health: His and hers. *Psychological Bulletin, 127,* 472–503.

Knapp, M., & Vangelisti, A. (2005). *Interpersonal communication and human relationships* (6th ed.). Boston, MA: Allyn & Bacon.

Stewart, L. P., Cooper, P. J., Stewart, A. D., & Friedley, S. A. (2003). *Communication and gender* (4th ed.). Boston, MA: Allyn & Bacon.

Takisha and William are locked into a tense discussion, the latest in a series of arguments about whether they will move to Minnesota. Takisha has been offered the job of her dreams: vice president of a training and development firm located in Minneapolis. William has never lived outside of Virginia, and he has no desire to do so now.

"This job is an excellent opportunity for me," Takisha says, repeating what she has told William before. "Can't you understand that?"

"I see that, but it's not an opportunity for me, and you don't see that," William replies. "You have a good job here. We both do. Why can't you let well enough alone?"

"Because it isn't good enough when I have such a big chance to advance."

"It is good enough, good enough for me, anyway!"

"But you can be a network technician anywhere. Your career doesn't depend on being here, so a move wouldn't damage your career. I can't go any farther in my job here. I can only advance if we move to Minneapolis. Not moving would damage my career."

"You have a fine career here. Why can't you just be satisfied and leave well enough alone?"

"You're not being reasonable."

"I am being reasonable. But life is about more than jobs. We can't live anywhere. This is our home." William paces as he speaks. "We don't belong in Minnesota."

"William, I know you're comfortable here. I know you love Virginia," Takisha says. "I can understand that. But can't you at least try living somewhere else? You might find you like it."

"I wouldn't like it. I don't need to try living there to know I won't like it. I hate snow and cold weather, and I don't like the hassles of a big city."

"So you're saying that a place means more to you than I do?" she demands.

"You said that, I didn't."

"That's the only conclusion I can draw if you refuse to move, knowing what it means to me." She moves closer to him. "Please work with me to make this happen."

"Stop trying to control me," he barks. "You're not going to roll over me just to get what you want."

"I'm not trying to roll over you. I'm trying to figure out how to come to some decision that works for both of us."

"I plan to stay here, with or without you." He clamps his jaw firmly and stares ahead at the wall.

"Sweetheart, you can't mean that," she says softly. "We can work this out if we really try."

William moves away and cradles his head in his hands. He doesn't speak.

"Don't go silent on me, William," she says. "The only way we can work this out is to keep talking."

"I'm talked out," he mumbles.

"But we haven't resolved the issue," she insists. "We have to keep talking until we work it out."

He shakes his head and doesn't speak.

"William, what would it take to persuade you to move to Minneapolis?" she asks. "What would make the move comfortable for you?"

"Nothing, I don't want to move." His voice is tense and tired.

"Well, that's not good enough. Come on, talk to me about what would make this move good for you."

"Nothing. I don't want to move period."

"Please don't be so inflexible," she asks. "There have to be ways we can work out something that suits both of us. How about an experiment? We'll move to Minnesota and commit to staying there for one year. At the end of that time, if you're not happy, we can reassess our options. How does that sound?"

"Just let me be," he says, moving across the room.

"How can I do that when we aren't through with this discussion?"

"We are through. I'm talked out," he says, his voice strained and his jaw muscles flexing tensely.

"William, not talking doesn't solve anything," she insists. "Please talk to me?"

"I can't talk about this now," he thunders and stomps to the door, opens it, walks out, and slams it behind him.

What is Takisha to think when William walks out on her and the argument? Often people in Takisha's position think the other person is refusing to deal with the conflict. They feel that the other person (William in this case) doesn't care enough about the relationship to work through problems. Takisha may feel that when William stomps out he is dismissing the importance of her career and is disrespecting their relationship.

But Takisha's feelings are only half the picture. What is William feeling? He may feel pressured by Takisha's demands for talk. He may feel she is trying to control him by manipulating him to do what she wants. He may not share Takisha's view that she's inviting him to collaborate. Also, he may not be comfortable talking about deep feelings, such as his attachment to Virginia and his anxiety about moving to an unfamiliar place.

Why does he walk out instead of working with Takisha to resolve the issue? Takisha perceives his departure as a sign that he doesn't care about her or the issue, but that may not be what leaving means to William. Perhaps he leaves because he cares so strongly about Takisha and the relationship that the discord between them is tearing him up. Perhaps he feels so strongly about not moving he is afraid he'll become belligerent, or even violent, if he doesn't leave. Perhaps he sees leaving as the only way to avoid letting the conflict degenerate into open warfare. Perhaps he sees nothing to be gained by staying and talking more because he doesn't know what else to say.

If Takisha understands how William perceives conflict, she might realize that his leaving is not a sign that he doesn't care about her career or their relationship. If William figures out that Takisha sees talking as a way to make them closer, maybe he will feel less pressured by her requests to talk. And perhaps if each of them learns that people have different ways of responding to conflict, they can better understand how each views conflict and why they both respond as they do.

UNDERSTANDING THE MISUNDERSTANDING

Psychologist Caryl Rusbult and her colleagues have studied how people respond to interpersonal conflict. Rusbult's work shows four basic responses to conflict. These are habitual responses that we learned at some point and now repeat without much thought or contemplation of alternative ways we might respond when tension surfaces in relationships.

The Exit-Voice–Loyalty-Neglect Model

Rusbult graphs responses to conflict in terms of whether they are active (assertive) or passive (yielding) and whether they affect relationships in ways that are constructive (preserve the possibility of continuing the union) or destructive (undermine the relationship and its future).

The exit response is to leave an argument or even end a relationship when conflict arises. William relied on the exit response when he stomped out on the conversation with Takisha. Another version of the exit response is what marriage counselor John Gottman calls "stonewalling." The person who stonewalls refuses to discuss problems and conflicts. The stonewaller may stick around, but he or she will not talk about problems. Exit, then, may be physical or psychological; either way, the person who exits ceases to be involved in the conflict. Exit is an active response because it is forceful. Because it doesn't allow people to resolve differences, however, it can damage relationships.

The neglect response occurs when a person denies or minimizes problems. When presented with a problem, the neglecter may say, "You're blowing this all out of proportion." William used the neglect response when he told Takisha that her career advancement was less important than other things in life. Neglecters often gloss over tensions and conflicts rather than deal with them. Because neglect is not forceful, Rusbult labels it passive. Because it doesn't address problems fully and with respect for each person's feelings, neglect can be destructive for relationships.

Loyalty responses involve quietly staying loyal to a partner and a relationship. Someone who uses this response may silently hope things will get better. Alternatively, she or he may think, "It could be worse" or "This doesn't matter a whole lot in the big picture." Loyalty may also be expressed by transferring anger or blame from the other person to oneself: "I should have known better." "I expect too much." Because loyalty doesn't assertively engage problems, it is passive. Because it assumes a relationship is worth continuing, it can have a constructive impact on relationships and people's feelings for each other.

The fourth response is voice, which is an active way to manage conflict. The voice response engages the conflict and invites the other person to collaborate in resolving it. "Let's talk about our problem" is a voice response. "I want to work this out with you" and "I'm willing to discuss the issue" are also voice responses. Because voice actively works to resolve problems, Rusbult considers it constructive for relationships.

In the example that opened this chapter, William used the neglect and exit responses, and Takisha relied on voice. According to Rusbult, their responses are typical of their respective sexes. Her research shows that men are more likely than women to respond with neglect or exit. Women, on the other hand, are more likely than men to choose voice and loyalty when conflict arises.

THE INFLUENCE OF GENDER

Some scholars think the different response tendencies of women and men reflect gender socialization. Psychologist Carol Gilligan maintains that women are socialized to value relationships and to use talk as a way of maintaining them. Masculine socialization typically places less emphasis on talk. As a result, many men have little or no training in how to talk about problems, especially problems that involve strong feelings. They may also feel frustrated if they can't fix a problem. Masculine socialization encourages men to fix things, to engage in instrumental activities that solve problems. If men feel they cannot do this when conflict erupts, they may communicate that the problem is unimportant or they may walk out on discussion or even the relationship.

Anne Campbell has studied links between aggression and gender. She reports that boys and girls typically are taught different meanings for conflict. She explains that girls are most often taught to respond to conflicts by talking (voice) and turning anger and disappointment inward (loyalty). Masculine socialization is more likely to encourage aggressive responses to conflict—asserting dominance to maintain control and self-esteem. Many boys are taught not to harm girls, however, so they may not feel able to respond aggressively in conflicts with women. It's not surprising, then, that men might choose to minimize conflicts (neglect) or leave when arguments erupt (exit) rather than risk losing control or acting aggressively toward women.

Further insight into the link between gender and responses to conflict comes from psychologist Eleanor Maccoby, who has studied socialization patterns typically experienced by girls and boys. Maccoby informs us that, at early ages, many boys are taught to derail tense interaction by threatening, inhibiting, contradicting, or topping a partner. William contradicted several of Takisha's statements and he issued a veiled threat to break up their relationship if she insisted on moving. He also showed little empathy with Takisha's feelings and desires. When these measures don't work, boys (and later the men they become) may feel they can't get control, so they exit rather than suffer outright defeat.

Girls, more often than boys, are taught to enable others in conversation. Typically, they learn to try to understand what others need and feel and to support others, even while disagreeing with them. Takisha expressed understanding of William's love of Virginia and his reluctance to move, and she tried to get him to talk with her about what he would need to be comfortable moving to Minneapolis.

John Gottman adds to our understanding of differences in how women and men typically respond to conflict. He maintains that men and women have different physiological reactions to tension and confrontation. During such times, men's blood pressure rises more quickly and stays elevated for longer periods of time than does women's. In other words, many men have a more intense physiological response to conflict than do women. Thus, it may cost [men] more than women to engage in conflict.

Working with his colleague Sybil Carrere, Gottman studied men and women in marriages in which they were in conflict about responsibilities for homemaking and child care…. Husbands often felt flooded by their wives' complaints. The men felt overwhelmed by criticisms and complaints. They felt psychologically and physiologically deluged and this disabled them from responding constructively. The women were less likely to feel flooded when they encountered negative emotions and criticism, and were more likely to feel that they could continue dealing with conflict.

Why do men and women differ so often in initiating and responding to discussions of problems? Carol Tavris, a social psychologist, suggests that women are expected by others and themselves to be "relationship experts," so it is their job to notice problems and to work to address and resolve them. Girls and later women, says Tavris, have the role of identifying and bringing up problems in relationships.

In childhood socialization, many girls learn how to talk about interpersonal tensions. Because they have experience in working through problems, dealing with conflict tends to be less uncomfortable for them psychologically and physiologically than it is for many men.

Psychologist Sharon Brehm extends Tavris's analysis by suggesting that women's socialization tends to make them sensitive to and aware of existing and potential problems in relationships. They may also see as problems events or conditions that men do not perceive or consider significant. In other words, women may feel a need to address issues that men don't perceive as difficulties, disappointments, and failed expectations. Brehm suggests that this difference may reflect women's higher expectations of relationships.

My own research confirms what we've discussed in this chapter. Several years ago I asked heterosexual women and men to describe how they responded to crises in their relationships. Although there weren't differences in the issues men and women cited as precipitating crises, there were clear differences in how they responded to the events. Men were more likely to deny that any difficulty existed (neglect) or to walk out (exit) when an acute problem erupted. Women consistently gave priority to voice as a means of responding to these extreme difficulties. If voice failed, many of the women in my study relied on loyalty—quiet allegiance to the relationship despite its problems.

I later replicated my study with lesbians and gay men. Again, I found that men tended to respond to crises by neglecting problems and especially by walking out of relationships. Again, the women gave priority to talking about problems, to working collaboratively to resolve issues or at least to understand each other. Caryl Rusbult and her colleagues confirm my findings by reporting that gender is more important than sexual orientation in shaping people's responses to conflict in relationships.

IMPROVING COMMUNICATION

The first step in dealing effectively with conflicts is to understand that people differ in how they view and respond to problems, tensions, and crisis. Someone who doesn't know how to talk about feelings and fears may not see voice as a useful or helpful response to conflict. A person who experiences substantial physiological discomfort when relationship tension arises may be less willing to engage in conflict than someone who is less physiologically taxed by it. A person who has been socialized to believe people should talk through differences may regard exit as a dismissive and counterproductive response to problems. On the other hand, someone who doesn't feel comfortable talking about problems may regard exit as a reasonable response to conflict.

Try to Understand Different Views of Conflict

William and Takisha might improve their communication if they realize they don't see conflict in the same way. To her, it's a call to engage, talk, and resolve problems. To him, it's a contest for control and he doesn't want to lose. In other words, they have different constitutive rules for what conflict is, or what it counts as.

The relationship would benefit if William understood that Takisha isn't trying to control him; that's not what arguments are about for her. The relationship would also be helped if Takisha understood that William feels pressured by her needs and her demands for talk and that he views conflict as a competition for power.

People who have different individual ways of responding to conflict can develop a variety of strategies for talking about tense topics without harming their relationships. I know of one couple much like William and Takisha. Like the men in John Gottman's studies, the man in this couple felt emotionally flooded when his wife brought up problems or complaints. He felt that she was trying to control him, to remake him into a person different from who he was. Early in their marriage, he would deny or minimize conflicts or he would stonewall. His wife relied on voice and was hurt continuously when he wouldn't talk with her. She interpreted his behavior as expressing a lack of caring about her and problems in their relationship.

When the couple's efforts to resolve their differences were unsuccessful, they sought therapy. After several months of counseling, each one began to understand how the other viewed conflict and why each of them responded in particular ways when tension arose in their relationship. Now when he feels emotionally flooded and unable to respond, he doesn't just leave. Instead, he says,

"I can't talk about it now, but I promise I will later when I've thought it through." This signals his wife that he does care about the issues and will discuss them—but later, after he's calmed down and regained the sense of control he needs. His response gives her the assurance she needs that he will collaborate with her to resolve the problem. It also gives him the time and space he needs to regain his emotional equilibrium.

Evaluate Your Responses to Conflict

Because our responses to conflict tend to be habituated, we seldom reflect on them. If we think about our ways of dealing with conflict, however, we may discover that they don't always serve us well. Realizing this provides us with an incentive to change how we act and what consequences follow.

An acquaintance of mine realized she was hurting herself and her relationship by not giving voice to her dissatisfactions and frustrations. As she explained to me, "They don't go away. They fester in me." She relied on the loyalty response virtually any time she encountered conflict with friends or romantic partners. Because that response did not enhance her self-esteem or her relationships, she worked to learn to voice her concerns assertively but not aggressively. She now feels that her relationships are more honest and healthy and she has greater self-respect.

Enlarge Your Response Repertoire

Another way to improve communication during conflict is to broaden your ways of responding to relationship tensions. Most of us have one or two habitual ways of reacting when problems erupt— behaviors for dealing with interpersonal tension that are almost automatic. Some of us consistently respond by trying to talk about the problems; others of us unfailingly react by refusing to discuss the issues or even by walking out on relationships.

Yet habitual ways of reacting to conflict are neither permanent nor absolute, and they may not be the most constructive ways for us to use. With commitment and patience, we can change our usual patterns of dealing with relationship tensions. Takisha might adopt the loyalty response so that William has some time to mull over issues before talking about them. William could commit to talking about his feelings about the move, difficult as that would be for him. The point is that we can choose to move out of the restrictive framework of our habitual responses to conflict. Doing so allows us to communicate in ways that are effective in a range of situations that invite diverse modes of response.

We don't change our habituated responses to conflict easily or immediately. To do so, we must make firm commitments to changing and we must develop patience. The first requirement for change is a serious commitment to learning new ways of viewing and responding to conflict. Unless you really want to change, you can't. You may find the motivation to do so, however, if you realize that your habitual ways of responding to conflict are not serving you or your relationships well.

The second requirement for change is patience. We need to be patient with ourselves and our partners. It's much more realistic to realize that the more we try a new style, the more comfortable and skillful we will be in using it. We also need to be patient with our partners. Like us, they have habituated responses to conflict and to our ways of dealing with it. When we change our approach to conflict, they may not immediately change how they respond to us. Given time and consistent effort to become proficient in new response styles, our partners and we will change the way we communicate about difficult issues.

Conflicts are part of relationships and human interaction. They're inevitable and they can be productive for us as individuals and for our relationships. Their productivity, however, depends on two conditions. First, we should recognize and respect different ways of responding to conflicts. Second, we should reflect on our own responses to conflicts and ask whether they are effective, honest, and respectful of ourselves and others. If not, we have the freedom to choose to become proficient in other modes of responding. We can change how we act and, if we do, we will influence changes in our partners and the relationships we collaboratively create and inhabit.

REFERENCES

Brehm, S. (1992). *Intimate relationships.* New York, NY: McGraw-Hill.

Campbell, A. (1993). *Men, women, and aggression.* New York, NY: Basic Books.

Gilligan, C. (1982). *In a different voice: Psychological theory and women's development.* Cambridge, MA: Harvard University Press.

Gottman, J. (1979). *Marital interaction.* New York, NY: Academic Press.

Gottman, J., & Carrere, S. (1994). Why can't men and women get along? Developmental roots and marital inequities. In D. Canary & L. Stafford (Eds.), *Communication and relational maintenance* (pp. 203–229). San Diego, CA: Academic Press.

Gottman, J., & Levenson, R. W. (1986). Assessing the role of emotion in marriage. *Behavioral Assessment, 8,* 31–48.

Gottman, J., Markman, H., & Notarius, C. (1977). The topography of marital conflict: A sequential analysis of verbal and nonverbal behavior. *Journal of Marriage and the Family, 39,* 461–477.

Maccoby, E. (1990). Gender and relationships: A development account. *American Psychologist, 45,* 513–520.

Rusbult, C. (1987). Responses to dissatisfaction in close relationships: The exit-voice-loyalty-neglect model. In D. Perlman & S. Duck (Eds.), *Intimate relationships: Development, dynamics, and deterioration* (pp. 209–238). London, England: Sage.

Rusbult, C., Zembrodt, I., & Iwaniszek, J. (1986). The impact of gender and sex-role orientation on responses to dissatisfaction in close relationships. *Sex Roles, 15,* 1–20.

Tavris, C. (1992). *The mismeasure of woman: Why women are not the better sex, the inferior sex, or the opposite sex.* New York, NY: Simon and Schuster.

Wood, J. T. (1986). Different voices in relationship crises: Contrasting reasons, responses, and relational orientations. In J. Ringer (Ed.), *Queer words, queer images: The (re)construction of homosexuality* (pp. 238–264). State University of New York Press. Albany NY.

QUESTIONS/THOUGHTS

1. Using Rusbult's model, which response to conflict do you usually use? After reading Wood's

article, do you want to change this response? Why or why not?

2. How does your gender affect your response to conflict? Give a specific example.

3. Watch a film in which romantically paired males and females experience ongoing conflicts. To what extent did their chosen styles reflect the gender patterns noted in the article?

Irresolvable Interpersonal Conflicts: Students' Perceptions of Common Topics, Possible Reasons for Persistence, and Communication Patterns

COURTNEY WAITE MILLER

Ongoing conflicts strain relationships. Revisiting an issue over and over again challenges partners, friends, and colleagues who find themselves caught up in difficult or unpleasant patterns in which they feel trapped. However, such conflicts are not unusual, especially in long term committed relationships or in involuntary relationships, such as those found in the workplace. In studying ongoing conflicts in marriages over four years, marital researcher, John Gottman, writes, "In looking at the videotapes of most of the cases, it was as if the couple had changed clothes and hairstyle, while continuing to talk about the same or analogous issues in precisely the same ways" (1999, p. 56). His research team found that 69 percent of the time these couples were disagreeing about a "perpetual problem" that they had struggled with for many years. The majority of these problems had to do with differences in personality or needs related to a core aspect of self-definition. When couples cannot find a way to dialogue with their perpetual problems, John Gottman believes that the conflict becomes gridlocked and the partners experience emotional disengagement. You may have experienced or observed such painful circumstances, when people you cared about got caught up in destructive continuous conflict cycles. *Such struggles may be considered part of the dark side of communication because they impair the ability of the relationship to function.*

Although friends and colleagues' ongoing, repetitive conflicts tend to be less dramatic and painful than couple conflicts, they also drain positivity and support from the relationship, creating tension and frustration for the parties involved. Less energy is directed toward sustaining the relationship as people regularly find themselves defensive and angry. Such battles impact their social circles of other friends or coworkers who learn to dread witnessing these encounters. If you find yourself in ongoing, repetitive conflicts you know the frustrations of this experience.

In the following article Courtney Waite Miller examines a specific type of ongoing conflict, one she refers to as irresolvable conflict. Such conflicts are based on the perception of at least one person that the issue will never be resolved. In other words, there is no way to bridge the differences, now or forever. If one party believes this, then that person sees no value in revisiting the issue. Miller provides her definition of irresolvable conflict and relates this to other descriptions of ongoing conflicts. Based on a study of undergraduate students, she discusses the types of issues that may be considered irresolvable, the reasons why they are perceived as never resolvable and, finally, she examines the related communication patterns. The three primary communication patterns include avoidance, argument prevention, and withdrawal.

As you read this chapter decide if you can identify any issues you would consider irresolvable and ask yourself, "What strategies have I used or observed to manage irresolvable conflicts or other ongoing, repetitive conflicts?

REFERENCES

Gottman, J. M. (1999). *The marriage clinic: A scientifically- based marital therapy.* New York, NY: Norton.

"Uncle Jack, I really wish you and Grandma would patch things up so that you can both come to my wedding. It would mean a lot to me to have you both there and know that you're close again."

"Sabrina, this isn't ever, *ever* going to be patched up. Do you understand me? Never. I'm not budging and she's not budging and that's just the way it's going to be. Aunt Lisa and I have already planned on not attending your wedding."

***

"John, there has to be a middle ground somewhere. I don't want to have a disagreement with you. Can't we work this out somehow?"

"You and I are never going to see eye to eye on this issue, Anne. No amount of talking is ever going to make me agree with you. Just save your breath [laughing]. Where do you want to go for dinner?"

***

"Mom, it's important to me that you respect my decision. Can we at least discuss this so I feel that you understand why I want to spend my life doing this?"

"You can talk about this career choice forever, but nothing you say will ever make me understand or support it. I don't want to spend your entire break from school arguing."

***

Have you ever experienced a situation similar to those above? If you are like me and a lot of people I've talked with, you probably have. When I discuss my research with friends and family, almost everyone responds with stories similar to those above.

As I'm sure most of you know from experience, conflict is a common occurrence in interpersonal relationships. Thankfully many interpersonal conflicts are short in duration (e.g., Vuchinich, 1987). However, sometimes we have arguments that seem as though they will last forever. When we have an argument such as those above or we experience multiple arguments about the same issue without getting any closer to a resolution, many of us conclude that the argument is impossible to settle. I call these arguments irresolvable interpersonal conflicts.

In irresolvable conflicts, at least one of the individuals involved believes the argument is impossible to resolve. In many cases, opposing parties agree that a conflict is impossible to resolve. However, both parties do not have to agree on a conflict's resolvability for it to be considered irresolvable. One may view a conflict as resolvable and another may view it as irresolvable. An individual might not even state explicitly that he or she believes a conflict is irresolvable. An individual might decide to keep this belief private and this does not matter in defining and irresolvable conflict. The definition rests solely on an individual's *perception* of irresolvability. The definition of an irresolvable conflict is a personal judgment. In other words, it is your perception that matters for you.

In my opinion, once you believe that a conflict is impossible to settle, you're experiencing an irresolvable conflict…and you will communicate accordingly. Your relational partner's perception of irresolvable conflict also will impact how he or she communicates with you. Experiencing an irresolvable conflict is certainly a walk on the dark side of interpersonal relationships, as described by Spitzberg and Cupach (1998).

I will now describe common topics of irresolvable conflicts, possible reasons why irresolvable conflicts persist, and the communication patterns that commonly occur in irresolvable conflicts. I also will address the relational impact of irresolvable conflicts. My research indicates that it is not just the presence of an irresolvable conflict that affects a relationship. Instead, it is the way in which individuals manage the conflict (Waite, 2004a). All of my findings are based on a study of students' conflicts in their dating or parental relationships. I will start with examples of common topics of irresolvable conflicts.

COMMON TOPICS OF IRRESOLVABLE CONFLICTS

When I first started researching irresolvable conflicts, I reasoned that only very important issues would become irresolvable. I assumed that a compromise could be reached for less important issues or, at the very least, individuals would believe that they could reach an agreement on less important issues if they were forced to do so. However, when I asked undergraduate students to describe an irresolvable conflict in their romantic or parental relationships, their descriptions were similar to those provided by individuals who described resolved conflicts or conflicts they believed they could resolve in the future.

Students perceived the issues at the heart of their irresolvable conflicts as not any more important than the issues involved in resolvable or resolved conflicts (Waite, 2004a). Some students described their issues as very important and some said their issues were not important at all. In reading students' descriptions, I identified serious issues and issues that were more routine. The following are examples of serious issues involved in irresolvable conflicts (Waite, 2004b):

- The topic is religion. I am a Christian and he [romantic partner] is Jewish. While we both believe in one God, we will never agree about his abilities or works in the lives of humans. This has also led to other debates such as evolution vs. creationism.
- My mother is extremely closed-minded on the subject of homosexuality. I have a man in my family who was my uncle by marriage. He divorced his wife because he is gay. My mother is convinced that he and his life partner are going to hell and she's not shy about that opinion at all.
- My parents are divorced and my father is currently dating someone who is considerably younger than he is and was a graduate student of his at one point. While she's very nice, I have issues with their age difference (57 versus late 30s) and the way their relationship began, as a teacher and student. My father does not see anything wrong with him dating someone younger and a former student and doesn't understand my issues with it.

As you can see, these individuals described difficult conflicts centered on religious and other personal beliefs. Religious/personal beliefs was the most common topic of irresolvable conflict described in both romantic and parental relationships. However, as I mentioned previously, not all irresolvable conflicts involved serious issues. Here are examples of less serious issues:

- The topic is habits and sleep patterns. I sleep late at night and get up late in the morning. My parents think I should sleep early, get up early.
- The disagreement is about how I manage my money. My mother is very meticulous about saving all her receipts and balancing her checkbook. I just don't have the time to do it and I don't see why it's important if I check my bank and credit card statements.
- My boyfriend pressures me to go out on weeknights and he doesn't agree that the fun should be saved for after the school week.

In these cases, the topics are more routine, everyday issues. Nonetheless, the individuals involved did not believe they would ever be able to resolve these conflicts. These examples show that even an unimportant issue can be perceived as irresolvable.

In addition to thinking that only very important issues would become irresolvable, I also thought that arguments on certain topics would evolve into irresolvable conflicts more so than others. I reasoned that it would be more difficult to resolve issues on differing beliefs, different personality traits, or other issues that are important to one's sense of identity. For example, John Gottman (1999) studies irresolvable conflicts in the context of marriages. He calls these conflicts perpetual problems and states that they often occur as a result of fundamental personality, cultural or religious differences, or essential needs of each spouse (Driver, Tabares, Shapiro, Nahm, & Gottman, 2003).

Contrary to my predictions, the topics of irresolvable arguments were very similar to the topics of resolvable and resolved conflicts. Students responding about conflicts in their dating relationships described conflicts about religious/personal beliefs, trust, and commitment. These three issues produced the most conflict. It did not matter whether students were describing irresolvable, resolvable, or resolved conflicts. Students reporting on conflicts in their parental relationships described conflicts about financial issues, religious/personal beliefs, and independence struggles. Again, it did not matter what type of conflict students were describing. These results show that arguments on just about any topic can be perceived as impossible to settle. So, if it's not the issue itself that determines perceived resolvability, then why are some disputes perceived as irresolvable when others are not? The answer might be in our beliefs about conflict.

POSSIBLE REASONS WHY IRRESOLVABLE CONFLICTS PERSIST

To research this idea, I asked undergraduate students why they believed they would never be able to resolve the conflict they described. More than half of the students thought that the conflict would remain unresolved because they believe individuals do not readily change their personal beliefs or

personalities. The following are examples of students' beliefs:

- This is an issue of values and personal beliefs. Religion is something that is deep-rooted and personal. Opinions about it rarely change.
- Our conflicting views are a result of the differences in who we are as people; we would have to radically change ourselves in order to resolve the conflict.
- What we want in life is strictly personal, so if we think differently about something, and at the same time are very set on that goal, it is impossible to change the way the other feels.
- This is a values/morals question and people rarely budge on those issues.

From reading these examples, we can see that many students think people do not easily change their beliefs or who they are as people. And, as a result, many students believe that irresolvable conflicts will remain unresolved. It is interesting to note that it's not the topic of conflict itself that makes a conflict irresolvable. Instead, students' beliefs about human nature lead them to conclude that a conflict is impossible to resolve.

These beliefs also reflect a sense of hopelessness. Many students seemed quite certain that the conflict was never going to be resolved. Would you continue to try to resolve a conflict you viewed as hopeless? Many of us would just throw up our hands and decide there is nothing we can do. We'd probably decide it's just not worth our time or stress to attempt resolution. However, if we don't even try to resolve a conflict, there is a pretty good chance that it is going to remain unresolved! In this way, believing an argument is irresolvable becomes a self-fulfilling prophecy.

On the bright side, knowing this information may help us avoid irresolvable conflicts in the future. We should remember that negative beliefs inhibit conflict resolution by discouraging resolution attempts. We might have a better chance of resolving a conflict if we maintain positive thoughts during the resolution process. This is related to the way we communicate in irresolvable conflicts.

COMMUNICATION PATTERNS IN IRRESOLVABLE CONFLICTS

Think about the three scenarios described at the beginning of this essay. In the first one, it is clear that Uncle Jack and Grandma are no longer on speaking terms. Their ties to each other as parent and child are present, but their day-to-day relationship and communication appears to be overshadowed by their relationship as opponents. This is one way irresolvable conflicts occur in relationships (e.g., Coleman, 2000, 2003).

In the second and third scenarios, the parties are ending their arguments and it is clear that at least one party in each conflict is convinced that the conflict will remain unresolved. In the second scenario, John makes his opinion clear to Anne and then asks where they should go for dinner. In the third scenario, the mother makes her position clear to her child and states that she does not want to spend her child's break from school arguing. We see that John and the mother would rather focus on their day-to-day relationships than work on resolving their conflicts. These examples show how irresolvable conflicts commonly exist within functioning relationships (e.g., Gottman, 1999). My research focuses on this type of irresolvable conflict—those that exist within an ongoing relationship.

I am particularly interested in the communication patterns involved in irresolvable conflicts within ongoing relationships. Gottman's (1999) research on perpetual problems in marriages suggests that it is not the presence of a perpetual problem that has an impact on relational quality. Instead, it is how a couple handles a perpetual problem that impacts relational quality. Although Gottman's research studies married couples, I believe this finding is applicable to other interpersonal relationships and my research indicates this. The way individuals manage an irresolvable conflict can have a big impact on how an irresolvable conflict affects a relationship.

Students who described irresolvable conflicts reported moderate levels of relational damage associated with the irresolvable conflict. Students who described resolved conflicts also described relational damage, but they described a bit less damage than students who reported on irresolvable conflicts.

More interestingly, students also exhibited communication patterns that likely help them endure the irresolvable conflict and resist attempts to resolve it. It is impossible that individuals believe that the relational costs of resolving a conflict are greater than the costs associated with continuing a conflict (Putnam & Wondolleck, 2003). Thus, they work to preserve the relationship despite an irresolvable conflict. Several communication patterns help individuals tolerate the irresolvable conflict within an ongoing relationship.

The first communication pattern I noticed was *topic avoidance* regarding the area of the irresolvable conflict. On average, the irresolvable conflicts in my investigation had persisted for 20 months at the time of my survey. One student reported an ongoing irresolvable conflict that already had lasted 10 years! Another student reported on an irresolvable conflict that had persisted for only 10 days at the time she completed my survey. However, on the whole, students did not continually argue about their irresolvable conflicts. Students reported an average of 13 arguments over the life of the conflict and reported that an average of seven weeks passed in between arguments regarding the irresolvable conflict. This indicates that individuals only sporadically argue about irresolvable conflicts (Waite, 2004a). One or both individuals likely engage in topic avoidance strategies in order to keep arguments from occurring more frequently. Here are some descriptions of topic avoidance that students provided:

- My parents avoid the topic as much as possible, but I am able to tell when they become angry about it.
- We both try to avoid the issue.
- This issue hasn't come up for some time.

The second communication pattern I noticed was *argument prevention*. Students indicated using moderate-to-high levels of preventative strategies such as actively trying to stop an argument from occurring or not allowing a small comment to result in a big argument. This strategy appears to be common when one person wants to continue discussing the issue and the other person had decided that he or she does not want to argue anymore. Unlike the examples above, the topic itself is not avoided. The topic is mentioned within the relationship, but at least one party works to avoid having arguments about the topic. The following are examples of students' preventative strategies:

- My partner tries to end the conversation immediately when I try to confront the issue.
- I know when he [my partner] is trying to get me to fight about this issue. I refuse to do it anymore.

The third communication pattern I noticed was withdrawal. From reading students' open-ended responses about what happens when they choose to argue about an irresolvable conflict, I saw that a large portion of the arguments ended with one party leaving the scene or refusing to continue discussion of the issue. This pattern is common in interpersonal conflicts. Benoit and Benoit (1987) reported that approximately 40% of the everyday argumentative episodes described by college students ended when the interactants stopped arguing or when one interactant left the scene. Similarly, Lloyd (1987) reported that 32% of disagreements described by dating couples ended when one partner left the scene or refused to continue discussion of the issue. Furthermore, Montemayor and Hanson (1985) reported that 50% of adolescents' arguments with parents or siblings ended with the interactants withdrawing without resolution. Here are some examples of withdrawal from my research:

- I state my points, then they [parents] provide their side. We argue rather intensely for a few minutes and then either party ends the argument by leaving.
- We both lay out our reasons for why we want our side of the issue and then drop the subject when it becomes frustrating.
- We try to rationally discuss it until one of just quits and says, "whatever."

In these examples, both parties actively engage in arguments regarding the irresolvable issue. However, it appears that individuals recognize the conflict is harmful to their relationships and, at some point within the argument, decide not to engage in a prolonged dispute. It seems that individuals decide to "agree to disagree" rather than to continue arguing. Leaving the scene or refusing to continue arguing is a quick method of enacting such an arrangement.

Do you notice any commonalities between topic avoidance, argument prevention, and withdrawal? All are aimed at limiting or containing communication about the irresolvable conflict. And, in fact, this might help individuals endure the presence of an irresolvable conflict in an important relationship. These strategies may also limit the amount of relational damage associated with an irresolvable conflict. However, none of the strategies are aimed at resolving the irresolvable conflict. As a result, all of these strategies probably contribute to prolonging irresolvable conflicts. In other words, the communication patterns individuals engage in during an irresolvable conflict in an ongoing relationship focus on relationship preservation at the expense of conflict resolution. It appears that many individuals would rather maintain a satisfying relationship than resolve the conflict.

Are these strategies successful? My data does not allow me to establish a causal link between these strategies and relational satisfaction. It is impossible to say with certainty that these strategies increase relational satisfaction during an irresolvable conflict. However, I can say that relational satisfaction for individuals experiencing irresolvable conflicts was very similar to satisfaction levels of individuals who described resolvable and resolved conflicts. This shows that individuals are able to tolerate the presence of an irresolvable conflict and maintain relational satisfaction. This is good news when we consider that these strategies likely will not lead to conflict resolution.

CONCLUSION

In thinking about these results, it is important to emphasize that the students in my study were college undergraduates. Most were 18–22 years of age. In addition, I asked students to report on conflicts in romantic or parental relationships so this study did not include irresolvable conflicts that occur in other relationships. Conflicts in other types of relationships might vary.

Even with those limitations in mind, I hope that this study has given you a greater understanding of irresolvable conflicts in ongoing relationships. Irresolvable conflicts can be about issues that are very important to the individuals involved or can occur as a result of differences in everyday issues. Our beliefs about conflict might encourage the existence of irresolvable interpersonal conflicts by discouraging resolution attempts. However, communication techniques such as topic avoidance, argument prevention, and withdrawal might allow individuals to tolerate the presence of an irresolvable conflict while maintaining high levels of relational satisfaction. Hopefully considering these issues will help you to see your experiences of irresolvable conflicts with a new perspective.

REFERENCES

Benoit, W. J., & Benoit, P. J. (1987). Everyday argument practices of naïve social actors. In J.W. Wentzel (Ed.), *Argument and critical practices: Proceedings of the fifth SCA/AFA conference on argumentation* (pp. 465–473). Annandale, VA: Speech Communication Association.

Coleman, P. T. (2000). Intractable conflict. In M. Deutsch & P. T. Coleman (Eds.), *The handbook of conflict resolution: Theory and practice* (pp. 428–450). San Francisco, CA: Jossey-Bass.

Coleman, P. T. (2003). Characteristics of protracted, intractable conflict: Towards the development of a meta-framework—I. First paper in a three-part series. *Peace and Conflict: Journal of Peace Psychology, 9*(1), 1–37.

Driver, J., Tabares, A., Shapiro, A., Nahm, E. Y., & Gottman, J. M. (2003). Interactional patterns in marital success or failure: Gottman laboratory studies. In F. Walsh (Ed.), *Normal family processes: Growing diversity and complexity* (pp. 493–513). New York, NY: Guilford Press.

Gottman, J. M. (1999). *The marriage clinic: A scientifically- based marital therapy*. New York, NY: Norton.

Johnson, K. L., & Roloff, M. E. (1998). Serial arguing and relational quality. *Communication Research, 25*(3), 327–343.

Lloyd, S. A. (1987). Conflict in premarital relationships: Differential perceptions of males and females. *Family Relations, 36,* 290–294.

Montemayor, R., & Hanson, E. (1985). A naturalistic view of conflict between adolescents and their parents and siblings. *Journal of Early Adolescence, 5,* 23–30.

Putnam, L. L., & Wondolleck, J. M. (2003). Intractability: Definitions, dimensions, and distinctions. In R. Lewicki, B. Gray, & M. Elliott (Eds.), *Making sense of intractable environmental disputes* (pp. 35–59). Washington, DC: Island Press.

Spitzberg, B. H., & Cupach, W. R. (1998). Dusk, detritus, and delusion: A prolegomenon to the dark side of close relationships. In B. H. Spitzberg & W. R. Cupach (Eds.), *The dark side of close relationships* (pp. xi–xxii). Mahwah, NJ: Lawrence Erlbaum.

Vuchinich, S. (1987). Starting and stopping spontaneous family conflicts. *Journal of Marriage and the Family, 49,* 591–601.

Waite, C. (2004a). *Intractable interpersonal conflicts* (Unpublished doctoral dissertation). Northwestern University, Evanston, IL.

Waite, C. (2004b). Irresolvable interpersonal conflicts. Unpublished raw data.

QUESTIONS/THOUGHTS

1. What verbal or nonverbal cues emerge in ongoing irresolvable conflicts that help you distinguish them from conflicts that are not repetitive?
2. Describe the use of one or more of the communication patterns described by the author in an ongoing irresolvable conflict with which you are familiar.
3. From your experience, identify three issues that are likely to be considered irresolvable and explain why you, or other individuals, consider them irresolvable.

4. Identify factors you believe are necessary if long term romantic partners or very close friends are to maintain significant relationships that involve irresolvable conflicts. Give a specific example in your answer.

Anti-Comforting Messages

DALE HAMPLE

No matter how hard you may try, there is no guaranteed, tried-and-true method for comforting someone when they are upset. Everyone has a different style of coping and responds best to varying types of comforting. You were socialized into ways to comfort others by your family members as well as friends. In some cases gender influenced this socialization as males often receive messages to avoid being feminine, and therefore sensitive, whereas females are encouraged to express their sensitivity. Therefore, some males learned that joking, one-liners, or general avoidance is a workable and appropriate way to get the other person to laugh or move on. Their female counterparts learned to talk things out and convey sensitivity. By young adulthood such communication rules become less powerful but, in many situations, individuals have difficulty conveying an appropriate sense of support when others are in emotional need. These are times that call for emotional support and when an inappropriate response can create relational frustration and hurt. As Brant Burleson (2003) so aptly puts it, "But seeking social support does not guarantee the receipt of sensitive, effective support" (p. 551). In describing how emotional

support relates to communication Burleson (2003) suggests, "It is useful to view emotional support as specific lines of communicative behavior enacted by one party with the intent of helping another cope effectively with emotional distress" (p. 552). Yet, some attempts at providing emotional support fail miserably because they tend to reflect the respondents' discomfort with displaying direct sensitivity and lack of a wide communication repertoire from which to select the appropriate response to an emotionally charged situation. Therefore the response to another's bid for support results in distance and frustration instead of providing a sense of comfort and understanding.

According to Dale Hample, there are very specific strategies that are almost guaranteed to make another feel worse, not better. Even with the best intentions, these "anti-comforting" styles often serve to discount, disregard, or diminish the feelings of someone in emotional distress, under the guise of words of support or assistance. Using the underlying tenets of face theory and confirmation, disconfirmation, and rejection, Hample frames this unusual communication circumstance and demonstrates how certain attempts at supportive messages *can be hurtful. Further, Hample depicts multiple examples of the differences between content level anti-comforting and relationship level anti-comforting. Through the descriptions of each type of anti-comforting, the ways to recognize and avoid anti-comforting in one's own interactions are made clear. Overall, this chapter offers a very interesting and detailed discussion of a pervasive yet illusive and often unrecognized issue in communication.*

As you read this chapter think about anti-comforting messages you have experienced and ask yourself the question, why did these messages fail and what might have been said or done differently?

REFERENCE

Burleson, B. (2003). Emotional support skills. In J. O. Greene & B. R. Burleson (Eds.), *Handbook of communication and social interaction skills* (pp. 551–594). Mahwah, NJ: Lawrence Erlbaum.

I've always really liked baseball, and I played slow pitch softball in a church league until I was nearly 50. I'm a right-handed hitter, but had realized many years ago that people like Ozzie Smith play on the left side of the diamond, and people like me play on the right. So I learned to hit to right field, and was pretty consistent at it. A couple of games into my final season, I decided to quit at the end of the summer. I hit a line drive between the first and second basemen, and as I trundled to first, the right fielder threw to the first baseman. I've always been pretty slow-footed, so the play was close. As the ball arrived, the umpire threw up his hands, but didn't call me out or safe. He shouted, "No play." Several of us were confused, so the umpire explained. Before the season had begun, the team captains had met and had decided on a new rule: outfielders couldn't throw runners out at first. As I drove home that night, I realized that the rule had probably been put in for me and a player on the Catholic team, who had the same game, age, and athletic makeup as I did. I felt a little embarrassed about it, and at the next game I made a couple of awkward comments about it to my team. I guess I was hoping for some sympathy or encouragement.

But it turns out that guys are guys whether they're on a church team or not, and all I got for my trouble was having the rule named after me.

When we think about our lives in the short term, we wish that things would always go smoothly, without crises, disappointments, or humiliation. But in the long term, we often benefit from those stressful or hurtful moments. I got over my short term feelings about the Dale Rule, and don't really regret having left behind a game that I was getting worse at. My golf game has improved considerably, and I enjoy having my weekend nights back. I have had other experiences that I don't wish to share, and several of those have made me a better person and father, even though the first moments of my enlightenment felt awful. In the episode when the rule got named, I was looking for some comforting. What I got instead was anti-comforting, even though it was intended in a good humored way. It's nice to know that the guys didn't think I was fragile—most of them actually have good interpersonal skills and would have treated me differently if they had thought it was needed—but I actually wanted a little bit of social support. When our lives hit bumps, that's what we all want from those around us, whether we're self-contained or delicate or somewhere in between.

People often find themselves in emotional need. Perhaps the problem is a very substantial one, such as a death in the family or a positive diagnosis of HIV, perhaps it seems huge in the moment but might dissipate with time, such as abandonment by a relational partner, and perhaps it's even more minor than the Dale Rule. But in varying degrees, and with varying justification, people sometimes need the aid of those around them. Those of us fortunate enough to have a supportive social network and to receive good quality comforting from others reap a number of substantial benefits: we are more at peace, we have better health, we find more satisfaction in our relationships, we feel better about ourselves, and we have a generally more positive outlook on life (see reviews in Burleson, 2003, or Goldsmith, 2004). When our emotional needs are not met, either by circumstances or by others, we suffer in some measure.

This essay is about talking to those in emotional need, whether that need is great or small. Forming such messages—deciding what to say and how to say it—is one of the most intricate of all communication skills. Unfortunately, most of what we say to others day to day really isn't consequential, and so we form the habit of simply expressing whatever first comes to mind, without much worry about getting it wrong. When comforting is called for, however, our messages are almost never neutral in their effects, and we have to overcome the routine habit of just talking without reflection. We can make things better, or we can make them worse. And what we say in those moments can reverberate for a surprisingly long time.

Some time ago, I got curious about what I'm calling anti-comforting messages. These are things that are intended as emotional support, but are so incompetent that they actually backfire. (The Dale Rule is a mild example.) I expressed my interest on crtnet@natcom.org, a discussion list for people (mostly faculty and graduate students) with advanced interests in communication, and invited others to send me examples. Eventually I compiled them and put them on my own website, (www.wiu.edu/users/mfdjh), where you can see the whole list. (If you have more examples, they will be welcome.) I will use these to illustrate the points I make here.

SETTING THE STAGE: BASIC PRINCIPLES OF INTERPERSONAL COMMUNICATION

Before plunging into the abyss of communication incompetence, we need to start by seeing why emotional support messages are so hard to accomplish properly. The first thing to notice is that every message has two levels of meaning, content, and relationship (Watzlawick, Beavin, & Jackson, 1967). Suppose I were to say, "go back one paragraph, and highlight the definition of anti-comforting messages." The content of that statement involves highlighting, paragraphs, and definitions. What the sentence means, more or less on its surface, is the content level of meaning. But the statement also has relational meanings, because

it implies who I am, who you are, and what our relationship is. Thus it has several other meanings as well: you need to be told what to highlight; I am entitled to tell you what to highlight; and you have to do what I tell you. If you're annoyed at my statement, we can probably trace your unrest to the relational implications of it, not its content. Every message projects a relationship between the two people. It can be a projection of dominance, as in the highlighting command, or it can suggest equality, caring, contempt, or any number of other things. Routine comments—those that are given and heard as routine, that is—generally don't create any new relational issues. But when people are in emotional need, things can be more labile.

Relationships are composed of people, or more precisely, of identities (Goffman, 1959, 1967). Each person has what we call positive face (Brown & Levinson, 1987), which consists of the positive things we want others to think about us. Commonly, we want to be seen as smart, friendly, good humored, and so forth, but sometimes we might want to be viewed as cold or dangerous. Even though the identity we want can change, we still intend that others see what it is, acknowledge it, and positively confirm it. The other person is doing the same thing, and there is a kind of unspoken social contract by which we each agree to support the other's identity if at all possible. We also have negative face, which is the desire to be unimpeded. We want to be free to act and think as we please. When events or people impede us, or try to, that is negative, and we resist it (Brehm, 1966). The same social contract applies here, too: we each try to avoid interfering with the other's freedoms. When circumstances or accident result in an affront to either negative or positive face, we often engage in facework to repair things: we apologize, we try to take it back, we give a compliment. All interpersonal communication involves a negotiation of identities, and this is done in part by the relational meanings of what we say, because these bear on face.

Three particular kinds of relational meaning are important (Watzlawick, Beavin, & Jackson, 1967). When we become aware of another person's projected identity, we can confirm it, reject it, or disconfirm it. To confirm the other's definition of self is to support it. If the other hints that she is a good student, we immediately compliment her studiousness or grades. Rejecting the other's identity means confronting it and disagreeing. If someone says he is adept at video games, we can refute that projection by suggesting that his little brother is better. Disconfirming a definition of self involves simply ignoring it. A spouse casually sets a new trophy on the dining room table, and the other spouse puts it in a box without comment or eye contact. These three relational meanings, as you might suppose, are in order of supportiveness: confirmation is most positive, following by rejection (at least the identity was noticed, after all), and disconfirmation is worst (the relational message being, "you don't exist"). Notice that there aren't any other possibilities. When you are drawn into a conversation, you have to do one of these three things (or perhaps more than one, in different degrees).

APPLYING THE BASIC PRINCIPLES TO MOMENTS OF EMOTIONAL NEED

Every moment of emotional hurt is unique, and every person is different. Still, there are some likely features that we should be alert to. First of all, the upset person is emotional and perhaps not thinking as clearly as usual. This is not the time to expect him or her to be perceptive about your intentions or feelings. In fact, when people are in the throes of depression or anger, they may well lash out with little provocation, or mistake a helpful overture for taunting. For this reason, Burleson (2003, p. 580) suggests that the support provider actually be explicit about wanting to help (e.g., "I'm on your side in this"). The person in need is likely to be especially sensitive to identity issues, because emotional pain inevitably creates a focus on self. And most of all, it is his or her moment, not yours. The support provider may have to put self in the background, and exclusively feature the other.

Second, different categories of things create emotional stress. A key consideration is whether the problem is manageable, that is, whether it can be fixed with constructive action. For instance, a

family member passing away is uncontrollable, and nothing instrumental can be done to reverse this (Davidowitz & Myrick, 1984, have studied bereavement support). In contrast, being stressed because of an upcoming public speaking responsibility is open to instrumental advice or assistance. Advice is out of place if the problem isn't manageable, but might be allowable if the problem is potentially malleable. Another consideration is whether the support provider can do something substantial to alleviate the problem. If a friend is late to work and you have a car, offering a ride might be more effective and appropriate than a conversation about feelings.

A third issue is that emotionally hurtful events don't come with obvious labels. Something that bothers one person might pass unnoticed by another. One friend might take a speeding ticket in stride, but another might be extremely upset by it. Whether the instigating event seems justifiable in its emotional effects is really irrelevant to the person who is hurt. It is his or her feelings that are at issue, not your independent judgment about how weighty the circumstances really are. Everything must be seen through the eyes of the person in need, if genuine comfort is to be provided.

Lastly, we should pause for a moment to consider the support provider. As I've implied, giving good emotional assistance isn't easy. As with any voluntary behavior, offering support depends on motivation and ability (Burleson & MacGeorge, 2002). If you don't really have a strong impulse to help, you may not be likely to do well even if you have a high level of skill. Adults can generally create a temporary artificial motivation to help others, though. Most of us can force ourselves to be nurturing, to go through the motions even if we are honestly indifferent, just because it seems to be called for in the moment. Ability deficits are harder to repair. The support provider has to be perceptive about others, has to form the right goals for the interaction, has to be able to think of appropriate and effective things to say, and has to be able to work them into the conversation.

What should the goals be? They need to be chosen with the other person in mind, and his or her wishes should be respected. If the distressed person wants information or advice, give it. If he or she wants to feel better, try to accomplish that. In the absence of reliable signals, though, here are some things to consider.

Identity and relationship issues are permanent considerations. Giving advice usually carries the relational message, "you're not as competent as I am, so I'll help you," which of course affronts both positive and negative face. "Correcting" the other's feelings, perhaps by suggesting that they are unjustified, is an insult to positive face. A great deal of facework is probably going to be necessary in any emotional support effort, and this may involve showing your own vulnerability, to make things seem more or less even. But even "this has happened to me, too" might have the implication of devaluing the other's feelings, and moving the spotlight to you. The problems that make people upset are rarely one-dimensional. The situation might well call for information, assistance, advice, and identity confirmation, and not just one of them. The support provider's goals should be flexible, and adaptable at every moment.

ANTI-COMFORTING MESSAGES

With these general considerations in mind, let us finally look over some examples of anti-comforting messages, and try to understand what went wrong. These were all sent to me with the understanding that one person had actually been trying to help the other, but the effort had backfired. (Some of the contributors were willing to share their names, and those credits are on my website. No one expected their story to be in a book.)

A common sort of episode was being abandoned by a relational partner. Here are some awful things to say.

- Don't take it so hard. She was a slut anyway.
- That's okay. You don't need him anyway.
- Come on, you know you had this coming. You were overdue for payback.
- I think she was a narc.
- He was always a jerk about you behind your back, telling everyone how bitchy you were

and how you tried to control him. Who needs that?
- Get over it. Everyone knows college relationships don't really last anyway.

Let's begin by noticing that any of these might have been well intentioned. They really are awful, but they don't necessarily arise from unfriendly intentions.

These remarks are similar in several ways. Consider the identity work they are doing for the upset person. They devalue his or her feelings ("don't take it so hard," "get over it") and suggest that they are illegitimate. In fact, the upset person was incompetent to have even been in this position ("she was a slut," "she was a narc"). In other words, not only are the current feelings wrong, but so were the original ones. Rather than having negative feelings, the injured person should be pleased ("you don't need him," "who needs that?"). All of these are actually damaging to the identity and feelings of the person who is already feeling hurt.

Some other instances of anti-comforting in this same circumstance just seem to miss the whole point, or to distort it.

- That's too bad. Wanna go out Friday?
- Aww, that's nothing! You know how I got dumped?
- Well, at least you are free to go on to graduate school now.
- I know exactly how you feel. My cat ran away from me once. I needed a few weeks to heal after that before I could get another cat.

The first example almost seems like disconfirmation, as though the support provider felt vaguely obliged to say something, but really just wanted to get on with things. The second message is genuinely disconfirming because it changes the conversational focus to the provider. The third one offers consolation of sorts, but does so by implying that the breakup is a good thing, not something to be legitimately mourned. And the last one devalues almost everything: the lost relational partner, the value of being in love (with a human), the stressed person's identity, and the durability of one's feelings.

To this point, we have been concentrating on the relational level of meaning, which bears directly on identities and relationships. But the content of what we say is important, too. If we are offering emotional support, it needs to be sincere. If we are sharing information, it needs to be accurate. If we provide advice, it needs to be wise. Here are some content problems.

- At a funeral home a women remarked to my father about my grandmother's death that it happened "for a reason." My father, tired and grief-stricken, responded, "and what would it be?"
- Look at it as a growth experience. This way, your first divorce won't hit you so hard.
- Wow, now that it is finally over, I can tell you she's been cheating on you, dude!
- You can't have everything you want in this life.

In the first case, we see a woman trying to give solace in a way that is common in some religious communities. But she mistook the man or his mood, and found herself being asked for proof and elaboration. She could not support her information. He must have seen her comment as superficial, empty, and devaluing. He might have felt that if she had truly cared, she would really have had something to say. The second example offers some advice on how to understand a relational breakup. But the advice is immature and insulting. On top of whatever the upset person was presently feeling, now divorced (and the "first" one, at that) has been piled on. The third message certainly provides information. But even assuming that it's true, it has not been very well adapted to the goal of being helpful. Rather than giving emotional assistance, the information provides other things to be upset about—having been so blind as to date a cheating woman, and having a friend who wouldn't tell you about it. The last example is a cliché. It isn't apparently adapted to the upset person or the circumstances. Aside from having very little content at all, its very commonness suggests insincerity—that the speaker felt he or she had to say something but didn't really care, so said the simplest and quickest thing that occurred. It really doesn't seem to show much interest.

CONCLUSIONS

This has been the opposite of a how-to essay. But often we can most easily see the right way to do things by looking at examples of failure (Petroski, 1985). If you would like to read more positive material, I can recommend Burleson's (2003) advice, as well as Goldsmith's (2004) careful studies of supportive conversations.

It is no wonder that people sometimes fail to give useful emotional support, even when they want to. The conversations may be highly charged, and both identities and relationships may be at risk to an unusual degree. A person who is in need is thereby vulnerable and sensitive, too. And the task of navigating through the various demands and goals is so risky that even the provider may feel in danger as well. Perhaps that is one reason that some people try to dodge this basic obligation of close relationships.

REFERENCES

Brown, P., & Levinson, S. C. (1987). *Politeness: Some universals in language usage.* Cambridge, England: Cambridge University Press.

Burleson, B. R. (2003). Emotional support skills. In J. O. Greene & B. R. Burleson (Ed.), *Handbook of communication and social interaction skills* (pp. 551–594). Mahwah, NJ: Lawrence Erlbaum.

Burleson, B. R., & MacGeorge, E. L. (2002). Supportive communication. In M. L. Knapp & J. A. Daly (Eds.), *Handbook of interpersonal communication* (3rd ed., 374–422), Thousand Oaks, CA: Sage.

Davidowitz, M., & Myrick, R. D. (1984). Responding to the bereaved: An analysis of "helping" statements. *Death Education, 8*, 1–10.

Goffman, E. (1959). *The presentation of self in everyday life.* Garden City, NY: Anchor.

Goffman, E. (1967). *Interaction ritual.* Garden City, NY: Anchor.

Goldsmith, D. J. (2004). *Communicating social support.* Cambridge, England: Cambridge University Press.

Petroski, H. (1985). *To engineer is human: The role of failure in successful design.* New York, NY: Vintage Books.

Watzlawick, P., Beavin, J. H., & Jackson, D. D. (1967). *Pragmatics of human communication: A study of interaction patterns, pathologies, and paradoxes.* New York, NY: Norton.

QUESTIONS/THOUGHTS

1. One predictable place to find examples of anti-comforting is in televised situation comedies. What makes them so funny in this context? If audiences have seen so many examples of this communication strategy, why do people continue to do it?

2. The general discussions of interpersonal communication and emotionally challenging situations give a number of principles for comforting properly. Identify five anti-comforting messages and construct appropriate messages to replace the anti-comforting ones. Identify the context for each message.

3. For the most part, comforting actually takes place in a conversation, rather than as a simple message. How would you try to participate in a conversation to give another person emotional assistance?

Intercultural-Intimate Conflict: Major Obstacles

STELLA TING-TOOMEY AND LEEVA C. CHUNG

The overall ethnic composition of the U.S. is changing rapidly. The increase in interracial/intercultural dating and marriage reflects this shift. By 2006, 7.1 percent of marriages involved partners who were from different racial groups or one spouse was Hispanic and the other was not (Lauer & Lauer, 2009). The 2000 Census data indicated that interracial couples accounted for 1.9 percent of married couples and 4.3 percent of unmarried couples (Simmons & O'Neill, 2001). Yet, Stanford University sociologist, Michael Rosenfeld (2007), stated that in 2005, more than 7 percent of married couples in the United States were interracial. This figure includes Hispanic as a separate category. Intercultural partnerships and dating couples would add significantly to this population. Yet, although there have been major shifts in attitudes toward these relationships, partners still struggle with challenges from outsiders as well as challenges from each other.

Couples who are visibly different encounter more reactions from strangers, particularly couples that reflect African American and Caucasian backgrounds. Such circumstances often increase the tensions these couples face. Yet, the stresses created by discussing issues of race or racism within the friendship and family environment or between the partners are most salient to couples.

As Anita Foeman and Teresa Nance indicated earlier, in Chapter 16, "From Miscegenation to Multiculturalism," there are four stages in the development of interracial romantic relationships: these include racial awareness, coping with social definitions of race, identity emergence, and maintenance. Moving through these stages requires extensive partner communication about race, identity, differences, challenges from others as well as high levels of self disclosure.

In her study of meanings for marriage and experiences within marriage Marianne Dainton (1999) interviewed a small number of African American, European American, and biracial couples. She found that the biracial couples identified marriage as "work" and "love" as the meaning of marriage more frequently than other couples. She speculates that "Perhaps these couples were also more likely to focus on their enduring emotional connection because of the societal disapproval of biracial relationships" (p. 156). These stresses may account for the fact that the lowest intermarriage rate is for African American and Caucasian couples.

Dating, partnerships, or marriage for couples of racial variations other than African American and Caucasian appear to have fewer stresses. Yet, in many cases, the extended family resists any challenge to the norm of marrying within one's background. For example, in Asian-Indian immigrant families, intermarriage may be viewed as "as a threat to the integrity of the family, culture, and faith" (Almeida, 2005, 382).

Creating intercultural romantic ties challenges partners to confront difficult issues early in their relationships, forcing them to hold significant conversations about identity, culture, and commitment; such conversations may serve to deepen significantly the bonds between the partners. As you read this chapter consider how you were taught to perceive interracial couples and whether or not your perceptions may need to be reconsidered.

REFERENCES

Almeida, R. (2005). Asian Indian families. In M. McGoldrick, J. Giordano & N. Garcia-Preto (Eds.), *Ethnicity and family therapy* (3rd ed., pp. 377–394). New York, NY: Guilford Press.

Dainton, M. (1999). African-American, European-American and biracial couples. In T. Socha & R. C. Diggs (Eds.), *Communication, race, and family.* (pp. 147–165) Mahwah, NJ: Lawrence Erlbaum.

Lauer, R. H., & Lauer, J. C. (2009). *Marriage & family: The quest for intimacy.* New York, NY: McGraw-Hill.

Rosenfeld, Michael (2007). The age of independence: Interracial unions, same-sex unions and the changing American family. Cambridge MA: Harvard University Press.

Simmons, T., & O'Neill, G. (2001, September). Households and families: 2000 (C2KBR/01-8). In Census 2000 brief. Washington, DC: U.S. Census Bureau, Department of Commerce. Retrieved December 18, 2004, from http://www.census.gov/prod/2001pubs/ck2br01-8.pdf

Intercultural dating or marriage is fertile ground for culture clash and shock. At the same time, it is a hopeful arena for honoring and reconciling cultural differences. According to a recent census report, there are more than 1.3 million racially mixed marriages in the United States. This tally does not include interethnic marriages (e.g., Bolivians and Peruvians) within the same race. The highest rate of intermarriage occurs between European American males and Asian American females, and the lowest rate is that between European American males and African American females (Wehrly, Kenney, & Kenney, 1999).

There are many sources of intercultural-intimate conflict. Intercultural-intimate conflict is defined as any antagonistic friction or disagreement between two romantic partners due, in part, to cultural or ethnic group membership differences. Some of the prominent conflict sources are cultural-ethnic value clashes…prejudice and racism issues, and raising bicultural and biracial children. This section examines prejudice and racism reactions in the everyday environment of the romantic couple. It also explores the different coping strategies that couples use to counter racist attitudes and includes a discussion of identity issues in raising a bicultural or biracial child.

ENCOUNTERING PREJUDICE AND RACISM

Of all the contrasts that interracial couples bring to their relationship, the most visible and inescapable is that of their ethnicity. Interethnic (or interfaith) couples of the same ethnicity can choose how and when they will reveal their differences to outsiders, but interracial couples display obvious visible differences. An African American and German couple is visually different because of their outward appearance: markers of skin color and facial features. Interracial couples must find different ways to cope with various family and social reactions as well as with each other's reactions toward the roles of their ethnic group membership in their relationship.

Although the emotional reactions from an outgroup member can range from complete acceptance to utter ostracism, the couple's reactions in considering race as a factor in their relationship can also range from deep understanding to total dismissal. Conflict often arises when intercultural and interracial couples have to deal with the dilemma of whether or not to talk about matters of race or racism in their surrounding environment and within their own relationship context.

Prejudice is about biased, inflexible prejudgments and antagonistic feelings about outgroup members. However, racism is about a personal/institutional belief in the cultural superiority of one race and the inferiority of other races (Jones, 1997). Racism also refers to the practice of power dominance of a "superior" racial group over other "inferior" races. Couples often encounter initial conflict when they speak to their respective parents about plans for marriage. Their respective families' reactions can range from responses of support, acceptance, rejection, or fear, to outright hostility. For example, let us look at Gina's family's response from the following interview excerpt (Gina is a White woman planning to marry a Black man):

> Well, when I told my parents, they both looked kind of shocked, and then my father sort of blew up. He was yelling and screaming and told me that I had just thrown my life away and was I happy about that. But the whole time, I didn't hear my mother say anything against us. Later, after my father went to bed, she came up to me and told me that while she couldn't go against my father's wishes, she just wanted to make sure that I was happy. (McNamara, Tempenis, & Walton, 1999, p. 76)

Consider James' family response (James is and African American man planning to marry a White woman):

> My father was absolutely against my marrying a White woman. He said I was a traitor to my race and that I was not giving Black women a chance at a wonderful life. He would not talk to Donna, would not see her under any circumstances, and we did not talk to each other for five years. (McNamara et al., 1999, p. 84)

For many White families, fear is the basic reason for the opposition to an interracial marriage.

Their reasons can include societal or community disapproval, fear for the general physical and emotional well-being of the couples, fear of ostracism, and self-esteem issues concerning their biracial grandchildren (Frankenberg, 1993). As one White woman commented:

> I am sitting in a small restaurant with my daughter, my husband, my grandson, and my son-in-law. I look at my two-year-old grandson. I have a warm feeling and think to myself, "This is my first grandchild." Then my pleasure dissolves into anxiety as I realize that everyone in the restaurant is looking at us. My grandson is brown. My son-in-law is black. And my daughter is no longer mine. (Crohn, 1995, p. 90)

In terms of societal reactions, one of the most common problems experienced by interracial couples is the blatant, open stares from strangers. In addition to the stares, prejudicial treatment by some restaurant servers and real estate agents and racism within their own workplace may deeply disturb the couple's relationship. For example, listen to Russell's (an African American husband) comments:

> We go into a restaurant, together, with our children. We will order the meal and when we are done, the waitress hands us separate checks. Like she is saying "There is no way you two could be together." And here we are sitting with our children, who are obviously fair-skinned: whom does she think they belong to? (McNamara et al., 1999, p. 96)

Finally, simply because the partners are in an intimate relationship, there is no guarantee that they are free of racism or matters of race in their own evolving relationship. In times of anger and conflict, couples may have expressed racial epithets or racial attitudes to vent their frustrated feelings, and these expressions can seriously hurt each other. Although some of the words may have been exchanged in a joking/teasing or sarcastic way during an intimate conflict, those words or phrases can be taken as hurtful, racist comments.

Sometimes a White partner's indifference to or ignorance of a racial issue may actually perpetrate a racist worldview. Gloria (an African American woman married to a White man) said in an interview excerpt:

> I told him someone yelled, "nigger." I was on the corner down there: I was with the baby, just driving by. And his first reaction is, "Well, what did you do to provoke that?" …And I thought, "That's the difference between being Black and White. Why would I have to do anything to provoke it?" (Rosenblatt, Karis, Powell, 1995, p. 240)

The White partner's insulated stance toward racism issues reflects his lifelong privilege of being a White male in a dominant, White society (see McIntosh, 1995). The concept of White privilege refers to the invisible systems that confer dominance or power resources on Whites. Thus, White males can walk down the street at night or drive their cars routinely without the need for awareness of potential racist remarks directed at them without cause, nor do they need to be particularly concerned with racial profiling issues by the police on the highways.

Fortunately, not all European American males have such a chilling, indifferent reaction to racism issues faced by their intimate partners. As Adam (a white male married to an African American female) commented:

> It takes being open to your own racism. It's all well and good to be sensitive to others in how they react to you, but you ought to be a little bit sensitive when you can and recognize your own mistakes, try to learn why what you've just said or done offended your partner…for example, there's an experience where Wanda would say, "Yeah, I understand that," and I say, "I don't understand it. What was happening? Help me out here." (Rosenblatt et al., 1995, p. 243)

When two intimate partners bring to their relationship strong identities as members of two different minority groups, they are hypersensitive to identity conflict issues. The following heated debate between Alan (with a strong sense of African American identity) and Sara (with a strong sense of Jewish identity) illustrates this point:

ALAN: How can you know what it means to be discriminated against? You grew up in a comfortable, safe neighborhood. You got to choose whether or not you revealed to others that you were Jewish. My ancestors were brought here as slaves.

SARA: I can't believe you're saying this stuff. You know that I lost great-aunts and great-uncles in the Holocaust. You don't have any monopoly on suffering. What right does the past give you to say how we lead our lives? (Crohn, 1995, p. 171)

Alan and Sara's identity conflict issues—cultural, racial, and religious identities—obviously tapped into very intense, core emotions in their own identity construction. They will need time to really get to know the identity of each other and to find meaningful ways to connect to each other's cultures as well as their own.

COUNTERING RACISM AND PREJUDICE: COPING STRATEGIES

In dealing with prejudice and racism outside their relationship, some couples may talk about racism issues as a lifetime project, whereas others dismiss them as inconsequential. Some reinforce the idea that to deal with prejudice issues, they have to learn to be honest about prejudices that they carry within themselves. Other couples try to keep matters of race a small part of their relationship and focus their attention more on love, grocery shopping, raising children, doing the laundry, washing the dishes, planning vacations, and handling all the details of a shared life (Rosenblatt et al., 1995). In addition to race issues, emotional issues (e.g., work stress, money, sex, housework, and a new baby) are the most common topics of marital squabbles (Gottman & Silver, 1999). These are the frequent "emotional tasks" that couples have to deal with in their everyday lives and that often reveal their very different cultural and personal perspectives on how to approach such issues.

Most interracial couples, however, have developed specific coping strategies to deal with recurring prejudice and race situations. These coping strategies include *ignoring/dismissing* (especially for minor offenses, such as staring or nasty comments), *normalizing* (thinking of themselves and appealing to others to treat them as "normal" couples with marital ups and downs), and *withdrawing* (avoiding places and groups of people who are hostile to interracial couples). In addition, they use *educating* (outreach efforts to help others to accept interracial couples), *confrontation* (addressing directly the people who insult or embarrass them), *prayer* (relying on faith to solve problems), and *humor* (adding levity in distressing situations) to ease or ward off the pains of racism (McNamara et al., 1999). Partners usually use ignoring/dismissal coping strategies to deal with minor threats but use more direct strategies—such as educating and confronting—when countering major racist comments or slurs.

Because the discussion of any racial or religious identity issue is so complex and emotionally charged, most couples actually avoid the topic altogether in their own relating process. However, refraining from dealing with identity issues (especially from the beholder's viewpoint) is like "buying peace for your relationship on a credit card. You may enjoy the temporary freedom from anxiety you 'purchased' by avoiding the difficult topics, but when the bill finally comes due, the 'interest' that's accumulated in the form of resentment and regret may be devastating" (Crohn, 1995, pp. 183–184). Partners in an intercultural-intimate relationship often wonder whether their conflicts are a result of genuine differences of opinion, personality clashes, cultural value differences, or the prejudiced attitude of one of the partners. To achieve a genuine understanding of these intertwined issues, couples have to learn to listen, to probe for accuracy, and to listen some more. As a final example, let us listen to the following comments by an African American male who is married to a White female:

> If I had to pick the perfect wife that I could have, she is very close to it.... She knows me better that anyone else...(and) she helps me a lot too.

I like to talk to her and trust her and the fact that we both trust each other was there from the start. I know that she is really sensitive to issues of race and that is because we have experienced so much together. But I also know how difficult that has been for her. So I always try to keep her feeling in the front of my mind. I can't do anything about my race, but I can do something about how it affects her, at least sometimes I can. She does the same for me, which means that we are always thinking of each other. That's one of the reasons why I think we have lasted for so long—we are a lot stronger because we are really sensitive to the problem (McNamara et al., 1999, p. 150).

A fundamental acceptance of the cultural-racial and religious aspects of a partner's identity and a mutual willingness to explore cultural codes, as well as a mutual openness in discussing racism issues, can facilitate greater relational satisfaction. Whether we are in an intimate intracultural or intercultural relationship, we will do well to regard each interpersonal relationship as if it is an intercultural one.

REFERENCES

Crohn, J. (1995). *Mixed matches: How to create successful interracial, interethnic, and interfaith marriages.* New York, NY: Ballantine/Fawcett.

Frankenberg, R. (1993). *White women, race matters: The social construction of whiteness.* Minneapolis: University of Minnesota Press.

Gottman, J., & Silver, N. (1999). *The seven principles for making marriage work.* New York, NY: Crown.

Jones, J. (1997). *Prejudice and racism* (2nd ed.). New York, NY: McGraw-Hill.

Kasselman, A., McNair, L.D. & Scheiedewind, N. (Eds.). (1995). *Women, images, and realities: A multicultural anthology.* Mountain View, CA: Mayfield.

McIntosh, P. (1995). White privilege: Unpacking the invisible backpack. In A. McNamara, R. P., Tempenis, M., & Walton, B. *Crossing the line: Interracial couples in the South*, (1999). Westport, CT: Praeger.

McNamara, R.P., Tempenis, M. & Walton, B. (1999). *Crossing the line: Interracial couples in the South.* Westport, CT: Praeger.

Rosenblatt, P., Karis, T., & Powell, R. (1995). *Multiracial couples: Black and white voices.* Thousand Oaks, CA: Sage.

Wehrly, B., Kenney, K. R., & Kenney, M. E. (1999). *Counseling multiracial families.* Thousand Oaks, CA: Sage.

QUESTIONS/THOUGHTS

1. What do you envision as the major communication tasks for romantic partnerships formed across ethnic and racial line? Identify a specific relationship created through cultural difference (e.g. racial/ethnic difference and any possible confounding factors, such as religion, language, etc.) and discuss some specific issues that the couple would have to address directly.

2. Interview members of a partnership that has been formed across racial or ethnic lines. Ask one or both persons to talk about the reactions of family and friends to their relationship, the differences that even surprised them as the relationship developed, and what they have learned from the experience. If you are currently in such a relationship, you may wish to discuss your own experience.

3. Why does the topic of racial differences seem so difficult to talk about in our society? Describe a conversation you had with someone from a different racial background, or a conversation you heard. Identify the factors that contributed to the effectiveness of that conversation or to the ineffectiveness of that conversation.

4. If you were to enter an interracial relationship, what are the factors in your background that your partner would have to learn and appreciate in order for the relationship to be successful from your standpoint?

28

Lying

MARK L. KNAPP AND ANITA L. VANGELISTI

Lying appears as one of the most complicated relational interaction patterns. Often thought of as deceitful, devious, or unethical, lying has also been considered the lesser of two evils—less painful than the truth. A complication of lying is the distinction between lies of commission, deliberately telling a falsehood to another, and lies of omission, neglecting to tell the whole story or telling selected information while withholding the most critical parts. Even when their intentions are admirable, people may misrepresent the truth to achieve their goals (Floyd, 2009). Many people decide whether to tell the whole truth and nothing but the truth, based on the possible outcome of that choice. In their writing on deception O'Hair and Cody (1994) discuss the valence or positive to negative directions of relational motives. They suggest, "Positive relational deception strategies are termed utility and usually focus on tactics intended to improve, enhance, escalate, and repair relationships" (p. 196). Often the utility motive is to promote intimacy or maintain a relationship. Messages may include agreeing with or complimenting other people, even when the message is a fabrication, in order to foster liking. Messages may include indications of disinterest in others in order to protect self from multiple romantic involvements. In countless cases deception has started with good intentions but eventually creates painful upheaval when the truth is revealed. Many communicators use a social exchange model when considering deception, weighing the costs and benefits of equivocation or deception in the short term and long term. These complexities confound labeling lying as strictly a dark side behavior.

Frequently, romantically involved partners will attempt to establish an expectation of total truthfulness, a goal that frequently puts the partners in conflict with other relational goals such as politeness, positivity, or supportiveness. Partners struggle with minor decisions about whether to respond honestly to the risky question "How do I look?" or to report that dinner was "terrific" even if the meat was overcooked and the sauce was burned. Sometimes they struggle with major decisions about whether to reveal fears of serious illness or the reality of a gambling problem. Often the perceived state of the relationship as well as the possible costs and rewards of such a disclosure determine the level of truthfulness provided.

The choice to enter certain occupations may consign one to continuous deception-oriented struggles. Police officers often mask the possible risks of certain assignments when talking with family members; doctors may find themselves downplaying the severity of certain illnesses in order to leave patients with some hope. Historically, many adoption workers refrained from telling prospective parents certain negative information about a potential child's background in order to foster a match. Educators may try not to discourage students' dreams even if they view them as highly unrealistic. As O'Hair and Cody so directly state it: "The person who is brutally honest will be a very lonely person" (p. 196).

Online dating serves as a site of major deception; lying is a common communication practice. With multiple e-mail addresses teenagers have multiple ways to engage in identity construction; variations in online names and a range of roles facilitate playing with the boundaries between truth and fantasy (Livingstone, 2009, p.101). In other cases, when creating a personal profile on a dating Web site, participants want to present an attractive profile, even if it is not fully accurate.

In the following article on lying Knapp and Vangelisti address lying in established relationships as well as the verbal and nonverbal processes of lie detection in these relationships. Wisely, they warn of the dangers of extreme levels of suspicion on any relationship. As you read this piece ask yourself the following questions: What did I learn about lying in my family of origin and how does that influence my behavior in close friendships and romantic relationships? Under what conditions is lying online an expected and acceptable behavior?

REFERENCES

Livingstone, S. (2009). *Children and the Internet.* Malden, MA: Polity Press.

O'Hair, H. D., & Cody, M. J. (1994). Deception. In W. R. Cupach & B. H. Spitzberg (Eds.), *The dark side of interpersonal communication* (pp. 181–214). Hillsdale, NJ: Lawrence Erlbaum.

At first glance, it may seem strange that we include lying as a behavior involved in maintaining a close

relationship. After all, honesty and close relationships go hand in hand. And some people report that honesty and trustworthiness are more desirable traits in a partner (for long- and short-term relationships) than almost any other—including an exciting personality, a good sense of humor, adaptability, dependability, kindness/understanding, and others.[1] And, as expected, people in close relationships report telling fewer lies to each other.[2] But most people realize that satisfying relationships somehow learn to appreciate and accommodate behavior that falls short of "the whole truth and nothing but the truth."[3] Decisions about truth-telling and lying are at the very heart of what constitutes a close relationship. For many, the familiar promise, "We won't lie to each other" is viewed as a covenant that will lead to and sustain greater intimacy. It is, however, worth noting that each partner may have different referents for what "agreeing not to lie" means. For instance, does it mean I have to tell you things that I know would hurt you and you probably wouldn't find out anyway? Does it mean I have to tell you I hate your outfit (if that's the way I feel) when you ask for my opinion? If I tell you I went to bed with another person, is it lying not to tell you the details? If acts of omission, exaggeration, vagueness, evasiveness, and substitution are all a part of the act of lying, then everybody lies. If we can't avoid lying, then what is the kind of behavior we are trying to avoid with the "we won't lie to each other" promise?

For most couples, the real issue is whether a lie will have a damaging effect on the relationship and whether the motivation for lying was well-intended or not. Thus, when contemplating a lie, the following questions seem to be key: (1) Will this lie help both of us? If the lie is solely for the benefit of one partner, it is more likely to be viewed negatively and incur more relationship damage. Liar motivation is at issue here. The couple's short- and long-range mutual goals are the focus. From this perspective, we would expect most of the lies of people in close relationships to be motivated by a desire to help their partner. And that seems to be the case.[4] Lies designed to protect their partner from hurt, to help them build or maintain their self-esteem, to assist them in accomplishing their goals, and to show concern for their physical and mental states are the most common lies told by the most committed partners. This doesn't mean that self-oriented lies don't occur in close relationships. In fact, sometimes "closeness" itself facilitates or prompts self-oriented lying when the fear of losing it is high and when one's partner makes it clear that there is a high probability that such lies will be forgiven.[5] (2) Is the lie consistent with the rules of fairness in the relationship? That is, does one's partner operate by the same rules you do? Liar intentions are the concern now. If both partners agree that certain classes of lies are okay but others are not (e.g., lying about one's sexual prowess may be okay, but lying about having lunch with an ex-lover may not), then lies in the forbidden categories will incur more relationship damage. Sometimes, of course, a couple either assumes the other knows what categories are okay and what are not or they have not discussed the issue specifically. Thus, when an intentional lie in a category one partner believes is not acceptable occurs, the liar may argue that he or she was not aware of the rule and that it won't happen again. This is one way fairness rules about lying are negotiated. (3) Does your partner (the lied to) believe you have his or her best interests at heart—both generally and in this specific situation? If the answer is yes, the lie is likely to do less damage to the relationship. Even in situations where the liar clearly violates the couple's agreed-upon norms for lying (e.g., lying about an affair), the damage to the relationship will be offset if the offender can convince his or her partner that the lie was consistent with other instances that indicated a concern for the partner's welfare.

The best predicator of relationship termination as a result of a discovered lie is the perceived importance of the information lied about. This explains why those people who are more involved/committed to their relationship are going to have a greater emotional reaction to lies that impinge directly on the relationship.[6]

The way that a liar and a lie detector behave in a close relationship is strongly influenced by certain conditions that are unlike those conditions that characterize less intimate relationships.[7]

The first characteristic has to do with the kind of *mutual influence* exerted by the partners to a close relationship. Even in lies to non-intimates, we may be more involved in the lie than we care to admit. It is easy to condemn lies that we feel we had no part in. but we can influence a person's decision to lie, and we can give tacit approval to it once it occurs. A familiar behavior of this type is the hostess who knows a guest is lying about "what a nice party this has been" but recognizes the intent is to avoid unpleasantness, so she cooperates in the deception. In other instances, a person may make it so clear that he or she is intolerant and inflexible regarding a certain behavior that this person's partner feels the necessity to lie when experiences with that behavior occur. Thus, we may be well advised to reflect on our own role in another's decision to lie before we determine how much punishment is deserved. Additionally, the role of the deceived in the deceiver's behavior is likely to affect the deceived person's motivation and accuracy in detecting the deception as well as the way the liar performs the lie. In close relationships, partners constantly negotiate interaction norms with the knowledge that each will play a role in the outcome. Lying is no different. When the outcome is an undesirable one, however, responsibility is frequently attributed to one's partner.

The second important characteristic of lies in close relationships concerns the increased possibility of *multiple exposure* to the lie. Lies to people we don't see that often do not require the same kind of development and/or repetition. This will surely affect the extent to which the liar will want to engage in lies of omission.

The third characteristic of intimates is that they are quite *familiar* with one another's behavior. This raises the question of detection accuracy. Most of the research on detection of liars has been done with people who don't know each other very well. This research indicates that an untrained observer, looking at and listening to a stranger without the aid of any mechanical equipment, will be able to identify liars about half or slightly better than half the time. The percentage of accurate identification is, in reality, probably lower due to the fact that it is easier to deceive a person who has no reason to suspect that he or she is being lied to, and much of the research conducted asks subjects to "identify this person as a deceiver or nondeceiver"—an instruction that immediately forewarns subjects of possible deception.

LIE DETECTION

Although research on detecting lying among friends and intimates is sparse, Comadena found intimates generally more accurate than acquaintances. Friends, however, may exhibit more accuracy than spouses.[8] Spouses are committed to a relationship that may last a long time and involves daily contact. As a result, they may be more likely than good friends to develop a desensitization to behavior associated with lying. People in close relationships don't expect their partner to lie, and there also may be a strong desire not to be an accurate detector, as this wife attests:

> Little by little things were happening that didn't make sense, but I can remember making excuses for them myself...I didn't want to believe there was anything to find out...so I was being deceived from two angles...I was deceiving myself...I didn't sit there when it was happening saying" I am just fooling myself." You know, I, I, as I said, I made up a lot of excuses, and really believed them...I didn't confide in anyone, too, because I was afraid of what they would tell me. I wanted to believe everything was going to be fine and I wasn't being deceived. If I told someone else they might tell me I was being deceived and I didn't want to hear that.... But as much as I wanted to be a detective and find him out, I didn't want to either. Because the truth, I was afraid more of the truth than living in the lie kind of.[9]

If intimates do want to detect the lies of their partners, they have several advantages. For example, in more intimate relationships the partners have a mental record or backlog for verbal checking and verification; further, they have a history of having observed the other in many different emotional situations. Hence, intimates should have a better idea of what behavior exceeds the boundaries of normality for their partner. Changes in behavior or activity patters often trigger partner alertness

if not suspicion. In addition, intimates have considerably more motivation to look closely for clues than acquaintances or mere observers. Although greater intimacy may give one an advantage in being able to perceive a partner's lies, greater intimacy may also make partners less attentive to the possibilities of lies.[10] Thus, unless intimates have a reason for expecting a lie, they may be less apt to notice it. The first lies to intimate partners are likely to be the easiest to get away with. After all, the relationship was built on trust, so there is no reason to be suspicious. Even if a lie goes undetected, it may still have a significant impact on the relationship.[11] For example, a person who has engaged in an important deception in a close relationship may get mad at himself or herself and take out their anger on their partner. Perceptions of their partner as being easily duped or as no more honest themselves may begin to take hold and alter feelings and discourse.

Although lie detection is no doubt an important skill on some occasions, there is always the danger of engaging in such acts too often. Those who go on a search-and-destroy mission for their partner's lies may find they have created more harm than good for the relationship. Suspicion can create suspicion to the point where neither person trusts the other and the lie detector has created the very thing he or she set out to destroy. In addition, it is likely that such a campaign against lies may only drive the worst offenders underground so they can refine their strategies. Besides, relationships often rely on certain kinds of deceptions for sustenance. To wipe out any ability to deceive another may wipe out some important structural foundations for the relationship. This doesn't mean we shouldn't probe, question, and investigate situations in which a lie seems to harm the relationship; it simply means we should try to preserve the assumption of truthfulness rather than replace it with an assumption of deceit. If you're like us, there are some things you'd rather no know the "truth" about.

Are there any behaviors that are always associated with lying behavior and nothing else? No. There are behaviors that liars in nonintimate relationships regularly exhibit, such as speech errors, higher pitch, more hesitations, fidgeting, etc., but intimates may attend to more idiosyncratic cues.[12] We know one person whose wife listens for a barely audible gulp after a statement that is already suspected of being an untruth—e.g., "I dropped by the office to do some work," whereas "I stopped by the jeweler to check on your ring" would be the true statement. It is usually wise to look for clusters of behavior rather than a single cue. To say, "I knew he was lying because he didn't look at me" is just as risky as saying "I knew he didn't have a large vocabulary because he used the word *liar* instead of *deceiver.*" In order to increase the probability that we are accurate in detecting deception, we should look for clusters of cues—does his or her lack of eye contact fit with other things you've observed such as nervous movement and speech errors?

Some data are known on what seems to be stereotyped categories for lying behavior. Liars, for instance, will sometimes be observed exhibiting a cluster of *anxiety responses* due to guilt or psychological distress. These may include such behaviors as blushing, shaking, gulping, perspiring, voice tremors, speech errors, using fewer different words, and sending shorter messages. Sometimes observers key their observations on what they consider to be *excessive responses.* As noted earlier, excessive responses go beyond the boundaries of normal behavior for the individual being observed. It may be that the person is too inactive or too active; it might be that he or she talks excessively or engages in pronounced pauses and silences; it might be that he or she makes excessive eye contact (staring) or no eye contact at all; or it may be that he or she answers seemingly nonthreatening questions with extremely defensive remarks—"You're a little late this evening, dear. Where have you been?" "CAN'T I HAVE ONE PEACEFUL MOMENT BEFORE I GET THE THIRD DEGREE! IF YOU WANT TO KNOW MY WHEREABOUTS EVERY MOMENT OF THE DAY, HIRE A PRIVATE DETECTIVE!" Another category people sometimes observe in liars is *incongruous responses.* Liars sometimes have a hard time keeping their stories straight. Verbally, a person may contradict some known

fact the receiver is aware of, or contradict his or her own earlier statement. Sometimes, incongruity is shown when a person is being very careful and trying to maintain control in a situation that doesn't call for such behavior. Nonverbally, we might see inconsistency—saying "I've always liked you" but exhibiting a host of nonverbal cues that attest otherwise. Finally, sometimes observers detect what might be called *indirect responses.* Verbal indirectness will take on the characteristics of some evasive tactics mentioned—answering a question with a question, changing the subject. A person could also show verbal indirectness through vagueness—fewer verifiable factual assertions, fewer references to a verifiable past, fewer self-oriented statements for which a person could be held responsible, and more broad, sweeping generalizations. Nonverbally, indirectness may be seen, among other things, by not maintaining a direct body orientation when talking to another person or simply by increasing the distance between oneself and the listener. It should be clear from the preceding that many of the behaviors typically associated with liars are also manifested by people telling the truth. Thus, it is advisable to gather as much information about the situation as possible before charging the other with lying.

Of course, lie detection in close relationships is not always wholly dependent on observing the behavior of one's partner. Some of the most common methods involved obtaining information from third parties and finding evidence that contradicts the liar's story.[13]

QUESTIONS

1. Reconstruct a recent disagreement you had with a close friend. Write down as completely as possible who said what in what sequence. Analyze the conflict using Hocker and Wilmot's ideas. To what extent did you use collaborative negotiation? Which of these strategies did you use, or might you have used?

2. Transcribe a difficult or painful argument from a movie with which you are familiar. Analyze the verbal strategies used by the participants. Prepare a list of suggestions you would make

to them in order to develop a more collaborative style.

3. Identify someone you believe demonstrates good communication skills and uses the language of collaboration. Carefully listen to that person engage in a problem solving discussion. Describe in detail how that person exhibited at least three of the following sensibilities: community concerns, cooperativeness, subjectivity, intuition, and emotion.

4. Try to identify one or two examples of "expanding the pie." Look for how what looked like a two-sided argument was resolved by finding a creative solution that left both parties pleased.

NOTES

1. S. Stewart, H. Stinnett, L.B. Rosenfeld, "Sex Differences in Desired Characteristics of Short-Term and Long-Term Relationship Partners." *Journal of Social and Personal Relationships* 17 (2000): 843–853; H. LaFollette and G. Graham, "Honesty and Intimacy," *Journal of Science and Personal Relationships.*

2. B.M DePaulo and D.A. Kashy, "Everyday Lies in Close and Casual Relationships," *Journal of Personality and Social Psychology.*

3. S.D. Boon and B.A. McLeod, "Deception in Romantic Relationships: Subjective Estimates of Success at Deceiving and Attitudes Toward Deception," *Journal of Social and Personal Relationships* 18 (2001): 463–476.

4. DePaulo and Kashy, 1998; S. Metts, "An Explanatory Investigation of Deception in Close Relationships." *Journal of Social and Personal Relationships* 6 (1989): 159–179; B.M. DePaulo and K. L. Bell, "Truth and Investment: Lies Are Told to Those Who Care." *Journal of Personality and Social Psychology.*

5. T. Cole, "Lying to the One You Love: The Use of Deception in Romantic Relationships." *Journal of Social and Personal Relationships* 18 (2001): 107–129.

6. S.A. McCornack and T.R. Levine, "When Lies Are Uncovered: Emotional and Relational Outcomes of Discovered Deception," *Communication Monographs* 57 (1990): 119–138.

7. D.E. Anderson, M.E. Ansfield, and B.M. DePaulo, "Love's Best Habit: Deception in the Context of Relationships." In P. Philippot and R.S. Feldman, eds. *The Social Context of Nonverbal Behavior* (New York: Cambridge University Press, 1999), pp. 372–409.

8. M.E. Comadena, "Accuracy in Detecting Deception: Intimate and Friendship Relationships." In M. Burgoon, ed. *Communication Yearbook 6* (Beverly Hills, CA: Sage, 1982), pp. 446–471. Also see S.A. McCornack and M.R. Parks, "Deception Detection and Relationship Development: The Other Side of Trust." In M.L. McLaughlin, ed., *Communication Yearbook 9* (Beverly Hills, CA: Sage, 1986), pp. 337–389.

9. L.F. Werth and J. Flaherty, "A Phenomenological Approach to Human Deception." In R.W. Mitchell and N.S. Thompson, eds. *Deception: Perspectives on Human and Nonhuman Deceit* (Albany, NY: SUNY Press, 1986), p. 296.

10. T.R. Levine and S.A. McCornack, "Linking Love and Lies: A Formal Test of the McCornack and Parks Model of Deception Detection," *Journal of Social and Personal Relationships* 9 (1992): 143–154.

11. B.J. Sagarin, K.v.L. Rhoads, and R.B. Cialdini, "Deceiver's Distrust: Denigration as a Consequence of Undiscovered Deception," *Personality and Social Psychology Bulletin.*

12. B.M. DePaulo, J.J. Lindsay, B.E. Malone, L. Muhelbruck, K. Charlton, and H. Cooper, "Cues to Deception." *Psychological Bulletin* 129 (2003): 74–118.

13. H.S. Park, T.R. Levine, S.A. McCornack, K. Morrison, and M. Ferrara, "How People Really Detect Lies." *Communication Monographs* 69 (2002): 144–157.

QUESTIONS/THOUGHTS

1. What criteria do you use to decide whether, and to what extent, you will tell the truth in friendship or romantic situations? How did you develop these criteria for yourself?

2. Think about a person who you interact with regularly. What are the nonverbal cues, sometimes

called leakage, that tell you the individual is equivocating or lying? How do you respond when faced with those cues?

3. Imagine you are socializing a young child (age 5–7) regarding honesty. What would you tell him or her about lying to other people? What kinds of situations might you discuss with this child?

4. Under what conditions do you believe it is acceptable to create variations of the truth when interacting with strangers online?

Reprinted from Mark L. Knapp and Anita L. Vangelisti, *Interpersonal Communication and Human Relationships*, 5th ed., pp. 261–268. Published by Allyn & Bacon, Boston, MA. Copyright © 2005 by Allyn & Bacon. Reprinted with permission.

Ending Relationships

Introduction

The life of any ongoing relationship is challenged by the developmental changes of each individual, pressures of commitments and school/career obligations, as well as efforts expended to maintain multiple relational ties. At any point in time, you may be building one or two relationships and loosening the bonds of a similar number. Geographic mobility separates friends, sometimes dissolving the relationship. Many relational partners opt to terminate their first or second marriages. Workplace mobility works against developing long-term friends at the office. Most relationships come apart through a process; dissolution is seldom the result of one major event.

Unlike the movie images of a huge fight followed by silence and distance, the majority of relationships end through a coming-apart process; other people or commitments take priority, differences reduce the pleasures of togetherness, and familiarity reveals critical points of tension. Relationships are terminated for many different reasons, some of which include: lack of openness and intimacy, lack of similarity, sexual incompatibility, need for autonomy and independence, money, boredom, social network. (Guerrero, Andersen & Afifi, 2001). When long-term relationships end, the sense of loss is acute. You may grieve the loss of a romantic partner or close friend for a long time.

Many models of relational dissolution exist. The stages of grief and mourning, originally conceived by Dr. Elizabeth Kübler-Ross (1970) to account for the experiences of dying patients and their families, have been applied to the death of relationships. These stages include (1) denial, (2) anger and blame, (3) bargaining, (4) depression, and (5) acceptance. For example, friends may deny that there are any really small or large issues that may lead to great anger or threats. Discussions of "Let's try to do better" or "I'll never say that again" represent bargaining. Sadness at the loss of a good friend is followed by a sense of acceptance.

Although listed in linear form, the feelings evoked by these stages may be experienced in many different ways.

Duck (1982) described four dissolution stages as Breakdown (dissatisfaction), Dyadic Phase (confrontation and negotiation), Social Phase (move to public level), and Grave-Dressing Phase (getting-over-it activities). You may remember that stage models are linear but that dialectical tensions operate as the "background noise." At periods of clear decline the dialectical tensions that serve as background move to the foreground as the struggles become overt and intense. Although there are multiple models describing relational decline, the model found here serves as the "other side" of the coming together stages of relationships. Communication practices characterize each of the five stages.

A significant number of studies have addressed issues of conflict and relational decline; only recently have scholars addressed topics such as betrayal, deceit, violence, stalking, or manipulation, often referred to as the "dark side." Previously most scholars focused on the positive and affirming features of interpersonal interaction, although conflict was addressed. Yet everyday life is also filled with relational hostility, aggression, deception or anger as well as relational catastrophes (Duck, 2004). In certain relationships the dark side emerges as predictable and dangerous; physical fights become the pattern, stalking replaces questioning, manipulation characterizes everyday interaction, and verbal abuse substitutes for discussion.

Certain communication acts reflect opposite sides of the same coin within relationships. Low-level dark side behaviors, such as jealousy, insincerity, gossip, lying, or avoidance are predictable and may even, paradoxically, strengthen some ties. Relational partners may use deception to keep from devastating the other, hurtful words may be the only way to get a friend's attention on a critical issue, and jealousy may convince another of the importance of the relationship. Duck (1994) argues that "the 'dark side' is integral to the experience of relationships, not separate from it" (p. 9).

Although certain behaviors are problematic rather than horrendous, the dark side must not be taken lightly. Examples of the horrors of the dark side may be found in the communication research related to physical and verbal abuse, obsessive relational intrusion, or sexual coercion. In some cases the behavior is linked to physical and/or psychological health issues, such as battering (Jacobson and Gottman, 1998). If you have ever lived with a violent individual, you have seen the dark side of interpersonal interactions in a very personal way.

Recently obsession in its many forms has received extensive scholarly attention. In their studies Cupach and Spitzberg (2004) define obsessive relational intrusion (ORI) as "the repeated pursuit of intimacy with someone who does not want such attentions" (p. 3). Stalking represents a severe form of ORI and has received growing attention. ORI behaviors range from mildly annoying acts, such a pestering someone for a date, leaving constant messages, or providing unwanted gifts or favors, to threatening acts, such as home invasion, physical abuse, verbal threats, or stalking. Sexual coercion represents a type of threatening act often experienced by young adults. In a world of "hookups," or "friends with benefits", desired personal boundaries may be ignored or misinterpreted, resulting in date rapes. In other cases, predatory stalkers "strategically plan sexual attack or coercion" (Cupach & Spitzberg, 2004)

Your interpretation of problematic behavior is tied, in part, to your gender, culture, and family experiences. If you grew up learning that deceit was the way to survive in your family, you may view it as functional and protective; if your upbringing stressed openness and truth at all costs, deceit might lead you to end a significant relationship.

In this section you will find a model of relational decline, an overview of the dark side, including its "seven deadly sins," a discussion of why marriages fail, and a study of dissolutional communication in breakup narratives. As you read these articles, think about the relationships in your life that have ended. To what extent do these authors' statements reflect your experiences?

REFERENCES

Cupach, W. R., & Spitzberg, B. H. (2004). *The dark side of relationship pursuit.* Mahwah, NJ: Lawrence Erlbaum.

Duck, S. (1982). A topography of relationship disengagement and dissolution. In S. Duck (Ed.), *Personal relationships: Vol. 4. Dissolving relationships* (pp. 1–30). New York, NY: Academic Press.

Duck, S. W.(1994). Strategems, spoils, and a serpent's tooth: On the delights and dilemmas of personal relationships. In W. R. Cupach & B. H. Spitzberg (Eds.), *The dark side of interpersonal communication* (pp. 3–24). Hillsdale, NJ: Lawrence Erlbaum.

Duck, S. (2004). *Human relationship* (4th ed.). Los Angeles, CA: Sage.

Guerrero, L. K., Andersen, P. A., & Afifi, W.A. (2001). *Close encounters: Communicating in relationships.* Mountain View, CA: Mayfield.

Jacobson, N., & Gottman, J. (1998). *When men batter women: New insights into ending abusive relationships.* New York, NY: Simon & Schuster.

Kübler-Ross, E. (1970). *On death and dying.* New York, NY: Macmillan.

Relational Decline

MARK L. KNAPP AND ANITA L. VANGELISTI

Earlier in this volume you read Mark Knapp and Anita Vangelisti's stages of relational development, or "coming together." Using the same theoretical perspective, these authors also discuss stages of "coming apart." The generalizations that applied to the "coming together" stages apply to the stages of "coming apart": (1) movement through stages is generally systematic and sequential; (2) movement may be forward; (3) movement may be backward; (4) movement is always to a new place; and (5) movement may be rapid or slow and (6) dialectical tensions serve as a background to each stage. Of course, there are occasions when one person unilaterally ends a relationship with little or no communication. Essentially, if there is not further contact, those relationships fall off the stage model discussed in this chapter.

Relationships experience decline, permanent or temporary, by inertia or by the choice of one or both partners. Relationships beset by inertia find themselves drifting as major time commitments, geographic separation, or serious personal concerns cause one or both to be unavailable. Thus, lack of ongoing connection renders the tie weaker and weaker.

Advice columnists regularly respond to readers' questions regarding how to end a relationship. Such explicit desire usually results in statements indicating a lack of interest, a major fight resulting from the less-involved individual's frustration, or significant efforts to disconfirm or ignore the other, such as not returning calls or e-mails. In partnerships, explicit desire usually results in separation or divorce.

Most models of relational decline follow similar patterns. In 1982 Steve Duck created a breakdown model that accounted for what happened after a relational breakdown. This model included four phases: intrapsychic (individual reflection), dyadic (partner confrontation), social (going public to others), and grave-dressing (healing and postmortems). Canary, Cody, and Manusov (2008) adapted Steve Duck's original work (1982) to develop a model of relational repair that attempts to explain how to intervene as the relationship disintegrates. For example, they suggest that during "The Breakdown Phase: Dissatisfaction with Relationship" partners might try to focus on the attractions in the relationship and try to reduce turbulence in the interactions. During the Social Phase and beyond *they might enlist public support by asking others to help them understand the breakup or enlist the aid of others to help save the relationship. Even in these painful circumstances most people follow rather predictable patterns.*

In this chapter, Knapp and Vangelisti describe five stages involved in relational decline: differentiating, circumscribing, stagnating, avoiding, and terminating. The discussion of each stage includes the types of communication (or lack of communication) involved throughout the decline of the relationship. Conversations and expressions that are characteristic of each stage are offered as examples throughout the chapter, along with corresponding behaviors (like arguing or ignoring) that are commonly seen as relationships come apart. For example, in the Terminating Stage, communication is characterized as more narrow, stylized, difficult, rigid, awkward, public, and hesitant, with overt judgments suspended. In the Differentiating Stage, communication is characterized by more breadth, efficiency, uniqueness, flexibility, smoothness, and spontaneity, and overt judgments are given. In other words, people communicate within a prescribed range of content, style, and language at different levels of intimacy.

Although many relationships reach the terminating stage, it is not acknowledged; lack of contact continues indefinitely until one or both persons realize it's over. Or, one learns a partner's status is now "single" on a Facebook wall. In other cases, there is a need for defined closure; this may be a divorce or a resignation from a workplace where both were employed.

Family breakups present special issues. In cases of divorce, when children are involved, formerly spouses are divorced "to" each other rather than" from" each other, because most ex-spouses develop a divorced relationship centered on their children's needs (Galvin, Bylund,& Brommel, 2008). A functional divorced relationship takes time and parental commitment, but it serves the children well.

As you read the following article, think about the relationships in your own life that have declined significantly or ended. Ask yourself, to what extent did those relationships follow the stages discussed in this chapter?

REFERENCES

Canary, D. J., Cody, M. J., & Manusov, V. L. (2008). *Interpersonal communication: A goals-based approach* (4th ed.). Boston, MA: Bedford/ St. Martin's.

Duck, S. W. (1982). A typography of relationship disengagement and dissolution. In S. W. Duck (Ed.), *Personal relationships: Vol. 4. Dissolving personal relationships* (pp. 1–30). New York: Academic Press.

Galvin, K. M., Bylund, C. L., & Brommel, B. J. (2008). *Family communication: Cohesion and change* (7th ed.). Boston, MA: Allyn & Bacon.

DIFFERENTIATING

Literally, to *differentiate* means to become distinct or different in character. Just as integrating is mainly a process of fusion, differentiating is mainly a process of disengaging or uncoupling. While individual differences are of some concern at any stage in the developing relationship, they are now the major focus and serve as a prelude to increased interpersonal distance. A great deal of time and energy are spent talking and thinking about "how different we really are."

Joint endeavors formerly described by "we" or "our" now assume a more "I" or "my" orientation. Previously designated joint possessions often become more individualized—"my friends," "my daughter," or "my bathroom." Communication is generally characterized by what distinguishes the two persons or how little they have in common. Differences may be related to attitudes, interests, personality, relatives, friends, or to a specific behavior such as sexual needs or picking one's nose. Individuals who persist in interaction at this stage perceive these differences as strongly linked to basic or core values. Hence, we would expect to see less conversation about certain central areas of personality that may reflect these basic values. Persons who move in and out of this stage develop a history of expectations for the manner in which such difficulties will be settled, even if it is simply an agreement to seal off the areas of potential conflict.

When an unusually intense siege of differentiating takes place following bonding, it may be because bonding took place before the relationship achieved sufficient breadth and depth. It may also be due to some unplanned individual or social changes that altered the data upon which the original commitment was made. Advocates of renewable-term marriage argue that couples would be more likely to face, discuss, and work out unexpected changes in their lives if the marriage bond was not a lifelong commitment—if "till death do us part" meant the death of the relationship rather than the death of the participants.

The most visible communication form of differentiating, or affirming individuality, is fighting or conflict, although it is possible to differentiate without conflict....

CIRCUMSCRIBING

At almost any stage of a relationship we can see some evidence of communication being constricted or circumscribed. In decaying relationships, however, information exchange qualitatively and quantitatively decreases. The main message strategy is to carefully control the areas of discussion, restricting communication to safe areas. Thus, we find less total communication in number of interactions as well as depth of subjects discussed, and communications of shorter duration.

Communication restraint applies to both breadth and depth. As the number of touchy topics increases, almost any topic becomes dangerous because it is not clear whether the new topic may in some way be wired to a previous area of static. When communication does take place, superficiality and public aspects are increasingly the norm. Communications related to one's basic values and hidden secrets may have a history of unpleasantness surrounding them; hence, we see a lot less information exchanged about "who I am and what our relationship is like." A corresponding decrease in expressions of commitment may be seen. When one person ventures such an expression, the echo response may not be so prevalent. "In spite of our differences, I still like you a lot." (Silence)

Familiar phrases typical of this stage include: "Don't ask me about that"; "Let's not talk about that anymore"; "It's none of your business"; "Just stick to the kind of work I'm doing and leave my religion out of it"; "You don't own me and you can't tell me what to think"; or "Can't we just be friends?" The last example is a suggestion that prescribes a whole new set of ground rules for permissible topics in the interaction.

When circumscribing characterizes the relationship, it may also have an impact on public social performances. Sometimes mutual social circles are also circumscribed, sometimes the presence of others is the only time when communication seems to increase—an effort to avoid being seen as not getting along. The following routine is not at all uncommon for some couples at this stage: Driving to a party, the two people exhibit mutual silence, empty gazes, and a general feeling of exhaustion. While playing out their party roles we see smiling, witticisms, and an orientation for being the life of the party. The trip home becomes a replay of the pre-party behavior.

STAGNATING

To stagnate is to remain motionless or inactive. Rather than orally communicate, participants often find themselves conducting covert dialogues and concluding that since they "know" how the interaction will go, it is not necessary to say anything. At this stage, many areas are closed off, and efforts to communicate effectively are at a standstill. Even superficial areas have become so infected by previous communicative poison that they are generally left untried. In a sense, the participants are just marking time.

Some of the messages that are sent reflect unpleasant feeling states through the medium of nonverbal behavior. Other messages are very carefully chosen and well thought out. Language choices and message strategies seem to come closer to those used with strangers, and the subject of the relationship is nearly taboo.... While there may be many covert judgments made, overt judgments are generally avoided.

Extended stagnating can be seen in many relationships: between alienated parents and children, just prior to divorce, just prior to the termination of a courtship, following unproductive small talk. The main theme characterizing this stage is "There is little sense bringing anything up because I know what will happen, and it won't be particularly pleasant." Experimentation is minimal because the unknown is thought to be known. It is during this time that each partner may engage in "imagined interactions."[1] These imagined dialogues will either take the form of narratives (e.g., "I'll say this and then she'll say this, and then...") or perceived actual dialogues (e.g., "I'll do it." "You don't have to." "Ok." "Ok, what?" "Ok, I won't." "Your typical attitude." "And *Your Typical Attitude!*"....)

You might legitimately question why people would linger at this stage with so many apparent costs accumulating. Most don't. But when persons continue interacting at this stage they may be getting some rewards outside of the primary relationship, through increased attention to their work or in developing another relationship. They also avoid the pain of terminating the relationship, which they may anticipate will be stronger than the current pain. Others may have hope that they can still revive the relationship. Still others may spend time at this stage because of some perverse pleasures obtained in punishing the other person.

AVOIDING

While stagnating, the participants are usually in the same physical environment and avoiding attempts to eliminate that condition. The rhetoric of avoidance is the antithesis of the rhetoric of initiation. Here, communication is specifically designed to avoid the possibility of face-to-face or voice-to-voice interaction. The overriding messages seem to be: "I am not interested in seeing you; I am not interested in building a relationship; and I would like to close the communication channels between us." In this sense, then, avoiding suggests a much more permanent state of separation than that communicated by most people in their everyday leave-taking.

When the need to communicate avoidance results from an intimate relationship gone sour, the particular messages may contain overtones of antagonism or unfriendliness. They are more likely to be direct and to the point. "Please don't call me anymore. I just don't want to see or talk to you." This bluntness may naturally evolve from other conditions as well, such as when one person wants to pursue the relationship and ignores the more subtle avoidance cues. These subtle or indirect cues may take the form of being consistently late for appointments or preceding each encounter with, "I can't stay long." Here the avoiding tactics are not motivated so much by dislike of the other as a lack of desire to expend time and energy pursuing a relationship. Sometimes an inordinate number of conflicting engagements can make the point: "I'm so busy I don't know when I'll be able to see you. Friday? I'm going home for the weekend. Monday? I have a sorority meeting. Tuesday? I have to study for a test," etc. etc.

In certain situations physical separation simply cannot be achieved, so a form of avoiding takes place in the presence of the other. It's as if the other person didn't exist. Not surprisingly under such conditions we find the receiver participating less in what interaction is available, not evaluating the other highly, and being less inclined to provide a reward to the other when an opportunity arises. The less obvious result of being ignored is the possibility of a lowered self-concept.[2]

TERMINATING

Relationships can terminate immediately after a greeting or after twenty years of intimacy. Sometimes they die slowly over a long period of time. The bonds that held the pair together wear thin and finally pull apart. The reasons behind such deterioration may be something obvious like living in parts of the country separated by great distance; or termination may just be the end result of two people growing socially and psychologically at different rates and in different directions. At other times, the threads holding two people together may be abruptly cut. It may be the death of one partner, radically changed circumstances, or an effort by one person to spare both of them the anticipated agony of a prolonged termination period.

Naturally, the nature of the termination dialogue is dependent on many factors: the relative status held or perceived between the two communicators; the kind of relationship already established or desired in the future; the amount of time allowed; whether the dialogue is conducted via the telephone, through a letter, or face to face; and many other individual and environmental factors.

Generally, however, we would predict termination dialogue to be characterized by messages of distance and disassociation. *Distance* refers to an attempt to put psychological and physical barriers between the two communicators. This might take the form of actual physical separation, or it may be imbedded in other nonverbal and verbal messages. *Disassociation* is found in messages that are essentially preparing one or both individuals for their continued life without the other—increasing concern for one's own self-interests, emphasizing differences. Obviously, the amount of distancing and disassociation will vary with the kind of relationship being dissolved, time available, and so on....

We would also predict that the general dimensions of communicative behavior reviewed earlier in this chapter would polarize more than ever around narrow, stylized, difficult, rigid, awkward, public, hesitant, and suspended judgments.

Finally, we would like to take a finding derived from the study of conversations and apply it to relationships. Thus, we would predict that termination dialogue would regularly manifest: (1) a summary statement; (2) behaviors signaling the impending termination or decreased access; and (3) messages that indicate what the future relationship (if any) will be like.[3] A summary statement reviews the relationship's history and provides the rationale for the imminent termination. Decreased-access messages clarify what is happening. Addressing the future avoids awkward interactions after parting. Even when dissolving a long-term relationship, the subject of being future friends or enemies must be addressed. "I'll always respect you, but I don't

love you anymore," or "I don't ever want to see you again!" Saying good-bye to a long-term relationship may take longer, especially if one party does not want to end it and seeks to delay the final parting....

NOTES

1. Imagined interactions may occur at other points in the relationship as well—and for different purposes. For example, a person may construct an imagined dialogue relative to a date or marriage proposal. See J. M. Honeycutt, K. S. Zagacki, and R. Edwards, "Intrapersonal Communication, Social Cognition, and Imagined Interactions." In C. Roberts and K. Watson, eds., *Readings in Intrapersonal Communication*. Birmingham, AL: Gorsuch Scarisbrick, 1989.

2. D. M. Geller, L. Goodstein, M. Silver, and W. C. Sternberg, "On Being Ignored: The Effects of the Violation of Implicit Rules of Social Interaction," *Sociometry* 37 (1974): 541–556.

3. M. L. Knapp, R. P. Hart, G. W. Friedrich, and G. M. Shulman, "The Rhetoric of Goodbye: Verbal and Nonverbal Correlates of Human Leave-Taking," *Speech Monographs* 40 (1973): 182–198.

QUESTIONS/THOUGHTS

1. Analyze a segment from a play, film, or TV show that deals with relationship termination. How does the communication of the relational partners progress through Knapp and Vangelisti's coming apart stages?

2. Using the stages of "coming apart," analyze a relationship in your life that was terminated. Could you tell it was ending before you heard the news? Try to remember exact words and nonverbal cues that occurred over time. What was the impact on others who were close to both persons?

3. Using the circumscribing and stagnating stages, create a list of 5–10 phrases that typify the type of interaction patterns, as well as predictable nonverbal messages that are typical of such stages.

4. Describe how relationships may be terminated online. Is the communication directed to the other person in the relationship or is it sent to multiple friends?

Adapted from Mark L. Knapp and Anita L. Vangelisti, "Stages of Relationships." In *Interpersonal Communication and Human Relationships*, 5th ed., pp. 43–47. Published by Allyn & Bacon, Boston, MA. Copyright © 2005 by Pearson Education. Reprinted with permission.

The Dark Side

BRIAN H. SPITZBERG

After a decade of growing attention to interaction patterns described under the label of "the dark side," most communication scholars address these types of interactions in their teaching and writings. Yet the concept of the dark side is quite fluid, reflecting its complexity and development over a limited period of time. Although individual scholars addressed many topics currently considered to fall under the dark side label, it was in 1994 that William Cupach and Brian Spitzberg produced their groundbreaking edited book, The Dark Side of Interpersonal Communication. This work challenged communication faculty and students to consider seriously a wide spectrum of problematic, challenging, and disruptive communication patterns; thus, topics ranging from sexual abuse to name calling gained prominence in communication literature. The book's title established the overarching reference point for future studies of multiple problematic topics that became known under the rubric of "dark side of communication" studies.

Yet Cupach and Spitzberg and subsequent writers address this topic in a highly nuanced manner, recognizing the difficulty in interpreting motives for certain seemingly negative behaviors as well as the possibility of unpredictable potentially beneficial outcomes from dark side communication interactions. The dialogue regarding how to conceptualize this issue continues. At this point the authorship team has produced two new books, The Dark Side of Close Relationships (1998) in which they address issues such as gossip, jealousy and envy, sexual coercion, and copdependence, and The Dark Side of Relationship Pursuit (2004), devoted solely to obsession and stalking. In addition, many other communication scholars have published articles and book chapters devoted to the topic.

In the following chapter Brian Spitzberg addresses the question, "What is the dark side?" by exploring what he calls the "seven sins" of the dark side. He also provides some history of the development of this research area. As you read this chapter the topic's complexities will become apparent. You may find yourself re-thinking positions you hold, such as how you view lying. Spitzberg provides a model for categorizing specific behaviors accordingly as presumptively/normatively constructive or destructive that reinforces the nuanced nature of the dark side. Finally he summarizes a range of dark side research topics currently being studied by *communication scholars. As you read this article, keep the following question in mind: Under what conditions might I view a dark or problematic interaction as having potential benefits for both communicators?*

REFERENCES

Cupach, W. R., & Spitzberg, B. H. (Eds.). (1994). *The dark side of interpersonal communication.* Hillsdale, NJ: Lawrence Erlbaum.

Cupach, W. R., & Spitzberg, B. H. (2004). *The dark side of relationship pursuit.* Mahwah, NJ: Lawrence Erlbaum.

Spitzberg, B. H., & Cupach, W. R. (Eds.). (1998). *The dark side of close relationships.* Mahwah, NJ: Lawrence Erlbaum.

The dark side of human possibility makes most of our history. But this tragic fact does not imply that behavioral traits of the dark side define the essence of human nature.

S. J. GOULD (1993).
Eight Little Piggies.

This essay is about the dark side of human behavior. The dark side is an integrative metaphor for a certain perspective toward the study of human folly, frailty, and fallibility. It is also a window into the realm of evil, corruption, and baseness. In the process of pursuing this metaphor, we find that the dark sides of our nature are integral to understanding the human condition, and perhaps, even to being human. Along the path that these pursuits take, it is not uncommon to experience a sense that we are peering from the wrong side of the prison bars. Our crimes and misdemeanors sometimes seem wholly just and necessary, and our acts of goodness often inadvertently murder the very morals they were intended to serve. Such are the paradoxes of the dark side.

The dark side has fascinated humans and scholars of the human condition at least throughout all of recorded history (see Pratt, 1994; Watson, 1995). But what is the dark side? Recently, Spitzberg and Cupach (1998) took up

the question, and suggested an initial, if yet incomplete, answer in the form of the "seven sins" of the dark side.

First, and perhaps most obvious, the dark side is about the dysfunctional, distressing, and destructive aspects of human interaction. Evil is mostly about violence (Baumeister, 1997), the intentional harming of someone or something valued by others. But at levels less than evil, we consider things dark when they impair the ability of someone to function (Charny, 1996). From grand failures to the malfunctioning of everyday plans to the grinding destructiveness of dysfunctional family interactions, we find frustration and pain in activities that are so impaired.

Second, the dark side can be found in deviance, betrayal, transgression, and violation. Morals and social conventions may be arbitrary, but they serve to preserve an order that is comforting if nothing else. Thus, rebellion against normative culture is viewed as a threat to the integrity of society, family, relationship, and the self's place in this order.

Third, the exploitation of the innocent is another of the shadows of the dark side. Child abuse, coercion, manipulation of the ignorant, and constraint of basic freedoms strike at our assumptions of individual autonomy and the social contract. Those who cannot help themselves must be protected from those who can. But human nature is not always so cooperative.

Fourth, the dark side is concerned with the unfulfilled, underestimated, and unappreciated endeavors of life. From the unborn to the unloved, from blemishes to blight, we decry the repression of what that might have been, especially when the potential for the positive is apparent.

Fifth, the dark side thrives in the presence of the physically unattractive, the ugly, the distasteful, and the repulsive. The loneliness of rejection, and the seductiveness of self-superiority sought through alienating others, are hallmarks of intergroup conflict, enemyship, and simple neglect. We make the enemy ugly in our eyes, and often, through social isolation and scape-goating, we make the ugly our enemies. In such manner, enemies may be created less by *their* own actions, and more by *our* own actions.

Sixth, objectification in humans represents the darkness wrought by dehumanization. We demean ourselves when we treat people through our symbols as things. There are some ways in which such symbolic reduction of people to objects is more damaging to our spirits than actual physical torture and violence. Bombadiers and warplane pilots drop bombs on "the enemy" rather than on families and villages. A thing is easier to exploit, to neglect, to abuse, and to kill, than is a kindred spirit.

Finally, the dark side reflects a fascination with the paradoxical, dialectical, mystifying aspects of human action. Time and again, our studies of topics on the dark side have revealed that those things we presume to be healthy and moral have their destructive forms and applications. Conversely, those shadowy insinuations of evil that appall our collective and individual senses often function in surprisingly positive ways.

Two simple examples can illustrate. Honesty, and its cousin clarity, are generally accepted as valued and moral goals. Yet, most people lie, even to their best friends and partners (DePaulo et al., 1996; Rodriquez & Ryave, 1990). Simple politeness requires considerable deviation from the truth (Bavelas et al., 1990). Leaders employ fundamentally ambiguous symbols (e.g., freedom, pride, prosperity) because they cannot hope to gain widespread consensus without them (Eisenberg, 1984). In stark contrast, everyone *knows* that child abuse is intrinsically dark. Yet, research has shown that some people find silver linings to this dark, invidious cloud (McMillen et al., 1995). Some victims of abuse find themselves more cautious, more resilient, more appreciative of life, or more responsible in child-rearing. This in no way is intended to justify activities such as child abuse or deception. Instead, it is intended to suggest that the human experience is far, far more complex in its functions than our simplistic moral paradigms typically permit us to admit, much less see.

These sins of the dark side illustrate that these shadows are probably far more prominent in our everyday lives than we often realize. One way of thinking about this is to consider two criteria of darkness: functional versus normative.

A communication process is functionally dark if it detracts from the ability of a person, relationship, or group to survive and thrive. Violence is a good example, because violence almost by definition threatens the victim's ability to survive, much less thrive (although, see Spitzberg, 1997). In contrast, a communication process is normatively dark if groups, societies, or cultures generally view the behavior as immoral, prohibited, or dysfunctional. Of course, both of these criteria have their opposite (i.e., functional brightness and normative brightness). If we cross these two criteria, there are three possible territories of the dark side, as displayed in Figure 1.

Evil incarnate is the most obvious domain of the dark side, and yet, in some ways, it is among the most difficult to populate. That is, there are few communication activities that are *purely* evil, both functionally and normatively. Perhaps the closest pure example would be rhetorical campaigns that incite terror or genocide. Next are behaviors that are productively bright, yet normatively dark. These are behaviors that a society or culture may consider wrong, but serve important functions. Obscenity might be a good example; it is generally considered inappropriate in everyday discourse, and yet it serves a variety of expressive

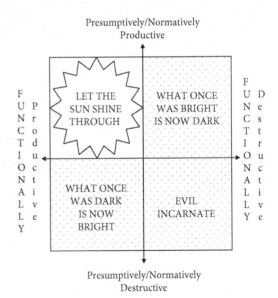

Figure 30-1

and regulatory functions in how we define our relationships with others. The third territory is the productively destructive but normatively productive domain. These are behaviors that groups consider appropriate but have destructive effects on other people, or other groups. For example, many gang-related communication activities are viewed as vital to their own group, but are destructive to the larger societal or community group in which they exist. Finally, there is the territory beyond the dark side, consisting of behaviors that are both functionally productive and normatively approved. As an interesting exercise, you may try to come up with a communication activity that is inherently "bright."

There are many potential applications of the dark side metaphor to the larger domain of human communication activity. A few illustrations that follow are provided merely to "whet the appetite" of scholars to take seriously the import of the dark side in their studies and creative pursuits. My reason for offering these illustrations is not to cast a morbid shadow upon our scholarly landscape, but instead to suggest avenues for bridging unrecognized connections among the communication arts and sciences.

The topics of concern to the dark side are often the same topics of interest to the media. I have been involved in research on the following: gossip, obscenity, double binds, mundane incompetence in communicating, equivocation, misunderstanding, failures of social support, unrequited love, relationship break-ups, loneliness, depression, co-dependency, embarrassment, privacy violations, jealousy, envy, infidelity, conflict, deception, hurtful messages, revenge, intimate violence, sexual coercion and rape, fatal attractions, stalking, and the pathology of normal families. These topics litter the talk show circuit, self-help literature, and one would be hard pressed to find a newscasts or entertaining movies without such topics. Deception, for example, is a major topic of screen characters, of rhetorical scholars studying political deception, of professionals studying ethics of public relations practitioners and advertising campaigns, and of scientists studying the accuracy of deception

detection. Crime, criminality, and the dark sides of human behavior, therefore, are "seductive" (Katz, 1988; Twitchell, 1989) in their ability to evoke curiosity and fascination. Collectively, however, we seem to have little sense about how all these dark and bright sides of our human condition fit together to make us human.

Traditionally, textbooks of human behavior have tended to recommend the virtuous aspects of action and belief. Thus, we are advised by most self-help and undergraduate communication textbooks to be honest, open, clear, articulate, attractive, trustworthy, trusting, cooperative, loyal, nonviolent, confident, assertive, fair, equitable, tolerant, empathic, and optimistic. We are encouraged to be humorous, to be leaders, and to develop heterosexual nuclear families. Yet, honesty can be destructive, openness embarrassing, attractiveness a curse, articulateness inefficient, trust, cooperation, and loyalty exploited, nonviolence a formula for failure, confidence and assertion unlikable, fairness and equity unreciprocated, tolerance taken advantage of, empathy abused, and optimism disappointed with dire consequences (Baumeister et al., 1996; Bochner, 1982; Cupach & Spitzberg, 1994; Fillion, 1996; Goldberg, 1993; Levitt et al., 1996; Parks, 1995; Ray, 1993; Rook & Pietramonaco, 1987; Spitzberg, 1993, 1994b). Leaders are not necessarily valuable in a world without followers (Conger, 1990; Gioia & Longenecker, 1994), humor and laughter can be employed in terribly demeaning and corrupting ways (Jenkins, 1994, Keough, 1990) and some of the most horrific crimes occur in ostensibly nuclear heterosexual families (Blount, 1982; Charny, 1996; Poster, 1978). In essence, the bright side is often darker than it seems.

For example, in the 1960s and early 1970s, assertiveness training became a craze. Researchers, mainly in the areas of counseling and clinical psychology, started conducting considerable scientific research to validate the value of such training. For about a decade everyone in the self-help, scholarly, and lay publics seemed impressed with assertiveness as a key to interpersonal health and self-actualization. Then some scholars decided it would be a good idea to ask the students' confederates and "recipients" of the assertion what they thought. It turns out that people on the receiving end of assertion tend to view it as effective, but not very likable or appropriate. In essence, thousands, perhaps tens of thousands of people were being trained to lose friends and influence people. And yet, everyone *knew* that assertion was one of the bright sides of social behavior. Are the risks of social engineering any less anytime Dr. Phil advises millions of viewers on television how to respond to a given personal situation?

Similar lessons can be derived from many other realms of the dark side. For example, we constantly are told the importance of reducing conflict, despite the fact that sometimes, what is most needed is to know how to start a conflict. We are told that empathy is an essential ingredient for good relationships. But empathy is probably destructive for negotiators and surgeons. We are told to be nonviolent, but we rarely begrudge someone violence in self-defense. We are told to be disclosive and open in relationships, even though such openness can be abused. We are told to be optimistic, and yet, lonely persons are those who expect more intimacy than they receive. Thus, the elderly tend to be less lonely than college-age populations, who expect too much in the way of intimacy (Russell, 1996). We are told that mutual understanding is essential to a good marriage. However, the research thus far is very qualified. The extent to which husbands and wives *think* they are understood, the more satisfied they are with their marriage. To date, there is very little evidence that *actual* accuracy of understanding and being understood are related to marital satisfaction. Indeed, there is even a tantalizing tidbit of evidence to the contrary. Spouses who *really*, accurately, understand each other may be *less* satisfied, presumably because they find more details over which disagreement and conflict can arise.

The point is that popular press, media, public, and scholarly opinion seems fascinated by the dark side because it reflects those aspects of our lives we collectively want to avoid (Putney, 1992). The irony is that the dark side is often not so dark, and the bright side to which we aspire is often darker than we care to believe. Thus, a question such as "Does violence in the media cause violence in society?" is only part of the relevant question. The other questions include issues such as: "Why do people seem drawn to or entertained by violence?" "Under what conditions is violence in the media harmful to society, and under what conditions is it helpful?" "How should the darker sides of our nature be theoretically and artistically integrated into our broader conceptions of ourselves?" Schoenewolf (1991) speaks of the "art" of hating, Spitzberg (1997) about the "competence" of violence, Katz (1988) about the seductions of crime, Sabini and Silver (1982) about the some of the functional ambiguities of life (e.g., flirtation), Volkan (1988) about the need to have enemies, Coser (1956) and Gilmore (1987) about the important social functions of conflict, and several authors have noted the many values of ambiguity (e.g., Bavelas et al., 1990; Spitzberg, 1993, 1994a).

The field of communication has a long tradition of studying topics on the dark side, although it has seldom explicitly viewed these topics as possessing common threads of connection with one another—threads that collectively define the nature of the dark side of human communication. There are many examples that illustrate the richness of the discipline, including research on ethics in public relations, advertising, and political communication; the impact of stereotyping, objectification, and paradoxical images of women portrayed in the mass media; internet addiction; the rhetorical strategies of terrorists and groups such as the KKK; the study of interpersonal conflict, sexual harassment, sexual coercion, safe sex (or the lack thereof), sexual assault, intimate violence, and stalking; as well as dozens of everyday types of communication on the dark side, such as deception, infidelity, rejection, relationship breakup, embarrassment, shame, guilt, anger, loneliness, depression, conversational dilemmas, hurtful messages, criticism, obscenity, and communicative aggression. Finally, many scholars are attempting to anticipate the role that communication media will have on our future. Will the new communication media provide the utopia so many advertisers seem to promise, or will they create a *dystopia*, in which the colder media of screens and keyboards and artificial intelligence make relationships less intimate and satisfying? Will the advent of an information economy mean that the information haves will exploit the information have-nots? Is it a brave new world in which privacy is a scarce commodity, or will communication media permit the creation of information islands in which people secure themselves in the telecommuting wombs of their homes? In short, the dark side is integral to the work that communication scholars do, but it has yet to be recognized as such.

The dark side offers tangible opportunities to understand the human condition (Duck, 1994; Duck & Wood, 1995). To date, we have tended to be too simplistic ideologically. Artistically, we tend to construct characters who are good or evil, but only occasionally do we get a really good characterization of someone capable of, even adept at, both. Scientifically, we tend to treat the bright side as intrinsically moral and the dark side as something to extricate from society, rather than seeking the many ways in which the dark side is an ally to desirable individual and social relations. We have reasonably elaborate understandings of serial killers and crimes of passion, but we have relatively little understanding of the wish to kill that may be in all of us. We have extensive programs of research on deception, and know almost nothing about how hurtful or dysfunctional honesty can be. Until such questions are taken seriously, by artists, professionals, and scholars, the answers will continue to elude us, and we will be less able to make legitimate choices in our public policies, much less our daily lives, in regard to social behavior.

REFERENCES

Baumeister, R. F. (1997). *Evil.* New York, NY: Freeman.

Baumeister, R. F., Smart, L., & Boden, J. M. (1996). Relation of threatened egotism to violence and aggression: The dark side of high self-esteem. *Psychological Review, 103,* 5–33.

Bavelas, J. B., Black, A., Chovil, N., & Mullett, J. (1990). *Equivocal Ccommunication.* Newbury Park, CA: Sage.

Berke, J. H. (1988). *The tyranny of malice: Exploring the dark side of culture.* New York, NY: Summit Books.

Blount, F. (1982). *The subversive family: An alternative history of love and marriage.* London, England: Jonathan Cape.

Bochner, A. P. (1982). On the efficacy of openness. In M. Burgoon (Ed.), *Communication yearbook 5* (pp. 109–124). New Brunswick, NJ: Transaction/International Communication Association.

Cerullo, K. A. (1988). What's wrong with this picture? Enhancing communication through distortion. *Communication Research, 15,* 93–101.

Chancer, L. S. (1992). *Sadomasochism in everyday life: The dynamics of power and powerlessness.* New Brunswick, NJ: Rutgers University Press.

Charny, I. W. (1996). Evil in human personality: Disorders of doing harm to others in family relationships. In F. W. Kaslow (Ed.), *Handbook of relational diagnosis and dysfunctional family patterns* (pp. 477–495). New York, NY: Wiley.

Conger, J. A. (1990). The dark side of leadership. *Organizational Dynamics, 19,* 44–55.

Coser, L. (1956). *The functions of social conflict.* New York, NY: Free Press.

Cupach, W. R., & Spitzberg, B. H. (Eds). *The dark side of interpersonal communication.* Hillsdale, NJ: Lawrence Erlbaum.

DePaulo, B. M., Kashy, D. A., Kirkendol, S. E., Wyer, M. M., & Epstein, J. A. (1996). Lying in everyday life. *Journal of Personality and Social Psychology, 70,* 979–995.

Duck, S. (1994). Stratagems, spoils, and a serpent's tooth: On the delights and dilemmas of personal relationships. In W. R. Cupach & B. H. Spitzberg (Eds.), *The dark side of interpersonal communication* (pp. 3–24). Hillsdale, NJ: Lawrence Erlbaum.

Duck, S., & Wood, J. T. (1995). For better, for worse, for richer, for poorer: The rough and the smooth of relationships. In S. Duck & J. T. Wood (Eds.), *Confronting relationship challenges* (pp. 1–21). Thousand Oaks, CA: Sage.

Eisenberg, E. M. (1984). Ambiguity as strategy in organizational communication. *Communication Monographs, 51,* 227–242.

Fillion, K. (1996). *Lip service: The truth about women's darker side in love, sex, and friendship.* New York, NY: HarperCollins.

Finkelhor, D., Gelles, R. J., Hotaling, G. T., & Straus, M. A. (Eds.). (1983). *The dark side of families: Current family violence research.* Newbury Park, CA: Sage.

Gilmore, D. D. (1987). *Aggression and community: Paradoxes of Andalusian culture.* New Haven, CT: Yale University Press.

Gioia, D. A., & Longenecker, C. O. (1994). Delving into the dark side: The politics of executive appraisal. *Organizational Dynamics, 22,* 47–58.

Goldberg, J. G. (1993). *The dark side of love: The positive role of our negative feelings--anger, jealousy, and hate.* New York, NY: Putnam's.

Gustafson, S. B., & Ritzer, D. R. (1995). The dark side of normal: A psychopathy-linked pattern called aberrant self-promotion. *European Journal of Personality, 9,* 147–183.

Harper, R. (1968). *The path of darkness.* Cleveland, OH: Case Western Reserve University Press.

Jenkins, R. (1994). *Subversive laughter: The liberating power of comedy.* New York, NY: Free Press.

Katz, J. (1988). *Seductions of crime: Moral and sensual attractions in doing evil.* New York, NY: Basic Books.

Keough, W. (1990). *Punchlines: The violence of American humor.* New York, NY: Paragon House.

Kursh, C. O. (1971). The benefits of poor communication. *Psychoanalytic Review, 58,* 189–208.

LaGaipa, J. J. (1990). The negative effects of informal support systems. In S. Duck (Ed.), *Personal relationships and social support* (pp. 122–139). Newbury Park, CA: Sage.

Levitt, M. J., Silver, M. E., & Franco, N. (1996). Troublesome relationships: A part of human experience. *Journal of Social and Personal Relationships, 13,* 523–536.

McMillen, C., Zuravin, S., & Rideout, G. (1995). Perceived benefit from child sexual abuse. *Journal of Consulting and Clinical Psychology, 63,* 1037–1043.

Moore, T. (1994). *Dark eros: The imagination of sadism* (2nd ed.). Woodstock, CT: Spring Publications.

Parks, M. (1982). Ideology in interpersonal communication: Off the couch and into the world. In M. Burgoon (Ed.), *Communication yearbook 5* (pp. 79–108). New Brunswick, NJ: Transaction.

Parks, M. R. (1995). Ideology in interpersonal communication: Beyond the couches, talk shows, and bunkers. In B. R. Burleson (Ed.), *Communication yearbook 18* (pp. 480–497). Thousand Oaks, CA: Sage.

Poster, M. (1978). *Critical theory of the family.* New York, NY: Seabury Press.

Pratt, A. R. (1994). *The dark side: Thoughts on the futility of life from the ancient Greeks to the present.* New York, NY: Carol Publishing.

Putney, M. J. (1992). Welcome to the dark side. In J. A. Krantz (Ed.), *Dangerous men and adventurous women* (pp. 99–105). Philadelphia: University of Pennsylvania.

Ray, E. B. (1993). When the links become chains: Considering dysfunctions of supportive communication in the workplace. *Communication Monographs, 60,* 106–111.

Rodriquez, N., & Ryave, A. (1990). Telling lies in everyday life: Motivational and organizational consequences of sequential preferences. *Qualitative Sociology, 13,* 195–210.

Rook, K. S. (1989). Strains in older adults' friendships. In R. G. Adams & R. Blieszner (Eds.), *Older adult friendship: Structure and process* (pp. 166–194). Newbury Park, CA: Sage.

Rook, K. S., & Pietromonaco, P. (1987). Close relationships: Ties that heal or ties that bind? In W. H. Jones & D. Perlman, *Advances in personal relationships: Vol. 1* (pp. 1–35). JAI Press. Stamford CT.

Russell, D. W. (1996). UCLS Loneliness scale (version 3): Reliability, validity, and factor structure. *Journal of Personality Assessment, 66,* 20–40.

Sabini, J., & Silver, M. (1982). *Moralities of everyday life.* Oxford, England: Oxford University Press.

Schoenewolf, G. (1991). *The art of hating.* Northvale, NJ: Jason Aronson.

Schotter, A. (1986). On the economic virtues of incompetency and dishonesty. In A. Diekmann & P. Mitter (Eds.), *Paradoxical effects of social behavior* (pp. 235–241). Heidelberg, Germany: Physica-Verlag Heidelberg Wein.

Sedikides, C., Oliver, M. B., & Campbell, W. K. (1994). Perceived benefits and costs of romantic relationships for women and men: Implications for exchange theory. *Personal Relationships, 1,* 5–21.

Spitzberg, B. H. (1993). The dialectics of (in)competence. *Journal of Social and Personal Relationships*, *10*, 137–158.

Spitzberg, B. H. (1994a). The dark side metaphor. *International Society for the Study of Personal Relationships Bulletin*, *11*, 8–9.

Spitzberg, B. H. (1994b). The dark side of (in)competence. In W. R. Cupach & B. H. Spitzberg (Eds.), *The dark side of interpersonal communication* (pp. 25–49). Hillsdale, NJ: Lawrence Erlbaum.

Spitzberg, B. H. (1997). Intimate violence. In W. R. Cupach & D. J. Canary (Eds.), *Competence in interpersonal conflict* (pp. 174–201). New York, NY: McGraw-Hill.

Spitzberg, B. H., & Cupach, W. R. (1998). Dusk, detritus, and delusion: A prolegomenon to the dark side of close relationships. In B. H. Spitzberg & W. R. Cupach (Eds.), *The dark side of close relationships* (pp. xi–xxii). Mahwah, NJ: Lawrence Erlbaum.

Tseëlon, E. (1992). What is beautiful is bad: Physical attractiveness as stigma. *Journal for the Theory of Social Behaviour*, *22*, 295–310.

Twitchell, J. B. (1989). *Preposterous violence: Fables of aggression in modern culture*. New York, NY: Oxford University Press.

Volkan, V.D. (1988). *The need to have enemies and allies: From clinical practice to international relationships*. Northvale, NJ: Jason Aronson.

Watson, L. (1995). *Dark nature: A natural history of evil*. New York, NY: HarperCollins.

QUESTIONS/THOUGHTS

1. Under what circumstances do you regularly encounter dark side interactions of a particular type, such as jealous rages, malicious gossip, or lying? What are the costs to at least one participant in the interactions? What, if any, possible benefits might this participant experience?

2. Describe a situation in which you, another person, or a fictional character enacted problematic, difficult, or destructive communication behaviors. What appeared to be the reason for this choice? What was the effect of the choice?

3. Online interactions may reveal the dark side as teenagers ridicule or threaten a peer. What distinguishes the impact of these online negative and hurtful messages from face to face harassment? To what extent are bullies more vicious online than in person?

4. Analyze a film or television special that depicts a relationships characterized by jealousy, verbal abuse, stalking or compulsive lying. Assess the impact of these negative communicative interactions of the victim.

Why Marriages Fail

JOHN GOTTMAN

John Gottman, internationally acclaimed marital and family researcher, suggests that the quality of communication is the best predictor of a successful marriage. The type of relationship spouses have affects their frequency of communication, their willingness to self-disclose, and their willingness to confront conflict rather than avoid it. Satisfaction is not necessarily created by any of these communication styles, per se. That is, different couple types are satisfied with different communication styles. Highly independent couples are satisfied with informational exchanges (self-disclosure, discussion of conflict, etc.), whereas more traditional couples enjoy togetherness, sharing, and similarity.

Gottman (1994) argues that couples who maintain a "magic ratio" of 5:1 positive feeling and interaction, to negative feeling and interaction between a husband and wife, avoid the risk of marital misery. Essentially, he says: "Accentuate the positive; don't eliminate the negative" (p.56.) His research reveals marriages that work are characterized by, (1) an overall level of positive affect, and (2) an ability to reduce negative affect during conflict resolution (Gottman, 1999a, p. 105). In his popular book,

The Seven Principles for Making Marriage Work (1999b), Gottman suggests that successful couples live by principles such as, turn toward each other instead of away, solve your solvable problems, and create shared meaning.

According to Gottman, couples that experience high levels of negativity risk losing their marriages. Such couples face the "Cascade of Dissolution" or moving downward through a pattern of criticism, defensiveness, contempt, and stonewalling that can devastate the marriage. He believes marriages can be restored and repaired if couples will learn and practice new skills, including communication skills. In the following article he provides an introduction to his research processes and describes the three very different types of functional marriages, the validating, volatile, and conflict avoiding. Partners in these marriages tend to use the 5:1 "magic ratio" interaction pattern of positivity to negativity; each partnership is characterized by highly positive experiences although the couple may fight actively or avoid conflict. John Gottman's research also reveals, "The Four Horsemen of the Apocalypse" or four disastrous ways of interacting that sabotage attempt to communicate with a partner;

these are criticism, defensiveness, contempt, and stonewalling.

The Gottman research team also developed an elaborate laboratory in which they could take physiological measures of individuals as they interacted with each other. For example, they were able to document the rise in heart beats per minute as couples argued and to recognize signs of "flooding" when the adrenaline gets so high that individuals cannot think calmly or really listen to the partner's point of view. Flooding creates defensiveness and a fight or flight reaction.

In some of his recent work John Gottman has addressed the difference between solvable problems and unsolvable or perpetual problems. He describes a study in which his team brought couples back into the laboratory four years later to talk about the major issue in their marriage. They found "69% of the time couples had the same problems and talked about them in the same way; 31% of the problems had been solved" (psychotherapy. net, 2000). Marital problems often reflect powerful patterns that are very difficult to change.

As you read this chapter ask yourself about your personal perceptions of "good" relationships: How willing am I to accept that successful marriages may be characterized by active conflict or avoidance of conflict? How willing am I to work to increase positivity in my partnership?

REFERENCES

Gottman, J. M. (1994). *Why marriages succeed or fail.* New York, NY: Simon and Schuster.

Gottman, J. M. (1999a). *The marriage clinic: A scientifically based marital therapy.* New York: Norton.

Gottman, J. M., & Silver, N. (1999b). *The seven principles for making marriage work.* New York, NY: Three Rivers Press.

Wyatt, R. C. (2001). An interview with John Gottman, Ph.D. *Psychotherapy.* Retrieved August 13, 2009, from http://www.psychotherapy.net/interview/John_Gottman

Every therapist knows how mysterious marriage can be—witness the apparently incompatible couples who seem to have more fights in a week than most spouses average in a year but still stay together for a lifetime, and even seem to be happy with each other. Or, at the other extreme, consider those couples who approach potential conflict like a fatal virus, dodging and hedging around disagreeable subjects, unable to openly discuss, let alone resolve, what would seem to be critical issues in their marriage. And yet, these same couples—frequently labeled "in denial" or "repressed" by the marital therapy profession—not infrequently raise families and merrily celebrate 30th and 40th wedding anniversaries in spite of doomsday prognoses.

The truth is that, for all our theorizing about how a good marriage coheres and a bad one unravels, few of us can claim to know very much about the mysterious inner workings of this most intimate relationship. The actual daily *stuff* of marriage—the slow accretion over the years of countless small, subtle but deeply telling patterns of interaction that make or break individual marriages—is still *terra incognita* to most of us, married couples and therapists included.

This news may come as a shock, considering the plethora of psychological prescriptions for fixing broken marriages, but until very recently, we did not know much more about the emotional and behavioral processes within marriage than we did about the physiology of sexual behavior before Masters and Johnson. And most of what we still claim to know comes from personal musings based on the idiosyncratic practice of individual therapists; almost none of our theory and practice is founded on empirical scientific research. This is not to say that therapists have not helped countless couples save their own marriages, or have not themselves accumulated a wealth of informal wisdom about marriage over the years. But the reasons that individual marriages succeed or fail remain mysterious, and much of the marital advice—whether it works or doesn't—has only the frailest of empirical foundations....

Twenty years ago, I made my own first forays into this new world of marital research. As a young therapist I felt stymied in my attempts to help a particularly troubled couple, whose therapy sessions inevitably disintegrated into bitter personal fights, over which neither they nor I had much control. On a hunch, I made a series of videotapes of the sessions, then had them watch the tapes with me and tell me what they had been feeling and thinking during certain moments of their filmed interaction.

Both the couple and I were astonished by the vividness and clarity on the tape of the pattern of criticism, contempt, and defensiveness they repeatedly fell into—a pattern of which they had been largely unaware and even I couldn't see clearly in session. While I still didn't know what to *do* to help turn them around, not only did the tape act as a kind of positive catalyst for them—it shocked them into working harder at hearing each other and trying to improve the way they spoke to each other—it gave me my life's work. I wanted to develop a science of marital interaction, a body of replicable data about the destructive emotional processes between spouses that, unless they were interrupted fairly early on, could reliably predict the dissolution of the marriage. In short, I wanted to be able to see, identify and intervene in these specific and observable patterns before they achieved critical mass.

From this more or less ad hoc beginning, I gradually developed, along with many colleagues, a complex multimethod research model for studying the interstices of marriage. Our data base has been drawn, over the last two decades, from 20 different studies based on the three videotaped conversations of 2,000 couples overall, correlated with electronically measured physiological responses and backed up by questionnaires and interviews. We have used a coding system for relating facial expressions to emotion, as well as measuring other indices of emotional expression, including voice and language, to demonstrate levels of affection, interest, amusement and joy as well as anger, sadness, fear, contempt and disgust at different points during the conversation. We have also watched and listened for specific kinds of verbal and physical behavior that communicated, for example, complaint, blame, criticism, whining, defensiveness, belligerence, and domineering. In addition, physiological data— heart rate, blood-flow rate, perspiration during stress, gross motor movement, and sometimes,

stress-related hormones in urine and blood—have been synchronized with observed interactions of the couples. We then have interviewed spouses about what they were thinking and feeling (and what they think their spouses were thinking and feeling) during specific moments of the taping. Finally, we have collected questionnaires and oral histories about the state of their marriages, their feelings of loneliness or togetherness, what they think and feel about each other, and what they think the other feels about them.

While we still have a long way to go before we truly understand the complex processes of marriage, we have gathered enough data about the way individual couples interact in marriages to develop a theory of the factors that, if they are not interrupted, put a couple on a trajectory toward divorce, one that grows steeper and more slippery {stet –authors'word}over time. We think there is evidence to show that if these negative patterns of interaction are not reversed in time, there is a point of no return, after which not much can be done to save the marriage.

Even without being able to fully identify and analyze the thousands of factors that go into the subtle and complex communication patterns between a couple, we believe we are still in a position to predict, based on our data, which couples are most likely to be divorced in the future. Of the 2,000 couples in our data base, we have followed 484 couples, many for as long as 10 years, testing four years after the initial interview for the impact of factors we thought might predict divorce and continuing to monitor them after that. We found such strong linkages between the information we had collected originally and the couples' marital status four and more years later—whether they had divorced or not—that we now feel confident about our abilities to predict the potential for divorce in particular kinds of marriages. Indeed, I can now tell from a brief interview with a couple, a few questionnaires and a portion of a videotape what the eventual fate of a particular marriage is likely to be. In fact, from just six variables from our standard Oral History interview, I can predict with 94-percent accuracy which marriages are headed for divorce.

We already have enough evidence to unseat some of the most venerable truisms of marital therapy, including what comprises a "good" marriage. The satisfactorily married couple, according to the conventional therapeutic wisdom, is first of all, deeply *compatible*: the spouses do not necessarily have to come from the same ethnic, religious, and class background (though it helps), but they must agree on important things—sex, money, religion, childrearing—and should be able to compromise on about everything else. Not that this couple doesn't argue—they do, but their arguments seldom get lowdown and dirty, or even very heated. When they disagree, they naturally and without prompting do exactly what therapists advise less compatible and more troubled spouses to do: recognize conflicts, acknowledge differences openly but address them honestly and calmly before they degenerate into shouting matches. Conventional wisdom says they listen respectfully and empathize with each other's point of view; they don't interrupt much and if neither can persuade the other to do this or that side of the issue, they negotiate a workable compromise. Not surprisingly, these couples look and sound a lot like two psychotherapists engaging in a dialogue.

Undoubtedly, this kind of union—what we call the validating style of marriage—usually works very well. And it is, therefore, not surprising that a wide range of marital theories and therapies—insight-focused, behavioral, psychoeducational—are geared to getting all troubled marriages to approximate this pattern. Certainly, viewing this style of marriage as the ideal has simplified the careers of marital therapists; their fundamental goal has been to help unhappily married couples get back to the bottom-line compatibility they are all presumed to have started with, if the marriage was ever viable in the first place. It followed then that either a lot of fighting or no fighting at all were both signs of a marriage on the rocks, that both indicated hidden agendas and unrecognized symbolic conflicts, which were undermining the marriage. Whichever it was—fighting or no fighting—the couple needed to uncover and "hash out" their differences, then come to a compromise so

they could achieve the kind of idyllic balance represented by the validating couple.

But from what we see in the laboratory, the idea that the only truly satisfying marriage is cast in the mold of the validating style is wrong. Likewise, the orthodox belief that compatibility is indispensable to marital happiness and the reduction of conflict is critical to saving troubled marriages is a myth.

Our research shows that it isn't the lack of compatibility that predicts divorce, but the way couples handle their inevitable *incompatibilities*; not whether they fight all the time or never fight at all, but the way they resolve conflicts and the overall quality of their emotional interactions in a marriage that determines its well-being—whether the good moments of mutual pleasure, passion, humor, support, kindness, and generosity outweigh the bad moments of complaint, criticism, anger, disgust, contempt, defensiveness, and coldness. In fact, after studying, tabulating, and analyzing probably tens of thousands of marital interactions in our data base, we have concluded that we can actually quantify the ratio of positive to negative interactions needed to maintain a marriage in good shape. And we found that satisfied couples, no matter how their marriages stacked up against the ideal, were those who maintained a five-to-one ratio of positive to negative moments. Whether they fought a lot or not at all, whether they seemed passionately engaged with each other or distinctly distant, and most important, whether or not they were compatible socially, financially, sexually—what counted was the overall *balance* of positive to negative.

This claim sounds entirely presumptuous: how can something with the mercurial, idiosyncratic, and labyrinthine dynamics of a marriage be reduced to a simple ratio of interactions? But much to our own surprise, we found that certain kinds of marriages that would seem doomed to failure according to standard therapeutic prognoses, were actually quite successful; what set these rule breaking, good marriages apart from others was their adherence to the five-to-one ratio.

Perhaps the most classic example of the presumably endangered marriage is the volatile type between spouses who apparently live to fight. These Punch-and-Judy couples have intensely emotional marriages, characterized by epic brawls, high levels of jealousy, prickly interactions, petty bickering, sarcastic asides, and hair-trigger tempers. Unlike the "compatible" couples that are the marital therapist's dream, these excitable couples do not fight fairly. When they argue, they go for the jugular, rarely listen to or empathize with their mates during the course of battle, and attempt to steamroller each other to their respective points of view.

And yet, that these couples engage in a lot more *sturm und drang* than most couples (and many therapists) could tolerate does not, of itself, mean they don't have good marriages. In a successful marriage of this type, for every nasty swipe, there are five caresses, so to speak. Indeed, far more than other marriages, however solid and satisfying, volatile marriages are inclined to be deeply romantic and frequently dramatic. And because the spouses tend, as one would expect, to be passionate and intense people, their relationship—when it is satisfying—can be much more exciting and deeply intimate than the marriages of less emotionally engaged people.

Of course, there are pitfalls to these volatile marriages. Neither spouse worries overmuch about hurting the other's feelings, nor do the two believe that discretion is the better part of valor. Thus, for these spouses, who readily wade into controversy and contumely, the five-to-one ratio is more dangerously vulnerable to shifting downward than for more cautious couples. And when they fly at each other without forethought, as they often do, they can inflict unforgivable wounds. Under external stresses—the birth of a baby, for example—the normally argumentative style of their marriage can deteriorate into endless bickering and quarreling, even violence.

At the opposite end of the spectrum of presumably "dysfunctional" marriages, at least according to received wisdom, are the imperturbable couples who cannot stand fighting—the conflict avoiders. When a potential disagreement raises its serpent's head, these conflict-avoidant or conflict-minimizing couples are more than

likely to step around it, eyes averted. Interviewing these couples, we found it extremely difficult to even find a subject of continuing disagreement between them, and had to settle for relatively trivial problems that may have caused an occasional twinge of discomfort. (One couple admitted that they disagreed once on whether to have chicken or pizza for dinner.) When differences cannot be smoothed over or ignored—sexual incompatibility, for example—they are likely to resolve them by *not* resolving them, concluding that although they recognize the conflict exists, they don't consider it as important as the many areas of common agreement they do share. In a sense, all of their conversations (they couldn't be called arguments) with us about differences between them ended in standoffs; they agree that they disagreed, but make no attempt to persuade each other. They simply agree to continue disagreeing, and then drop the subject.

According to standard theories of marital therapy, the union of this couple, even more than the first, is doomed. Compatibility seems to have become too much of a good thing, as it were, and they are terrified of disagreement. Their unacknowledged conflicts, while "repressed" and "denied," so goes the standard theory, feed a deep, toxic undercurrent of hostility and rage. The prognosis for these couples is that either the spouses will become quietly antagonistic strangers living separate parallel lives in the same household, or, according to the "volcano" theory of marital interaction, the repressed fury (which, it is often assumed, must be there) may explode into outright violence.

Our research shows these "doomed" marriages survive. The reason is that these couples, just like the volatile spouses, share an interactive ratio of five positive to one negative moment. While they have fewer negative interactions, they also have fewer positive ones. The difference is that their relationships are less emotional than the volatile marriages. They are less likely to fight passionately, but also less likely to love passionately. Instead of a marriage that resembles a raging torrent, theirs looks like a calm lake. They are likely to be *truly* compatible, as well paired as matching bookends. Often they come from the same social and economic background, hold similar beliefs about religion, values, childrearing practices, financial issues, and the like. They share a sense of their marriage as a kind of secure bastion, a solid fortress of "us," so strong a bond that they can afford to overlook disagreements. Probably for centuries, traditional marriages resembled this type; the married couple, as unbudgeable a social institution as church and state could make them, didn't require romance, or even active companionship, to shore up a union considered by nature, law, and religion indissoluble.

Of course, these marriages also have their weaknesses. Because these couples allow so little negativity into their interactions, they may not be able to deal effectively with disagreements that cannot be ignored or evaded, in which case they may live with a good deal of unresolved misery and frustration. In an effort to avoid any confrontation at all, they also tend to undermine intimacy and, as a result, they may see their marriage become rather cold and distant. While they have fewer negative interactions, they also have fewer positive ones. Nonetheless, like the volatile couples, these conflict-minimizing pairs also have a very good shot at making and keeping a good, solid marriage for life—in spite of the fact that they, too, do not follow the marital "rules" of the therapeutic trade.

In fact, we found such consistency of success for all three types of marital unions—validating, volatile, and conflict avoiding—if they maintain the five-to-one ratio that we are inclined to consider it a universal constant. Like any other living thing, the marital relationship must sustain a kind of emotional ecological balance in order to survive. Marriages seem to thrive on, proportionately, *a little* negativity and *a lot* of positivity. The total amounts vary substantially from style to style, but the proportion between the pluses and minuses must remain the same. One couple's successful marriage exhibits a lot of both negative and positive affect, another shows moderate amounts of negativity and positivity and the third, small amounts of each—but all will show the same ratio.

Just as striking, however, is the strong possibility emerging from our studies that *only* couples from one of these three affective styles seem able to maintain the necessary ratio for a satisfying marriage. It seems, in short, that lasting marriages come in three discrete types, and that there are no in-between types that work well or last very long. The fighting styles of each individual spouse probably reflect deeply entrenched personality traits and worldviews; a conflict between styles may well represent fundamental disagreement on the very constitution of happy versus miserable marriages. So, if a validator (temperamentally disposed to calmly and rationally work problems out) or a conflict-minimizer (content to let problems remain unresolved) marries a volatile type (who thrives in the heat of passionate battle), serious problems in the marriage are almost foreordained. Typically, the volatile spouse (often the wife) first feels puzzled and impatient, then patronized and frustrated, finally frustrated and maddened by her validator or conflict-minimizing husband's refusal to go *mano a mano* with her. The more moderate and reasonable he is, the more irritable, insulting, and furious she becomes, driving him to defensive retreat, silent contempt, and cold hostility. It seems from our studies that one or the other spouse would have to make a very concerted and probably difficult attempt to change his or her style of fighting, which might mean transforming some very basic personal attitudes, as well.

Paradoxically, successful couples *are* compatible—but not in the way traditionally suggested by marital therapy theory. As it turns out, the spouses within each different style are compatible fighters; they do implicitly agree on the way they will disagree, on how they will traverse the rough terrain they inevitably cross on their trek through marriage.

Our research suggests that while disagreements and fights are not pleasant, and no couples except the volatile seem to enjoy them, they are necessary in some degree to all good marriages. Recognizing disagreement and engaging in it, even if it is never settled or no compromise is reached, helps couples cope with difficult issues, while enriching and stimulating both of them. We speculate that the function of negativity, including anger, in marriage is to create a dynamic rather than static equilibrium between spouses; certain forms of negativity are like spice that keep relationships from going flat. Anger, when directed at a particular issue and expressed without contempt or global criticism, is healthy, perhaps even necessary. We have found in our studies that while angry exchanges made both spouses unhappy during the period when they were happening, they correlated with long-term marital satisfaction. Blunt, straightforward anger seems to immunize marriages against deterioration.

Not all forms of negativity are equal, however, in the ecology of marriage, and we have observed that some are clearly more dangerous, more toxic than others. The five-to-one ratio is a measure of a satisfying marriage; that couples experience it at one point in their marriage is no guarantee that they can count on it forever. From what we can see, no marriage of any type—even one exhibiting a healthy five-to-one ratio of positive to negative interactions—can long sustain itself once four particularly corrosive personal exchanges have insinuated themselves into the relationship. These four processes—criticism, defensiveness, contempt, and stonewalling—I call the "four horsemen of the apocalypse" because they seem to have the inherently destructive power of a virus or a cancer; if they are not checked, they can colonize and ultimately destroy a relationship.

Although every couple engages in the terrible four from time to time, they need to be aware lest they begin gradually to occupy a growing proportion of normal fights and disagreements. Therefore, both couple and therapists need to understand the sometimes subtle, but always critical, difference between less damaging forms of negativity and the terrible four. Anger and disagreement, for example, are quite distinct from criticism and contempt. In the former, a husband might say, "I'm upset that you didn't balance the joint checkbook. The bank called today about two bounced checks, and I was very embarrassed." In the latter, his remarks would be less specific, more global, aimed less at his spouse's actions, more toward her very being. "As usual, you screwed up our checkbook and humiliated me. You're no rocket scientist, but I'd think you could learn to do some simple addition and subtraction." It is not the anger that makes this attack destructive, it is the derision and gratuitous insult added to it. She not only made a mistake, she *always* makes mistakes and is kind of stupid, to boot.

Clearly, the walls are already closing in on these two, leaving no room for maneuvering into a more tolerable mutual exchange. Typically, they would trade attacks until one or the other, probably the wife, started screaming and the husband would engage horseman number four—stonewalling. He would "remove himself" emotionally or physically—refuse to answer or look at her, or storm out of the room.

Stonewalling is a characteristically male thing to do; in one of our samples of couples, we found that 85 percent of our stonewallers were male. And, in the course of our research, we have made some startling discoveries about the physiological differences between men and women that account for this disproportion.

Marital strife has a significant physiological as well as psychological component, which shows up differently between men and women during arguments. At the onset of a fight, men become more intensely upset physiologically than women—measured in terms of higher heart rate and blood pressure—and they remain distressed for a longer time—long after their wives have calmed down. Probably this difference in wiring had evolutionary survival benefits: the prehistoric male of our species, to protect the female and her young, had to be more alert and physiologically responsive to external danger than she did—more ready to attack and fight or flee in the face of environmental danger. In modern life, this propensity to higher arousal is not nearly so adaptive; it feels terrible, and to avoid the acute distress it causes, men are likely simply to shut themselves down, refuse to respond, try, as much as possible, to turn themselves into unfeeling stone. But this pain-reducing strategy is terrible for marriage. The stonewalling, as it turns out, increases the woman's feelings of unpleasant physiological arousal more than anything else her spouse does, much more than shouting back, for example.

This physiological gender difference may help explain some of the truisms about male and female styles of fighting in marriage—why women are more likely to be "emotional" during a fight and pursue their mates with complaints, criticisms and demands, while men tend to engage in rationalizations, avoid the subject, withdraw into silence and impassivity, or physically retreat. In fact, our research confirmed that men engage in such maddeningly avoidant behaviors (to their wives, at least) precisely because they are much more unpleasantly physiologically aroused by a fight than their wives.

On the other hand, we also found that in happy marriages, the widely touted theory that men are less emotionally expressive than women was *not* confirmed in our research; in fact, we found that, by and large, in satisfying marriages, there are no gender differences in emotional expression: men are as likely to share their most intimate emotions as women. Surprisingly, in happy marriages, men are more likely to reveal personal information about themselves—dissatisfaction with the self, hurts, dreams, aspirations, reminiscences—than their wives. And when these men are angry, they don't stonewall, but openly let their wives know what they are feeling—which, again, is much less stressful for their wives than stubborn withdrawal. Unfortunately, marriage is still about the only outlet for emotional expression in the lives of most men. Whereas wives usually have a fairly wide support network outside the marriage of friends and relatives, husbands, in essence, only disclose to their wives—and nobody else. It is not surprising, then, that unhappily married men are deeply lonely.

What is surprising is that we found that men who did housework were likely to be more happily engaged and involved in their marriages than men who did not, and less lonely, less stressed, *and* less likely to be sick four years after the initial meeting with them in the laboratory. Tested as a separate factor in men, doing housework, by itself, was related to lower heart rate, less physiological arousal in general, and better health four

years later. Clearly, what is measured here is not the fabulous, curative powers of housework, but the mutual and supportive engagement of spouses in good marriage—not such a startling fact on its own, but astonishing in that it is expressed so clearly in physiology, in the very life and well-being of the body.

Unhappy marriage is not physically good for either spouse, though the actual effects differ according to gender. Men are inclined to withdraw from marital interaction to buffer themselves from physically stressful feelings of arousal—to a certain extent, this mechanism protects them. But years spent warding off emotional and physiological feelings of being flooded by their wives' anger—the use of enormous stores of energy for continual stonewalling and withdrawal—take a very high toll on men's physical health.

Conversely, women actually become sick after too many years of figuratively knocking their heads against a stone wall—trying to get a response from someone who relentlessly refuses to respond. In fact, we found that the husband's contempt in marriage predicted, over time, a wife's susceptibility to illness; for example, by counting the number of a husband's facial expressions of contempt for his wife, we could correctly estimate the number of infectious diseases she would have over the next four years.

It is an unpalatable, but unescapable, truth that some marriages cannot and should not be saved. Not only do patterns of toxic marital interaction keep the body in a state of unhealthy physical arousal, they create a psychological climate of helpless misery—neither spouse *can* surmount the negativity and hostility that have seeped into virtually every shared marital interaction. Our study shows a physiological linkage between spouses—in the laboratory, physiological responses of each spouse can be predicted by those of the other. In other words, in negative interactions, something like a complex feedback loop occurs between spouses, which includes the back-and-forth exchange of negative physiological arousal, psychological misery, and destructive behavior. The repeated trauma of the marital interactions has not only become, in a sense, "hard-wired" into the physiology, but these bone-deep states of arousal can no longer be willfully controlled. Couples at the end of these marriages are unable to muster the cognitive and social abilities that, in less damaged relationships, could see them through to better times.

In good marriages, couples can readily repair the damage done during fights and the inevitable fallow periods (there are times, probably, when every spouse secretly wonders if the marriage hasn't been a terrible mistake) just in the mutually soothing exchanges that make any relationship flow. But these repair mechanisms no longer work in badly ailing marriages; there is literally nothing the couple can talk about, no subject, no common interest that is not fully colonized by the all-absorbing state of their mutual contempt and defensiveness. The range of available positive exchanges has so shriveled, and the negativity grown so cancerous, that both spouses have literally lost the ability to breathe and move normally in each other's presence; their muscles tense, their hearts beat harder, they feel they are suffocating.

At this point, we believe efforts to save the marriage are more likely to be disastrous than helpful. The partners are overwhelmed by a sense of failure, hopelessness and mutual alienation; they have been at war so long that there is no common ground left between them. Not only is it fatuous to suggest that they just "try harder" at this juncture, it may be bad for their health—witness our data suggesting that staying in a hostile, distant marriage actually compromises the immune system, increasing susceptibility to illness.

Furthermore, while divorce is never desirable, the research of Andrew Cherlin, Mavis Hetherington, and others suggests that it is probably better for children, as long as coparenting tasks are well-managed, than a marriage reduced to a vicious intermingling of mutual hostility and loneliness. The evidence from research I am currently doing reinforces this position. It appears that a well-managed divorce, in which both spouses were helped therapeutically to separate with some degree of calm and dignity and make reasonable mutual childcare arrangements, is better for children than forcing them to live in the donnybrook of their parents' terrible marriage....

The conclusions that have emerged from this large body of research show that "what everybody knows" is not always true—attempts to turn perfectly good, conflict-minimizing or volatile marriages into the validating-style marriages that therapists prefer are unsuited to the real spouses in those real relationships.

A good theory of marital dissolution—why it happens—must accurately predict which couples are most at risk long before the ultimate slide. Until recently, it would have seemed foolish to think that anything as complex, personal and idiosyncratic as marriage adhered to predictable patterns. And yet, it seems to be so. When we ask enough questions, when we deeply and carefully observe the smallest piece of behavior, we find in the most apparently chaotic marriages an intricate, but ultimately predictable, web of patterns at work. As we study marriage with the same respect and the same attention to detail that natural historians apply to the apparently inchoate confusion of nature, we come up with the same amazing discovery—human relationships, like other natural processes, are not random and unknowable, but appear to obey certain laws. Science, which might be called the study of natural laws, will not compromise the fundamental mystery of the heart, any more than science will eliminate the mystery of spring because the processes of germination and photosynthesis are understood. But with every new bit of knowledge about the couples who come into our laboratory, we increase our ability to help them and ourselves fulfill in all of our lives the original promise inherent in love's beginning.

QUESTIONS/THOUGHTS

1. Think about a romantic relationship that you know well and you consider highly successful. How are positive and negative messages managed in this relationship? To what extent does it reflect the 5:1 positivity to negativity magic ratio?

2. What would communication in your "ideal" marriage be like? Compare your ideal with that of a classmate of the opposite sex.

3. Give an example of a real or fictional relationship in which one partner engages in

stonewalling. How does he or she enact stone-walling? How does the partner react when that happens?

4. Interview a couple that you believe has a well-functioning relationship. Ask each partner for perceptions about why their relationship appears to work well, the efforts that either person makes to take care of the relationship.

Excerpted from John Gottman, "Why Marriages Fail," In *The Family Therapy Networker*, pp. 41–48. Copyright © 1994 by The Family Therapy Networker. Reprinted with permission.

"The Worst Part Is, We Don't Even Talk Anymore": Post-Dissolutional Communication in Break-Up Stories

JODY KOENIG KELLAS AND SAI SATO

The phrase "And they lived happily after" does not capture the experience of most romantic pairs who break up. Even the question, "Can't we just be friends?" may not evoke a positive response. Most adults have experienced a number of romantic breakup conversations and dealt with the aftermath of these discussions. There are many possible outcomes, ranging from maintaining a close friendship to experiencing stalking or threatening actions (Harvey and Weber 2002). Although a great deal is known about divorce and long-term interactions among ex-spouses (Hetherington & Kelly, 2002), far less is known about romantic breakups.

Much of the existing research relies on personal narratives because they capture the meaning of the experience for the respondents. According to Wells (1986), "Constructing stories in the mind—or storying, as it has been called—is one of the most fundamental means of making meanings...stories are one of the most effective ways of making one's own interpretation of events and ideas available to others" (p. 194).

Although the breaking up experience receives extensive attention in popular magazines and online chat rooms as well as on television and in films, only a limited number of studies have examined the follow-up experiences of young romantic relationships that have ended. Everyone is familiar with the "classic" break-up story: the couple fights, they break up, go their separate ways, and never speak again. Nevertheless, while most of us have witnessed or experienced this kind of break-up, it is certainly not the way that all couples end their relationships. For many, some ongoing communication occurs, often because the individuals continue to encounter each other through friendship networks, school, or work commitments.

Recent research identifies four different post-breakup relational trajectories and ten categories of turning points (Koenig Kellas, Bean, Cunningham & Cheng, 2009). The first, Linear Process, reflects a rather flat progression; the level of commitment tended to remain consistent over time. The second, Relational Decline, is characterized by a downward progression; each turning point resulted in a drop in commitment. The third, Upward Relational Progression, refers to relationships that rose in commitment over time. Finally, the fourth, Turbulent Relational Progression, depicts a somewhat tumultuous post-dissolutional experience.

As Jody Koenig Kellas, who has studied the impacts of relational breakups for over a decade, and Sai Sato report in this chapter, there are many couples who continue speaking to one another after their romantic relationship ends, and according to the research, this communication significantly impacts how the couple adapts and heals from relationship dissolution. They open the chapter with their personal stories, discuss the post-dissolutional issues, introduce the role of narrative in understanding these relationships, and analyze post-dissolution narratives.

As you read this chapter think about the questions: What are the advantages or disadvantages to continuing to interact with one another after ending a romantic relationship? What are the unspoken new rules for communication developed by many people who maintain regular contact after the breakup?

REFERENCES

Graham, E. E. (1997). Turning points and commitment in post-divorce relationships. *Communication Monographs, 64*, 350–368.

Koenig Kellas, J., Bean, D., Cunningham, C., Cheng, K.Y. (2008). The ex-files: Trajectories, turning points, and adjustment in the development of post-dissolutional relationships *Journal of Social and Personal Relationships, 25*(1) 23–50.

Harvey, J. H., & Weber, A. L. (2002). *Odyssey of the heart* (2nd ed.). Mahwah, NJ: Lawrence Erlbaum.

Hetherington, E. M., & Kelly, J.(2002). *For better or for worse: Divorce reconsidered.* New York, NY: Norton.

Wells, B. (1986). *The meaning makers.* Portsmouth, NH: Heinemann Press.

When I (Jody) was 16, I fell in love for the first time with a boy named Justin. It had all the great attributes of a first love—it was fun, exciting, and the feeling of butterflies surfaced in my stomach every time I knew I was going to see him. And, the best part was, we had been best friends before we started dating so we easily moved into a deeper closeness and into the kind of rich talks that accompanied our new bond. At the time, we, and our friends, saw us as a pair that would be connected forever, and in many ways we did a lot of growing up together. Eventually, however, as many young relationships do, ours came to an end when my family's cross-country move separated us, and we discovered that maintaining a long distance relationship at 16 was too difficult. Justin met a girl that lived in his own zip code, ended the relationship, and in the process, gave me my first broken heart.

I could end my story here, leaving a neat and packaged, albeit sad conclusion to a narrative about my first love and first "real" break-up. That would be, however, simplifying the complex set of communicative interactions that ensued immediately following the break-up and the many interactions that have continued over the years between Justin and me.

I share with you my own story as an exemplar of the idea that our relationships—and the communication that comprises them—do not simply end with the words "I think we should break up" or "I don't think we should see each other anymore." Instead, many relational partners continue communicating after the "state-of-the-relationship-talk" that ends the romantic relationship in an effort to understand what happened and/or construct a new sense of what the relationship will be now that they are no longer romantically involved. Indeed, even though it may have been easy in some ways for Justin and me to stop talking—we did live 3,000 miles apart after all—both of us made a concerted effort to continue calling one another. During many phone calls and visits, we attempted to make sense of why what seemed like a lasting relationship had to end and to repair the damage that our relationship had encountered so that it could continue on in friendship form.

Of course, not all communication following a break-up is so friendly, characterized by concerted effort, or harmonious. When my first love Yoshi and I (Sai) broke up, we were separated by many miles as well, but our post-dissolutional communication looked very different from Jody and Justin's. Yoshi broke up with me over an international phone call, leaving me shocked and betrayed. The communication after the breakup was bitter as I gradually grew angry at Yoshi, and Yoshi grew distant from me. Our post-dissolutional communication quickly came down to a few e-mail exchanges in which I exaggerated about my new boyfriend and Yoshi asked for some of his possessions back. With the advancement of technology, relationship dissolutions are now happening online through e-mails and Facebook (e.g., Starks, 2007), in addition to the conventional means such as face-to-face or phone conversations. As we saw in Sai's breakup story, we can also assume that individuals choose to use these computer-mediated technologies, not only to terminate their relationships, but also to communicate with their ex-partners after their breakups.

Despite the fact that many people do continue communicating with their former partners in a variety of forms, the current models used to explain relationship dissolution concentrate primarily on the communication that leads up to and culminates in the "official" termination (e.g., Knapp & Vangelisti, 2000). Other researchers look at the communication following the break-up that takes place outside the relationship (e.g., gravedressing, Duck, 2005). Scholars have recently started examining why former partners stay in contact after their breakups (Masuda, 2005), and the quality of post-dissolutional relationships among heterosexual and homosexual romantic partners (Koenig Kellas, Bean, Cunningham, & Cheng, 2008; Lannutti & Cameron, 2002). Research on narratives of relationship dissolution indicates that *whether or not* and *how* people continue talking after they break up matters to them and may affect how well they deal with the relationship's end. More specifically, Koenig Kellas and Manusov (2003) found that people used "current communication status" as conceptual yardsticks to evaluate the break-up process and/or to describe their present emotions. This seemed to be an integral part of the stories provided by a majority of the people in that study. In this essay, we will share with you what we found when we looked deeper into those stories to explore the importance of what we call *post-*

dissolutional communication (PDC), or the interaction that takes place between former partners after the break-up of a romantic relationship.

THE IMPORTANCE OF STUDYING POST-DISSOLUTIONAL COMMUNICATION

Relationship dissolution, particularly for young adults, is a regular and often difficult part of the relationship life cycle. Models of relationship development and dissolution document the centrality of communication in the process of leading to, negotiating, and confirming relational dissolution (e.g., Altman & Taylor, 1973; Baxter, 1984; Duck, 1982; 2005; Knapp & Vangelisti, 2000). Duck's (2005; Rollie & Duck, 2006) model of relationship dissolution, for example, explains that people go through five processes when ending a relationship as they face uncertainty in the course of dissolution as well as needs to prepare for future relationships. First, during the *intrapsychic processes*, individuals start to feel resentment and dissatisfaction regarding their partners and the relationship, and these negative feelings are often expressed through social withdrawal. In this phase, individuals weigh the strengths and weaknesses of the relationship in an effort to make decisions about whether to break-up or stay together. Second, individuals confront their partners with their dissatisfaction during the *dyadic processes* and, together, they discuss options of repairing or ending the relationship. Since the partners may openly express their discontent with each other, these processes can be hurtful. In the third, or *social processes*, individuals share either their unhappiness with the relationship and seek counsel from friends and family, or announce the decision to break up with members of their social networks. Due to the act of "going public", communication patterns in the partners' social networks change, and the relational problems become more difficult to deny (Rollie & Duck, 2006). Fourth, during the *grave-dressing processes*, individuals create accounts and stories that explain why the relationship ended, in ways that allow them to rebuild their social self-image. Finally, during the *resurrection processes*, individuals prepare for the different future. This preparation process centers around rebuilding their self-image as desirable partners, through sharing self-enhancing stories about breakups, advice seeking, and so forth. Communication models of relationship dissolution such as Duck's, as well as a large body of research that examines the reasons why relationships end (e.g., Amato & Previti, 2003; Metts & Cupach, 1986) and the tactics people use to end them (e.g., Baxter, 1982; Cody, 1982), all present communication as integral to the process of relational decline and eventual dissolution. We know less, however, about the role that communication plays between partners after the break-up has occurred. It is worthwhile to learn more about the way people communicate with partners after the deterioration of a romantic relationship for a couple of other reasons.

First, the ending of a romantic relationship does not necessarily constitute the end of the relationship between partners altogether. Few would suggest, for example, that once the couple ends the romantic relationship that the relationship in all aspects ceases to exist. If nothing else, the storytelling literature suggests that the relationship lives on through the stories about it or the dissolution process (Weber, Harvey, & Stanley, 1989). Even when they end, relationships may continue to live in the communication and memories about them.

Terminated romantic relationships do not, however, only continue to exist in the memory of its partners. Experience and research suggest that former partners communicate after the break-up in a variety of ways. Indeed, Koenig Kellas et al. (2008) studied post-dissolutional turning points and found that 174 participants reported 787 turning points in their post-dissolutional relationships (PDRs) suggesting the prevalence of this relationship phase. Some ex-partners remain friends (Lanutti & Cameron, 2002; Masuda, 2005; Metts, Cupach, & Bejlovec, 1989), and some continue to argue long after they have officially ended their bond (Weiss, 1975). Other people might try to remain civil, whereas others try to reconcile. Romantic relationships may cease to be romantic, but the relationship between the two partners

may continue in a different size, shape, and/or form (Koenig Kellas et al., 2008). Weiss (1975) demonstrates this in his research on the accounts that people provide for why they get divorced. He argues that "Separation is an *incident* in the relationship of spouses, rather than an ending of that relationship. It is a critically important incident, to be sure: an incident that ushers in fundamental changes in the relationship. But it is not an ending" (p. 83, emphasis added). Similarly, Masuda (2005) found in his research on non-marital PDRs that "relationship dissolution does not stop all relational interactions" (p. 114). Indeed, many of his interviewees emphasized the irreplaceability of their PDRs by stating, "She[He] is a part of my life" (p. 121). Lannutti and Cameron (2002) also demonstrated in their research that individuals' liking for their former partners was a positive predictor of interpersonal contact and emotional intimacy in both homosexual and heterosexual PDRs. In other words, relationship dissolution does not necessarily constitute the "death of the dyad." Communication facilitates the relationship that emerges afterward. For example, although not all couples put the same amount of time and effort into maintaining a friendship as Justin and Jody did (in fact many people we've talked to find it much too difficult or downright strange!), communication is central to understanding the relationships that still exist after the break-up. These might be surviving, struggling, dwindling relationships or relationships that only exist in the memories and stories of individual members. Whatever the case, examining this process offers an even more detailed picture of the relational life cycle.

A second reason that understanding communication in PDRs is important is because for most people, the ending of a significant romantic relationship is a difficult and sometimes traumatic experience. How people communicate about traumatic experiences, such as relational loss, may help to explain how they adjust to the experience. One of the reasons it may be difficult to adjust and come to terms with the relationship ending is because of the companionship and attachment the relationship offered. Attachment is an enduring feature of love, providing the security of no longer feeling lost and lonely in the world (Weiss, 1975). Following a break-up, however, people struggle with losing a companion and, sometimes, with feelings of being alone. People may even experience "separation distress" or the anxiety and loneliness associated with the lost attachment (Weiss, 1975).

When people end a significant attachment, they have to renegotiate a sense of how they communicate with their former partners and renegotiate a sense of themselves. Stephen (1984) argues that "everyday conversation between couple members, about their past, about the affairs of the day, and about their hopes and plans for the future, is thought to gradually form a basis for the development of a highly integrated 'couple reality'—that is, an intimate, dyadic world view" (p. 4). Breaking up threatens, if not destroys, the continuation of this world view and the conversations that help to create what he calls "symbolic interdependence" (Stephen, 1984, p. 4). After a breakup, some people wish to maintain a sense of identity that keeps them close to the couplehood. Others "battle toward an autonomous self" (Weiss, 1975, p. 73). Either of these extremes, or what lies between them, gets negotiated in the processes associated with PDC. Koenig Kellas et al. (2008) found four different patterns of negotiating PDR commitment, including Linear Process (steady, and primarily low, levels of commitment to the PDR), Relational Decline (a pattern in which ex-partners began with high levels of commitment to the PDR that steadily declined over time), Upward Relational Progression (an increase in commitment and friendship over time), and Turbulent Relational Progression (a pattern characterized by, sometimes extreme, ups and downs). They also found that those who reported linear PDRs also reported significantly higher levels of adjustment to the breakup than participants with any other PDR trajectory pattern. Acknowledging different strategies and reasons for maintaining PDRs, Masuda (2005) argued that attachment to former partners is not necessarily troublesome as long as it does not become an obsessive preoccupation about them.

On this ground, establishing a successful PDR can be considered one of the effective strategies of coping with relationship dissolution. Different types of communication between former partners might significantly influence one's break-up experience and their ability to cope with the loss of self and other in the process.

In sum, communication often continues between former partners, and communication between partners may play a hand in how people adjust to relationship loss. With these reasons in mind, and with a desire to better understand communication in this aspect of the relationship life cycle, we conducted a study on the type and quality of communication that people report characterizing their PDRs.

POST-DISSOLUTIONAL COMMUNICATION IN STORIES OF RELATIONSHIP DISSOLUTION

One place to investigate PDC is in the stories that people tell about their break-ups. Narratives have been shown to be important and consequential forms of explaining and understanding the dissolution of romantic relationships among both married and non-married populations (Cupach and Metts, 1986; Harvey & Fine, 2005; Harvey, Orbuch, & Weber, 1992; Koenig Kellas & Manusov, 2003; Weber, et al., 1989; Weiss, 1975). The ability to construct and tell the story of a break-up enables the teller to make sense of the events (Weiss, 1975), increase self-esteem and control over the events (Weber et al., 1989), and has been linked to tellers' adjustment to the relationship's end (Koenig Kellas & Manusov, 2003). Harvey and Fine (2005) summarized five functions of the account-making process that are relevant to PDC contexts: (a) experiencing the release of emotion about the breakup; (b) attributing blame and responsibility about the breakup; (c) trying to clarify one's interpretation about the breakup; (d) seeking to provide information about the breakup; and (e) receiving advice about future relationships. In other words, narratives of relationship dissolution allow people to create plot, develop characters, and assign responsibility in a way that communicates for themselves and others how and why the relationship ended. Moreover, these narratives "both reflect experience and also shape subsequent experiences" (Harvey & Fine, 2005, p. 198). Therefore, these types of stories are good sites for understanding how communication factors into the dissolution process, and what happens between partners after the break-up has occurred. For example, one individual who laments about missing the talks that he and his girlfriend used to have (e.g., "I really miss talking to her, but she won't return my calls") might have more difficulty coming to terms with the break-up than an individual who is on "good terms" with his former partner or someone who is happily out of contact with that person (e.g., "We don't talk anymore which is the best thing for both of us").

Types of Post-Dissolutional Communication

In order to better understand PDC, we researched the types of communication people used with former partners and whether or not these types of communication related to adjustment. In the study, 90 college-age participants were asked to provide a written narrative describing the dissolution of a romantic relationship. Specifically, participants were instructed to "Please tell the story of a break up of one of your significant romantic relationships." After completing the story and some questions about who had initiated the break-up, how long it had been since the relationship ended, and current relationship status, participants completed a measure of post-relational adjustment. Adapted from the Fisher Divorce Adjustment Scale (FDAS), this 100-item self-report questionnaire measures individual adjustment (including feelings like anger, self-worth, disentanglement from the former partner, and grief) to relationship dissolution.

After the data were collected, the narratives were examined to see how tellers addressed the issue of PDC, or communication with their former partner following the break-up. It was found that people engaged in several different types of communication with their former partners, including (1) positive communication,

(2) occasional/circumstantial communication, (3) rare, awkward, or negative communication, (4) absence of communication, and/or (5) no mention of communication.

Positive Communication. Despite the fact that people were writing about a relationship that they or their partner decided to end because the romantic side of it wasn't working, many of them reported that they not only continued to communicate with their former partner, but also communicated with them in positive ways. One type of positive communication was *friendly post-dissolutional communication*. A number of people described wanting to stay friends with their ex-boyfriend or girlfriend. For example, one person said, "I guess we actually pulled off that whole…let's just be friends thing." Staying friends and communicating positively with the partner after the break-up might depend on what the relationship was like before the two people started dating. For example, Metts et al. (1989) found that both disengagers and disengagees claimed to have stayed friends with their former partner if they had been friends prior to becoming romantically involved. Certainly for Justin and Jody, salvaging our friendship was the biggest motivation for continuing to talk after we broke up. Other people's positive communication went beyond remaining friends and communicating with former partners in ways that revitalized the romantic relationships. Those engaging in *rekindled romantic communication*, said things like "For the next three months we dated other people and meanwhile maintained our friendship. We came to realize we were meant to be together." Stories describing this type of communication often described an important conversation, realization, or instance of forgiveness as being essential to rekindling the romantic relationship.

Occasional/Circumstantial Communication. Many people, in their stories, explained that communication continued, although only occasionally with their former partner. This type of communication was often determined or motivated by routine, or common activities. For example, many described their interactions with their former partner as *circumstantial communication*. One woman said, "We are friends, but I am not in contact with him unless he is home [from school]," indicating that she only communicates with him when it is convenient. People engaging in circumstantial communication reported not putting much effort into communicating with their ex-boyfriend or girlfriend. Other people did make an effort to talk to the other person, but not with the same regularity as when they had been dating. People engaging in *occasional communication* tended to say things like "We talk maybe once a week, or every other week." There was a sense that people using this type of communication felt the need to maintain some kind of connection, but that it was a muted version of the communication that existed before. Finally, a number of stories characterized PDC in terms of *sexually motivated communication* (e.g., "This summer we went with friends to the beach and again had sex, which happens about every two weeks now"). A number of the people in our study reported that although the romantic relationship had officially ended, couples continued to interact through regular sexual encounters. One woman ended her story by saying "Afterward, we had flings where we would go out on weekends and kiss and play 'dating couple' again for about six months." This type of communication tended to be characterized by casual and occasional connection.

Rare, awkward, or negative communication. A third type of PDC involved rare or negative interactions, akin to the type we described about Sai and Yoshi. Some people, for example, reported *one-sided or unsuccessful attempts at communication.* This type of communication was often characterized by one person's desire to maintain a friendship or rekindle the romance and another person's refusal to accept his or her attempt. One woman, who was particularly hurt by her boyfriend's actions leading to the break up, said, "He called me every night for a month…I stopped returning his calls and eventually the pain went away." Another woman acknowledged her own unreturned attempts at maintaining contact by saying, "the 'trying to be friends thing' never actually worked. Once in a while, I try to reach him to see how he is doing, but it just seems as though he is not interested in pursuing a

friendship at this time." These stories suggest the importance of both parties' willingness to continue communication. For couples in which both parties agreed to continue communicating, it was often with *awkward or superficial communication*. In these types of encounters, people described a need or obligation to continue talking, but they also acknowledged the difficulty associated with reframing communication in the new relationship. For example, one man said "We tried to stay friends after, but it was just too awkward, so we stayed away from each other…. We talk occasionally, but it is still hard to know what to say." Other types of rare/awkward/negative communication included *rare communication* (e.g., "Since then, we hardly talk"), *ambiguous communication* (e.g., "We haven't remained very close"), and *harassing communication* (e.g., "he threatened me, would drive by my house, and wouldn't come near our friends"). These types of communication occurred often in the break-up stories written by participants in our study. People seemed to struggle frequently with wanting to, or feeling obligated to, continue communicating with the former partner, but also experiencing the awkwardness or potentially harmful ramifications of doing so.

Absence of communication. It may be that people who were unwilling to endure awkward feelings or rare, negative encounters were those who reported no longer communicating with their former partners. Some people simply stated at the end of their stories things like, "We haven't talked since." Others described the events that led up to the break-up in ways that conveyed them as motivators for not talking anymore. For example, one woman told a story about breaking up with a man because he had started dating someone else while she was away on vacation. She ends her story with: "…we ended up having a fight and ended the relationship on bad terms. I went off to college and all I know about him is that he is now a dad and lives with the girl he was seeing while I was on my trip." Some people reported never talking again, but communicating through other mediums, such as e-mail, that were less threatening, but allowed closure. One man explains that "because of the way I left the situation, we didn't talk again (ever). Behind her back I took some slanderous shots at her which I now regret saying and have since written her letters of apology."

No mention of post-dissolutional communication. Finally, others in their stories made no mention of whether or not they still communicated with their ex-boyfriend or girlfriend. These stories did not necessarily seem qualitatively different in content than the other stories, but did seem to end differently, making less or little sense about how, or if, PDC affected the break up experience.

Post-Dissolutional Communication and Adjustment

The five types of PDC illustrate that people deal with relational termination in different ways. As mentioned before, one reason it's important to study PDC is because it might help us understand how people adjust to the decline of romantic relationships. In the current study, we also investigated if these different types of communication helped to explain how adjusted people felt to the break-up. Results indicated that it didn't seem to be the type of PDC (e.g., positive, occasional) that related to overall adjustment, but rather whether or not people mentioned communication in their stories. In other words, there was a significant trend toward higher adjustment for people who mentioned PDC in their stories versus those who didn't. Thus, although adjustment did not differ according to *how* one communicates with one's former partner, it did differ based upon *whether or not tellers mention PDC* within their stories.

From a communication perspective, this trend is important. It suggests that metacommunication—or communication about communication—may matter in the process of adjusting to the relationship. People who talked about how they communicated with their former partner were more likely to be adjusted than those did not discuss PDC. This may be explained in a couple of ways. First Pennebaker's (e.g., 1997) work on disclosure suggest that writing or talking about traumatic events relates positively to health such that people who talked about their problems tend to

experience fewer health problems than those who ruminate about them. It may be that the participants in the study, consciously or unconsciously, recognized the value of communication in their relational lives and, by mentioning PDC in their stories, demonstrate an acknowledgement of its potential impact. Those who didn't mention communication may not value its potential for helping them to adjustment to the dissolution and thus may not have included this part of the break-up in their stories.

Second, communication seemed to be an important part of sense-making in the story. In other words, acknowledging the fuller relationship life cycle from relationship development to dissolution and beyond, seemed to reflect a fuller understanding of the process overall. Some research has argued that stories help people make sense of events, gain a sense of control, and search for closure and understanding (Weber et al., 1987). Explaining PDC in the story probably provides a more complete account (Koenig Kellas & Manusov, 2003) of the process and may help tellers gain more control and understanding over the events.

Post Dissolutional Communication and Anger

The study results also showed that there was a link between how people reported communicating with their partner and how angry they felt at that person. Specifically, people's anger went down as the amount and quality of the communication with their former partner went up. In other words, the more positive the communication they had, the less angry people were with their former boyfriend or girlfriend. The biggest difference existed between people who didn't talk to their former partner any longer and people who were on "good terms" or engaged in positive communication with their former partner. Intuitively, this is not surprising. Those who engage in positive communication likely have little reason to be angry, whereas those who don't talk to their former partners might very well have chosen not to because of the anger they felt toward that person. For example, one woman described the fact that she and her former partner no longer talk *in terms of* his infidelity and her anger:

> He kept telling lies and I could never catch him in them. One day a girl who I knew he was once involved with confronted me. We mapped out numerous times he had given one of us an excuse to see the other. She thought that it was all my fault and blamed me. I got very angry with him and ended our relationship in an angry yelling match. We haven't talked since.

Alternatively, individuals might be angry *because* they don't speak. Another woman describes her "perfect" relationship with a boy she considered to be her best friend. She depicts their relationship as very close, but complicated by the fact that she had gone off to college while he was still in high school. She explains the break-up and the lack of communication as not *motivated* by anger, but rather confusion, and seems upset *based on the fact that they no longer communicate*:

> ...Paul and I talked for a long time. We both cried. He said "Pam, I love you so much. But this is so hard for me because I'm so confused. I think you're the one I want to marry but I need to make sure. We just need some time apart so that when we get back together we'll have no doubts." So anyways, we talked every few days for a week. Then we just stopped talking. I always hear him asking about me from friends. I think someday he'll come back to me. But right now he's confused.... This has been so hard for me. I did terrible in school last quarter because I was so depressed....

These stories differ significantly in tone from those who maintain positive communication with the former partner.

Struggling with Post-dissolutional Communication

Despite the fact that those who engaged in positive communication felt less anger toward the other person, most of the stories that depicted positive communication indicated that it was not "all roses" from the beginning of the break-up.

Ultimately, participants in this study described a number of struggles associated with breaking up in which PDC played a starring role. These included struggles with forgiveness, guilt, concern for the other person, and freedom. Although breaking up was fairly seamless for some people, for many others negotiating PDC was a difficult, *and* important, part of the process.

Many of the people in the study described PDC in terms of *guilt*, *regret* over the circumstances of the break-up, and *concern* for the other person. After struggling in his relationship for sometime, one man described his break-up and his feeling of regret for how his behavior influenced their interactions afterward. He said:

> I was in a bad mood that day to begin with and practically blew up over the phone without thinking. She hung up. To this day, I still regret that one thing I did. I've moved on but still wish we could be good friends. Even though we still see each other when I go home, it's just not the same anymore. Oh well, that's life I guess.

This young man seems to accept the awkward nature of their communication as part of the break-up process, but also acknowledges the regret associated with how he acted and the ramifications for PDC with his ex-girlfriend. Other people expressed the tension between feeling relieved about the break-up and feeling concerned for the other person. A woman who felt trapped by her boyfriend described PDC in terms of that tension by explaining:

> I felt very free but did feel some guilt because I did care about him very much, just no longer romantically. We've been able to, after time, move our relationship toward friendship. There seems to be no tension between us as far as hard feelings go but if I spend prolonged periods of time with him I get that same stressed and trapped feeling.

This woman, and many others who wrote about their break-ups, experienced tensions between feelings of *freedom* and *guilt*, as well as the role that PDC plays in mediating that tension.

Several other stories revolved around the complicated process of becoming friends or maintaining positive communication following the break-up. For example, two of the stories reflected themes of *forgiveness*, with one man talking to his former girlfriend because she admitted she was wrong and another woman reporting being friends after she forgave her partner for harassing her at the beginning of the break-up. Some people vacillated between romantic and platonic relationships, breaking up and getting back together before deciding to be friends. Still others report rekindling the romantic relationship. At times, many of the struggles associated with PDC accompanied stories that ended in positive communication or rekindling the romantic relationship. One woman describes the complexities associated with breaking up, getting back together, and eventually becoming friends:

> ...so we broke it off.... We did not speak to each other for a while and it was uncomfortable seeing him at times, though once we started talking the tension would die down a bit. A few months after we broke up, we got back together and then broke it off for good not long afterwards. After this second break-up it was more mutual, but it was still hard. We didn't communicate for about a month and then we would talk about once a month on the phone just to keep in touch. We ended up being friends.

The stories of positive communication indicate that the categories of PDC are not mutually exclusive, and that the process of communicating on good terms with a former partner does not appear to be an easy one.

Finally, in addition to feelings of guilt, concern, forgiveness, freedom, and the complications associated with staying friends or getting back together, people reported that PDC can also be just generally *painful* for some people, particularly when there is a feeling that it is out of one's control. For some people, continuing to communicate is painful. For example, one woman said "I am okay today if I don't see him. But that is almost impossible considering we are in the same major and end up with at least one class together. Everyday it gets a little easier, but there will always be that pain. When I see him, I have to get past

that initial attraction and think of why we can't be together." For others, not communicating is painful. This was the case for a woman who lamented, "Now we've lost our closeness. I used to be able to confide all of my emotions and feelings in David. Now he only answers my letters superficially. I feel very sad to think about him."

Post-dissolutional Communication and Time

After reading about the adjustment, anger, and struggles associated with PDC, you may be thinking, "I bet time plays a big role in determining how much or the ways in which people communicate." If so, you're right! Different types of PDC were associated with different amounts of time since the break-up. People experience break-ups differently according to a number of situational factors. Weiss (1975) suggests that time often plays a determinant role in the continuing relationship of former partners, with those immediately following the dissolution maintaining feelings of obligation toward the former partner or a need for that partners' companionship.

For our participants, significant differences existed between people that no longer talked to their former partners and all other types of PDC. In other words, those who occasionally talked, engaged in rare/awkward communication, or those who didn't mention whether or not they communicated had been broken up for a significantly less amount of time than those who no longer talk at all. The biggest difference existed between those who no longer talk and those who continued to talk occasionally or circumstantially. This suggests that as time passes, fewer people talk to their partners, whereas the beginnings of dissolution seem to be characterized by occasional communication.

One man, who reported breaking up with his girlfriend just 2 ½ months prior to telling this story explains their ensuing occasional communication:

> ...Since we broke up, I feel like I am free and that I can do whatever I want. I still care for her, but feel that I made the right decision for me, and

what I need to do. We talk maybe once a week, or every other week, but it is definitely hard for her though. I wish her the best and for some reason, I know she will hang around and wait for me to come back. If I do, I do, but things will have to change, and she will have to have lived life and experienced some more things.

This excerpt reinforces the idea that PDC is a complex process, influenced by the tensions of guilt and freedom, satisfaction and concern for the other person. It also supports Weiss' (1975) contention that people often stay in contact with their former partners based on feelings of guilt and a sense of loyalty to the partner. This young man expresses happiness with his decision, but concern for his former girlfriend. The results of this study may suggest that as time goes on, these feelings of guilt and obligation diminish—perhaps due to new experiences, lovers, and/or communication—in a way that may explain why people who have been broken up for the longest amount of time no longer speak to their former partners. Interestingly, those that report positive communication with their former partner had been broken up for an average of 22 months, second only to those who don't talk anymore (an average of 36.12 months). It seems as though, in the long run, people either tended to stay friends, or stop talking altogether.

CONCLUSION

In this essay, we have described the complex process of post-dissolutional communication. People engage in a variety of different types of communication with their former partners and the study reported here indicates that PDC does in some ways relate to or reflect the process associated with adjustment to relationship dissolution. Those who mentioned communication in their stories tended to be more adjusted than those who did not; those who don't talk tended to be more angry than those who do talk, at least in some capacity; people struggle with how to communicate with their former partner and often vacillate between types and feelings like guilt, concern, freedom, and regret; and, finally, time

helps to differentiate between the types of PDC. An examination of specific stories indicates that the process of communicating with former partners following a break-up can range from simple to complex. In some cases, partners end communication altogether with the break-up. Others fluctuate between different types of communication before arriving at a comfortable relationship.

In addition to these findings and more recent research on the topography and correlates of PDRs (e.g., Koenig Kellas et al., 2008; Lanutti & Cameron, 2002; Masuda, 2006), further understanding the progression or regression of communication following a break-up may add detail to models of relationship development and dissolution and, moreover, help people like you and us to better understand the processes and functions of non-marital PDC. Stories provide rich sites for viewing the sense-making process associated with relationship disengagement. This essay provides an initial examination of how PDC is described and helps to facilitate that sense-making process.

REFERENCES

Altman, L. & Taylor, D. A. (1973). *Social penetration: The development of interpersonal relationships.* New York, NY: Holt, Rinehart & Winston.

Amato, P. R., & Previti, D. (2003). People's reasons for divorcing: Gender, social class, the life course, and adjustment. *Journal of Family Issues, 24,* 602–626.

Baxter, L. A. (1982). Strategies for ending relationships: Two studies. *Western Journal of Speech Communication, 46,* 233–242.

Baxter, L. A. (1984). Trajectories of relationship disengagement. *Journal of Social and Personal Relationships, 1,* 29–48.

Cody, M. J. (1982). A typology of disengagement strategies and an examination of the roles intimacy, reactions to inequity, and relational problems play in strategy selection. *Communication Monographs, 49,* 148–170.

Duck, S. (1982). A typology of relationship disengagement and dissolution. In S. Duck (Ed.), *Personal* relationships: Vol. IV. Dissolving personal relationship (pp. 1–30). New York, NY: Academic Press.

Duck, S. W. (2005). How do you tell someone you're letting go? A new model of relationship break up. *The Psychologist, 18*, 210–213.

Harvey, J. H., & Fine, M. A. (2005). Social construction of accounts in the process of relationship termination. In M. A. Fine & J. H. Harvey (Eds.), *Handbook of divorce and relationship dissolution* (pp. 189–199). New York, NY: Routledge.

Harvey, J. H., Orbuch, T. L., & Weber, A. L. (1992). Introduction: Convergence of the attribution and accounts concepts in the study of close relationships. In J. H. Harvey, T. L. Orbuch, & A. L. Weber (Eds.), *Attributions, accounts, and close relationships* (pp. 1–18). New York, NY: Springer-Verlag.

Knapp, M. L., & Vangelisti, A. 2000. *Interpersonal communication and human relationships* (4th ed.). Boston, MA: Allyn & Bacon.

Koenig Kellas, J., Bean, D., Cunningham, C., & Cheng, C. (2008). The ex-files: Trajectories, turning points, and adjustment in the development of post-dissolutional relationships. *Journal of Social and Personal Relationships, 25*, 23–50.

Koenig Kellas, J., & Manusov, V. (2003). What's in a story? The relationship between narrative completeness and tellers' adjustment to relationship dissolution. *Journal of Social and Personal Relationships, 20*, 285–307.

Lannutti, P. J., & Cameron, K. A. (2002). Beyond the breakup: Heterosexual and homosexual post-dissolutional relationships. *Communication Quarterly, 50*, 153–170.

Masuda, M. (2005). Perspectives on premarital post-dissolution relationships: Account-making of friendships between former romantic partners. In M. A. Fine & J. H. Harvey (Eds.). *Handbook of divorce and relationship dissolution* (pp. 113–132). New York, NY: Routledge.

Metts, S., & Cupach, W. R. (1986). *Disengagement themes in same-sex and opposite-sex friendships*. Paper presented to the Interpersonal Communication Interest Group, Western Speech Communication Association, Tucson, AZ.

Metts, S., Cupach, W. R., & Bejlovec, R. A. (1989). I love you too much to ever start liking you: Redefining romantic relationships. *Journal of Social and Personal Relationships, 6*, 259–274.

Pennebaker, J. W. (1997). *Opening up: The healing power of expressing emotions* (Rev. ed.). New York, NY: Guilford.

Rollie, S. S., & Duck, S. (2006). Divorce and dissolution of romantic relationships: Stage models and their limitations. In M. A. Fine & J. H. Harvey (Eds.), *Handbook of divorce and relationship dissolution* (pp. 223–240). Mahwah, NJ: Lawrence Erlbaum.

Starks, K. (2007). Bye bye love: Computer-mediated communication and relational dissolution. *Texas Speech Communication Journal, 32*, 11–20.

Stephen, T. D. (1984). Symbolic interdependence and post-break-up distress: A reformulation of the attachment construct. *Journal of Divorce, 8*, 1–16.

Weber, A. L., Harvey, J. H., & Stanley, M. A. (1989). The nature and motivations of accounts for failed relationships. In R. Burnett, P. McGhee & D. D. Clarke (Eds.), *Accounting for relationships: Explanation, representation, and knowledge* (pp. 114–133). London, England: Methuen.

Weiss, R. S. (1975). *Marital separation*. New York, NY: Basic Books.

QUESTIONS/THOUGHTS

1. To what extent are Koenig Kellas' description of former partners' experiences similar or different from what you have experienced or observed in post-breakup interactions? What category, if any, would you have expected to be included that did not appear in this article? Explain the interactional dynamics of that category.

2. Analyze a film or television show that depicts post-breakup interaction and describe it according to one or more of the categories included in this article.

3. What links would you expect to find between dialectical theory and the experiences of the college-age respondents in the post-dissolution stage? How might that relate to the former partners' struggles with communication?

4. How important do you believe post-dissolution communication is in dealing with a breakup? Give reasons for your position.

Contexts

A. Family

INTRODUCTION

Family life is a universal human experience, yet, because of the unique communication patterns in each family system, no two people share the exact same family experience. Even siblings have different family experiences due to the transactional nature of communication. The combination of personality, experiences, age, and gender of each child and each parent impacts their relationship. Because family is such a powerful influence in each person's life, it is important to examine family interaction patterns in order to understand the communication dynamics of this powerful life-shaping entity. Members' communication patterns serve to construct as well as reflect familial experience; essentially, you create your families just as you are created by these families.

Although you may not agree with these beliefs, some commonly held beliefs about families and family communication include:

1. There is no "right" way to be a family. There are many types of families and numerous ways to relate within each family type. Each family must struggle to create its own identity as it encounters positive and negative experiences.

2. Communication serves to constitute as well as reflect family life. It is through talk that persons construct their identities and negotiate their relationships with each other and the rest of the world. This talk also serves to indicate or reflect the state of family relationships.

3. Communication is the process by which family members work out and share their meanings with each other. Members create a family relational culture as well as individualized relational ties with parent(s) and any siblings.

4. Families are part of multigenerational communication patterns. Family members

are influenced by the patterns of previous generations as they create their own patterns, which will influence future generations.

5. Well-functioning families work at managing their communication patterns. Such families develop the capacity to adapt to and create change, to share intimacy, and to manage conflict (Galvin, Bylund & Brommel, 2008).

No single, widely agreed upon definition of the term "family" exists. Traditionally, blood and legal ties determined family membership; currently, families may be viewed more broadly as *"networks of people who share their lives over long periods of time bound by ties of marriage, blood, or commitment, legal or otherwise, who consider themselves as family and who share a significant history and anticipated future of functioning in a family relationship"* (Galvin, Brommel, and Bylund, 2008, p.6). Given the multiple variations of family structures, members are defining themselves for themselves through their interactions. At the same time, issues such as longevity, legal flexibility, personal choice, ethnicity, gender, geographic distance, and reproductive technology are impacting traditional biological and legal conceptions of the family. Therefore, we dismiss the "traditional" vs. "nontraditional" family distinction. Today scholars are concerned with how family members define themselves as families to outsiders as well as how they use communication to explain their family to themselves. This constitutive approach to creating a family challenges old conceptions (Whitchurch and Dickson 1999). We take a broad, inclusive view of families, encompassing countless variations of family forms and numerous types of interaction patterns.

It is important to distinguish between two types of family experience—current families and families of origin. Families in combination beget families through the evolutionary cycles of coming together and separating. Thus, each person may experience life in different families, starting with his or her family of origin. *Family of origin* refers to the family or families in which a person is raised. Noted family therapist Virginia Satir (1988) stresses the importance of the family of origin as the blueprints for *peoplemaking*. She suggests that blueprints vary from family to family. Some blueprints result in nurturing families, some result in troubled ones. Multigenerational patterns, those of more than two generations, are considered part of the blueprint (Hoopes 1987). Family of origin and multigenerational experiences are crucial in the development of communication patterns in current families.

The systems perspective provides insight into family functioning and family communication. This perspective maintains that individuals do not exist in a vacuum; rather, individuals are linked in ways that make them interdependent. Each individual is part of an overall *family system*, affecting and being affected by that system. You cannot fully understand a person without knowing something about his or her family. An individual's behavior becomes more comprehensible when viewed within the context of his or her family system. For example, an individual's behavior may appear strange to you but, if you understand the whole family context, your perceptions may change. What may be viewed as problematic behavior in one setting may be functional in another context.

Within any system, the parts and the relationship between those parts form the whole; changes in one part will result in changes in the others; as events touch one member of the family, other members are affected by the change. From the systems perspective you analyze families by paying attention to the relationships among members, as opposed to focusing on each individual. Patterns of relating, making decisions, sharing affection, or handling conflict may vary slightly or greatly among different families. Yet each family finds its own way to establish communication patterns reflecting their identity.

Families serve as your first communication classroom. According to Richard West and Lynn Turner (2006), "Family relationships school us in how to communicate, how to relate to others, and whether and how to commit ourselves to significant others" (p. x). If you contrast your family to a friend's family you may be able to see the different patterns that reflect the upbringing of your friend's parents or parent figures.

As you read this section think about the families you know well, or about fictional families, and try to identify key communication patterns that seem to contribute to the family's identity and to its members' ways of relating to one another as well as to people outside the family.

REFERENCES

Galvin, K. M., Brommel, B. J., & Bylund, C. (2008). *Family communication: Cohesion and change* (7th ed.). Boston: Allyn & Bacon.

Hoopes, M. (1987). Multigenerational systems: Basic assumptions. *American Journal of Family Therapy, 15*, 196–205.

Satir, V. (1988). *The new peoplemaking.* Mountain View, CA: Science and Behavior Books.

Turner, L. H., & West, R. (2006). Preface. In L. H. Turner & R. West, *The family communication sourcebook* (pp. ix–xx). Thousand Oaks, CA: Sage.

Whitchurch, G., & Dickson, F. C. (1999). Family communication. In M. B. Sussman, S. K. Steinmetz, & G. W. Peterson (Eds.), *Handbook of marriage and the family* (2nd ed., pp. 687–704). New York, NY: Plenum Press.

Family Ground Rules

ELIZABETH STONE

It is likely that you can recall being told stories about your family as you were growing up. It's also very likely you heard the same stories over and over again. Family stories bind the family together; the predictability and patterns reinforce family identity. These stories provide your personal history, indicate what is expected of you as a family member, and ground your identity. According to Elizabeth Stone (2004) family stories exert a force and influence on the listeners' lives, revealing what we owe to those who went before us.

Family stories serve the following functions as they carry important messages to family members: (1) to remember, (2) to create belonging and reaffirm family identity, (3) to educate current members and socialize new members, (4) to develop family culture and (5) to provide stability by connecting generations and (6) to entertain. (Galvin, Bylund & Brommel, 2008). These stories may be told on holidays, at special family occasions or when a family or member is facing adversity. They serve as keys to understanding what it means to be a member your family.

Specialized research on family stories indicates the importance of adoption stories that construct the meaning of how children were born, separated from birth parents, and integrated into their adoptive families (Krusiewicz & Wood, 2000). Families of varied ethnic backgrounds tell stories in order to entertain, inspire, reminisce, and teach (Bylund, 2003).

Family narrative researchers pay careful attention to how stories are told—Does one person tell or are stories share? When and where are stories told? In their exploration of family storytelling practices, Langellier and Peterson (2006) report that researchers often focus on gender, for example noting that mothers may tell birth stories differently to daughters than to sons or that single mothers or stepmothers tell stories that place them in normative narratives of motherhood.

You might wish to gather your own family stories. Zeitlin and his coauthors (1982) suggest that every family has its heroes, rogues, mischief makers, survivors, saints, and sinners. And each of these characters has an interesting story. Stories of courtship, feuds, lost fortunes, and immigrations are all "grist for the mill." An example of the beginning of a story-collecting process is found in the following quote:

My child's fifth-grade class had just finished a Grandparent Day celebration and the teacher *asked my parents to attend school and be interviewed by all my child's class. I was amazed at the questions the children asked—all the way from "How did you meet?" to "What did you do in World War II?" My father told the story of selling his colt to get the money for my mother's diamond engagement ring. The horse sold for $75, which, at that time was a lot of money. I learned more about my parents that day than I had ever known.*

In the following excerpt from her book, Black Sheep and Kissing Cousins: How Our Family Stories Shape Us, *Elizabeth Stone details the impact of family stories—particularly on relationships in the family. Through an analysis of several family narratives, including a few of her own, the author explains how stories convey a family's rules and expectations to its members. She elaborates on "types" of family stories in general, what they mean, whom they are about (usually men), and who conveys them (usually women). Stone develops the issue of proximity as an example of how families convey their values about togetherness and separation. Such stories and their prevalence in all families serve as the "cornerstone of family culture." As you read this excerpt, think about the question: How have the meanings of your own family stories influenced your life?*

REFERENCES

Bylund, C. L. (2003). Ethnic diversity and family stories. *Journal of Family Communication, 3,* 215–236.

Galvin, K. M., Bylund, C. L., & Brommel, B. J. (2008). *Family communication: Cohesion and change* (7th ed.). Boston, MA: Allyn & Bacon.

Krusiewicz, E. S., & Wood, J. T. (2001). "He was our child from the moment we walked into that room: Entrance stories of adoptive parents." *Journal of Personal and Social Relationships, 18,* 785–803.

Langellier, K. M., & Peterson, E. E. (2006). Narrative performance theory: Telling stories, doing family. In D. O. Braithwaite & L. A. Baxter (Eds.), *Engaging theories in family communication: Multiple perspectives* (pp. 99–114). Thousand Oaks, CA: Sage.

Zeitlin, S., Kitkin, A., & Baker, H. (1982). *A celebration of american family folklore.* Washington, DC: Smithsonian Institute.

In 1890, my grandfather, Gaetano Bongiorno, came to New York from the Lipari Islands off the coast of Sicily. He was a young man of eighteen, serious and somewhat stolid, but also big and hardworking. Like many Southern Italian men of the time, he was a "bird of passage," a man who had come here to work so he could earn money for his family back home, rather than to settle down here. Over the years, he had a variety of jobs, among them piloting a barge and working as a longshoreman loading and unloading the ships that came into Brooklyn harbor. After work, he would go home to Union Street, where he lived with the two married sisters who had preceded him here. It was even cozier than that; Gaetano's two sisters had married two brothers and those brothers also happened to be first cousins.

The years went by, and Gaetano showed no sign of returning to Italy or marrying and settling down here, either. By 1905, he was already thirty-three. One day in the mail, however, a letter came. Along with it was a photograph of his cousin Annunziata, the youngest sister of Gaetano's sister's husbands.

Gaetano was taken with the photograph of this young woman, and as his sisters had been badgering him to marry, he decided to try to arrange a marriage with her. And so Gaetano sailed to Sicily, went to his uncle, Annunziata's father, and asked for permission to marry her. My grandmother was agreeable to marrying Gaetano. She was fifteen. The idea of marriage seemed very grown-up to her, and the prospect of coming to live in America was exciting. Besides, my grandfather was tall and redheaded, and his looks appealed to my grandmother. So the betrothal was arranged and the marriage soon followed.

In 1905 my grandfather and his bride returned to Union Street and his two sisters and two brothers-in-law, and there they *all* lived until Gaetano and Annunziata could find a place on Union Street of their own. And thus it was that two sisters and a brother married two brothers and a sister and all lived right on top of each other on Union Street in Brooklyn.

The story of how my grandparents had come to marry was often told in my family, and what it said to me was that family was so important that one should even try to marry within the family. I remember at four or five having already decided which of my male first cousins I would eventually marry. The whole story, including my grandfather's Union Street living arrangements, also told me that the essential unit was the extended family. The nuclear family—a couple and their children—tucked itself into the larger unit.

While my conclusions about whom I ought to marry were unwarranted, there was no doubt that the story implicitly laid down other rules about what family members should do for each other. The fact that my grandfather had lived with his two sisters and their families for years on end was expressed without comment. There was nothing extraordinary about it, nothing even especially laudatory. That was what family members did for each other.

And yet this story could so easily have been told another way, with another meaning. My grandmother was the youngest of twelve children, almost all of whom had left Sicily in the hopes of better prospects elsewhere. A few had come here, a few had gone to Australia, and still others to South America. The story, with a twist in tone, could have become a lament about the Bongiorno *diaspora*, the disintegration of family. Perhaps the insistence on family unity and the belief in Bongiorno closeness was an implicit defense against—and emotional denial of—the fragmentation which had left my great-grandparents alone in one place while their children were scattered elsewhere around the world. But the facts of a family's past can be selectively fashioned into a story that can mean almost anything, whatever they most need it to mean. Homage to family unity was apparently what my family needed, and so that's the story the Brooklyn Bongiornos made for themselves out of selected bits of their collective experience.

By the time I was four or five, I was convinced that the bulwark of family could protect me from death itself. There was a little boy my age named Vincent who lived next door to my East Fifth Street cousins. One hot August day, he had come to a family birthday party. Within a week of the birthday party, Vincent was dead of spinal meningitis. I remember that my aunts thereafter decided that only cousins could come to our birthday parties. Though everyone remembered Vincent's death, no one else remembered my aunts' decision to close the birthday party ranks. Perhaps I invented it. Just a few weeks after Vincent died, I was hospitalized myself with polio and certainly needed to think that I could find in my family a magical protection. I was also sure that my full recovery was due to my aunt's *novenas*. In fact my gratitude went entirely to her and not at all to the doctors or whomever she addressed in her prayers.

There is no doubt that we learn about the idea of family and how to be a member of a family from our families. Much of our instruction is mute: the experience of living in a family tells us what we can expect from relatives and what we owe them. But family stories are one of the cornerstones of family culture; they throw what may be mute and habitual into sharp relief. By their presence, they say what issues—from the most public and predictable to the most private and idiosyncratic— *really* concern a given family.

Family stories in fact are not just secondhand accounts of someone else's experience. To the listeners, the stories can be experiences in themselves, and as such they exert a force and influence of their own, sometimes so that the listeners are quite conscious of what's going on, but usually more subliminally. But one thing is certain: given that a story is told in the context of family life, its meaning is circumscribed; when there are clusters of stories gnawing on a given theme, the meaning is more limited, even if no explicit gloss is ever given.

The family, of course, doesn't invent itself or its concerns but is sculpted by class, by the times, and by ethnicity as well as by the combination of individual personalities that comprise it. My family's conviction that the collective welfare of the family is more important than the goals of any one individual—which is the subtext of the story of my grandfather in America—may be unusual in American culture but is, or was, typical of Italian-American culture. There was once a study, done among schoolchildren of varying ethnic backgrounds, that asked whom they would share with if they were given a million dollars. The children named friends as well as charitable organizations as beneficiaries. It was only the Italian-Americans who distributed their hypothetical gift entirely within the family.

Family stories reach into even more private realms of experience to warn and instruct, however subliminally. They tell us about the decorum and protocol of family life—what we owe and to whom, what we can expect and from whom, in time or money or emotion. From the stories we hear, we learn matters of both substance and style.

HOME IS WHERE, WHEN YOU HAVE TO GO...

I want right at the outset to talk about an imbalance in family stories about the family. There is no lack of men in family stories at all. They appear plentifully—as returning soldiers or prosperous lens grinders or guileless immigrants, as errant schoolboys or black sheep or heroes who save the townspeople from drowning in the flood. But men do not feature prominently as family members acting in their familial role. And they often do not tell their own stories. Instead, their stories come down the generational pike riding sidesaddle, via their sisters, mothers, wives, or daughters.

Family stories—telling them and listening to them—belong more to the women's sphere. When I interviewed married couples, it was not unusual for the woman to know more of her husband's family stories than he did, usually because she'd heard them through her mother-in-law. In this way, despite the convention of patrilineality, the family is essentially a female institution: the lore of family and family culture itself—stories, rituals, traditions, icons, sayings—are preserved and promulgated primarily by women.

On a statistical level, women's prominence in the family is apparent. The number of female-headed families has grown dramatically in our time. In 1983, 5.7 million families were headed by women, which meant that 22 percent of all children were growing up with just one parent, usually the mother. The increase in such families is usually attributed to the increase in divorce, the American inclination to self-fulfillment at the price of commitment and self-sacrifice, and the greater number of women in the work force.

But it seems to me that men's hold on the family and the family's hold on men first began to be challenged with the beginning of the Industrial Revolution. Industrialization was responsible for creating the first widespread division between the public world and the world of home.

Men inherited the world, and when they came home they told stories of work and identified themselves essentially in that fashion, while women were left to keep the family going. Family stories, telling them and listening to them, grew out of the way people lived and to some extent still live. Family stories are often told in an almost ritual fashion, for instance at holiday family dinners, but they are also told incidentally, because someone says something that sparks someone else's memory in the course of daily living, while both are making the beds, cooking the meal, or folding the laundry, and these tasks remain essentially although not exclusively women's work. As a result, through the universe of family stories, we glimpse a world in which women play a more substantial role than men and come through far more untarnished. Thus family stories are the obverse of more public and codified cultural genres in which men invariably play the more dominant and flattering roles.

I didn't begin this research by thinking of family stories as a women's genre, but the men I interviewed first alerted me. Says twenty-six-year-old B. C. Heinz, who grew up in Indiana, "From everything I've studied or seen, I would expect the men to be the storytellers. In tribes the *griots* who tell the family genealogy are always men, but that's not my experience. If I want family history, I go to the women. I want to hear about men, I still go to the women. It's my aunts who tell stories about my father. Never my father himself."

Ben Rindt, an Illinois businessman in his fifties, observed that in his family the storyteller was his great-uncle and almost all his stories were about men and their adventures—on the prairies, in the farmyard, in the stock market. After telling me a particularly dramatic story about his great-grandfather's experience in a wagon train attacked by Indians, he concluded that these were not really *family* stories at all. "If you only see men on a wagon train, that's an expedition, an adventure," Rindt mused. "But women are necessary to represent us as people. If women are there, it means families are there, and it means people are really suffering."

The first and cardinal rule of family life, as embodied in family stories, is that when people are *really* suffering, you can count on the family. Family stories about the Depression that exist in every American family survive not because they're dramatic (they're usually not) but because they're exemplary—the family's celebration of itself for coming through.

Then there's the matter of sickness, affliction, and death. As a nation, no matter how mobile we are and no matter how often we've heard that the family is defunct, we do seem to live with the legacy of the stories we've heard—that it's the responsibility of family to come to the aid of those in trouble.

In family stories, as in practice, the responsibility falls more heavily on the women, who probably are listening more closely anyhow. Whatever details, the flavor of our narrative legacies is not very different now from what it was fifty years ago when Ma Joad in John Steinbeck's *Grapes of Wrath* took her aging mother on the road westward to California, ministering to her as she grew weaker and frailer and finally died.

The ideal of caring for aging parents is sufficiently strong that even the most undeserving aging parents can ride its coattails. Rowena Court, born and raised in Texas, tells a story about her grandmother and her great-grandfather that makes the point. "My great-grandfather," she begins, "abandoned his family when his kids were still young. He disappeared, and the family thought he was dead. One day when Nanny was about thirty years old, her father showed up at her front door. She was married and had kids of her own by then. She said 'Who are you?' And he said, 'I'm your father, and I need some place to stay. I'm dying and I need someone to take care of me.' And she did. First she nursed him, and when he died, she buried him." Home is where, when you have to go there, they have to take you in."

Family stories such as this continue to exert a force on the way we live now. They establish the ideal that we depart from only at the price of our own guilt. Only 5 percent of the nation's elderly are in nursing homes. Even among the very old— eighty five and over—77 percent remain outside institutions. For aging family members who live on their own, family bonds do seem to hold up. According to the National Institute on Aging, 80 percent of the elderly see "a close relative" every week. Equally consistent with the family stories, the emotional responsibility continues to fall on the women in the family, usually the daughters, but occasionally the daughters-in-law as well.

Such loyalty is by no means automatic or the inevitable consequence of propinquity. It's based on a deep stratum of belief which the family works unceasingly to instill. After all, it is rarely the case that unrelated people who spend enormous amounts of time together at work or in the neighborhood will continue the connection if their circumstances change.

Family members may have no more in common with each other than they do with neighbors or coworkers, so the fact that family members almost always keep their connections no matter what, means somebody's been doing something to make sure that these connections survive. It is a relationship supported by an idea that kinship matters profoundly.

Of all the family bonds that we expect to hold up under duress—mother or father to child, child to mother or father, sibling to sibling—the mother-child bond is, for reasons of both biology and social practice, the most invincible, the most mythic. Anthropologist Robin Fox believes the essential irreducible family unit is nether extended nor nuclear but just the pair of a mother and her child.

Indeed there is a "Pieta" genre of family stories involving a suffering child (usually a son) and a ministering mother that appears in family after family. In Irene Goldstein's story the most striking motif is maternal sacrifice, and indeed a whole family's sacrifice, at a very, very high cost. The mother is Irene's grandmother Irena, and the son is Kurtzie, her father's younger and slightly retarded brother.

> This is a big story, and it's about how my grandmother was basically the reason that my father's whole family didn't get out of Austria at the start of World War II. The story was that the whole family had gotten visas to go to Palestine in 1935—everyone, that is, except Kurtzie. They wouldn't give one to Kurtzie because he was retarded. My grandmother said if Kurtzie didn't go, she wasn't going, and as a result the entire family said that they weren't going. And so the whole family died. That's seven people—my grandmother, my grandfather, my father's oldest brother, his wife, my father's oldest brother's son, my father's fiancee, and Kurtzie. Only my father survived.

> That story is certainly about loyalty, blind loyalty. I know that one of the things that was told to me was that my grandmother loved her retarded youngest son most of all and could not bear to leave him behind. In this story, my grandmother Irena also seems a totally mythical character, at least in the sense that she didn't seem to be in touch with the kinds of things that other mothers were in touch with like cooking or dirty diapers. What comes through is a totally idealized notion of the maternal, the maternal perhaps as envisaged by a Victorian. Loving, sacrificing. For my father, she was no ideal, and I think he tried to integrate some of what he imagined her qualities to be into himself.

What is so striking about Irene Goldstein's story is that it makes clear how willing family members are to sacrifice—or repress—their own point of view in favor of the collective familial point of view. Irene's father lost an entire family, a fiancee, and almost his own life because his mother was steadfastly loyal to her young retarded son. Somewhere

he must have questioned whether it was worth it, somewhere he must have felt enraged at his own losses. It is inconceivable that this same scenario could have played itself out as it did with a group of unrelated individuals. But day by day and story by story, the family teaches us that such extremes of altruism and self-sacrifice are, if not customary, at least not astounding.

If the mutual bonds between mothers and children are the hardiest, then perhaps the most fragile are the ones between siblings, especially brothers, since they are often beset with both emotional reserve and rivalry. If there is any twosome in a family likely to drift apart, it is a pair of brothers.

And so the family stories that are meant to emphasize the extreme importance of family connections and coming through for one another often focus on brothers. The most common celebrates the ideal, those occasions when brothers under siege act as they ought to. From her mother, Jane Gilbert often heard the story of a long-dead ancestor who fought for the South during the Civil War.

> His name was Hubert and he was a prisoner of war, or maybe he was just in a hospital, with his brother. Both of them were soldiers and both were wounded and put in the same bed. The brother died and Hubert spent two days lying in bed with the corpse of his brother. On the surface this is a horrible story, but it was never told as something to make you shudder or go ugh. To me it had something to do with closeness and sticking with your family, even if they're not alive anymore. They told this story with a kind of pride, or strength—that they lay there in that bed and one of them was dead and one was alive. The way I always envisioned it was that the live one, Hubert, even though he was feverish, he didn't want anyone to know his brother was dead. He wanted to keep his brother with him.

The chafing part of family loyalty, of course, is that it often involves delaying or forsaking one's own individual wishes. In fact the tension between individual desire and collective weal is present in almost all realms of human life. The family, as an inherent partisan of the good-of-the-many, mostly offers stories in support of its own interest, though paradoxically these stories are told by the very individuals who may have had to subordinate themselves.

PROXIMITY

All families agree that when someone's life is on the line, the family has to do something, but in other realms there are more differences between one family and the next. What about how close to one another grown family members should live? As one man I interviewed put it, "One of the messages was 'Don't go too far.'"

What rules, however veiled, do other families have about such matters? Erik Erikson, in *Childhood and Society*, believes that in nineteenth-century American frontier families, the young, sons especially, had to be raised in a way that wouldn't keep them from pursuing their manifest destiny. Better, then, to have rather elastic family ties that wouldn't bind, because one way or another, the value of exploring, getting up and going, had to be instilled and take precedence over staying huddled together on the same acreage.

Margo Henson, a poet in her forties, is a New Yorker born and bred, but her interior life and her poetry are filled with her maternal ancestors, the Lugers, a prairie family such as Erikson had in mind. Small and pale, with thick, loosely plaited red hair and green eyes, she sits with me over lunch one day and talks these ancestors back to life. She speaks of their bombazine dresses and their fascinators so intimately that one could almost imagine she herself had worn them just yesterday.

The issue of sons moving on is very much a theme in her stories, and its urgency, especially as it relates to the economic survival of the nuclear family, comes through strongly in the first story she tells.

My mother's family were the Lugers. A bunch of the Luger boys came from somewhere outside Vienna, where they already had a furniture store, to Minneapolis to start another one. The other brothers all had boys but my great-grandmother proceeded to produce six girls—Anne, Olivia, Clare, Julia, Amelia, and Elizabeth—before she

got to the two boys, Peter and Fred. So then my great-grandmother said to her husband, "What is going to happen to our girls? When we die, what is going to happen? Your brothers have nothing but boys. Are they going to take care of our girls, because our girls can't work in the store? We have to do something!"

What they did was to pack the whole family into the back of the Conestoga wagon, leaving the other Luger boys and their families behind, and to head across the Northwest Territory to Fargo, which was just a beginning town at the time. And they set up their own store. Somewhere along the line, they also lived in Wabash and in Reed's Settlement on the Mississippi.

It's clear that in the Henson scheme of things, family proximity, for the sons at least, is not a major value, and even more, that the nuclear family must take precedence over the extended family.

What about the daughters? Are they free to get up and go? The beginnings of an answer lie in two other "traveling" stories Margo Henson tells.

These are both traveling stories. One is that my great-aunt, when she was three or four, decided to leave home. She made up her mind to run away and she just packed herself up and left. When she got to the edge of town, she found a little boy who was wandering around, not knowing what he wanted to do that day. So my aunt picked him up and the two of them went off across the prairie together. They weren't picked up till about five or six hours later. There's a newspaper photograph of the two of them that I have which is entitled 'The Runaways.'

The other story is about another one of my great-aunts. This is when they were living on the Mississippi and my aunt was about ten. She had read about New Orleans and had been fascinated by it. And there she was living on the Mississippi River and knowing that New Orleans was at the end of it! It was winter and the Mississippi was frozen. So my aunt talked three friends into skating down the Mississippi to New Orleans. They took off and weren't discovered until rather late that night, very cold and extremely frightened on the banks of the Mississippi.

Are these just "cute" stories of failed and foiled runaway daughters? Margo Henson thinks not. "This is the matriarchy telling its own story. There were a lot of women in that family, and they all lived very constricted lives, especially because only two of my great-aunts married. They were better than middle class. My great-grandfather made quite a bit of money and raised his young women very well. They were all given artistic educations.

"Great-Aunt Anne was the painter in the family and, so the story goes, wanted to go to Paris but was not allowed to. She was quite a good painter, too. Maybe not brilliant, but well above the maidenly average in the 1800s. My great-aunt Clare played the harp, and she always wanted to go to Ireland and travel around on the back of a cart and play in villages."

"Instead, they spent their lives working at the family store—Olivia was bookkeeper for near fifty goddamn years. The others did various things—taking stock, selling in the store. I felt they had these little cameo lives, but there was all of this enormous energy that never got used, that was waiting for some kind of release. I feel that very strongly."

So the initial family ground rule, which gave sons permission to move on but kept the daughters at home, thwarted, with nothing to look back on but childhood runaway foibles, became transformed so that the succeeding generations—Margo and her mother—would receive a very different instruction.

As Margo says, "I have a very strong feeling of imperative. My opportunities in life have this push behind me from these women who never had the chance. In fact I feel a responsibility to go and do what they had not done." And Margo Henson has acted on that "imperative" persistently. Every summer she sets off for somewhere, sending postcards the way Hansel scattered bread crumbs.

She has also drawn on the ground rule that one *must* get up and go when the issue is the economic well-being of the family. She married in her twenties and had one son. But when he was eight or nine, Margo and her husband divorced. For a while she taught writing in various New York City

colleges, but in the late 1970s, when colleges were tightening their belts and reducing their faculty, the jobs dried up.

Since she had primary financial responsibility for her son, by then a senior in high school, she found a solution—an unconventional one, but one her great-aunts would probably have approved of. She found a live-in tenant to stay with her son in their brownstone in Brooklyn, and for herself she found a series of artist-in-residence positions at colleges around the country, six weeks here, six weeks there, a weekend at home in Brooklyn whenever possible.

In Rachel Kalber's family, the issue of how near family members must stay or how far they can go is also a vital one, and so the family has a small cluster of stories that huddle around the theme, worrying it and examining it.

The first story has to do with her father, a Russian Jew by birth, who, says Rachel, came from a long line of rabbinical scholars and teachers. Like his male antecedents before him, he was as a young child sent by his family to a distant village to study Talmud. In the context, the importance of becoming a Talmudic scholar is so great that it supersedes the value of staying geographically close to the family.

At the time that this story takes place, Chaim Kalber had been away from his family studying Talmud for eight or nine years. Says Rachel Kalber:

My father left his home in the Ukraine when he was nine years old. He was the child chosen to be sent away to study. So he went and studied at the yeshiva and slept in the synagogue on the floor and ate meals on charity.

Then when my father was seventeen or eighteen, he was conscripted into the czar's army. This was World War I, and he was a corporal or a sergeant. At one point he was told there were a bunch of soldiers that had run away—AWOL—and that he had to take them back to be jailed. Walking along with the group, he realized that one of them was a Jew. He began talking to this man, asking what had happened, why he had run away. The man said that his father was sick and close to death and that, since he had not been granted a leave, he had to run away. My father started to ask him where he came from, and it turned out that the man was my father's brother!

What I felt when I heard this story was, "Oh, the things I take for granted—the family closeness, knowing what's happened in the family." These things were denied my father. To be so far away that you couldn't recognize your own brother and would have to find out in this horrible way that your own father was dying—it was a very brutal world that my father was telling me about, and it made me feel my good fortune: the fact that I was secure and nested, that I'd always know who my father and mother were, that I'd always know how my brother looked.

While on the face of it, the story seems to underscore the fragmentation of the family, it is to the Kalbers a cautionary tale, describing how dreadful—but not how forbidden—it is to be so separated from family. As Rachel hears the story, it has a mystical cast to it, demonstrating that, miraculously, family members will somehow find each other, no matter what.

The subtlety of the Kalber family instruction is that it insists that family members be closely involved—telepathic becomes the ideal—but it does not insist that they live geographically in one another's midst. The additional point is that Judaism and, by its extension, education are so important that it is permissible to sacrifice immediate family closeness for undertakings related to either.

A second Kalber family story reiterates the instruction that its members share in an almost telepathic intimacy. Again, this is a story that Rachel first heard from her father.

The year was 1918 or 1919, the year of a terrible pogrom in the Ukraine. My father, by then working for the Central Jewish Organization, had been sent to collect all the children orphaned by the pogrom and to bring them to a central place.

He came back to his home village to discover that the cossacks had tried to hang his mother and sister, but that they had been cut down in time to save their lives. [After an episode in which Rachel's father was almost killed by the cossacks, he collected the orphans and traveled with them to a town about one hundred miles away.]

An aunt of his was living there. She said, "How is your mother? Is your mother all right?" She said she'd had a dream two weeks before in which she saw my father's father running. [He had in fact died at the start of World War I.] In the dream, my father's aunt said to him, "Yakov, why are you running?" And he said, "I'm running to save my wife. I have to save her. And the children." My father then told his aunt the story about how his mother and sister had been hung and then cut down. My father always cried when he told this story. He was very moved.

This story was a staple in the Kalber repertoire. "I first heard this story as a child," says Rachel Kalber, "and have heard it often since then. What I got from it was that the Jews were always in danger, and that there was some way in which our family would rescue us. Even my father's run-in with his brother was a miraculous reunion. There was no way you could really lose the family, even if they died. Family was all, and you couldn't break that connection."

The constellation of values that these stories promulgate has guided the family for several generations now. When Rachel's parents came to this country, they settled in Florida for a while, where Rachel and her brother were born. When Rachel was fourteen, she was allowed to go to New York to attend a school superior to those in Florida. "Like my father, I was the child chosen to study," she says. Now Rachel Kalber is the mother of a daughter of her own, who is on the verge of entering college. Though Rachel is divorced and has full responsibility for child support, there is no question in her mind that her daughter will go away to college. For an education, even a secular one, she knows that her parents will contribute.

In *Habits of the Heart*, sociologist Robert N. Bellah and his colleagues coined the phrase "communities of memory" to characterize those groups whose members' affiliation was based not only on current similarities but on a more rooted historical affiliation. Among these "communities of memory" they included the family. "Families," they wrote, "can be communities, remembering their past, telling the children the stories of parents' and grandparents' lives, and sustaining hope for the future…." Family stories certainly do this. In fact the implication of what Bellah and his colleagues had to say is that the mere existence of family stories—whether happy or unhappy—exerts a binding cohesive force.

But family stories do even more. For good and for ill, they delineate the rules and the mores that govern family life, rules that succor and support as well as rules that chafe uncomfortably; rules that are out in the open as well as those that operate only by stealth. Indeed, family stories go a step further and define the family, saying not only what members should do, but who they are or should be.

QUESTIONS/THOUGHTS

1. Who are the primary storytellers in your family—men or women? Older or younger relatives? How did this come to be the practice?

2. What are the family themes and family rules embedded in your family stories? What do they tell you about what it means to be a (family name)?

3. Begin your own collection of family stories. You will need a tape recorder or video camera. Simply find relatives to interview and begin. It's best to prepare a list of questions before the interview. Open-ended questions are best because they stimulate ideas and trigger memories. At the beginning of the interview, record the date, location, and names of the people.

Once you start asking questions, let the conversation develop naturally. Below are some sample questions.

> What is your birthdate? Where were you born?
> What were your parents' grandparents' names? What did they do for a living?
> What one special thing do you remember about each of them?
> Where did you go to school? What did you like most about school? What did you like least?
> What was your favorite activity as a child?
> Describe the house (or town) you grew up in.
> What was your most memorable birthday?
> What made you afraid when you were a child?
> How did you meet your spouse? Describe your first date.
> What has changed most in your lifetime?
> If you could live your life over, what would you do differently?

4. Describe how family members tell stories jointly. Who starts a particular story? How does another person enter the storytelling? Do the tellers trade off sections or does one person tend to tell most of the story while the other interjects comments? Do certain members "own" certain stories? Where and when are those stories told?

Adapted from Elizabeth Stone, "Family Ground Rules." In *Black Sheep and Kissing Cousins*, pp. 15–31. Copyright © 1988 by Elizabeth Stone. Reprinted by permission of Transaction Publishers, Inc.

Claiming Family Identity Communicatively: Discourse-Dependent Families

KATHLEEN M. GALVIN

In the 21ˢᵗ century fewer families can be described by discrete categories such as stepfamily, biological family, single parent family, or adoptive family, due to overlapping complexities of connections. Family interactions patterns are increasingly unpredictable due to the diversity of family forms. Although scholars attempt to define families, Baxter and colleagues (2009) assert that scholars must examine how laypersons conceptualize "family." Their research reveals that perceptions of family status increased with the presence of children, intactness, co-residence of family members, marriage, heterosexualiy (in the absence of children), and non-fictive kin union. This remains an important area for future study because U.S. family forms continue to shift.

People continue to marry across their lifespan; many experience third or fourth weddings. Stepfamilies, formed through remarriage or cohabitation, generally reflect divorce and re-commitment, although an increasing number are formed by single mothers marrying for the first time. Little is known about ex-stepfamily relationships although increasing numbers of children live in second or third stepfamilies.

Single-parent families continue to increase. Today, women under 30 who become pregnant for the first time are more likely to be single than married. Increasingly, single women and men become parents through adoption and new reproductive technologies. Gay and lesbian committed couples and families are becoming more visible due, in part, to a greater willingness of same sex partners to identify their lifestyle. A growing number of same-sex couples report children present in their home: about 21% of partnered lesbians and 5.2 % of partnered gays (Black, Gates, Sanders & Taylor, 2000).

More families are being formed, in part, through adoption. The practice of international adoption continues to expand; over 20,000 children a year are adopted internationally (Kreider, 2003). Many of these families become transracial through the adoption process. Open adoption is emerging as the common domestic form, creating an ongoing adoption triangle—the adoptee, the birth parent(s), and the adoptive parent(s) with variable contact among members.

Intentional families, families formed without biological and legal ties, are maintained by members' self-definition. These "fictive" or self-ascribed kin become family by choice, performing family functions for one another. The next-door neighbors who serve as extended kin, the best friend who is considered a sister, or other immigrants from the same homeland are examples of fictive kin.

The processes by which intentional families are formed reflect a transactional definition of family, that is, "a group of intimates who generate a sense of home and group identity and who experience a shared history and a shared future" (Koerner & Fitzpatrick, 2002 p. 71).

Currently fewer people report membership in families fully formed through lifelong marriages and biological offspring; many experience multiplicities of connections. The complexities are captured in a discussion of the label gay and lesbian families: "Should we count only families in which every single member is gay?...Or does the presence of just one gay member color a family gay?" (Stacey, 1999, p. 373). The same question must be asked about labeling families as adoptive, blended or step, single parent, and so on.

The current diversity of family presents communication challenges for its members who must manage their family identity communicatively. Members find themselves explaining their family to outsiders who challenge their claims of relatedness; sometimes members have to reaffirm for themselves what makes them a family. Members of certain family forms create and alter language to manage interactions. For example, stepchildren may engage in code-switching as they talk about and to family members (Koenig Kellas, LeClair-Underberg, & Normand, 2008).

In the following article Kathleen Galvin presents a number of communication strategies used by family members to manage their identity both outside the family as well as inside the family. She suggests that members of families formed outside of full biological or adult legal ties will be called upon to address their family's identity. When addressing outsiders, the family members may rely on strategies of labeling, describing, legitimizing and defending; when talking with each other, family members may rely on naming, discussing, narrating, and creating rituals. As you read this article

consider the question: What strategies have you used, or observed others using, in an attempt to address family identity and how effective were these attempts?

REFERENCES

Baxter, L. A., Henauw, C., Huisman, D., Livesay, C. B., Norwood, K., Su, H., & Wolf, B. (2009). Lay conceptions of "family": A replication and extension. *Journal of Family Communication, 9*, 170–189.

Black, D., Gates, G., Sanders, S., & Taylor, L. (2000). Demographics of the gay and lesbian population in the United States. *Demography, 37*(2), 139–154.

Koenig Kellas, J., LeClair-Underberg, C., & Normand, E. L. (2008). *Journal of Family Communication, 8*, 238–263.

Koerner, A. F., & Fitzpatrick, M. A. (2002). Toward a theory of family communication. *Communication Theory, 12*, 70–91.

Kreider, R. M., & Simmons, T. (2003, October). Marital status: 2000. (C2KBR-30). *Census 2000 special reports*. Washington, DC: U.S. Census Bureau, U.S. Department of Commerce.

Stacey, J. (1999). Gay and lesbian families are here; all our families are queer; let's get used to it. In S. Coontz (with M. Parson, & G. Raley) (Eds.), *American families: A multicultural reader* (pp. 372–405). New York, NY: Routledge.

Although all societies and cultures have webs of kinship relationships, the structures of which change across time and cultures (Garey and Hansen, 1998), U.S. families represent the forefront of familial redefinition due to the multiplicity of emerging, ever-changing, kinship patterns. As families become increasingly diverse, *their definitional processes expand exponentially rendering their identity highly discourse-dependent.* Family identity depends, at least in part, upon members' communication with outsiders, as well as with each other, about how they make sense of themselves as family.

All families engage in some level of discourse-driven family identity building, less traditionally formed families are more discourse-dependent, engaging in recurring discursive processes to manage and maintain identity. A growing number of U. S. families are formed through differences, visible or invisible, rendering their ties more ambiguous to outsiders as well as to themselves whereas, in other cultures, families are still identified by similarities. Circumstances such as ongoing connections to a birthmother and adoptive parents, visual differences among members, siblings' lack of shared early childhood experiences, same-sex parents, a solo parent and a "seed daddy," or ties to ex-step relatives, create ambiguity necessitating active management of family identity. These definitional concerns surface as members face outsiders' questions or challenges regarding the veracity of members' claims of relatedness, or experience a need to revisit their familial identity at different stages of individual or familial development. The greater the ambiguity of family form, the more elaborate the communicative processes needed to establish and maintain identity.

High discourse-dependent families engage regularly in external as well as internal boundary management practices. Times of stress and/or boundary ambiguity challenge family boundaries because expectations of inclusion and support are less clear in self-ascribed or ambiguous relations than in families formed and maintained through traditionally recognized biological and adult legal ties.

What serves as the basis of family? Minow (1998), identifies the key question as, "Does this group function as a family?" arguing that the issue is not whether a group of people fit the formal, legal definition of a family, but "whether the group of people function as a family; do they share affection and resources, think of one another as family members, and present themselves as such to neighbors and others?" (p. 8). Communicative practices contribute to family functioning, especially in families formed, fully or partly, outside of traditional means.

FAMILY DIVERSITY
Families in the first half of the 21st century will alter irrevocably any sense of predictability as to what "being family" means. These families will:

1. Reflect an increasing diversity of self-conceptions, evidenced through structural as well as cultural variations, which will challenge society to abandon any historical, nucleocentric biases, unitary cultural assumptions, traditional gender assumptions, and implied economic and religious assumptions.

2. Live increasingly within four and five generations of relational connections. Escalating longevity, changing birth rates and multiple marriages or cohabitations will reveal long-term developmental patterns, ongoing multiple intergenerational contacts, generational reversals, and smaller biological-sibling cohorts.

3. Continuously reconfigure themselves across members' lifespan as choices of individuals or subgroups create new family configurations through legal, biological, technological, and discursive means, impacting members' family identity (Coontz, 1999; Galvin, 2004b).

Further examination of these claims provides a picture of current family life.

Fewer families can be depicted validly by discrete categories or unitary terms, such as stepfamily, biological family, single parent families, or adoptive families, due to overlapping complexities of connections.

DISCOURSE AND FAMILY IDENTITY
We need richer concepts and tools both to make sense of increasingly complex family forms, as well as to address questions such as: "How are we to characterize the most important relationship processes in such families? When do we need to expand our lexicon to address the new relationships and issues challenging such families?" (Grotevant, 2004, p. 12). From a social construction standpoint, "Our languages of description and explanation are produced, sustained, and/or abandoned within processes of human interaction" (Gergen, Hoffman & Anderson, 1996,

328 PART VII: CONTEXTS

p. 102). Discourse processes are relevant to families because, through interaction and language, individuals, within their family context, collectively construct their familial identity and the realities in which they live (Stamp, 2002).

Family communication scholars claim families are based on, formed, and maintained through communication, or "our families, and our images of families, are constituted through social interaction" (Vangelisti, 2002, p. xiii), necessitating studies that "employ definitions of the family that depend on how families define themselves rather than definitions based on genetic and sociological criteria" (Fitzpatrick, 1998, p. 45). Over time, as diversity increases, communicative definitions of family will be privileged over structural definitions, requiring new models for talking about and studying families (Whitchurch & Dickson, 1999). Discourse-dependency is not new; what *is* new is that discourse-dependent families are becoming the norm.

Discourse-dependent family members manage identity across external boundaries through practices such as labeling, explaining, legitimizing, and defending familial identity. Concurrently they manage internal boundaries through practices such as labeling, discussing, narrating, and ritualizing. Usually the necessity for such practices depends on the degree of difference reflected within the family form.

EXTERNAL BOUNDARY MANAGEMENT PRACTICES

When families appear different to outsiders, questions and challenges arise. Family members tend to engage in a process of managing the tensions between revealing and concealing family information on the assumption that they control access to their private information (Petronio, 2002). Yet little is known about how families with differences manage their boundaries. For example, researchers have not yet examined the strategies that gay and lesbian parents use "to shelter their children from negative experiences, to help children cope with instances of prejudice, to build resilience in their children…" (Peplau & Beals, 2002, p. 244). Moreover, the practices of parents who build

families through new reproductive technologies remain invisible. The following section describes a set of communication strategies commonly found in popular literature as well as academic and professional sources.

Labeling

Titles or positions provide an orientation to a situation or problem; for example, identifying the familial tie when introducing or referring to another person. The constitutive approach invites questions such as: What do we want a familial relational label to communicate? To whom? How will others view that label?

Relational labels orient familial ties such as "brother" or "step-grandmother." When transitions occur, the specific meaning of certain names must be linked to the person-in-relationship. For example, among the many communicative tasks a man faces in becoming a stepfather is negotiating a definition of the step-father/step-child relationship (Jorgenson, 1994). Frequently this involves overt or covert negotiations about whether to refer to him as "My mother's husband," "Brad," "My stepfather," or "My other Dad"; each choice reveals a different sense of connection (Galvin, 1989). Because language serves as a constituent feature of cultural patterns embedded within a relationship, changing the language alters the relationship (Gergen, Hoffman & Anderson, 1996).

Titles and labels establish expectations. When a stepmother looks the same age as her stepson, two siblings represent different races, or "Grandma Carl" is male, creating a relational definition becomes challenging. Today's families are confronted with circumstances unimaginable to earlier generations: How does one reference his sperm donor or the surrogate mother who carried her?

Explaining

Explaining involves making a named family relationship understandable, giving reasons for it, or elaborating on how it works. When someone's non-hostile curiosity seems to question the stated familial tie, explanation is a predictable response. Remarks such as, "How come you don't speak

Korean?" or "How can you have two mothers?" are commonplace for some individuals. An explanation for an international adoptee's lack of facility in her native language may include "My parents are Irish, so I didn't learn any Korean" (Galvin & Wilkinson, 2000, p. 11). When a playmate challenged her young son because he did not have a "Daddy," Blumenthal (1990/1991) explained the concept of a Seed Daddy to the boys—"a man who is not really a parent, but one who helps a woman get a baby started" (p. 185). Finally, negotiating parenthood within a heterocentric context creates issues for same-sex partners faced with educating others about their family but who are often frustrated by the task (Chabot & Ames, 2004).

Legitimizing

Legitimizing invokes the sanction of law or custom: it positions relationships as genuine and conforming to recognized standards. Legitimizing occurs when one's relational ties are challenged, creating a need to provide information that helps another recognize the tie as a genuine, familial link. Adoption agencies regularly prepare parents of families formed through transracial and/or international adoption for questions such as, "Is she your real daughter?" Adoption Learning Partners http://www. adoptionlearningpartners.org online adoption education community, provides new parents with alternative responses to such an intrusive question. These include: "No, she's my fake daughter." "Yes, she's really mine," or "Yes, we're an adoptive family." The response is chosen on the basis of the parent's interaction goals and/or the child's age and ability to understand the interaction. Gay or lesbian parents make reference to outside sources that legitimate their family, such as books that depict their family as genuine (*Heather Has Two Mommies* or *Daddy's Roommate*) or well-known figures who represent gay male or lesbian parents.

Defending

Finally, defending involves shielding oneself or a familial relationship from (this should not be indented) attack, justifying it or maintaining

its validity against opposition. Defending is a response to hostility or a direct challenge to the familial form. For example, Garner (2004), the daughter of a gay father, depicts the difficulty of listening to constant messages from media, politicians, religious leaders, teachers, and neighbors claiming gay people are bad or sinful. She describes the specific complications for her nephew when a teacher or friend asserts, "That's impossible. You can't have grampas in the same house. Which one is REALLY your grampa?" (n.p.). Parents who adopt transracially must be prepared for questions such as, "Couldn't you get a White child?" or "Is she one of those crack babies?" (Adoption Learning Partners, http://www.adoptionlearningpartners.org). Defending responses may arise from sheer frustration. Annoyed by hearing the question, "How can you two be sisters?" a pair of Asian and Caucasian teenage sisters decided, "When we got the question…we would respond 'the mailman' and walk away" (Galvin & Fonner, 2003). Children in cohabiting stepfamilies face challenges such as, "He's not your real stepfather if your Mom didn't marry him." Advice columnists regularly respond to questions about how to deal with similar invasive comments or questions.

INTERNAL BOUNDARY MANAGEMENT PRACTICES

Members of families formed through differences engage in ongoing communication practices designed to maintain their internal sense of family-ness. These practices include: naming, discussing, narrating, and creating rituals.

Naming

Naming also plays a significant role in the development of internal family identity. Names or titles present issues within family boundaries as members struggle to indicate their familial status. Sometimes names are decided and never re-visited; in other cases, the familial ties and labels become a source of ongoing negotiation. Naming a child, especially an older child, or a child adopted internationally and/or transracially, presents a challenge. Children arrive with names reflecting their birth family and/or birth culture. An international adoptee captures the loss involved when her Korean name was replaced by an American one, saying "That was really all I had when I came to this country: that name. And my parents overlooked it and chose another one" (Kroll, 2000, p. 18).

Open adoption provides a unique set of linguistic challenges, given the lack of terminology for any extended family members in the adoption triangle. Stepfamily members confront the question, "What do I call you?" Answers are confounded by the "wicked stepmother" myth, conflicting loyalties between biological parents and stepparents, and the lack of conventional names for a stepparent's extended family. Stepchildren may choose a name honoring a stepparent's parental role, such as a hyphenated last name or using biological terms such as "Pop" or "Moms," dissimilar from their name for the biological parent. Gay or lesbian parents confront the issue of inclusive language, or how they wish to be referred to by their children, because linguistic labels do not include the non-biological parent easily. Some lesbian pairs consider taking one last name, either having one take on the other's name or creating a new name. Those who changed names report it was to establish a public family identity or to strengthen their presence as a couple or family (Suter & Oswald, 2003).

Discussing

The degree of difference among family members impacts the amount of member discussion of their family situation. Lesbian parenting partners encounter decisions regarding how to become parents, who will be the biological mother, and how to decide on a donor (Chabot & Ames, 2004). In many cases donors are chosen because of their physical appearance since "Looking related suggests family, which helps communicate a shared family identity" (Suter, Bergen, Daas & Parker, 2004). Gay male parents experience variations on these issues such as adoption or gestational carriers.

A blended family must develop its identity and "create a shared conception of how their family is to manage its daily business" (Cherlin & Furstenberg, 1994, p. 370). A study of blended family development found that some of the families "used direct communication, such as regular family meetings, to air issues surrounding the adjustments to becoming a family" (Braithwaite, Olson, Golish, Soukup & Turman, 2001, p.243). Concerns regarding belonging result in conversations ranging from grandparent gift-giving, designated space for non-custodial children, signing official school papers, or rights to discipline.

A child's entrance into a family through adoption or new reproductive technologies necessitates an ongoing series of talks across years as the child's ability to comprehend information results in varied depths of explanation. Currently, sequential, age-appropriate, discussions of adoption have replaced the earlier "one big talk" as children's informational needs change as they reach new developmental milestones (Wrobel, Kohler, Grotevant & Mc Roy, 2003). Transracially adopted children begin to question the physical differences between themselves and other family members at an early age. Parents in families formed through assisted reproductive technology raise questions about how to discuss their children's origins.

Narrating

Every family tells stories, however, families formed through differences experience more complex storytelling processes. McAdams (1993) suggests that a person's story "brings together the different parts of ourselves and our lives into a purposeful and convincing whole" (p. 12). Over time "we tell and retell, to ourselves and to others, the story of who we are, what we have become, and how we got there, making and remaking a story of ourselves that links birth to life to death . . . ." (Jorgenson and Bochner (2004) p. 516). Because family stories are "laced with opinions, emotions, and past experiences, they can provide particularly telling data about the way people conceive of their relationships with family members" (Vangelisti, Crumley & Baker, 1999). Everyday narratives create a powerful scaffold for a family's identity.

Creation or entrance stories answer the question, "How did this family come to be?" They include accounts of how the adult partners met or how an individual chose to become a parent, as well as birth and adoption narratives. In cases of adoption the entrance story sets the tone for a family's adoption-related communication; it is the beginning of an ongoing dialogue between parents and their children (Wrobel, et. al, 2003). In addition, "How the (adoption) story is told and retold in the family can have lasting consequences for the child's adjustment and well-being" (Friedlander, 1999, p.43). Cooper (2004) depicts the development of her stepfamily through three types of stories—stepfamily, blended family, and bonus stories—each reflecting a stage in the family's move toward deeper joining.

Many families formed through differences suppress or lose their narratives. Just as many divorced families and stepfamilies lose the original parental love stories, certain adoptive parents struggle with the extent to which an adopted child's painful birth family background should be told to family members. Uncertain parents may fabricate some pieces of the story to avoid discussing infertility or donor insemination.

Creating Rituals

Families accomplish their "emotional business" as they enact rituals (Bossard & Boll, 1950). A typology of family rituals includes major celebrations, traditions such as reunions, vacations, and birthdays, and mundane routines (Wolin and Bennett, 1984). Although most families develop rituals, those formed through differences struggle with what to ritualize, and which rituals from previous family experiences should be continued or terminated.

Family rituals provide opportunities for stepfamilies to define family membership on multiple levels of connection, although they require sensitivity and negotiations. In their study of blended families, Braithwaite, Baxter & Harper (1998) found members engaged in rituals, or "important communicative practices that enable blended family members to embrace their new family while still valuing what was important

in the old family environment" (p. 101). Family members described enacting new rituals, not imported from a previous family, rituals that were imported unchanged, rituals that were imported and adapted. Respondents also reported that some new rituals lasted and some failed, demonstrating that becoming a family is an ongoing process. Gay and lesbian stepfamilies face creating an identity without the traditional courtship and marriage rituals, creating ambiguity about the new family for all members (Lynch, 2000).

Adoptive families may celebrate arrival days as well as birthdays; in international adoption the family may adopt some celebrations from a child's birth culture. Birth family members may be invited to share a holiday or a tradition. Some children report rituals of pulling out adoption papers and looking at them, or attending a summer culture camp (Fujimoto, 2001).

MULTIPLE IDENTITIES

As noted earlier, most families cannot be described in unitary terms; many are formed through multiple differences. For example, white, lesbian mothers of two African American boys reported the following common (non-hostile) questions from the boy's preschool peers: "'Why are you black and she white?' or 'Why is he black and you white?'" As the boys aged they encountered variations on the question, "Why do you have two moms?" (Fine & Johnson, 2004). These authors detail the multiple objectified identities ascribed to them as parents in a family created across race and gender borders. Black lesbians experience "triple jeopardy" by virtue of race, gender, and sexual orientation, with racism as the most stressful challenge (Bowleg, Huang, Brooks, Black & Burkholder, 2003).

The concept of family is changing visibly and invisibly, but irrevocably. When family identity is involved, language follows lived experience. This language, managed within and across boundaries, reflects individual's personal or observational experiences. Contemporary families, living in a world of normative instability and definitional crisis, depend increasingly on discourse to construct their identities.

REFERENCES

Adoption Learning Partners http://www.adoption-learningpartners.org

Blumenthal, A. (1990/91). Scrambled eggs and seed daddies: Conversations with my son. *Empathy: Gay and Lesbian Advocacy Research Project, 2*(2), 185–188.

Bossard, J., & Boll, E. (1950). *Ritual in family living.* Philadelphia: University of Pennsylvania Press.

Bowleg, L., Huang, J., Brooks, K., Black, A., & Burkholder, G. (2003). Triple jeopardy and beyond: Multiple minority stress and resilience among black lesbians. *Journal of Lesbian Studies, 7,* 87–108.

Braithwaite, D. O., Baxter, L., & Harper, A. M. (1998). The role of rituals in the management of the dialectical tension of "old" and "new" in blended families. *Communication Studies, 49,* 101–120.

Braithwaite, D. O., Olson, L. N., Golish, T. D., Soukup, C., & Turman, P. (2001). Becoming a family: Developmental processes represented in blended family discourse. *Journal of Applied Communication Research, 29,* 221–247.

Chabot, J. M., & Ames, B. D. (2004). It wasn't "Let's get pregnant and go do it": Decision making in lesbian couples planning motherhood via donor insemination. *Family Relations, 53,* 348–356.

Cherlin, A. J., & Furstenberg, F. F. (1994). Stepfamilies in the United States: A reconsideration. *Annual Review of Sociology, 20,* 359–381.

Coontz, S. (1999). Introduction. In S. Coontz (with M. arson, & G. Raley) (Eds.), *American families: A multicultural reader* (pp. ix–xxxiii). New York, NY: Routledge.

Cooper, P. J. (2004, April). *Step? Blended? Bonus? Looking back to look forward: Legacies, myths and narratives of stepfamilies.* Paper delivered at the Central States Communication Association Convention, Cleveland, OH.

Fine, M., & Johnson, F. (2004). Creating a family across race and gender borders. In A. Gonzalez, M. Houston, & V. Chen (Eds.), *Our voices: Essays in culture, ethnicity, and* communication (pp. 240–247). Los Angeles, CA: Roxbury.

Fitzpatrick, M. A. (1998). Interpersonal communication on the Starship Enterprise: Resilience, stability, and change in relationships for the twenty-first century. In J. Trent (Ed.), *Communication: Views from the helm for the 21st century* (pp. 41–46). Boston, MA: Allyn & Bacon.

Friedlander, M. L. (1999). Ethnic identity development of internationally adopted children and adolescents: Implications for family therapists. *Journal of Marital and Family Therapy, 25,* 43–60.

Fujimoto, E. (2001, November). *South Korean adoptees growing up in white America: Negotiating race and culture.* Paper presented at the National Communication Association Convention. Atlanta, GA.

Galvin, K. M. (2004). The family of the future: What do we face? In A. L. Vangelisti (Ed.), *Handbook of Family Communication,* 675–607. Mahwah, NJ: Lawrence Erlbaum.

Galvin, K. M., & Fonner, K. (2003, April). *"The mailman" as family defense strategy: International/ transracial adoption and mixed siblings.* Paper presented at the Central States Communication Association Convention. Omaha, NE.

Galvin, K. M., & Wilkinson, K. M. (2000, November). *That's your family picture?! Korean adoptees communication management issues during the transition to college.* Paper presented at the National Communication Association Convention. Seattle, WA.

Garey, A. I., & Hansen, K. V. (1998). Analyzing families with a feminist sociological imagination. In A. I. Garey & K. V. Hansen (Eds.), *Families in the U.S.: Kinship and domestic policies* (pp. xv–xxi). Philadelphia, PA: Temple University Press.

Garner, A. (2004). Families like mine. Retrieved from http://www.familieslikemine.com/faq/index.html

Gergen, K. J., Hoffman, L., & Anderson, H. (1996). Is diagnosis a disaster? A constructionist trialogue. In F. W. Kaslow (Ed.), *Handbook of relational diagnosis and dysfunctional family patterns* (pp. 102–118). New York, NY: Wiley.

Grotevant, H. D. (2004). Comments. *Relationship Research News International Association for Relationship Research, 2*(2), 12.

Jorgenson, J. (1994). Situated address and the social construction of "in-law" relationships. *The Southern Communication Journal, 59,* 196–204.

Jorgenson, J., & Bochner, A. P. (2004). Imagining families through stories and rituals. In A. Vangelisti (Ed.), *Handbook of family communication* (pp. 513–538). Mahwah, NJ: Lawrence Erlbaum.

Kroll, M. L. (2000). My name is…In M. W. Lustig & J. Koester (Eds.), *Among us: Essays on identity, belonging, and intercultural competence* (pp. 18–23). New York, NY: Longman.

Lynch, J. M. (2000). Considerations of family structure and gender composition: The lesbian and gay stepfamily. *Journal of Homosexuality, 40,* 81–95.

McAdams, D. P. (1993). *Stories we live by: Personal myths and the making of the self.* New York, NY: Guilford Press.

Minow, M. (1998). Redefining families: Who's in and who's out? In K. V. Hansen & A. I. Garey (Eds.), *Families in the U.S.* (pp. 7–19). Philadelphia, PA: Temple University Press. (Originally in 1991 *University of Colorado Law Review, 62* (2), 269–285).

Peplau, L. A., & Beals, K. P. (2002). The family lives of lesbians and gay men. In A. Vangelisti (Ed.), *Handbook of family communication* (pp. 233–248). Mahwah, NJ: Lawrence Erlbaum.

Petronio, S. (2002). *Boundaries of privacy: Dialectics of disclosure.* Albany: State University of New York Press.

Stamp, G. H. (2002). Theories of family relationships and a family relationships theoretical model. In A. L. Vangelisti (Ed.), *Handbook of family communication,* (pp. 1–30). Mahwah, NJ: Lawrence Erlbaum.

Suter, E. A., Bergen, K. J., Daas, K. L., & Parker, J. H. (2004, November). *Communicative construction of lesbian family through rituals and symbols.* Paper presented at the National Communication Association Convention, Chicago, IL.

Suter, E. A., & Oswald, R. F. (2003). Do lesbians change their last names in the context of a committed relationship? *Journal of Lesbian Studies, 7,* 71–83.

Vangelisti, A. L. (2002). Introduction. In A. L. Vangelisti (Ed.), *American families: A multicultural reader* (pp. xiii–xx). Mahwah, NJ: Lawrence Erlbaum.

Vangelisti, A. L., Crumley, L. P., & Baker, J. L. (1999). Family portraits: Stories as standards for family relationships. *Journal of Social and Personal Relationships, 16,* 335–368.

Whitchurch, G. G., & Dickson, F. C. (1999). Family communication. In M. Sussman, S. K. Steinmetz, & G. W. Peterson (Eds.), *Handbook of marriage and the family* (2nd ed., pp. 687–704). New York: Plenum.

Wolin, S., & Bennett, L. (1984). Family rituals. *Family Processes, 23,* 401–420.

Wrobel, G. M., Kohler, J. K., Grotevant, H. D. & McRoy, R. G. (2003). The family adoption communication (FAC) model: Identifying pathways of adoption-related communication. *Adoption Quarterly, 7,* 53–84.

QUESTIONS/THOUGHTS

1. What are circumstances in which family members find themselves challenged to communicatively elaborate on their family identity to those outside the family? Explain how the interaction unfolded.

2. Under what circumstances have you, or others you know, found it important to address the issue of family identity with other members of the family? Explain why the issue arose and how the interaction unfolded.

3. What strategies do you think are missing from this article? Give some examples.

4. Interview someone from a stepfamily or a family headed by two fathers or two mothers. Ask your respondent to describe the ways members refer to each other within the family and how they introduce the adults to persons outside the family. Specifically focus on terms of address.

Adapted from Galvin, K.M. (In press). "Diversity's impact on defining the family: Discourse-dependency." In R. West and L. Turner (Eds.) FAMILY COMMUNICATION: A REFERENCE OF THEORY AND PRACTICE. Thousand Oaks, CA: Sage Publications.

Adult Siblings' Use of Relational Maintenance Behaviors Across the Sibling Lifespan

SCOTT A. MYERS

Siblings represent the people you are going to know for most of your life and who will share many of your major life milestones. Safer (2002) eloquently expresses the centrality of this relationship saying: "No future tie is exempt from their influence; relations with them are the prototype for friendships, romances, and professional connections with coworkers, rivals, and collaborators for the rest of your life" (p. 39). Sibling relationships change significantly over time as individuals move through developmental stages. These changes occur in three stages: childhood-adolescence, early and middle adulthood, and old age (Goetting, 1986). During these stages most siblings provide one another with companionship and social support.

In childhood the older siblings often function as caregivers and teach social and other skills to younger siblings. The support or nurturing of older siblings reduces the influence of negative life events on children's social adjustment (Conger & Conger, 2002). In adulthood the frequency of interaction may decline, depending on geographical distances and the pressures of raising children. A review of the dynamics of siblings across the lifespan reports that even if interaction is infrequent, older adult

siblings maintain a symbolic relationship by recalling shared incidents and providing a sense of continuity as well as emotional and instrumental support (Nussbaum, Pecchioni, Robinson, and Thompson 2000). In the final stage, old age, the sibling relationship often takes on greater significance as friends and other family members die. Older siblings help one another review life events and face current ones.

Yet, the sibling tie is involuntary and permanent, not voluntarily chosen the way friends are chosen (Mikkelson, 2006). Therefore, sibling relationships may reflect greater variation in styles of connection. Gold (1986) studied older sibling relationships and discovered five types: intimate (14 percent of the relationships studied), congenial (30 percent), loyal (34 percent), apathetic (11 percent), and hostile (11 percent). These percentages reveal the strength and importance of older sibling relationships in many families.

How do siblings maintain their relationships throughout adulthood? In the following article Scott Myers describes some of his personal experiences with adult sibling ties as he introduces a wide range of studies that shed light on how adult siblings exhibit relational maintenance behavior, and then suggests a number of behaviors that siblings employ to stay connected. Notice the finding that adult siblings report that the use relational maintenance behaviors more strategically than routinely, or they use these behaviors intentionally and consciously to keep the relationship intact. Clearly, this sends the message of working to preserve this family tie. As you read this article, consider your sibling relationships and the methods you use to maintain them. Ask yourself the question: To what extent do my siblings, or siblings I observe, actively engage in communicative efforts to sustain the sibling tie? Think carefully about the importance of this sibling tie in your life because,"Ultimately they are the only surviving witnesses to your intimate history. Nobody else will remember your childhood" (Safer, 2002, p. 39).

REFERENCES

Conger, R. D., & Conger, K. J. (2002). Resilience in Midwestern families: Selected findings from the first decade of a prospective longitudinal study. *Journal of Marriage and the Family, 64,* 361–373.

Goetting, A. (1986). The developmental tasks of siblingship over the life cycle. *Journal of Marriage and the Family, 48,* 703–714.

Gold, D. T. (1986). Sibling relationships in retrospect: A study of reminiscence in old age. Unpublished Doctoral dissertation, Northwestern University, Evanston, IL.

Mikkelson, A. C. (2006). Communication among peers: Adult sibling relationships. In K. Floyd & M. T. Morman (Eds.), *Widening the family circle* (pp. 21–35). Thousand Oaks, CA: Sage.

Nussbaum, J. E., Pecchioni, L. L., Robinson, J. D., & Thompson, T. L. (2000). Relationships with siblings in later life. *Communication and aging* (2nd ed.). Hillsdale, NJ: Lawrence Erlbaum.

Safer, J. (2002). *The normal one: Life with a difficult or damaged sibling.* New York, NY: The Free Press.

INTRODUCTION

Take a moment and reflect on your relationships with your siblings. I have three siblings: Michelle, who is three years younger than me; Susan, who is five years younger than me; and Mark, who is seven years younger than me. Some of my fondest memories of my childhood center on the time spent with my siblings. Together, the four of us explored the neighborhood on our bicycles and Big Wheels, starred in talent shows for our parents and grandparents, took turns being cops and robbers as well as cowboys and Indians, formed our own rock band, and forged friendships among GI Joe, Barbie, Donny and Marie, and the Sunshine Family. Holidays always took on a special meaning as we sat around the kitchen table, decorating sugar cookies at Christmas and coloring eggs for Easter. Sad times were equally shared, such as when our gerbil Squiggy died and our dog Skippy was hit by a car. Everyday tasks, such as walking each other to school and pleading with our parents to be allowed to stay up late on Saturday nights, were completed as a unit of four.

As we grew into adolescence, the activities changed, but our time spent together did not. Instead of spending time playing, we now spent time engaging in household chores, fulfilling school responsibilities, and working. Cooking dinner and cleaning up afterwards became a carefully orchestrated routine, equally shared and rotated among the four of us. One of us would clear the table, one of us would put away the leftovers and unused dishes, one of us would wash the dishes, and one of us would dry the dishes. Whoever cleared the table also had to sweep the floor and whoever put away the leftovers also had to wipe off the table and the stove. The completion of other household chores, such as laundry and mowing the yard, was negotiated. At school, we participated in several activities together, in part because there were usually two of us in the same school at the same time and in part because these were activities we mutually enjoyed. In high school, these activities included being on the school newspaper and yearbook staffs (I was editor my senior year; Michelle, Susan, and Mark were, at some point, reporters), participating in the school musicals (Michelle always had a starring role while Susan, Mark, and I were cast as "extras"), and being members of the forensics team. Sports (Susan and Mark were the athletes of the family;

Michelle and I were content with watching) and cheerleading (Michelle was a cheerleader all four years in high school; Susan was a cheerleader for two years) also were shared activities. In the summer, it wasn't unusual to find between two and four of us detasseling corn and rouging beans for a local farmer.

Once the four of us graduated from high school and entered and graduated from college, we still managed to spend some time together, but it wasn't as frequent or in the same manner as it was when we were younger. Romantic relationships, jobs, and friendships dominated our time, which required us to negotiate the ways in which we maintained contact with each other. Communication became relegated to telephone calls; relaying messages and updates through our mother; the occasional card or letter; and mutually agreed upon attendance at holiday events, family reunions, and extended family functions such as weddings and funerals. Within the past 15 years, life events such as the deaths of my father and my brother Mark; the marriage, divorce, remarriage, and second divorce of my sister Michelle; the births of Michelle's children; and my mother's demise in health have forced us to renegotiate not only the ways in which we maintain contact with each other, but also the tasks that have surfaced as a result of each event. This time, however, we are doing so as a unit of three.

RELATIONAL MAINTENANCE BEHAVIORS

The aforementioned examples illustrate a concept known as relational maintenance behaviors. Relational maintenance behaviors are defined as the actions and activities used to sustain desired relational definitions (Canary & Stafford, 1994). In other words, relational maintenance behaviors are the things that people do or say in order to keep their relationships alive. Commonly used in heterosexual and gay and lesbian romantic relationships (Dainton, 2007; Guerrero & Bachman, 2006; Haas & Stafford, 1998; Rabby, 2007; Stafford & Canary, 2006) as well as in cross-sex and same-sex friendships (Guerrero & Chavez, 2005; Messman, Canary, & Hause, 2000), relational partners use a host of behaviors to keep their relationship in existence, in a specified state, in satisfactory condition, or in repair (Dindia & Canary, 1993). Furthermore, as Dainton and Stafford (1993) noted, these relational maintenance behaviors either can be used strategically (i.e., used consciously and intentionally to maintain the relationship) or routinely (i.e., used unconsciously and unintentionally as a means to maintain the relationship).

One of the most widely recognized typologies of relational maintenance behaviors has been conceptualized by Stafford and Canary (1991). This typology consists of five relational maintenance behaviors used by romantic partners: positivity, openness, assurances, networks, and tasks. *Positivity* involves interacting with the partner in a cheerful, optimistic, and uncritical manner. *Openness* includes directly discussing the nature of the relationship and disclosing one's desires for the relationship. *Assurances* are messages that stress an individual's continuation in the relationship. *Networks* involves both relational partners interacting with or relying on common affiliations and relationships. *Tasks* requires partners to perform responsibilities specific to the relationship. Continuing this investigation, Stafford, Dainton, and Haas (2000) identified two additional relational maintenance behaviors—conflict management and advice—used by marital partners. *Conflict management* refers to behaviors that consist of understanding, forgiveness, and patience. *Advice* centers on providing social support to a partner.

Dainton and Stafford (1993) identified an additional seven relational maintenance behaviors. These behaviors are joint activities, talk, mediated communication, avoidance, antisocial, affection, and focus on self. *Joint activities* consists of activities in which both partners participate as a way to spend time together. *Talk* refers to verbal communication that is centered more on topic breadth than topic depth. *Mediated communication* involves any form of communication that is not face-to-face. *Avoidance* refers to the evasion of one partner or a particular topic. *Antisocial* involves the use of behaviors considered to be socially unfriendly or unacceptable. *Acceptance* consists of illustrating displays of fondness for the partner. *Focus on self* revolves around behaviors that are self-directed, but are intended for the good of the relationship.

Across marital relationships, dating relationships, and friendships, the use of relational maintenance behaviors varies. Among romantic partners, assurances are used more frequently than other relational maintenance behaviors (Guerrero & Bachman, 2006; Stafford & Canary, 2006); among friends, positivity (Messman et al., 2000) is used more frequently than other relational maintenance behaviors. Positivity, openness, assurances, and tasks are used more often by romantic partners and family members than by friends or coworkers (Canary, Stafford, Hause, & Wallace, 1993). Joint activities are used more frequently by dating couples than by married couples (Dainton & Stafford, 1993). Friends also use several relational maintenance behaviors—such as humor and gossip, avoidance of negativity, and no flirting—that are not used by romantic partners (Guerrero & Chavez, 2005; Messman et al., 2000). Together, these results indicate that both the frequency and the type of relational maintenance behaviors used by relational partners depend on the type of relationship in which the partners are involved.

RELATIONAL MAINTENANCE BEHAVIORS IN THE SIBLING RELATIONSHIP

Within the past decade, researchers have turned their attention to the study of relational maintenance behaviors in adult sibling relationships. Adult siblings are considered to be "permanent but flexible members of [their] social networks, whose roles…are renegotiated in light of changing circumstances and competing obligations" (White, 2001, p. 557). As part of this research community, I have conducted a series of studies with my undergraduate students, my graduate students, and my colleagues on the relational maintenance behaviors used by adult siblings. To date, our collective research has concluded that not only do adult siblings use relational maintenance behaviors in their relationships, but that the use of these relational maintenance behaviors is associated with

a variety of positive feelings (i.e., liking, trust, commitment, satisfaction, solidarity, and psychological closeness) directed toward their siblings (Eidsness & Myers, in press; Goodboy, Myers, & Patterson, 2009; Myers, Brann, & Rittenour, 2008; Myers, 2001, 2008; Myers & Goodboy, 2009; Myers & Members of COM 200, 2001; Myers & Weber, 2004). This research can be divided into three segments: the initial foray into the identification of adult siblings' use of relational maintenance behaviors, the exploration of adult siblings' use of relational maintenance behaviors across the sibling lifespan, and the role relational maintenance behaviors play in functional adult sibling relationships.

INITIAL IDENTIFICATION OF ADULT SIBLINGS' USE OF RELATIONAL MAINTENANCE BEHAVIORS

In the first study (Myers & Members of COM 200, 2001), we (my undergraduate students enrolled in a communication research methods course I was teaching and I) examined the extent to which siblings use each of the five relational maintenance behaviors identified by Stafford and Canary (1991). Using a sample of 262 adult siblings who ranged in age from 18 to 90 years, we found that although siblings use all five of these relational maintenance behaviors, they do have a preference for using some relational maintenance behaviors over other relational maintenance behaviors. Specifically, we found that siblings report using (in descending order) tasks, positivity, assurances, networks, and openness.

Surprisingly, the most frequently reported relational maintenance behavior used by siblings was *tasks*. Recall that tasks involve both partners participating in and sharing responsibility for tasks unique to the relationship (Canary & Stafford, 1992). For adult siblings, tasks may be an important relational maintenance behavior for two reasons. First, adult siblings may use the tasks relational maintenance behavior as a way to fulfill their familial obligations, particularly because adult siblings are expected to serve as a source of support and responsibility across the lifespan (Connidis, 2005) and often are committed to helping each other morally, emotionally, and financially throughout their lives (Kahn, 1983). These obligations may be magnified once adult siblings start families of their own; in addition to the parental or spousal roles that they play, they also must contend with the new roles (e.g., aunt or uncle, sibling-in-law) that emerge within the context of the extended family. These roles can be strengthened or weakened through attendance at holiday events and celebrations of family member milestones such as birthdays, graduations, weddings, and anniversaries or having to address issues such as divorce, remarriage, and conflict with sibling's spouses. Adult siblings also have to confront issues associated with the care and well-being of their parents, requiring siblings to work together as caregivers (Matthews & Rosner, 1988). Although these tasks may not always be perceived as enjoyable, these tasks may be considered instrumental to siblings during adulthood. Second, it is possible that siblings consider staying in touch with each other as a task. Connidis and Campbell (1995) reported that sibling contact becomes more of a task as siblings marry and start families of their own. At the same time, siblings tend to stay in greater touch when they live geographically closer together (Lee, Mancini, & Maxwell, 1990).

For some siblings, the quality of their relationship may be reflected through the use of the *positivity* relational maintenance behavior. Positivity, which is defined as communicating in a cheerful, optimistic manner (Canary & Stafford, 1992), may explain why siblings are communicatively satisfied in their interactions with each other. When siblings report high amounts of communication satisfaction in their interactions with each other, they indicate that these interactions lack verbal aggression and teasing (Martin, Anderson, Burant, & Weber, 1997). Satisfied siblings also report greater feelings of solidarity, self-disclosure, and trust with each other (Myers, 1998). In a study conducted with another group of undergraduate students (Myers et al., 1999), certain dimensions of relational communication were found to be related to sibling communication satisfaction. We discovered that siblings who are cooperative and supportive, are willing to listen as well as speak,

act involved in the interaction, share demographic and attitudinal attributes, and remain calm and poised impact positively their siblings' perceived communication satisfaction. The bottom line is that when siblings are relationally and communicatively satisfied, they make an effort to behave in ways that demonstrate their commitment to each other (Myers & Bryant, 2008). Some examples of these behaviors include participating in shared hobbies, having the same interests, and merging their groups of friends.

The third most frequently used relational maintenance behavior was *assurances*. Assurances center on partners either implicitly or explicitly stressing their desire to remain involved in the relationship (Canary & Stafford, 1992). Because the sibling relationship is involuntary, it might be expected that siblings would not utilize this relational maintenance behavior. However, there is evidence that suggests siblings are interested in engaging in communication that stresses their commitment to each other. For example, my undergraduate students and I found that when siblings establish relational intimacy, they treat each other as equals, establish rapport, engage in self-disclosure, and regard each other as friends during their interactions (Myers et al., 1999). As such, siblings stress their commitment to each other when they engage in communication that not only is emotionally and affectionately supportive (Rittenour, Myers, & Brann, 2007), but indicates an interest in maintaining the relationship. In another study, my colleague Ronda Knox and I (Myers & Knox, 1998) found that regardless of sibling age, siblings use affectively-oriented skills (i.e, communication skills centered on the management of affect) at a higher rate than non-affectively-oriented skills (i.e., communication skills centered on the management of communication activity). Affectively-oriented skills, such as providing comfort and being supportive, are perceived to be used more frequently by siblings than nonaffectively-oriented skills, such as being able to tell jokes and stories. We concluded that siblings use affectively-oriented skills at a higher rate because providing each other with psychological and social support is one way to indicate an interest in remaining emotionally involved in the relationship.

Assurances also may be a by-product of the emotional attachment siblings feel with one another. Siblings who feel closer emotionally confide in each other, talk to each other on the telephone, and see each other in person more often than siblings who are less closer emotionally (Connidis & Campbell, 1995). This mutual confiding also is one reason why some siblings consider each other to be best or close friends (Connidis, 1989b; White & Riedmann, 1992) and why siblings feel responsible for each other's welfare (Lee et al., 1990). Siblings who feel close to each other also interact more frequently and with a greater breadth and depth of topics (Rocca & Martin, 1998).

Networks, which involve both partners relying on common affiliations and relationships (Canary & Stafford, 1992), may be one relational maintenance behavior that always is present over the sibling lifespan. Nicholson (1999) found that as youngsters and adolescences, siblings form alliances with each other and these alliances are considered to be a functional part of family life. He identified several reasons why siblings develop alliances. Two reasons—"to improve, develop, or reconcile relationships with someone" and "to do something together" (p. 12) —are particularly relevant to sibling relational maintenance. Not only do siblings have rules for creating an alliance, but they also develop sanctions and penalties for siblings who break these rules. As siblings move into adulthood, their alliances may be dependent on their marital and parental status. For example, Connidis (1989a; Connidis & Campbell, 1995) found that unmarried adults, childless adults, and widowed adults remain in greater contact with their siblings than married adults and adults with children. Unmarried and childless adults also rely on their siblings for social, emotional, and instrumental support more so than married adults and adults with children (Campbell, Connidis, & Davies, 1999; Miner & Uhlenberg, 1997). Thus, the extent to which siblings depend on each other or spend time together may exert a positive influence on the manner in which they choose to maintain their relationships.

The least frequently used relational maintenance behavior was *openness*. Openness, which involves direct discussions about the relationship (Stafford et al., 2000) and allows for the expression of feelings, thoughts, and emotions (Canary & Stafford, 1992), may not be as central to the sibling relationship due to the fact that the sibling relationship cannot be terminated. Unlike romantic relationships that rely on intimacy and self-disclosure to stimulate and sustain growth, siblings can (and will) remain siblings regardless of emotional involvement and/or investment. Although self-disclosure is considered to be an important behavior in intimate relationships, sibling self-disclosure is used primarily to convey information and to receive information from one another (Dolgin & Lindsay, 1999). Pulakos (1989) reported that young adult siblings tend to be more open with their friends than with each other on a number of topics, including money, sex, romantic partners, childhood memories, and important decisions; parents/siblings is the only topic discussed more with siblings than friends. As such, openness may not be a frequently used relational maintenance behavior because openness is not essential to maintaining the sibling bond. Although Floyd (1997) discovered that the breadth and depth of sibling self-disclosure is related positively to perceptions of liking, loving, and commitment, it is possible for adult siblings to be satisfied with their interactions without engaging in a wide breadth or depth of self-disclosure (Myers, 1998).

ADULT SIBLINGS' USE OF RELATIONAL MAINTENANCE BEHAVIORS ACROSS THE SIBLING LIFESPAN

Because adult siblings often are separated by geographic distance and their contact may be limited to mediated communication (e.g., telephone, e-mail) or infrequent visits (e.g., holidays, family reunions, and vacations), my colleagues and I were interested in whether the use of these relational maintenance behaviors remains constant or fluctuates across the stages of the sibling lifespan. Researchers (Arnett, 1998; Goetting, 1986) have posited that the adult sibling relationship progresses through three stages. The first stage is emerging adulthood, which occurs when individuals are between the ages of 18 to 25 years (Arnett, 2000). During this stage, individuals begin to distance themselves physically and emotionally from their siblings, increase their dependence on their friends and their romantic partners, and decrease their involvement (e.g., time, interaction) with their siblings (Arnett, 2001; Pulakos, 1989; Scharf, Shulman, & Avigad-Spitz, 2005). In a study using a sample of 153 emerging adult siblings, we (Eidsness & Myers, in press) found that they reported using (in descending order) the tasks, positivity, networks, assurances, and openness relational maintenance behaviors with their siblings.

The second stage is early and middle adulthood, which occurs when individuals are between the ages of 26 to 54 years (Myers & Goodboy, 2006). In this stage, individuals no longer reside with their families of origin and become actively involved with a family of their own that has formed through marriage or cohabitation or for economic reasons (Goetting, 1986). During this stage, individuals adopt an ambivalent stance regarding their sibling relationships: on one hand, they view their sibling relationships as less obligatory (White, 2001) due to a strong focus on their own marital relationships, their children, and their careers (Connidis, 1992); on the other hand, they consider their siblings to be peers and friends (Van Volkom, 2006). In a study using a sample of 122 early and middle adulthood siblings, we (Myers et al., 2008) found that early and middle adulthood siblings reported using (in descending order) the tasks, positivity, networks, assurances, and openness relational maintenance behaviors. The fact that early and middle adulthood siblings report that tasks is the most frequently used relational maintenance behavior is interesting, given that they no longer reside in the same home with their siblings and they often are separated by time and distance. However, it is likely that adult siblings remain loyal to each other, which Gold (1989) characterized as a sense of family obligation rather than a sense of personal involvement. Loyal siblings provide instrumental support

(e.g., childcare, transportation, and household help), assist in times of family crises, and attend family events; they also continue to provide each other with emotional and psychological support in addition to serving as sources of affirmation and advice (Boland, 2007; Depner & Ingersoll-Dayton, 1988; Goetting, 1986; White & Riedmann, 1992). Thus, sibling loyalty during this stage may explain why early and middle adulthood siblings use tasks most frequently to maintain their relationships.

The third stage is late adulthood, which occurs when individuals are age 55 or older (Myers & Goodboy, 2006), are no longer responsible for their offspring, and (may) have entered into retirement from their vocation (Goetting, 1986). During this stage, the sibling relationship takes on a renewed importance and individuals resolve their sibling rivalries, validate their sibling relationships by engaging in shared reminiscence, and intensify their emotional bond (Cicirelli & Nussbaum, 1989; Goetting, 1986). In a study using a sample of 193 late adulthood siblings, we (Goodboy et al., 2009) found that they reported using (in descending order) the positivity, tasks, conflict management, assurances, advice, networks, and openness relational maintenance behaviors with their siblings.

Collectively, these findings support the notion that adult siblings' use of relational maintenance behaviors remains constant across the three stages of the sibling lifespan. To further corroborate this finding, as well as to identify whether adult siblings use relational maintenance behaviors unique to the sibling relationship, I (Myers, 2008) conducted a study with a sample of 640 adult siblings whose ages ranged from 18 to 82 years. They were asked to indicate the extent to which they used 53 behaviors to maintain their sibling relationships. From this list of 53 behaviors, factor analysis resulted in the emergence of five relational maintenance behaviors specific to the adult sibling relationship: confirmation, tasks, networks, avoidance of negativity, and humor. (Recall that the positivity, openness, assurances, networks, and tasks relational maintenance behaviors used by adult siblings were originally derived from research conducted on romantic partners.) *Confirmation* refers to the behaviors siblings use to validate their involvement in each other's lives and stress their commitment to the relationship, *tasks* refers to the shared activities in which siblings engage to fulfill their obligations and responsibilities to both each other and their family of origin, *networks* refers to the social and group memberships shared by siblings, *avoidance of negativity* refers to siblings' intentional avoidance of behaviors that might contain criticism or evaluation, and *humor* refers to the behaviors that siblings use to amuse and entertain each other.

Generally, adult siblings' use of these five specific relational maintenance behaviors were found to remain constant across the three stages of the sibling lifespan with three exceptions: emerging adult siblings use the humor relational maintenance behavior more frequently than late adulthood siblings, early and middle adulthood siblings use the tasks relational maintenance behavior more frequently than emerging adult siblings, and late adulthood siblings use the avoidance of negativity relational maintenance behavior more frequently than emerging adult siblings. Furthermore, it was found that adult siblings are more likely to use these five relational maintenance behaviors—regardless of the stage of the sibling lifespan—when they remain committed to each other, trust and like each other, and are satisfied with their relationships.

THE ROLE RELATIONAL MAINTENANCE BEHAVIORS PLAY IN FUNCTIONAL ADULT SIBLING RELATIONSHIPS

Aside from the frequency with which adult siblings use specific relational maintenance behaviors, four other general research findings garnered from this collective body of research are worth acknowledging. First, female siblings generally use relational maintenance behaviors at a higher rate than male siblings and female-female sibling dyads generally use relational maintenance behaviors at a higher rate than male-male sibling dyads or cross-sex sibling dyads (Myers & Members of COM 200, 2001). Second, adult siblings involved in intimate sibling relationships generally use

relational maintenance behaviors more frequently than adult siblings involved in congenial, loyal, or apathetic sibling relationships and use a greater number of communication channels (e.g., face-to-face, telephone, and e-mail) to maintain their relationships (Myers & Goodboy, 2009). Third, whether early and middle adulthood siblings use relational maintenance behaviors is dependent, in part, on if they are psychologically close with their siblings and if they are motivated to communicate their caring for and appreciation toward their siblings (Myers et al., 2008).

Fourth, adult siblings report that they use relational maintenance behaviors more strategically than they do routinely (Myers, Byrnes, Frisby, & Mansson, 2009). Recall that when individuals use relational maintenance behaviors strategically, they do so intentionally and consciously as a means to preserve their relationships; when they use relational maintenance behaviors routinely, they do so without putting much thought into why or how they use the behaviors. We posited that adults use relational maintenance behaviors strategically more so than routinely as a way to purposely remain connected to their siblings. Because sibling contact wanes once siblings reach emerging adulthood, strategically engaging in relational maintenance behaviors enables siblings to seemingly remain involved in each other's lives despite limited contact, time spent together, or other relational (e.g., romantic partner, children) demands. For example, although I do not speak with my sisters frequently on the telephone and our e-mail communication is sporadic, one way in which I strategically choose to maintain our relationship is to send holiday cards (often accompanied by gifts) every Halloween, Valentine's Day, and Easter to Hailey and Jenna (Michelle's children) and to Pepsi, Sage, and Bella (Susan's dogs, whom she considers to be her children). Doing so signifies to them that not only am I committed to maintaining our relationship—even though we do not talk that often—but also that I cherish my relationships with their children, whom undoubtedly maintain the most important presence in their lives.

CONCLUSION

Through communication, individuals can use a variety of behaviors to maintain their relationships. The adult sibling relationship is no exception. Although the sibling relationship is involuntary, most siblings have a commitment to the relationship that extends beyond sustaining obligatory, familial ties (Cicirelli, 1991) because feeling good about a sibling is a rewarding experience (Bedford, 1995). By using relational maintenance behaviors, siblings are able to provide emotional, moral, and psychological support; fulfill familial responsibilities; engage in shared activities; and remain involved in each other's lives. The use of these behaviors may indeed explain why the sibling relationship is important to adults (Van Volkom, 2006), why the sibling relationship is generally considered to be a positive experience (Pulakos, 1987), and why adult siblings are committed to maintaining this relationship (Crispell, 1996).

REFERENCES

Arnett, J. J. (1998). Learning to stand alone: The contemporary American transition to adulthood in cultural and historical context. *Human Development, 41*, 295–315.

Arnett, J. J. (2000). Emerging adulthood: A theory of development from the late teens through the twenties. *American Psychologist, 55*, 469–480.

Arnett, J. J. (2001). Conceptions of the transition to adulthood: Perspective from adolescence through midlife. *Journal of Adult Development, 8*, 133–143.

Bedford, V. H. (1995). Sibling relationships in middle and old age. In R. Blieszner & V. H. Bedford (Eds.), *Handbook of aging and the family* (pp. 201–222). Westport, CT: Greenwood Press.

Boland, S. (2007, March). *Social support and sibling relationships in middle adulthood.* Paper presented at the annual meeting of Eastern Psychological Association, Philadelphia, PA.

Campbell, L. D., Connidis, I. A., & Davies, L. (1999). Sibling ties in later life: A social network analysis. *Journal of Family Issues, 20*, 114–148.

Canary, D. J., & Stafford, L. (1992). Relational maintenance strategies and equity in marriage. *Communication Monographs, 59*, 244–267.

Canary, D. J., & Stafford, L. (1994). Maintaining relationships through strategic and routine interactions. In D. J. Canary & L. Stafford (Eds.), *Communication and relational maintenance* (pp. 1–22). New York, NY: Academic Press.

Canary, D. J., Stafford, L., Hause, K. S., & Wallace, L. A. (1993). An inductive analysis of relational maintenance strategies: Comparisons among lovers, relatives, friends, and others. *Communication Research Reports, 10*, 5–14.

Cicirelli, V. G. (1991). Sibling relationships in adulthood. In S. K. Pfeifer & M. B. Sussman (Eds.), *Families: Intergenerational and generational connections* (pp. 291–310). New York, NY: Haworth Press.

Cicirelli, V. G., & Nussbaum, J. F. (1989). Relationships with siblings in later life." In J. F. Nussbaum (Ed.), *Life-span communication: Normative processes* (pp. 283–299). Hillsdale, NJ: Erlbaum.

Connidis, I. A. (1989a). Contact between siblings in later life. *Canadian Journal of Sociology, 14*, 429–441.

Connidis, I. A. (1989b). Siblings as friends in later life. *American Behavioral Scientist, 33*, 81–93.

Connidis, I. A. (1992). Life transitions and the adult sibling tie: A qualitative study. *Journal of Marriage and the Family, 54*, 972–982.

Connidis, I. A. (2005). Sibling ties across time: The middle and later years. In M. L. Johnson (Ed.), *The Cambridge handbook of age and ageing* (pp. 429–436). Cambridge, England: Cambridge University Press.

Connidis, I. A., & Campbell, L. D. (1995). Closeness, confiding, and contact among siblings in middle and late adulthood. *Journal of Family Issues, 16*, 722–745.

Crispell, D. (1996). The sibling syndrome. *American Demographics, 18*(8), 24–31.

Dainton, M. (2007). Attachment and marital maintenance. *Communication Quarterly, 55*, 283–298.

Dainton, M., & Stafford, L. (1993). Routine maintenance behaviors: A comparison of relationship type, partner similarity and sex differences. *Journal of Social and Personal Relationships, 10,* 255–271.

Depner, C. E., & Ingersoll-Dayton, B. (1988). Supportive relationships in later life. *Psychology and Aging, 3,* 348–357.

Dindia, K., & Canary, D. J. (1993). Definitions and theoretical perspectives on maintaining relationships. *Journal of Social and Personal Relationships, 10,* 163–173.

Dolgin, K. G., & Lindsay, K. R. (1999). Disclosure between college students and their siblings. *Journal of Family Psychology, 13,* 393–400.

Eidsness, M. A., & Myers, S. A. (2008). The use of sibling relational maintenance behaviors among emerging adults. *Journal of the Speech and Theatre Association of Missouri, 38,* 1–14.

Floyd, K. (1997). Brotherly love II: A developmental perspective on liking, love, and closeness in the fraternal dyad. *Journal of Family Psychology, 11,* 196–209.

Goetting, A. (1986). The developmental tasks of siblingship over the life cycle. *Journal of Marriage and the Family, 48,* 703–714.

Gold, D. T. (1989). Sibling relationships in old age: A typology. *International Journal of Aging and Human Development, 28,* 37–51.

Goodboy, A. K., Myers, S. A., & Patterson, B. P. (2009). Investigating elderly sibling types, relational maintenance, and lifespan affect, cognition, and behavior. *Atlantic Journal of Communication, 17,* 1–9.

Guerrero, L. K., & Bachman, G. F. (2006). Associations among relational maintenance behaviors, attachment-style categories, and attachment dimensions. *Communication Studies, 57,* 341–361.

Guerrero, L. K., & Chavez, A. M. (2005). Relational maintenance in cross-sex friendships characterized by different types of romantic intent: An exploratory study. *Western Journal of Communication, 69,* 339–358.

Haas, S. M., & Stafford, L. (1998). An initial examination of maintenance behaviors in gay and lesbian relationships. *Journal of Social and Personal Relationships, 15,* 846–855.

Kahn, M. D. (1983). Sibling relationships in later life. *Medical aspects of human sexuality, 17,* 94–103.

Lee, T. R., Mancini, J. A., & Maxwell, J. W. (1990). Sibling relationships in adulthood: Contact patterns and motivations. *Journal of Marriage and Family, 52,* 431–440.

Martin, M. M., Anderson, C. M., Burant, P. A., & Weber, K. (1997). Verbal aggression in sibling relationships. *Communication Quarterly, 45,* 304–317.

Matthews, S. H., & Rosner, T. T. (1988). Shared filial responsibility: The family as the primary caregiver. *Journal of Marriage and the Family, 50,* 185–195.

Messman, S. J., Canary, D. J., & Hause, K. S. (2000). Motives to remain platonic, equity, and the use of maintenance strategies in opposite-sex friendships. *Journal of Social and Personal Relationships, 17,* 67–94.

Miner, S., & Uhlenberg, P. (1997). Intragenerational proximity and the social life of siblings after midlife. *Family Relations, 46,* 145–154.

Myers, S. A. (1998). Sibling communication satisfaction as a function of interpersonal solidarity, individualized trust, and self-disclosure. *Communication Research Reports, 15,* 309–317.

Myers, S. A. (2001, November). *A typological analysis of sibling relational maintenance behaviors.* Paper presented at the meeting of the National Communication Association, Atlanta, GA.

Myers, S. A. (2008, November). *An investigation of relational maintenance behaviors across the adult sibling lifespan.* Paper presented at the meeting of the National Communication Association, San Diego, CA.

Myers, S. A., Brann, M., & Rittenour, C. E. (2008). Interpersonal communication motives as a predictor of early and middle adulthood siblings' use of relational maintenance behaviors. *Communication Research Reports, 25,* 155–167.

Myers, S. A., & Bryant, L. E. (2008). The use of behavioral indicators of sibling commitment among emerging adults. *Journal of Family Communication, 8,* 101–125.

Myers, S. A., Byrnes, K., Frisby, & Mansson, D. A. (2009, November). *Adult siblings' use of affectionate communication as a relational maintenance behavior.* Paper presented at the meeting of the National Communication Association, Chicago, IL.

Myers, S. A., Cavanaugh, E. K., Dohmen, L. M., Freeh, J. L., Huang, V. W., Kapler, M. R., Leonatti, A . . . . (1999). Perceived sibling use of relational communication messages and sibling satisfaction, liking, and loving. *Communication Research Reports, 16,* 339–352.

Myers, S. A., & Goodboy, A. K. (2006). Perceived sibling use of verbally aggressive messages across the lifespan. *Communication Research Reports, 23,* 1–11.

Myers, S. A., & Goodboy, A. K. (2009, April). *Relational maintenance behaviors, relational characteristics, and communication channel use among adult siblings.* Paper presented at the meeting of the Eastern Communication Association, Philadelphia, PA.

Myers, S. A., & Knox, R. L. (1998). Perceived sibling use of functional communication skills. *Communication Research Reports, 15,* 397–405.

Myers, S. A., & Members of COM 200. (2001). Relational maintenance behaviors in the sibling relationship. *Communication Quarterly, 49,* 19–34.

Myers, S. A., & Weber, K. D. (2004). Preliminary development of a measure of sibling relational maintenance behaviors: Scale development and initial findings. *Communication Quarterly, 52,* 334–346.

Nicholson, J. H. (1999, November). *Sibling alliance rules.* Paper presented at the meeting of the National Communication Association, Chicago, IL.

Pulakos, J. (1987). Brothers and sisters: Nature and importance of the adult bond. *Journal of Psychology, 121,* 521–522.

Pulakos, J. (1989). Young adult relationships: Siblings and Friends. *Journal of Psychology, 123,* 237–244.

Rabby, M. K. 2007. Relational maintenance and the influence of commitment in online and off-line relationships. *Communication* Studies, *58,* 315–337.

Rittenour, C. E., Myers, S. A., & Brann, M. (2007). Commitment and emotional closeness in the sibling relationship. *Southern Communication Journal, 72,* 169–183.

Rocca, K. A., & Martin, M. M. (1998). The relationship between willingness to communicate and solidarity with frequency, breadth, and depth of communication in the sibling relationship. *Communication Research Reports, 15,* 82–90.

Scharf, M., Shulman, S., & Avigad-Spitz, L. (2005). Sibling relationships in emerging adulthood and in adolescence. *Journal of Adolescent Research, 20,* 64–90.

Stafford, L., & Canary, D. J. (1991). Maintenance strategies and romantic relationship type, gender and relational characteristics. *Journal of Social and Personal Relationships, 8,* 217–242.

Stafford, L., & Canary, D. J. (2006). Equity and interdependence as predictors of relational maintenance strategies. *Journal of Family Communication, 6,* 227–254.

Stafford, L., Dainton, M., & Haas, S. (2000). Measuring routine and strategic relational maintenance: Scale revision, sex versus gender roles, and the prediction of relational characteristics. *Communication Monographs, 67,* 306–323.

Van Volkom, M. (2006). Sibling relationships in middle and older adulthood: A review of the literature. *Marriage & Family Review, 40,* 151–170.

White, L. (2001). Sibling relationships over the life course: A panel analysis. *Journal of Marriage and Family, 63,* 555–568.

White, L. K., & Riedmann, A. (1992). Ties among adult siblings. *Social Forces, 71,* 85–102.

QUESTIONS/THOUGHTS

1. Dainton and Stafford (1993) noted that relational maintenance behaviors can be used either strategically or routinely. Would you consider your use of relational maintenance behaviors with your siblings to be primarily strategic or routine? Give examples of each.

2. Describe sibling alliances you have witnessed or experienced. What accounted for the development of the alliances? What communicative strategies were used to

reinforce the alliances and/or to keep other siblings at a distance?

3. As you move through the three stages of the sibling lifespan, how might your *use* of relational maintenance behaviors change? How might your *choice* of relational maintenance behaviors change?

4. To what extent is your use of relational maintenance behaviors with your siblings dependent on your gender or your siblings' gender? Explain how gender influences your relational maintenance practices.

Mother–Child Play: Collaboration or Power Struggle?

STEVEN R. WILSON, FELICIA ROBERTS, AND ELIZABETH A. MUNZ

"The stretching of family boundaries begins in childhood" (Karraker & Grochowski, 2006, p. 346). One of the most complicated aspects of raising children involves letting go, allowing a child to make the next move toward independence. For most parents this is a bittersweet process; for some parents letting go becomes a highly conflictual process. When children are young, renegotiation of power involves subtle shifts managed through verbal and nonverbal communication by parents and their offspring. "The pushes and pulls among family members as they work together to meet individual and family needs require negotiation" (Karraker & Grochowski, 2006, p. 346). Yet, in healthy families, the end goal is to empower every family member.

Negotiating family power does not come easily to all parents. Although some parents make very conscious choices about raising children, many rely on their family-of-origin or cultural patterns to raise the next generation without considering any alternatives. In certain cases, positive outcomes result; in other cases, struggles abound. The transactional nature of relationships, or the mutual influence process, serves as the unpinning

for the connection and interaction between a parent and a child. Therefore, styles of play or conflict may work well for one parent-child dyad and become problematic for another one, even in the same family.

Family power struggles are natural and even healthy as long as one person is not always overpowered. Part of parenting involves "letting go" as a child struggles to learn new ways to gain independence. Physically abusive parents are characterized by the following patterns in face-to face family interactions: (1) frequency, duration, intensity and sequencing of negative parenting behaviors, (2) verbal aggression and physical aggression are linked, (3) abuse reflects how parents form/ pursue interaction goals, (4) thinking and feeling differently during family interaction and (5) holding distorted perceptions of their child as an interaction partner (Wilson, 2006).

In the United States corporal punishment, such as slapping, hitting, grabbing, or shoving is declining; it is highest with younger children and declines through adolescence (Olson, DeFrain & Skogrand, 2008). Do you believe these changes might contribute to the use of verbal aggression? If so, what might be done to also reduce the amount of verbal aggression?

REFERENCES

Karraker, M. W., & Grochowshi, J. R. (2006). *Families with futures.* Mahwah, NJ: Lawrence Erlbaum.

Olson, D. H., DeFrain, J., & Skogrand, L. (2008). *Marriage & families: Intimacy, diversity and strengths.* New York, NY: McGraw-Hill.

Wilson, S. R. (2006). Child physical abuse. In K. M. Galvin & P. J. Cooper (Eds.), *Making connections: Readings in relational communication* (4th ed., pp. 260–265). New York, NY: Oxford University Press.

The mother and child relationship represents one of the most powerful human bonds. Such a connection is seen as uniquely special; many consider it a cornerstone for a child's well-being and development. Yet, just because persons in a relationship hold the label of "mother" or the label of child does not predict with accuracy the nature or quality of their tie.

For many, the word "play" brings back fond childhood memories. Although difficult to define precisely, researchers have identified several typical elements of play, including that it is: (a) intrinsically self motivated (done for the satisfaction of doing it), (b) freely chosen by participants (children forced into an activity are unlikely to view it as play), (c) pleasurable, (d) non-literal (often involves an element of make-believe), and (e) actively engaged in, physically and/or psychologically (Hughes, 2010). Through play, children use their creativity and imagination, practice adult roles, learn to work in groups and manage conflict, address fears in a non-threatening environment, and discover their own interests (Ginsburg, 2007). Children sometimes play alone, but often play with siblings, peers, parents, and other adult caretakers. By joining their children in play, parents have the chance to see the world through their child's eyes while communicating that they are responsive and involved with their child (Ginsburg, 2007).

Although play is "fun" rather than "serious," observing parents and children playing together can reveal important insights about the parent–child relationship. We have studied how mothers who self-report a tendency towards verbal aggressiveness play with their children. We found that they often try to control the interaction rather than following their child's lead. In other words, a tendency to be verbally aggressive is associated with broader patterns of parenting that may undermine children's self-esteem or encourage oppositional child behavior even in situations that are supposed to be fun. To clarify this point, we provide a brief background on verbal aggression, describe our own research on parent–child play, and discuss what the findings tell us about the role of communication in defining healthy parent–child relationships.

VERBAL AGGRESSION AND PARENTING

Infante and Rancer (1996) define verbal aggression as behaviors that attack another's self-concept in order to inflict psychological pain (e.g., feelings of humiliation or embarrassment). They distinguish verbal aggression from argumentation: the former occurs when parents attack their child personally whereas the latter occurs when parents explain why they disagree with their child's ideas. Examples of verbal aggression include calling a child "dumb," "lazy," or "no good" as well as yelling or swearing at a child.

Although all parents say things that they later regret, many studies have found that frequent parental verbal aggression is associated with negative outcomes for children, including low self-esteem, depression and anxiety, having trouble making friends, getting into fights with other children, and poor school performance (Moore & Pepler, 2006; Solomon & Serres, 1999; Teicher, Samson, Polcari, & McGreenery, 2006; Vissing, Straus, Gelless, & Harrop, 1991). These studies show that: (a) parental verbal aggression is associated with negative outcomes for children even after controlling for parents' physical aggression (e.g., slapping, shoving), (b) the frequency of parental verbal aggression is as good—if not a better—predictor of negative outcomes for children as is parental physical aggression, and

(c) these negative outcomes occur regardless of whether children are in preschool, elementary school, or high school.

In the communication discipline, a large body of research has focused on trait verbal aggression (VA), or individual differences in people's general tendency to be verbally aggressive. Most studies measure people's trait VA using Infante and Wigley's (1986) verbal aggressiveness scale, which asks respondents to rate whether statements such as the following are true of them: "When individuals are stubborn, I use insults to soften their stubbornness" and "If individuals I am trying to influence really deserve it, I attack their character." Parents who score high on this measure are thought to be extremely sensitive to situational stressors (e.g., a child who repeatedly ignores his/her parent's reminders that it is bed time) and hence more prone to using verbal aggression. Parents high in trait VA report being angry with their children more often and spanking their children more frequently compared to parents who score low on the scale (Bayer & Cegala, 1992, Roberto, Carlyle, & McClure, 2006).

Although parents who self-report a tendency to be verbally aggressive may be most likely to act directly on this predisposition (i.e., attack their child verbally) when faced with situational stressors, the predisposition may be evident in other ways that parents behave even in situations that are much less stressful. Our own research has investigated differences in mother-child play when mothers are high versus low in trait VA.

MATERNAL TRAIT VA AND MOTHER–CHILD PLAY

In our research, we observed 40 mothers playing with one of their children between the ages of 3 and 8 years (Roberts, Wilson, Delaney, & Rack, 2009; Wilson, Roberts, Rack & Delaney, 2008). Mothers were recruited from two social service agencies in a large metropolitan area and paid $50 for participating. On average, mothers were 31 years and had completed 13 years of education. About two-thirds described their ethnic background as "African American," 20% as "Hispanic/Latina" and the rest as "European American," "Asian American,"

or "Other." About 60% were single mothers who lived with their children, extended family, and/or an unmarried partner. Flyers advertising the study (approved by our university) were posted at the social service agencies, and mothers contacted us to set a time to complete the study.

Upon arriving at the social service agency, each mother was videotaped playing with her child for approximately 12 minutes. A blanket was placed on the floor of a conference room and a box of toys (e.g., puzzles, blocks) was placed on the blanket. A camcorder on a tripod was set in the corner to videotape the play. The mother and child were told that they could play with one or several toys in any order that they chose. They were asked to stay on the blanket so that they would be in range of the camera. After 10 minutes, a researcher knocked on the door and said it was time to clean up. The mother had been instructed to put the toys back into the box at that point, making sure her child helped clean up. This cleanup period lasted about 2 minutes. Upon completing the play session, the mother responded to several questionnaires including the trait VA scale, after which we answered questions and thanked the mother and child for participating.

Initially we trained undergraduate coders to count the number of commands and suggestions each mother used during her play period (Wilson et al., 2008). Commands take the form of imperatives, such as "Take that out of the box" or "Help momma clean up." Suggestions propose a course of action for the child (or mother and child) in the form of a statement, such as "Let's do this" to "You gotta put it in the right hole" (explaining how to use a toy). Coders also identified any instances of verbal aggression or statements in which a mother communicated overt disapproval of her child (e.g., "You're lazy," or "It's no wonder your little brother doesn't like to play with you"). Other undergraduates were trained to rate the degree to which each child was cooperative during the play period. Child cooperation was defined as the degree to which the child's actions were in harmony with the apparent wishes of the mother, and demonstrated by behaviors such as a child complying with the mother's commands/suggestions as well as asking questions rather than demanding his/her own way. None of the undergraduate coders knew which mothers had scored high or low on the trait VA scale.

Several interesting findings emerged from these initial analyses. First, verbal aggression did not occur in these play-time interactions. The 40 mothers performed virtually no verbally aggressive behaviors as they played with their children. This may reflect that mothers were being videotaped, their children were actively engaged with new toys, and the play sessions were only 12 minutes long. The play periods did not contain the types of situational stressors (e.g., repeated child noncompliance) that would elicit verbally aggressive behavior. A second, key finding is that although mothers were not verbally aggressive, those mothers who scored high on the trait VA scale still used far more commands and suggestions during the play periods compared to mothers who scored low on trait VA. It is important to clarify that all mothers gave commands and suggestions as they played, but mothers high in trait VA did so especially often. For example, the 10 mothers who scored highest on the trait VA scale on average made more than 5 commands or suggestions during each minute of their play period, whereas the 10 mothers who scored lowest on trait VA made about 3 commands or suggestions per minute. Finally, children of mothers high in trait VA were rated as less cooperative than children of mothers low in trait VA. This occurred despite the fact that observers did not know which mothers were high or low in trait VA and even though most children appeared to enjoy the play.

Given these initial findings, we wondered: what were mothers high in trait VA doing with all those commands and suggestions? When low trait VA mothers made commands or suggestions, were they doing similar things? To answer these questions, we selected the four mothers from the overall sample who scored highest on the trait VA scale and the four who scored lowest for more detailed analysis (Roberts et al., 2009). The two subgroups were similar in terms of mothers' age, ethnicity, and education, and both contained preschool and elementary school-aged children. We created

detailed written transcripts for all eight play sessions, taking note of what mothers and children said and also nonverbal features such as vocal pitch, pauses, and gestures. We analyzed what child behaviors led up to mothers' commands and suggestions, what mothers were trying to accomplish with them, and how children responded, looking for differences that consistently distinguished high vs. low trait VA mothers.

Based on these follow-up analyses, we concluded that mothers high in trait VA not only used commands and suggestions more often than low trait VA mothers, they also approached the activity of "play" itself differently. High trait VA mothers tended to treat the play session as a "task" to be managed, and attempted to control the choice of activities and the manner in which activities were done. Low trait VA mothers tended to treat the play session as something to be done collaboratively with the child (i.e., play for play's sake), and hence used a variety of actions including commands and suggestions to support their child's playful pursuits.

Comparing how two mothers—one high in trait VA and the other low—initiate a new activity with their child should help illustrate this difference (for more examples, see Roberts et al., 2009). Excerpt 1 occurs at the start of the play period involving a high trait VA mother and her three-year old son. The mother (M) pulls a shape sorter from the box, but her child (C) is not particularly interested and keeps trying to return to the box of toys.

Excerpt 1 (Dyad 21)

1.	M: Wanna play with mommy?	*M pulls out shape sorter from box*
2.	C: Uh huh.	
3.	M: Come on.	
4.	(2 second pause)	*C turns back to box of toys*
5.	M: Come here let mommy show you.	*M's hand on C's shoulder, M squeezes and*
6.	*pulls slightly back*	
7.	M: Wait a minute.	*M removes toy from C's hand*

8. M: This next, okay?

9. C: M hm

10. M: Come right here. Put it right here.   *C again turns back to box of toys*

11. C: Look. Wait a minute.   *M puts her hand on child's lower arm and pulls toward her; C straightens his arm and lifts it out of her grasp*

In this example, the child already had pulled out a container of Lego blocks from the toy box, but his mother instead invites him to play with a different toy that she has selected: the shape sorter (line 1). Although the child initially accepts her invitation (line 2), his attention quickly returns to other toys in the box. The mother then uses a series of commands (lines 3, 5, 7–8, and 10–11) along with physical touch (lines 5–6 and 11–13) to prevent her son from moving towards other toys. Her verbal and nonverbal behavior indicate that her focus is on completing a particular game that she has chosen, and her son's interest in other toys is not encouraged. In the process, she sets up a power struggle in terms of who will decide what activities are to be performed.

Excerpt 2 involves a low trait VA mother and her 6 year old daughter. After putting together puzzles, they are transitioning to a new activity: drawing/writing on a pad of paper.

Excerpt 2 (Dyad 31)

1. C: Yeah. I wanna write some markers.

2. M: Here go some paper.

3. C: Kay.

4. M: What are we gonna do.   *M now has paper pad in her lap.*

5. C: We're gonna write   *C opening marker case*

6. M: We're gonna write your name then we're gonna draw.   *M & C set paper and markers on blanket in front of them*

7. M: I'm gonna write on one.

8. You're gonna write on one.   *M tears off a sheet of paper.*

9. C: Kay.

10. M: Watcha wanna write?

11. C: I don't know.

12. M: Or what you wanna draw?

13. (5 second pause)   *C kneels down in front of paper.*

14. M: Here you can write on this.   *M hands C pad, M picks up puzzle*

15. I'll write top of here.   *and puts her single sheet on it.*

16. C: I'm gonna write my name with a red marker.

17. M: I'm gonna draw.

18. C: I'm gonna write my name first. I'm gonna write my last name too.

In this example, the low trait VA mother does make several commands and suggestions (lines 6–7, 9, and 15). Yet this example differs in important ways from the first one. Here, the mother's commands and suggestions help set up a drawing activity (e.g., lines 15–16, where the mother gives them both something on which to draw) that she and her daughter have jointly chosen. The mother asks several questions to solicit her daughter's input (lines 4, 11, 13) and some of her suggestions elaborate on her daughter's answers (e.g., lines 5–6). By the end of the excerpt, the child describes her unique part of the activity (she's going to write both of her names even though her mother has started to draw). The daughter does not resist her mother's suggestions, perhaps because the activity is constructed collaboratively with the mother organizing some details while also inquiring about her daughter's plans or preferences.

IMPLICATIONS

Mothers who score high versus low in trait VA differ not just in how much verbally aggressive behavior they direct towards their children but also in how they orient to positive interactions such as play. Our research has implications for understanding the nature of trait VA, including what the trait VA scale actually measures (Infante & Wigley, 1986). Rather than only being hypersensitive to situational stressors, parents who score high on trait VA appear to be very sensitive to power or control even during positive parent-child interactions. High trait VA mothers in our study appeared to frame play sessions as situations in which they needed to take control as opposed to playing with their child for play's sake (Wilson et al., 2008). Our findings also may help explain at least part of the reason why children, as they get older, tend to be less satisfied with the parent-child relationship if their parents are high in trait VA (Beatty & Dobos, 1992). Play is supposed to be fun, but what messages do parents communicate to their child by playing in ways that downplay their child's preferences and limit their child's autonomy?

At a more practical level, our findings suggest that high trait VA parents would benefit not just from learning about the harmful nature of verbal aggression, but also from programs in which parents are encouraged to practice following their child's lead and side-stepping unnecessary power struggles with their children during play. One such parenting education program is the Incredible Years which was designed by Carolyn Webster-Stratton at the University of Washington (Webster-Stratton, Reid, & Hammond, 2001). The program helps parents develop positive relationships with their children, including children with conduct disorders. Training programs such as the Incredible Years would profit from considering how learning child-directed play may be especially valuable for particular types of parents such as parents who are high in trait VA.

REFERENCES

Bayer, C., & Cegala, D. (1992). Trait verbal aggressiveness and argumentativeness: Relationship with parenting style. *Western Journal of Communication*, 56, 301–310.

Beatty, M. J., & Dobos, J. A. (1992). Relationship between sons' perceptions of fathers' messages and satisfaction in adult son-father relationships. *Southern Communication Journal*, 57, 277–284.

Ginsburg, K. R. (2007). The importance of play in promoting healthy child development and maintaining strong parent-child bonds. *Pediatrics*, 119, 182–191.

Hughes, F. P. (2010). *Children, play, and development* (4th ed.). Thousand Oaks, CA: Sage.

Infante, D. A., & Rancer, A. S. (1996). Argumentativeness and verbal aggressiveness: Recent theory and research. In B. R. Burleson (Ed.), *Communication yearbook 19* (pp. 319–351). Thousand Oaks, CA: Sage.

Infante, D. A., & Wigley, C. J. (1986). Verbal aggressiveness: An interpersonal model and measure. *Communication Monographs*, 53, 61–69.

Moore, T. E., & Pepler, D. J. (2006). Wounding words: Maternal verbal aggression and children's adjustment. *Journal of Family Violence*, 21, 89–93.

Roberto, A. J., Carlyle, K. E., & McClure, L. (2006). Communication and corporal punishment: The relationship between parents' use of verbal and physical aggression. *Communication Research Reports*, 23, 27–33.

Roberts, F., Wilson, S. R., Delaney, J. E., & Rack, J. J. (2009). Distinguishing communication behaviors of mothers high and low in trait verbal aggressiveness: A qualitative analysis of mother-child playtime interactions. In D. D. Cahn (Ed.), *Family violence: Communication processes* (pp. 155–178). Albany, NY: State University of New York Press.

Solomon, C. R., & Serres, F. (1999). Effects of parental verbal aggression on children's self-esteem and school marks. *Child Abuse & Neglect*, 23, 339–351.

Teicher, M. H., Samson, J. A., Polcari, A., & McGreenery, C. E. (2006). Sticks, stones, and hurtful words: Relative effects of various forms of child maltreatment. *American Journal of Psychiatry*, 163, 993–1000.

Vissing, Y. M., Straus, M. A., Gelless, R. J., & Harrop, J. W. (1991). Verbal aggression by parents and psychosocial problems of children. *Child Abuse & Neglect*, 15, 223–238.

Webster-Stratton, C., Reid, M. J., & Hammond, M. (2001). Preventing conduct problems and promoting social competence: A parent and teacher training partnership in Head Start. *Journal of Clinical Child and Adolescent Psychology, 30,* 283–302.

Wilson, S. R., Roberts, F., Rack, J. J., & Delaney, J. E. (2008). Mothers' trait verbal aggressiveness as a predictor of maternal and child behaviors during playtime interactions. *Human Communication Research, 34,* 392–422.

QUESTIONS/THOUGHTS

1. What is trait VA and what is the impact of trait VA on children? Why might some parents consider verbal aggression to be necessary parenting behavior?

2. What are examples of verbally aggressive behavior? Are parents who are high in trait VA always verbally aggressive with their children? Why or why not?

3. What did the authors learn about the relationship between trait VA and how mothers' interacted with their children during play?

4. The authors conclude that mothers high in trait VA may use more commands because they view play as a task to be controlled compared with mothers low in trait VA who view play as a collaborative activity. What are some other reasons why mothers high in trait VA may use more commands?

B. Friends

INTRODUCTION

Friendship is clearly one of the most important contexts of interpersonal communication. Ever since childhood you have depended on friends to be your companions, listen to you, play with you, challenge you with different ideas, and teach you new things. Yet, as the articles in this section indicate, friendships are complicated. They take time, effort, patience, and commitment. Ongoing friendships are characterized by relational maintenance behaviors such as positivity, openness, commitment, and shared activities. Most friendships involve exchanging relational currencies and mutual self-disclosure.

Friendship changes across the lifespan. Peers are extremely important in our early years and during adolescence. Males' development generally occurs in larger groups with changing membership. Females tend to focus on friendships with one or two individuals. As children grow up in the U.S., friendship and peer acceptance become increasingly important; less time is spent with family. High school students and traditional college students find themselves regularly surrounded with friends and potential friends; as people age, they report that it becomes harder to make new friends.

In his book *Seinlanguage,* Jerry Seinfeld (1993, 159) captures the difficulty of making new friends after age 30:

> You're not interviewing, you're not looking at any new people, you're not interested in seeing any applications. They don't know the places, they don't know the food, they don't know the activities....
>
> Of course when you're a kid, you can be friends with anybody. There were almost no qualifications. If someone's in front of my house now, that's my friend, they're my friends, that's it. "Are you a grown-up. No? Great, c'mon in!

Even adults may take friends for granted, but once they move to a new town, change jobs, or lose a friend, they may find it takes great effort to make new friends. A columnist writing about the difficulty of finding friends in her 40s, was deluged with letters from readers reporting similar frustrations and a shared sense of estrangement (Paul, 1995). Many adults said that their lack of children kept them from community connections; others believed they were outsiders because of snobbishness, their newcomer status, or regional norms. One person wrote, "I've often felt that I'm standing outside looking through a window at a party to which I wasn't invited." From a *social exchange* perspective, connected individuals do not foresee rewards in adding new friends, whereas those without friends feel the costs of being isolated all too keenly. Today many people find and maintain friends through the Internet.

Although a valued friendship may appear to be easy to maintain, long-term, meaningful friendships take effort. According to Kory Floyd (2009), friendships have five common characteristics; they are voluntary, rule governed, usually formed between peers, differ by sex, and have a life span. There may be variations on these characteristics based on particular circumstances. A college athlete may become friends with a coach over four years and the tie is maintained for decades. Cross-sex business colleagues may find a friendship through countless hours of working on the same accounts. But most friendships operate according to spoken or unspoken rules that both understand.

Given the nation's history of immigration, American friends may depend on their close friends for social support and companionship whereas, in other countries, the extended family may fulfill more of these needs. Friends are often considered part of the voluntaristic family and, as such, may be seen as more important than distant blood relatives (Galvin, 2006).

As you read this section, consider how your own friendships have developed as you have matured. Has what you value in a friend changed? How have work or school commitments affected your ability to maintain or make new friends? How have factors, such as gender, age, or new technologies, impacted your friendship networks?

REFERENCES

Floyd, K. (2009). *Interpersonal communication*. New York, NY: McGraw-Hill.

Galvin, K. M. (2006). Diversity's impact on defining the family. In L. H. Turner & R. West (Eds.), *The family communication sourcebook* (pp. 3–19). Thousand Oaks, CA: Sage.

Paul, M. (1995, August 20). Lonely? Don't feel like the Lone Ranger. *Chicago Tribune* 6 pp. 1, 6.

Seinfeld, J. (1993). *Seinlanguage*. New York, NY: Bantam Books.

Being There for Friends

WILLIAM K. RAWLINS

In all stages of life, people rely upon their friends for help, support, commitment, love, and acceptance. However, the definition of what makes a good friend changes with age. Children could be best buddies with someone just because they were invited to their birthday party, or shared their chocolate chip cookie at lunch. And although the feelings of affection and bonding are no less important, there are usually much more challenging and complex ways to earn friendships for adults. According to Steve Duck (2007), "Your friendship obliges you to perform certain kinds of supportive actions and the persuasion to perform them is inherent in the acceptance of the role of friendship" (p. 165). The maintenance of adult friendships, as discussed in this chapter, depends upon the idea of "being there" for each other—"each other" being the operative term. This is often where social exchange theory comes into play; friendships are likely to thrive when both parties experience benefits.

Sometimes "being there" for others involves companionship. In his book, Friendship: An Exposé, author Joseph Epstein describes friendship as "the strongest of relationships not bound by or hostage to biology, which is to say, blood." (p. 2) and

emphasizes the importance of conversation among friends. He asserts that,"The best talkers are those who are devoted to keeping the conversation going. These same people frequently turn out also to be the best listeners" (p. 173). Although sharing activities and establishing rituals contribute to friendship maintenance, being able to really talk to each other about important issues and feelings move a friendship to another level of connection.

William (Bill) Rawlins suggests that "being there for friends" means different things to different individuals. Friendship research indicates individuals have varied goals for their friendships. For example, individuals with a strong focus on intimacy in their same-sex friendships exchange high levels of social support and self disclosure. They are also more likely to engage in constructive methods of resolving conflict (Sanderson, Rahm & Beigbeder, 2005). Those not seeking such strong intimacy are likely to contribute less social support and self disclosure in their friendships.

The following article highlights the distinction between agentic and communal relationships. In general, agentic friendships are begun rationally or conveniently based on joint activities or *projects. They are characterized by independence and maintained as long as the benefits outweigh the costs. The term "agentic" characterizes workplace friendships that are pleasant and satisfying but which fade if one member leaves. It also characterizes friendships limited to a particular activity, such as watching ballgames, playing video games, or shopping. Communal friendships, on the other hand, may develop through convenience or personal attraction and are characterized by mutual responsibilities or obligations, strong emotional attachment, and loyalty. Contact, openness, and cooperation characterize communal friendships. As you might guess, female relationships are more often communal, while male relationships are more often agentic.*

In this reading, Rawlins addresses the similarities and differences between male and female friendships, offering examples and explanations for how these relationships begin and are managed throughout adulthood. As you read this article, consider how your friendships have changed since you entered adulthood and ask yourself the question: What does the phrase "being there" for friends mean to you?

REFERENCES

Duck, S. (2007). *Human relationships* (4th ed.). Los Angeles, CA: Sage.

Epstein, J. (2006). *Friendship: An exposé.* New York, NY: Houghton Mifflin.

Sanderson, C. A., Rahm, K. S. & Beigbeder, S.A. (2005). The link between the pursuit of intimacy goals and satisfaction in close same-sex friendships: An examination of the underlying processes. *Journal of Social and Personal Relationships, 22,* 75–98.

When things are on an "even keel" with family and at work, it is easy to take friends for granted, but when things go poorly or well in life, people want their friends to "be there" to talk to and to help or to celebrate. Reflecting the folk wisdom, "a friend in need is a friend indeed," and "a friend is someone who multiplies our joys and divides our sorrows," being there when needed was the measure

of true friendship for these adults. Lamentably, this gift of presence, so vital for friendship, is typically metered within a larger social problematic of coordinating life structures. One's closer friends are persons that one "makes the effort" to contact regularly; one "goes out of one's way" to see them and to "stay in touch"; and they do the same. One pursues other types of friendships largely in conjunction with the common schedules, activities, and role requirements of work, neighboring, or in the larger community. Network researchers have called the former type relationships of commitment and the latter, convenience (Feld, 1984).

But what is the nature of the commitment of close friends in adulthood? How is it communicatively and behaviorally accomplished, given two friends' concurrent involvement in their respective, multiple, social realms and their often conflicting needs for independence from and dependence on each other in managing their lives? With some overlap, differing commitment practices composed and expressed agentic or communal tendencies even in these adults' close friendships. And, with a few clear exceptions, the males' accounts of committed and close friendships exhibited agentic themes and the females' communal ones. Whereas both men and women expected close friends to be there to help and talk to them, by and large, they etched these needs differently in time and tangible encounters.

Mutual needs for assistance and discussion are routine matters in communal friendships. "Regular contact" means habitual as well as conscientious attempts to spend face-to-face time together as often as possible, weekly if not more frequently. In the interim, phone calls and sometimes notes or cards keep the friends abreast of evolving day-to-day concerns, moments of self-doubt, and minor or major triumphs or challenges at work or with one's children. Friends' daily lives are always sufficient grist for conversation, and whether a person "just" wants to talk or needs ready advice or relief, a close friend will "be there" for her or him. Commitment in these bonds is special precisely because it reflects a mundane and relatively continuous interweaving of lives.

Although also important in communal bonds, commitment in agentic close friendships is expressed by someone actually or potentially "coming through" when it is "really" needed, "in a pinch," "when the chips are down." Though "regular contact" is also part of such agentic commitment, the words mean something different as the time between interactions specifically devoted to the friendship may vary widely according to its circumstances. Individuals may see each other quite frequently at work, for example, yet have difficulty scheduling "quality time" or discretionary opportunities to speak or spend time together "as friends." The basic independence and separation of lives maintained in agentic friendships usually mean that "regular contact" is more drawn out in time than in communal ones and less organized around everyday concerns. Consequently, the commitment described in close agentic friendships evinces a "heroic" flavor. One feels or learns that one can count on a friend for counsel or help in moments of need, and tacitly indicates reciprocal availability. But these moments are typically conceived as transcending ordinary problems and requiring special effort on the friend's part. Ironically, this very conception may make friends less inclined to seek each other out because they may not want to admit to having such problems or to trouble the friend. Meanwhile, both friends may feel they can count on each other should a "real" need arise.

The differences between communal and agentic senses of commitment are amplified by their usual emphases on the contradictory motives of affection versus instrumentality. Communal friends envision their joint availability and obligations as growing out of caring for each other as intrinsically valued human beings within a shared relationship that comprises a worthwhile end-in-itself. Although both friends benefit from their involvement and efforts on each other's behalf, these actions do not fundamentally derive from a calculation of reciprocal return. Rather, each person views their friendship as a basic existential condition of their ongoing individually yet interdependently conducted lives such that the friend's happiness or sadness directly affects self's well-being.

The allegiance of agentic friends stems more from instrumental needs and reciprocated capacities for practical and emotional relief. Continuing affection and involvement with each other are important, but remain primarily contingent on personal availability and other priorities. Emphasizing individual freedom and rights, agentic friends dislike the concept of obligation in the sense of mutual responsibility applied to friendship. They want to avoid feeling dependent on one another, and they are not comfortable "owing" others, including friends, anything. Ironically, although this mutual stance seems to inhibit sustained integration and interconnection of lives, the intermittent quality of such friendships invokes instrumental assistance at important junctures or "out of the blue" phone calls or letters to attest to their continuity.

Despite variations in agentic and communal emphases in their practices, all of these adults' friendships required time together, either face-to-face or over the phone. Consequently, being there for one's friend usually demanded "making" or "taking time" for him or her. Time constraints were cited throughout the interviews as causing problems between friends. Kathleen's remarks are typical:

> The most trouble? I suppose that it might be time. I would have to say that ever since I had Ginny, having to share time with her and with my husband and with my job, that I find lesser and lesser time to develop or spend time with other people. And so that's probably why I find I spend more time with people like at work and stuff, because they are there, you know, and I can talk to them during the day.

Time limitations compel persons to revise their conceptions or expectations of friendship and/or combine them with work affiliations. But availability due to lack of time can find friends adversely interpreting each other's actions, according to James:

> When we're in a bad mood, it's easy to think that if the other person doesn't have the time or take

the time to listen, then that means we're of less value as a friend. And that snowballs to the point where you think this person isn't interested in you.

Um, the biggest problem I have, I guess, in friendly relationships is making the time away from everything else that we do to, to cultivate it, to make sure the person understands that I care, and that I'm willing to listen. Sometimes you have to schedule that, you know, just like everything else. And if you approach it as an effort and as, I don't want to say as work, but it takes a lot of effort, I think, to make sure that you're maintaining a friendship.

The adult time crunch can make developing or cultivating friendships resemble another job, requiring scheduling and effort to make them "work." Even when one's basic premise is caring, as James implies above, the pressures of larger social configurations convert the words describing friendships into instrumental and cost effective predicates. Consider David's comments:

Probably competition for time certainly strains commitments, even though I think friends have to understand. I don't think friends demand the time, but I think when you're caught up and getting on with your lives and all the other things that go on around you that take time, the time that you don't have available for your friends I think can eventually become a strain. It's an investment of time.

David's references to "competition for" and "investment of time," coupled with James' previous allusions to a friend's "interest" and "valuing" call to mind a principle of economics that, "The rate of interest is the price of time" (Hicks, quoted in Brown, 1959, p. 273). How much time can someone afford to "invest" in a friend? Might that time be better "spent" elsewhere, in effect, yielding a better return on one's investment? How does one justify "interest" in another person for his or her own sake within such a dominant utilitarian

calculus? The prevalence of such language in "accounting for" problems among friends reveals how thoroughly economic assumptions permeate these persons' thinking about friendship, even when attempting communal ones, and ultimately how little control they have over their schedules as enactments of the values of their surrounding social systems.

Consequently, friends must understand their constricted availability to each other throughout adulthood. But resentments persist and dissolve attachments when supposedly close friends "let me down when I needed help," or could not "be there" or "show up" for weddings, anniversaries, reunions, or parties. They also begrudge friends who do not understand why they cannot "make it" to specific activities, events, or functions. People end up judging their friends' availability according to a combination of negotiated expectations, relational precedents, and the priorities and associated schedules of their respective life structures. Even so, because of the definitive anticipations and instances of close friends either being there or not during distressing or joyous moments, crucial events in one's adult life usually involve one's "true" friends and pivotal events affecting friends will rearrange one's own endeavors....

REFERENCES

Brown, N. O. (1959). *Life against death*. Middletown, CT: Wesleyan University Press.

Feld, N. (1984). The structured use of personal associates. *Social Forces, 62*, 640–652.

QUESTIONS/THOUGHTS

1. Would you characterize your friendships as generally agentic or communal? Describe one example of each, focusing specifically on how communication patterns reflect the nature of the friendship.

2. Develop a rationale for the importance communal friendship across the lifespan.

3. If one person characterizes her/his friendship differently than the other characterizes it

(agentic vs. communal), how might that affect their relationship? Give an example.

4. Using a social exchange framework, examine a friendship that you know well and lists some of the costs and benefits each person receives from the other. Who appears to receive more rewards? More costs? Explain why you believe this relationship has lasted according to social exchange theory.

Urban Tribes

ETHAN WATTERS

At a time in which the age of first marriage is increasing and more individuals are choosing not to marry, the rise of a large group of young single adults is shifting the conception of friendship. No longer do the majority of Twentysomethings split off into married couples and romantic pairs, experiencing friendships through a partnered lens; friendship and social life is enacted in groups, frequently a continuation of the collegiate experience. Although some group members may be partnered, the greatest numbers are single. Often these young adults are living in urban areas, great distances from their families of origin, leaving them highly dependent on friends for social life as well as care and support. For most of them, this is life between families; for others, it is the beginning of the rest of their relational life.

This generation of 20 year olds to 30 years olds, or slightly older, is the first to use Web-based social networking to make friends and find business associates. They go online to websites such as Facebook or MySpace and encounter opportunities to build networks of friends. In many cases the online connections develop into face-to-face connections. In addition, other opportunities to meet new people appear through speed dating services, social networking parties, and interest groups formed around interests such as volleyball or wine tasting.

Although this friendship phenomenon had been evolving for over a decade, it became a recognized reality with the publication of Urban Tribes, a title coined by its author, Ethan Watters (2004). Attempting to capture this group experience he writes: "We were a curious new breed, those of us treading water in the cities—outside of our families of origin and seemingly unwilling to begin families for ourselves. We were interested in (often devoted to) our careers and avocations, but we stayed strangely off the social map in other ways" (p. 19). Moving from analyzing his own personal tribe, Watters moved on to explore this friendship phenomenon in cities across the country. Throughout his travels he uncovered a wide range of very different tribes but, most provided a place to meet the needs of friends, almost like an extended family.

Although novel in title, the "urban tribe" is not new in concept. These small societies formed through friendships and mutual interests are common in densely populated urban areas, where people come to find their own community in a sea of *diversity. Using examples and feedback from his research on such groups, Watters explains how these societies collaborate, form, and maintain themselves. The establishment of rituals and the creation of individual roles are key elements of each tribe's survival and management, which Watters depicts in great detail. In addition he highlights the concept of a group's "clustering coefficient" or a way to tell if your friendship circle is diffuse or dense. Finally, Watters summarizes his findings with a discussion of patterns in tribe characteristics and behavior—which proved consistent even across cultures—revealing a fascinating new perspective on the nature of friendship networks in urban areas.*

When members of some tribes enter marriage or committed partnerships with non-tribe members relational challenges may occur. There may be a struggle between the partners regarding the role of the tribe or members of the tribe my not fully accept the new partner. Yet for most couples, partners will likely satisfy certain intimacy needs outside of the committed relationship (Olson, DeFrain, & Skogrand, 2008). Such circumstances tend to necessitate multiple conversations between the partners or with other friends about how to balance significant connections.

You may or may not have experience with such groups but, as you read this chapter, ask yourself the following question: What communication-related benefits or costs may arise from active social involvement in an urban tribe?

REFERENCES

Olson, D. H., DeFrain, J., & Skogrand, L. (2008). *Marriages & families: Intimacy, diversity, and strengths.* New York, NY: McGraw-Hill.

Watters, E. (2003). *Urban tribes: A generation redefines friendship, family, and commitment.* New York, NY: Bloomsbury.

Flush with the idea that I had discovered in my urban tribe something true about my generation, I rushed the idea into print....

Fear of being beaten to the punch was not the only reason I worked quickly. I was also anxious to share the idea, because it seemed like good news. The idea that my group of friends comprised more than the sum of the parts represented a dawning realization that my life, which had so often felt like a talentless, improvisational dance, might have more of a structure than I had perceived. To be in your thirties and still be feeling your way along, still figuring things out, was sad and disconcerting, so I held tenaciously to any notion that suggested my life had momentum.

Unfortunately, in my haste to share the idea, I got some things wrong. Writing for the esteemed *New York Times Magazine,* I described the urban tribe as "a tight group with unspoken roles and hierarchies, whose members thought of each other as 'us' and the rest of the world as 'them'." I was soon to learn that this summary was fundamentally inaccurate....

Through the Internet, my article on tribes had been shared from friend to friend around the world. Although most of the people who e-mailed me were from the United States, people e-mailed me to tell me about their tribes in India, England, Australia, Canada, and even Karachi. Many of my correspondents expressed surprise that other people were living like they were, in small societies formed by friendships and mutual interests....

Because there were things about tribes that made them hard to see from the outside, they were illusive as a national trend. Tribes did not have membership rolls or official meetings. No parent or mentor had taught or encouraged the formation of these groups. No organization sponsored the national convention of urban tribes.... Because there was no recognized social trend toward this behavior, the sensation of being in such a social entity was singular. "We thought we were the only ones" was a common refrain of my correspondents....

While some urban tribes began through specific activities or pre-existing friendships, for the most part it was a puzzle to figure out why or how they have formed into a group. Many people who wanted to tell me about their tribes had trouble tracing the origins. The beginnings of tribes often seemed to be happenstance—roommate answered ads or acquaintances struck up in cafes. "Outsiders who see our tight bond often ask us, 'How did you all meet?'" wrote Kevin from Dallas. "It's difficult to answer because there was no specific circumstances that led to the formation of our tribe. We became friends through a variety of connections, such as friends of friends. Somehow we were magnetically drawn to each other.".…

Others also reported that the strength of the bond within the group could not be adequately explained through either the connections that brought them together in the first place or any shared interests or avocations. "No activity or trait defines us," Chuck from Cleveland wrote after I asked him what was unique about his group. "It's just a wonderful collection of individuals who genuinely care about each other. We ourselves are the only cool thing.".…

Those who wrote to tell me about their tribes were nearly all college educated. I had predicted this because the marriage delay was greatest among people who stayed in school longer, especially those who went for postgraduate degrees and the demanding careers that lead from them. It made sense to me that the more time one spent outside a traditional family, the more likely it was that one would form a social entity to take its place.

In general the groups that formed from college (or sometimes high school) friendships tended to be more demographically uniform in age, race, and income. The groups that formed later, during the swirl of adult city life could sometime match the remarkable diversity of those communities. Chris, a graphic designer in L.A., marveled at his group's mix. "When we go out to dinner we look like the UN," he wrote of his group of fifteen. "There are Blacks, Italians, Thais, Filipinos, Mexicans, Colombians, Jews, Indians. Nobody seems to care about anyone else's background.".…

It occurred to me that I might find meaningful commonalities among the tribes by examining the roles people within them took on. At first this appeared promising, for my correspondents identified dozens of roles within their tribes. Interestingly, few of my correspondents identified one person in their groups as the leader, de facto or otherwise. However, there was almost always at least one "organizer" (sometimes called "mother figure," "party planner," or "social director"), who appeared to earn this designation over time by successfully bringing people together or putting in the time to plan the logistics of trips and gatherings. Assuming this person was the chief of the tribe would be wrong. Having held the organizer's role off and on in my own tribe, I knew that from personal experience. The role of organizer commanded little special respect or privileges. If you wanted to be the one to go to the grocery store to gather food, or if you wanted to manage the e-mail list and make the phone calls to tell people where to show up, the role of organizer was yours for the taking.…

There was often another group member (usually but not always a woman) who acted as "advice giver" (called by some the group "therapist" or "shoulder to cry on"), who would console and counsel friends, particularly on the subject of romantic relationships. In one case this person was called "Switzerland" because he not only counseled individuals but also had a knack for smoothing rifts between members. Other roles people identified included "innovators," who came up with new projects for the group, and "assistant in charge of details," who followed the directions of the organizer. Other roles identified by those who wrote me included "comedian" and "deal negotiators," who could step forward when someone in the group needed help negotiating a promotion or a home purchase. There was "the worrier," who kept the group from doing dangerous things, and "the chaperone" who, in a slightly different manner, helped individuals make the choices they wouldn't regret the next morning. Women sometimes identified certain female friends as their "guardians" or "bodyguards," who could, usually just by their presence, ward off unwanted advances or make them feel safer when exploring new areas of town or unfamiliar social situations. There was also sometimes a firebrand, or "life of the party," someone other people wanted to be around because he or she could draw people out of their shells and milk the most from social situations.

There were often two or three "children" in a group. These were not literal children, but adults who seemed always in trouble or in need. "The cynic" seemed to be the one variation of "the child." The cynic had the disgruntled demeanor of a two-year-old, and other group members seemed to enjoy spending large amounts of time trying to improve the cynic's mood. While you might think that groups would avoid such personalities, these "children" appeared to offer something of a group activity. The "child" would show up on a camping trip having managed to pack only hot chocolate mix. While such habits were exasperating, providing the "child" with food and shelter for the weekend made for a challenging, and ultimately enjoyable, group project. The organizer and the assistants in charge of details would rally and prove their acumen. This challenge was made more meaningful by the stories told later about the weekend. Often it was the boneheaded actions of the "children" that became the groups' most beloved stories to retell.

As I studied people's descriptions of these roles, some enticing patterns emerged. It was clear that there needed to be a certain balance between some roles. There were no groups with all cynics or, for that matter, all organizers or all advice givers. Some general ratios became apparent. The organizers, assistants in charge of details, and advice givers usually out numbered the children and cynics by at least a four-to-one ratio. Christina, from Raleigh, North Carolina, described such a balance: "Libby is the hostess. Mark always cooks huge dinners. Sylvia is the cruise director, always with an eye on the events calendar to rally the tribe to attend certain cool events. Jenny hosts annual Christmas parties. And then there's Bill, who shows up to everything with his dog and six-pack."....

It seemed to me, however, that the fact people with tribes took on roles at all was something that made these groups of friends distinct. It appeared that taking on a role of some sort allowed each individual to effect a little extra gravity on the group. The gravity manifested by the organizers, those who took the time to pull people together, was the most obvious. But all the other roles

functioned similarly. That people took on roles encouraged my suspicion that these groups were not just random collections of friends but functioning social entities.

CLUSTERING AROUND THE CORE

There was another way these groups tended to differ from other, looser groups of friends one might have had in college or at other points in life—they had what social scientists call extremely high "clustering coefficients." This is the idea: you take all the people in your social circle and up all the possible connections that could exist if absolutely every one of your friends had a personal relationship with every else in your social circle. Next you add up the number of people in your social circle that actually do have a personal relationship with someone you know. Your group's clustering coefficient is the number of people who actually know each other divided by the total number who could possibly know each other. So if you have six friends there is a possibility of a total number of fourteen connections within that group. If all fourteen connections actually exist, then you have fourteen divided by fourteen, or one. Your social circle couldn't be more clustered. If ten of those fourteen connections exist, your group has a clustering coefficient of 0.71. The closer your coefficient is to one, the more friends your friends share.

As I learned about tribes across the country, it became clear that their clustering coefficients were quite high. The individual friendships that made up these tribes could not be understood, I came to believe outside the complexity of these interlocking friendships. Try to examine a single friendship while ignoring the other interlocking relationships the friends share, and the thing you wanted to examine might vanish. It was the high clustering coefficients that kept some of these relationships together....

Many people told me similar stories of maintaining ties through their tribes with people they otherwise would not have had as friends. High clustering coefficients create dense groups that bond friendships—both friendships that would exist outside the groups and many more that would not. Because of intensely high clustering coefficients, friendships in tribes sometimes defy what you'd normally expect of friendships, namely, that they are always reciprocal, positive relationships which are freely entered into and relatively freely exited from. With highly clustered groups, which friendships you are bound to often becomes as much of a group decision as a personal one....

In describing the dynamics of their groups, many people also talked of tight "core groups" of four to twelve who were surrounded by "affiliate members," "stragglers," or "outliers" who might double or triple the size of the core group. Sometimes groups had ways of clearly stating who was a core member and who was not. Often this communication took the form of who was invited to certain events. Frieda from Oakland described how her group's weekly dinners were structured to delineate between core members and affiliates....

In terms of how membership ebbed and flowed, these groups were not cultish in the least. In fact, they seemed uniquely designed to assimilate new members and to create social situations during which new people could be mixed in with older members. What kept the clustering coefficient high was that new people would almost immediately meet all other members of the group. Over time, most of these groups appeared to have extremely porous borders, with people joining and drifting away frequently. Janice, twenty-two, a part of a thriving Oakland tribe of technoheads, learned that at the outer edges of her group, "most people are not 'forevers.' Most people come to teach us and learn from us and off they go."

QUESTIONS/THOUGHTS

1. What do you see as advantages and/or disadvantages of a strong commitment to life within a social friendship network, or urban tribe, when you are a young single adult?
2. What communication skills would be particularly important if one is to function effectively within a strong friendship network?
3. How might living in an urban tribe for a number of years affect the nature of members' new ties to romantic partners?
4. To what extent can active use of multiple digital media substitute for physical proximity when creating an urban tribe?

Reprinted from Ethan Watters, *Urban Tribes: A Generation Redefines Friendship, Family, and Commitment*, pp. 40–53. Copyright © 2003 by Bloomsbury.

Communication in Cross-Sex Friendships

LEA P. STEWART, PAMELA J. COOPER,
ALAN STEWART, AND SHERYL FRIEDLEY

From the college dormitory, to the military training fields, to the corporate boardroom, the intermixing of men and women of equal status and similar personal goals has resulted in the development of male/female friendships. Until recently, adult friendships were characterized as same-sex relationships, except in the cases of couple friendships. Today, as men and women study together, plan organizational strategy together, and travel together professionally, their proximity and similar status contribute to the development of **cross-sex** non-romantic friendship. In addition, as people marry later in life, men and women in their twenties and thirties often socialize in large mixed-sex groups, such as the urban tribes discussed in the previous chapter.

Cross-sex friendships can be very rewarding (Werking, 1997) as males and females share their different perspectives and enjoy activities together. Yet, they can be stressful as these friends encounter challenges unlike those they find in same-sex friendships. In addition to the basic sexual challenge, or negotiating expectations about the role of sex in their friendship, they find themselves struggling with managing their emotional bond, given the socialization they received as children regarding male/female relationships. These friends also have to manage their public presentation because such friendships are questioned by others who assume these are romantic ties.

As the following article suggests, little research has examined these types of relationships. When research has been conducted, the emphasis has been on whether cross-sex friendships differ from romantic friendships.

Friendship research suggests that males and females describe friends similarly. That is, both males and females describe a friend as someone who is supportive, encouraging, and trustworthy, someone with whom to share intimacies and who is fun to be with (Duck & Wright 1993; Sapadin 1988). Yet research also suggests that although males and females describe a friend in similar ways, they participate in friendships differently. Thus, cross-sex friendships can be difficult to maintain.

Yet, for those people who beat the odds, and manage to establish a cross-gendered friendship, there are, according to the authors of this chapter, unique ways in which they balance communication and behavior to make the relationship work. Stewart and her associates explore why cross-sex *friendships occur less frequently than same-sex friendships and have shorter longevity. In examining this issue, they address the communication variables of conflict, intimacy and self-disclosure, and communicator style. The authors then illustrate strategies for change that make such friendships possible, incorporating how to avoid and/or manage the aforementioned problem areas. Finally, a brief summary wraps up the chapter.*

Given the complex nature of cross-gender friendships, they take more effort and communication to maintain. As you read this piece, reflect on the male/female friendships that you have witnessed or experienced and ask yourself the question: How might conflict and self-disclosure have contributed to the success or failure of these friendships?

REFERENCES

Duck, S., &Wright, P. (1993). Examining gender differences in same-gender friendships. *Sex Roles, 28*, 1–19.

Sapadin, L. (1998). Friend and gender: Perspectives of professional men and women. *Journal of Social and Personal Relationships, 6*, 387–403.

Werking, K. (1997). *We're just good friends: Women and men in nonromantic relationships.* New York, NY: Guilford Press.

While romantic relationships and same-sex friendships have received considerable research attention, male/female platonic friendships have not (Kaplan & Keys, 1997). This lack of research may result, in part, from the fact that societal norms discourage friendships between females and males. Think of all the movies and television shows in which the main characters begin as friends and inevitably end up in a romantic relationship. Nevertheless, platonic friendships do exist and are worthy of further examination.

As one reads the literature on cross-sex friendships (friendships between women and men), a recurrent theme seems to be the difficulty of these friendships (Rawlins, 1993). As Swain (1992) says:

> Since cross-sex friendship is not a clearly defined or expected social relationship it is often interpreted in terms of heterosexual love relationships. For example, many heterosexual love relationships begin as platonic friendships, thus promoting a view of cross-sex friendships as a stage of development in the coupling process, rather than as a legitimate relationship in and of itself. When an adolescent develops a friendship with a cross-sex friend, family members often tease, hint at, or praise the person for establishing a possible heterosexual dating, sexual, or love relationship. Claims that "we're just good friends" are often viewed as withholding information, or as an indication of embarrassment or bashfulness about the sexual content of the relationship. (p. 154)

In general, cross-sex friendships occur less frequently than same-sex friendships and have shorter longevity (Swain, 1992). Males report more cross-sex friendships than females (Rawlins, 1992). Sapadin (1988) reports that men rate their cross-sex friendships as more enjoyable and nurturing than their same-sex ones, although they rate both similar in perceived intimacy. In contrast, women rate their same-sex friendships as more intimate, enjoyable, nurturing, and higher in overall quality than their cross-sex ones. Further, they feel much more nurtured by their female friends, in both personal and career areas than by male friends (Sapadin, 1988, p. 401).

Why are cross-sex friendships difficult to achieve and to maintain? Several possibilities come to mind. The first one is the one we've already alluded to: society's lack of acceptance of this type of friendship. Rawlins (1993) suggests that cross-sex friendships are socially "deviant." Often others simply won't believe the "just good friends" explanation of cross-sex friendship.

In addition, sexual attraction is often present in platonic friendships, especially for men (Kaplan & Keys, 1997). Because our societal norm for friendship is same-sex friendship, we may have difficulty understanding how a male and female can be just good friends, particularly in light of what we know about the differences between male same-sex friendships and female same-sex friendships.

This brings us to a second possibility, differing attitudes toward friendship. Remember our earlier discussion about same-sex friendships. In terms of intimacy, females tend to show intimacy through self-disclosure, while males are more likely to base their intimate friendships on shared activities. Another difference in attitudes relates to romantic involvement and sexual activity. Women often believe that men's motive for friendship is sexual and are, therefore, reluctant to form friendships with men if they have no desire for a more romantic involvement (Rose, 1985). A final factor influencing cross-sex friendships concerns emotional needs. If, as our research suggests, men look to women rather than to other men to meet their emotional needs (Rand & Levinger, 1979), and women think men cannot meet their emotional needs and so form female friendships (Gilligan, 1982), then a cross-sex friendship may be difficult to maintain.

Closely related to the different perceptions of how best to meet emotional needs, Rubin (1983) finds that males have a more difficult time recognizing the feelings of another person. This is particularly true when the other person is female. Women, on the other hand, are better able to recognize others' emotions. This ability is evidenced by the fact that women use more affectionate touch, expressions of empathy, and feedback after disclosure than men (Buhrke & Fuqua, 1987). As Ivy and Backlund (1994) suggest, differences in the recognition of feelings can create problems for cross-sex friends if an imbalance is perceived in the amount of emotional support one derives from the relationship.

COMMUNICATION

Conflict, intimacy and self-disclosure, and communicator style have been studied in cross-sex friendships. We will examine briefly each of these issues.

Conflict

Every relationship has conflict. However, in some ways, men and women handle conflict differently. If conflict or tension occurs in cross-sex friendships, women are more likely to blame themselves for relational failures and credit others for relational successes (Martin & Nivens, 1987). Also, if problems arise, women are more likely than men to end the relationship. Men are more likely to ignore relational problems by focusing on positive aspects of the relationship.

A recent study on deception (Powers, 1993) sheds some light on why females might choose to end a relationship that is difficult. Women tend to be more sensitive to relational deception than men. In addition, women evaluate the character and competence of a deceiver lower than do men. If a woman discovers deception has occurred, she may decide to end the relationship because deception is so unacceptable to her. (See also Levine, McCornack, & Avery, 1992).

Intimacy and Self-Disclosure

Dindia and Allen (1992) examined more than 200 studies on self-disclosure and found that women self-disclose more than men. It is important to take into account whether the conversational partners are male or female since women disclose more than men in same-sex dyads but do not disclose more than men when they are talking with a man.

In terms of disclosure in cross-sex friendships, men report that they disclose more intimate information to women than they do to other men. Women, however, claim they disclose more intimate information to other women (Aukett, Richie, & Mill, 1988). In addition, there are some interesting differences in the nature of disclosure in cross-sex friendships compared with disclosure in same-sex friendships (Hacker, 1981). Specifically, unlike self-disclosure in same-sex friendships, there is no significant difference in the amount of disclosure between men and women in cross-sex friendships. Instead, differences emerge in the nature of the self-disclosure between men and women. For example, when talking to female friends, men tend to confide more about their weaknesses while they *enhance* their strengths (Stephen & Harrison, 1985). Women tend to confide about their weaknesses and *conceal* their strengths.

To illustrate this disclosure pattern, consider the following scenario. Don is very upset with his boss. Lately, every proposal he presents to her is turned down. Don discloses this information to his co-worker and friend, Karen. During Don's disclosure he tells Karen all the wonderful things he has done for the company during the last year. He dismisses the fact that he hasn't done as well this year and blames his boss for not knowing a good idea when she sees one. In reply, Karen admits that she too has had some of her proposals turned down, but fails to mention that three out of her four proposals have been accepted and used.

These two different disclosure patterns are reflective of common gender ideology. Men are expected to assume a superior or dominant position through disclosure, so they include and even enhance their strengths when they confide to women about their weaknesses. Women are expected to facilitate the disclosure process by playing a subordinate role in which they confide only their weaknesses and discuss none of their strengths. This superior-subordinate role relationship often found in cross-sex conversation indicates that women may be dominated in cross-sex conversation while men are more likely to dominate the conversation (Rubin, Perse, & Barbato, 1988; Tannen, 1990).

Goldsmith and Dun (1997) asked college students to respond to typical problems encountered by their friends, including failing an exam, registration problems, or being "dumped by a boyfriend or girlfriend." Contrary to the stereotype that women are concerned with emotions while men are concerned with problem solving, when asked to talk about a problem both men and women spent the same amount of time talking about what action to take. Men, however, did use more time to discuss the problem and more of that talk dismissed or denied the other person's problem. Neither men nor women talked much about emotions but focused more on the problem presented.

Communicator Style

Communicator style refers to "the way one verbally and paraverbally interacts to signal how literal meaning should be taken, interpreted, filtered, or understood" (Norton, 1978, p. 99). Such characteristics as dominant, animated, relaxed, attentive, open, and friendly often are used to describe a person's communicator style, and these characteristics contribute to a person's effectiveness in the communication process.

When men and women are asked to describe their own communicator styles, they report minimal differences (Staley & Cohen, 1988). For example, of all the variables that constitute communicator style, women perceive themselves as more animated than men, and men perceive themselves as more precise than women. Both men and women rate themselves similarly on all other aspects of communicator style (Montgomery & Norton, 1981). Thus, both men and women claim they have more similarities than differences in their communicator style. In addition, both men and women report similar self-perceptions concerning stylistic characteristics considered to be indicators of effective communication.

Although men and women claim that they use a similar communicator style, their actual behavior is perceived differently. Women generally use a communicator style that others consider attentive and open, but men are more likely to use a style perceived by others as dominant, relaxed, and dramatic (Montgomery & Norton, 1981; Tannen, 1990). These perceived communicator styles coincide with gender stereotypes. For example, as we discussed earlier in this chapter, females are perceived to be facilitators of communication. Both attentiveness (letting other people know they are being heard) and openness (receptivity to communication) facilitate the interpersonal communication process. Being dominant (taking charge of the interaction), dramatic (manipulating verbal and nonverbal cues to highlight or understate content), and relaxed (anxiety-free) convey control in the communication process—a control often associated with status and power.

Most research that examines the communicator style actually used by men and women in cross-sex friendships focuses primarily on men's use of dominance as a means of controlling the communication. Specifically, this dominance includes men talking more than women, men receiving more positive evaluations for their performance in dialogue from both men and women, and perceptions of greater male influence (Berger, Rosenholtz, & Zelditch, 1980; Tannen, 1990). But dominance may be affected by the other person's level of dominance. Davis and Gilbert (1989) found that when high-dominant women were paired with low-dominant men, the women took a leadership role 71 percent of the time. However, when high-dominant women were paired with high-dominant men, the women assumed the leadership role only 31 percent of the time. Thus, high-dominant men are somewhat more likely to become leaders than high-dominant women.

Language choice in conversations between cross-sex friends also indicates differences in perceptions of male and female communicator styles. In general, there is a tendency for females to judge verbs used in interpersonal communication with friends as more emotional than men do; in contrast, males tend to judge verbs used in interpersonal communication with friends as more reflective of control (Thompson, Hatchett, & Phillips, 1981). For example, a women may characterize her own behavior toward a man as protecting him (intending to communicate positive emotions), but she may be surprised when he responds to her actions in terms of the control he perceives her communication conveys. For a man, protecting may imply that the protector is stronger and the person needing protection is weaker.

In conclusion, amount and type of disclosure are important in creating and maintaining gender ideologies in cross-sex friendships. As in same-sex friendships, disclosure (and specifically self-disclosure) is essential to the development of cross-sex friendships. Although men and women use an equal amount of disclosure in mixed-sex friendships, women's disclosure is more self-related and more intimate in traditional terms than men's disclosure. In relationships where men and women are of equal status, both men and women perceive that more disclosure occurs. Perhaps more important in this discussion, however, is the introduction of differences in the communicator styles used by men and women in cross-sex friendships. A variety of language strategies— including duration of speech, language choice, and interpretation—reflect and reinforce gender stereotypes in these relationships.

IMPLICATIONS AND CONSEQUENCES OF GENDER IN FRIENDSHIPS

In examining friendship, one observation is apparent: traditional gender ideologies associated with male and female communication remain relatively consistent in friendships. In general, females disclose more and are perceived as using a communicator style that is facilitative and expressive. Males disclose less and are perceived as using a communicator style that is seen as controlling and instrumental.

Within same-sex friendships, women are more likely to focus on topics related to people: self, family, and friends. Female friends encourage disclosure in their interactions and provide a supportive communication climate to facilitate disclosure. Expressive and facilitative behaviors are typically associated with traditional gender stereotypes for women. It is not surprising, then, that these behaviors are prevalent in female interactions and are often the focus for the study of communication among women. Men are more likely to focus on topics related to status, power, and competition. They may avoid rather than facilitate disclosure, usually to control the focus and direction of the interaction. These functions are consistent with gender stereotypes for men.

Many men and women also continue to maintain traditional gender ideologies as communicators in cross-sex friendships. Many men tend to use communication behaviors that reinforce images of power, status, and control, while women tend to use communication behaviors that reinforce images of expressivity and facilitation. Although men both initiate and receive more verbal communication in cross-sex friendships, the participants seem to compromise on certain topics. In conversations among college undergraduates, men tend to speak less about competition and physical aggression, while women tend to speak less about home and family than they would in same-sex groups (Aires, 1987). In cross-sex friendships, women initiate more topics (facilitation), but men decide which of those topics will be discussed at length (control). In cross-sex friendships, men's topics and language choices are more task-oriented (instrumental), and women's topics and language choices are more personal and emotional (expressive). Women generally encourage disclosure (facilitation), and men are more likely to avoid disclosure (control). When men and women do disclose, men disclose strengths and conceal weaknesses (superiority), while women disclose weaknesses and conceal their strengths (subordination). These communication behaviors reinforce traditional gender stereotypes from both men and women.

STRATEGIES FOR CHANGE
Given our changing society, corresponding change in the basic interpersonal relationship of friendship is inevitable. The mobility of our population makes it likely that you will initiate, maintain, and terminate both same-sex and cross-sex friendships many times throughout your life. While these social changes reflect the quantity of friendships you may develop in a lifetime, the quality of those relationships is the far more important issue to consider.

A growing shift away from traditional masculine and feminine gender ideologies is beginning to change the nature of our interpersonal relationships by introducing ambiguity and uncertainty into our friendships. We need to create ways to cope with the evolving roles available to women and men because of changing social conditions, and we should be willing to redefine and renegotiate changes in the roles typically associated with friendship. Effective communication in our friendships will allow us to negotiate changing behaviors that can enhance relationship satisfaction (Petronio, 1982). Consider the following suggestions to facilitate adaptation and change in your friendships.

Develop a Supportive Climate for Change
Because any change in relationships carries with it an implicit message of dissatisfaction from the one seeking change, it is important that one or both parties in a friendship avoid feeling defensive or threatened by the possibility of change.

Using communication that creates a supportive climate establishes a positive context for change. Likewise, viewing change as an opportunity to create a mutually satisfying relationship rather than as an attack or a negative assessment of current definition of the relationship is essential to the process of change. For example, someone who asks a housemate to do more of the housework may believe that their relationship is very positive but that more active participation from the housemate in doing household chores would give them more time to spend in social activities together.

If you find yourself in a relationship that you want to change, try to use communication strategies that encourage your friends to describe their feelings about your relationship and their role in your friendship. Suggest a willingness on your part to cooperate in a mutual problem-solving orientation that will help establish a communication climate supportive of change. Do not judge or evaluate feelings; rather, describe or attempt to understand those feelings. Do not imply your superior ability to define change, but emphasize equal participation by both parties in this process. Do not manipulate or control the defining and negotiation process; instead, approach it as a mutually directed process involving both parties in the relationship. Creating a defensive communication climate rather than a supportive one will only serve as a barrier to negotiating relational change.

One of the best ways to facilitate supportive change in a friendship is to engage in new activities that help produce a closer relationship. Go to a movie together. Volunteer to serve meals to the homeless. Participate in a community clean-up day. People who share enjoyable, worthwhile activities together strengthen the bonds of their friendship.

Encourage Effective Disclosure Patterns
Earlier we noted differences in disclosure patterns for males and females. Women traditionally tend to disclose about self and about personal topics for the purpose of serving expressive and affiliate needs. Men tend to disclose about task- or goal-oriented topics for the purpose of serving

instrumental needs. Perhaps one of the greatest frustrations expressed by women in cross-sex friendships is that men do not disclose on the expressive or feeling level. While men may find it difficult to alter the nature of their disclosure, they may become comfortable disclosing about self in interpersonal relationships where trust has been established.

Since men appreciate this type of disclosure from women in relationships, men obviously value it. Men may strive to share their feelings more openly with their close friends when increased disclosure is appropriate, and women may facilitate and positively reinforce such disclosure in their relationships.

Women may also respect men's desire to refrain from disclosure. As long as the absence of disclosure is an indication of satisfaction with the relationship and not a control tactic, men's lack of disclosure should not be criticized. Tavris (1992) suggests that women appear to: "be better than men at intimacy because intimacy is defined as what women do; talk, express feelings, disclose personal concerns. Intimacy is rarely defined as sharing activities, being helpful, doing useful work, or enjoying companionable silence. Because of this bias, men rarely get credit for the kinds of loving actions that are more typical of them" (p. 100).

Communicator Style Awareness

As we examined friendship, we noted some differences between men and women in their communicator styles. Women generally initiate topics in an attempt to facilitate conversation. Men may subtly control interaction because they often choose the topics that will be discussed more fully during the course of the conversation. Women use verbal and nonverbal turn-yielding cues to facilitate the continuation of interaction with men, but men often use avoidance strategies to control the continuation or discontinuation of a conversation. Women tend to be more adept at encoding and decoding the nonverbal cues that are related to expressiveness. Men tend to use a style that enhances the instrumental functions within a relationship.

Although the traditional male-female relationship in most communication situations has reflected male dominance and female subordination, these traditional roles are changing. Any power structure in a relationship may be satisfying if it is negotiated by the people involved. Examine the power structures in your friendships and assess your satisfaction with them.

Relationships that reflect patterns of communication based on inequality and difference are said to be *complementary* in nature. Much like a parent-child relationship, complementary patterns of communication generally imply a superior-subordinate relationship. Relationships that reflect patterns of communication based on equality and similarity are said to be *symmetrical* in nature, such as among peers who form friendships based on equality. For example, one person in a relationship may be responsible for organizing social engagements outside the home while the other is responsible for organizing the daily activities within the home. While the complementary pattern of communication may be closer to traditional gender stereotypes, where men dominate and women are subordinate, the symmetrical pattern of communication is more closely aligned with the independent or nontraditional relationships. In these relationships, all participants are committed to growth and change in the relationship based on the recognition that there will be equal input from everyone into that growth process.

These two patterns of communication establish clearly dichotomous categories of power in relationships. The reality, however, is that most relationships probably reflect both of these power structures at various times and on various issues. Rather than using only complementary or only symmetrical patterns of communication, consider the benefits of using both at given times in your relationship. Consider a variety of communication options so that no person is superior or subordinate all the time. For example, in an apartment, one of the roommates may buy the food and do most of the cooking while another pays the bills and is responsible for cleaning the kitchen. In this instance, both of them serve the instrumental function of decision maker at different times and concerning different decisions. At the same time, symmetrical patterns of communication based on equality in a relationship should become apparent. Relationships that employ a combination of both complementary and symmetrical communication patterns within the relationship are said to be using a *parallel* communication pattern. Again, the key to redefining and changing a friendship is being open to a variety of communication choices, adopting a parallel pattern of communication that is both complementary and symmetrical at appropriate times and in appropriate situations.

SUMMARY

Interpersonal relationships found in friendships are developed, maintained, and terminated through the process of communication. Because of the intimacy that can develop in these relationships, they may provide us with the ultimate opportunity for personal satisfaction in our communication with others. Men and women, however, may communicate differently in these relationships. An examination of the communication occurring in these interpersonal relationships generally confirms the traditional gender ideologies associated with communication between men and women in other situations. Women may be more likely to use expressive and facilitative behaviors, while men may use instrumental and control strategies.

REFERENCES

Aires, E. (1987). Gender and communication. In P. Shaver & C. Hendrick (Eds.), *Sex and gender* (pp. 149–176). Newbury Park, CA: Sage.

Aukett, R., Richie, J., & Mill, K. (1988). Gender differences in friendship patterns. *Sex Roles, 19,* 57–66.

Berger, J., Rosenholtz, S. J., & Zelditch, M., Jr. (1980). Status organizing processes. In A. Inkeles , N.J. Smelser & K. H. Turner (Eds.), *Annual review of sociology* vol. 6, (pp. 479–508). Palo Alto, CA: Annual Reviews.

Buhrke, R. A., & Fuqua, D. R. (1987). Sex differences in same- and cross-sex supportive relationships. *Sex Roles, 17,* 339–351.

Davis, B., & Gilbert, L. (1989). Effect of dispositional and situational influences on women's dominance expression in mixed-sex dyads. *Journal of Personality and Social Psychology, 57,* 294–300.

Dindia, K., & Allen, M. (1992). Sex differences in disclosure: A meta-analysis. *Psychological Bulletin, 112,* 106–124.

Gilligan, C. (1982). *In a different voice: Psychological theory and women's development.* Cambridge, MA: Harvard University Press.

Goldsmith, D., & Dun, S. (1997). Sex differences and similarities in the communication of social support. *Journal of Social and Personal Relationships, 14,* 317–337.

Hacker, H. M. (1981). Blabbermouths and clams: Sex differences in self-disclosure in same-sex and cross-sex friendship dyads. *Psychology of Women Quarterly, 5,* 385–401.

Ivy, D., & Backlund, P. (1994). *Exploring gender speak: Personal effectiveness in gender communication.* New York, NY: McGraw-Hill.

Kaplan, D., & Keys, C. H. (1997). Sex and relationship variables as predictors of sexual attraction in cross-sex platonic friendships between young heterosexual adults. *Journal of Social and Personal Relationships, 14,* 191–206.

Levine, T. R., McCornack, S. A., & Avery, P. B. (1992). Sex differences in emotional reactions to discovered deception. *Communication Quarterly, 40,* 289–296.

Martin, V., & Nivens, M. K. (1987). The attributional response of males and females to noncontingent feedback. *Sex Roles, 16,* 453–462.

Montgomery, B. M., & Norton, R. W. (1981). Sex differences and similarities in communicator style. *Communication Monographs, 48,* 121–132.

Norton, R. W. (1978). Foundation of a communicator style construct. *Human Communication Research, 4,* 99–112.

Petronio, S. S. (1982). The effect of interpersonal communication on women's family role satisfaction. *Western Journal of Speech Communication, 46,* 208–222.

Powers, W. (1993). The effects of gender and consequence upon perceptions of deceivers. *Communication Quarterly, 41,* 328–337.

Rand, M., & Levinger, N. J. (1979). Implicit theories of relationship: An intergenerational student. *Journal of Personality and Social Psychology, 37,* 645–661.

Rawlins, W. K. (1992). *Friendship matters: Communication, dialectics, and the life course.* Hawthorne, NY: Aldine de Gruyter.

Rawlins, W. K. (1993). Communication in cross-sex friendships. In L. P. Arliss & D. J. Borisoff (Eds.), *Women and men communicating: Challenges and changes* (pp. 51–70). Fort Worth, TX: Harcourt Brace Jovanovich.

Rose, S. M. (1985). Same- and cross-sex friendships and the psychology of homosociality. *Sex Roles, 12,* 63–74.

Rubin, L. B. (1983). *Intimate strangers: Men and women together.* New York, NY: Harper and Row.

Rubin, R. B., Perse, E. M., & Barbato, C. S. (1988). Conceptualization and measurement of interpersonal communication motives. *Human communication Research, 14,* 602–627.

Sapadin, L. A. (1988). Friendship and gender: Perspectives of professional men and women. *Journal of Social and Personal Relationships, 5,* 387–403.

Staley, C. C., & Cohen, J. L. (1988). Communicator style and social style: Similarities and differences between the sexes. *Communication Quarterly, 36,* 192–202.

Stephen, T. D., & Harrison, T. M. (1985). Gender, sex-role identity, and communication style: A Q-sort analysis of behavioral differences. *Communication Research Reports, 2,* 53–61.

Swain, S. (1992). Men's friendships with women: Intimacy, sexual boundaries, and the informant role. In P. Nardi (Ed.), *Men's friendships* (pp. 153–172). Newbury Park, CA: Sage.

Tannen, D. (1990). *You just don't understand: Men and women in conversation.* New York, NY: William Morrow.

Tavris, C. (1992). *The mismeasure of women.* New York, NY: Simon and Schuster.

Thompson, E. G., Hatchett, P., & Phillips, J. L. (1981). Sex differences in the judgment of interpersonal verbs. *Psychology of Women Quarterly, 5,* 523–531.

QUESTIONS/THOUGHTS

1. Think of a cross-gendered friendship that is close to you (either your own or a friend's) and discuss some of the benefits and challenges of that relationship.

2. Analyze your own cross-sex friendships in terms of conflict, intimacy, self-disclosure, and communication styles.

3. Interview two persons, ages 50 or older, and ask them what they learned about having cross-gender friendships when they were young adults. Also, ask them to describe characteristics of a current cross-gender friendship in which they are a participant.

C. Technology

INTRODUCTION

You were introduced to the terms Digital Natives, Digital Settlers, and Digital Immigrants (Palfrey & Gasser, 2008) earlier in the book. Digital Natives were born after 1980 when social technologies came online; this group has access to digital technologies and the skills to use them. Digital Settlers grew up in an analog–only world and worked to develop sophisticated technology skills, although they also rely heavily on analog forms of communication. Digital Immigrants, usually born well before 1980, remain less comfortable in this digital environment and find the digital environment less intuitive and manageable than either the Digital Natives or Settlers. You are managing your life in a complex digital world, no matter which label may apply to you. Whereas "Digital Natives change the personal information they share over the Internet all the time as they change their sense of self and how they wish to portray themselves" (Palfrey & Gasser, 2008, p. 32), others may engage in self portrayals much more selectively.

Every year new communication technologies expand your possibilities for interaction. Computers, cell phones, and Sidekicks serve as linchpins for everyday business communication. Many friendships are maintained through IM and text messaging as well as through Facebook, blogs, and electronic gaming. You may develop friendships online and learn personal information about acquaintances, friends or friends of friends by reading their blogs. Family pictures and news circulate on e-mail or are posted on websites. Regardless of how impersonal you may believe these technologies to be, they will continue to have a profound impact on human communication in general, and on your personal communication practices specifically.

Computer-mediated-communication (CMC) differs from face-to-face interaction. It is text-based, primarily linguistic; asynchronous or synchronous; potentially anonymous; and lacking nonverbal and/or standard social cues. Users can "talk" without disclosing their names or embarrassing themselves or their families, all on the safety of their screens. Online status, gender, physical appearance, body position, speech patterns, facial expressions, and dress all take a backseat to linguistic expression. Today that world has changed. In fact, although "The dominant theories related to interpersonal relations presently are premised on the absence of visual or other nonverbal cues" (Walther & Ramiriz, 2010, p.267), those theories have been seriously challenged due to technological advances. You may chat on Skype while smiling at a grandparent, download pictures from your camera, and then digitally alter those pictures before posting them on a dating website or on your Facebook page.

In Chapter 4, Theories of Relational Communication, Richard West and Lynn Turner asserted that technological advances have challenged our understandings of interpersonal communication, particularly the processes of developing and maintaining interpersonal relationships. No longer must first meetings occur face to face or on the telephone; strangers, such as future college roommates, may talk on Skype or exchange photos on their cell phones long before the school year starts. They may also read each others' blogs or connect regularly on Facebook, all of which reflects the reality that technology plays a major role in our relational life.

Not only do individuals interact with each other, but entire communities are created online. Individuals may join the community for the sense of connectedness it provides or for the information available through its members. Internet "communities" allow people around the world to discuss anything from alcoholic addiction to environmental regulations. Such communities depend on the regularity and commitment of members. As early as 1993, Howard Rheingold argued that, to form an online community, "A core of people must believe in the possibility of community and keep coming back to that amid the emotional storms in order for the whole loosely coupled group to hold together at all" (p. 53). Today online communities form around issues of interpersonal social support and knowledge exchange. Parents of autistic children will find support websites; adults whose parents suffer from Alzheimer's will find the same.

Concerns about personal dependence on these new technologies, as well as concerns about privacy, continue to grow as new media become increasingly pervasive. Whether by requirement or choice, some people appear unable to separate themselves from the technological world. In fact some teenagers may send and receive 500 text messages a day (Miller, 2009) while others spend countless hours playing games with players from across the globe.

The friendship development process is being transformed. Many college students meet new friends in cyberspace rather than in classes or dormitories. For example, Facebook.com has contributed to the development of networks of friends across the country and the globe. Even students on the same campus may interact online for weeks before ever having a face to face conversation, meeting only after they have seen their friend's photo, read their information profile and chatted about everything from mutual acquaintances to religion and politics. Sites such as eHarmony.com or Match.com serve young and old adults in their search for new romantic relationships; members of urban tribes attribute some of their tribes' membership growth to online relationships. Participants in these exchanges interact in code, translating letter configurations such as LOL, CTN, GG, or BBL fluently.

Studies of social networks suggest that the Six Degrees of Separation concept, the idea that all people are connected to each other through six other people, is being transformed by the Three Degrees of Influence Rule (Christakis & Fowler, 2009). This rule suggests that what you do or say ripples through your network impacting your friends (one degree), your friends' friends (two degrees) and your friend's friends' friends (three degrees). Therefore your words and actions affect a very wide range of people. In return, you are influenced by many people you have never met.

Professional relationships continue to evolve. Corporate employees report living in a 24/7 connected world in which they are continuously accessible to members of their organization; e-mails or text messages arrive at 9 p.m. requesting a report at tomorrow's 8:30 a.m. meeting; managers expect employees to carry their company cell phone on vacation "in case of a problem." Teachers and parents e-mail each other, online grade books and class websites provide parents with continuous access to information about their child's school work and classroom life. Currently some schools provide parents with continuous visual access to their children's classrooms.

The extent of an individual's dependence on such technology raises concerns. Some experts believe active technology users can become addicted to their continuous access to e-mail, cell phones, or other interactional technologies. The need to be technologically connected creates dependency. For example, some rural campsites report a drop in the number of visitors as well as a reduction of time spent on site because visitors wish to return to their Internet and cell phone access (Canfield, 2005).

In her thoughtful essay addressing how computers change the way users' think, MIT professor, Sherry Turkle, argued that computerization has impacted everything from an understanding of privacy, to taking things at "interface value", to the sharing of feelings. She concludes, "If we take the computer as a carrier of a way of knowing, a way of seeing the world and our place in it, we are all computer people now" (Turkle, 2004, p. B28). As you read the articles in this section, think about your present or future as a member of an online relationship or community. What are the advantages and disadvantages of such a technology dependent lifestyle? ? How have these technologies impacted your interaction with others?

The following section contains only new articles; the world of mediated communication is changing so rapidly that printed material tends to be outdated very quickly. The first selection provides an overview of some of the current technologies and their uses, the second selection serves as a challenge to consider the impact of the Internet on social tolerance in the future. The final chapter is an update of a selection writer for the book by a college senior reflecting on communication theories and concepts in light of her experience. Four years later, she has written a piece describing her current mediated world of work and relationships.

REFERENCES

Canfield, C. (2005, July 4). Is camping losing outdoors appeal? *Chicago Tribune*, p. 2.

Christakis, N. A. & Fowler, J H. (2009). Connected: The surprising power of our social networks and how they shape our lives. New York, NY: Little, Brown and Company.

Guernsey, L. (2001, October 18). Please don't e-mail my dad, Mr. Weatherbee. *New York Times*, pp. D1–D8.

Miller, C. C. (2009, August 26). Twitter? That's so, like, for grown-ups. *New York Times*, pp. B1–B2.

Palfrey, J. & Gasser, U. (2008). Born digital: understanding first generation of Digital Natives. New York, NY: Basic Books.

Rheingold, H. (1993). *The virtual community: Homesteading on the electronic frontier*. New York, NY: HarperCollins.

Turkle, S. (2004, January 30). How computers change the way we think. *Chronicle of Higher Education*, pp. B26–B28.

Walther, J. B., & Ramirez, A. (2010). New technologies and new directions in online relating. In S. W. Smith & S. R. Wilson (Eds.), *New directions in interpersonal communication research* (pp. 264–284). Thousand Oaks, CA: Sage.

Technology and Interpersonal Communication

RICHARD WEST AND LYNN H. TURNER

Much of life is managed online these days. Virtual greeting cards acknowledge family birthdays, teenage friends interact through animal avatars, teachers and parents clarify children's assignments, a senior citizen blogs about the children in the school where he volunteers, and a cancer survivor runs a support group online for other survivors. Individuals spend hours each day online, conversing, blogging, playing games, running a home business, taking classes, creating websites, or surfing to see what others are doing or creating.

Recreation frequently involves the Internet. Some individuals spend hours in Second Life where a "Digital Native could reinvent herself many times over without leaving her bedroom, much less her village" (Palfrey & Gasser, 2008, p. 20). Others develop screen names and interact in dating websites representing themselves in a variety of ways. Others make time to provide support to others through illness support groups and websites. Others play chess with friends around the world.

Today, the Internet plays a significant role in managing organizational life. In their book, Groundswell, Charlene Li and Josh Bernoff (2008) offer advice to organizational leaders on how to *turn customers into partners through social technologies. They define "groundswell" as "A social trend in which people use technologies to get the things they need from each other, rather than from traditional institutions like corporations" (p. 9), and argue that three news trends are creating a challenge for corporations: "people's desire to connect, new interactive technologies, and online economics" (p. 11).*

Contemporary customers are blogging, interacting on social networking sites (SNS), collaborating on wikis, and reacting to each other through forums and reviews. Corporate leaders who ignore the buzz and conversations about their products and services are placing their organizations in jeopardy. If they don't read the blogs that praise or criticize their products, or know that a video on YouTube is bashing their service, or know how their company is being described on Wikipedia, they miss the opportunity to address problems immediately, capitalize on great ideas or praise, or refute misconceptions.

Recently, a frustrated airline passenger whose guitar was damaged during his trip believed he was ignored by the employees to whom he complained.

In a bid to get some attention he wrote and posted a song on YouTube depicting his plight, causing enormous embarrassment to the airline. This triggered an avalanche of sympathetic reactions from former passengers that further damaged the airline's image. Li and Bernoff (2008) stress the need for organizations to decide how they wish to develop an outstanding customer relations program. Among their ideas for gaining customer satisfaction, the authors describe how corporate leaders should track and react to blogs or wikis that refer to their organization. In addition they should tweet to customers about new products, sales, and opportunities as well as to see what is on their minds.

In the following chapter, Richard West and Lynn Turner address issues related to the presentation of self online and relational maintenance through technology. After describing the growing presence of avatars, digital fictional, and fantasy representations of a user in a virtual world, they address four assumptions of how people present themselves online and the use of identity markers. Then they review similarities and difference between online and offline relationships and conclude with an overview of the "language" of online relationships. You will find many examples of how life online is experienced. As you read this chapter, keep in mind the need to question what you see or hear as you enter chat rooms, dating sites, or support groups. Virtual worlds support fantasy and provide protection for users who wish to disguise themselves.

The Internet world provides access to people, places, and experiences you might never have in the offline world. You are able to communicate with others from around the globe who may be quite similar or remarkably different from yourself. You may give and receive assistance from others, engage in spirited competitions and conversations, and encounter ideas and information that challenge you. These authors want their readers to use the Internet wisely, appreciating its benefits and its dangers.

REFERENCES

Li, C., & Bernoff, J. (2008). *Groundswell*. Boston, MA: Harvard Business Press. Palfrey, J. & Gasser,

U. (2008). Born digital: Understanding the first generation of Digital Natives. New York, NY: Basic Books.

THE INTERNET: CONNECTING NOW

...Sherry Turkle (1995) reminds us that people online develop a "cyber-self" and that in "virtual reality, we self-fashion and self-create" (p. 180). The following story reported by Alexandra Alter (2007, August 10) in the *Wall Street Journal* illustrates this point:

> On a scorching July afternoon, as the temperature creeps toward 118 degrees in a quiet suburb east of Phoenix, Rick Hoogestraat sits at his computer with the blinds drawn, smoking a cigarette. While his wife, Sue, watches television in the other room, Mr. Hoogestraat chats online with what appears on the screen to be a tall, slim redhead (p. W1).

Rick is part of a growing virtual world called Second Life, which, according to Alter, is a fantasyland in which a synthetic identity plays itself out in intriguing ways. Mr. Hoogestraat has become so entranced with Janet Spielman, the "redhead" with whom he has a "second life", that he has asked her to become his virtual wife. Alter writes that "The woman he's legally wed to is not amused" (p. W1).

This story underscores the growing presence of *avatars*, a digital fictional and fantasy representation of a user in a virtual world. Avatars have become dynamic interjections into people's relational lives. Alter (2007) quotes Edward Castronova, a telecommunications expert, who encapsulates the concern of many people in relationships with avatar-obsessed partners: "There's a fuzziness that's emerging between the virtual world and the real world" (p. W8).

We will begin with a brief explanation of a few assumptions associated with the way identities are managed online, and then we sort out some of the identity markers available to those in electronic relationships. As you review this section of the chapter, keep in mind that much of it can be framed by *signaling theory*, which proposes that people have qualities that they wish to present to others. Your participation on an online site may be accompanied with technical expertise, particular language, and/or "bells and whistles." For instance, as Marcia places a personal ad on a dating website in order to attract a college-educated mate, she may use language that is clear and precise and have a personal biography of her accomplishments. Further, she may not want a great deal of flashy or twinkling icons, instead choosing to be more professional in her approach. In this way, Marcia is signaling her desire for a particular "type" of person, If she were looking for a "drinking buddy," Marcia would likely use a much different approach.

ASSUMPTIONS OF ONLINE PRESENTATIONS OF THE SELF

Understanding a few assumptions of how individuals present themselves online will expand your thinking about the self and its relationship to technology. With each of the assumptions we describe, we draw comparisons to face-to-face (FtF) encounters.

Assumption 1: The Computer Screen Can Deceive

When people are online, they often pretend to be someone or something they are not. Online dialogues can lead to deceitful presentations. Men can become women who want to talk to other women. Convicted felons can pose as young girls or boys interested in Miley Cyrus or Zac Efron. The unemployed can become corporate CEOs, and CEOs can present themselves as unemployed...or someone else. For example, several years ago, John Mackey, the CEO of Whole Foods, disguised himself as another person and wrote anonymous attacks online against his company's biggest competitor. Under the name "Rahodeb" (an anagram based on his wife, Deborah's name), Mackey predicted bankruptcy for Wild Oats, and stated that its stock was overpriced. Eventually, Whole Foods received government permission to buy Wild Oats, but this episode remains a cloud over the company.

In face-to-face encounters, being deceitful to such an extent is usually much tougher. We can't lie about our biological sex, and we can't claim to be a tall and toned person when we are short and stocky. Our conversations with others are in the present; they are not delayed or responded to later, as are our online dialogues. If we ask a question, we expect a response. If we don't get a response, we may walk away from the encounter. Although chat rooms are in "real time," people can choose when they'd like to respond. Researchers have referred to the "real time" communication as *synchronous communication*, or communication between the sender and receiver taking place at the same time. If the sender and receiver do not have to synchronize before and after each communication exchange, they are engaged in *asynchronous communication*.

Assumption 2: Online Discussions Often Prompt Introspection

Imagine that Bob and Shelly e-mail each other about what they thought of the midterm exam. Shelly tells Bob that she thought it was pretty easy, but Bob thought it was pretty tough. As Bob reads Shelly's email, he starts to think about why he and Shelly each had different perceptions. They had studied together, after all. Before responding to the e-mail, Bob starts to think about the material he didn't understand. "Yeah," he thinks, "there was some stuff I just didn't get." E-mail, in this situation, inspired Bob to think about his own study habits, an introspective behavior that might not have occurred without his friend's prompting.

Not every e-mail elicits this self-assessment. Yet, when we do e-mail someone, we frequently engage in something similar to an internal dialogue. Think about when a supervisor e-mails an employee requesting a meeting as soon as possible but offer no specifics. Or, consider a time when a partner sends you an e-mail wanting to break up, yet fails to explain why. These instances provoke us to reflect on both the message and our response to that message.

With FtF communication, this same introspection and self-dialogue is not as apparent. First, we often don't take the time to think about the words of another *while they are being stated*. Stopping to think about what another person was saying in the middle of a conversation would likely bring the conversation of a halt. We are not trained or conditioned to pause or stop conversations in this way. Instead, we typically mentally replay and analyze conversations once they are over. Most of our interpersonal encounters move rather freely from one point to another, with little reflection time.

Assumption 3: Online Discussions Promote Self-Orientation

…When communicating online, we tend to value our way of doing things. Working on and with the computer is essentially a personal endeavor. We search out people, websites, and chat rooms in which we are interested. If others wish to contact us, we make a choice whether or not we want to respond to their overture. In electronic relationships, keep in mind that one or both individuals may either choose to reply or not to reply. Because we have no physical proximity, we are not compelled to interact. People communicate at their own convenience.

We typically must be collaborative in our conversations while FtF. Although we can choose to say nothing, our silence…can communicate a great deal. In addition, when we are speaking in person, there is give and take, questions require answers, and out answers usually result in further dialogue. People cannot avoid the ongoing and transactional nature of communication in face-to-face conversations. And like FtF conversations, out conversations vis-à-vis CMC are transactional.

Assumption 4: Self-Disclosure Occurs Online

The process of revealing aspects of yourself to another is not confined to face-to-face conversations. Research shows that self-disclosure occurs online and that some people reveal quite a bit through electronic communication (Miura, 2007). Particularly with blogs, self-disclosure is at a premium…. When people self-disclose, they are inclined to give people important pieces of information about themselves. Further, we know that self-disclosure tends to increase intimacy.

Some people feel comfortable disclosing online because they don't have to deal with immediate reactions of disgust, disappointment, or confusion. Individuals may find it easier to reveal emotionally laden information in a technological medium. The problem, according to Susan Barnes (2003), is that *postcyberdisclosure panic (PCDP)* can set in. PCDP is a situation in which someone discloses personal information in an email message or on a message board only to experience significant anxiety later because the discloser begins to think about the number of people who could have access to that message. For instance, if Fran e-mails a coworker about her past problems with alcohol, that information has the potential to be passed (even inadvertently) to others, both in and out of the workplace. Interestingly, people may reveal information about themselves online that they would never reveal while face to face, perhaps because the computer screen is an impersonal object that doesn't have the capacity to show emotion.

The self-disclosure conversations we have with people while FtF can be dramatically different from those we engage in via e-mail. In face-to-face interactions, we have to contend with facial reactions. We are often asked to clarify our thoughts or disclosures, and we may find it difficult to simply leave. We can't "turn off" another person as easily as we can turn off out computer screen. Self-disclosure in person generally causes an immediate reaction, which is something we don't necessarily have to deal with while online….

IDENTITY MARKERS ON THE INTERNET

On the Internet, individuals typically communicate who they are through identity markers. An *identity marker* is an electronic extension of the self. Two primary identity markers exist on the Internet: screen names and personal home pages.

Screen Names

As in face-to-face relationships, online relationships inevitably require introductions. Yet, unlike in interpersonal relationships, we can introduce ourselves online by using names that are odd, silly, fun, editorial, or outright offensive. These screen names are nicknames and often serve to communicate the uniqueness of the sender of a message. Many screen names function as a way for communicators to protect their identities from others until more familiarity and comfort develops.

People use a wide variety of screen names. Some are shaped by fiction (>madhatter< or >hobbit<), others by popular culture (>AmIdol< or >TRUMPthis<), and still others by a desire to reinforce personal values (>WARRingOUT<). Haya Bechar-Israeli (1996) observes that many people place a great deal of importance in their screen names and nicknames and that they invest a great deal of thought in their creation. According to Bechar-Israeli, "References to collective cultural, ethnic, and religious themes in nicknames might indicate that the individual belongs to a certain social group." (p. 12) Her research shows that rather than frequently changing their names, people tend to keep their names for a period of time, which underscores the fact that they commit themselves to a screen identity.

At first glance, screen names may seem unimportant in building an electronic discussion and relationship. However, unlike your name (which was probably given to you at birth), screen names are created by the individual and reflect some degree of creativity, a value that others may consider important when encountering people online. And despite the relative stability of screen names, people can change their names much more easily in virtual life than in real life. If you encounter someone who is verbally offensive online, you can leave a chat room, establish a different name, and reenter the chat room under an entirely different alias (remember our earlier story of the CEO of Whole Foods). Even wigs and cosmetic surgery can't achieve such a transformation so quickly! Finally, most of our given names at birth (for example, Joe, Luisa, Natalie) communicate little to others. On the other hand, screen names give others insight into people's interests or values. A screen name such as >STALKU< can tell other a lot... screen names that are appropriate for some aspects of our like may be inappropriate for others.

Personal Home Pages

If an individual wants to communicate a great deal of personal information, a personal home page may be the first step. Personal home pages, sometimes called web pages, present a number of features that depict who the person is, such as information on personal hobbies and genealogy; photographs of the person and his or her family members, friends, pets, and home; and links to groups with advocacy causes or contacts.

Communicating one's identity via a personal home page is often enlightening to others. Personal websites can contain information that may be deliberate or accidental. First, as is the case with personal interactions, people may strategically present themselves in a certain way on their personal web pages. Digital photos, slick graphics, funky fonts, interesting links, and creative screen names may communicate a sense of organization, creativity, insight, and invitation. These sorts of intentional markers may be consciously presented on web pages so that others have a comprehensive understanding of who the person is and can find out a bit about his or her attitudes, beliefs, and values. The message is clear: "I'm a person you want to meet. I've got it together online. You can imagine how together I will have it when you meet me." However, some personal home page designers would to well to remember a corollary of Murphy's law: If nothing can go wrong, it will anyway! Someone may have the best intentions of communicating clarity and authenticity, but they go awry. Consider the following greeting on a personal home page: "Welcome to my home page. I hoop you get a kick out of reading the different stories me." Or, what about the web page that has inadvertently been linked to a pornographic website? And then there are personal home pages that have so much personal information on them that it feels like an episode of Dr. Phil. When people encounter spelling errors, accidental links to websites, and over-disclosing, they may skip over a home page rather than engage it. As in face-to-face encounters, although we mean well, the words (and pictures and links) sometimes come out wrong.

Screen names and home pages are just two ways that individuals communicate their identity on the Internet. By now you should have a clear sense of how the Internet functions in online dating and how the self influences the process of electronic relationships. We now explore the interplay between communication technology and our interactions with others.

COMMUNICATION TECHNOLOGY AND RELATIONAL MAINTENANCE

Communication between and among individuals is forever changed because of technology. People are not able to initiate, maintain, and terminate relationships through technological means. Years ago, to get a date with someone, you had to meet in a common place, such as a laundromat, church, grocery store, bar, or classroom. Today, if you're *wired* with the right *hardware*, a *mouse* will help you *google* a date on *cupid.com*. The effects of technology on our interpersonal relationships are unprecedented, unpredictable, and unstoppable.

Our interpersonal communication and our relationships with others are influenced by online technology. Indeed, communication technology is changing the way we look at relationships. In that spirit, we first explain the role that online relationships play in our lives, and then look at how people develop their virtual relationships into face-to-face relationships.

The Electronic and Face-to-Face Relationship

Researchers have examined the association between electronic and interpersonal communication (e.g., Pauley & Emmer-Sommors, 2007). This scholarship has helped to differentiate between online relationships and traditional relationships. Succinctly noting why inline dating is a good idea, Judith Silverstein and Michael Lasky (2004) observe that "traditional dating is fundamentally random" (p. 10). What they mean is that during the dating stage, people tend to "stumble" onto others at a social gathering. You might find yourself in the right place at the right time and meet the right person. Or, you might not. Regardless, this way of meeting people involves a lot of luck.

However, developing an online relationship is not as random; online dating" reverses

the standard tiles of dating" (Shin, 2003, p. D2). Silverstein and Lasky (2004) note a number of advantages to meeting someone online:

- Many people online are available and seeking companionship.
- Before you exchange personal information, you have he power to secure a profile of the other person.
- You know something about how the other person thinks and writes.
- You know how to contact him or her.
- You have the chance to exchange email and talk on the phone without ever revealing your identity.
- You can do all of this for less than what it might cost for a typical first date, like dinner at a moderately priced restaurant.

In addition, many online dating services help match people who have similar qualities, interests, and relationship goals, increasing the chances that you will meet someone with whom you are compatible. Let's look at an example to explain how an online relationship might develop. After a breakup with his partner, Willy decides to post a personal ad and photograph with an online dating service. In a few days, he receives more than twenty inquiries from women all over the state. One woman in particular, Lena, is especially appealing to Willy. He e-mails Lena, she e-mails back, and he soon discovers that she shares one of his interests—she, too, is an amateur skier. After an ongoing exchange of e-mail (in which they communicate their dating history, feelings about family, and other personal details), they swap phone numbers. Soon, they are talking every night. After several weeks of phone calls, Willy and Lena decide to set up a time to meet. Meeting strangers online and forming the sort of virtual relationship that Willy and Lena have formed is what Warren St. John (2001) calls "*hyperdating*," which is the development of an online relationship at "lightning speed" (p. D1).

At what point do we move from an online relationship to a face-to-face relationship? First, the all-important telephone call begins the process of moving from the computer screen to a live voice. The wise use of the phone is critical. As

Silverstein and Lasky (2004) conclude, "The phone can hurt you or help you in online dating" (p. 237). As with all communication technology, the effectiveness and usefulness of the telephone can vary. Necessary cautions such as caller ID blocking and not disclosing personal details about one's self are essential. Ensuring that another person is not lying to you is also paramount. Remember, all communication has the potential to have a dark side.

THE "LANGUAGE" OF ONLINE RELATIONSHIPS

...Language is the primary way that people communicate with each other.... The language of the Internet is unique. When we put that language in the context of interpersonal relationships, we have a recipe for an interesting electronic relationship. We capture some of this uniqueness here by exploring abbreviated language, graphic accents, and blogging.

Abbreviated Language

Because technology is often used while people are on the go, it makes sense to use abbreviated language for efficiency in online relationships. People commonly use abbreviations such as ASL (age/sex/location), AFK (away from keyboard), PAW (parents are watching), HAND (have a nice day), S^ (s'up – what's up?), A3 (anyplace, anytime, anywhere), SETE (smiling ear to ear), and one of our favorites, FMTYEWTK (far more than you ever wanted to know). One challenge with abbreviated language is that both the sender and the receiver have to understand the abbreviations. An additional challenge is that abbreviated language does not often lead to shared meaning. If you don't understand an acronym, will you ask its meaning? How do you go about getting clarification? Abbreviated language occurs quite a bit in text messages and its usage suggests the texter's familiarity with the person he's texting. If that familiarity is not there, this abbreviated wording may prevent meaning from being communicated.

Graphic Accents

Some writers talk about CMC as a "lean" medium for interaction. Users try to compensate for this spareness by using graphic accents...emoticons, such as smiley faces, are used to communicate emotions. An *articon* is a picture used in an electronic message; it can be downloaded from a website or created with keyboard characters. Researchers have discovered that using graphic icons can elaborate on the words being used. For example, Diane Witmer and Mary Lee Katzman (1997) discovered that emoticons and articons helped clarify for the reader the meaning of the written word. They also concluded that both men and women use graphic accents sparingly. Perhaps they feel that their words and abbreviations are sufficient. The use of emoticons and articons will become more frequent as computer graphic programs become more sophisticated and Internet users continue to download websites filled with faces, bodies, and objects depicting various emotions. In fact, on the horizon is an ever-growing list of artwork that, unlike most emoticons, does not require you to tilt your head, but rather allows you to look at the icon straight on:

(::[]::)   @(*o*)@   =^.^=

Band-Aid for comfort koala for playfulness/cute cat for frisky

These kinds of graphic accents show creativity and, when used by both communicators, allow for shared meaning. Although it may be easier for some to express their feelings via technological displays, eventually two people have to meet before they can facilitate an intimate bond.

Blogging

In our electronic relationships with others, we may also keep or read blogs. As many of you already know, a blog is a running commentary—a journal on the Internet—that usually includes personal thoughts and feelings about a particular topic or individual. Blogs detail everything, including information about family, work, and personal heartaches. Andrew Sullivan (2002) notes that blogs are "imbued with the temper of the writer." Blogging is a technological intrapersonal and interpersonal experience. It is intrapersonal in nature because the authors are communicating something about themselves every time they write something for others to read. Blogging is also an interpersonal experience because others may comment on what is written or may be directed to Internet links relevant to the conversation taking place.

Especially given Web 2.0, writing your thoughts and feelings for public consumption should be done cautiously. For example, blogging about work colleagues (also known as gossip!) can come back to haunt you (Armour, 2007). Imagine, for instance, blogging about a coworker's decision to elope or chatting about his mental illness. Further, as a result of search engines, remember that the original blog is often quickly placed on the Internet. Finally, keep in mind one fundamental tenet of this course: Communication is irreversible. Once you blog, that information is available and regret, remorse, or anxiety will not take back the words you post. Clearly, there are ethical considerations associated with such disclosures.

REFERENCES

Alter, A. (2007, August 10). Is this man cheating on his wife? *Wall Street Journal*, pp. W7–W8.

Armour, S. (2007, September 10). Office gossip has never traveled faster, "thanks" to tech. *USA Today*, p. 1B.

Barnes, S. B. (2003). *Computer-mediated communication: Human-to-human communication across the Internet*. Boston, MA: Allyn & Bacon.

Bechar-Israeli, H. (1996). From <Bonehead> to <CloNehEAd>:" Nicknames , play and identity on the Internet relay chat. Retrieved October 21, 2007, from http://www.ascusc.org/jcmc/vol11/issue2/bechar.html.

Miura, A., & Yamashita, K. (2007). Psychological and social influences on blog writing: An online survey of blog authors in Japan. *Journal of Computer-meditated Communication*, 12. Retrieved from http://jcmc.indiana.edu/vol12/issue1.

Palfrey, J. & Gasser, U. (2008). Born digital: understanding first generation of Digital Natives. New York, NY: Basic Books.

Pauley, P. M., & Emmers-Sommer, T. M. (2007). The impact of internet technologies on primary and secondary romantic relationship development. *Communication Studies, 58,* 411–427.

Shin, L. (2003, May 9). Ah, sweet mystery of email. *New York Times*, p. D2.

Silverstein, J., & Lasky, M. (2004). *Online dating for dummies*. Indianapolis, IN: Wiley.

St. John, W. (2001, April 21). Young, single and dating at hyperspeed. *New York Times*, pp. D1, D2.

Sullivan, A. (2002, May). The blogging revolution. *Wired*. Retrieved March 15, 2008, from http://wired.com/wired.archive

Turkle, S. (1995). *Life on the screen: Identity in the age of the Internet*. New York, NY: Simon and Schuster.

Witmer, D. F., & Katzman, M. L. (1997). On-line smiles: Does gender make a difference in the use of graphic accents? Retrieved December 22, 2007, from http://www.ascusc.org/jmc/vol2/issue4/witmer1.html

QUESTIONS/THOUGHTS

1. Identify the three most common reasons you use the Internet for communicative purposes. To what extent do your interactions involve actual people you know or persons you have met only online. How would you characterize two of the relationships you have with the persons you know only through on online relationship? What do these relationships provide for you?

2. To what extent do you believe online discussion promotes introspection and self-orientation? Give reasons and examples in your answer.

3. Go to the home page of someone you do not know well. What does the nature and design of the home page tell you about the person? To what extent does the home page motivate you to learn more about, or meet, this individual? Explain your answer.

4. Interview three or four people of different ages and genders about why they use the Internet and what benefits or frustrations they encounter from going online. Compare their answers. Indicate what particular responses surprised you, if any.

The Future of the Internet III: The Internet and the Evolution of Social Tolerance

LEE RAINIE AND JANNA ANDERSON

In the early years of Internet development questions were raised about the long-range impact of this technology on how individuals would interact online and whether the technology would bring very diverse people closer together through their interactions or whether the technology would serve to fragment users into small, tight groups of similar others. When James Carey, a communication scholar, was asked about the impact of the new technologies on human life, he replied, "The consequences of technology are always profoundly contradictory; contradiction is of the essence in technology, not just some accidental byproduct of the historical process" (Arakaki Game, 1998, p.127). To support this point he cited writing on the impact of the printing press that drove down some borders while erecting others. (It provided greater possibilities for communication across class barriers but hardened the divide between vernacular languages, leading to greater intellectual differences). The rise of the Internet has stirred similar concerns about its impact on interpersonal connectedness across groups, large and small, as well as nations, and world regions.

Shedletsky and Aitken (2004) explore the role of the Internet in creating linkages among users. They suggest that "As you try out a certain discussion group, you may find that you clash with some of the ideas or people you encounter. You could just keep trying different groups until you find just the right bunch of people who think like you" (p. 94). They describe how you can winnow down the types of people you encounter by revealing information about yourself that can be used to locate similar others. In addition, cookies can track your online activity and a central system can analyze the information to target information and entertainment that match your interests. Think about the Facebook process. When you agree to "friend" another person, you are provided with a set of other possible friends of your newly acquired friend. The implied meaning suggests, "If you are friends with X, then X's friends are likely to be people similar to the person you already friended." Or, similarities attract!

In an attempt to anticipate the long range impact of the Internet, members of the PEW Internet and American Life Projects set out to survey technology stakeholders and critics to assess scenarios about the future of the Internet in the world of 2020. Some 578 Internet activists, builders, and commentators, *as well as 618 stakeholders, responded to questions on issues such as the evolution of privacy, identity and forgiveness, the evolution of mobile Internet communication and the evolution of the Internet user. In the following selection you will encounter the responses of this expert group as they attempted to assess scenarios about the future of the Internet. This segment contains the group's thoughts on the impact of the Internet's influence on social tolerance. Respondents read the prediction that opened with the sentence, "Social tolerance has advanced significantly due in great part to the Internet" and was followed by a short scenario of life in 2020 congruent with the prediction. After you read the full prediction, but before you read the responses contained in the following piece, take a minute to consider how might have responded if you had been selected as a respondent.*

REFERENCES

Arakaki Game, J. (1998). Communication, culture and technology: An Internet interview with James W. Carey. *Journal of Communication Inquiry, 22,* 117–130.

Shedletsky, L. J., & Aitken, J. E. (2004). *Human communication on the Internet.* Boston, MA: Allyn & Bacon.

THE FUTURE OF THE INTERNET III

A survey of experts shows they expect major tech advances as the phone becomes a primary device for online access, voice-recognition improves, and the structure of the Internet itself improves. They disagree about whether this will lead to more social tolerance, more forgiving human relations, or better home lives....

Scenario 2: The Internet and the Evolution of Social Tolerance

Prediction and Reactions

PREDICTION: *Social tolerance has advanced significantly due in great part to the Internet. In 2020, people are more tolerant than they are today, thanks to wider exposure to others and their views that has been brought about by the Internet and other information and communication technologies. The greater tolerance shows up in several*

Expert Respondents' Reactions (N=578)

Mostly Agree 32%
Mostly Disagree 56%
Did Not Respond 13%

All Respondents' Reactions (N=1,196)

Mostly Agree 33%
Mostly Disagree 55%
Did Not Respond 11%

Note: Since results are based on a nonrandom sample, a margin of error cannot be computed. The "prediction" was composed to elicit responses and is not a formal forecast

metrics, including declining levels of violence, lower levels of sectarian strife, and reduced incidence of overt acts of bigotry and hate crimes.

OVERVIEW OF RESPONDENTS' REACTIONS

A majority of respondents disagreed with the proposed future. Many say while there is no doubt the Internet is expanding the potential for people to come to a better understanding of one another it also expands the potential for bigotry, hate, and terrorism, thus tolerance will not see net gains. They believe that the natural human tendencies to congregate with like-minded allies and act in tribes is too potent to be overcome by technology tools that expand communication and the flow of information. Still, about a third agreed with the premise, optimistic that gains will be made, while adding the qualifier that negative agendas will always also be well-served by advances in communications technologies.

More than half of respondents mostly disagreed with the idea that the Internet will help inspire a significant increase in social tolerance. A representative response came from Adam Peake, a policy analyst for the Center for Global Communications and a leader in the United Nations-facilitated World Summits on the Information Society and Internet Governance Forums. "Not in mankind's nature," he wrote. "The first global satellite link-up was 1967, BBC's Our World: the Beatles 'All You Need Is Love,' and we still have war, genocide, and assassination (Lennon's poignantly)."

Jamais Cascio, the founder of Open the Future, active in the Institute for Ethics and Emerging Technologies, commented, "Sadly, there's little evidence that greater observational exposure to one's 'enemies' automatically reduces hostility and increases tolerance. In many cases, it does the opposite, especially if that observational exposure is controlled or manipulated in some way."....

Fred Baker, Cisco Systems Fellow, Internet Society and IETF leader, and an architect of the Internet, wrote, "Human nature will not have changed. There will be wider understanding of viewpoints, but tolerance of fundamental disagreement will not have improved."

And Tom Vest, an IP network architect for RIPE NCC Science Group, expert on Internet protocol policy, and consultant for the Organization for Economic Cooperation and Development, commented, "Absent some major external shock, effective education on the kind of global scale necessary to make this one come true will take much longer than 15 years. On average, people will not be much more tolerant/intolerant (or educated/ignorant) than they are today."

Matt Gallivan, senior research analyst for National Public Radio in the US, wrote, "Sharing, interacting, and being exposed to ideas is great and all, but saying the Internet will eventually make human beings more tolerant is like saying that the Prius will reverse global warming; a little too much of an idealistic leap in logic. People are people are people. And people are terrible."

Philip Lu, vice president and manager of research analysis for Wells Fargo Bank Internet Services, commented, "Just as social networking has allowed people to become more interconnected, this will also allow those with extreme views (who would otherwise be isolated) to connect to their 'kindred' spirits elsewhere. Therefore, I am not optimistic that violence will go down."...

And Frederic Litto, president of the Brazil Distance Learning Association, wrote, "Much to the contrary, all our advancement in knowledge about evolution, human cognition, and medical diagnostics and treatment have done little to reduce human stupidity, hate, and violence. We may advance indefinitely into new worlds of technological competence and globalized knowledge about one another, but there's no guarantee that universal education, sophisticated flows of communication, and international organizations attempting to reduce intolerance and acts against peace, will be entirely successful...."

SOME SAY THE INTERNET WILL ACCELERATE OR EXPAND FRAGMENTATION AND REINFORCE PREJUDICES

A number of respondents said the Internet's capabilities enhance the opportunities for people with ill will and violent agendas. "Are you kidding?" responded Dan Larson, CEO of PKD Foundation. "The more open and free people are to pass on their inner feelings about things/people, especially under the anonymity of the Internet—will only foster more and more vitriol and bigotry."

Many expressed concerns over the use of networked communications to further the goals of groups that sometimes leverage the differences between themselves and others to gain unity. "I see more anger in society, more carelessness, less regard for rules of civility and behavior," wrote Alexis Chontos, Webmaster for the Art Institute of Pittsburgh. "There will be greater crime, an increase in the 'you owe us' mentality, less tolerance, more sectarianism, more hate crimes (religion against religion)."

Fred Ledley, founder and chairman of Mygenome, was even more certain of the negatives. "The Internet is a danger to social tolerance," he wrote. "The easy distribution of hate and propaganda through the Internet allows dissemination of hateful material that would not previously have received attention. Worse, it makes it harder to appreciate what is fringe behavior by a small number of individuals, and what represents a true movement or organization. The prevalence of anti-semitic propaganda on the Web is a frightening example of what the Web can sustain."...

Bernardo Huberman, senior fellow and director of the Social Computing Lab at HP Laboratories, commented, "Have you been on the Internet? It allows people to find their own insular communities that are outside the criticisms of others. See: furies." An anonymous participant added, "There will be more tolerance on a whole, which will only aggravate extremists even more." And another added, "By bringing people of every background together, the immediate effect is more and bloodier wars, perhaps not on the battlefield, but certainly in social movements and politics."

Many shared the view that people will spend less time in face-to-face communications, and that this will damage their ability to have empathy and relate well to others. "Insofar as the virtual world permits less actual interaction, then individuals with dangerous biases will have no cause to question their beliefs" wrote one anonymous contributor.

MANY RESPOND THAT THE INTERNET WILL CONTRIBUTE TO THE EXPANSION OF TOLERANCE AND INTOLERANCE

Many mostly disagreed with the scenario because the Internet, like all technologies, serves both good and evil human motives equally well. "Although I believe the Internet is a net positive for tolerance and sociability, its impact will be gradual, even generational, and although positive on balance, it will also contribute to the cohesion and separateness of intolerant (and worse) subgroups," responded Tom Hughes, COO at The Connors Group, a financial markets information company.

"Polarization will continue and the people on the extremes will be less tolerant of those opposite them," wrote Don Heath, Internet pioneer and former president and CEO of the Internet Society. "At the same time, within homogenous groups (religious, political, social, financial, etc.) greater tolerance will likely occur...I hope I am wrong."...

Richard Osborne, Web manager for the School of Education & Lifelong Learning at the University of Exeter, responded, "Humans are basically tribal and they will simply use the new virtual spaces to create new tribes or solidify and enhance existing ones. Knowing more about someone online could just as easily lead to less tolerance as opposed to more—because you can read their views more fully you might find this enhances your dislike."

SOME SAY THE INTERNET IS MAKING A POSITIVE DIFFERENCE, ALLOWING PEOPLE TO COME TO A BETTER UNDERSTANDING

Still, some respondents agreed with the scenario. "I do see a long, slow road of improvement," wrote Paul Jones, director of ibiblio.org, based at the University of North Carolina-Chapel Hill. An anonymous participant commented, "Levels of sectarian strife and overt bigotry and hate crimes will peak after 2020 (not before) in response to this wider exposure and increased public presence of cultural minorities."

"One can only hope," wrote BuzzMachine blogger Jeff Jarvis. "I wouldn't go so far as predicting world peace through the Internet. Sadly, there will always be fanatics and criminals.... But I do at least believe that the Internet's ability to bridge nations and divides and bring together individuals can only be positive.".…

"Increased access to information about different people will enhance our understanding of different cultures and promote greater intercultural sensitivity," wrote Gary Kreps, chair of the department of communication at George Mason University. "People will recognize similarities in values and goals and use these shared values as a basis for coordination and cooperation."

Joe McCarthy, self-described "principal instigator" at MyStrands, formerly principal scientist at Nokia Research Center in Palo Alto, wrote, "Yochai Benkler's book *The Wealth of Networks* shows how the Internet can help transform economics and society, and enable more people to be both self-sufficient and entrepreneurial. As more people are able to truly engage in this increasingly inclusive economy, there will be less violence. We'll all come to see that 'everyone's a customer'...and that everyone's a potential trading partner (on an individual, not just a national, stage)."

"I believe that as Derrick de Kerckhove so aptly named it, the Internet has created a global, connected intelligence," wrote Barry Chudakov, principal of the Chudakov Company, a marketing strategies firm. "And while this connecting can be used to foment hate and divisiveness, the larger use of the Internet is to create intelligent communities. Further, one can encounter voices within these communities that build awareness of wider views than one may have known before. So it is the community-building, the focusing of shared interest, that has the potential at least to allow more and varied voices to be heard. Whether this will indeed result in greater tolerance and declining levels of violence and strife… let's just say there is great potential for that to happen."

DO OUR TOOLS SHAPE US OR DO WE SHAPE OUR TOOLS? THE QUESTION OF TECHNOLOGICAL DETERMINISM

This question drew the attention of several respondents who are attuned to the concept known as "technological determinism." A dominant view holds that advances in technology are the driving force behind social change and that they carry inherent effects—that our tools are vital to how we act and who we are. This view is referred to as technological determinism by those who argue against it—they say technological innovation is mostly shaped by society through the influence of economic, political, and cultural motivations.

"It would be marvelous if this were to happen, but be wary of attributing deterministic effects to the Internet and other ICTs, never mind assuming they will change human nature in this short a time scale," wrote Victoria Nash, of the Oxford Internet Institute, formerly a fellow at the Institute of Public Policy Research.

Benjamin M. Ben-Baruch, senior market intelligence consultant and applied sociologist for Aquent, wrote, "First, I disagree with the notion that social tolerance has advanced or increased. Second, I disagree with the notion that either technology or education tend to increase tolerance. There is, as far as I can discern, no body of evidence that supports such notions. To the extent that evidence exists, it supports the notion that both education and technology can be used to increase tolerance but only under conditions that

All Respondents' Reactions (N=1,196)

Mostly Agree 33%
Mostly Disagree 55%
Did Not Respond 11%

Note: Since results are based on a nonrandom sample, a margin of error cannot be computed. The "prediction" was composed to elicit responses and is not a formal forecast

are unlikely to be replicated broadly across large populations (at least in the foreseeable future)."

"To credit the Internet would be overly technologically deterministic," responded Christine Boese, information architect for Avenue A-Razorfish. "There are aspects of both greater and lesser social tolerance online. If the technology tends to lead cultures in any particular direction, it is leading to greater polarization of extremes, and less of the middle. Does greater tolerance constitute the middle? Not in this case. The extremes find support for their views online, more so than in the less-connected, face-to-face world, so bigots find their views reinforced and even the far extremes of social relativists find their views reinforced…. Is everyone really entitled to his or her own opinion, or are there very real and socially-constructed methods to evaluate whether some opinions and views are indeed superior to others? I believe the latter…."

REFERENCES

Rainie, L., & Anderson, J. (2008, December 14). The future of the Internet III. *Pew Internet & American Life Project.* Retrieved August 5, 2009, from http://www.pewinternet.org/Reports/2008/The-Future-of-the-Internet-III.aspx

QUESTIONS/THOUGHTS

1. What was your first reaction when you read the full prediction? Write what you would have answered in a paragraph.

2. Under what conditions have you "gone outside your comfort zone" in making connections with persons quite different from yourself? What motivated you to connect with these individuals? Were the results of the efforts satisfying enough that you would repeat this connection effort with others?

3. To what extent have you witnessed changes toward "others" as interaction online created shifts in attitudes toward others holding beliefs or attitudes very different from your own? Cite examples.

4. How might the fragmentation of the Web into subgroups of likeminded people be changed? What avenues might be created to bring people into more direct dialogue about their differences?

Communicating in a Connected World

KATRINA SHONBECK

The world of communication technology contin-ues to explode. Many of you are "Digital Natives" and have grown up in a world of computers, digital games, MP3s, avatars, and Internet friends. On the other hand, some technology experts argue that not all young people, born after 1980 are Digital Natives because "Digital Natives share a common global culture that is defined not by age, strictly, but by certain attributes and experiences related to how they interact with information technologies, infor-mation itself, one another, and other people and institutions" (Digital Natives, 2009).

Younger people who grew up with computers are at the forefront of this communication revo-lution. Significant personal messages are commu-nicated increasingly online. According to Barker (2005), "Message boards, personal websites, list-servs, and blogs have become virtual soapboxes for brooding over and boasting about the kind of news—disease and death, cheating boyfriends and new boyfriends, job raises and losses..."(2D). In the past such information was communicated through more private channels, such as phone calls, face to face interaction or letters, if it was communi-cated at all. Part of using these new mediated

opportunities involves not only learning to use the hardware but to learn the language of relating in a new medium. For example, instant messag-ing (IM) requires developing a new vocabulary of acronyms for high speed message delivery as well as an understanding of the etiquette involved in real time access online. Twitter, a free social network-ing tool developed in 2006 allows users to send and read messages (tweets) or text based posts of up to 140 characters. Blogging has exploded as a public means of self expression. And, of course, there's "Twittorati," which reveals what top bloggers are tweeting about and how these trends compare to Blogosphere trends. Many digital immigrants struggle to understand and use these technologies effectively whereas the natives speak fluently and quickly.

Such online involvement requires a commit-ment of time, energy, and a willingness to learn new approaches. You could have written a vari-ation on this chapter's essay. Issues such as age, gender, educational experiences, culture, eco-nomic status, and computer skills would render your essay different from the author's. But you live in a wired world and, whatever your age and background, this reality impacts your interpersonal interactions with some or most of the significant people in your life. In some cases it brings you closer to certain individuals or groups; in other cases it isolates you from potentially important connections.

This is a special final piece. Katrina Shonbeck wrote the last chapter for the 4th edition of this book when she was a senior in college. It was titled, "Thoughts on CMC by an E-mailer, IMer, Blog Reader, and Facebooker." After graduation she joined a large advertising and technology corporation where her Internet knowledge and skills expanded dramatically. In the current piece she discusses how she depends on digital communication in multiple areas in her everyday life. She also cites numerous studies about the impact of such digital media on all our lives. As you read this chapter, imagine how you might have written a version of it relying on your personal experiences.

REFERENCES

Barker, O. (2005, August 1). Web spins personal laundry. *USA Today*, pp. 1D–2D.

Digital Native. Retrieved August 11, 2009, from http://www.digitalnative.org/wiki/Main_Page

Jalichandra, R. (2009, July 7). We've launched Tweetorati—Discover where blogs and tweets converge [Web log message]. Retrieved from http://technorati.com/weblog/

Prensky, M. (2001). Digital natives, digital immigrants. *On the Horizon*, 9(5).

As a twenty five year-old marketing professional, computer-mediated communication (CMC) isn't an alternative communication channel for me—it's a way of life. In fact, I have more logins to more communication services online than I can keep track of: Gmail Chat, Blogger, Twitter, Facebook, LinkedIn, YouTube. And these are only the services I use most often. In the past I have also had accounts with AOL Instant Messenger, MySpace, Match.com, MeetUp, Yahoo! Groups and Google Groups. I grew up during the rise of the personal computer and the Internet so it's easy for me to take CMC for granted. But as a former communication

Table 42-1

CMC Channel	% Usage Increase	Time Period
Blogging	8%	2002–2008
Social Networking	28%	2005–2008
Watching Online Video	19%	2006–2008

student, I must remember that e-mail, instant messaging, blogging, microblogging, social networking, and video sharing have, in fact, drastically changed the way people communicate.

In March of 2000, 46% percent of Americans used the Internet; now approximately 75% do (Pew Internet and Life Project. *Usage Over Time* Spreadsheet). With this increase in Internet usage, we also see an increase in the percentage of Americans using the internet to communicate with others. Americans' usage of the two oldest forms of online communication—email and IM—has not increased in the last several years, but blogging, microblogging, social networking, and watching online videos has increased over the last several years (see table above). (Pew Internet and Life Project. *Usage Over Time* Spreadsheet).

As these new communication tools continue to emerge, we must look at different examples to better understand how they're changing the way people communicate. In this chapter we will explore some of the ways CMC changes our communication, from expressing everyday updates, sharing major life events, meeting new people, and starting new relationships.

To me, communication around "everyday updates" could mean talking to a friend about a daydream I had on the bus, a conversation I had at work, or the party I went to over the weekend. You can often find examples of this kind of information in your friend's IM away message, Twitter post, or Facebook status update. Before CMC options existed, it would have been impossible for you to share these fleeting updates with your entire network. Chances were, only the people you talked to on a very regular basis would know you at this micro level. With CMC, however, you can quickly and easily syndicate this kind of information to your entire social network. This

Table 42-2

	Millennials (14–25)	Total
Maintaining a profile on a social networking site	76%	48%
Contributing to a blog (not my own) by adding comments or postings	42%	27%
Maintaining my own blog for others to read about myself and my opinions	34%	17%
Uploading my own videos on YouTube	24%	12%
Uploading my own videos to a Website other than YouTube	20%	10%

micro-update phenomenon might seem like the norm to you as a college student because, statistically speaking, you are, and have been, a power user of these kinds of technologies compared to the entire US population of Internet users. See table above (Deloitte, 2009):

What does this mean in terms of communication theory? Let's look at two theories in the context of everyday updates.

SOCIAL PENETRATION THEORY

Given the trivialness of this kind of information, you might be thinking this is the kind of public information you would share during the orientation or exploration stage in Social Penetration Theory. Altman and Taylor's Social Penetration Theory states that "interpersonal exchange gradually progresses from superficial, nonintimate areas to more intimate, deeper layers of the selves of the social actors," (Altman & Taylor, 1973). But are everyday updates really an example of SPT? I will argue that this kind of information differs slightly from the public information you'd share with others in an early stage of a relationship because everyday updates have an expiration date. Everyday updates are only accurate in the here and now and they are forever being replaced with new updates. When meeting someone new, you're probably not going to mention a passing thought you had three weeks ago, but rather what you study, where you work, or your favorite hobbies.

COMMUNICATION PRIVACY MANAGEMENT THEORY

According to CPM theory, "when people disclose, they manage a friction—a push and pull—of revealing or concealing private information,"

(Baxter & Braithwaite, 2008). For me, this friction is ever present when I'm updating my status messages and blogs. I need to ask myself if the information I'm posting is truly mine to post. For example, let's pretend my friend has decided to try an Internet dating website and calls me for advice on what to put on his profile. When updating my blog later that day, I need to remember that his decision to join a dating website is his news, not mine, and he might not want me sharing it with our mutual friends. Just because he didn't say not to talk about it, doesn't mean he wants the world to know either. On more than one occasion, I've been asked to edit blog posts or remove videos from YouTube because the people involved didn't want certain information shared in the public domain—even information and videos that I considered harmless.

Sharing news online is very different than sharing news using more traditional methods. Once you post information online, it can live indefinitely. You may remove the content later, but you don't know who may have copied and pasted it elsewhere, or forwarded it to a friend. Additionally, once information is online, it is easily passed to a large audience very quickly, unlike letter writing or talking on the phone or face-to-face. This efficiency is a double-edged sword. On the one hand, the speed and ease with which we can post everyday updates and consume this information—within a wider social network than ever before—is mind-boggling. But with this content explosion we must also remember that not all information is ours to share and information posted online is hard, if not impossible, to delete permanently.

Major life events are also being communicated differently with the advent of CMC. I'll focus on two life events to illustrate my point: weddings and children.

WEDDINGS

In the past, phone trees may have been a bride's only hope to spread the news of her engagement to her second cousin twice removed who lives abroad. Now, thanks to CMC and websites like TheKnot.com, there's another way. If you've known someone getting married recently, you may have heard of TheKnot.com, a wedding website that boasts "8 out of 10 US brides planning a wedding are active on [their] network," (*The Knot Advertising*, 2009). One of TheKnot.com's popular features is the wedding website builder which allows the engaged couple to communicate their engagement story and wedding details to a wide group of people. Think of it as a blog on steroids with one subject: the wedding. This wedding website often displays links to the couple's registry to "eliminate the social stigma and confusion that usually surround communicating registry details,"(Evite, 2003).

But wedding websites aren't the only place you can find wedding details. Evite.com and other electronic invitation services allow people in the wedding party to send invitations to events surrounding the wedding with greater ease. Instead of looking up mailing addresses, companies like Evite.com allow you to copy your email contacts directly into their website so you can quickly send invitations to wedding showers, bachelor/bachelorette parties, and the rehearsal dinner.

Another interesting tool that couples can use to communicate with their wedding party is the Dress Your Wedding tool from David's Bridal. This electronic wedding attire planner is targeted to brides and it allows her to create and then dress virtual simulations of herself and her wedding party. My sister is currently using this tool while planning her wedding. Given her bridesmaids are scattered around the country and they can't all go shopping with her, she will send her bridesmaids different simulations to get their feedback before settling on a color and style. Her bridesmaids can then find local David's Bridal shops in their own cities and be fitted for their dress.

With interactive tools like wedding websites, electronic invitations, and wedding attire planners, traditional wedding planning processes and communication are changing. Will there come a time where you no longer expect a phone call announcing your former college roommate is engaged and instead get sent a link to her wedding website from Facebook? Or instead of anticipating a hand-written invitation to a bridal shower, you look for the invite in your inbox? Or dress shopping with the bride in person is replaced with virtual, online shopping?

CHILDREN

Like weddings, my friends who have had children use blogs, social networking sites, and video sharing sites to keep in touch with both close and distant friends. Using CMC, parents can inform their social network of their children's growth, accomplishments, and important updates. Starting with pictures of their bellies and ultrasounds and continuing through childhood, some parents choose to post this content to blogs and social networking websites to share the lives of their children with their friends. If I want to know the most recent word my college friend's child has said, I only have to look as far as her Facebook wall. From her wall, it's easy enough to find the information I'm looking for, comment on the word-of-the-day, and ask how she's doing. Because social networking commenting is an asynchronous activity, meaning the communication isn't happening real-time like on IM, she can respond when she has time. In fact, the people with whom US digital moms communicate online with the most are their friends, with 83% of them using social networking to achieve this goal, ("People with Whom..." 2008).

Uploading videos of one's children is also a popular online activity. In fact, 32% of US Internet users upload video clips monthly and 72% watched a video clip in the last month making video bigger than blogging or social networking, (eMarketer.com, 2009). If you search for videos tagged with the word "baby" on YouTube millions of results return. In fact, several of the most popular videos on YouTube were posted by parents who captured their child's funny or endearing moments. As I'm writing this chapter, "Hahaha," a video of a baby laughing posted by user BlackOleg, has received over 83 million views. And it's not only babies that get YouTube attention. "David After Dentist" a video of a 7-year-old after his trip to the dentist posted by user booba1234 has received over 21 million views on the original video. While the vast majority of family videos do not achieve this level of stardom, video is an excellent way for parents to communicate with their network. First, to meet parents' concerns about privacy, most video sites allow users to set privacy rules so parents can determine who gets to watch their child's first steps, or kindergarten graduation. Second, online video is by no way a one way dialogue between parents and their network. Video viewers, the recipients of video communication, can leave comments on videos or submit their own videos in response.

While video websites foster asynchronous communication, video chat or video messaging is synchronous, meaning it happens real-time. Video chat like Skype and iVideoChat use video from a webcam and your web browser to connect the participants. Video chat first started to become popular in 2004 and interest is steadily increasing as broadband adoption continues to grow. I'm discussing this technology in this section because my friends have found the service very helpful when communicating with distant friends and family members, and their youngsters. Because video is visual as well as auditory, this form of CMC is the closest thing we have to face-to-face communication. This technology is so nascent, very few studies have explored how people are using video chat and how this usage affects their relationships with the other participants. Clearly, this is a subject that communication researchers should further explore.

Using social networking, online video, and video chat, more people are able to communicate their child's development with their network. But is this CMC a reciprocal dialogue? Certainly in the case of video chat, all the participants are communicating in one fashion or another. But what about users receiving these updates on social networks, or watching these videos online? Are the recipients of these updates merely listening or are they contributing to the dialogue through various

commenting features? Keep these questions in mind as you continue reading this chapter.

Up until this point, I have discussed some of the many ways CMC is used to maintain relationships; yet CMC has also changed the ways that people meet and begin relationships. When I was in high school, I still expected a "crush" to ask for my number, but he often proved himself over a witty round of emails or chats on IM first. Once upon a time, courtship and flirting happened strictly in person in person; now a computer serves as the catalyst for this rite of passage, helping single individuals everywhere save face during the awkward phase of defining "what are we?" or in the unfortunate event that their interest might be met with rebuff. In this last section, I will focus on social networking websites to illustrate how CMC has changed the way we communicate at the beginning of a relationship in some ways, while still upholding many existing norms.

When Facebook came to my college campus in 2005, it seemingly changed the rules of dating forever. How many of us have heard people say something along the lines of "How long do I have to wait after the party before I can friend everyone I just met so I can see their profiles and figure out if they're single?" But "facebook stalking" for relationship statuses (even if it successfully helps us avoid an awkward conversation about the long-distance girlfriend) isn't the only way social networking is changing the way we communicate at the beginning of a relationship.

Let's take a deeper look at Facebook stalking. According to Urban Dictionary, Facebook stalking is "A covert method of investigation using facebook.com. Good for discovering a wealth of information about people you don't actually know," ("Facebook Stalking" def. 1). Unlike actual stalking, Facebook stalking is generally considered harmless because users set their own privacy boundaries around who can see their profile and what information they want to post about themselves.

What's interesting to me about this "investigation" is that it allows users to learn more about other people without having to communicate with them (aside from the initial "friend request" process). On the surface, this may seem to violate the central premise behind social penetration theory: that closeness develops over a gradual period of self disclosure. By perusing someone's social networking profile, I can, more often than not, learn many of the same things I'd learn from them during the first couple of dates without the other person being present. From what they self disclose on the general information page, I can learn their relationship statuses, political preferences, favorite hobbies, music, books, and movies. By looking through their pictures and their wall, I can get a pretty good sense of the kinds of people they like to hang out with, what they like to do on the weekends, their personal styles. But does reading someone's social networking profile equate to closeness? I would argue that it does not because it takes two people for real closeness to occur.

Say you meet someone new at a party. You're introduced and chat briefly, but at the end of the party you both go your separate ways. The next day your send him a friend request to be social. He spends the next 20 minutes pouring over your profile before deciding to friend you back. It turns out you both like the same music and have the same political interests. He accepts your friend request and the flirting begins. First you make a crack about his profile picture. He writes a witty response and after a couple rounds of commenting he messages you and asks if you want to go get dinner on Friday night.

In this example, you're able to pre-qualify the person with whom you're going on a date. While he's not a credit card application, it is safe to say that there is a better chance that you two will hit it off because you already have common ground to build upon. So why is it that we still discuss these superficial details at the beginning of a relationship? To begin, whether or not you're using a social network to communicate, you can't be sure that the other person has absorbed all the details in your profile. Second, you need to be sure that the information you read accurately captures the other person. While I wouldn't describe this phase as "fact checking" per se, that's basically what it boils down to.

Another way CMC has changed the way we start relationships is more overt than the flirting and first date request I described on social networks above: online dating. In the last decade, singles have flocked to online dating websites in the millions: eHarmony boasts over 20 million registered users (Hoovers, 2009a) and Match.com claims over 15 million registered users, (Hoovers, 2009b). Like traditional social networking websites, interested singles create profiles describing their various views and interests. However the goals between these two services are quite different. Whereas the majority of US Internet users use social networking sites to stay connected with friends (89%) (Lenhart, 2008), users registering on dating websites have one main goal in mind: meet *new* people.

In many ways, online dating upholds existing communication theory. For example, when creating online dating profiles, or any social network for that matter, users engage a great deal in face management. You may not have thought about it this way before, but you manage your face, or "the conception of self that each person displays in particular interactions with others," (Cupach & Metts, 1994) when you decide what pictures to post, what activities to share, and what interests to list. You also manage your face through your communication with others on the site. Your timeliness and grammar greatly affect the perception others have of you.

Online dating also challenges communication theory. The getting-to-know you narrative differs between people meeting in person versus online. To begin, the narrative may not even start with words when meeting someone online. It may start, instead, with a symbol. Online dating websites often use symbols to indicate initial interest in someone. Like a "poke" on Facebook, you can send "winks" on Match.com and "smiles" on Lavalife. From personal experience, when I was a member of Match.com I chose to wink at people I was interested in before writing an e-mail to them. This tactic saved me time and effort because if he didn't wink or message me back, I ended communication.

Second, I've found the narrative is often more direct when getting to know someone on an online dating website vs. in person. On my profile, I clearly stated what I was "looking for." I specified how far away he should live, how old he should be, and what kind of relationship I was looking for. If someone messaged me and he didn't fit my criteria, I very politely, but directly, explained that it just wasn't going to happen.

Finally, eHarmony's "Guided Communication" is perhaps the best example of changing communication practices. Using this service, two matches can break the communication ice by opting into a computer-mediated service that facilitates answer to 5 multiple choice questions, 10 "Must Haves" and 10 "Can't Stands", and several open-ended questions. After the process is over, you can choose to enter into "open communication," using eHarmony's proprietary messaging system.

CONCLUSION

Now that we've looked at how CMC has changed the way we communicate everyday updates, major life events, and how we start new relationships, how does CMC uphold or challenge traditional communication theory? Well, I would argue this is an impossible question at this level of generality because everyone uses various CMC channels differently. For example, what I might consider private information and only share with close friends, others may consider public information and post on their Facebook status message. So think about the question a different way: How does CMC uphold or challenge traditional communication theory in your life? These are questions scholars of communication must address in today's connected world.

- Dialectic Theory: Are you more, less, or equally willing to share information you consider private over CMC channels?
- Social Penetration Theory: When you meet someone new, does closeness still follow a gradual process of self-disclosure? What if one person posts in a blog blog and the other doesn't?
- Social Exchange Theory: How do you decide who you're "friends" with online? Does it involve a cost-benefit analysis? What would

prevent you from accepting a friend request online?

- Face Negotiation Theory: Is your online presence one of the ways you manage your face? How do you decide what to choose as your profile picture? Do you believe others make judgements about you based on your social networking profile?
- Communication Privacy Management Theory: How do you decide what information to share online? Have you ever removed information at a friend's request?

REFERENCES

Altman, I., & Taylor, D. (1973). *Social Penetration: The Development of Interpersonal Relationships.* New York: Holt, Rinehart, and Winston.

Baxter, L.A., & Braithwaite, D.O. (2008). *Engaging Theories in Interpersonal Communication: Multiple Perspectives.* California: Sage Publications, Inc.

Cupach, W. R. and S. Metts. (1994). *Facework.* Thousand Oaks, CA: Sage Publications.

Deloitte, "State of the Media Democracy Third Edition," January 2009.

Emarketer.com. (2009). *Global Web Index* conducted by Lightspeed Research. Retrieved from http://totalaccess.emarketer.com/Article. aspx?R=1007111

Evite. (2003, June 11). *The Knot and Evite Say "I Do" to Online Invitations for Wedding-related Events.* [Press Release]. Retrieved from http://www.evite. com/pages/gt/press/pressReleases/070103.jsp

"Facebook Stalking" def 1. In www.UrbanDictionary. com. Retrieved May 25, 2009 from http:// www.urbandictionary.com/define.php?term= facebook+stalking

Hoover's Inc. (2009). *eHarmony.com*, Inc. Retrieved June 2, 2009 from http://premium.hoovers.com/sub-scribe/co/overview.xhtml?ID=fffrrcrrhscsrrtxyy

Hoover's Inc. (2009). *Match.com, LLC.* Retrieved June 2, 2009 from http://premium.hoovers.com/ subscribe/co/competitors.xhtml?ID=fffrfktxxfy sfsfxsc

Lenhart, A. (2008). Pew Internet Project Data Memo: Adults and social network websites. Retrieved from http://www.pewinternet.org/~/media//Files/

Reports/2009/PIP_Adult_social_networking_data_memo_FINAL.pdf.pdf

"People with Whom US Digital Moms Communicate Online, by Channel, October 2008 (% of respondents)." Razorfish and CafeMom, "Digital Mom" conducted by InsightExpress, February 2, 2009. Retrieved from http://totalaccess.emarketer.com/Chart.aspx?R=82583&Ntt=moms+online&No=23&xsrc=chart_head_sitesearchx&N=0&Ntk=basic

Pew Internet and Life Project. *Usage Over Time* [Data file]. Retrieved from http://www.pewinternet.org/Data-Tools/Download-Data/Trend-Data.aspx

The Knot Advertising. Retrieved May, 24, 2009 from http://www.theknotinc.com/the-knot-advertising/national-advertising-the-knot.aspx

QUESTIONS/THOUGHTS

1. How do your digital media experiences differ from those of the author? In one to two pages describe how you would write your version of this essay based on your experience.

2. Choose one or two of current digital opportunities (Twitter, IM, blogging), or an emerging one with which you are familiar, and describe how the communication theories discussed earlier in the book are relevant, or irrelevant, when one uses such technology. Use examples of the digital form as part of your answer.

3. Interview someone who is, at best, a reluctant Digital Immigrant. Ask him or her to talk about the reasons for resisting moving more fully into the digital world. Try to discover whether there is personal resistance to this major change or personal, practical issues, such as money or training, which keeps the individual from becoming more fully engaged in communicating with others through a range of digital options.

4. What do you see as an intriguing emerging new technology? In what ways will it contribute to the ongoing Communication Revolution?

Growing Toward Greatness: Reaching Your Communication Potential

There is a children's story by Mem Fox entitled *Wilfrid Gordon McDonald Partridge.* It tells the story of a little boy who lives next door to an old people's home. He learns that his best neighborhood friend, Miss Nancy Alison Delacourt Cooper, is now in that home and has lost her memory. So Wilfrid sets out to help her find it. He asks other residents of the old people's home, "What's a memory?" and he receives various answers: "something that makes you laugh," "something that makes you cry," something that makes you warm," "something from long ago," "something as precious as gold." Wilfrid gathers up things—a puppet, his grandfather's war medal, a warm chicken egg, a seashell, and something as precious as gold—his football. He puts everything in a basket and takes it to Miss Nancy. As Wilfrid gives her each article, she remembers something from her past, and when he gives her the football, she remembers Wilfrid and all the fun they had. As a result, their relationship becomes strong and vibrant again.

The message of this story links to the message of this book—relational success lies in creating ways in which both persons feel recognized and connected. Highly functioning relationships are life-giving and life-affirming. Such relationships contribute to good health, a strong self concept, and a sense of future connectedness and commitment.

Relationships characterized as life-giving and life-affirming do not just happen; they take attention, effort, and commitment, a small price to pay for the rewards that result. Many of you are good communicators; some of you hope to be better communicators. All of you have the potential to be great communicators. This entails consciously relying on the stages of communication competence development (repertoire, selection, enactment and evaluation) and making ongoing adaptations in order to maintain each important relationship in your life. Fortunately, the repertoire of significant communications skills is available to everyone, but developing those skills, common to great communicators, takes conscious effort and practice.

Through the readings in this text I hope that you have discovered some new ways to view relationships—their joys as well as their struggles. I also hope that you have come away with a new set of "lenses," to better understand communication in your own relationships and to become more analytical as you observe the relationships of others. May you make deeper and stronger relational ties as you make connections between the thoughts and theories of academic scholars and your own communication knowledge and skill. And may these ties be life-giving and life-affirming for you.

Kathleen M. Galvin

INDEX

CPSIA information can be obtained
at www.ICGtesting.com
Printed in the USA
BVOW03s1112041216

469362BV00011B/8/P